PERSONNEL MANAGEMENT

A HUMAN RESOURCES APPROACH

The Irwin Series in Management and the Behavioral Sciences

L. L. Cummings and E. Kirby Warren   *Consulting Editors*
John F. Mee   *Advisory*

Personnel Management

A Human Resources Approach

LEON C. MEGGINSON
Research Professor of Management
University of South Alabama

Fourth Edition • 1981

RICHARD D. IRWIN, INC.   Homewood, Illinois   60430
Irwin-Dorsey Limited   Georgetown, Ontario   L7G 4B3

The first two editions were published under the title:
Personnel: A Behavioral Approach to Administration
The third edition was published under the title:
Personnel and Human Resources Administration

© RICHARD D. IRWIN, INC., 1967, 1972, 1977, and 1981

ISBN 0-256-02511-8

Library of Congress Catalog Card No. 80-84543

Printed in the United States of America

1 2 3 4 5 6 7 8 9 0 K 8 7 6 5 4 3 2 1

To

William A. Megginson,
who provided me with my pride in the past;
and to
Tom, Gayle, and Arwen,
John, Nancy, and Justin,
Bill and Peggy,
and Jay,
who are my hope for the future.

Preface

This fourth edition of *Personnel Management: A Human Resources Approach* is the result of comments and suggestions from the many teachers and students who have used the first three editions. Those editions were successful because they covered the areas of greatest concern to personnel managers. This edition continues that approach, examining in depth subjects such as the improving role of personnel management, the effects of the environment on the organization and individual employees, how the legal environment affects personnel—especially employment opportunities for all groups—employee health and safety, improving the quality of work life, career management, and the effect of unions on personnel.

Because recent events have made conventional personnel practices and programs obsolete, this edition is the most extensive revision made in the material up to this time. Changes are occurring so rapidly that the concepts and conclusions of four years ago must be updated and modified. Therefore, the material has been revised, combined, and condensed to add or increase the coverage of new and more meaningful subjects and developments, while reducing or eliminating the less important material. Two chapters have been added. Chapter 10 deals with the quality of work life, which is now becoming so important, while Chapter 12 covers performance evaluation, including some of the newer techniques. At the same time, the material in the 25 old chapters has been combined so that there are only 20 chapters in this edition. Also, the number of parts has been reduced from eight to seven.

Some of the new subjects included in this edition are communication, career opportunities in personnel (including the American Society for Personnel Administration's accreditation program), the relationship between the personnel department and operating departments, employee privacy, sexual harassment, personnel actions resulting from employee appraisals, and stress resulting from the working environment. Greater emphasis is placed on equal employment opportunity and affirmative action for women, minorities, the handicapped, older workers, and veterans. Organizational development, design and redesign of work, varying work schedules, retirement, personnel research, and evaluation of the personnel program are also treated in greater detail.

There is also a more logical organization and arrangement of the material. A model based on the systems approach is used to develop a smooth and logical integration of the material. The effects of the external environment and the internal organization for performing the personnel function are covered in Part One.

As before, an overview of the legal environment is given early in the text to stimulate awareness of its influence on the performance of the personnel function. This material can be referred to as the various functions affected are discussed later in the course.

Parts Two through Five develop and explain the functions performed by personnel managers—selecting and developing employees, improving employee performance, compensating employees, and industrial relations. Part Six pulls the material together, emphasizing the need for, and use of, personnel research and evaluation of the entire personnel program.

The chapters are organized and presented according to the programmed learning concept. First, learning objectives are stated, along with a list of some important words and terms you should know or learn. These are italicized in the text so that they can be found easily. Frequent and descriptive subheadings are used to break the flow of material and serve as an outline to help you learn the material. The theories, concepts, and ideas are presented in regular type. Illustrative anecdotes, examples, and research findings are set off and printed in a different typeface to dramatize the practical applications of the material. The summary and conclusions are intended to help you see if you have achieved the learning objectives. Finally, there are one or two problems at the end of the chapter that illustrate the material covered.

There are a number of cases in Part Seven that should help you apply the ideas you have learned. They are true cases involving real organizations, people, and events. Placed at the end of the text, they show that the various personnel functions are integrated and cannot be considered in isolation. Of the 14 cases, 2 are new.

As the subtitle of the text implies, this edition continues the heavy emphasis on the concept that the people in organizations should be regarded as human resources. Behavioral science research findings are again used extensively. The number of footnote citations is kept to a minimum to prevent clutter and distraction in reading, but a list of references is provided at the end of each chapter to suggest possibilities for further reading if the subject interests you. At schools with a strong organizational behavior course, the material in Chapters 10 and 11 may be omitted without losing the continuity of the material; yet the material in them provides a human resources approach to these organizational behavior subjects.

In conclusion, this is an exciting and stimulating time to be involved with personnel and human resources management! Events of the past few years have revolutionized the performance of the personnel function and led to more creative, interesting, and rewarding experiences. Present events indicate that the next few years will present even more stimulating, challenging, and rewarding—but frustrating—opportunities for those in the field. In essence, a "people revolution" is under way, and it is changing the very nature of organizational life and the performance of the personnel function.

These are the ideas that are developed in this text. Previous editions have integrated the knowledge of the behavioral scientists with the existing pragmatic and practical field of personnel management. That approach is reemphasized in this edition, which concludes that (1) personnel is now a dynamic, forceful, and integral part of management, (2) there is a fairly well defined body of generally useful behavioral and technical knowledge that future managers should know in order to perform the personnel function successfully, and (3) there is a promising future for those interested in entering the personnel field.

Acknowledgments

So many people have been involved in producing this book that it is impossible to acknowledge the contribution of each one. The contributions of some, however, are so great that they must be mentioned. My students have made many helpful suggestions, especially about the organization of the material. Participants in supervisory and executive development programs, and other practicing managers, have provided the cases and examples, as well as suggestions for updating the text material.

I am greatly indebted to Terrell F. Pike, chairman, Department of Management; Carl C. Moore, director, Business Resources Center; and Donald C. Mosley, dean, College of Business and Management Studies, all at the University of South Alabama, for their encouragement, understanding, and support.

Invaluable assistance in the form of critical evaluations and suggestions was provided by Edward L. Harrison of the University of South Alabama; O. Jeff Harris of Louisiana State University; Rosemary Pledger, University of Houston at Clear Lake City; Donald Bolon, Ohio University; Gladys Gershenfeld, Philadelphia College of Textiles and Science; and George W. Jacobs, Middle Tennessee State University.

L. L. Cummings, University of Wisconsin-Madison and E. Kirby Warren, Columbia University, provided many suggestions and much encouragement.

Linda Furru and Philip Turnquist provided invaluable research and editorial assistance for this edition. Peggy P. Megginson contributed several of the drawings that enhance the text material. I am greatly indebted to them for their help.

To Suzanne S. Barnhill and Joclaire L. Waldorf, who unselfishly gave of their time and effort to translate my dictation and longhand into the final typed manuscript, goes my unqualified appreciation.

While all of these people made definite contributions toward improving this edition of the text, any limitations or shortcomings in the book, and any errors remaining, are mine.

Finally, my wife, Jayne, and my son, Jay, paid the price for this book to be written. For this, I thank them.

Leon C. Megginson

Contents

to recruit potential employees. Methods used to recruit new employees. College recruiting. Recruiting special groups.

Importance of selection. An effective selection procedure. Establishing selection policies. Establishing selection criteria, predictors, and techniques. Gathering and evaluating information about applicants. Making and communicating the decision to accept or reject.

Importance of employee development. Establishing development objectives. Assigning responsibility for development. Identifying development needs. Factors needed for effective development programs. Conducting the development programs. Evaluating effectiveness of development programs. Influence of EEO on training and development.

Determining the need for managers. How to identify managerial talent. Requirements for effective management development. Methods used to develop managers. Organizational development. Evaluating management development. EEO and management development.

How work is managed. Job dissatisfaction and efforts to overcome it. Designing and redesigning jobs. Varying the work schedule.

Using managerial leadership. Communicating with employees. Motivating employees. Improving employees' self-perception.

Role of performance appraisals in a personnel system. Why do appraisals? Who should do the appraising? How should appraisals be done? Making performance appraisals more effective. Personnel actions resulting from appraisals.

Role of counseling. Areas requiring counseling. Need for discipline. Authority for administering discipline. How discipline is administered under the judicial due process. Areas with unique discipline problems.

Growing awareness of occupational safety and health. OSHAct's role in maintaining safety and health. Protecting employee health. Protecting employee safety.

PART ONE

Personnel Management in Perspective

Take away all our factories, our trade, our avenues of transportation, and our money, but leave me our organization, and in four years, I will have reestablished myself.
ANDREW CARNEGIE

What do you think the great industrialist meant by this statement? What did he mean by "our organization"? Do you agree with his conclusion?

An organization is not the factories, trade, transportation, money, or other physical resources. Instead, it is the people, or human resources, who are linked together through a formal structure, process, and managerial leadership. People are vital to an effective personnel management program. It is only through selecting, developing, utilizing, motivating, rewarding, and maintaining capable people that an effective organization can exist.

The main goal of most organizations is to produce goods or provide services effectively. Some other goals are to provide employment and satisfaction to employees, benefits to the public, and a return to owners.

These objectives can best be achieved by combining the needed financial, physical, and human resources into an efficient production system. For that system to function effectively, however, a well-developed personnel system is needed to select, develop, utilize, reward, and maintain capable people. This is the concept expressed by Andrew Carnegie.

The personnel system suggested in this book is based upon the systems concept, as shown in Figure I-1. This concept will be explained in more detail in Chapter 2. But there are a few things you need to know about it at this time. First, notice in the figure that personnel management takes place in two different types of environment. The external environment consists of all the factors outside the organization that directly or indirectly affect it. The internal environment is made up of all the elements within the organization.

Personnel management, in the form of inputs, processes, and outputs, takes place within the framework established by these environments. These environments, shown by the dark shading, are covered in this part. As most of the internal constraints are discussed in other courses, they will not be covered in much detail.

Within this perspective we begin the study of personnel management. The following subjects are covered in the chapters shown.

1. The Improving Role of Personnel Management
2. Organizing and Developing an Effective Personnel System
3. The Evolution of a New Work Force
4. How the Legal Environment Affects Personnel Management

FIGURE I–1
Environments in which personnel management is performed

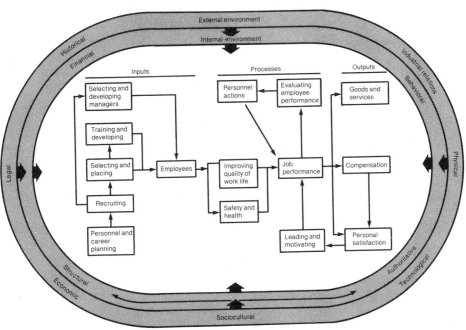

CHAPTER ONE

The Improving Role of Personnel Management

Learning Objectives

After studying the material in this chapter, you should be able to:

1. Define personnel management.
2. Describe the improving position of personnel management.
3. Explain why the position has improved.
4. State some consequences of this improving position.
5. Describe some career opportunities in personnel.
6. Explain how to prepare for a career in personnel.

Some Important Words and Terms

Personnel management	Career path
Human resources	Accreditation
Behavioral science	*Occupational Outlook Handbook*

Your production and your personnel problems are one and the same problem. You cannot solve one without the other.
GLENN GARDINER

Outline of the Chapter

DEFINITION OF PERSONNEL MANAGEMENT
THE IMPROVING POSITION OF PERSONNEL MANAGEMENT
       Previous Low Position
       Now, an Improved Position
       Consequences of the Improved Position
CAREER OPPORTUNITIES IN PERSONNEL MANAGEMENT
       Operating or Personnel Route to Management?
       Career Paths to Becoming a Personnel Manager
       How to Prepare Yourself
       Employment Opportunities
       Salaries to Expect

General Motors has long been noted for its efficient organization and the styling of its cars. Its personnel and industrial relations, however, were once considered weak. The same managers who negotiated contracts with the union and administered them also performed all other personnel activities.

This changed in 1971 when industrial relations were delegated to one executive. All other personnel functions were turned over to a "Vice President of Human Resources." Dr. Stephen H. Fuller, a former professor at the Harvard Business School and the president of the Asian Institute of Management, was made responsible for all personnel activities except industrial relations.

This action by a leading firm indicates the increasing importance being given to personnel and human resources management. Many other institutions are elevating the personnel function to a high level. The chief executive officers (CEOs) are now saying, "Check it out with personnel first," before instituting a program, locating a new facility, or making any major decision involving employees.

The changed position of Reuben Krigsman, manager of personnel research at Union Carbide Corporation, emphasizes this point. He used to initiate about 90 percent of all his contacts with top management. Now, they come to him on their own initiative about 90 percent of the time.[1]

DEFINITION OF PERSONNEL MANAGEMENT

One of the problems in teaching personnel management is what to call it and how to define it. Some terms that have been used are: *personnel, the personnel function, manpower management, personnel administration, industrial relations, employee relations, human resources administration, personnel and human resources administration, personnel and industrial relations* (PAIR), and *personnel management.*

Personnel management is the term preferred in this book. But, to avoid repetition, the other terms will also be used. *Personnel management* is defined for this text as: *the performance of all managerial functions involved in planning for, recruiting, selecting, developing, utilizing, rewarding, and maximizing the potential of the human resources of an organization.*

According to this definition, all managers, at all levels, in all organizations, perform the personnel function. That is the only way there can be a logical, unified, and meaningful, yet broad and complete personnel program.

Personnel managers may be assigned the duty of coordinating specific personnel programs and functions. But this does not relieve the other managers of

[1]"Personnel Widens Its Franchise," *Business Week*, February 26, 1979, p. 121.

their duty to perform personnel functions. Also, as will be seen later in the chapter, all managers—from the CEO to first-line supervisors—are responsible for different aspects of personnel management.

What are the human resources of an organization? There is no adequate definition of the term. In this book the term *human resources* refers to *the sum total of all the inherent abilities, acquired knowledge, and skills represented by the aptitudes, attitudes, and talents of an organizational work force.*

The theories and practices discussed in this book apply to *all types of organization, including business firms, governments, schools, hospitals, civic groups* (such as united community charities), *and churches.*

A church with about 5,000 members, a budget of about $1.2 million, and a staff of about 25 full-time (and an equal number of part-time) professional, clerical, food service, and maintenance personnel has a full-time professional business administrator. Along with her other duties, she performs the personnel function. While she is directly supervised by the pastor, the objectives, procedures, and other personnel matters are set by the personnel committee. This group is composed of men and women of the church. Yet the day-to-day personnel activities are handled by the administrator.

THE IMPROVING POSITION OF PERSONNEL MANAGEMENT

In order to understand the improving role of the personnel function, we need to compare current changes with past practices. Historically, personnel managers and their departments have suffered from a perceived low position. Figure 1-1 illustrates the improving position of personnel managers and their jobs.

Previous Low Position

The perceived low position of personnel management resulted from at least three causes. They were: (1) disrespect for the function and those performing it, (2) low position in the organization, and (3) lack of expertise in performing the function.

Inadequate funding. The weak position of personnel departments caused them to suffer during times of budget cutting. While the results of many other costs are direct and visible, the benefits of personnel management are indirect and often go unrecognized. For example, it is hard to see the relationship between the cost of undertaking a comprehensive job enrichment effort and improved profits. Because of this difficulty, the personnel department is one of the first areas to be cut in hard times and one of the last to be increased when conditions improve.

FIGURE 1-1
The improving position of the personnel function as reflected in job titles

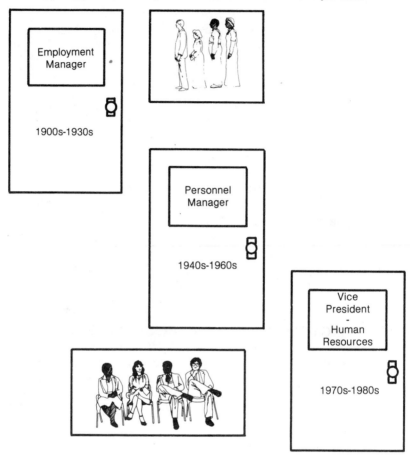

Source: Adapted from "Heritage of the Personnel Profession," a 35mm slide/cassette presentation developed by the Personnel and Industrial Relations Association of Wisconsin for the 31st Annual Conference of the American Society for Personnel Administration.

Such management actions are particularly shortsighted. While the cost of human resources is about 40 to 70 percent of the total costs in most businesses, personnel staff costs tend to be only about 1 to 2 percent of their total costs.

For example, a 1979 survey of personnel executives who were members of the American Society of Personnel Administrators (ASPA) and the Bureau of National Affairs (BNA) Personnel Policies Forum (PPF) found that the personnel department budget was only 1 percent of the average firm's total budget.[2] This amounted to $330 for every employee of the typical American company. (See Table 1-1 for other data.)

---

[2]"Personnel Activities, Budgets and Staffs: 1978 and 1979," ASPA-BNA Survey no. 38, *Bulletin to Management*, no. 1531 (July 5, 1979).

TABLE 1–1
Personnel department budget as a percentage of costs

	Personnel budget (1978 median figures)		Companies with no separate personnel budget (percent of companies in each category)
	As percent of total payroll	As percent of total company budget	
All companies	2.3	1.0	28
By industry			
Manufacturing.	2.5	1.0	37
Nonmanufacturing	3.2	1.3	20
finance	3.2	1.3	22
Nonbusiness.	1.0	0.6	16
health care.	1.1	0.7	14
By size			
Up to 249 employees	6.3	1.7	67
250–499 employees.	2.3	1.7	41
500–999 employees.	2.2	1.0	28
1,000–2,499 employees	2.3	1.0	14
2,500 employees or more.	2.0	0.5	10

Source: Reprinted by special permission from *Bulletin to Management,* copyright 1979 by The Bureau of National Affairs, Inc., Washington, D.C.

There was only one full-time personnel staff person for every 100 employees.

These findings suggest that productivity should increase if firms improved their personnel departments in hard times instead of slashing them. This, in turn, should lead to more effective and relevant personnel action programs that could have a great effect on organizational performance.

Another result of their low position was the reluctance of personnel managers to present advanced ideas to top management. Top managers, in turn, refused to accept new ideas. According to one chief executive officer, it was shortsighted of top management not to do something about the need for change. Yet, he said, "when such ideas are proposed, personnel often leads the opposition."[3] This tendency has contributed to the personnel managers' low position.

Lack of qualified personnel.   Another result of this low position has been the difficulty of getting highly qualified people to enter the field.

Research found that, of the people sent to Harvard's Advanced Management Program just before 1975, only 37 of the last 1,500 (with 6 from

---

[3]"PAIR Potpourri," *Personnel Administrator* 23 (February 1978):35.

"Just how lonely is it at the top? I'm very gregarious."

Reprinted by permission *The Wall Street Journal*

government, 4 from the oil industry, and 2 from a single company) were from the personnel or industrial relations area.[4]

Now, an Improved Position

All this is now changing! The personnel function—and its performance—is being viewed as an essential and integral part of an organization. A recent study found that human resource matters take up to 20 percent of top management's time. By 1983, they are expected to take up 30 percent.[5]

Top management knows that in order to meet changing needs personnel management and the people who perform it must be given a high position. This means that they must be given—or must acquire—(1) increasing respect, (2) higher position in the organizational structure, and (3) improved expertise.

Increasing respect.   Personnel managers are now gaining added respect in the leading business firms, as the following example shows:

Until 1976, the personnel department at Standard Brands routinely did hiring and firing, handled labor relations, kept personnel records, handled employee benefits, and saw that people were paid on time. It was placed well below finance, marketing, and planning in the organizational structure. It had little impact on the firm's future.

---

[4]See Fred K. Foulkes, "The Expanding Role of the Personnel Function," *Harvard Business Review* 53 (March–April 1975):71–84, for the results of these studies. This article is one of the best written recently on the improving role of personnel. You are strongly urged to read it!

[5]Van M. Evans, "Recruitment Advertising," *Personnel Administrator* 23 (December 1978):30.

Now, it is the "human resources department," headed by Madelyn P. Jennings, a corporate vice president. It has over twice as much responsibility and four times its previous staff.[6]

Personnel is moving up the organizational ladder.   In the past, the personnel department has been placed at a low level in the organization. This has tended to restrain line managers from seeking help from personnel specialists. If several personnel people must be contacted to solve a problem, the system discourages people from going to the department for help. Yet the size and reporting level of personnel departments are not as important to their effectiveness as the role assigned to them, their own internal organization, and the caliber of their staffs. This is shown in the following example:

In a study of a large nonprofit organization, 61 managerial and staff-level employees did not include personnel in their lists of five most important units contributing to the success of the organization. Yet, in later interviews, these same people were quick to point out how effective the personnel unit had been in selecting the people who had developed the organization and made it unique. When asked the cause of the organization's success, one manager said, "I work very closely with the director of personnel; it is a very important function."[7]

While other managers were dealing with difficult problems such as financing, pollution control, and building complex production facilities, personnel managers were often seen as doing necessary but unimportant work. They performed routine and detailed activities such as "keeping the union out," handling employment details, doing wage and salary surveys—to show why increases could not be given—and handling employee welfare programs.

Consequences of personnel's low position.   This failure to involve personnel people in the key issues led to frustration for them as well as for top management. The personnel function was often staffed by untrained people who weren't needed elsewhere. The results were low status and prestige for personnel managers and their departments.

Causes of increasing prestige.   Now, both external and internal pressures are forcing top managers to reconsider not only the nature of personnel services they ought to provide but also the role of personnel in their organizations. This thought was expressed by one executive in the ASPA-BNA survey this way:

The personnel activity within our company has grown in stature and recognition [during the past year] as a result of several factors—(1) high cost of labor and benefits, (2) negative impact of government monitoring of business, and (3) planning for future manpower needs. During 1979, a full-time personnel professional was added to the corporate staff and reports to

---

[6]"Personnel Widens Its Franchise," p. 116.

[7]Richard L. Pattenaude, "Increasing the Importance of Personnel: A Strategy," *Personnel Journal* 54 (1975):451–53.

the president. Prior to this time the highest level personnel positions reported to divisional vice presidents.[8]

Better use of personnel people.   If personnel departments are to help their organizations, there must be more knowledgeable, competent, and committed personnel executives who are alert to what others in the organization expect of them. Also top managers must be more aware of how to use personnel departments effectively.

Top managers now seem willing to use their personnel directors and staffs better. They are choosing able people and giving them freedom to carry out their expanded role.

For example, in a large U.S. financial company, a young man with no background in personnel work but capable of learning quickly was asked to head the personnel function. A top official of the firm said the person selected was "one of the three people who might become president of this company. We wanted to try him out by giving him some experience in personnel for two or three years."

Improving expertise of personnel managers.   The abilities of personnel managers and specialists are also changing. In the past, line managers were often "kicked upstairs" to the personnel department. Sometimes this was to reward them for good performance elsewhere, even though their experience there might not have prepared them for personnel work. Sometimes, too, poor line managers were transferred to personnel because this was considered a less important area, where performance was less crucial than in their line department. When unsuccessful operating managers are made personnel managers, they cannot command the needed respect of other line managers.

Some personnel managers are inadequate.   Research shows that some personnel people lack knowledge of, or interest in, broader organizational matters. Moreover, as the following study shows, some CEOs also lack these qualities.

A management consulting firm found that the two most common organizational weaknesses in personnel management were:

1. Personnel managers were often inadequate and could not foresee the problems that could trouble the company, or they misjudged the possible effects of the problems.
2. Personnel managers recognized the problems but received little or no support from above and had no authority to do anything about the problems.

---

[8]"Personnel Activities, Budget and Staffs: 1978 and 1979."

It was concluded that, in almost every case where weaknesses existed, the presidents did not understand or did not accept their own accountability for personnel management.[9]

But most personnel managers are well qualified—and satisfied. A study by O. Jeff Harris indicated that, contrary to popular belief, most top-level personnel people are well qualified.[10] Harris sent a questionnaire to 200 directors of personnel at the corporate, divisional, and plant levels of business firms throughout the United States. It sought information about the managers' qualifications, traits, interests, and background.

The study reached the following conclusions:

1. Most personnel directors view their work with some degree of permanence and tend to have a strong desire to remain in it.
2. About a third of today's personnel directors have spent their entire business careers in personnel work. The others entered the personnel field from widely differing business positions.
3. Most of them hold at least a bachelor's degree from a college or university, and some hold advanced degrees. Their college majors vary widely, but most of those with degrees have taken at least a few basic personnel-oriented courses.
4. The training received by most personnel managers from their companies before they are made responsible for performing the personnel tasks is limited. Apparently training is received after they accept the responsibility or is gained through self-training.

Another study indicated that 70 percent of personnel managers wish to remain in the personnel field, while only a small minority view it as a stepping-stone to line management.[11]

A team of researchers from Korn/Ferry and UCLA found similar results.[12] They studied the executives of the *Fortune* 500 top firms. The average personnel manager was a 53-year-old white male with BA and MBA degrees. He had worked to pay half of his school expenses and felt that his formal education had helped in his career. He had been with the same firm for 15 years and had relocated only three times in his working career. If he were starting over again, he would pursue the very same, or a similar, career.

---

[9]"Who's Responsible for Personnel Policy?" *Iron Age,* January 11, 1968, pp. 21 ff.

[10]O. Jeff Harris, "Personnel Administrators—The Truth about Their Backgrounds," *MSU Business Topics* 17 (Summer 1969):22-29.

[11]Julius Rezler, "Role of Industrial Relations Centers in the Education of Personnel Managers," *Personnel Journal* 50 (1971):64-68.

[12]John Sussman, "Profile of the Successful Personnel Executive," *Personnel Administrator* 25 (February 1980):77-82.

FIGURE 1-2
Growth in personnel and labor relations jobs

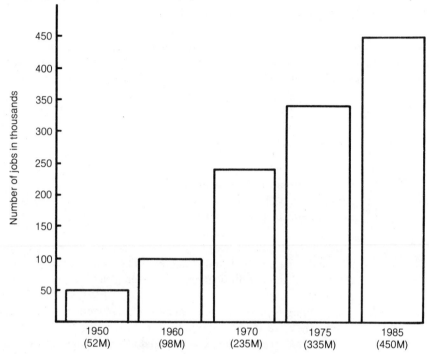

Source: Reprinted from the April 1979 issue of *Action* with permission of The American Society for Personnel Administration.

Consequences of the Improved Position

There are many results of this new position. But the most important ones are: (1) top management has accepted the situation, (2) personnel managers are using new knowledge and techniques, and (3) the field is expanding rapidly, so that there are many career opportunities, as shown in Figure 1-2.

Top management has accepted the situation. A special panel was set up by *Personnel Journal* to discuss the need for innovative and creative human resources management for today's and tomorrow's changing workplace. The most significant finding was that top managers are beginning to accept the dignity and work of the new personnel professionals as the limiting factor to continued growth and survival.[13]

The new personnel director of an operating division of a communications firm was appointed to the job with new and expanded responsibilities.

---

[13]"The New Personnel Professional: Responsive to Change," *Personnel Journal* 58 (1979):17-19.

She was told to "select and develop people who can run this company so as to assure our retirement pay."

Personnel managers are using new knowledge and techniques.   Personnel managers are aware that the function is moving beyond the traditional and classical activities into the broader area of overall human resources management. Yet the term *human resources* is not simply a new label to be attached to traditional personnel departments. Instead, it is a new and exacting role. It places personnel managers in challenging situations where they can make critical decisions. To the new breed of personnel people, this is the chance to strengthen the influence and impact of their departments and get them into the mainstream of the management process, where they belong.

The executive in charge of personnel at Dow Chemical Company reports directly to the president and is a member of the board of directors. Among other things, he is responsible for corporate administration and global product planning.

Yet the true value of this new human resources management lies in its ability to respond effectively to performance objectives and chances for growth. This assures that the right people with the proper mix of knowledge and skills will be in the right place, at the right time, and at the right cost to achieve the organization's objectives.

Because of the impact of the behavioral sciences, personnel managers are now using such complex and advanced techniques as assessment centers, executive career planning and development, organization development (OD), personnel research, and job enrichment.

The role of the behavioral sciences.   As you can see, the use of the behavioral sciences has helped personnel management develop. A working definition of a *behavioral science* is *a systematized body of knowledge about how people behave, why they behave as they do, and the relationship between people's behavior and their environment.*

The behavioral sciences include *economics, psychology, sociology,* and *cultural anthropology.* The research findings of this group have helped personnel managers to understand, predict, and influence employee behavior.[14]

Playing the new role.   Personnel managers are beginning to play a central role in managing the more progressive organizations. The proper role of personnel managers has grown from emotional ideas of "human relations" to the hard and advanced ideas of organizational growth and planned change.

The personnel manager of a department store with over 400 employees and $1 million sales reports directly to the two owners of the firm. She handles all parts of recruiting, selecting, training, developing, compensat-

---

[14]Stephen S. McIntosh, "Social Scientist Meets Industrial Practitioner," *Personnel Journal* 53 (1974):38–44.

ing, and maintaining the work force. She also helps the owners with organizational planning and development. Policy statements on such matters as attendance, hours, benefits, and bypassing lines of authority are issued by her. Her ideas are sought on setting up new branch stores. She promotes people to managerial positions and even discharges people for violating certain rules.

The field is expanding rapidly.   Top managers now seem willing to expand personnel departments, to staff them with more capable people, and to pay them more.

According to one study, personnel departments of American firms grew in size from an average of 6.2 employees in 1976 to 8.5 in 1978. The average personnel budget grew from $133,000 in 1976 to $178,000 in 1978, a 34 percent increase.[15]

Another study found that "human resources continue to grow as a corporate concern."[16] Demand for personnel specialists jumped 13 percent from 1977 to 1978. Average salaries increased 13 percent, and those of some critical specialists jumped 20 percent or more.

CAREER OPPORTUNITIES IN PERSONNEL MANAGEMENT

You should be impressed by now with the present and future importance of personnel management. You should also know from the examples given that it is a satisfying field. A recent study confirmed this. Personnel managers, as a group, were very well satisfied with most aspects of their job. Seventy percent said they were satisfied with their jobs as well as their social relationships and personal lives.[17]

There is now a search for *human resources experts*, just as there has long been awareness of the need for experts in other areas. The position description in Figure 1-3 shows what these experts must be able to do. Do you think you could qualify now or in the near future? Whether you can fill this job or not, there are many career opportunities in personnel, as you saw from Figure 1-2.

Operating or Personnel Route to Management?

As shown earlier, personnel management is performed by all managers. As you can see from Figure 1-3, the head of the personnel department works

---

[15]*The Wall Street Journal,* July 17, 1979, p. 1.

[16]*The Wall Street Journal,* September 26, 1978, p. 1.

[17]J. L. Rettig and R. F. McCain, "Job Satisfactions of Personnel Managers," *Personnel Administrator* 23 (September 1978):23–26.

FIGURE 1-3
Position description: Large Western Hospital

Position Description:
Large Western Hospital

Job Title: Director of Personnel Services   Date: 2-4-76

Department: Personnel   Position No.: ___

Responsible to (give position): Executive Vice President—Administrator

JOB SUMMARY

Under the general direction of the Executive Vice President—Administrator is responsible for the employee relations program of the hospital. Shares with line management the responsibility for achieving an optimal balance between high utilization of the hospital's human resources and staff satisfaction, through creation of a positive work environment which provides a high level of service to patients.

BASIC FUNCTIONS AND RESPONSIBILITIES	EST. PERCENT OF TIME
1. Develops and maintains an effective and sensitive program of recruitment and screening to provide the hospital with qualified employees and to encourage career ladder development by promotion of employees within the organization when appropriate. Provides an effective position control system.	
2. Provides a wage and salary program insuring equitable employee compensation based upon job relationships within the hospital, and in relation to comparable positions in other hospitals and industries in the area. Develops and maintains a system of position descriptions.	
3. Responsible for administering the employee benefits program including liaison with the Credit Union. Periodically reviews benefits and makes recommendations necessary to maintain a program comparable with those of other employers in the area.	
4. Develops, maintains and communicates written personnel policies, including grievance procedure and performance appraisal policies, that are equitable, meet the needs of both the employees and the hospital, and are clearly stated and uniformly administered.	
5. Represents hospital, with consultation and advice of the Senior Vice President, in negotiation of collective bargaining agreements. Administers negotiated contracts.	
6. Assures compliance with federal, state, and local regulations relating to employment practices and wage and salary administration.	

FIGURE 1-3 *(continued)*

BASIC FUNCTIONS AND RESPONSIBILITIES	EST. PERCENT OF TIME
7. Administers the Employee Health Service. Contracts for a Medical Director to provide pre-employment health screening and the employee health program.	
8. Responsible for communication of all personnel policies and benefits to employees, utilizing the services of the department heads and the Department of Public Affairs.	
9. Administers the hospital employee safety program and works with the Workers' Compensation carrier to develop an effective program.	
10. Responsible for retention, security, and control of relevant and meaningful data pertaining to individual employees, former employees and applicants and controls the release of such information.	
11. Responsible for providing educational services to include employee orientation, management development and supervisory training, audiovisual and medical photography, and conference room scheduling.	
12. Develops systems for analysis of manpower data that provides meaningful management information to appropriate line managers.	
13. Participates on hospital policy committee and represents administration on medical staff committees as requested.	

(Date)	Signature of Writer
(Date)	Signature of Approver

Source: *Personnel Management* Report No. 472 (Washington, D.C.: The Bureau of National Affairs, Inc., 1980), pp. 251: 124-25.

closely with other departments and managers to see that the personnel function is performed effectively.

As you study the material to follow, your interest in one of these two areas may be stimulated. If so, the material should help you in making up your mind.

In general, if you prefer working with people in a direct, personal way, then you may want to perform the personnel function as a supervisor or manager in some other department.

If, though, you choose to seek a personnel department position, it is not easy to do so directly. For every recruiter seeking personnel specialists, there are dozens looking for potential managers in other areas. Therefore, you may still get managerial experience and learn the organization and its jobs as a line manager.

It is possible to overcome this employment handicap by doing advanced graduate study. Most MBA or MPA programs offer a major in personnel.

Career Paths to Becoming a Personnel Manager

There are at least three levels of personnel positions in large organizations: (1) entry, or specialist, level, (2) second level, or managers of functional branches of personnel, and (3) the major personnel executive. Some of these job opportunities and their career paths are shown in Figure 1-4. A *career path is the*

FIGURE 1-4
Typical personnel jobs in large organizations

Employee benefits supervisor—Coordinates and administers employee benefit programs relating to vacations, insurance, pensions, and other mutual benefit plans.

Employee counselor—Assists employees in understanding and overcoming social and emotional problems; also helps employees appraise their interests, aptitudes, and abilities.

Employment interviewer—Interviews job applicants, records and evaluates such information as job experience, education and training, skills, knowledge and abilities, physical and personal qualifications, and other pertinent data for classification, selection, and referral.

Job analyst—Collects, analyzes, and develops occupational data concerning jobs, job qualifications, and worker characteristics required to perform jobs.

Labor relations director—Organizes, directs, and coordinates industrial relations functions; these activities include dealing with personnel problems relating to absenteeism, turnover, grievances, strikes, and demands made by labor.

Personnel recruiter—Travels to areas geographically distant from organizational operations and interviews applicants for position openings.

Test administrator—Administers tests and interprets the results; rates applicants and makes recommendations for employment based on the test results.

Training director—Organizes, administers, and conducts training and educational programs for purposes of employee development and improving employee performance.

Training representative—Evaluates training needs in order to develop educational materials for improving employee performance; prepares and conducts training for organizational personnel.

Wage and salary administrator—Establishes and administers the wage evaluation system in the organization to insure that the pay system is equitable and that it meets government regulations, organizational policy, and agreements with labor unions.

Source: Lloyd L. Byars and Leslie W. Rue, *Personnel Management: Concepts and Applications* (Philadelphia: W. B. Saunders Co., 1979), p. 28.

route one takes in going upward from one job to the next until the chosen job is achieved.

Entry level.   The many jobs at the entry level are specialized ones. The titles of such jobs include job analyst, EEOC specialist, personnel forecasting and planning specialist, employment interviewer, personnel trainee, industrial relations specialist, testing specialist, pension analyst, training specialist, and personnel research analyst. In addition, there are professional positions such as nurse, labor lawyer, doctor, psychologist, and safety engineer.

These jobs are available if you exert yourself. Many major firms, such as General Electric, have formal training programs in these jobs, especially in personnel planning and equal employment opportunity (EEO).

Second level.   The people at this level are middle managers who supervise functions such as EEO, personnel planning, recruiting, and industrial relations. The right to these jobs must be earned by proving one's ability.

Top level.   As shown throughout this chapter, these jobs are located at the top of the organization. They carry titles such as vice president—human resources, director of personnel, corporate personnel director, and manager of personnel and industrial relations.

Climbing the career ladder.   Some possibilities for career progress are shown in Figure 1–5. Your actual movement up the path will depend on your abilities, preparation, and creative efforts.

How to Prepare Yourself

The way to prepare yourself for a personnel position is to (1) get a degree, (2) read professional and scholarly journals, (3) attend nonacademic programs, (4) join professional associations, and (5) become accredited.

Get a degree.   One way to prepare yourself is to get at least a bachelor's degree. (It is better to get a master's degree in the personnel field.) Courses in colleges of business or other courses that directly relate to the personnel area should be taken either for degree credit or for extra credit.

Read professional and scholarly journals.   You should do a great deal of reading in professional and scholarly journals. Some suggested journals are: *Personnel, Personnel Administrator, Personnel Journal, Human Resources Management, Public Personnel Management, Personnel Psychology, Monthly Labor Review, Industrial Relations,* and *Labor Law Journal.*

Attend nonacademic programs.   You should attend seminars, short courses, conferences, and other nonacademic programs.

Join professional associations.   Join professional associations as soon as you qualify. Some of the more popular ones are: the Human Resources Division of the American Management Association, the American Society for Personnel Administration (ASPA), the American Society for Training and Development (ASTD), the Industrial Relations Research Association (IRRA), and the International Personnel Management Association.

Become accredited.   In the mid-1970s, the ASPA set up the ASPA Ac-

FIGURE 1-5
Some sample career paths in personnel departments

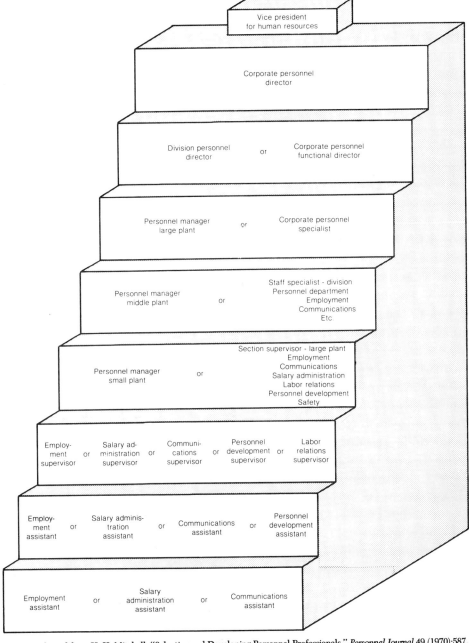

Source: Adapted from H. H. Mitchell, "Selecting and Developing Personnel Professionals," *Personnel Journal* 49 (1970):587.

creditation Institute at its headquarters in Berea, Ohio.[18] The program assumed that (1) there is a common body of knowledge in human resources management, and (2) it could be shown, by testing, whether a person had that knowledge.

A person can become an Accredited Personnel Specialist (APS) in a specialized functional area or an Accredited Personnel Manager (APM). At a higher level, one can become an Accredited Personnel Diplomat (APD) or Accredited Executive in Personnel (AEP).

Accreditation is when a person receives a certificate showing that he/she has successfully completed an examination on the required body of knowledge.

Employment Opportunities

The best source of information about future job openings in personnel is the U.S. Department of Labor's *Occupational Outlook Handbook*. The 1978–79 edition said that the number of personnel and industrial relations jobs will grow faster than the average for all groups, at least until 1985.[19]

The *Handbook* indicated that one reason for this growth was government action in personnel areas, especially in equal employment opportunities, occupational safety and health, and pension protection.

There will be more job openings in state and local governments than in private firms. This is a result of the growth of public unions.

The "Labor Letter" on page 1 of *The Wall Street Journal* each Tuesday frequently has information on job openings in specialized areas.

Salaries to Expect

The salaries of top personnel executives range from $23,000 in firms with less than 500 employees to more than $45,000 in those with at least 10,000, according to a recent survey of 724 employers by *Personnel Journal*.[20]

A majority of 2,000 chief executives of top business and financial institutions said they paid their chief personnel executives equal to, or more than, the pay for top legal, administration, and manufacturing executives.[21]

The Korn/Ferry-UCLA study found that the average top personnel executive in the *Fortune* 500 earned a cash compensation (base salary and bonuses) of over $94,000 per year in 1979.[22] This did not include the normal employee benefits provided to senior-level managers.

---

[18]Wiley Beavers, "Accreditation: What Do We Need that For?" *Personnel Administrator* 20 (November 1975):39–41.

[19]U.S. Department of Labor, *Occupational Outlook Handbook*, 1978–79 ed., Bulletin no. 1955 (Washington, D.C.: Government Printing Office, 1979).

[20]*The Personnel Department*, Report no. 470 (Washington, D.C.: Bureau of National Affairs, 1979), pp. 251:151.

[21]*The Wall Street Journal*, October 10, 1979, p. 1.

[22]Sussman, "Profile of the Successful Personnel Executive."

SUMMARY AND CONCLUSIONS

In the late 1960s and early 1970s, personnel departments became more important. The reasons for this were: (1) the growth of government regulation of almost every aspect of personnel, (2) the need for increased employee productivity, for there was less profit to invest in more labor-saving equipment, and (3) the need to conserve an organization's human resources.

The chief executives came to see the need for using their people better, and finding more capable people, in order to have more profit. This required experts in personnel positions.

The personnel function has been held in low repute. It has had a bad self-image and fallen short of achieving its potential contribution to organizations. Now all this is changing for the better! The expert knowledge and special talents of personnel managers now permit them to have greater authority over the personnel function wherever it is performed in the organization. Personnel management is also looked upon as an integral part of all administrative and managerial activities, including setting objectives and motivating employees to achieve them.

The position of personnel has improved because it is now being viewed as an important part of an organization and plays a key role in meeting changing needs. Therefore, personnel management and the people who perform it must be given a high position. This means that they must be given (1) more respect and (2) a higher position in the organizational structure. They must also improve their knowledge and abilities.

There are more capable, more committed, and better informed personnel managers who are alert to what others in the organization expect of them. Top managers are more aware of how to use the personnel departments more effectively and more willing to give them the freedom needed to carry out their expanded role. Personnel managers are using new behavioral science knowledge and techniques. Moreover, the field is expanding rapidly, so that there are many career opportunities.

There are career opportunities in personnel at the entry level, second level (managers of functional branches of personnel), and top level (the major personnel executive).

You can prepare for a career in personnel by (1) getting a bachelor's or master's degree in the personnel field, (2) reading professional and scholarly journals, (3) attending seminars, short courses, conferences, and other non-academic programs, (4) joining professional associations as soon as you qualify, and (5) becoming accredited by some professional group.

QUESTIONS

1. Distinguish between (1) the personnel function, (2) personnel management, and (3) the personnel department.
2. Briefly discuss the factors that led to the previous low status of personnel management.

3. Briefly discuss the factors that led to the present higher position of personnel management.

4. How have the behavioral sciences led to improved personnel management?

5. How do you reconcile the fact that there are career opportunities in personnel management with the difficulty of getting entry-level jobs?

6. Do you agree or disagree that there is a future for you in personnel? Defend your answer.

7. How would you advise a fellow student to prepare for the personnel field?

PROBLEM

The New Employment Manager

The Record Corporation employed about 4,000 workers, 85 percent of whom were women. The plant had an extremely high turnover rate, requiring the employment of around 1,500 people a year just to replace those who left.

The employment department was headed by James Butler, who reported to Carl West, the general manager. There were 20 people in the department. Of these, 15 were management-level women who interviewed job applicants. The other 5 were clerical employees.

Mr. Butler was hired into his position after completing his military service. His test scores were high, his interview showed that he was achievement-oriented, and his records in the personnel curriculum of a small liberal arts college placed him high in his graduating class. Mr. Butler thus seemed a "natural" for the position.

Soon, however, Mr. West found it necessary to talk to him about his poor follow-up and indecisive approach to the job. Mr. Butler said that he did not know exactly what his job was or how he was to handle it.

For a short period there was some improvement. Then Butler's subordinates began to complain, saying, "We just can't get an answer out of him, and he doesn't seem to know what to do."

Butler became more withdrawn from his subordinates and others in the plant. He showed little interest in his subordinates or in working with managers in other departments. In general, he lost control of his job by being involved with routine aspects of shuffling papers and doing detailed work rather than the functions of managing.

Questions

1. What do you think of the selection and placement of Mr. Butler?

2. Is it feasible to put a person directly into a position as employment manager? Explain.

3. What should be the relationship between an employment manager and other managers?
4. What should the responsibilities and duties of a personnel manager be?

SUGGESTED READINGS FOR FURTHER STUDY

Austin, David L. "Portrait of a Personnel Executive: More Participation." *Personnel Administrator* 23 (August 1978):58–63.

Driessnack, Carl H. "Financial Impact of Effective Human Resources Management." *Personnel Administrator* 24 (December 1979):62–66.

Fottler, Myron D., and Norman A. Townsend. "Characteristics of Public and Private Personnel Directors." *Personnel Management* 9 (1977):250–58.

Foulkes, F. K., and H. M. Morgan. "Organizing and Staffing the Personnel Function." *Harvard Business Review* 55 (May–June 1977):142–54.

Henderson, J. A. "What the Chief Executive Expects of the Personnel Function." *Personnel Administrator* 22 (May 1977):40–45.

Hoffman, Frank O. "Identity Crisis in the Personnel Function." *Personnel Journal* 57 (1978):126–32.

Kenny, Roger. "The Future Top Personnel Executive." *Personnel Administrator* 23 (December 1978):17–19.

Locker, Arthur R. "Growing Professionalism: Three Contributing Factors." *Personnel Administrator* 22 (May 1977):54–56.

Petitpas, George. "Internationalization of Professional Personnel Associations." *Personnel Administrator* 23 (April 1978):18–19.

"Selection and Performance Criteria for a Chief Human Resources Executive . . . A Presidential Perspective." *Personnel* 54 (May–June 1977):11–21.

Smith, Abbot. "How to Select Human Resource People." *Training and Development Journal* 32 (July 1978):46–48.

"The Specifications for a Top Human Resources Officer . . . A Personnel Symposium." *Personnel* 55 (May–June 1978):24–31.

U.S. Civil Service Commission. *Planning Your Staffing Needs: A Handbook for Personnel Workers.* Stock No. 006-000-01020-2. Washington, D.C.: Government Printing Office.

CHAPTER TWO

Organizing and Developing an Effective Personnel System

Learning Objectives

After studying the material in this chapter, you should be able to:

1. Explain how an effective personnel program is an integrated system.
2. Describe how to develop an effective personnel program.
3. Explain the shared responsibilities for performing the personnel function.
4. Define the types of authority used by personnel managers.
5. Explain the relationship between the type and size of an organization and the way its personnel department is organized.

Some Important Words and Terms

Systems concept
Coordinated personnel program
Staff authority
Lines of authority

Functional authority
Unity of command principle
Contingency approach

Every program involving people is actually a line responsibility—but that does not mean that . . . personnel . . . should simply turn the problem over to the line and leave them to figure it out.
JAMES D. PERLEY

Outline of the Chapter

PERSONNEL MANAGEMENT IS A TOTAL SYSTEM
FUNCTIONS PERFORMED BY PERSONNEL MANAGERS
      Earlier Research Findings
      Current Research Findings
DEVELOPING AN EFFECTIVE PERSONNEL PROGRAM
      Identifying Organizational Objectives
      Setting Up an Effective Organization
      Studying the External and Internal Environments
      Planning, Recruiting, Selecting, and Developing Employees
      Maximizing Employee Performance
      Compensating Employees
      Dealing with Unions and Employee Associations
      Performing Other Creative Activities
      Establishing Procedures for Evaluating the Personnel Function
      Need for a Coordinated Approach
ORGANIZING A PERSONNEL DEPARTMENT
      Roles Played by Personnel Managers
      Relationship Between Personnel and Other Departments
      Who Is Responsible for What?
      Types of Authority Used by Personnel Managers
      Some Ways of Organizing Personnel Departments

A department of the state government planned to employ a personnel officer to handle the personnel activities for about 700 employees. Previously,
personnel work had been performed by various individuals under the direction of the department director, Mr. Hicks. Employee records had been filed
with the accounting division. The division chiefs had been responsible for
handling the personnel paperwork in their respective divisions. Now that
several new programs were about to get under way, the director felt that
the division chiefs could be more effective in their specialized fields if they
were relieved of the duties related to personnel work.

Bill Norris, a personnel technician with vast experience in both federal
and state civil service, was transferred to the department to occupy the
newly created personnel officer position.

A meeting of the division chiefs was promptly called. Bill was introduced
by Mr. Hicks as "the man who will be taking over our personnel problems."
The division chiefs thought that Bill would relieve them of the time-con-
suming duties they disliked. They offered him their cooperation and assistance.

During the meeting, Mr. Hicks explained that Bill would establish a personnel program that would provide for "the best use of our people, and
insure more efficient work." He also told Bill, "You're the personnel expert,
not the division chiefs or I."

Bill's office was located next to the director's. They shared a receptionist who did Bill's priority work but was supervised by Mr. Hicks. The clerical
work was to be done by a Steno Clerk II who was already doing most of the
personnel clerical duties.

Do you see any problems with this arrangement? Do you think the program will be effective?

This case shows the need for a well-developed and organized personnel
program in any type of organization. The material in this chapter is designed
to show you how to organize and develop an effective personnel system.

PERSONNEL MANAGEMENT IS A TOTAL SYSTEM

According to the *systems concept, the parts of a unit, body, or group are so
interrelated, interacting, and interdependent that when one part is acted upon,
the others are also affected.* The parts of any system are: (1) the environment
within which it operates, (2) inputs into the system, (3) processes performed,
and (4) outputs.

As you can see from Figure 2-1, the personnel function in most organizations is such a total system. The external environment within which the personnel function takes place is shown in the outer circle. You can see that the
overall ethical-philosophical, physical, technological, sociocultural, economic,
legal-authoritative, and historical environments affect personnel management.

FIGURE 2-1
Personnel management as a total system

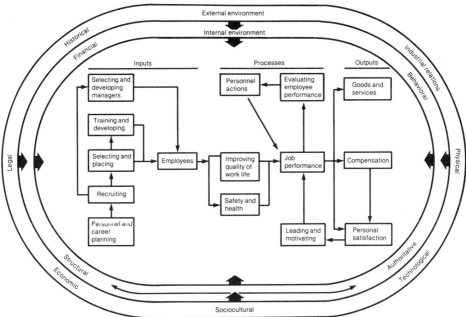

It is very much influenced by what happens in the "outside world." In fact, very little that happens "out there" does *not* affect the performance of the personnel function. These environments are discussed throughout this part.

Personnel management is also part of the organizational, or internal environment, as shown in the next circle in the figure. If anything happens to the finances, authority structure, or behavior of an organization, it affects the personnel function—for better or for worse. We will look at the authoritative and structural part of this system in this chapter. The behavioral part is covered in all parts of the text. Financial aspects are found in Part IV.

The inner circle shows *inputs* being *processed* into *outputs*. Although these components are shown in a straight progression (with →), they may interact in many other ways and directions. The next four parts will discuss these inputs, processes, and outputs.

This model is based upon the assumption that personnel management is (1) a comprehensive, human resources related activity, (2) directly concerned with "bottom-line" results, (3) part of general management activities, and (4) dependent upon top management's support.[1]

---

[1]Elmer H. Burack and Edwin L. Miller, "A Model for Personnel Practices and People," *Personnel Administrator* 24 (January 1979):50–56.

FUNCTIONS PERFORMED BY PERSONNEL MANAGERS

There is no agreement about what functions should be performed by personnel managers or departments. However, we will look at some research findings to see what functions are—or should be—performed.

The findings of four studies are given to show the relative importance of the functions. The first study was done in 1966, while the others were done in 1979. The differences will dramatize the changes that have occurred during the late 1960s and 1970s.

Earlier Research Findings

An early study by the National Industrial Conference Board (NICB) asked personnel managers to list what they thought were the most important overall functions they performed. Table 2-1 shows the percentages of managers including each function in the list. Notice the failure to even mention governmental relationships.

TABLE 2-1
Functions considered important by personnel managers

Function	Percentage of managers listing the function
Management development, personnel planning, and/or organization planning..................	97
Labor relations	87
Compensation and benefits	64
Recruitment and employment....................	63

Source: Allen R. Janger, *Personnel Administration: Changing Scope and Organization*, Studies in Personnel Policies, No. 203 (New York: National Industrial Conference Board, 1966), p. 16.

Current Research Findings

A study by Information Sciences, Incorporated asked a group of chief personnel executives to list the *principal functions they performed.*[2] Their answers (with the percent answering) were: (1) compensation—82 percent, (2) benefits and retirement plans—68, (3) personnel planning and development—63, (4) recruitment and selection—58, (5) labor and industrial relations—54, (6) equal employment opportunity (EEO) and affirmative action (AA)—44, (7) employee relations and communications—44, (8) organization planning and development—23, and (9) safety and health—23.

---

[2]*Inside Human Resources Management* (Montvale, N.J.: Information Sciences, Inc., 1979).

A survey of members of the American Society for Personnel Administration and/or the Personnel Policies Forum of the Bureau of National Affairs was discussed in Chapter 1. One purpose was to find out which functions were performed by personnel departments. Table 2-2 shows which of the activities had (1) all, (2) some, or (3) none of their costs or responsibilities charged to the personnel department.

Another study surveyed Arizona executives who supervised personnel managers in their firms and line managers who were served by those personnel managers to find out what functions and activities they considered "desirable."[3] The findings were similar to those of the other studies.

The executives were *quite willing for the personnel department to be responsible for:* (1) EEO and affirmative action, (2) wage and salary activities, (3) staffing, (4) training and development, and (5) similar activities. They were *less willing* to let the personnel people handle: (1) industrial relations, (2) layoffs and discharges, (3) job design, (4) safety and OSHAct, and (5) promotions.

The personnel managers *wanted to handle:* (1) EEO and affirmative action, (2) wage and salary activities, (3) staffing, (4) training and development, and (5) grievances. They *did not want to be in charge of:* (1) food service, (2) buildings and grounds, (3) industrial relations, (4) medical services, and (5) athletic and social activities.

DEVELOPING AN EFFECTIVE PERSONNEL PROGRAM

Within this overall personnel system, and considering the activities to be performed, what type of personnel program would be most effective? In developing any personnel program, one must perform the following functions:

1. Identify organizational objectives.
2. Set up an effective organization.
3. Study the external and internal environments.
4. Plan for, recruit, select, and develop capable people.
5. Maximize employee performance.
6. Compensate employees.
7. Deal with unions and employee associations.
8. Perform many specific creative activities.
9. Set up procedures to evaluate the performance of the personnel function.

An overview of these parts of a personnel program will be given here. The details of the first two functions will be covered in this chapter. The third is discussed in detail in Chapters 3 and 4. The others will be covered in the rest of the book.

---

[3]Harold C. White and Michael N. Wolfe, "The Role of Personnel Administration," *Arizona Business*, November 1979, pp. 3-7.

TABLE 2–2
Activities included in personnel departments

Activity	Percent of all companies ($N = 573$)			
	Costs (or responsibility) allocated to personnel			
	All	Some	None	Not applicable
Personnel records and reports.................	92	7	1	°
Personnel research	87	3	1	9
EEO/affirmative action	82	15	2	1
Wage and salary administration...............	80	16	3	1
Insurance benefits administration	79	13	8	°
Unemployment compensation administration	73	14	12	1
Job evaluation.............................	72	21	4	3
Vacation/leave procedures	71	17	11	1
Workers' compensation administration..........	67	17	11	1
Preemployment testing.......................	66	8	2	24
New employee orientation....................	66	27	5	2
Promotion/transfer/separation procedures	66	27	6	1
Recruiting/interviewing/hiring	66	31	3	0
Health and medical services	63	14	13	10
Recreation/social/recognition programs.........	57	24	10	9
Counseling programs	57	19	4	20
College recruiting...........................	55	16	4	25
Preretirement programs......................	54	6	3	37
Employee relations/discipline	54	40	4	2
Pension/profit sharing plan administration.......	53	29	13	5
Performance evaluation	52	36	9	3
Employee attitude surveys....................	51	9	3	36
Union/labor relations........................	49	16	4	31
Tuition aid/scholarships......................	46	16	28	10
Human resource planning	43	34	5	18
Relocation services administration	43	15	13	29
Employee communications	43	42	13	2
Supervisory training	41	42	14	3
Executive compensation......................	39	22	25	14
Management development.....................	34	43	14	9
Safety programs/OSHA compliance............	33	38	24	5
Community relations/fund drives..............	32	30	29	9
Food services	30	7	37	26
Management appraisal/MBO	30	28	15	27
Thrift/savings plan administration..............	26	11	10	53
Suggestion systems	26	14	10	50
Security/plant protection.....................	25	11	56	8
Skill training, nonmanagement.................	19	37	33	11
Stock purchase/option plan administration	18	11	12	59
Public relations.............................	16	26	50	8
Company library............................	12	6	37	45
Payroll processing...........................	11	28	60	1
Administration services (mail, PBX, etc.)........	9	15	73	3
Maintenance/janitorial services................	6	6	82	6

Source: Reprinted by special permission from *Personnel Activities, Budgets and Staffs: 1978 and 1979*, copyright 1979 by The Bureau of National Affairs, Inc., Washington, D.C.

Identifying Organizational Objectives

Personnel managers need to satisfy the objectives of (1) employees, (2) the public, including customers, governments, and advocacy groups, and (3) owners, of both private and public organizations. As the objectives of these groups sometimes conflict, personnel managers need to balance their demands as well as possible.

Employee objectives. Personnel managers try to provide pleasant working conditions, satisfying group relationships, and room for individual growth and development. However, these must be based on adequate income and economic security.

The public's objectives. Customers want efficient production of desired goods and services, at a cost they can afford to pay. Advocacy groups are demanding safer products and healthy working conditions and a more careful and frugal use of physical resources in order to prevent pollution and depletion of resources. They also want equal employment opportunities for minorities, women, the handicapped, veterans, and older workers. Governments, of course, seek tax revenues and compliance with laws.

Owners' objectives. Owners of private firms ask managers to perform effectively so that adequate profits are made. Even public institutions want managers to do cost-benefit analyses in order to have the best use of scarce resources.

Setting Up an Effective Organization

Personnel managers are now being asked to help design more effective organizational structures and relationships. (Some aspects of this will be covered in Part 3.) Also, as will be seen later in this chapter, they are expected to design their own departments to best serve other parts of the organization.

Studying the External and Internal Environment

When you study Chapters 3 and 4, you will see how much environments affect the personnel function. Personnel managers need to know as much as is feasible about both external and internal environments. They should also share that knowledge with other managers.

Planning, Recruiting, Selecting, and Developing Employees

As seen earlier, personnel managers usually perform the staffing activities. They are directly responsible for determining job and work requirements and setting personnel qualifications. Then employees must be recruited, selected, and trained. Finally, personnel managers help provide for management succession in their organizations. These activities are discussed in Part 2.

Probably the most accepted and basic personnel activity is educating, training, and developing employees. Special emphasis is now being placed on career planning and development, especially management development.

Maximizing Employee Performance

Getting the most out of employees is quite important, for our complex environment now makes it harder than ever to motivate employees to be productive. The entry of former unemployables into the work force also demands better management counseling and guidance. From the personnel point of view, this function involves helping line managers establish an environment that encourages output, serve as a counselor to difficult and troubled employees when required, maintaining health and safety, and appraising and evaluating employee performance. This function is covered in Part 3.

Compensating Employees

The compensation function is also important, for it involves developing an effective wage and salary plan. There should be some effort to share productivity gains with employees. In addition, employee benefits are becoming a major element in rewarding employees to join and remain with the organization. Part 4 covers this aspect of personnel.

Dealing with Unions and Employee Associations

Employees often have a dual allegiance. They are loyal to the employer, but they often belong to employee and labor associations. These groups demand loyalty as well. They include the traditional labor unions as well as newer groups such as professional associations. These groups have a great effect on employee abilities, attitudes, and performance. An important function of personnel executives is to establish—and maintain—cooperative relationships with these groups, as shown in Part 5.

Performing Other Creative Activities

Personnel managers are using their new higher status, knowledge, and skills to perform many new and creative activities. These include:

1. Conducting attitude surveys and performing other communications programs.

2. Studying the effectiveness of changing work hours, groupings, and life-styles.
3. Designing and redesigning jobs, including instituting job enrichment programs.
4. Helping employees plan and develop their careers.
5. Doing organizational planning and developing organizational changes and modifications, including instituting and administering OD programs.
6. Performing work analyses.
7. Acting as liaison between the organization and outside government and activist groups.
8. Conducting personnel and behavioral research and specialized studies.

Establishing Procedures for Evaluating the Personnel Function

As will be seen in the final part of this book, there must be some form of control over the personnel function—as over all other management functions. Effective planning for the previous functions should also provide the bases for evaluating them.

Need for a Coordinated Approach

The previous discussion emphasizes that a *coordinated personnel program* is needed, for the personnel function is an integrated system. Therefore, the personnel function cannot be separated from other organizational activities. Whatever happens in the organization affects the personnel program, while any change in the personnel program influences the organization.

ORGANIZING A PERSONNEL DEPARTMENT

As the opening quotation and case show, personnel management is a shared responsibility, based on the line-staff concept. The chief executive officer (CEO) is responsible for setting and carrying out personnel policies. From there, responsibility flows down through the line managers. But they cannot perform the function alone. They need the help of the personnel staff.

Roles Played by Personnel Managers

Therefore, personnel managers usually play two roles. First, they serve as *staff experts* to advise and guide the CEO and other managers on personnel matters.

Table 2-3 shows that this is now being done by personnel managers in the Bureau of National Affairs' Personnel Policies Forum. Sixty-two percent report directly to the CEO, and 21 percent report to the senior vice president.

Second, personnel managers are *heads* of *a vital service department* that helps the other managers perform their personnel activities.

The personnel director of a small manufacturing firm put it this way: "Department heads and the personnel manager have equal status. Cooperation is very good in carrying out the company's personnel policies and programs."

We will look at four aspects of personnel department organization:

1. The relationship between the personnel and other departments.
2. Who is responsible for what.
3. Types of authority used by personnel managers.
4. Some ways of organizing personnel departments.

Relationship Between Personnel and Other Departments

Until recently, personnel departments were mainly run by labor relations experts who tried to keep the unions from taking away "management rights." Usually the department consisted of a strong leader assisted by many lower level specialists in areas such as testing, recruiting, hiring, and compensation. Managers in other departments were confused by having to go to various different specialists to get things done.

Need for cooperation. Line managers were frustrated; they wanted to improve performance but could not. They tried practical things to increase output—changing lay-out, better methods, improved tools, and changing hours of work. Yet they were dealing with job-related factors, which showed up quickly in profits, if at all.

Line supervisors wanted more output. But they could not see any benefit in transferring one of their best workers to another unit, or promoting a good producer out of the unit, or sending a poor performer away for training. These did not show up directly in improved output. Instead, the supervisor would wind up with poorer workers.

What was needed was an effective personnel department, staffed with capable people, with the authority and desire to go out and help the other managers. This can be done in one of two ways.

Helping line managers. In larger organizations, the personnel manager and his or her department can do many creative activities themselves. At the corporate level, they can do surveys, research, planning, testing, and training. They can deal with government agencies, institute organizational change, propose an MBO program, and provide needed information to the line managers.

TABLE 2-3
Authority and responsibility of the top personnel executive

Practice	Percent of companies					
	By industry			By size		All companies
	Manufacturing	Nonmanufacturing	Nonbusiness	Large	Small	
Head of department reports to—						
Company's highest official........	71	60	21	54	68	62
Vice president	15	33	15	28	15	21
In formulating and administering personnel policies, the top personnel executive—						
Is virtually on own authority	10	9	9	7	11	9
Needs approval only of top-level management (president, vice president)........	74	78	62	75	70	72
Executes the program only after consultation with and approval of line management........	15	2	6	10	8	9
Functions within an established framework approved by management........	18	13	27	16	20	19
Other........	2	7	3	5	3	4
Top personnel executive participates in overall company planning and policy determination........	97	85	68	85	86	86

Note: Percentages add to more than 100 because of multiple responses.
Source: The Bureau of National Affairs, Inc., BNA Policy and Practice Series: *Personnel Management*, Report No. 472 (Washington, D.C.: Bureau of National Affairs, 1980), p. 251:104.

Other members of the personnel department can then go out and help line managers carry out these personnel programs.

Performing the activities. In smaller organizations, line managers want to do many of these creative and innovative things but do not have the expertise or time. They are so involved with increasing production that they must concentrate on the usual incentives—wage increases, discipline, contests, and so forth. In those cases, the personnel people can perform many of the personnel activities for them. They can also give the line managers human relations training and try to improve their skills, attitudes, and knowledge. Personnel managers in small organizations must be generalists as well as specialists in personnel activities.[4]

Who Is Responsible for What?

A constant problem in personnel management is: Who is responsible for what? Personnel people cannot be fully effective unless they know what activities they are to manage, who is to assist them, to whom they report, and who reports to them. They need to know within what limits they may operate, over what activities they have authority, and to what degree they will be held accountable for performing those duties.

As will be emphasized throughout this book, *all managers are responsible for performing the personnel function.* And *performing the personnel function is the responsibility of all managers.* The job of personnel managers is to see that this is done well, rather than doing it themselves. One practicing manager explained the problem by saying, "While personnel management is a staff function, it is line management's responsibility."

In general, the role of each group of managers is as follows:

1. *Top management* sets personnel objectives and policies and does long-range planning and organizing.
2. *Middle managers* control the operating procedures needed to achieve the personnel objectives and carry out the personnel policies of top management.
3. *First-line supervisors* interpret the policies to the employees, adjust grievances, influence attitudes, direct work, and, in turn, interpret the employees' interests to higher management.
4. *Personnel managers* help all of them by providing expert advice, guidance, and assistance. This trend is increasing, as the previously mentioned Arizona study shows.[5]

Responsibility of line managers. Line managers cannot delegate their responsibility for the personnel function by appointing a staff personnel person. Line managers would probably prefer to do many of the functions themselves

---

[4]See Robert C. Gruver, "Personnel Management in the Small Organization," *Personnel Administrator* 23 (March 1978):38–44.

[5]White and Wolfe, "The Role of Personnel Administration."

(as shown in the opening case). To do so, they would need policy guidance concerning the various personnel activities and the chance to get the needed help from the personnel department. With its support, in the form of policy, advice, and service, the line would even accept some increased control over its personnel-related performance.

Top management.   The personnel function has been neglected by top management in comparison with the time, effort, and money devoted to other aspects of their operations. Now the task of setting objectives and policies to guide other managers in performing this function is being more effectively carried out. What has not been recognized, though, is that *top management frequently does not know precisely what it wants done in the personnel field.* It does, however, know *what it does not want.* It *does not want* costly turnover, a class action EEOC suit, or the loss of its most promising people.

Middle managers.   Middle managers must help top management perform its duties. To do this, they receive the programs and policies from above. They then interpret them to subordinates who are to implement them. They also make the needs of subordinates known and understood by top management.

First-line supervisors.   These are probably the most important individuals in achieving the objective of effective personnel management. They direct, supervise, control, and otherwise manage the activities of the workers. Thus, day-to-day aspects of the personnel function must be performed by first-line supervisors.

As lower level workers have little or no chance to see higher level managers, their only contact is usually through their supervisors. Therefore, the supervisor represents "management" to the employees. The actions, attitudes, and methods used by the supervisor are interpreted as being those of the organization.

The manager of a large department with 65 employees had to replace one of the four supervisors who was retiring. On Friday afternoon, he offered the job to the person he considered most capable and asked her to think about it over the weekend. When the new supervisor came in on Monday, she said, "I used to think of us in the department as *we*, versus the supervisors, who were *they.* Now I'm one of *them*, and I must change my way of thinking."

Responsibility of the personnel manager.   The personnel function should be placed in the highest levels in the organization. One person should be responsible for it, and that person should have the aggressive backing of top management. The personnel executive should then be held directly accountable to the CEO for developing policies and procedures to permit the most effective use of human resources so the organization's needs and goals will be met.

Table 2–4 shows that this is now being done. In the BNA Personnel Policies Forum, 93 percent of the firms have "a single administrator" who heads the personnel function. Notice that over half of these are vice presi-

TABLE 2-4
Structure of the personnel/industrial relations function

Practice	Percent of companies					
	By industry		Nonbusiness	By size		All companies
	Manufacturing	Nonmanufacturing		Large	Small	
Single administrator heads the personnel function.	94	96	88	92	94	93
Title of the person in charge of personnel						
Vice president	25	36	6	43	33	24
Director of personnel	20	24	47	18	35	28
Personnel manager	23	13	9	7	24	17
Director, industrial relations	18	4	0	7	11	9
Director, human resources	6	4	6	7	5	6
Other	0	7	18	7	6	6
Employee relations manager/director	2	7	6	7	3	4
Name of the department						
Personnel	59	62	71	48	75	63
Industrial relations	16	7	0	13	6	9
Employee relations	5	9	6	13	1	7
Human resources	8	7	12	13	5	9
Other	3	9	3	3	6	5

Number of managerial/professional persons reporting to
head of personnel department*

Zero	7	13	15	2	18	11
One	25	5	24	3	29	18
Two	10	5	3	5	11	9
Three	12	22	24	13	14	18
Four	7	16	15	13	10	12
Five	13	2	3	16	—	7
Six	3	5	—	7	—	3
Seven	2	7	9	10	1	5
Eight	2	2	—	3	—	2
Nine	2	2	—	3	—	2
Ten	2	2	—	3	—	2
Eleven	2	—	—	2	—	1
Twelve	2	—	—	2	—	1

Note: *Percentages do not add to 100 because of nonresponses from companies with more than one official responsible for P-IR activities.
Source: The Bureau of National Affairs, Inc., "Organization of the P-IR Department," BNA Policy and Practice Series: *Personnel Management*, Report no. 472 (Washington, D.C.: Bureau of National Affairs, 1980), p. 10.

dents or directors of personnel. It is interesting that almost two-thirds of the departments are now called *personnel departments.*

Types of Authority Used by Personnel Managers

A former weakness in performing the personnel function was that personnel managers had only staff authority to advise their superiors. They had no real authority to see that their advice was carried out. Now they are being given a new and stronger type of authority, namely, *functional authority.*

Staff authority.   As you probably know, *staff authority is the right to give advice and guidance to one's immediate superior and to recommend how suggestions should be put into action.* Either the superior or the staff specialist may start this process. If the superior feels a need for counsel, the staff person is asked for it. If the staff member thinks the superior needs advice about a personnel matter, it is offered. The superior then uses line authority to carry out the suggestion. This advisory relationship is shown in Figure 2-2.

This arrangement rarely works in actual practice. Instead, *lines of authority* (chains of command) are often bypassed. This results in conflict between the line—which has formal authority—and staff, which can only use specialized competence. Organizations can no longer rely solely on this arrangement to reach their objectives. Current practice is changing in the direction of a more shared relationship based on the use of functional authority.

Functional authority.   The functional concept, which was developed by Frederick W. Taylor, the father of "scientific management," was initially less appealing than the line-staff concept. Now functional authority is emerging as one of the important forms of authority. It is felt that in the near future it might be the dominant form in personnel relations.

Functional authority is the right given to staff personnel to demand compliance with methods, procedures, policies, and timing of one specialized function of the organization. It is found in areas requiring special knowledge, such as accounting, personnel, and research. The responsible executives have authority over *how* and *when* the special function will be performed, regardless of

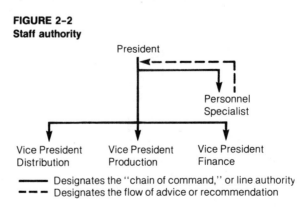

FIGURE 2-2
Staff authority

Designates the "chain of command," or line authority
Designates the flow of advice or recommendation

where it is performed in the organization. They have the authority to tell other operating and staff managers not under their command how that activity is to be performed. A workable definition of *functional authority,* as it applies to personnel, is *the right of personnel managers to use limited line authority over a personnel function that is part of the duties of other executives who are not normally subordinate to them.* Figure 2–3 shows how this relationship works.

Possibility of conflict. The major criticism of this system is that it tends to disregard the *unity-of-command principle.* This principle states that every activity must have a manager with complete authority and responsibility for its achievement. And yet there is no real violation of the unity-of-command principle in the use of functional authority.

In addition to having authority over policy decisions and procedural questions, the users of functional authority frequently have authority over other matters. In real life, we usually have many superiors. This is true in the home, at school, and on the job. Many people tell us what to do.

A study of 71 firms found the problem of possible line-staff conflict to be small. Personnel managers spent around 90 percent of their time on activities such as supervising subordinates, planning activities, and gathering and providing information. Only 10 percent of their time was left to exercise control over the personnel actions of other managers or departments.

FIGURE 2–3
Functional authority

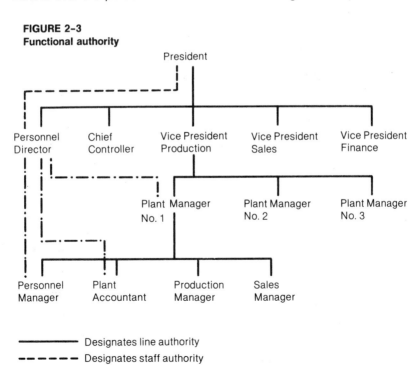

─────────── Designates line authority

▬ ▬ ▬ ▬ ▬ Designates staff authority

▬ · ▬ · ▬ · Designates functional authority over how and when
a given function will be performed

Top-level personnel managers perceived the conflict between them and line managers as low. There was general agreement that personnel managers should have a stronger role in organizational decision making. Yet the personnel managers' desires were stronger than the line managers'. This indicates that there is potential conflict in this area.[6]

Some Ways of Organizing Personnel Departments

Behavioral scientists have adopted the contingency approach to organization structure. In essence, the *contingency approach* says: *There is no one best form of organization, but if certain changes occur that affect the size of the organization or the type of employee, then its structure should change accordingly.*

That is the approach to organizing the personnel department followed by the more progressive managers. Here are several concepts, with examples, of what might happen to the organization of personnel departments if certain things happen. The concepts are based on the assumption that *the performance of the personnel function varies according to the type and size of the organization.*

First, personnel management *in small groups,* especially in service-type institutions, tends to be spontaneous and flexible.

Figure 2-4 illustrates a *typical* personnel department in a small manufacturing firm. The following case shows how personnel is organized in a small service-type institution:

A nursing home with around 50 rooms has about 70-75 professional and other employees. The personnel function is performed by the assistant administrator, who also carries the title "personnel manager." She does the personnel planning, recruiting (including putting ads in the papers and contacting employment agencies), interviewing, hiring, and orienting of

FIGURE 2-4
Organizational chart for the personnel department of a manufacturing corporation with 300 employees

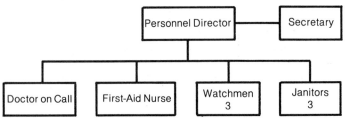

Source: The Bureau of National Affairs, Inc., *The Personnel Department*, Personnel Policies Forum Survey no. 92 (Washington, D.C.: Bureau of National Affairs, 1970), p. 17.

---

[6]James A. Belasco and Joseph A. Alutto, "Line-Staff Conflicts: Some Empirical Insights," *Academy of Management Journal* 12 (1969):469-77.

new workers. The personnel manager arranges rates of pay and holidays and vacations. She handles complaints and does other activities. The paperwork involving payroll, reports to government agencies, and other clerical details is handled by a computer service.

Second, with increasing organization size and numbers of employees, and where the operations must be cost effective, personnel management tends to become more difficult. It requires well-defined objectives, policies, procedures, rules, and regulations. Therefore, the problem for personnel managers is to achieve the advantages of size without reducing productive capacities and satisfactions.

A typical personnel department in a medium-sized, nonmanufacturing firm is shown in Figure 2–5. The following case shows how personnel work is performed in a medium-sized service firm:

In a medium-sized government office, the personnel administrator reports directly to the administrator. She is advised by a committee composed of the personnel manager of a local chemical plant, a professor of personnel management, an insurance agent, the owner of a small marketing firm, and a physician. She is responsible for setting objectives, establishing personnel programs, and handling the technical aspects of the personnel function. In turn, she has a training director, an employment director, a manager for a child-care center, and four other people reporting directly to her.

Third, in larger, more complex operations, the organization structure becomes much more extensive and specialized (see Figure 2–6).

In summary, the "best" organizational structure for a personnel department depends on (1) the size of the organization, (2) the type of industry involved, (3) the complexity of operations, (4) the importance assigned to

FIGURE 2–5
Organizational chart of the employee relations department of a nonmanufacturing corporation with 1,000 employees

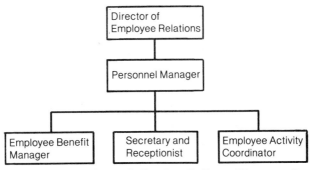

Source: The Bureau of National Affairs, Inc., *The Personnel Department*, Personnel Policies Forum Survey no. 92 (Washington, D.C.: Bureau of National Affairs, 1970), p. 17.

FIGURE 2-6
Xerox Corporation's Information Group personnel organization

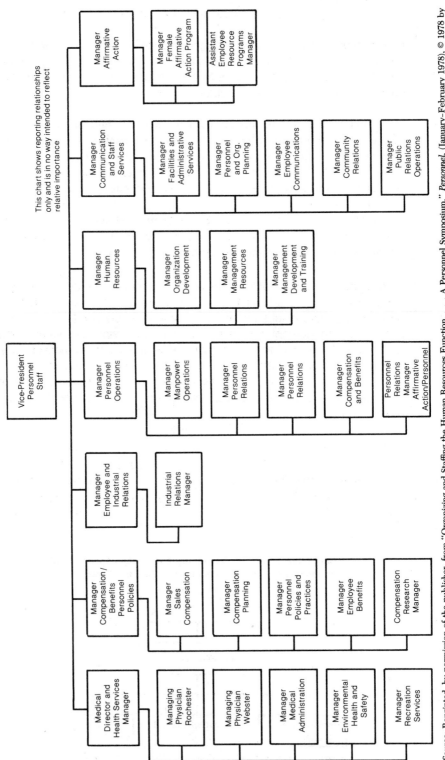

This chart shows reporting relationships only and is in no way intended to reflect relative importance

Source: Reprinted, by permission of the publisher, from "Organizing and Staffing the Human Resources Function. . . . A Personnel Symposium," *Personnel*, (January–February 1978), © 1978 by AMACOM, a division of American Management Associations, p. 18. All rights reserved.

efficiency, and (5) management's belief in the importance of the personnel function.

SUMMARY AND CONCLUSIONS

An effective personnel program is an integrated system. All elements in the external environment influence the performance of the personnel functions, either directly or indirectly.

The internal environment determines (1) the *inputs* (planning, recruiting, selecting, training, and developing people), (2) the *processes* (leading, communicating, motivating, appraising, evaluating, rewarding, and maintaining people in their job performance), and (3) the *outputs* (personal satisfaction, goods, and services).

An effective personnel program should include the following functions:

1. Identify organizational objectives.
2. Set up an effective organization.
3. Study the external and internal environments.
4. Plan for, recruit, select, and develop capable people.
5. Maximize employee performance.
6. Compensate employees.
7. Deal with unions and employee associations.
8. Perform many specific creative activities.
9. Set up procedures for evaluating the performance of the personnel function.

Personnel management is a shared responsibility, as follows:

1. *Top management* sets personnel objectives and policies and does long-range planning and organizing.
2. *Middle management* controls the operating procedures needed to achieve objectives and carries out the policies of top management.
3. *First-line supervisors* interpret the personnel policies to the employees, adjust grievances, influence attitudes, direct work, and, in turn, interpret the employees' interests to higher management levels.
4. *Personnel managers* assist all of them by providing expert advice and guidance.

Personnel managers use (1) *staff authority,* which is the right to give advice and guidance to one's immediate superior and to recommend how suggestions should be put into action, and (2) *functional authority,* which is the right of personnel managers to use limited line authority over a personnel function that is part of the duties of other executives who are not normally subordinate to them.

The type and size of organization influences how its personnel department is organized:

1. Personnel management in small groups, especially in service-type institutions, tends to be spontaneous and flexible.

2. With increasing organization size and increasing numbers of employees, and where the operations must be cost-effective, personnel management tends to become more difficult and to require well-defined objectives, policies, procedures, rules, and regulations.
3. In larger, multiplant operations, the organization structure becomes much more complex and specialized.

QUESTIONS

1. Do you think that personnel management is really an integrated system? Explain your answer.
2. How do the major functions of personnel management relate to each other?
3. Who should be responsible for performing the personnel functions? What are the relationships between the responsibilities of each of them?
4. What kinds of authority should personnel managers have in performing their responsibilities?
5. What effects do size, number of employees, and type of industry have on the organization of a personnel department?

PROBLEM

The Division Chiefs' Rebellion*

Bill spent his first week reviewing the varied aspects of the department's work. He met with each of the division chiefs to discuss their areas of work and some of their personnel problems. Bill soon found that there were strong political feelings influencing promotions into the higher levels of the department.

Some of the personnel folders that had been checked out of the accounting department's files by some of the division chiefs had not been returned for centralized filing in Bill's files. He requested that the folders be returned. Most of the chiefs felt that Bill was trying to undermine their authority and refused to return them. At Bill's request, Mr. Hicks told the division chiefs that Bill was in charge of personnel records, and the folders should be returned immediately. Bill got the folders back, but the division chiefs appeared to avoid him afterward.

A year later, the state Civil Service began its usual audit of the department. Following a briefing session, the Civil Service auditor asked for appointments with the division chiefs. Bill told her that he doubted that several of them

---

*See the case at the beginning of the chapter for earlier details.

would be available, as they were seldom in their offices. This sounded to the auditor as if these people were figureheads who were on the department's payroll without any formal duties. In fact, they were out traveling through the state most of the time. When they found out what Bill had said, the chiefs angrily complained to Mr. Hicks, who severely reprimanded Bill.

Bill resigned the next week. Mr. Hicks abolished the personnel office and assigned its duties to a lawyer in the newly created legal division.

Questions

1. How can you explain the problems of the personnel officer?
2. What would you have done differently if you had been Bill? Mr. Hicks?
3. Would you have abolished the personnel office? Explain your answer.

SUGGESTED READINGS FOR FURTHER STUDY

Anthony, William P., and Edward A. Nicholson. *Management of Human Resources: A Systems Approach to Personnel Management.* Columbus, Ohio: Grid Publishing Co., 1977.

Brewer, Richard. "Personnel's Role in Participation." *Personnel Management* 10 (September 1978):27–29.

Conference Board, Inc. *Monitoring the Human Resource System.* New York: Conference Board, 1977.

Desatnick, Robert, and Margo Bennett. *Human Resource Management in the Multinational Company.* New York: Nichols Publishing Co., 1978.

Foulkes, F. K., and H. M. Morgan. "Organizing and Staffing the Personnel Function." *Harvard Business Review* 55 (May–June 1977):142–54.

Greene, Walter E. "Visible Management Planning." *Personnel Administrator* 22 (January 1977):35–37.

Harschnek, Robert A., Jr., Donald J. Petersen, and Robert L. Malone. "Which Personnel Department Is Right for You?" *Personnel Administrator* 23 (April 1978):58–60.

Henderson, J. A. "What the Chief Executive Expects of the Personnel Function." *Personnel Administrator* 22 (May 1977):40–45.

Janger, Allen R. *The Personnel Function: Changing Objectives and Organization.* Conference Board Report no. 712. New York: Conference Board, 1977.

The Personnel Management Function—Organization, Staffing and Evaluation. Personnel Bibliography Series, no. 91. Washington, D.C.: U.S. Civil Service Commission Library, 1977.

Schein, Edgar H. *Human Resource Planning and Development: A Total System.* Boston: Massachusetts Institute of Technology, A. P. Sloan School of Management, 1978.

Seamans, Lyman H., Jr. "Establishing the Human Resource System Data Base." *Personnel Administrator* 22 (November 1977):44–49.

CHAPTER THREE

The Evolution of a New Work Force

Learning Objectives

After studying the material in this chapter, you should be able to:

1. Explain why you need to study the evolution of personnel management.
2. Describe how selected historical periods have changed the environment in which personnel management occurs.
3. Explain how this new environment has led to technological developments that have caused human resources to be more important.
4. Explain why the work force has expanded and is expected to continue expanding.
5. Describe the new types of jobs being performed.
6. Describe the new types of workers being managed.

Some Important Words and Terms

Guild system	Baby boom
Industrial Revolution	Great American dream
Scientific management	Equal employment opportunity (EEO)
Hawthorne experiments	Affirmative action programs (AAPs)
Fringe (employee) benefits	Social responsibility
GI Bill	Employment ratio

Presently the younger generation will come knocking at my door.
HENRIK IBSEN, *The Master Builder*

Only the fullest use of today's technology will see us through this century, and only the discovery of new technology will stave off disaster beyond that.
The Quiet Revolution

Outline of the Chapter

Shortly after World War II ended, two veterans used the GI Bill to establish a small plumbing firm. They hired several craftsmen to do plumbing, heating, and wiring of both residential and commercial buildings. Their business grew steadily until the beginning of the Korean conflict in 1950. Then the demand for their services increased rapidly, but they could not keep up with the demand because of the shortage of workers.

As they were unable to recruit trained craftsmen, they started their own training program. This worked well until the mid-1960s. Then many of the people they had trained left them, for they preferred the easier work, better benefits, and greater security offered by the larger firms and government jobs in the area. It was hard to attract new trainees, as they did not like the "dirty working conditions" and "degrading jobs."

In the mid-1970s, the firm finally abandoned its service activities and became a supplier of equipment and supplies.

This case shows some of the lessons that can be learned from a study of the evolution of today's new work force. It also shows why the personnel management job is now more difficult—despite improvements in its role and position.

The computer system in the United States now employs about 5 million people to operate and service around half a million computers.

According to the 1979 *Employment and Training Report of the President,* 60 percent of the growth in employment in the United States in 1978 was caused by 1.9 million adult women entering the work force. Employment of adult men increased by only 1.3 million.

These facts indicate the new types of jobs and employees that have evolved in the United States. These employees now provide personnel managers with many of their opportunities and challenges.

WHY STUDY THE EVOLUTION OF PERSONNEL MANAGEMENT?

As shown in Chapter 1, personnel managers are now very important in their organizations. And there are now new types of jobs and employees to be dealt with. In order to do this most effectively, you—as a future personnel manager—need to understand the changes that have led to the development of personnel management and the new work force.

By studying what has happened in the past, you should be better prepared to be an effective personnel manager in the future. You will understand the management of human resources better if you understand the following premises:

1. The environment has a direct influence on human behavior and job performance, but the effect may be either positive or negative.
2. Today's work environment is very different from yesterday's.

3. The environment in which you will work as managers will be very different from and more difficult than today's environment.
4. The future environment is now being shaped by the events you have seen and are now seeing.

Thus the future performance of the personnel function can be made more effective by studying its historical background. A short historical review will help you and other managers avoid repeating past mistakes.

THE EVOLUTION OF PERSONNEL MANAGEMENT

Although personnel management as a field of study is relatively new, many of the ideas and practices upon which its current theory is based began long ago. For example, the minimum wage rate and incentive wage plans were included in the Babylonian Code of Hammurabi around 1800 B.C. The Chinese had originated the principle of division of labor (specialization) as early as 1650 B.C., and they understood the effects of labor turnover by 400 B.C. The Chaldeans were using incentive wage plans by around 400 B.C.

Personnel management did not evolve in one smooth movement. Instead, there were times when development progressed rapidly, primarily because of external forces. And personnel managers have usually followed, not led, in making these changes. It is suggested that personnel people should (1) anticipate problems and new developments affecting human resources and (2) assume positive leadership in managing these resources.[1]

Origins of Personnel Management

Personnel management really began with the guild system that developed in the towns and cities of Europe and with the Industrial Revolution that followed.

The guild system. The development of crude manufacturing forced laborers from their homes, where they were self-sufficient, to the cities, where they were not. This movement led to the *guild system.* There were clear-cut distinctions between the master craftsmen, the journeymen, and the apprentices. The *masters* were the owners of the shops that employed the traveling *journeymen,* who were applying their learning in order to become skilled. *Apprentices* were young learners who usually worked for their board, lodging, and a small allowance. During the initial stages of the system, all three classes of workers were a closely knit social group. Their success depended on their working together.

Personnel management actually began during this period, as the system

---

[1]See Edward J. Giblin, "The Evolution of Personnel," *Human Resource Management* 17 (Fall 1978):25–30, for further details.

involved selecting, training, developing, rewarding, and maintaining workers.
Wage and salary administration and collective bargaining over wages and
working conditions were much in evidence under this system.

The Industrial Revolution.   The *Industrial Revolution* evolved from the
guild system. Changes in manufacturing were required by a new economic
doctrine and by the invention of new tools, processes, and machines. The
economic doctrine was based on the French concept of *laissez faire, laissez
passer*,[2] which was the beginning of the free enterprise system.

The material benefits of the Industrial Revolution were great, and people's
standard of living increased. Yet there was a price to pay for the benefits.
Workers were crowded into a work environment with many machines in
small, dingy, dirty factories. Many psychological problems resulted from over-
long working hours, monotony, fatigue, noise, strain, and the ever-present
danger of accidents.

A gap opened between the owners and the employees, and it was impossible to maintain the personal bond that had existed before. The new machines
made it practical to employ women and very young children to replace men.

"Father of personnel management".   One man emerged as the father of
modern personnel management. Robert Owen, a Scottish mill owner, believed that environment influenced the growth and performance of workers.
In order to increase workers' output, their environment should be improved
to provide better living and working conditions.

Owen organized model villages next to his cotton mills. He introduced
shower baths and toilets in the factories. Factories were cleaned and painted
and had windows for light and ventilation. Day schools for children and night
schools for older workers were set up. He raised the minimum age for employing children to 11 years and shortened their work day to ten hours. Later,
he abolished child labor entirely.

Unfortunately for the development of personnel management, Owen's re-
forms were abandoned after his death.

Effects on personnel management.   The events of that period which are
still influencing personnel are: (1) the change in the method of production
from manual to machine operations, and (2) the separation of owners, managers, and their employees began.

Personnel Management in the American Colonies

Many of the forces of early colonial life exerted an important influence on
economic, cultural, social, religious, and political aspects of our lives. They
continue to strongly influence personnel management.

What happened.   The Industrial Revolution did not occur in the United
States at the same time as in Europe. The colonies were in a primitive stage of

---

[2]The term meant that people should be permitted to produce or sell what they pleased and
to go where they wished.

Courtesy of Bettman Archive

agriculture, industry, and commerce. About nine out of ten colonists earned their living by farming. As land was plentiful and available to anyone with the initiative and energy to clear and use it, economic growth was stimulated. Capital was scarce, but *labor was the scarcest of the productive factors.* As is true in such economic situations, the scarcest resource carried the highest price, and labor was more valuable than either land or capital.

Industrial development was slow in the colonies, but beginning with the revolutionary war—and especially after the War of 1812—there was an increasing emphasis on industrial development rather than agricultural. As capital began to accumulate and the industrial system grew, there was an increased need for labor. This need was met by an expanding population, resulting from a high birthrate and increased immigration.

Effects on personnel management.   The main effect on personnel was the recognition of the importance of human resources. Since workers were scarce, they were in a superior position, so employers invested in land and capital in order to improve and conserve the output of labor.

The Period of Industrialization

The events that began in 1861 had a great effect on personnel. First, the Civil War assured that this country would have a strong central government. Second, it followed that business firms and labor unions would also be large and powerful.

What happened.   The period between the Civil War and World War I saw an expansion in all aspects of life. There was a rapid movement to the West, with a resulting growth in population and transportation. New industries, such as mining, ranching, and communications, sprang up. Also, commerce and industry emerged and led the United States to become the world's greatest industrial power.

The corporate form of organization began to replace the proprietor and/or partnership type of ownership. This led to a further widening of the gap between the workers and owners. However, because big business began to dominate and exploit consumers and workers, Congress passed the *Sherman Antitrust Act* in 1890. The act limited the power of owners and managers. It is still the basic law regulating management's activities.

Although labor unions had been active since the 1780s, they had little success until this period. The American Federation of Labor (AFL) was organized in 1881 and reorganized in 1886. It was the leading labor organization until 1955, when it merged with the Congress of Industrial Organizations (CIO). By 1913, labor was so powerful that it was granted its own separate place in the president's cabinet, the Department of Labor. The following year, the *Clayton Act* exempted labor unions from prosecution under the *Sherman Antitrust Act*.

In 1881, Frederick W. Taylor began the studies that resulted in the principles of *scientific management*. These principles were: (1) determine the best way to do each job, (2) select the best people, (3) train them to do the job effectively, and (4) reward them with financial incentives. These are still the concepts upon which the effective use of human resources is based.

When workmen's compensation laws were passed in the early 1900s, safety personnel were hired to protect workers. These people soon branched out into other personnel fields.

Effects on personnel management.   The two main effects on personnel were: (1) manufacturing replaced agriculture, forestry, mining, and fishing as the main source of employment, and (2) a strong central government, the corporate form of business, and strong national labor unions became accepted.

World War I and the "Roaring Twenties"

The period from 1914, when World War I began in Europe, until 1929 saw the development of modern personnel management. The long-term effects on the personnel function cannot be overemphasized.

What happened.   The first significant effect of the war was an increase in the demand for labor that far exceeded the available supply. Part of the demand was met by the million or more women who entered the labor force at that time. Many of them never left it. By 1920, women accounted for 21 percent of the labor force.

Personnel departments set up in plants manufacturing war supplies gave a great boost to improving personnel management. The Committee on Classification of Personnel was set up in the U.S. Army. This led to the use of job analysis, job specifications, testing, interviewing, and rating systems.

Labor turnover and mobility became significant factors. For the first time, large numbers of employees were uprooted from their jobs and homes and shown new opportunities for jobs and living. Labor stability has never been the same since! Later, the popularity of the automobile, which was made possible by Henry Ford's use of the assembly line technique and interchangeable parts, added to this mobility. The lessons of the Industrial Revolution and Taylor's principles of management were blended to become the foundation of the tremendous productive capacity of World War II.

The position of workers and the unions that represented them improved. Labor leaders were appointed to most of the boards and committees that were established.

The 1920s was a period of sustained prosperity. Total production increased twice as fast as the population and output per employee increased by the same amount. Prices remained relatively stable while the cost of production declined. Real wages increased.

From 1924 to 1932, the *Hawthorne experiments* began the behavioral science movement. The effects of changes in the physical environment led to studies of psychological and social effects of groups. It was concluded that organizations are social systems, as shown in Figure 3-1.

Employee-management cooperation, through worker representation plans, was used to increase production, adjust grievances, and improve the material and social well-being of workers. While new personnel policies and the new approach to human administration were adopted by the more enlightened employers, it should not be assumed that all managers followed this approach.

The foundation for the human relations movement was laid, for both management and labor realized that individual employees were really important.

Effects on personnel management.   The effects of this period on personnel were: (1) improved role of unions, (2) mobility of labor, including the migration from rural to urban areas (except for the reverse migration of the 1930s, this movement has continued until today), (3) entry of women into the industrial work force, and (4) a changing lifestyle, especially the love affair between the American people and the automobile.

The Great Depression

The period of "perpetual prosperity" ended on October 29, 1929, when stock prices plunged 40 points to usher in the Great Depression.[3] The events that followed are still influencing personnel management.

What happened.   In 1933, a new administration headed by Franklin D. Roosevelt began passing laws affecting all aspects of business, including personnel management. For example, the *National Labor Relations Act* (NLRA) made collective bargaining compulsory for the employer and significantly increased union membership. The *Social Security Act* provided unemployment insurance, old-age pensions, and disability and death benefits. The *Fair Labor*

---

[3]If you would like a better understanding of this period and its continued effect upon your life, read Gordon Thomas and Max Morgan-Witts, *The Day the Bubble Burst: A Social History of the Wall Street Crash of 1929* (New York: Doubleday, 1979).

FIGURE 3-1
The organization as a social system

Photo courtesy of Western Electric Photographic Services

In the world-famous book about the Hawthorne Studies, *Management and the Worker,* Theresa Layman Zajac, center in both photos, was described as "Operator Number Three." She was 16 when the renowned Relay Assembly Test Room experiment began. Almost everything is different at today's Hawthorne Works but Relay Assembly—and Theresa's enthusiasm—continued in 1974.

Standards Act regulated the minimum wage and the maximum hours of work for employees.

Probably the most significant event of the period, however, was the Supreme Court's decision in *National Labor Relations Board* v. *Jones and Laughlin Steel Corporation* (1937). The Court declared that the NLRA was constitutional, and that manufacturing within a state was included in the "interstate commerce clause" of the Constitution. As a result, the government was in a position to become more involved in personnel management activities.

In spite of the laws, union activities, and other efforts, unemployment was still a problem. The number of unemployed persons declined from 13 million (about 25 percent of the total labor force) in 1933 to 9 million (about 17 percent) in 1939. Still, the unemployment problem was not solved until World War II began in Europe.

Effects on personnel management.   The main effects of this period on personnel were: (1) people became more interested in personal and job security, (2) collective bargaining replaced individual bargaining between the workers and management, (3) employee's "right" to jobs took priority over the owner's right to property, and (4) an abnormally low birthrate led to a shortage of workers in the 1950s and 1960s. These changes led to an emphasis on newer management philosophies and styles.

World War II and the "Fabulous Fifties"

Not only did World War II revolutionize the political and social worlds. It also greatly altered personnel management by modifying the work force and the work environment.[4]

What happened.   Many jobs associated with the war effort were in highly technical fields, such as optics, electronics, and aeronautics. New skills and techniques were needed to fill these jobs with employees of new types and to motivate them to greater productivity. Industrial psychology, industrial sociology, cultural anthropology, and operations research were extensively used. These efforts greatly improved the practice of personnel management.

Although wages and prices were legally controlled, the law of supply and demand was still at work. Employers could not use wage increases to attract workers. Instead, they offered *fringe benefits* (now called *employee benefits*), such as free meals, transportation, work clothes, and housing, as well as paid time off for reasons such as meals and coffee breaks, sick leave, holidays, and vacations.

The *electronic computer* was developed to help us acquire and use knowledge. But it also modified personnel management by changing ways of work-

---

[4]See "40 Years Later: World War II's Impact on Mankind," *U.S. News & World Report*, September 10, 1979, pp. 65-71, for a discussion of this period and its effects today.

ing, organizational structures, the types of employee needed, and the method of attracting employees.

In order to reduce the effects of an increasing supply of workers relative to a declining demand at the end of the war, Congress passed the *Servicemen's Readjustment Act* of 1944. This *GI bill* provided returning veterans with free training and educational opportunities and low-interest loans to buy houses and go into business. The resulting increase in the quantity and quality of knowledge made it possible to develop and expand technologically oriented industries. It also increased the number of technical and professional jobs.

The *increased education of women* between 1940 and 1950 led to their economic independence and increased participation in the work force.

No discussion of this period would be complete without a discussion of the *baby boom* beginning in 1946. At about the same time, Dr. Spock was writing his baby book. Many young and inexperienced parents interpreted it as advising them to give children what they wanted so they would not feel rejected. Some people feel that the large number of children, changed parental attitudes, and the affluence of the young people led to the "new breed" of workers now entering management positions.

Entirely new industries and changes in old ones modified industrial and occupational patterns. Air conditioning, synthetic fibers, frozen food and drinks, prepackaged foods, "wonder drugs," miniaturization, electronics, and other industries increased the demand for—and the requirements of—employees with higher level skills and knowledge. Single-family homes were mass produced rather than constructed individually. Later, single-family dwellings gave way to apartments, townhouses, and condominiums.

After the Korean conflict (1950-53), there was a quiet period of peace and prosperity that was unique in recent history. During the "Fabulous Fifties," television began to supplant movies and radio as a means of entertainment—and a source of employment.

Some of the factors during this period that changed the work environment and the work force were: (1) the interstate highway system, which led to the tremendous production and use of automobiles and encouraged the leisure industry, (2) the *great American dream*, according to which, if you obtained an education, especially a college degree, your future was assured, (3) the aerospace industry, resulting from—and leading to—the expansion of scientific and technical knowledge and the beginning of whole new industries, (4) increased education at all levels and in all fields, and (5) the declining birthrate, beginning in 1957, which is now reducing the growth in the work force.[5]

These factors and others—such as affluence—led to "unwarranted expectations" on the part of young people, blacks, and women, and to their belief that utopia had arrived. This, in turn, resulted in the shock, disillusionment, agitation, upheavals, and convulsions of the 1960s and early 1970s.

---

[5]The birthrate has been declining since 1800, except for the 1947-57 period. There were 3.76 children per woman in 1957, but only 1.75 in 1976. This will lead to tight labor markets in the late 1980s, because "the generation arriving at working age is smaller, thus providing fewer workers." *The Wall Street Journal,* April 10, 1979, p. 1.

FIGURE 3-2
White-collar and service jobs increasing, but blue-collar and farm jobs declining

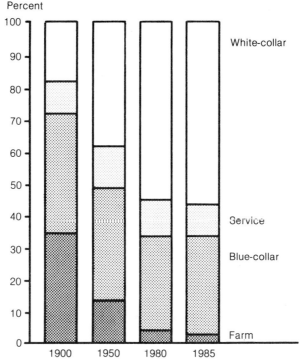

Source: "The U.S. Economy in 1980: A Preview of BLS Projections," *Monthly Labor Review*, April 1970; and *Employment and Training Report of the President* (Washington, D.C.: Government Printing Office, 1979).

Effects on personnel management. The effects on personnel were: (1) increasing importance of the computer, (2) new technology and education creating new industries, which required new and higher level occupations, (3) emphasis on employee benefits, and (4) the continuing shift from agriculture and blue-collar employment to service and white-collar jobs (see Figure 3-2).

The Period of Activism

The period from the early 1960s to the present can be characterized as one of *activism*.

Movements during the period. There were several streams of activity, or *movements*, running through this period. They have drastically and unalterably changed the performance of personnel management.

Equal employment opportunities. An early movement was the "civil rights" theme, or *equal employment opportunities* (EEO) for minorities and poverty groups. It began with Executive Order 10925 in 1961. The women's liberation movement also greatly improved the position of female workers. Later, *affirmative action programs* (AAPs) were also required for older and handicapped workers and for veterans. These movements helped these groups in all aspects of economic activity, especially in hiring, training, and promotion to managerial positions.

Unionization of public, professional, and farm personnel. Another movement was the unionization of government, professional, and farm employees. This trend began with Executive Order 10988 in 1962. It was followed by executive orders and state and federal legislation so that public employee unions are the fastest growing unions.

Technological development. The race to the moon started by Kennedy in 1961 and achieved under Nixon in 1969 greatly increased employment, especially in higher level jobs. Also, whole new industries resulted from space technology.

Help for poverty groups. The "war on poverty" begun by Johnson in 1965 has resulted in the ability of many individuals and families to survive without being in the work force. This phenomenon led to an increase in jobs related to public and private welfare activities. It also resulted in more purchases of goods and services by this group. This then increased the demand for other workers.

Youth movement. The teen-age culture developed during this time. The younger generation emphasized (1) their rights and privileges, (2) the purchasing power of the group, which opened up mass markets for new products and services, and (3) countercultures, which rebelled against their parents' generation, the Establishment, and prevalent lifestyles.

Social responsibility. Finally, the growth of advocacy groups in the areas of ecology, safety, consumerism, and employment of minority groups vitally influenced the personnel function. It caused employers to be more aware of their *social responsibility* to these groups and society in general.

Effects on personnel management. It is hard to isolate the effects of this period on management, the work environment, and the work force, as we are too near it to be objective. However, the following trends are evident: (1) technological developments are making human resources more important, (2) there are new types of job to be performed, and (3) there are new types of workers to manage.

TECHNOLOGICAL DEVELOPMENTS ARE MAKING HUMAN RESOURCES MORE IMPORTANT

Technological developments are still occurring, especially in the areas of ecology, health and safety, and automation. Yet, as our economy is based on technical and service industries, the human resources are becoming ever more important. Let us see how these developments and new jobs are increasing the value of human resources.

FIGURE 3-3
Innovative automation: A mechanical "mailboy" makes its rounds

Source: "Blue-Collar Robots," *Newsweek,* April 23, 1979, pp. 80-81.

Jobs Are Becoming More Technological

In the past, technological growth has created jobs. However, it now appears that machines may be capable of replacing people in some work situations. Almost entirely automatic systems are being used in producing goods—and services (see Figure 3-3).[6] Personnel people must deal with both the favorable and unfavorable results of these developments.

Favorable results. Some of the favorable results of technology are higher output, greater employment, and a general upgrading of jobs.

---

[6]Japan has 13,000 of the world's 17,500 industrial robots, while the United States has only 2,500, says one expert. Japan has 70 firms making robots (to 27 in the U.S.) and a $50 million research program to produce "completely unmanned, robot-operated factories." *The Wall Street Journal,* March 4, 1980, p. 1.

Technological progress has *increased production*, cut costs, improved service, generated new products, and improved quality.

For example, in the industrialized countries, productivity has averaged an increase of about 3 percent per year during the last 25 years. In Japan, the increase has been 15 percent.

Actual unemployment as a result of automation is not common; *increased employment* is the rule. For example, despite the rapid movement toward office mechanization, there is little evidence that any substantial number of workers have been thrown out of jobs.

The Stanford Research Institute found that when seven firms automated, some workers were transferred within the same firm, some retired, but no one was laid off.[7]

In general, there is an *upgrading of jobs* and a decrease in the number of unskilled, routine jobs. Employees are used more effectively, for the machines do more of the boring and tedious work. Employees should be able to do more interesting and creative work.

The *Dictionary of Occupational Titles* listed around 17,000 jobs when it was first published in 1939. Since then, it has added over 18,000 new job titles, mostly in new fields, such as computers, electronics, and space travel.

Unfavorable results.   Among the negative results of these changes are job displacement and strained group feelings. Many *employees* who might have been able to perform the more technically advanced jobs *have been displaced.* They were not physically, mentally, educationally, or emotionally able to adapt to the new type of work.

Group feelings are strained by technological changes. There is less interaction between people when many machines run by people are replaced with one—or a few—large unit(s) run by another machine. The social system is disturbed by these developments.

Human Resources Are Becoming More Important

It is well known that just having enough physical and financial resources does not make an organization successful. Instead, an adequate supply of human resources—in the form of well-educated, trained, developed, and motivated people—is needed.

---

[7]See U.S. Department of Labor, *Management Decisions to Automate,* Manpower/Automation Research Monograph no. 3 (Washington, D.C.:Government Printing Office, 1965), p. 7, for these and other results of automating.

In 1970, a firm that sold to the military had excess capacity and workers at the end of the Vietnam War. It greatly cut its work force, laying off many skilled and experienced craftsmen and technicians. When the recession was over in early 1972, its demand quickly increased. But it had to turn down orders, as it could not find able people to replace those it had let go. Most of them had taken other jobs.

Thus, as human resources account for such a large proportion of economic output, there is much room for increasing productivity through the intelligent use of these resources.

Need to conserve human resources.   The material in this book is based on the assumption that *the main goal of any organization is to use its human resources to the greatest extent feasible in order to achieve its goals.* Another assumption is that *the effectiveness of an organization is determined by the caliber of its human resources.* This thought is well expressed in the following example:

A hurricane severely damaged a luxury hotel. The owner said, "I'm glad it destroyed just our buildings. We can rebuild them in less than a year. But it would take us from three to five years to rebuild our staff."

Need for interaction of resources.   A word of caution is needed at this point. While human resources are quite important, output results from the interaction of human resources with financial and physical factors and technology.

It is not a question of machines *or* workers, for they need each other. The use of machines tends to make difficult jobs easier and impossible jobs possible. People work best on jobs with just the right amount of difficulty. If a job is too easy, they become bored. If it is too difficult, they become fatigued, discouraged, and frustrated to the point of quitting.

Machines are needed to produce goods.   People are becoming less important in the direct production of goods. Capital—in the form of technology, machines, tools, and automation—is the main productive factor in that area. Machines can often produce goods better, faster, and at a lower cost. When production is predictable and controllable, and when uniform output is required, a machine system is probably better than manual operations.

People are needed for flexibility and creativity.   However, automated systems tend to be inflexible. Therefore, if flexibility is desired, or if the job is critical, manual operations or human support for the machine is needed. So, until machines are more nearly perfect than at present, when creativity or flexibility is needed, or a vital decision must be made, some member of the human race will still be needed.

A firm in Los Angeles installed a computer to take care of accounting details and financial analyses. When there was a severe breakdown of the computer, the firm had to hire 11 people to do its work. A newspaper

"We've decided to rehire you—the machine we bought to replace you won't work either."

Reprinted by permission *The Wall Street Journal*

People are still important!

headline read: "Computer Has 'Nervous Breakdown'/Replaced by 11 People."

While many lower level skills are disappearing, the demand for skilled, creative, and responsible workers is increasing. While a relatively few scientific, technical, professional, and managerial personnel are bringing about increased productivity through their creative efforts, *there has been a shift in the use of human resources from producing goods to performing services.*

EMPLOYMENT IS INCREASING AND CHANGING IN NATURE

There have been three significant changes in employment in the last three decades in the United States. First, the proportion of adults working is the greatest on record. Second, the proportion of workers producing goods has decreased relative to those performing services. Third, the proportion of blue-collar workers has declined relative to white-collar employees. Also, technical and professional jobs have multiplied.

Greater Proportion of Adults Working

In 1978, the *employment ratio*—the percentage of 16-year-and-over citizens holding jobs—reached 58 percent, the highest on record (see Figure 3-4). This trend is expected to continue.

FIGURE 3–4
Employment ratio (over two decades)

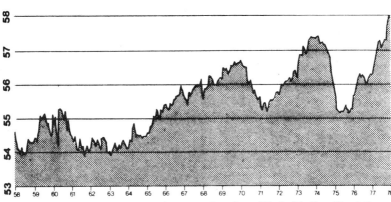

Source: Alfred L. Malabre, Jr., "More and More People Seek—and Find—Jobs Even Though Unemployment Rate Stays High," *The Wall Street Journal*, January 18, 1978, p. 42.

The Bureau of Labor Statistics estimates that about 16 million new jobs will be created in this decade, as compared to 19 million during the 1970s. The decline results from the lower birthrate.[8] There will be around 47 million job openings, including the new jobs and replacements for those leaving the work force.

Shift from Goods-producing to Service-performing Jobs

There has been a definite shift away from goods-producing to service-performing and government jobs (see Figure 3–5). As you can see from Figure 3–6, this trend is expected to continue until 1990, at least for service and goods-producing employment.

In general, jobs in private households, agriculture, and mining will continue to decline as a percentage of all employment (see Figure 3–6). Manufacturing and government's share of employment will decline slightly. Big gains are expected in office, service, and sales jobs, which will be the biggest employers, with manufacturing and government following.

Shift From Blue-collar to White-Collar and Service Occupations

There has been a marked shift from blue-collar to white-collar jobs, as shown in Figure 3–2. The greatest shift was to technical and professional jobs.

Over half of all jobs are now white-collar positions. These are expected to increase to around 52 percent by 1990. About a third of the jobs are blue-collar, while around 14 percent are service types.

Notice in Figure 3–6 how few people are in agriculture. About 3 percent of the adult work force can now feed the remaining 97 percent of the adults, all

---

[8]*AP* bulletin, December 28, 1979.

FIGURE 3–5
Percentage distribution of total employment (counting jobs rather than workers) for selected years

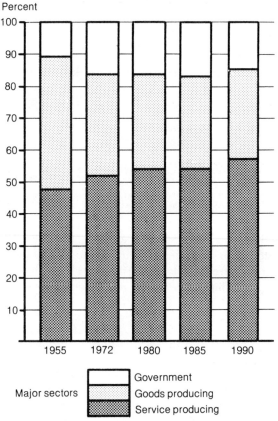

Percent

1955   1972   1980   1985   1990

Major sectors

Government
Goods producing
Service producing

Note: Government includes all federal, state, and local civilian employees. Goods producing includes agriculture, mining, construction, and manufacturing. Service producing includes transportation, communications, public utilities, trade, finance, insurance, real estate, and other services.

Source: *Monthly Labor Review* 96 (December 1973):40; and *Employment and Training Report of the President,* 1979.

the children, and still have food left over to export. This percentage is expected to decline to about 2 percent by 1990 if present trends continue.

Figure 3–7 shows that the leading occupations by 1985 will be (1) clerical workers, (2) professional and technical personnel, (3) operatives, (4) service workers, (5) craft and kindred workers, and (6) managers and administrators.

THERE ARE NEW TYPES OF EMPLOYEE TO MANAGE

If you become a manager, you will have to deal with a "new breed" of employees. It is a very diverse group. A record 41 percent are women, while 10 percent are black. They are younger, as 23 percent are under 25 years old. They are also more affluent. The average worker's real spendable income

FIGURE 3-6
The shift from goods-producing to service-performing jobs is continuing

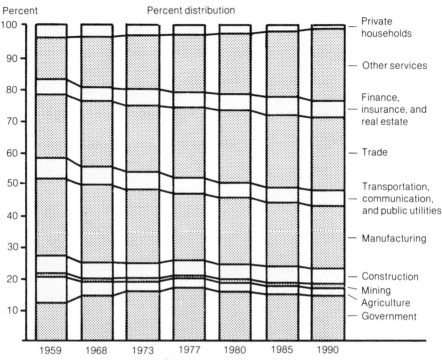

Source: "Industry Output and Employment," *Monthly Labor Review* 102 (April 1979): p. 12.

has risen 9 percent since 1960. Working spouses have raised median family income to a record $17,500. There are now two wage earners in 63 percent of all families.

They are better educated. In 1959, 30 percent of the work force had an elementary education or less. Now this group accounts for only 10 percent. High-school graduates increased from 30 to 40 percent of the work force and college graduates from 10 to 17 percent.

The new workers have more leisure time. Hours of work have declined, and vacations and holidays are more generous. The average office worker gets 10 paid holidays a year, as against 7.8 in 1960.

Workers are more mobile.[9] The typical worker in 1963 kept a job for 4.6 years. Now he or she changes jobs every 3.6 years.

Figure 3-8 shows some examples of these new employees performing services, along with the more traditional employees.

---

[9]See Carl Rosenfeld, "Occupational Mobility During 1977," *Monthly Labor Review* (December 1979):44-48, for a discussion of how age, sex, education, occupation, and other factors influence mobility.

FIGURE 3–7
Total employment by occupational group as a percentage of total employment by selected years, 1975, 1980, 1985

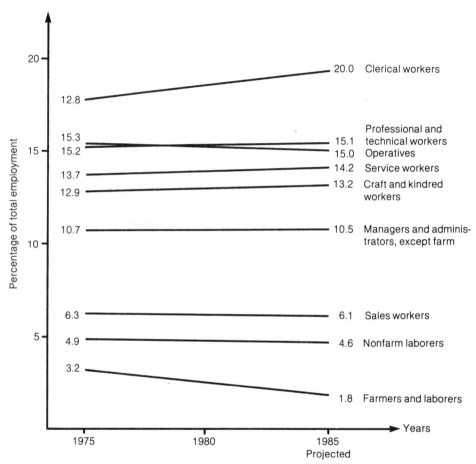

Source: Compiled from *Employment and Training Report of the President* (1979), p. 362, table E-10.

There Are More Younger, Female, and Minority Workers

There are more younger, female, and minority workers in the work force you are entering. They will greatly influence the performance of the personnel function.

There are more younger workers.   The workers are now younger than before. But this is changing. The "baby bust," or decreasing birthrate, which began in the late 1950s, is resulting in an older population, as the average age increased from 26 in 1966 to about 30 in 1980. This trend, along with the increase in the mandatory retirement age to 70, is expected to cause the average age of employees to increase by 1985.

FIGURE 3-8
Examples of the new employees

Source: American Telephone and Telegraph Company, *1977 Annual Report,* cover.

There are more minorities.   The racial mix of today's employees is also changing. The proportion of blacks in the work force increased from around 10 percent in 1970 to around 12 percent in 1980. The real progress, though, was in the improved position of these employees in the technical, professional, and managerial ranks.

There are more women.   You can see the progress made by women by looking at Table 3-1 and Figure 3-9. Notice that only three out of ten employees were female in 1950, but now over four out of ten are. About two out of three new jobs in the late 1970s were filled by women. The number of

FIGURE 3–9
Women's share of jobs is increasing

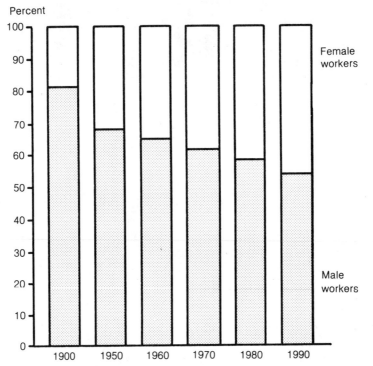

Source: Computed from the *Employment and Training Report of the President* for various years.

women workers aged 25–34 increased over two and one-half times as fast as
men workers the same age from 1966 to 1976.[10]

The jobs women hold are being upgraded. Although women are still concentrated in "women's" jobs, they are beginning to move up into higher level
positions.

An interesting trend to watch is the percentage of adult men and women
who are in the work force. From 1960 to 1979, the percentage for men
declined from about 87 to 80. The percentage of women in the work force
increased from about 38 to 51.

The Workers Are Better Educated

Workers are now better educated than the general public. And those who are
employed are more highly educated than the unemployed.

Direction of the changes.   Around 75 percent of the work force have
completed high school, and about 20 percent have finished four years of

---

[10]"The Effect of Demographic Factors on Age-Earnings Profiles," *Human Resources* 14
(Summer 1979):3.

TABLE 3-1
Working women are increasing their influence in all aspects of work

Year	Number (millions)	Percentage of labor force	Participation rate (percent)	°
1950	18.4	30	34	28
1960	23.2	33	38	39
1970	31.6	37	43	49
1977	40.1	40	48	56
1980	—	42	51	—
1985	50.1	44	55	—
1990	54.4	45	57	—

°Labor force participation rate of working wives with school-aged children.
Source: *U.S. Working Women: A Chartbook* (Washington, D.C.: Government Printing Office, 1975), ch. 2; *Manpower Report of the President* (1975), p. 57; and *Employment and Training Report of the President* (1979), pp. 295, 354, 355, 358.

college. Blacks have increased from 7 percent of all students on college campuses in 1970 to 11 percent.[11] Also, 51 percent of all college students are women.[12]

Figure 3-10 shows that there will be even more educated persons by 1990. Younger, better educated workers are replacing the older, less well-educated ones who are leaving the work force.

Consequences of the changes.   There are several consequences of these changes. First, increased knowledge has *raised the productive capacity of employees* and consequently *increased their earning capacity*. Second, this knowledge has tended to *limit the employment opportunities of the unskilled and the uneducated* and caused them to become unemployable or unpromotable. Third, increased education has led to greater *mobility* and *high turnover*. In the past, the proportion of 18- to 24-year-olds who changed jobs had been at least twice as high as that of the population as a whole.

Fourth, personnel managers face a problem of *employee alienation and frustration*. We have convinced our young people that education is the best route to increased status, power, and income. But increasing numbers of college-trained youth are now bumping into the reality that pyramids narrow at the top. It has been estimated that perhaps 5 million college graduates will be unemployed or underemployed by 1985.

Finally, there is some question of the quality of education being received by some students.

They Are More Independent

The historical review showed that the status of workers has undergone, and continues to undergo, great change. They have achieved many of the same

---

[11]*U.S. News & World Report,* March 19, 1979, p. 18.
[12]"More Women," *Parade,* March 30, 1980, p. 28.

FIGURE 3-10
**Percentage of civilian labor force with at least
four years of high school and at least four
years of college, by age, 1970 actual and 1990
projected**

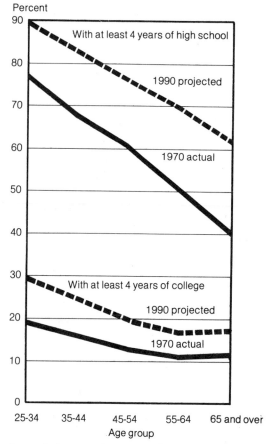

Percent

90

With at least 4 years of high school

80

1990 projected

70

60

1970 actual

50

40

30

With at least 4 years of college

1990 projected

20

1970 actual

10

0

25-34   35-44   45-54   55-64   65 and over

Age group

Source: *Employment and Training Report of the President,* 1979.

benefits that owners, professionals, and managers had in earlier times—such as
retirement benefits, insurance programs, a guaranteed annual income, and
time off with pay.

Management can no longer assume that present or potential employees are
completely dependent on a given employer—or even *any* employer—for survival. In fact, with the various social programs now available, *not working* is
one possible choice! Thus managers must depend more on persuasion and
positive motivation and less on financial incentives or the use of managerial
authority.

"I graduated Cum Laude, whatever that means."

Reprinted by permission *The Wall Street Journal*

They Are Motivated Differently

The new employees are motivated differently. They seek jobs that satisfy the higher needs for creativity, achievement, prestige, and self-expression. Also, *they want rewards now instead of having to work for years for some distant goal.*

Economic incentives were at one time considered the prime motivators. It is now known, though, that factors such as personal dignity, security, recognition, creative and challenging work, responsibility, achievement, and participation are also important motivators. Therefore, the problem is *not* a question of whether these employees desire the economic benefits *or* the nonmonetary benefits, but that they demand *both* in order to be satisfied with their work.

SUMMARY AND CONCLUSIONS

It is important for you to understand historical background, for it determines the environment in which personnel management occurs. Most personnel policies and practices had their origin in the past. By understanding the evolution of changes, managers should be better able to adapt to the new work environment and work force.

The environmental factors discussed indicate that personnel managers should plan for technologically oriented production systems and service-type organizations in the future. Before 1870, we were an agricultural nation, as more workers were engaged in agriculture and extractive industries than all others. From then until 1966, we were an industrial nation, as more workers were producing manufactured products than were engaged in farming and extractive industries. Since then, we have become a service-type economy, for more people are now employed in nonmanufacturing activities than in manufacturing, construction, transportation, and agriculture. This trend is expected to continue—or even accelerate—during the rest of this century.

Also, white-collar employees, especially clerical, technical, and professional employees, are replacing blue-collar and farm workers. This trend is expected to continue.

These changes will require a different type of personnel executive in the future, for there must be a more humanistic approach to performing the personnel function. This is especially true of rewarding and motivating the new employees. This new breed of workers is younger, has more female and minority workers, and is more highly educated.

QUESTIONS

1. Just how important is a knowledge of history to the study of personnel management? Explain.
2. What effects of World War II do you see in personnel practices today? Explain.
3. Take any one of the movements during the "period of activism" and explain what is currently happening to it. Is it growing, slackening, or remaining stable?
4. Does technological development have a detrimental effect on employment? Why or why not? What are the real problems of employment as far as it is concerned?
5. What changes in our work environment have brought about the changes in the work force discussed in this chapter?
6. White-collar workers have displaced blue-collar workers as the largest occupational grouping. What are some implications for personnel managers?
7. Employment in goods-producing industries is declining relative to that in service-performing ones. What are some possible consequences for personnel managers?
8. What are some possible consequences of the new breed of employees?

PROBLEM

The Returnee

A speaker asked a group of supervisors in a large hospital to recount a managerial situation that had caused them a problem. A head nurse answered as follows:

My problem has been trying to readjust to hospital life. In 1948, I left the nursing profession to be a housewife and mother. I returned to hospital work only seven years ago and have had a problem adjusting to the changes that have occurred.

During those years at home, I remained a member of the professional associations and subscribed to two nursing journals in an effort to try to keep abreast of the changing trends. I also read anything that pertained to my profession.

After returning to work, I worked for a very smart head nurse. She was quite helpful in trying to get me acquainted with the latest equipment and methods.

I suppose the hardest thing was getting used to the new type of people working in hospitals. When I had nurses' training, we were taught always to be "strictly professional" when on duty. Thus, I had to adjust to the new relaxed attitude and permissiveness that prevail in our hospital.

I thought I did very well and really enjoyed my work until I was asked to be head nurse in my department. I accepted the position reluctantly and with reservations. I love to work with people but the job of being head nurse, or supervisor, is a lonely one. I like to teach or instruct but do not like to be a "foreman" and to have to watch and point out errors and mistakes that are made through carelessness.

Questions

1. What does this situation tell you about the changing work environment?
2. What does it show about the "new breed" of employees?
3. How would you advise the head nurse to act as a supervisor, if you were the personnel manager at the hospital?

SUGGESTED READINGS FOR FURTHER STUDY

Allen, Robert E., and Timothy J. Keaveny. "Does the Work Status of Married Women Affect Their Attitudes toward Family Life?" *Personnel Administrator* 24 (June 1979):63–66.

Drucker, Peter. *Managing in Turbulent Times.* New York: Harper & Row, 1980.

"Employers 'Sensitive' to Dual Careers Gain Competitive Edge, Experts Say." *MBA Executive* 8 (January 1979):10–11.

Gale, Deborah. "Minority Report." *MBA*, February 1978, pp. 32–33.

"Labor's Big Swing from Surplus to Shortage." *Business Week*, February 20, 1978, pp. 75–77.

Malabre, Alfred L., Jr. "More and More People Seek—and Find—Jobs Even though Unemployment Rate Stays High." *Wall Street Journal*, January 18, 1978, p. 42.

Phillcher, William W., and William S. Fox. "Race, Class, and Perceptions of Affluence." *Sociological Focus* 10 (October 1977):375–80.

Rodriguez, Orlando. "Occupational Shifts and Educational Upgrading in the American Labor Force between 1950 and 1970." *Sociology of Education* 51 (January 1978):55–67.

Rout, Lawrence.   "Office Output: White-Collar Workers Start to Get Attention in Productivity Studies." *Wall Street Journal,* August 7, 1979, p. 1.

"Service Industries: Growth Field of '80s." *U.S. News & World Report,* March 17, 1980, pp. 80–83.

Woodworth, Margaret, and Warner Woodworth.   "The Female Takeover: Threat or Opportunity." *Personnel Administrator* 24 (January 1979):19–28.

CHAPTER FOUR

How the Legal Environment Affects Personnel Management

Learning Objectives

After studying the material in this chapter, you should be able to:

1. Explain why the legal environment is so important to personnel managers.
2. Identify the laws, executive orders, and regulations that establish the legal environment for the following personnel functions:
   a. Equal employment opportunity (EEO)
   b. Safety and health
   c. Compensation and hours of work
   d. Income maintenance
   e. Industrial relations
   f. Privacy.
3. Describe the efforts that have been made to provide EEO for minorities.
4. Explain what employers must do to provide EEO for different groups.
5. Explain some of the problems involved in complying with the legal environment.
6. Explain how personnel managers can cope with the legal environment.

Some Important Words and Terms

Legal environment
Interstate commerce
Fair employment practices commission
   (FEPC)
Affirmative action (AA)
Affirmative action program (AAP)
*Uniform Guidelines on Employee
   Selection Procedures*
Equal employment opportunity (EEO)

Bona fide occupational qualification
   (BFOQ)
Class action suits
Systemic suits
Handicapped person
Workers' compensation
Overtime
Unemployment insurance

We hold these truths to be self-evident, that all men are created equal, that they are endowed by their Creator with certain unalienable Rights, that among these are Life, Liberty and the Pursuit of Happiness.
The Declaration of Independence

Outline of the Chapter

BACKGROUND
THE LEGAL ENVIRONMENT IS BECOMING MORE IMPORTANT TO
      PERSONNEL MANAGERS
      Reasons for Growing Government Involvement
      Government Now Considered to Be a Major Partner
HOW EQUAL EMPLOYMENT OPPORTUNITY LEGISLATION GREW
      States Took Corrective Action
      Presidents Issued Executive Orders
      Congress Began to Pass Laws
      EEO Is Now an Accepted Part of Personnel Management
EQUAL EMPLOYMENT OPPORTUNITY REQUIREMENTS
      For Women and Minorities
      For Older Workers
      For the Handicapped
      For Veterans
      EEO and Religious Beliefs
ENFORCEMENT OF EEO LAWS
      By the EEOC
      By the OFCCP
      Setting Up Affirmative Action Programs (AAPs)
SAFETY AND HEALTH
      Workers' Compensation Laws
      Occupational Safety and Health Act
COMPENSATION, HOURS OF WORK, AND HOLIDAYS
      Laws Affecting Compensation
      Laws Affecting Hours of Work
INCOME MAINTENANCE
      Social Security Act
      Employee Retirement Income Security Act (ERISA)
INDUSTRIAL RELATIONS LAWS
PRIVACY

COPING WITH THE LEGAL ENVIRONMENT
Practical Problems Involved
Ways of Coping with the Laws

In early 1979, Sears, Roebuck and Company filed a class action suit against ten agencies—including the Office of Federal Contract Compliance Programs (OFCCP) in the Department of Labor and the Equal Employment Opportunity Commission (EEOC). The suit charged that conflicting laws and regulations discriminate against women and minorities.

The purpose of the suit, according to Sears officials, was to straighten out conflicting federal laws and regulations that make it almost impossible to comply with all legal requirements. For example, laws requiring the employer to give veterans preference in hiring and prohibit forced retirement before age 70 conflict with laws requiring affirmative action to hire minorities and women.

Sears said it had tried to comply with equal employment opportunity laws; progress had been made in hiring women and minorities, and a five-year old plan (Mandatory Achievement of Goals) offered better jobs to women and minorities. Yet the firm had been named in 1,500 federal charges and complaints since 1965.

In May 1979, the U.S. District Court in Washington threw out the suit. On October 1, 1979, Sears filed an appeal with the U.S. Court of Appeals for the District of Columbia (which was still pending at time of publication).[1]

Later, the EEOC sued Sears for a broad range of discriminatory acts against women and minorities. The suit was based on a six-year investigation, 1,700 documents submitted by Sears, and 20 statistical reports drawn from the data.[2]

As a result, Sears announced that it would no longer accept federal contracts, even though it meant a loss of $20 million each year.[3]

This case shows the problem(s) personnel managers have in conforming to the *legal environment,* which consists of *the laws affecting personnel management and the way they are enforced.* This legal-political environment sets the limits within which personnel management is performed.

This chapter will show how the trends discussed in the previous chapter have made it more difficult for managers to perform the personnel function.

---

[1]*Washington Vantage Point,* November 1979 (American Society for Personnel Administration, Washington, D.C.).

[2]"Firing Up the Attack on Job Bias," *Business Week,* June 25, 1979, pp. 64–68.

[3]"The EEOC May Settle Its Case Against Sears, " *Business Week,* August 20, 1979, pp. 4–5.

BACKGROUND

To a certain extent, managers brought the problems on themselves. Because firms often did not do what was needed to aid and protect employees, governments stepped in.[4]

For example, employers fought against workers' compensation laws when they were first passed shortly after 1900. They said the laws would violate the "master-servant doctrine," whereby workers accepted, as a condition of employment, the dangers that went with the job. Now workers' compensation laws are in effect in all the states.

Now, however, most personnel managers are finding that the regulations are forcing them to do what they should have done before—make personnel policies and practices more rational, objective, and effective.

It is not easy to select the most important laws, orders, and regulations that determine the legal environment. On the other hand, to cover all of them would only confuse you—and fill the rest of this book! Therefore, this chapter will give only an overview of the most important ones. They are discussed now so that you can refer to them as you study the subject further. More details will be added in later chapters as each personnel function is discussed.

THE LEGAL ENVIRONMENT IS BECOMING MORE IMPORTANT TO PERSONNEL MANAGERS

The Tenth Amendment to the U.S. Constitution gives the individual states the powers not specifically granted to the federal government. The states, therefore, have passed laws and developed their own legal and political constraints upon the performance of the personnel function.

The Constitution also gives Congress the right to pass laws affecting interstate commerce. The president also has the right to issue executive orders affecting government operations. Both have turned out many significant and far reaching regulations affecting personnel management.

Reasons for Growing Government Involvement

The original concept of *interstate commerce* was the movement of people or goods across state boundaries. This limited the role of the federal government in personnel activities until 1937. Then, in *National Labor Relations Board* v. *Jones and Laughlin Steel Corporation* the Supreme Court decided that manu-

---

[4]Bill Twinn, "The Discriminating Manager," *Management Today,* November 1979, pp. 65–70.

facturing goods within a state was also interstate commerce. After that, the
federal government was in a position to get more involved in the employer-
employee relationship, which it is now doing.

Another reason for the change in the role of the government is that the
world in which the personnel function is carried out is becoming more complex. Now most economic activities are more involved, as there is mass production, distribution, transportation, education, communication, and con-
sumption.

Government Now Considered to Be a Major Partner

Most people now view government as a partner with labor and management.
With the rapid increase in research and development costs, decisions affecting
economic growth now fall heavily upon business and government.

For example, around 60 percent of all scientific research and development in the United States—such as that of computers, nuclear energy, and
aerospace technology—has been financed and/or done by the federal
government.

HOW EQUAL EMPLOYMENT OPPORTUNITY LEGISLATION GREW

Before World War II, discrimination was generally accepted. Most managerial and other desirable jobs were held by white males. Women, minorities, the
aged, and handicapped people were placed in jobs with lower status—and
lower pay—and remained there.

States Took Corrective Action

During the late 1930s, many industrial states set up *fair employment practices
commissions* (FEPCs), which tried to prevent discrimination. Personnel managers were pressured to change their employment policies and practices.
There was much progress, but the laws were passive, as they only tried to
prevent unfair practices.

Presidents Issued Executive Orders

From then on, all presidents have issued executive orders forbidding employers with government contracts to discriminate against minorities, as shown:

1941   President Roosevelt issued Executive Order 8808.
1951   President Truman issued Executive Order 10308.

1953   President Eisenhower issued Executive Order 10479.

1961   President Kennedy issued Executive Order 10925.

Many business people tried to comply with these orders. They adjusted their recruiting, selection, training, and development practices to try to prevent discrimination.

In 1961, the top business leaders formed the National Alliance of Businessmen (NAB) to operate the Job Opportunities in the Business Sector (JOBS) program. This was a joint effort by business and government to provide meaningful jobs for the hard-core unemployed. But, as few qualified people applied for the job openings, there was little they could do.

Congress Began to Pass Laws

Congress tried to help minorities become qualified by passing the *Manpower Development and Training Act* in 1962. This law provided for training and development to make unemployed and underemployed people more employable.

However, the *affirmative action (AA)* stage of EEO did not begin until Congress passed the *Civil Rights Act* of 1964 (CRA), and President Johnson issued Executive Order 11246 in 1965 (amended by Executive Order 11375 in 1967). As a result, personnel managers had to do more than see that their employment practices were not unfair. They had to develop *affirmative action programs* (AAPs) to actively seek and promote minorities and women into better positions.

EEO Is Now an Accepted Part of Personnel Management

Next, agencies such as the EEOC, OFCCP, and others shown in the following tables, were set up to enforce the laws. In 1968, the EEOC, OFCCP, Civil Service Commission, and Department of Justice issued a set of *Uniform Guidelines on Employee Selection Procedures*.[5] These guidelines, which help employers comply with EEO regulations, are used by all relevant enforcement agencies.

The courts are now judging the legality—and meaning—of these regulations and the way they are enforced, as you will see throughout this text. In general, the regulations are being upheld.

But a law is not fully effective until it is accepted by the public. As we will now see, EEO has become an accepted part of personnel management.

---

[5]See "Adoption by Four Agencies of Uniform Guidelines on Employee Selection Procedures (1978)," *Federal Register* 43 (August 25, 1978), pp. 38290-38315, for these guidelines.

Source: Reprinted from the October, 1978 issue of *Action* with permission of the American Society for Personnel Administration.

EQUAL EMPLOYMENT OPPORTUNITY REQUIREMENTS

Equal employment opportunity (EEO) can be defined as *providing an equal opportunity to all employment practices and benefits to everyone.*

As shown in the Sears case, it is not easy to provide EEO. There are many differing laws and regulations that must be considered. There are now laws providing EEO for (1) minorities—including blacks, Spanish-surnamed Americans, Orientals, and American Indians, (2) women, (3) older workers, (4) veterans, and (5) the handicapped. These are summarized in Table 4-1.

For Women and Minorities

The basic law providing EEO for women, minorities, and those with special religious beliefs is the *Civil Rights Act*, as amended by the *Equal Employment Opportunity Act* of 1972.

Before reading any further, test your knowledge of EEO laws. Assume you are an employer, how would you answer the questions in Figure 4-1? The correct answers are under the figure.

The **Civil Rights Act.**   The CRA makes it unlawful for any *employer* to discriminate against any person because of race, color, religion, sex, or national origin. This applies to (1) hiring and firing, (2) wages, terms, conditions, or privileges of employment, (3) classifying, assigning, or promoting employees, (4) assigning the use of facilities, and (5) training or retraining. Covered employers must display the attached poster (Figure 4-2).

It is also unlawful for any *employment agency* to express any limitations or preferences based on one of these factors. Nor can it discriminate in receiving applications or classifying or referring for employment.

Labor organizations cannot exclude or expel from membership or discriminate against any person on the basis of race, color, religion, sex, or national origin. Nor can they cause or attempt to cause an employer to discriminate.

TABLE 4-1
Legal influences on equal employment opportunity (EEO) and affirmative action (AA)

Laws	Coverage	Basic requirements	Agencies involved
Title VII of Civil Rights Act, as amended by Equal Employment Opportunity Act	Employers with 15 or more employees, engaged in interstate commerce, federal service workers, and state and local government workers	Prohibits employment decisions based on race, color, religion, sex, or national origin; employers must develop affirmative action programs (AAPs) to recruit women and minorities	Equal Employment Opportunity Commission (EEOC)
Executive Order 11246 as amended by Executive Order 11375	Employers with federal contracts and subcontracts, with 50 or more employees, or with contracts over $50,000	Requires contractors to take affirmative action, including goals and timetables, to recruit, select, train, utilize, and promote minorities and women	Office of Federal Contract Compliance Programs (OFCCP), in the Labor Department
Age Discrimination in Employment Act	Employees from age 40 to 70, except selected high-salaried executives and tenured faculty	Prohibits employment discrimination, including mandatory retirement before 70 (or 65 for those exempted)	EEOC
Vocational Rehabilitation Act	Employers with federal contracts of $2,500 or more	Prohibits discrimination and requires contractor to develop AAPs to recruit and employ handicapped persons	OFCCP
Vietnam Era Veterans Readjustment Act	Employers with federal contracts	Require contractors to develop AAPs to recruit and employ Vietnam era veterans	OFCCP

Source: Extracted from BNA's Policy and Practice Series, *Fair Employment Practices* (Washington, D.C.: Bureau of National Affairs).

FIGURE 4-1
Test your knowledge of EEO laws

An employer. . .	True	False
1. Can refuse to hire women who have small children at home.	_____	_____
2. Can generally obtain and use an applicant's arrest record as the basis for non-employment.	_____	_____
3. Can prohibit employees from conversing in native language on the job.	_____	_____
4. Whose employees are mostly white or male, can rely solely upon word-of-mouth to recruit new employees.	_____	_____
5. Can refuse to hire women to work at night, because it wishes to protect them.	_____	_____
6. May require all pregnant employees to take leave of absence at a specified time before delivery date.	_____	_____
7. May establish different benefits—pension, retirement, insurance and health plans—for male employees than for female employees.	_____	_____
8. May hire only males for a job if state law forbids employment of women for that capacity.	_____	_____
9. Need not attempt to adjust work schedules to permit an employee time off for a religious observance.	_____	_____
10. Disobeys the Equal Employment Opportunity laws only when it is acting intentionally or with ill motive.	_____	_____

Source: Equal Employment Opportunity Commission, Washington, D.C. *Answers:* The answers to all ten is "false." The *Civil Rights Act* makes it illegal for an employer to discriminate on the basis of race, religion, color, sex or national origin.

You can see that the law is very broad and involves almost all personnel policies and practices.

Two areas involving women that are now causing many problems are (1) how to treat sexual harassment on the job[6] and (2) how to handle women's rights to jobs with reproductive hazards.[7] The only time sex can be used as a basis for selecting a person is when there is a *bona fide occupational qualification* (BFOQ) requiring a specific sex.

---

[6]See Sandra Sawyer and Arthur A. Whatley, "Sexual Harassment: A Form of Sex Discrimination," *Personnel Administrator* 25 (January 1980):36–38, for steps management must take.

[7]Guidelines are now being proposed on this issue. In general, a firm is presumed to be guilty if it denies women's rights to jobs without proof of hazard. See "Avoiding Sex Bias," *Business Week*, February 18, 1980, p. 74.

FIGURE 4-2

equal igualdad
employment de oportunidad
opportunity en el
is the empleo
law es la ley

Private Industry, State, and Local Government	Title VII of the Civil Rights Act of 1964, as amended, prohibits job discrimination because of race, color, religion, sex or national origin. Applicants to and employees of private employers, state/local governments, and public/private educational institutions are protected. Also covered are employment agencies, labor unions and apprenticeship programs. Any person who believes he or she has been discriminated against should contact immediately **The U. S. Equal Employment Opportunity Commission (EEOC)** **2401 E St., N.W.** **Washington, D. C. 20506** or an EEOC District Office, listed in most telephone directories under U. S. Government.	**Industrias Privadas, Gobiernos Locales y Estatales**	El Título VII de la Ley de Derechos Civiles de 1964, enmendado, prohíbe la discriminación en el empleo por razón de raza, color, religión, sexo o nacionalidad de origen. La ley protege a los empleados y solicitantes de empleo en empresas privadas, gobiernos estatales y locales e instituciones educacionales públicas y privadas. También abarca las agencias de empleo, sindicatos de trabajadores y programas de aprendizaje. Cualquier persona, tanto hombre como mujer, que crea que ha sido objeto de discriminación debe escribir inmediatamente a **The U. S. Equal Employment Opportunity Commission (EEOC)** **2401 E St., N.W.** **Washington, D. C. 20506** o a cualquier oficina regional de EEOC, las que se encuentran en las guías telefónicas locales bajo el nombre de: U. S. Government.
Federal Contract Employment	Executive Order 11246, as amended, prohibits job discrimination because of race, color, religion, sex or national origin and requires affirmative action to ensure equality of opportunity in all aspects of employment. Section 503 of the Rehabilitation Act of 1973 prohibits job discrimination because of handicap and requires affirmative action to employ and advance in employment qualified handicapped workers. Section 402 of the Vietnam Era Veterans' Readjustment Assistance Act of 1974 prohibits job discrimination and requires affirmative action to employ and advance in employment (1) qualified Vietnam era veterans during the first four years after their discharge and (2) qualified disabled veterans throughout their working life if they have a 30 percent or more disability. Applicants to and employees of any company with a federal government contract or subcontract are protected. Any person who believes a contractor has violated its affirmative action obligations, including nondiscrimination, under Executive Order 11246, as amended, or under Section 503 of the Rehabilitation Act should contact immediately **The Employment Standards Administration** **Office of Federal Contract Compliance Programs (OFCCP)** **Third and Constitution Ave., N.W.** **Washington, D. C. 20210** or an OFCCP regional office, listed in most telephone directories under U. S. Government, Department of Labor. Complaints specifically under the veterans' law should be filed with the Veterans' Employment Service through local offices of the state employment service. All complaints must be filed within 180 days from date of alleged violation.	**Empleos En Compañías Con Contratos Federales**	La Orden Ejecutiva Número 11246, enmendada, prohíbe la discriminación en el empleo por razón de raza, color, religión, sexo o nacionalidad de origen y exige acción positiva para garantizar la igualdad de oportunidad en todos los aspectos del empleo. La Sección 503 de la Ley de Rehabilitación de 1973, prohíbe la discriminación en el empleo contra personas que sufran de impedimentos físicos o mentales y exige acción positiva en el empleo y promoción de personas que sufran de impedimentos físicos o mentales, siempre que reúnan las condiciones indispensables para el desempeño del empleo. La Sección 402 de la Ley de 1974 de Asistencia para el Reajuste de los Veteranos de la Era de Vietnam, prohíbe la discriminación en el empleo y exige acción positiva en el empleo y promoción de (1) veteranos de la era de Vietnam, durante los primeros cuatro años después de haber sido separados del servicio activo, siempre que reúnan las condiciones indispensables para el desempeño del empleo (2) ciertos veteranos que tengan un 30 por ciento o más de impedimentos físicos o mentales mientras puedan trabajar, siempre que reúnan las condiciones indispensables para el desempeño del empleo. La ley protege a los solicitantes de empleo y empleados de cualquier compañía que tenga un contrato o subcontrato con el gobierno federal. Cualquier persona que crea que uno de estos contratistas no ha cumplido con sus obligaciones de tomar acción positiva, incluyendo la de no discriminar, bajo la Orden Ejecutiva 11246, enmendada, o bajo la Sección 503 de la Ley de Rehabilitación, debe escribir inmediatamente a **The Employment Standards Administration** **Office of Federal Contract Compliance Programs (OFCCP)** **Third and Constitution Ave., N.W.** **Washington, D. C. 20210** o a cualquier oficina regional de OFCCP, las que se encuentran en la mayoría de las guías telefónicas bajo: U. S. Government, Department of Labor. Las reclamaciones específicamente comprendidas bajo la ley de veteranos, deben de dirigirse a Veterans' Employment Service por medio de las oficinas locales del servicio de empleo del estado. Todas las reclamaciones deben de ser registradas dentro de los 180 días subsequentes a la fecha del supuesto acto de discriminación.

U.S. Department of Labor
Employment Standards Administration
Office of Federal Contract Compliance Programs

OFCCP-1420
(October 1976)

"Can't those Equal Opportunity people leave well enough alone??"

Reprinted by permission The *Wall Street Journal*

Bona fide occupational qualification?

The limits of the law are effectively set by the funds available for enforcement and the fervor of the chairman[8] of the EEOC.

Executive Order 11246. Executive Order 11246 was issued by President Johnson in 1965, just nine months after the CRA went into effect. It was amended by Executive Order 11375 in 1967. These orders require that contractors doing business with the federal government include in their contracts

---

[8]Eleanor H. Norton, who now heads up the agency, prefers to be called the "chair."

an agreement not to discriminate on the basis of race, color, religion, sex, or national origin. They must also agree to take affirmative action to employ minorities and females. Any firm providing over $10,000 of services to the government is *considered to be a contractor,* whether or not there is actually a contract. Over 300,000 contractors are now covered by these orders.

For Older Workers

During the 1960s, the children born during and after World War II began to enter the job market. This caused a general decline in the hiring of older workers. To protect them, Congress passed the *Age Discrimination in Employment Act* (ADEA) in 1967 to prevent discrimination against individuals between the ages of 39 and 65. The law was amended in 1978 to prevent forced retirement (except for tenured faculty and selected high salaried executives) before 70 years of age. There is no age limit in government.

This law may be the "sleeper" in the entire EEO field. The population is getting older, and people are now working longer.

Another aspect of this law and the CRA is that Help Wanted ads can no longer use terms such as "recent college grad," "girl Friday," "salesman," or "bellboy."

For the Handicapped

The *Vocational Rehabilitation Act,* passed in 1973, prohibits employers with federal contracts from discriminating against the handicapped. A *handicapped person* is defined as anyone with a physical or mental disability that substantially restricts major activities such as walking, seeing, speaking, working, or learning. Disabilities covered by the law also include alcoholism, cancer, diabetes, drug addiction, heart disease, and mental illness, among others.

Research has shown that most perceptibly handicapped people will perform (over their entire career) as well as the nonhandicapped, if they have a supportive vocational environment.[9]

Any private contractor or state or local agency receiving federal money must prepare an affirmative action program to find and hire the disabled, if they can do the job.

For Veterans

The *Veterans' Readjustment Act* of 1974 provides for job counseling, training, and placement service for veterans. In addition, it requires firms with federal

---

[9]Ray B. Bressler and A. Wayne Lacy, "An Analysis of the Relative Job Progression of the Perceptibly Handicapped," *Academy of Management Journal* 23 (1980):132–43.

contracts to have AAPs for recruiting and hiring disabled and Vietnam veterans.

EEO and Religious Beliefs

The EEOC's proposed rules on religious accommodations are particularly troubling to personnel managers. First, they require the employer to "bend over backwards" to avoid assigning employees to work on any day that violates their religious beliefs. Second, the definition of religion includes "sincerely held moral or ethical beliefs." This will be hard to apply.[10]

ENFORCEMENT OF EEO LAWS

Enforcement of the EEO laws is currently spread over several agencies. However, the most important ones are the Equal Employment Opportunity Commission (EEOC) and the Office of Federal Contract Compliance Programs (OFCCP).

By the EEOC

Effective July 1, 1979, the EEOC was given the sole authority to enforce the CRA and ADEA. In addition, it is to direct and coordinate EEO enforcement policies, standards, and procedures of all involved federal agencies. All other agencies that enforce EEO laws must submit their guidelines and enforcement procedures to the EEOC 60 days before they are to become effective. The head of the EEOC is to take any conflicts between the agencies directly to the White House.

The EEOC is composed of five members appointed by the president and approved by the Senate.

How it works.   The commission performs two basic functions. First, it investigates complaints of discrimination. If it finds they are justified, it seeks a full remedy by the process of conciliation or through the courts. Second, it promotes programs of voluntary compliance to put the idea of EEO into actual practice. The commission is concerned with discrimination by four major groups: private, public, and educational employers; public and private employment agencies; labor organizations; and joint labor-management apprenticeship programs.

At first, the agency tried to protect individual workers by bringing lawsuits against specific firms. Then it started filing *class action suits* to protect large groups, such as women. Now *systemic suits*, which bring charges against an

---

[10]See John M. Norwood, "But I Can't Work on Saturdays," *Personnel Administrator* 25 (January 1980):25–30.

entire company, are being used in addition to individual and class action suits. (This is the type of suit brought against Sears in the opening case.)

Now, let us look at some examples of how the EEOC has enforced the laws to protect women, minorities, and older workers.

How it protects women. The big push against sex discrimination was the AT&T consent decree. In 1970, the Federal Communications Commission (FCC) was hearing a Bell System request for an interstate rate increase. The EEOC brought charges before the FCC that the system's hiring and promotion practices were discriminatory. After two years of testimony and bargaining, an agreement was reached on January 18, 1973, between AT&T, the EEOC, and the Department of Labor. The company agreed to set up an affirmative action program (AAP) to remedy past discrimination.

Under the AAP, women college graduates hired between July 2, 1965 (the effective date of the CRA), and 1971 would be sent to assessment centers to be assessed as possible managers. If found qualified, they were to receive back pay from the time they had become eligible for the management position. Women and minorities holding craft jobs were to receive salary adjustments. The net result was that, while total employment increased by only 15 percent, black employment increased 44 percent and Spanish-surnamed employment 93 percent; about 7,000 women were put in jobs formerly held by men; and 4,000 men took jobs usually held by women.[11]

In spite of these efforts, there is still much discrimination, as the following example shows:[12]

A study of 26 organizations found that equal employment opportunities and efforts to get rid of discrimination were "low priorities." Some managers even said that they did discriminate against women—or intended to.

How it protects minorities. Discrimination is not always the result of open agreement among employers. Instead, they sometimes profess beliefs that convince them that minorities are less productive and are satisfied with lower job levels. Then, when management channels them into those jobs, discrimination results.

This type of practice led to one of the most significant cases involving minorities—the Detroit Edison case. The company and the unions involved were charged with using "word of mouth" hiring and seniority practices that effectively maintained the existing white labor force. The company and unions denied the charges. But blacks and other minorities held a very small percentage of the more desirable, highly skilled, and higher paying jobs, while making up 44 percent of the population of the city of Detroit. In 1973, the court

---

[11]See Ethel B. Walsh, "Sex Discrimination and the Impact of Title VII," *Labor Law Journal* 25 (1974):150–54, for further details. It also provides an excellent summary of how these laws are enforced.

[12]Pauline Glucklich and Margery Powell, "Equal Opportunities: A Case for Action in Default of the Law," *Personnel Management* 11 (January 1979):28–30.

ordered Edison to pay $4 million, and Local 223 was fined $250,000 in punitive damages.[13]

How it protects older workers.   The ADEA, though passed in 1967, was
not really enforced until the middle of 1974. Then Standard Oil of California
signed a consent decree in a federal court, at a cost of about $2 million. The
firm was charged with trying to save labor costs by clearing out the ranks of
older, more experienced—and therefore higher paid—employees. Some of
the employees were not rehired, for they were tested and found unable to
perform their jobs properly. Yet they were paid back wages because they had
been fired, not on the basis of their inability to do the job, but because of their
age.

By the OFCCP

The OFCCP is responsible for enforcing Executive Order 11246, the *Vocational Rehabilitation Act,* and the *Veterans' Readjustment Act* of 1974. The
secondary responsibility for enforcement rests with each of the contracting
and compliance agencies. The Secretary of Labor can bar offenders from
further contracts with the government. The individual agencies can then decide to terminate existing contracts if they choose.

In July 1979, the Secretary of Labor barred Uniroyal, Inc., from holding
future federal contracts because it had discriminated against female workers at one of its plants. The firm had received $37 million in contracts with
the Defense Department in 1978. The Defense Department and other federal agencies were left to decide whether or not to cancel existing contracts.[14]

The OFCCP's enforcement power was increased in 1979, when its staff for
implementing the laws was raised from 200 to 1,400. It then began to enforce
the laws more aggressively.

Several actions have been taken against firms accused of bias against
the handicapped. Some of the defendants were (1) a Hawaii construction
firm, for refusing to hire a worker with a back problem, even though he had
worked in construction for three years, (2) American Airlines, for suspend-
ing an epileptic, and (3) Northwestern University, for firing a cancer patient.

On the other hand, the Supreme Court set limits on application of the
Rehabilitation Act when it said a nursing school did not have to accept a
student who could not hear.

---

[13]See Beverly K. Schaffer and Sherman F. Dallas, "Racial Bias: The Detroit Edison Case,"
Labor Law Journal 25 (1974):570–77, for further details.

[14]See "Uniroyal Barred from Holding Federal Orders," *The Wall Street Journal,* July 2, 1979,
p. 1, for further details on how these orders are applied.

Setting Up Affirmative Action Programs (AAPs)

As indicated, EEO laws require organizations to have effective AAPs. These have also been accepted by top managers and the Supreme Court.

A survey of nearly 300 top executives found that most of them take affirmative action seriously and integrate it into their systems. But half of them questioned whether present government goals are attainable. They also felt that the agencies should emphasize EEO *results* rather than *methods*.[15]

The Supreme Court ruled in 1979 that AAPs voluntarily agreed to by employers and unions to provide employment opportunities for minorities are legal. Brian Weber, a white employee, claimed that the 60 percent quota established by Kaiser Aluminum and the United Steelworkers for black trainees in craft training programs was reverse discrimination. The Court ruled that it was not unlawful for voluntary programs to "discriminate . . . because of . . . race" to "eliminate traditional patterns of racial segregation."[16]

As AAPs are now such an important part of the personnel function, you should be familiar with the basics involved in setting one up.

The most important measure of an AAP is its effectiveness, in terms of results. To be successful, it should include at least the following steps:

1. Establish a strong commitment to the program.
2. Set up strong company policies.
3. Assign responsibility for the program to a top company official, and give him or her adequate authority.
4. Analyze the present work force to identify areas where minorities, women, and the handicapped are underutilized.
5. Set up meaningful programs to achieve the goals.
6. Make every manager responsible and accountable for helping to meet the goals.
7. Develop effective systems to monitor and measure progress regularly.

Issue an affirmative action statement. Top management should issue a firm statement of personal commitment to the importance of and legal obligations for EEO as a goal. The statement should at least say that:

1. EEO for all persons is a legal, social, and economic requirement for the organization.
2. EEO requires special affirmative action to overcome the effects of past discrimination.

---

[15]See "Affirmative Action Is Accepted by Most Corporate Chiefs," *The Wall Street Journal,* April 13, 1979, p. 1, for further details.

[16]*Weber* v. *Kaiser Aluminum (and United Steelworkers),* as reported in *Washington Vantage Point,* July 1979 (American Society of Personnel Administration, Washington, D.C.).

3. The policy will affect *all* employment practices.
4. Achievement of EEO goals will have positive results through using *all* human resources more effectively.

Assign responsibility for the program.   The importance given to an AAP is indicated from the start by the individual placed in charge and the authority the position carries. If a qualified minority or female manager heads the program, it may offer a good role model for present and potential employees.

An EEO/AA program must be a shared responsibility. Where it has been assigned mainly to the personnel department, it has not worked.[17] Instead, the line managers, from the CEO to the first-line supervisors, must be made responsible—and trained in how to assure compliance.

Analyze employment and utilization of women, minorities, and the handicapped.   At present, some groups are underutilized in certain areas of the work force. Personnel managers, or their designated AAP directors, should analyze and identify major job classifications and the number and percentage of minority, female, and handicapped employees currently in each unit and subunit.

EEO officers are requiring managers to vigorously seek out people for particular jobs. This is required by Revised Order no. 4. Figure 4–3 shows how to determine whether minorities and women are available.

Set up meaningful programs to achieve goals.   In general, AAPs should include (1) making good-faith efforts to recruit and promote women, minorities, the handicapped, and veterans, including recruiting through state employment services, (2) limiting the questions that may be asked in employment applications and interviews, (3) determining available percentages of women, minorities, and the handicapped in the local labor force, (4) setting up goals and timetables to recruit them, and (5) avoiding testing unless it meets established guidelines.

Develop systems to monitor and measure progress.   The most important measure of an AAP is its results. All other activities are meaningless unless the end product is a measurable improvement in hiring, training, and promoting these individuals in all parts of the organization.

SAFETY AND HEALTH

State laws and procedures have usually set and enforced safety and health standards. Now, however, this has changed. Providing for occupational safety and health is now one of the most significant areas of federal public policy. We will look at only two aspects here (see Table 4–2). The details will be covered in Chapter 14.

---

[17]Craig W. Cole "Decentralizing EEO Management: How to Share the Responsibility," *Personnel Administrator* 24 (August 1979):17–19 and 42–43.

FIGURE 4-3
How to determine whether minorities and women are available

The Eight-Factor Analysis

The eight-factor analysis used to determine the availability of minorities and women for particular job groups is based on the following factors.

Minorities	*Women*
1. The minority population of the labor area surrounding the facility.	1. The size of the female unemployment force in the labor area surrounding the facility.
2. The size of the minority unemployment force in the labor area surrounding the facility.	2. The percentage of the female work force as compared with the total work force in the immediate labor area.
3. The percentage of the minority workforce as compared with the total workforce in the immediate labor area.	3. The general availability of women having requisite skills in the immediate area.
4. The general availability of minorities having requisite skills in the immediate labor area.	4. The availability of women having requisite skills in an area in which a contractor can reasonably recruit.
5. The availability of minorities having requisite skills in an area in which the contractor can reasonably recruit.	5. The availability of women seeking employment in the labor or recruitment area of the contractor.
6. The availability of promotable and transferable minorities within the contractor's organization.	6. The availability of promotable and transferable female employees within the contractor's organization.
7. The existence of training institutions capable of training persons in the requisite skills.	7. The existence of training institutions capable of training persons in the requisite skills.
8. The degree of training the contractor is reasonably able to undertake as a means of making all job classes available to minorities.	8. The degree of training the contractor is reasonably able to undertake as a means of making all job classes available to women.

Note: From Revised Order 4, SS60-2.11.
Source: "Affirmative Action through Hiring and Promotion: How Fast a Rate?" by Berwyn N. Fragner, *Personnel* November–December 1979, © 1979 by AMACOM, a division of American Management Association, p. 68. All rights reserved.

TABLE 4-2
Legal influences on safety and health

Laws	Coverage	Basic requirements	Agencies involved
Workers' compensation laws (as passed by each state)	Varies by state; generally, employees or private nonagricultural firms, with work-related accidents or illnesses causing temporary or permanent disabilities, or death	Income benefits are usually about two-thirds of employee's weekly income, plus payments for medical and hospital care and rehabilitation activities; survivor benefits are paid for fatalities; funding is through (1) self-insurance, (2) private insurance carriers, or (3), state insurance systems; in (2) and (3), rates based on employer's experience rating	Various state agencies
Occupational Safety and Health Act	Employers engaged in interstate commerce with one or more employees, except those covered by Atomic Energy Act and Federal Mine Safety Act	Employees must be provided a place of employment free from recognizable hazards that might cause serious illness, injury, or death; employers and employees must comply with the safety and health standards issued by OSHA	Occupational Safety and Health Administration, (OSHA), in the Labor Department Occupational Safety and Health Review Commission (OSHRC) National Institute for Occupational Safety and Health (NIOSH)

Workers' Compensation Laws

All states now have laws requiring *workers' compensation,* which *specify a scale of benefits workers will receive for specific losses—such as an arm—and a percentage of salary they will receive for injuries.* There is also coverage of medical care and training for rehabilitation. The key factor is that the cost of such coverage to each firm varies with its safety record. This provides an incentive to encourage safety.

Federal standards are now set for these laws.

Occupational Safety and Health Act

The federal *Occupational Safety and Health Act* of 1970 (OSHAct) assumed much of the authority and responsibility for providing for health and safety. The law covers *every* employer in interstate commerce but specifically excludes federal, state, and local government employees and employees covered by other federal safety and health laws. The poster shown in Figure 4-4 must be prominently displayed.

OSHAact was passed in 1970 and went into effect April 28, 1971. The act was drawn up because of the failure of state governments, labor, and management to provide safe and healthy working conditions.

The purpose of the law is "to assure so far as possible every working man and woman in the nation safe and healthful working conditions and to preserve our human resources."

It is administered by (1) the Occupational Safety and Health Administration (OSHA), Department of Labor, (2) the Occupational Safety and Health Review Commission, and (3) the National Institute for Occupational Safety and Health.

COMPENSATION, HOURS OF WORK, AND HOLIDAYS

For a long time there have been many state and federal laws regulating wages and hours. They are now an accepted and well-understood part of personnel management. Only an overview of them is presented here, as they will be covered in greater detail in Part 4.

Laws Affecting Compensation

At the national level, there are many laws affecting compensation (see Table 4-3). They fall into two groups—those setting basic wage rates and those requiring equal pay. These are discussed in detail in Chapter 15.

Laws setting basic rates of pay. The basic wage and hour law is the *Fair Labor Standards Act* of 1938 (FLSA), as amended. Under this law, Congress sets a specific minimum wage for all employees engaged in interstate commerce or in the production of goods for interstate commerce, for employees of hospitals and schools, and for certain government employees. The minimum was originally 25 cents per hour. The basic work week was 40 hours, and "time and a half" was to be paid for all hours over 40 per week. The 40-hour week still prevails, but amendments have increased the minimum hourly wage

FIGURE 4-4

job safety and health protection

The Occupational Safety and Health Act of 1970 provides job safety and health protection for workers through the promotion of safe and healthful working conditions throughout the Nation. Requirements of the Act include the following

Employers: Each employer shall furnish to each of his employees employment and a place of employment free from recognized hazards that are causing or are likely to cause death or serious harm to his employees; and shall comply with occupational safety and health standards issued under the Act.

Employees: Each employee shall comply with all occupational safety and health standards, rules, regulations and orders issued under the Act that apply to his own actions and conduct on the job.

The Occupational Safety and Health Administration (OSHA) of the Department of Labor has the primary responsibility for administering the Act. OSHA issues occupational safety and health standards, and its Compliance Safety and Health Officers conduct jobsite inspections to ensure compliance with the Act.

Inspection: The Act requires that a representative of the employer and a representative authorized by the employees be given an opportunity to accompany the OSHA inspector for the purpose of aiding the inspection.

Where there is no authorized employee representative, the OSHA Compliance Officer must consult with a reasonable number of employees concerning safety and health conditions in the workplace.

Complaint: Employees or their representatives have the right to file a complaint with the nearest OSHA office requesting an inspection if they believe unsafe or unhealthful conditions exist in their workplace. OSHA will withhold, on request, names of employees complaining.

The Act provides that employees may not be discharged or discriminated against in any way for filing safety and health complaints or otherwise exercising their rights under the Act.

An employee who believes he has been discriminated against may file a complaint with the nearest OSHA office within 30 days of the alleged discrimination.

U.S. GOVERNMENT PRINTING OFFICE:

Citation: If upon inspection OSHA believes an employer has violated the Act, a citation alleging such violations will be issued to the employer. Each citation will specify a time period within which the alleged violation must be corrected.

The OSHA citation must be prominently displayed at or near the place of alleged violation for three days, or until it is corrected, whichever is later, to warn employees of dangers that may exist there.

Proposed Penalty: The Act provides for mandatory penalties against employers of up to $1,000 for each serious violation and for optional penalties of up to $1,000 for each nonserious violation. Penalties of up to $1,000 per day may be proposed for failure to correct violations within the proposed time period. Also, any employer who willfully or repeatedly violates the Act may be assessed penalties of up to $10,000 for each such violation.

Criminal penalties are also provided for in the Act. Any willful violation resulting in death of an employee, upon conviction, is punishable by a fine of not more than $10,000 or by imprisonment for not more that six months, or by both. Conviction of an employer after a first conviction doubles these maximum penalties.

Voluntary Activity: While providing penalties for violations, the Act also encourages efforts by labor and management, before an OSHA inspection, to reduce injuries and illnesses arising out of employment.

The Department of Labor encourages employers and employees to reduce workplace hazards voluntarily and to develop and improve safety and health programs in all workplaces and industries.

Such cooperative action would initially focus on the identification and elimination of hazards that could cause death, injury, or illness to employees and supervisors. There are many public and private organizations that can provide information and assistance in this effort if requested.

More Information: Additional information and copies of the Act, specific OSHA safety and health standards, and other applicable regulations may be obtained from your employer or from the nearest OSHA Regional Office in the following locations:

Atlanta, Georgia
Boston, Massachusetts
Chicago, Illinois
Dallas, Texas
Denver, Colorado
Kansas City, Missouri
New York, New York
Philadelphia, Pennsylvania
San Francisco, California
Seattle, Washington

Telephone numbers for these offices, and additional Area Office locations, are listed in the telephone directory under the United States Department of Labor in the United States Government listing.

Washington, D.C.
1977
OSHA 2203

Ray Marshall

Ray Marshall
Secretary of Labor

U. S. Department of Labor

Occupational Safety and Health Administration

TABLE 4–3
Legal influence on compensation and hours of work

Laws	*Coverage*	*Basic requirements*	*Agencies involved*
Public Construction Act (Davis-Bacon Act)	Employers with federal construction contracts, or subcontracts, of $2,000 or more	Employers must pay not less than the wages prevailing in the area as determined by the Secretary of Labor; overtime is to be paid at one and one-half times the basic wage for all work over 8 hours per day or 40 hours per week	Wage and Hour Division of the Labor Department
Public Contracts Act (Walsh-Healy Act)	Employers with federal contracts of $10,000 or more	Same as above	Same as above
Fair Labor Standards Act (Wage and Hour Law)	Private employers engaged in interstate commerce, and retailers having annual sales of $325,000; many groups are exempted from overtime requirements	Employers must pay a minimum of at least $3.35 per hour; and at the rate of one and one-half times the basic rate for work over 40 hours per week; and are limited (by jobs and school status) in employing persons under 18	Same as above
Equal Pay Act	All employers	Men and women must receive equal pay for jobs requiring substantially the same skill, effort, responsibility, and working conditions	EEOC
Service Contracts Act	Employers with contracts to provide services worth $2,500 or more per year to the federal government	Same as Davis-Bacon	Same as Davis-Bacon

Source: Extracted from The Bureau of National Affairs, Inc., BNA Policy and Practice Series: *Wages and Hours* (Washington, D.C.: Bureau of National Affairs).

to its present rate of $3.35. Of course, Congress can change the rate as it pleases.

The *Davis-Bacon Act* of 1931 covers employees of construction firms with government contracts or subcontracts in excess of $2,000. The *Walsh-Healey Act* of 1936, also called the *Public Contracts Act*, covers employees of any employer with a government contract in excess of $10,000. These laws set labor standards that require the payment to covered workers of the "prevailing wages" in the area—as determined by the Secretary of Labor. The company must also pay no less than one and a half times the employee's basic rate ("time and a half") for *overtime*, that is, for over eight hours worked in one day or over 40 hours in a given week.

A new aspect of compensation is the use of "voluntary" wage and price guidelines, which will be covered in detail in Chapter 15.

These laws are administered by the Wage and Hour Division of the Labor Department.

Laws requiring equal pay.   Public policy now requires equal pay for all employees engaged in the same type of work, regardless of the group they belong to. Until the passage of the *Equal Pay Act* of 1963, public policy on equal pay was found only at the state level. This law is now enforced by the EEOC.

The CRA prohibits pay discrimination due to race, color, religion, sex, or national origin. The ADEA forbids pay discrimination against persons from 40 to 70 years of age. The *Vocational Rehabilitation Act* protects the handicapped against pay discrimination.

Employers must display the poster shown in Figure 4-5.

Laws Affecting Hours of Work

The FLSA not only regulates the hours worked by adults (one and a half the base pay for all hours over 40 per week), it also limits minors aged 14 to 16 to three hours of work per day when school is in session and eight hours per day at other times. They cannot work over 40 hours per week.

The other federal laws require overtime after eight hours per day or 40 per week.

Most states had laws pertaining to work hours of women, but they have been decreed by the courts to be in conflict with federal laws.

INCOME MAINTENANCE

Although there are many laws providing for and protecting employees income (see Table 4-4), only two will be mentioned here. These are the *Social Security Act* of 1935 and the *Employee Retirement Income Security Act* of 1974 (ERISA), also called the *Pension Reform Act*. They will be discussed in detail in Chapter 17.

FIGURE 4–5

Attention
Employees

**Your Rights Under the Fair Labor Standards Act
(Federal Wage and Hour Law)**

The Act Requires . . .

Minimum Wage*

of at least:

$2.90 per hour

Beg. 1/1/80 - $3.10/hr.
Beg. 1/1/81 - $3.35/hr.

beginning January 1, 1979

This minimum wage applies to workers engaged in
or producing goods for interstate commerce or employed
in certain enterprises.

Overtime Pay

at least 1-1/2 times your regular rate of pay for all
hours worked over 40 in one workweek.

Note: The act contains exemptions from the
minimum wage and/or overtime pay requirements
for certain occupations or establishments.

Equal Pay for Equal Work**

The equal pay provision prohibits sex discrimination in the payment of wages to men and women
performing equal work in the same establishment.
The provision does not prohibit wage differentials
between employees of the same sex.

Child Labor

You must be at least 16 years old to work in most
nonfarm jobs; at least 18 to work in nonfarm jobs
declared hazardous by the Secretary of Labor.
Youths 14 and 15 may work in various jobs outside
school hours under certain conditions. Different rules
apply to agricultural employment.

Enforcement:

The U.S. Government may bring civil or criminal
action against employers who violate the act. In
certain actions, courts may order payment of back
wages. Employers may be fined up to $1,000 for
each violation of the child labor provisions. The act
prohibits an employer from discriminating against
or discharging you if you file a complaint or
participate in a proceeding under it.

State laws:

When a state law differs with the Fair Labor
Standards Act, the law providing more protection
or setting the higher standard applies.

Additional information:

Consult your telephone directory under U.S.
Government, Department of Labor.

or write:

U.S. Department of Labor
Employment Standards Administration
Wage and Hour Division
200 Constitution Avenue, N.W.
Washington, D.C. 20210

---

*Certain full-time students, student learners, apprentices, and
handicapped workers may be paid less than the applicable
minimum but only under special Department issued certificates.

**Effective July 1, 1979, equal pay enforcement will be
transferred from the Wage and Hour Division to the Equal
Employment Opportunity Commission.

U.S. Department of Labor
Employment Standards Administration
Wage and Hour Division
200 Constitution Avenue, N.W.
Washington, D.C. 20210

The law requires employers to display this
poster where employees can readily see it.

WH Publication 1088
Rev. January 1979

TABLE 4-4
Legal influence on income maintenance

Laws	Coverage	Basic requirements	Agencies involved
Social Security Act	Employees of private firms, state and local governments, and schools and hospitals	Disability benefits to disabled workers and their children Retirement benefits after age 65 (or at reduced rates after 62) to worker and spouse Survivor's benefits to widow with dependent children under 18, widow over 62, and dependent children under 18 Health insurance for persons over 65 (Medicare) Funded by payroll tax on employer, employee, and the self-employed	Social Security Administration
Employee Retirement Security Act (Pension Reform Law)	All employee benefit plans of employers engaged in interstate commerce, with 25 or more employees	Benefit plans must meet certain minimum standards for employee participation, vesting rights, funding, reporting, and disclosure Plans must be funded on an actuarily sound basis Vested benefits are to be insured through Pension Benefit Guaranty Corporation	Department of Labor Internal Revenue Service Pension Benefit Guaranty Corporation

Source: Extracted from F. Ray Marshall, Allan G. King, and Vernon M. Briggs, Jr., *Labor Economics*, 4th ed. (Homewood, Ill.: Richard D. Irwin, 1980), especially chap. 17.

Social Security Act

The *Social Security Act* of 1935 provides for a federal old-age and survivor's insurance program, along with a federal-state system of *unemployment insurance*. It provides assistance for the aged, the blind, and dependent children who need help. The act provides monthly life insurance payments to the widow and dependent children of a deceased worker. In 1965, disability insurance was added. In 1966, health insurance benefits (commonly known as Medicare) and other benefits for retired employees were added.

The law is administered by the Social Security Administration.

Employee Retirement Income Security Act (ERISA)

Another federal law aimed at protecting employees' rights and pension programs is having a tremendous impact on personnel work. ERISA requires all private firms with retirement programs to meet federally imposed standards. No company is required to have a plan. If it does, however, the plan must be financially sound and easily understood by the plan's participants. Also, firms with plans that cover 100 or more employees must submit detailed descriptions of the plans and annual reports to the Department of Labor. This also applies to other employee welfare benefit plans.

The act is the primary responsibility of the Department of Labor. Plans must be submitted to the administrator for approval. Yet the plans must also be approved by the Internal Revenue Service (IRS) in the Treasury Department, and the Pension Benefit Guaranty Corporation must approve the plans it insures.

INDUSTRIAL RELATIONS LAWS

The basic federal labor law of the land is the *National Labor Relations Act* of 1935 (NLRA), also referred to as the *Wagner Act*. It has been amended by several subsequent acts but primarily by the *Labor-Management Relations Act* of 1947 (LMRA), also referred to as the *Taft-Hartley Act*, and the *Labor-Management Reporting and Disclosure Act* of 1959 (LMRDA), also referred to as the *Landrum Griffin Act*. Title VII of the *Civil Service Reform Act* of 1978 applies to most federal employees. These laws, which are summarized in Table 4–5, will be covered in detail in Part 5.

It is difficult to condense these laws into a few statements. They essentially do three things: (1) permit workers to form or join unions of their own choosing without fear of prosecution under the antitrust laws (included in Section 7 of the NLRA), (2) limit the rights and discretion of management by having working conditions determined jointly at the bargaining table rather than by management alone, and (3) limit the rights of unions.

The judicial powers of the act are vested in a five-person National Labor Relations Board (NLRB). Its administrative duties are handled by a general

TABLE 4–5
Legal influence on industrial relations

Laws	Coverage	Basic requirements	Agencies involved
Railway Labor Act	Nonmanagerial employees of private railroads and airlines	Employees are free to choose their own representative for collective bargaining, and to settle disputes by mediation, arbitration, and emergency boards	National Mediation Board National Railroad Adjustment Board
Norris-LaGuardia Act	Nonmanagerial employees of private firms	Prohibited courts from issuing injunctions against nonviolent union activities. Outlawed contracts forbidding union activities	Judicial system
National Labor Relations Act, as amended (Wagner Act)	Nonmanagerial employees in nonagricultural private firms not covered by the Railway Labor Act, and postal employees	Employees have right to form or join labor organizations, (or to refuse to), to bargain collectively through their representatives, and to engage in other concerted activities such as strikes, picketing, and boycotts; these are unfair labor practices which the employer and the union can't engage in	National Labor Relations Board (NLRB)
Labor-Management Relations Act, as amended (Taft-Hartley Act)	Same as above	Amended NLRA; permitted states to pass laws prohibiting compulsory union membership; set up methods to deal with strikes affecting national health and safety	NLRB Federal Mediation and Conciliation Service

Source: Extracted from F. Ray Marshall, Allan G. King, and Vernon M. Briggs, Jr., *Labor Economics*, 4th ed. (Homewood, Ill.: Richard D. Irwin, 1980), especially chap. 16.

TABLE 4-5 *(continued)*

Laws	*Coverage*	*Basic requirements*	*Agencies involved*
Labor-Management Reporting and Disclosure Act (Landrum-Griffin)	Same as above	Amended NLRA and LMRA; guarantees individual rights of union members in dealing with their union; requires financial disclosures by unions	U.S. Department of Labor
Executive Order 10988, as amended, and Title VII of Civil Service Reform Act	Nonmanagerial federal service employees and agencies except military and postal personnel	Employees may bargain collectively through their own representatives on noneconomic and nonstaffing issues; grievances require arbitration	Federal Labor Relations Authority

counsel. All six members are appointed by the president, but by law the general counsel is to be independent of the other five.

PRIVACY

Privacy on the job is emerging as one of the hottest issues for personnel managers. It will probably be even more significant in the future.

Seven states have passed laws permitting employees in the private sector to see their personnel records. They also require rules of confidentiality for personnel records. Federal employees and those in nine states now have this right.

Surveys are now being done to see whether guidelines can be set up voluntarily or should be legislated.[18]

COPING WITH THE LEGAL ENVIRONMENT

Most personnel managers have accepted the laws mentioned in this chapter—with varying degrees of reluctance. And most managers abide by the law, voluntarily or otherwise. Yet there are many practical problems involved in conforming to these public policies.

---

[18]Alan F. Westin, "What Should Be Done about Employee Privacy?" *Personnel Administrator* 25 (March 1980):27–30.

Practical Problems Involved

Some of the practical problems involved are (1) conflicts in laws and enforcement decisions and (2) the time, effort, and cost of conforming.

Conflicting laws and decisions.   It can be seen that these laws lend themselves to conflict. For example, some state laws conflict with federal regulations.

Conflicts also arise between federal laws and regulations. For example, the courts must decide between equal employment rights and the seniority rights of employees with union-management agreements under the NLRA. For most unions any attempt to replace seniority with minority rights is a declaration of war, for seniority is one of the most basic union beliefs.

The controversy is still raging, with seniority apparently winning. In 1977, the Supreme Court ruled that an otherwise "neutral" seniority system does not violate the job bias provisions of the CRA, even when it continues past job discrimination.

The cost of conforming.   In addition to the legal conflicts, there is also a great cost involved. Each law requires that employees and potential employees be notified of its coverage. This is usually done by means of posters on bulletin boards, letters, memos, and direct oral communication. These all involve time, effort, and expense.

A speaker at a personnel management conference had finished speaking on government involvement in personnel work. Someone asked the question, "What is the most important thing I should do in order to comply with the regulations you mentioned?" The answer was, "Get a *big* bulletin board!"

Another thing that bothers many personnel managers is the need to send reports to the regulatory agencies. For example, the EEO laws require the completion of an Employee Information Report, Form EEO-1 (see Figure 4-6). According to many personnel managers, this is the most unpleasant aspect of government involvement.

The Office of Management and Budget estimated that Americans would spend 786 million hours, or 3.5 hours per person, filling out federal forms during 1979.

Another problem is the volume of laws and regulations that personnel managers should know. The *Code of Federal Regulations* reports laws passed by Congress. In 1977, it had 75,000 pages, up 39 percent from 1970. The *Federal Register*, which daily publishes new rules and regulations put out by regulatory agencies, had 65,603 pages, up 227 percent.

FIGURE 4-6

Standard Form 100
(Rev. 12/78)
O.M.B. No. 124-R0011
Approval Expires 12/79
100-210

EQUAL EMPLOYMENT OPPORTUNITY
EMPLOYER INFORMATION REPORT EEO-1

Joint Reporting Committee

- Equal Employment Opportunity Commission
- Office of Federal Contract Compliance Programs

Section A — TYPE OF REPORT
Refer to instructions for number and types of reports to be filed.

1. Indicate by marking in the appropriate box the type of reporting unit for which this copy of the form is submitted (MARK ONLY ONE BOX).

(1) ☐ Single-establishment Employer Report

Multi-establishment Employer
(2) ☐ Consolidated Report
(3) ☐ Headquarters Unit Report
(4) ☐ Individual Establishment Report (submit one for each establishment with 25 or more employees)
(5) ☐ Special Report

2. Total number of reports being filed by this Company (Answer on Consolidated Report only) _____

Section B — COMPANY IDENTIFICATION *(To be answered by all employers)*

OFFICE USE ONLY

1. Parent Company
  a. Name of parent company (owns or controls establishment in item 2) omit if same as label

a.

Name of receiving office	Address (Number and street)

b.

City or town	County	State	ZIP code	b. Employer Identification No.

2. Establishment for which this report is filed (Omit if same as label)
  a. Name of establishment

c.

Address (Number and street)	City or town	County	State	ZIP code

d.

b. Employer Identification No. _____ (If same as label: skip.)

3. Parent company affiliation
(Multi-establishment Employers Answer on Consolidated Report only)
  a. Name of parent—affiliated company   b. Employer Identification No. _____

Address (Number and street)	City or town	County	State	ZIP code

---

Section C — EMPLOYERS WHO ARE REQUIRED TO FILE   *(To be answered by all employers)*

☐ Yes ☐ No   1. Does the entire company have at least 100 employees in the payroll period for which you are reporting?

☐ Yes ☐ No   2. Is your company affiliated through common ownership and/or centralized management with other entities in an enterprise with a total employment of 100 or more?

☐ Yes ☐ No   3. Does the company or any of its establishments (a) have 50 or more employees AND (b) is not exempt as provided by 41 CFR 60-1.5. AND either (1) is a prime government contractor or first-tier subcontractor, and has a contract, subcontract, or purchase order amounting to $50,000 or more, or (2) serves as a depository of Government funds in any amount or is a financial institution which is an issuing and paying agent for U.S. Savings Bonds and Savings Notes?

NOTE: If the answer is yes to ANY of these questions, complete the entire form, otherwise skip to Section G.

FIGURE 4-6 *(continued)*

SF 100 Page 2

Section D — EMPLOYMENT DATA

Employment at this establishment--Report all permanent, temporary, or part-time employees including apprentices and on-the-job trainees unless specifically excluded as set forth in the instructions. Enter the appropriate figures on all lines and in all columns. Blank spaces will be considered as zeros.

JOB CATEGORIES	OVERALL TOTALS (SUM OF COL. B THRU K) A	MALE					FEMALE				
		WHITE (NOT OF HISPANIC ORIGIN) B	BLACK (NOT OF HISPANIC ORIGIN) C	HISPANIC D	ASIAN OR PACIFIC ISLANDER E	AMERICAN INDIAN OR ALASKAN NATIVE F	WHITE (NOT OF HISPANIC ORIGIN) G	BLACK (NOT OF HISPANIC ORIGIN) H	HISPANIC I	ASIAN OR PACIFIC ISLANDER J	AMERICAN INDIAN OR ALASKAN NATIVE K
Officials and Managers											
Professionals											
Technicians											
Sales Workers											
Office and Clerical											
Craft Workers (Skilled)											
Operatives (Semi-Skilled)											
Laborers (Unskilled)											
Service Workers											
TOTAL											
Total employment reported in previous EEO-1 report											

(The trainees below should also be included in the figures for the appropriate occupational categories above)

| Formal On-the-job trainees | White collar | | | | | | | | | | |
| | Production | | | | | | | | | | |

1. NOTE: On consolidated report, skip questions 2-5 and Section E.
2. How was information as to race or ethnic group in Section D obtained?
   1 ☐ Visual Survey   3 ☐ Other — Specify ....
   2 ☐ Employment Record   ....
3. Dates of payroll period used –

4. Pay period of last report submitted for this establishment

5. Does this establishment employ apprentices?
   This year? 1 ☐ Yes 2 ☐ No
   Last year? 1 ☐ Yes 2 ☐ No

Section E — ESTABLISHMENT INFORMATION

1. Is the location of the establishment the same as that reported last year?
   1 ☐ Yes 2 ☐ No 3 ☐ Did not report last year 4 ☐ Reported on combined basis
2. Is the major business activity at this establishment the same as that reported last year?
   1 ☐ Yes 2 ☐ No 3 ☐ No report last year 4 ☐ Reported on combined basis
3. What is the major activity of this establishment? (Be specific, i.e., manufacturing steel castings, retail grocer, wholesale plumbing supplies, title insurance, etc. Include the specific type of product or type of service provided, as well as the principal business or industrial activity.

OFFICE USE ONLY

e.

Section F — REMARKS

Use this item to give any identification data appearing on last report which differs from that given above, explain major changes in composition or reporting units, and other pertinent information.

Section G — CERTIFICATION (See Instructions G)

Check one
1. ☐ All reports are accurate and were prepared in accordance with the instructions (check on consolidated only)
2. ☐ This report is accurate and was prepared in accordance with the instructions.

Name of Certifying Official	Title	Signature		Date
Name of person to contact regarding this report (Type or print)	Address (Number and street)			
Title	City and State	ZIP code	Telephone Area Code / Number	Extension

All reports and information obtained from individual reports will be kept confidential as required by Section 709 (e) of Title VII
WILLFULLY FALSE STATEMENTS ON THIS REPORT ARE PUNISHABLE BY LAW. U.S. CODE TITLE 18, SECTION 1001

Ways of Coping with the Laws

As this is the legal environment within which personnel managers function, how can they cope with it? There are several things that can be done, such as:

1. Learn as much as possible about the laws.
2. Challenge detrimental or harmful laws.
3. Become involved in the legal-political system.
4. Find a better legal environment—if possible.
5. Accept the laws and comply.

Learn all about the laws. Managers can learn as much as possible about the laws, how they affect their business, what is required to be in compliance, and to what extent the law might even be to their advantage. For example, the targeted jobs tax credit program can be used to train employees—and save on taxes.[19]

Challenge undesirable laws. A second approach is for management to challenge any law or regulation that it thinks is detrimental or harmful. That is what Sears is now doing, as shown in the opening case. Admittedly, this is a costly procedure and probably will require a trade or professional association, or a group of individuals, to pool their resources to challenge the laws.

Become involved in the system. A third method is to become involved in the legal-political system. The new Campaign Practices Law permits organiza-

"The motion has been made and seconded that we obey the law."

Reprinted by permission *The Wall Street Journal*

---

[19]See F. Ray Marshall, "Targeted Jobs Tax Credit Program," *Personnel Administrator* 25 (January 1980):46–47, for an example of this.

tions to set up political action committees (PACs). A group of 50 people can form such a committee to raise and use funds the same way COPE and other union political action committees do.

Another way is to become involved in the election process and help to get people who will be favorable to one's point of view appointed to the administrative bodies that administer the laws.

Find a better environment. It may be possible to locate where there is a better legal-political climate. Many states have passed laws favoring business in order to attract new firms. As payroll costs are so important to most firms, one might seek states that have workers' compensation, unemployment insurance, and related laws that are not "antibusiness."

A firm could move to a state that has a right-to-work law, so that it will not have so many—or at least the same—problems with unions.

Accept the laws and comply. Finally, managers may decide that it is advisable to accept the laws and live with them. Therefore, they will do all that is necessary to be in compliance with the environment.

SUMMARY AND CONCLUSIONS

Personnel policies and procedures are increasingly being influenced by government legislation, orders, regulations, and court decisions. Very few personnel activities are exempt from this influence. Therefore the most important laws that provide the legal environment in which personnel managers operate are presented early in the text. This gives you an overview of how they affect personnel management. Also, you can refer back to this chapter as you study the functions involved.

The areas of government involvement causing personnel managers the greatest concern are (1) equal employment opportunity, (2) occupational safety and health, (3) compensation, (4) income maintenance, (5) industrial relations, and (6) privacy.

Personnel managers have moved from being almost completely free to do as they pleased, to passive and reluctant compliance with the letter of the law, to affirmative action to achieve the spirit of the law—in most cases.

The unfavorable actions of some personnel people contributed to the growing government involvement. These regulations, however, forced managers to have a more rational, systematic, and research-based approach to the personnel function. Now, though, many personnel managers are confused and frustrated by what they consider to be an overzealous enforcement of some of the regulations.

EEO is required for women, minorities, veterans, the handicapped, and older workers. The laws and orders involved are Title VII of the *Civil Rights Act*, Executive Order 11246, *Veterans Readjustment Act*, *Vocational Rehabilitation Act*, and *Age Discrimination in Employment Act*.

The main laws affecting safety and health are the state workers' compensation laws and the *Occupational Safety and Health Act*.

The *Fair Labor Standards Act* sets minimum wages, overtime pay, and hours of work for most employees. The *Davis-Bacon Act* and *Walsh-Healy Act* set wages and hours for government contractors.

The *Equal Pay Act* requires that women be paid the same as men for doing the same general type of work.

Income maintenance is provided by the *Social Security Act* in the form of disability pay, retirement, and unemployment compensation, as well as survivor's benefits. The *Employee Retirement Income Security Act* tries to protect employees' private pensions.

Personnel managers can cope with these laws by (1) learning how to use the laws to their advantages, (2) challenging "unreasonable" laws, (3) becoming involved in the political system, (4) finding a better legal environment, or (5) accepting the laws.

QUESTIONS

1. Do you think that employee privacy will be as important in the future as indicated? Explain.
2. How would you describe the effects of the legal environment on the personnel function?
3. Do you think the present level of government involvement is desirable or not? Explain.
4. Do you think the complexity of this environment will increase, decrease, or remain about the same in the near future? Explain.
5. How would you evaluate the suggestions for coping with the increasingly complex legal environment?
6. As a personnel manager, how would you cope with this environment?

PROBLEM

The Affirmative Action Plan (AAP) Manual

XYZ Company has an AAP manual of 25 pages, from which the following statements were taken:

I. Policy Statement

It is our policy to provide equal opportunity in all terms, conditions, and privileges of employment. This policy applies to all qualified applicants and employees without discrimination because of race, color, religion, sex, age, national origin, or handicap—except as provided for by law. We insist that our managers promote effective utilization of all minority, women, and handicapped applicants and employees through a positive and continuing AA program at all levels and in every office, region, and department of the company.

Yet, AA efforts are to be based on the requirement that the best qualified person in the applicant pool be selected. No personnel decisions will be based on a candidate's sex, race, or other nonrelated job factor.

Steady progress has been—and continues to be—made throughout the company as women and minorities continue to be promoted to higher level positions.

II.   Women

Our goal is to correct underrepresentation of women in better jobs. Our plan is to ensure that women are included in selection pools for hiring, training, and promotion, and that they be fully considered for positions commensurate with their abilities and desires. Our efforts are especially directed toward greater representation of women in management positions. At the end of 1979, 12 percent of the women employed were in management positions.

III.   Minorities

Our objective is to take positive steps to correct any underrepresentation of minorities. The number of minority individuals available in the surrounding community is to be used as the guideline for hiring at the entry level.

IV.   Handicapped

We have employed handicapped workers for many years. Individuals covered by our plan are to be qualified handicapped persons who, with the company's reasonable accommodation for their handicap, are capable of performing a particular job.

The AAP includes many provisions for active recruitment, implementation, and monitoring systems, analysis, and reporting.

Questions

1.   What are your reactions to this AA?
2.   Does it seem to conform to all legal requirements? Explain.
3.   Would you change it in any respect? Explain.

SUGGESTED READINGS FOR FURTHER STUDY

Brookmire, David.   "Designing and Implementing Your Company's Affirmative Action Program." *Personnel Journal* 58 (April 1979):234–37.

Brown, Robert J.   "Making the Promise of OSHA a Reality." *Labor Law Journal* 29 (February 1978):68–71.

Burton, Gene E., and Dev S. Pathak.   "101 Ways to Discriminate against Equal Employment Opportunity." *Personnel Administrator* 22 (August 1977):42–45 and 48–49.

Crickmer, Barry.   "Regulation: How Much Is Enough?" *Nation's Business* 68 (March 1980):26–33.

Dhanens, Thomas P.   "Implications of the New EEOC Guidelines." *Personnel* 56 (September–October 1979):32–39.

Linenberger, Patricia, and Timothy J. Keaveny.   "Age Discrimination in Employment: A Guide for Employers." *Personnel Administrator* 24 (July 1979):87–98.

Lynn, Naomi, and Richard E. Vaden. "Toward a Non-Sexist Personnel Opportunity Structure—The Federal Executive Bureaucracy." *Public Personnel Management* 8 (July–August 1979):209–15.

Miller, Ernest C. "An EEO Examination of Employment Applications." *Personnel Administrator* 25 (March 1980):63–69 and 81.

McFeeley, Neil D. "Weber versus Affirmative Action." *Personnel* 57 (January–February 1980):38–51.

Pati, Gopal C., and Edward F. Hilton, Jr. "A Comprehensive Model for a Handicapped Affirmative Action Program." *Personnel Journal* 59 (February 1980):99–108.

Schliebner, Joan Johnson, and Joy Sandberg. "Record Retention and Posting Requirements of the Federal Government." *Personnel Administrator* 24 (April 1979):54–59.

Somers, Patricia A., and Judith Clementson-Mohr. "Sexual Extortion in the Workplace." *Personnel Administrator* 24 (April 1979):23–28.

PART TWO

Selecting and Developing Employees

Full many a gem of purest ray serene
The dark unfathom'd caves of ocean bear:
Full many a flower is born to blush unseen
And waste its sweetness on the desert air.
THOMAS GRAY, "Elegy Written in a Country Churchyard"

Within the environment discussed in Part 1, personnel managers must develop an effective work team if they are to achieve organizational goals. This requires (1) recruiting and selecting the right type and number of needed personnel, (2) maximizing their potential through training and developing them, and moving them into positions where they can operate most productively, (3) utilizing their abilities, (4) appraising, evaluating, and rewarding their performance, and (5) maintaining them until they leave the organization.

The specific topics covered, and the chapters in which they are discussed, are:

5. Personnel Planning and Career Management
6. Recruiting Personnel
7. Selecting Employees
8. Training and Developing Employees
9. Management Development

The first two of these activities are discussed in this part. Figure II-1 shows how these activities fit into the overall personnel system.

FIGURE II-1
Selecting and developing employees

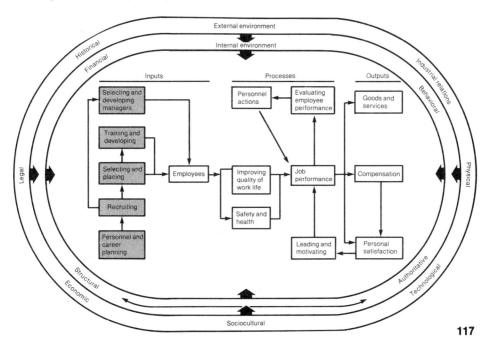

CHAPTER FIVE

Personnel Planning and Career Management

Learning Objectives

After studying the material in this chapter, you should be able to:

1. Explain the importance of personnel planning.
2. Describe how personnel planning is done.
3. Explain the need for developing an action plan to carry out personnel planning.
4. Show how career management and personnel are related.
5. Explain why career management is now so important.
6. Describe the requirements for career management to be effective.

Some Important Words and Terms

Personnel and human resource planning
Overall personnel requirements
Job analysis
Job description
Job specification
Personnel inventory

Personnel planning replacement chart
Net new personnel requirements
Action programs
Career management
Career
Career planning
Career development

No amount of sophistication is going to allay the fact that all your knowledge is about the past and all your decisions are about the future.
IAN H. WILSON

Outline of the Chapter

IMPORTANCE OF PERSONNEL PLANNING
What Is Personnel Planning?
Why Do Personnel Planning?
STEPS IN PERSONNEL PLANNING
Studying Long-range Objective and Plans
Determining Overall Personnel Requirements
Taking Inventory of Present Personnel
Determining Net New Personnel Requirements
Developing Action Programs for Filling Needs
Using Computerized Systems
HOW CAREER MANAGEMENT IS RELATED TO PERSONNEL PLANNING
Why the Emphasis on Career Management?
More Emphasis on Career Changes
Career Management Is Involved in All Personnel Functions
REQUIREMENTS FOR EFFECTIVE CAREER MANAGEMENT
Integrate Career Management with Personnel Planning
Make It a Cooperative Effort
Assign Definite Responsibility for Coordinating Career Management

In the mid-1970s, there was a chronic national shortage of medical technologists. This was also true at a pathology laboratory near a large university.

The pathologist who operated this medical testing laboratory employed around 30 technologists. As his demand was rising faster than the supply of well-trained technologists, he worked with a local hospital and the university to develop a degree program for technologists. In addition, he had a policy of only hiring wives of college students, if they were available. As the employees tended to leave after three or four years to follow their husbands, he had a continually improving caliber of personnel from the university and the incoming wives.

Of course, this case is not typical. But it does illustrate the two main thoughts of this chapter: (1) the need for personnel planning and how to do it and (2) career management.

As you can see from Figure 5-1, career management and personnel planning are closely related. As the organization plans its human resource needs, it can also plan how to help employees advance their career plans.[1] Both types of planning provide for the orderly succession of talented people who are then ready for advancement. Career and personnel planning provide the organization with an orderly approach to moving women and minorities rapidly into positions that satisfy EEO guidelines.

IMPORTANCE OF PERSONNEL PLANNING

Personnel planning is becoming one of the most important personnel functions. In a recent survey, 85 percent of chief executives listed it as "one of the most critical management undertakings for the 1980s."[2] In fact, the more progressive employers already have such programs.

Several companies, such as IBM, Xerox, Exxon, First National City Bank, J. I. Case, Tenneco, General Foods, Union Carbide, American Express, and General Electric, have set up refined, companywide personnel planning systems.

What Is Personnel Planning?

Personnel and human resource planning is the process of translating overall organizational objectives, plans, and programs into an effective work force to achieve specific performance.

---

[1]S. Breaux Daniel, "The Complementarity of Human Resource Planning and Career Planning," unpublished report, University of South Alabama, May 30, 1979.

[2]"Wanted: A Manager to Fit Each Strategy," *Business Week*, February 25, 1980, p. 166.

FIGURE 5-1
How personnel/human resource planning and career management are related

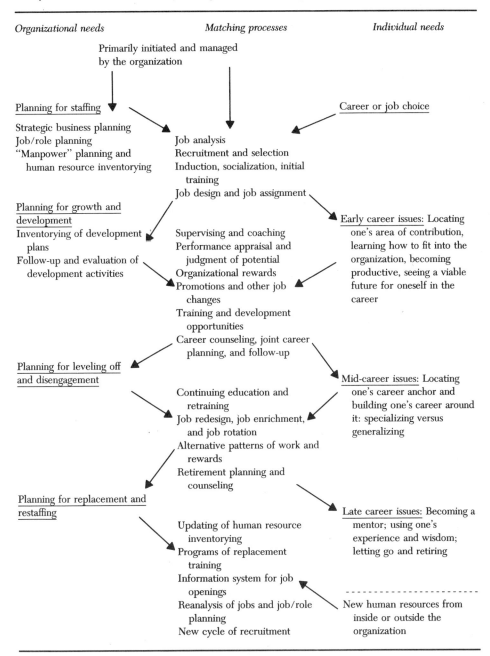

Source: Reprinted from Increasing Organizational Effectiveness through Better Human Resource Planning and Development by Edgar H. Schein, *Sloan Management Review* 19 (Fall 1977): 7 by permission of the publisher.

FIGURE 5–2
How personnel/human resource planning and career planning and development fit into the staffing function

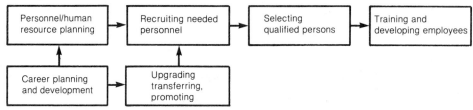

Figure 5–2 shows how personnel planning and career management fit into the staffing function of the personnel system.

In the past, personnel planning has been mainly involved with personnel recruitment, selection, and placement. But present trends in human resource planning are to involve *all of the personnel functions*. It is used in:

1. Designing and redesigning jobs.
2. Determining job requirements.
3. Recruiting and selecting.
4. Maximizing employee potential.
5. Utilizing, rewarding, and maintaining the work force.
6. Dealing with unions and employee associations.

Why Do Personnel Planning?

While human resource planning has been infrequently, or inadequately, used in the past, several factors are currently leading to a renewed interest in it.

Forces leading to personnel planning. Federal contract compliance, including programs for hiring women, minorities, older and handicapped workers, and veterans, has contributed to this trend. Also, the (1) shortage of experienced and capable managers, (2) expense involved in hiring, developing, and maintaining employees, (3) cost of using personnel ineffectively, (4) growth of knowledgeable workers—and increasing obsolescence of present personnel, and (5) emphasis on human resource accounting—all these have increased the move to introduce or improve planning.

Yet the methods being used still vary from elementary "guesswork" about short-range supply and demand to highly sophisticated systems. The latter use computer-based data banks to meet current needs or help managers plan for a long-range matching of supply and demand for expected occupational categories and job skills.

At Owens-Corning Fiberglas, employee planning is highly individualized. In a program set up under a new Human Resources Department, the total career of each salaried employee is followed from hiring to retirement. A computerized data bank of each employee's skills, education, experience, and other information is used as a basis for career planning, guidance, and appraisals. Each person's skills are analyzed and matched to the firm's needs.[3]

Objectives of personnel planning. Organizations cannot count on finding talented people just when they need them. Instead, planning and searching for qualified talent must be done continuously. Systematic steps must be taken in order to assure that a pool of talent will be ready when needed. Consequently, the objectives of personnel planning are to:

1. Relate human resource needs to the overall activities of an organization.
2. Make long-range estimates of specific—as well as general—needs.
3. Maximize the return on investment in human resources.

Organizations needing planning. Ironically, all else being equal, the organizations that need human resource planning most are those in which it is most difficult to do.

1. The more rapidly expanding groups need it more than those with a stable work force or a work force that is expanding gradually or predictably.
2. Organizations with a high proportion of the more expensive scientific, technical, professional, and managerial personnel should do more and better planning than those with many nonmanagerial workers.
3. Technologically oriented organizations need planning more than those using existing knowledge in order to match an inadequate supply of capable personnel with escalating demand.
4. The more responsive organizations are to their total environment, the more they need planning, especially those that use more sophisticated techniques and longer time frames.

Because of expanding technology in performing open-heart surgery and the development of related equipment to care for the patients, a progressive hospital planned and opened a Coronary Care Unit (CCU). There were not enough qualified people available to staff it. After "borrowing" from the limited supply of personnel in the Intensive Care Unit (ICU), there were only enough to allow one quarter of the equipped beds to be used when it opened. Even after a year, only half the beds were being used.

5. Organizations covered by government regulations must—in order to be in compliance—do human resource planning in almost all areas of personnel activities.

A national chemical company had several hundred products being produced at six plants. It tripled its personnel department's training staff and

---

[3]Jon Healey, "Big Push in Manpower Planning," *Dunn's Business Review* 104 (November 1974):106.

brought in consultants to comply with EEOC and OFCCP regulations. They took three years to do a functional job analysis for all nonexempt personnel. The results, used for recruiting, selecting, developing, and rewarding personnel, have been accepted as valid.

6. As shown in the previous case, the more diversified the products produced or services provided, the greater the need for planning.
7. The larger the organization is, the more it needs—and has the financial and personnel resources to do—longer range and more sophisticated planning.

Organizing for personnel planning.   There is little agreement about where the human resource planning function should be located in the organization. However, the personnel manager cannot do it alone. An integrated approach is more effective, as shown in Figure 5-3. Usually the personnel department does the overall planning and coordinates the activities of the operating managers.

If there is no personnel planning system, how do you begin one? Probably the best way to start is by inventorying existing personnel and expertise to see what shortages currently exist. This should provide a base from which to start doing more advance planning.

There is no rule of thumb about what you should do, but the system that fits you and your organization is the one you should use.

FIGURE 5-3
Responsibility for personnel planning in the Bureau of National Affairs' Personnel Policy Forum companies

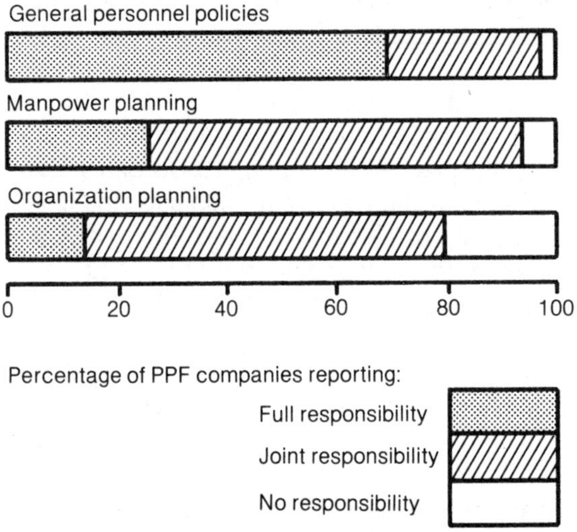

Source: The Bureau of National Affairs, Inc.: "The Personnel Department," BNA Policy and Practice Series: *Personnel Management* (Washington, D.C.: Bureau of National Affairs, No. 244), p. 251:21.

FIGURE 5-4
Steps in a human resource planning system

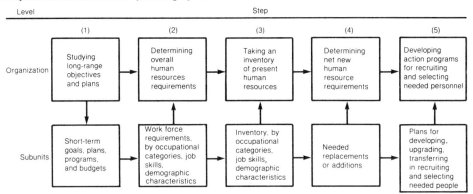

STEPS IN PERSONNEL PLANNING

The system of personnel planning proposed in this text is the six-step system shown in Figure 5-4. As shown, it operates at two levels. First, objectives and plans are made at the organization level and sent to subunits at lower organizational levels. Next, data from all the subunits are summarized and submitted up the line to the top manager.

Studying Long-range Objectives and Plans

Personnel planning begins with an evaluation of organizational objectives and plans. The primary use of personnel planning is to provide the organization with the people needed to perform the activities that will achieve the organization's goals. Therefore, the objectives and plans at all levels of the organization provide the basis for determining personnel needs.

The objective of most public institutions is to provide a service to the public. Therefore, the cost of human resources is not as important as in private firms.

The objectives of private firms may be *both economic and social.* While trying to increase profits, increase share of market, and produce a better product at a lower price, the firm may also try to hire minorities and women, clean up the environment, improve safety, and be socially responsive. Yet such programs tend to divert physical, financial, and human resources from the primary economic mission.

Standard Brands' new human resources department, headed by vice president Madelyn Jennings, has grown fourfold in three years. The primary reason for its growth in size and importance is its assignment of the firm's first manpower planning system. It is "directly tied to carrying out corporate strategies."[4]

Determining Overall Personnel Requirements

The second step in human resource planning is predicting the need for—and the availability of—people with the characteristics needed to perform present and future jobs. Therefore, the organization's *overall personnel requirements*—in terms of occupational specialties, job skills, and demographic characteristics—should be forecast. In multiunit organizations, this starts with the individual units and progresses to the organizational level. See Figure 5-5 for a model used at the departmental level in one division of a major corporation, which can serve as a guide in determining unit requirements.

The key to effective forecasting is to begin with cause-and-effect relationships. In other words, there is a need to know what factors determine the supply of and demand for workers. Second, as many factors are beyond its control, management cannot plan the changes in those variables. However, a forecast can still be made by anticipating possible changes in the uncontrollable factors and projecting their possible effect on the organization's personnel needs.

There are two procedures involved in determining overall requirements. First, there is the process of determining the job needs, including personal characteristics required of any employee to perform each job, such as training time, aptitudes, temperaments, interests, physical capacities, and ability to adjust to working conditions.

Second, the number of people needed to do all the jobs is based on the volume of work to be done and the number of people needed to do each job.

Determining job needs. *Job analysis* is the process used to determine what each job is and what is required to perform it. Job analysis can be defined as the process of gathering information and determining the elements of a job by observation and study. Job analysis also records details concerning the training, skills, required efforts, qualifications, abilities, experience, responsibilities, and so forth that are needed to perform the job.

A *job description* is then prepared from the results of the analysis. A job description lists the duties, responsibilities, and working conditions of the job. It details the relationships between the particular job as it exists and the other jobs with which it is associated. When it contains statements of mental, physical, and other demands required of a person to perform the job, it is called a *job specification.*

Determining the number of people needed. The second part of this step is to determine the number of people needed in each of the job and skill catego-

---

[4]"Personnel Widens Its Franchise," *Business Week*, February 26, 1979, p. 116.

FIGURE 5–5
Model of a departmental personnel forecasting system

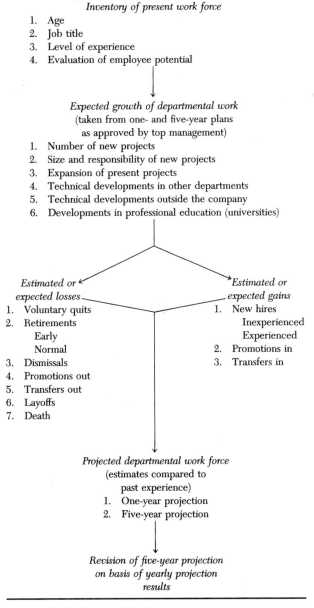

Inventory of present work force
1. Age
2. Job title
3. Level of experience
4. Evaluation of employee potential

Expected growth of departmental work
(taken from one- and five-year plans
as approved by top management)
1. Number of new projects
2. Size and responsibility of new projects
3. Expansion of present projects
4. Technical developments in other departments
5. Technical developments outside the company
6. Developments in professional education (universities)

Estimated or
expected losses
1. Voluntary quits
2. Retirements
   Early
   Normal
3. Dismissals
4. Promotions out
5. Transfers out
6. Layoffs
7. Death

Estimated or
expected gains
1. New hires
   Inexperienced
   Experienced
2. Promotions in
3. Transfers in

Projected departmental work force
(estimates compared to
past experience)
1. One-year projection
2. Five-year projection

Revision of five-year projection
on basis of yearly projection
results

Source: Richard D. Peterson, "The Growing Role of Manpower Forecasting in Organizations," *MSU Business Topics*, Summer 1969, pp. 7–14. Reprinted by permission of the publisher, Division of Research, Graduate School of Business Administration, Michigan State University.

THE WALL STREET JOURNAL

SANTA'S WORKSHOP

HELP WANTED:
SYSTEMS ANALYST
SOLID STATE PHYSICIST
ANALOG DESIGNER

"I can remember when all we needed was someone who could carve and someone who could sew."

Reprinted by permission *The Wall Street Journal*

ries. In making this analysis, the personnel planner should consider the business cycle, the stage of development of the individual and the organization, the rate of turnover, the absence rate, sales volume, and many other factors.

Taking Inventory of Present Personnel

The next step is to take a *personnel inventory* of present employees to see if the organization can fill its needs from within. This may be done simply or elaborately. But it does need to include the same data as the predicted requirements. Included in the inventory are the present duties of your people, as well as the skills they possess—as indicated by their educational attainments, past work experience, and participation in training and development programs. This may be done for individual employees or for just the positions involved.

Inventories such as this enable the personnel manager to match the skills in the organization to overall personnel requirements. It is uneconomical to recruit, hire, and train new people when the needed skills are already on hand. Often, internal changes can be made at much less cost.

An overall personnel inventory, by positions, is helpful in total organizational planning. It can indicate whether the organization is ready to undertake new programs and can help estimate the cost of hiring more human resources.

The more progressive organizations have some form of promotion table such as the *personnel planning replacement chart* shown in Figure 5-6. Each

FIGURE 5-6
Personnel planning replacement chart

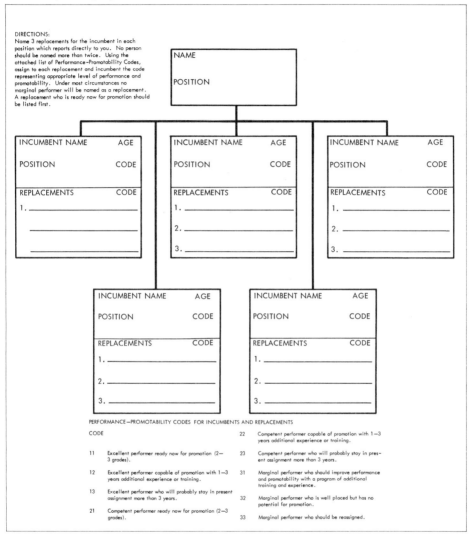

position on the chart is coded according to the incumbent's readiness for promotion.

The inventory—and resulting recruiting plans—must consider expected promotions, transfers, and other internal adjustment. Next, labor turnover, including retirements, deaths, discharges, disability, quits, and others, is estimated. From these analyses, the number of persons to be recruited is estimated, as shown in the following example.

Bell System economists have forecast that by the year 2000 there will be 265 million telephones in the United States. And the Bell System will be handling about 800 billion calls a year, including 14 times as many long-distance messages as are now handled. Bell System employment will increase by another half million persons as a result of these changes.

Determining Net New Personnel Requirements

The difference between *overall personnel requirements* and the *personnel inventory* becomes the *net new personnel requirements* to be filled. This becomes the personnel objective for the planning period. It is the basis for action programs to recruit new employees. However, other factors—such as the timing of personnel needs, age and experience variations, sex and race, and planning lead time—may also influence recruiting plans.

Figure 5-7 illustrates a simplified model that can be used to determine net demand for management personnel. This model must be supported by three other models for determining "internal supply," "external supply," and "demand."

Developing Action Programs for Filling Needs

Human resource planning includes designing and implementing *action programs* to assure that the organization's personnel needs are met. These programs emphasize selecting and developing human resource skills; but they

FIGURE 5-7
Variables determining the net demand for management personnel

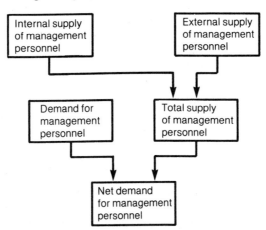

Source: N. S. Deckard and K. W. Lessey, "A Model for Understanding Management Manpower: Forecasting and Planning," *Personnel Journal* 54 (March 1975):169. Reprinted by permission from *Personnel Journal*, copyright March 1975.

also involve *all* the personnel functions, including utilizing and maintaining personnel.

Changes in personnel programs may take the form of expanding, adjusting, or reducing the work force—or a combination of these.

A point of departure in these programs is analyzing present personnel capabilities to see if some needs can be met through internal adjustment, such as promotions, transfers, or upgrading.

Action programs during periods of contraction are very difficult, especially for the many "plateaued executives." These managers, who were hired during periods of expansion or replacement, may have reached middle or upper ranks. They expect to progress further with the firm's expansion. Yet, when there is a period of recession, there is no place for them to go—except out.

Another vulnerable group are people hired for special programs. What do you do with them when the job or program is over? Allowing turnover and attrition to absorb such individuals is desirable, and temporary layoffs are preferable to permanent layoffs followed by later rehiring. "Efficiency" and "fairness" should be balanced.

Education, training, and development are other major action programs for meeting the organization's skill requirements.

As will be seen throughout this book, government-decreed programs—such as affirmative action programs—are increasingly being used in this step.

Using Computerized Systems

While computerized data systems are useful for advanced personnel planning, most organizations cannot afford these systems—nor do they need them. Any system that provides the needed data is adequate. Yet a computerized personnel information retrieval system should be investigated with a cost-benefit analysis. Potential applications to personnel research and employee planning and control are numerous.

HOW CAREER MANAGEMENT IS RELATED TO PERSONNEL PLANNING

Another rapidly expanding personnel activity is *career management*, which is the effort to combine ways of achieving organizational goals and objectives with helping employees advance their own careers.[5] It includes career planning and career development.

A *career* is the sequence of work-related attitudes and behaviors experienced during a person's life.[6] *Career planning* is the process of choosing occu-

---

[5]Several terms are used to refer to this activity, including *career planning, career guidance, career development* and *career planning and development*. The term I prefer is *career management,* but the others will be used interchangeably to avoid repetition.

[6]These definitions are based upon Douglas T. Hall, *Careers in Organizations* (Pacific Palisades, Calif.: Goodyear, 1976).

pations, organizations, and routes one's career will follow. *Career development* is engaging in the developmental activities required to attain career goals.

Why the Emphasis on Career Management?

Employers now realize that both the organization and its employees benefit from career management. There are many reasons for this new interest. They include: (1) affirmative action programs, (2) employees' heightened expectations on their jobs, (3) highly talented and skilled employees are in short supply and the market to attract and keep them is very competitive, and (4) management realizes it is in its best interests to improve the employees' quality of life, in order to reduce turnover, minimize unionization, and improve job performance.[7]

But employees are no longer willing to rely solely on the organization for career progress. Instead, they want a greater role in shaping their careers, for there are more opportunities available to individuals previously excluded. Women and minorities see new avenues opening up, and more of them are pursuing their careers with the same fervor of their white male counterparts.

More Emphasis on Career Changes

Increased life expectancy, changes in the work environment, and new patterns of career opportunities have caused more employees to reexamine their career plans. Most employees will spend over four decades as members of the labor force. During that time, their original ambitions change, and so do their career patterns.

Historically, individuals have typically chosen one of two career routes: (1) to specialize in a particular field, i.e., gain depth, or (2) to generalize, i.e., gain breadth in that field. Today, however, more people are making career changes into totally unrelated fields. They change directions not because they are forced to, or because they have failed at their jobs, or because of fear and desperation, but because of widening interests and heightened self-awareness.[8]

But not only are people no longer willing to commit themselves to one career, they are even less willing to commit themselves to one organization— as will be discussed in Chapter 12. This tendency, along with the increasing need for skilled and experienced scientific professions, technical, and managerial personnel (see Chapter 3), increases the need for personnel and career planning.

---

[7]James Walker, "Does Career Planning Rock the Boat?" *Human Resources Management* 17 (Spring 1978): 2–7.

[8]Marlys Hanson, "Career Development Responsibility of the Manager," *Personnel Journal* 56 (September 1977):443.

Career Management Is Involved in All Personnel Functions

Career management is not only related to personnel planning. It is also important in recruiting and selecting, training and developing, leading and motivating, and compensating employees.

Supervisors have tended in the past to identify subordinates with potential and then try to develop and promote them. As will be seen in Chapter 9, this mentor-protégé relationship has worked in the past. But no longer can personnel managers assume that senior officials can or will discover the right persons, or that junior managers will find their place in the promotional ladder.

REQUIREMENTS FOR EFFECTIVE CAREER MANAGEMENT

The requirements for career management to be effective are to (1) integrate it with personnel planning, (2) make it a cooperative effort, and (3) place definite responsibility for it.

Integrate Career Management with Personnel Planning

As shown in Figure 5-1, career planning must be an integral part of personnel planning if it is to succeed.[9] Individual employees will find it difficult to plan their future, unless the organization first does personnel planning. If management does not know what positions will be open and when, career management cannot be realistically maintained.

As discussed earlier, personnel planning involves looking at current employment trends and predicting how they will affect future human resource needs. As you have already seen, some of these trends are (1) increasing levels of education and affluence, (2) new attitudes toward work, (3) desire for participation in decision making concerning jobs and future careers, (4) employee loyalty shifting to the profession rather than to the organization, and (5) the desire for more flexible—and desirable—work situations.

As these trends are discussed throughout this book, they will not be discussed at this time. In general, though, management is responsible for providing employees with challenging career opportunities within the organization and offering information about current and future job opportunities—as determined by these trends.

Make It a Cooperative Effort

Career management can provide mutual benefits for both employees and management. For employees it can mean a conscious and continuous effort to

---

[9]Sam Gould, "Career Planning in the Organization," *Human Resource Management* 17 (Spring 1978):8.

FIGURE 5-8
Cooperative nature of career management

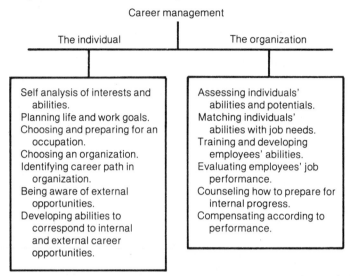

Career management

The individual	The organization
Self analysis of interests and abilities. Planning life and work goals. Choosing and preparing for an occupation. Choosing an organization. Identifying career path in organization. Being aware of external opportunities. Developing abilities to correspond to internal and external career opportunities.	Assessing individuals' abilities and potentials. Matching individuals' abilities with job needs. Training and developing employees' abilities. Evaluating employees' job performance. Counseling how to prepare for internal progress. Compensating according to performance.

adapt and adjust personal development to changes in environmental needs. For management it provides a systematic method for combining or integrating the many personnel functions, such as recruiting and selection, training and development, promoting and transferring, and compensating employees.

While the *primary responsibility* for career planning and development must rest with the individual, the organization can help employees grow and develop in many ways, as shown in Figure 5-8.

Management's responsibilities.   To have an effective career management program, management must commit itself not only to more effective personnel planning, but also to specific activities and the employees' planning process. Management must accept more responsibility for identifying and tracking candidates, for designing appropriate education and training programs, and for notifying employees of opportunities and paths for advancement and development. It must set definite objectives for such programs.

Some firms may stress career planning for highly skilled technicians—either to have them remain skilled as the technology advances, or to have them gain experience across operating divisions.

General Electric stresses career planning as a basis for development.

IBM stresses career planning as a basis of promoting from within.

Information on career paths, job requirements, and feedback on their current performance and personal capabilities are integral elements of a career planning system. As will be shown in Chapter 12, performance appraisal and feedback alone can establish a more realistic base for the individual's planning. Not only must the options be highly visible, but also the employees must be aware of what steps to take and what the logical progressions are. The employer must tell employees how long it will take to develop their skills, the frequency at which the desired positions become available, and the number of other employees who will compete for the position. In fact, the key to effective career planning is to *develop more realistic—not inflated—career expectations*. Finally, management must accept the fact that it may lose some good employees whose best interests are served elsewhere.

Some organizations are now asking their managers and expected future managers to state their career goals in writing. Other employers are offering *life planning courses* to employees in mid-career so that they can plan more thoughtfully for the future.[10]

One firm asked its people to define their next two desired jobs in the company. Then the personnel staff assisted the individuals to achieve their career goals by reaching those positions.

Employees' responsibilities. The ultimate responsibility for career planning and development rests with the individual. Management cannot force an individual to plan, for career planning is essentially a personal process of planning one's working life. As shown in Figure 5–8, individuals need to (1) do a careful self-evaluation, (2) set attainable goals and objectives, (3) evaluate how realistically these objectives match the employer's needs, (4) look at career paths, and (5) develop an action program to reach career goals. Such a program will more likely receive the organization's support in career development.

Employees must be willing to accept the fact that they may have to look outside the organization to fulfill their personal objectives. They must then decide whether to take action in moving outside the organization or to modify career goals to fit within the organization while still providing adequate satisfaction.

Some employers, such as Cleveland Trust Company, have included an "outplacement service" as part of their career development program. The main purpose is to aid management in terminating unacceptable workers. But it also serves those who feel they will have to leave the organization in order to reach their personal objectives.

Generally, however, employees will find that their key objectives, perhaps with slight modification, can be met within the organization. Then a career strategy will develop. The employee, with help from the personnel department, will have to identify the key tasks necessary to achieve career objectives. He or she must organize resources to achieve them.

---

[10]Fred K. Foulkes, "The Expanding Role of the Personnel Function," *Harvard Business Review* 53 (March–April 1975):71–84.

Assign Definite Responsibility for Coordinating Career Management

To be effective, career management requires that someone with appropriate authority be made responsible for coordinating the efforts of the individuals and organization. This is usually done by the personnel executive. The employee development division of the personnel department could be given this authority. The relationship would therefore be:

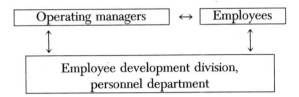

This arrangement would (1) increase development opportunities for employees seeking advancement, (2) reduce chance of unrealistic and overly optimistic planning by the employee, (3) make management aware of information affecting personnel planning, and (4) assure more professional assistance in personal career planning.

SUMMARY AND CONCLUSIONS

Personnel and human resources planning has been neglected but is now increasing in importance. Some reasons for the change are (1) a shortage of capable executives, (2) the changing industrial and occupational mix, (3) cost, and (4) new tools for analyzing cost-benefits.

The objectives of human resource planning are to relate personnel needs to organizational activities, estimate general long-range and specific short-range needs, and maximize return on investment in human resources.

Personnel planning is primarily involved with designing and redesigning jobs, determining job requirements, recruiting and selecting personnel, and maximizing employee potential.

The steps in human resource planning are (1) establishing organizational objectives and plans, (2) determining *overall* personnel requirements, (3) inventorying present personnel, (4) determining *net* new personnel needs, and (5) setting up action programs for filling needs, including affirmative action programs (AAPs).

According to a Chinese proverb, "Behind every able person there are always other abler people." This is true of career management, which is becoming an important part of personnel management. First, it helps meet organizational and individual goals. Second, it tends to increase employees satisfaction and increase their sense of dignity. Finally, it tends to reduce labor turnover and lower personnel costs.

Individuals may, and should, begin career planning before they get their first job. Yet, the work situation in which they find themselves, and the rate and extent of their personal development, can greatly modify their original career plans. With work experience, individuals can better understand their personal needs, career options, realistic opportunities available, and internal and external career paths that will help achieve career objectives.

The process of career planning and development is linked to personnel and human resource planning in many ways. Management must have its own strategic plan for human resources that relates to its other plans for the organization. If management does not know where it is and where it is heading relative to its human resources, it not only cannot expect employees to plan well but also will likely frustrate any career planning they may do.

Personnel planning and career management are simply two sides of the same coin. Personnel planning is the organization's effort to achieve the development and effective utilization of its employees. This also involves career management. Career planning and development are the employees' effort to develop and achieve their objectives within the framework of the organization's objectives.

QUESTIONS

1. If personnel-human resource planning is so important, why is it not done more extensively and better?

2. Earlier, the term *personnel planning* was used to refer only to determining job specifications and the number of employees to be hired. Do you think that is the correct concept, or is the more extensive and inclusive concept used in this text the correct one? Explain.

3. Are there changes you would suggest in the planning procedure advocated in this text? Explain.

4. What should management's responsibility be for employee career planning and development? Explain.

5. Who in the organization should be responsible for coordinating career management? Explain.

6. Is it really so important to relate career management and personnel planning? Explain.

PROBLEM

The Obsolete Employee

Henry was hired 20 years ago by a chemical firm. He had a general degree in chemistry, which fit the firm's needs at that time. As Henry was a mediocre employee, he was transferred from one meaningless job to another.

Recently two things happened which presented Henry's present supervisor with a difficult choice. First, new owners were trying to change from producing one product, fertilizer, to developing and producing a large variety of chemical components. Second, a recession made it difficult to retain Henry and several similar employees while hiring new graduates who could help them diversify.

Henry's supervisor went to Tammy Thompson, the personnel manager, with the problem.

Questions

1. If you were the personnel manager, what would you advise Henry's supervisor to do about him? Explain.
2. How would you set up a personnel planning program for the firm?
3. If you were Henry, what would you do? Explain.

SUGGESTED READINGS FOR FURTHER STUDY

Baker, C. R.   "Personnel and Organization Structures: Factors in Planning." *Managerial Planning* 25 (May 1977):26–28.

Burack, E. H., and T. G. Gutteridge.   "Institutional Manpower Planning: Rhetoric versus Reality." *California Management Review* 20 (Spring 1978):13–22.

Burton, Wendel W.   "Manpower Planning in an Inflationary Period." *Personnel Administrator* 24 (August 1979):33–38.

Cotton, Chester, and Richard Fraser.   "On-the-Job Career Planning: The Organization's Approach." *Training and Development Journal* 32 (February 1978):20–24.

Craft, J. A.   "Federal Influence in Manpower Programming: An Analysis of Recent Initiatives." *Labor Law Journal* 29 (March 1978):168–77.

Drucker, Peter F.   "Planning for 'Redundant' Workers." *Personnel Administrator* 25 (January 1980):32–34.

Miller, Ernest.   "Human Resource Executives and Corporate Planning: A Personnel Symposium." *Personnel* 54 (September–October 1977):12–22.

Moore, Lynda L.   "From Manpower Planning to Human Resource Planning through Career Development." *Personnel* 56 (May–June 1979):9–16.

Morgan, Marilyn.   *Managing Career Development.* New York: D. Van Nostrand Co., 1980.

Nemec, Margaret M.   "Networking: Here's How at Equitable." *Personnel Administrator* 25 (April 1980):63–64.

Seybolt, John W.   "Career Development: The State of the Art among the Grass Roots." *Training and Development Journal* 33 (April 1979):16–20.

Souerwine, Andrew.   "Career Strategies: Planning for Personal Achievement—the Job: Commitment to Activities." *Management Review* 67 (March 1978):52–61.

CHAPTER SIX

Recruiting Personnel

Learning Objectives

After studying the material in this chapter, you should be able to:

1. Explain who should be responsible for recruiting.
2. Name the internal and external sources of employees and show why each would be used.
3. Describe the methods used to recruit personnel.
4. Explain why college recruiting is so important, and some problems with its use.
5. Describe the needs of special groups to be recruited: women, minorities, older workers, the handicapped, and veterans.

Some Important Words and Terms

Recruiting
Source of supply
Upgrading
Transferring
Promoting

Job posting
Endicott Report
Coöp program
Bona fide occupational qualification
   (BFOQ)

Here lies a man who knew how to enlist in his service better men than himself.
Andrew Carnegie's Epitaph

Outline of the Chapter

WHAT IS RECRUITING
RESPONSIBILITY FOR RECRUITING
      In Small Firms
      A Shared Responsibility
DEVELOPING SOURCES FROM WHICH TO RECRUIT POTENTIAL
      EMPLOYEES
      Educational Institutions as Sources of Personnel
      Internal Sources
      External Sources
METHODS USED TO RECRUIT NEW EMPLOYEES
      Employee Referrals
      Advertising
      Scouting
      Electronic Assistance
      Other Methods
      Which Method to Use
COLLEGE RECRUITING
      Reasons for Using
      What Recruiters Look for
      What Influences Recruiters' Success
      What Influences Applicants' Job Choice
      Some Special Approaches Used
RECRUITING SPECIAL GROUPS
      Women
      Minorities
      Older Workers
      The Handicapped
      Veterans

During the spring of 1958, recruiters from a large national firm were on campus interviewing but making no job offers because of a bad recession. At the same time, the local plant was laying off graduates hired during the preceding three years. The students were so upset by this obvious inconsistency that even today the firm has a bad name on campus, and students are reluctant to interview with it.

After the planning is done, and when the type and number of employees needed is known, recruiting begins. Figure 6-1 shows how recruiting fits into the staffing function.

WHAT IS RECRUITING

Recruiting is the term applied to the phase of personnel management that involves reaching out and attracting a supply of people from which to select qualified candidates for job vacancies. An effort is thus made to attract potential employees with the necessary characteristics and in the proper quantities for the jobs available.

Recruiting is based on the job needs, as developed from personnel planning, as discussed in Chapter 5. It results in selection, which will be covered in Chapter 7.

FIGURE 6-1
How recruitment fits into the staffing function

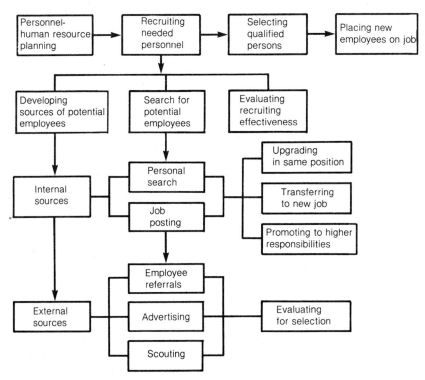

There are three phases of recruiting: (1) developing sources from which to seek potential employees, (2) the actual recruiting, or seeking out the needed people, and (3) evaluating the effectiveness of recruiting activities (see Figure 6–1). These activities are discussed in this chapter.

RESPONSIBILITY FOR RECRUITING

Although each manager is partially responsible for recruiting personnel, the more successful employers place the responsibility for it in the personnel department. Specifically, there should be one person at the top level of all organizations who is charged with this duty. This is usually the personnel executive, who is responsible for coordinating all recruiting strategies and activities with operating managers.

In Small Firms

In small business firms, the task of recruiting is usually undertaken by the firm's owner, a member of management, or an outside agent.

Small organizations must recruit outstanding people who are versatile, flexible, and expert in their field. They usually hire the person for a specific position. If the job is not done properly, the person must be replaced with someone who can do it, for these employers cannot afford to "carry" unproductive employees. In recruiting, these firms should emphasize the benefits of a variety of experiences, the opportunity to make an early contribution, and the opportunity for quick advancement they will have.

A Shared Responsibility

But, whether the organization is small or large, recruiting cannot be done by any one individual. Instead, the responsible person usually asks for the support of others. Assistance may be provided by the employees, the union, employment agencies, and consultants.

Figure 6–2 shows where responsibility for recruiting was placed among the employers making up the Bureau of National Affairs (BNA) Personnel Policies Forum (PPF).

DEVELOPING SOURCES FROM WHICH TO RECRUIT POTENTIAL EMPLOYEES

The extent of an organization's recruiting efforts and the sources of supply used depend on (1) the number and types of positions to be filled, (2) the labor market conditions prevailing in the local area, and (3) the type of industry involved.

FIGURE 6–2
Responsibility of personnel departments for recruiting in selected organizations

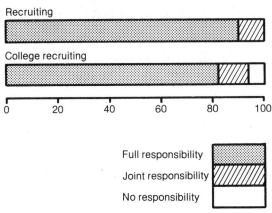

Source: The Bureau of National Affairs, Inc., "The Personnel Department," BNA Policy and Practices Series: *Personnel Management* (Washington, D.C.: Bureau of National Affairs) 251:21.

There is a greater chance of locating better qualified applicants if several sources are used. A knowledge of where to find new employees and how to recruit them is important in supplying personnel.

Source of supply is the places, agencies, and institutions to which recruiters go to seek potential employees to fill job needs. There are only two practical sources from which to seek employees: (1) from among present workers and (2) from the outside. Ultimately, all employees come from some educational institution. This source will be discussed first because of its importance to employees and their employers.

Educational Institutions as Sources of Personnel

As schools provide the required basic education and generalized training, they form the indirect reservoir from which all employees are obtained. Yet the actual recruitment may be from some other source. (It is assumed that some of the applicants may not have completed their work at an educational institution but may have dropped out of it.) This connection between recruitment and educational background can best be understood by seeing how employees progress through an organization.

Figure 6–3 shows the theoretical flow of employees through a hypothetical organization. They enter the system at the lower part of their occupational grouping. They then work at that job for a period of time, are promoted to supervisory or managerial positions, or leave for many reasons.

The figure also shows that employees enter the firm at different organizational levels. The skilled, semiskilled, unskilled, and operative employees tend to enter at lower wage levels and job classifications than the clerical, sales, and

FIGURE 6-3
Theoretical flow of personnel through a hypothetical organization

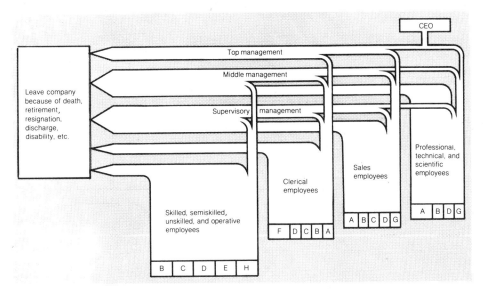

professional, technical, and scientific employees. Also, each group tends to enter the organization at a successively higher level than the previous group. Therefore, the higher level employees have a better chance for advancement than the lower level employees.

Although there are exceptions, there is a tendency for operative employees to progress only to the level of supervisor or middle management. Clerical and sales personnel tend to become supervisors and middle-level managers and even progress into top management. Professional, technical, and scientific employees tend to move through the supervisory, middle, and top levels of management. The chief executive officer usually comes from their ranks.

Internal Sources

Although the ultimate source of all personnel is some educational institution, a given position is filled either by movement from within the organization or by recruitment from outside. Most positions are filled from internal sources.

There are three methods of obtaining employees internally, namely, through *upgrading* the employee currently holding the position; *transferring* an employee from a less desirable or rewarding job elsewhere in the organization; or *promoting* someone from a lower level position. These will be discussed in detail in Chapter 12.

Reasons for using internal sources. It is only logical to try to fill job openings, especially supervisory ones, from among present workers before going outside the organization. Internal sources are often considered better than external ones, because filling jobs internally tends to:

1. Raise the morale of employees.
2. Save money and time, through reduced hiring and training costs.
3. Be more effective, as it is easier to evaluate those who are known than some stranger from the outside.

If the organization maintains a suitable record of the progress, experience, and service of its employees, and if transfer and promotions are based upon measured merit, this argument is valid.

Reasons for not using internal sources.   The chief weaknesses of the internal source are:

1. Danger of inbreeding, which may cause a lack of new ideas, knowledge, and enthusiasm.
2. Lack of available qualified candidates, as when there are many vacancies and during periods of rapid expansion.
3. Reluctance of supervisors to recommend their best employees for promotion or transfer, as they then have to train new ones.
4. Reluctance of employees to apply for job openings for fear that, if they are turned down, their supervisor will be angry at their desire to transfer.

Using job posting and bidding.   If the internal source is used, the best way of doing it is by job posting and bidding. With *job posting,* all job openings are announced by the employers, and all eligible employees can apply for them. When there is a union, all employees can bid on the job opening, and the one with the most seniority gets it.

The federal government now accepts this method of filling higher positions as one way of achieving equal promotional opportunities. While posting is not required by the EEOC and OFCCP, it is one of the factors looked for when there is a complaint of discrimination.[1] In the absence of this procedure, the organization must prove that its procedure isn't discriminatory.

External Sources

All job openings in growing organizations must ultimately be filled from the outside. Positions vacated through upgrading, promotions, or transfers must, in turn, be filled from outside sources.

The specific sources used to recruit new employees will depend upon the jobs to be filled, as well as other factors. But some of the regular sources used are former employees, unsolicited applications, unions, employment agencies, temporary help, and others.

---

[1]See Robert M. Fulmer and William E. Fulmer, "Providing Equal Opportunity for Promotion," *Personnel Journal* 53 (1974):491–97.

Former employees. Some employers keep a roster of former workers as a potential source of trained employees. If the worker left voluntarily and for a good reason, is in good standing, and is seeking reemployment—or can be encouraged to return—this source might be used. However, it tends to be static, as the chances are good that the former employee has failed to grow or maintain competence.

The General Insurance Company of Houston regards returning workers as among its most loyal employees.

Unsolicited applications. Unsolicited requests for employment are frequently received through the mail or at the employment office. Such applications should be considered if the person's qualifications appear to meet the employer's needs. However, this source requires greater use of the selection procedure than applicants from other sources, as there has been no preselection or screening.

An exception to this is in the "Silicon Valley," an electronics center near San Francisco. The recruiting efforts of all the firms attract many promising applicants. Around 90 percent of those who just "walk in" receive jobs.

Unions. In some areas and industries, employers rely heavily on unions as a source of workers. This is particularly true in skilled trades where the union has part of the responsibility for apprenticeship training programs.

This source is used in the construction and shipping industries, where it is convenient for the employer and is permitted by labor laws. It is also used by many small firms that cannot maintain a personnel staff, yet have variable demand and high turnover. Some examples are transportation, contract maintenance, clothing, and food service.

Private employment agencies. Private employment agencies are increasingly being used as a source of personnel. Some of these agencies are now specializing in only one type of personnel—operations, clerical, managerial, and so forth. Also, they are highly regulated in many states.

For example, Louisiana passed a law in 1975 requiring private employment agencies to offer their clients a 90-day no-fault guarantee. The act requires the agency to charge the applicants no more than 20 percent of the normal fee if their employment is ended for any reason in less than 90 days.

In general, a properly qualified agency is a good source. It knows the market, the skills available, the skills sought by the employer, and the abilities and records of its client employees. Since agencies have done much of the preliminary screening, their recommendations are valuable. Under this arrangement, a fee is paid—usually by the applicant.

Private agencies are used extensively for white-collar and technical employees but very little for blue-collar jobs.

For example, one researcher found that only 19 percent of the placements by these agencies in Iowa were in blue-collar positions.[2]

Public employment agencies.   Another source of workers is the Job Service. This service is operated by the states in cooperation with the U.S. Department of Labor's Employment and Training Administration [through the U.S. Employment Service (USES)].[3] Public agencies are important sources of unskilled, semiskilled, and skilled workers, particularly for production and service jobs. Now they are moving more into the clerical, technical, and professional areas.

Effective use of these agencies requires that the employer give the agency definite job specifications. The agency also needs to do more preliminary screening of potential employees. These agencies are quite important as a result of public policies affecting recruitment, selection, training, and development of minority groups.

Temporary help.   Many companies are now using an alternative source of supply in the form of part-time workers. This source takes two forms. (These will be discussed in greater detail in Chapter 10.) First, people who wish to work less than full time—such as retired persons, students, homemakers, and workers with time to spare—may be called upon during rush periods.

Second, leased personnel can be used during rush periods or for part-time jobs. Under this arrangement, the employer obtains from some outside firm employees who specialize in performing a given service. This method is useful in clerical and maintenance operations for which an employee with a given specialty can be hired by the hour or day. Also, it is often used in the janitorial field where office buildings (and even some manufacturing plants) use the personnel of a janitorial service firm on a fee basis.

The benefits to the company are reduced hiring and salary expenses, minimized turnover, less record keeping, lower benefits cost, and better use of highly paid employees. However, before this method can be used, management must decide what to do with any workers displaced by leasing, whether the proper skills are available in the right quality and quantity, and whether the union contract permits it. As full-time employees tend to resent being replaced by part-time people, the best time to begin using such a source is when normal attrition occurs.

A New York temporary replacement service sought women with "rough, red, dry-hand problems" on behalf of an ad agency. The hint of possible TV fame "really played into a lot of people's fantasies," for more than 200 women signed up for auditions. One caller asked, "Do you need a mother and a daughter?"

---

[2]See Jack W. Skeels, "Perspectives on Private Employment Agencies," *Industrial Relations* 8 (February 1969):151–61, for clarifying details.

[3]This service may also be listed under the state government in telephone directories as Employment Security Division or State Employment Service.

Other sources. Various types of school are used as sources of supply along with other sources. For example, some sources of blue-collar workers are *vocational-technical schools, manufacturer's training schools, competing firms, veterans,* and *immigrants.*

White-collar workers are often obtained from *business colleges, schools and colleges, correspondence schools, professional, fraternal, and religious organizations,* and *competing firms.* While there is an ethical question involved, the last source is particularly useful for recruiting sales personnel.

A unique approach is used by one firm in selecting its sales personnel. It hires college dropouts, for its experience has shown that these individuals, if carefully selected, make good, productive sales personnel with management potential. Such young people generate a lot of enthusiasm at being given a second opportunity to achieve success.[4]

Sources used in recruiting scientists, engineers, and technical personnel. It was found by 131 selected firms that the best methods of recruiting scientists, engineers, and technical personnel are *employee-referral programs, newspaper advertising,* and *specialized employment agencies.*[5] Of the firms questioned, 49 percent said that referrals by employees gave excellent results, while 29 percent said that ads in newspapers and the use of consultants and executive recruiters were equally effective.[6]

Sources used in recruiting managerial personnel. As there are so many factors and variables involved in recruiting managerial personnel, the sources will be discussed in Chapter 9, along with an analysis of selection, training, and development methods used.

METHODS USED TO RECRUIT NEW EMPLOYEES

Methods of recruiting new employees vary with each organization and recruiter. However, they usually include (1) employee referrals, (2) advertising, (3) use of consultants, and (4) special programs.

Employee Referrals

Present employees usually know the requirements of jobs to be filled and the personal requirements needed of people to fill them. Thus they can assist in

---

[4]"Why This Company Hires—and Trains—College Dropouts," *Business Management* 26 (May 1964):56–58 and 94.

[5]"How They Recruit Scientists and Engineers," *Business Management* 26 (April 1964):28.

[6]This may be changing. Most respectable recruiters will not "raid" a client for whom they have obtained a manager. But their very success makes it difficult to find possible recruits without going to current or former clients. See "How Success Cramps the Headhunters' Style," *Business Week,* May 5, 1980, pp. 66–69.

recruiting by suggesting possible employees. Research has shown that the suggestions and comments of current employees can be a major factor in determining who is best suited for a particular job.

For example, in a study of the Chicago labor market, it was found that the most widely used channels of recruitment were informal. *Employee referrals* were the most popular method. Of the employers interviewed, 85 percent favored this method.[7]

Referred workers tend to be more successful than the average. The quality of the referrals, however, depends on the morale of the employees, the accuracy of information, and the closeness of the referring friend. Occasionally, when there is a great shortage of skilled personnel, a firm will offer a bonus to its employees to stimulate their extra effort.

A hospital was short 75 nurses. It offered a $300 cash bonus to anyone recommending a qualified nurse who was not employed by a competing hospital. The first $150 was paid when the nurse accepted employment. The rest was paid after the new employee had been on the payroll for six months. There was a net increase of 40 nurses during the first year.

This system does have drawbacks. There is more chance of cliques and informal work groups being formed. Also, if the jobs involve handling money, there is the danger of collusion among friends and relatives.

Advertising

The following ad appeared in the Help Wanted section of the *Chicago Daily News* of April 11, 1887.

WATCHMAKER WANTED
with references who can furnish tools.
State age, experience, and salary
required.
T39, Daily News

The ad was placed by Richard Sears and answered by Alvak Roebuck.[8]

Display and want ads in a newspaper are the most common—and least expensive—forms of advertising. However, there are other media employed,

---

[7]Joseph C. Ullman, "Employee Referrals: Prime Tool for Recruiting Workers," *Personnel* 43 (May–June 1966):30–35.

[8]Champ Clark, "Classified Ads that Click," *Money*, December 1975.

such as trade, specialty, and professional journals. Radio, billboards, television, and recordings at special events, such as professional meetings and conventions, are also used.

Reasons for popularity.   Advertising is popular for very practical reasons. No other method is so flexible, relatively inexpensive, and effective over a period of time. Another reason is that people seem naturally to turn to recruiting ads when looking for jobs.

A study by *Electronic News* asked its technical readers: "When you want to change jobs, what are the first things you do?" Nearly three out of four answered: "First, I read the recruitment ads. . . ."[9]

Want ads are so important in recruiting workers that they indicate the business cycle. The National Industrial Conference Board's index of such ads, shown in Figure 6-4, shows us going into the 1980 recession.

Making advertising more effective.   As advertising is so important, we should see what makes it effective—or ineffective. According to one research study, most advertisements are more concerned with the *quantity of replies*

FIGURE 6-4
How index of want ads shows the business cycle
Source: *The Wall Street Journal,* April 30, 1980, p. 1.

Help-Wanted advertising rose in April to 115 percent of the 1967 average from 112 percent a month earlier, the Conference Board reports.

[9]Van M. Evans, "Recruitment Advertising in the 80s," *Personnel Administrator* 23 (December 1978):22.

than the *quality of applicants.*[10] The most effective advertising copy for college graduates and for scientific and technical personnel was found to be geared to their educational level. It was also specific about the placement and conditions of employment for the applicants and the opportunities available to them.

Some outstanding individuals who were recruited through ads are: Tom May, president of Lockheed Georgia Company and vice president of Lockheed Aircraft Corporation; Harlow Curtice, former president of General Motors; former Michigan governor George Romney; former U.S. Secretary of Commerce Luther Hodges; the late Walt Disney; and Marion Sadler, former president of American Airlines.

Scouting

A group of potential employees that deserves special attention is that composed of college graduates. The question is not whether to hire them or not, because with the present state of technology, an employer must hire them for certain positions in order to survive, especially for the more technical jobs. Because of the importance of this method, a complete section will be devoted to it.

Another form of scouting is the use of search firms to recruit scientific, technical, professional, and managerial personnel. However, they can be used as recruiters of potential employees in any job with high demand and low supply.

Electronic Assistance

Automation is now helping recruit people. The computer aids the recruiter by hastening the flow of information and by securing hard-to-gather data.

There are many ways the computer can help with recruiting. It can:

1. Help determine which job characteristics go with which personal preferences to find the best "fit."
2. Be hooked up to a telephone network to help private employment agencies locate the person with the desired qualifications.
3. Assign daily jobs when several variables are involved.

The more progressive organizations are now installing computerized data systems. In general, they attempt to allow the user to perform selected recruitment-related functions, such as:

---

[10]William A. Douglas, "Job Recruiting Ads: Why Do They Get Stepchild Treatment?" *Printers Ink*, March 11, 1960, p. 90.

"I'm Fred Johnson from Personnel, Miss Forbes, and I just had to see if you were all your punch cards said you were."

Source: *Saturday Review*, February 1, 1964.

1. Identifying the "ideal" candidate (if any).
2. Considering the marginal (yet acceptable) ones.
3. Determining the area/extent of candidates' inadequacies.

Citibank uses a computerized job-employee matching system, called "Jobmatch."[11] In essence, positions in the bank are on one program. Data about each employee are on another. When an employee wishes to transfer, his or her record is matched with possible job openings. When there is a job opening, employee records are searched to see if anyone in the bank can fill the position.

Other Methods

Some other methods that can be used to recruit people from the outside are: (1) field trips, with the chance to talk to out-of-town company representatives, (2) job hotlines, which appeal to the job seeker's desire for immediate action while exerting minimum effort, (3) career centers, and (4) open houses.

---

[11]Paul Sheibar, "A Simple Selection System Called Jobmatch," *Personnel Journal* 58 (January

G. D. Searle and Company invited job seekers in for refreshments, a film on the company, and preliminary job interviews. The firm expected to fill 20 secretarial and clerical positions from the 75 persons who showed up for the event, which had been advertised on radio and in local newspapers. The technique cost less per person hired than using personnel agencies or running long-term ads.[12]

Which Method to Use

More research is needed to determine which recruiting method is best. While many studies conclude that the relative cost of each method, economic conditions, type of industry, and jobs to be filled should be considered, more answers are needed.

More than 80 percent of companies in one survey used classified ads to recruit professional and managerial employees. Three-fourths used them to find sales people. Nearly 70 percent used the ad method to find office workers. But, after want ads, employment agencies are most likely to be used to find management personnel (75 percent) and professional and technical employees (71 percent).

For clerical and service workers, employers are more likely to hire "walk-ins"—persons who come looking for work on their own. Hiring walk-ins is the best method with blue-collar workers.

For recruiting minority workers, 33 percent rated community agencies best, 30 percent listed employee referrals, and 20 percent cited employment agencies.[13]

COLLEGE RECRUITING

College recruiting is the technique most often used for recruiting scientific, technical, professional, and managerial personnel. In fact, it is the major source of these personnel.

Reasons for Using

This method is used for two primary reasons. First, campuses are the best source of higher level personnel. In fact, more high-level employees are recruited by this method than from all other sources.

Second, it is easier to evaluate an applicant through a personal interview. It is also cheaper and more effective for the recruiter to go to the campus than to bring the applicants to the firm's headquarters.

---

[12]*The Wall Street Journal,* April 23, 1978, p. 1.
[13]*The Wall Street Journal,* September 11, 1979, p. 1.

A growing number of firms with foreign operations are seeking applicants from the countries where they operate. The most plentiful and most reliable places to recruit them are college campuses.

What Recruiters Look for

There are many things recruiters look for. But the most important ones are (1) educational abilities and (2) personal qualities.

Educational abilities.   The primary emphasis is still on the bachelor's degree for most sales, scientific, and technical positions. It is also adequate for many professional positions, such as for accountants, economists, engineers, and positions in statistics and finance. For managerial positions, though, the emphasis is shifting to MBAs—especially those with a technical undergraduate degree.

Personal qualities.   There is little agreement about what recruiters seek in college graduates. However, a survey of personnel managers in New York and Hawaii found a strong and consistent preference for graduates who were (1) people-oriented, (2) business-oriented, and (3) quantitatively oriented.[14] The survey also found that few graduates were meeting the executives' expectations. Only 1 out of 132 found 80 percent or more of the graduates meeting expectations.

TABLE 6–1
Reasons why employers do not offer jobs to certain graduates

Factors	Frequency of mention of each negative factor
Negative personality or poor impression: more specifically, lack of motivation, ambition, maturity, aggressiveness, or enthusiasm........................	110
Inability to communicate—poor communication skills.................	62
Lack of competence—inadequate preparation	56
Low grades—poor grades in major field ...	38
Unidentified goals.....................	32
Unrealistic expectations	28
Lack of interest in the type of work.......	25
Unwillingness to travel or relocate........	23
Poor preparation for the interview........	14
Lack of work experience................	10

Source: Frank S. Endicott, *The Endicott Report—1980: Trends in the Hiring of College Graduates* (Evanston, Ill.: The Placement Center, Northwestern University, 1979), p. 8.

---

[14]The details of the research can be found in Alfred G. Edge and Ronald Greenwood, "How Personnel Managers Rank the Importance of Various Educational Factors in Business Administration Graduates," *Marquette Business Review* 17 (Fall 1973):113–19.

The *Endicott Report* of employment trends for 1980 college graduates also showed what recruiters looked for. Notice in Table 6–1 how much emphasis is given to attitudes and personal relationships by recruiters from 166 firms.

What Influences Recruiters' Success

The personality and ability of the person who does the recruiting, the methods used, and the surroundings in which the recruiting takes place affect the quality of those selected and whether they stay with the firm.

These conclusions were verified in a study of 112 first- and second-year MBAs at Cornell. The effects of the recruiter's traits, behaviors, and attitudes on job candidate interview evaluations and probabilities of accepting a job were studied.[15] The best interviewers were perceived as (1) having more interest and concern, (2) seeing the candidates' strengths and weaknesses, (3) being younger and more successful, and (4) offering better chances of a higher starting salary.

Robert Brocksbank, of Mobil Oil, opens job interviews with the question, "Did you get our letter inviting you to interview with Mobil?" This personal letter from the firm's chief college recruiter is one reason he is known as one of the "best known and most respected industrial recruiters in the black community."[16]

What Influences Applicants' Job Choice

In general, college students consider the following factors in job selection: job appeal, potential for advancement, location, salary, and the organization.

Table 6–2 shows the reasons why college graduates accepted jobs with 164 firms. Notice the heavy emphasis placed on the more intrinsic job values. The reasons students gave for rejecting the firms' offers are shown in Table 6–3. Here, the emphasis tended to be on the extrinsic values.

Some Special Approaches Used

A method of recruiting that has found favor in some areas is the *Coop Program*. Using this method, employers contact the college and arrange to employ students on a prearranged scheduled basis. In this way, managers can observe prospective employees in on-the-job activities. In turn, the students

---

[15]C. P. Alderfer and C. G. McCord, "Personal and Situational Factors in the Recruitment Interview," *Journal of Applied Psychology* 54 (August 1970):377–85.

[16]"A Corporate Recruiter Searches the Campuses for 'The Right People,'" *The Wall Street Journal*, March 27, 1979, p. 1.

TABLE 6-2
Reasons why college graduates chose their company, as reported by 164 employers

Reasons	*Frequency of mention*
Type of work: challenging assignments, working conditions, diversity of exposure	110
Opportunity for advancement, progress, and growth . . .	84
Location—job near home	65
Salary	52
Reputation of company, company image, growth and stability of company	50
Personal relations in company, response to people the graduate met	46
Company training program including tuition reimbursement for graduate study	38
Benefits	17
Kind of industry	15
Size of company	7

Source: Frank S. Endicott, *The Endicott Report—1980: Trends in the Hiring of College Graduates* (Evanston, Ill.: The Placement Center, Northwestern University, 1979), p. 6.

get experience in their chosen fields of work as they actually exist. Upon graduation, the student and the organization can agree on future employment—if desired.

Other approaches to recruiting are *career weekends, summer internships,* and *closed-circuit TV.*

Some college placement offices have a supply-demand problem. Too many

TABLE 6-3
Reasons why graduates reject company offers, as reported by 164 employers

Reasons	*Frequency of mention*
Company location, size of community	115
Salary	97
Type of work, job assignments	63
Desire for faster promotion, more responsibility	28
Lack of interest in the industry	25
Reluctance to travel or to relocate	18
Desire for greater opportunity for graduate study	12
Work schedules, overtime	9
Benefits	9
Size of company	6
Housing	5

Source: Frank S. Endicott, *The Endicott Report—1980: Trends in the Hiring of College Graduates* (Evanston, Ill.: The Placement Center, Northwestern University, 1979), p. 7.

students want to interview with too few recruiters. This sometimes leads to all-night vigils outside the placement office. Some schools now use lotteries or computer "chance" selection to get away from the "first come, first served" system.

RECRUITING SPECIAL GROUPS

The planning, recruiting, and selection policies and practices of just a few years ago are obsolete! Most employers now make a vigorous effort to recruit women, minorities, older workers, the handicapped, and veterans.

This is especially true of small companies. The overall increase in employment for 1979 was 3.2 percent. Yet hiring by small firms rose about 10 percent. Their employment of women increased 11 percent and of minorities by about 16 percent.[17]

Women

While women have been a significant part of the American labor force for over a century, their roles have been changing during recent decades. Their number, percentage of the total labor force, participation rate, and percentage of working mothers with school-aged children have increased. Refer back to Table 3-1 to see these increases. As you can see from the table, in 1978, for the first time in history, there were more adult women in the work force than were out of it.

Research has shown that the three primary arguments against equal employment—men's and women's *work*, their *traits*, and their *nonwage costs*—are not valid.[18]

In order to have a job qualified for one particular sex, there must be a *bona fide occupational qualification* (BFOQ), which means that *only* a member of that sex can perform the job. There can also be no group characteristics arbitrarily applied to any and every member of the group, for each person shall be treated as a separate entity. Also, there is a new trend to take sex designations out of job titles. The Census Bureau has reclassified many jobs by removing the suffix *-men* in the title and replacing it with *workers* or *operators*.

Changing worklife pattern. There has been a drastic shift in women's worklife pattern. Some of the changes are:

1. A larger proportion is working at each age.
2. A smaller proportion is leaving the labor force during the prime child-bearing years.

---

[17]"Labor Letter," *The Wall Street Journal*, December 4, 1979, p. 1.

[18]See Dwight P. Flanders and Peggy E. Anderson, "Sex Discrimination in Employment: Theory and Practice," *Industrial and Labor Relations Review* 26 (April 1973):938–55, for this and other research results.

3. More are coming in during the middle-age period.
4. A larger proportion of wives and mothers are working.

In 1978, the average working woman could expect to be in the work force for about 23 years of her life. Also, almost two-thirds of women workers were single, widowed, divorced, or separated, or had husbands with less than $10,000 income.

Sharon Parker, of the National Commission on Working Women, reported: "The most spectacular increase in labor force participation has been for women 25 to 34 years of age. . . . This is remarkable, for over 70 percent of women in this age group are married, live with their husbands, and have children under age 18 at home."[19]

A side effect of employing working mothers—and fathers—is that many employers are providing day care centers for preschool children. This has led to reduced absenteeism, turnover, complaints, and grievances. It also pro duces "peace of mind," which leads to improved work performance.

Changing occupational patterns.   There has been an increase in the number of women employed in service work (outside of homes) and in professional and technical workers—particularly in teaching and health occupations. There has been a decrease in private household work and a slight decrease in sales and operation. However, as Figure 6-5 shows, women are still concentrated in the "feminine" stereotyped jobs. That means working as secretaries and typists, retail clerks, bookkeepers, teachers, and waitresses. This, too, is changing, as the following example shows:

Between 1960 and 1977, the percentage of women accountants rose from 17 to 28 percent; the percentage of physicians rose from 7 to 11 percent; and the percentage of lawyers and judges increased from 4 to 10 percent.

A study of the occupational aspirations of a sample of high school seniors indicated that occupational differences will probably continue in the future.[20] In general, female students aspired more toward the professional and technical areas than the males. The male students chose the managerial occupation more than the female students.

Other changes.   There is also an industry concentration. Women tend to be employed in services, finance, government, and trade. They represent a majority of the employees in services and finance.

Unemployment.   Women have tended to have higher unemployment rates

---

[19]Kristin Goff, "Working Women Challenge U.S. Stereotype," Associated Press wire story, January 1, 1980.

[20]Myron D. Fottler and Trevor Bain, "Sex Differences in Occupational Aspirations," *Academy of Management Journal* 23 (1980):144–49.

FIGURE 6–5
Women are underrepresented as managers and skilled craft workers

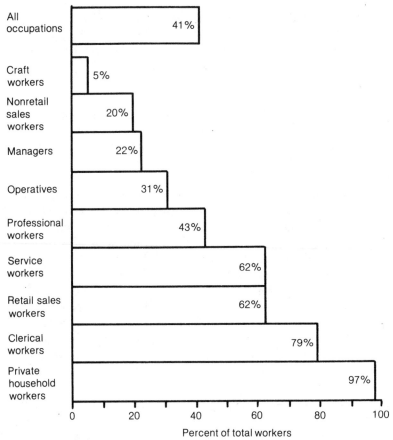

Source: Toni Trinchese, "Success," *Educational Horizons,* Winter 1979, p. 73. Prepared by the Women's Bureau, Office of the Secretary, from 1977 annual average data published by the Bureau of Labor Statistics (U.S. Department of Labor). Reprinted from *Educational Horizons,* 1979, 57(2), by permission of author & Pi Lambda Theta, Inc.

than men. This seems to be related to women's movement in and out of the labor force. While their commitment to work is increasing—and for many may be just as strong as men's—much of their unemployment is still related to reentry into the labor market.

Turnover. It has been accepted that turnover (especially the quit rate) and absenteeism among women were so high that men should be hired if stability was needed. Now, research shows that these are dropping for females, not only when compared to their earlier rates, but also when compared with male levels.

Dual job holding. More women are now dual job holders. It was estimated that about 1.3 million women held more than one job in 1978. This was up from 0.6 million in 1970. The number of men in this category dropped from 3.4 to 3.2 million.[21]

Future status of women.   Several conclusions can be reached concerning the future status of women in the labor force. Their number and participation rates will increase. Their share of jobs will also increase, particularly in technical and professional, managerial, and service (except household) occupations.

Minorities

As shown in Chapter 4, public policy has long been to encourage recruiting minorities. However, the policy has been truly implemented only during the last decade. Federal, state, and local governments now require equal employment opportunities for these groups. Also, the personnel function has been reoriented to include these individuals in personnel planning and recruiting.

Blacks.   Blacks have made considerable progress during the past decade in their efforts to move upward on the ladder of occupational status. They are still overrepresented—relative to whites—in the blue-collar and service occupations and underrepresented in the white-collar ranks. Yet the disparity has been significantly reduced since the EEO laws have been enforced.[22]

The proportion of black men in the more desirable, highly paid job categories has shown slight but steady progress. No less than one out of five blacks worked in white-collar occupations in 1964. Now about one in three blacks has a white-collar job. Substantial gains have been made within the professional, managerial, and sales ranks, but the greatest gains have been in the clerical field, with almost a doubling of their share of the market.

There has also been significant upward progress within the blue-collar group. Large numbers of blacks have left the ranks of the unskilled and entered the operative and craft trades. There has also been a great reduction in the proportion of blacks in service occupations, particularly private households. There the number employed has been cut by more than half.

The proportion of all male employees who are black has doubled in accounting, engineering, medicine, and drafting.

While blacks have a higher unemployment rate than whites, one study showed that variables other than race or color might be the cause. It was shown that the excess black unemployment might be related to differences in educational attainment, academic achievement, age, and legal constraints. It also reflects their occupational, industrial, and regional distribution in the labor force.[23]

---

[21]"Labor Letter," *The Wall Street Journal*, May 22, 1979, p. 1.

[22]*The Social and Economic Status of the Black Population in the U.S., 1974* (Washington, D.C.: Government Printing Office, 1975), p. 60.

[23]Curtis L. Gilbray, "Investment in Human Capital and Black-White Unemployment," *Monthly Labor Review* 98 (July 1975):13-21.

Spanish-speaking workers. Workers of Hispanic origin represent roughly 5 percent of the U.S. population. They are now our second largest minority group. By 1985, they are expected to be the largest group of minority workers. While professional and white-collar workers—and even prosperous businesspeople—are numbered among the Spanish-speaking, far too many are poorly paid laborers.

Spanish-speaking Americans tend to be severely disadvantaged in comparison to the dominant Anglo population. While their status is roughly equal to blacks in income, occupational status, and unemployment, in education they are far worse off.

As shown in Table 6–4, the occupational distribution of Spanish-speaking workers is similar to that of blacks. They are concentrated in occupations with high unemployment rates. Their higher unemployment rates are also related to (1) the greater number of young workers in the Hispanic labor force, (2) lower levels of education—sometimes compounded by language problems, and (3) greater concentrations in the West, where unemployment tends to be higher.

Lack of facility in English and other cultural differences—including a partially self-imposed ethnic isolation common to earlier generations of immigrants—leave many Spanish-speaking people outside the mainstream of economic opportunity.

Their precarious economic position is underscored by the nature of the jobs they hold. Over half of them are in unskilled and low-paid blue-collar, service, and farm jobs. Only a third of them hold white-collar jobs, compared with over half of all Americans.

TABLE 6–4
Employment of white, black, and Spanish-speaking Americans, by occupation group, 1978 [percentage distribution]

Occupation group	Total	White	Black	Spanish-speaking
Total				
Number (000)	94,373	83,836	8,925	4,801
Percentage	100.0	100.0	100.0	100.0
White-collar workers	50.0	51.8	33.5	32.4
Professional and technical	15.1	15.5	10.0	7.5
Managers and administrators (except farm)	10.7	11.4	4.2	5.9
Sales workers	6.3	6.7	2.5	3.9
Clerical workers	17.9	18.0	16.8	15.1
Blue-collar workers	33.4	32.9	39.0	46.6
Craft and kindred	13.1	13.7	8.9	13.4
Operatives	15.3	14.6	16.0	21.2
Nonfarm laborers	5.0	4.6	8.6	8.1
Service workers	13.6	12.3	25.2	16.9
Farm workers	3.0	3.0	2.3	4.1
Civilian population, 16 years and over (000)	158,941	139,580	16,641	7,639

Source: *Employment and Training Report of the President* (1979), (Washington: Government Printing Office, 1979), p. 260, Table A–16.

Older Workers

For a long time it was popular to reject those over 40 years of age for employment. This practice now violates the *Age Discrimination in Employment Act.*

The arguments for not hiring older workers are (1) physical deterioration, (2) the expense of employee benefits, (3) the problem of tenure, and (4) lack of ability. Yet experience has shown that it is useful to hire people over 40 years of age for several reasons. These include:

1. Greater experience and better judgment in decision making.
2. More realism about personal goals and abilities, as they have satisfied many of their personal needs and thus are able to concentrate more on their job.
3. Ability to understand and influence others.
4. Less risk, as the older person's potentialities can be more easily determined from his or her performance record.
5. Reduced training time, as their previous experience is easily transferable, especially into management positions.
6. Proven value, as older workers have proven their abilities.

Carcross Company, in Taunton, Massachusetts, tries to hire older workers. Of 160 employees, 46 are over 55, and 21 are over 65. The owner, age 76, found in a survey that those over 55 were rated ''more reliable and efficient.''[24]

The Handicapped

The physically, mentally, emotionally, and socially handicapped have difficulty finding jobs. Employers feel there are no jobs these people can do, or that they will have more accidents. These feelings are usually not true.

With some effort and expense—which may be reimbursed—jobs can be found. The important consideration is *not* what workers *can't do* but what they can do. Through selective recruiting and placement, employers can hire the handicapped.

Veterans

As shown in Chapter 4, many programs were designed to help veterans returning from Vietnam. Apparently they worked, at least for the older vets. The rapidly changing age composition of the veteran group has been an important factor in the decline of their unemployment rate. As most Vietnam era

---

[24]"Employer Tells Why He Hires Older Persons," *AARP News Bulletin* 20 (November 1979):7.

veterans were separated from the armed forces several years ago, they have now entered age groups with generally lower unemployment rates. Consequently, the proportion of veterans in the 20-to-24-year age group, where the jobless rate is relatively high, is now much smaller.

Nevertheless, employers must—and should—still actively recruit these workers.

SUMMARY AND CONCLUSIONS

Recruitment means reaching out and attracting a supply of people from which to select qualified candidates for job vacancies. Theoretically, the ultimate source of all personnel is some educational institution. But the immediate source of applicants for given jobs is either progression within the organization or recruitment from the outside.

The three sources from which employees can be obtained internally are upgrading, transferring, and promoting. The usual methods used to recruit from within are job posting and bidding.

The usual external sources used to fill positions are (1) former employees, (2) unsolicited applications, (3) unions, (4) employment agencies, both private and public, and (5) temporary help. Some commonly used methods of recruitment are (1) employee referrals, (2) advertising, (3) scouting or campus recruiting, and (4) electronic assistance in recruiting.

Campus recruiting is used because it is the best source of high level personnel. It is cheaper and more effective for the recruiter to go to the campus. In general, college recruiting is used more by large- and medium-sized organizations than by smaller ones.

Today's college students look for potential for advancement, appealing jobs, salary, and security.

Special attention is being given to recruiting women, minorities, older workers, the handicapped, and veterans.

Like the other aspects of personnel and human resource management, recruiting is undergoing tremendous changes. Increasingly, public policy will determine recruiting practices and the supply sources used, rather than organizational needs and policies. Yet, in the long run, this may prove to be more beneficial if it forces a more effective personnel system.

QUESTIONS

1. What are some of the methods used in recruiting?
2. What are the advantages and disadvantages of using employee referrals?
3. Do you view public policy as having a greater or lesser effect upon recruiting now than in 1970? Explain.

4. Do you agree with the theoretical flow of personnel in an organization and its implications for the personnel selection function? Explain.
5. What are the three methods of securing employees internally? What are the advantages and disadvantages of each method?
6. Why is it important to use external sources of employee supply?
7. What are the various external supply sources of employees? What are the advantages and disadvantages of each?

PROBLEM

Companywide Seniority

The Welcom Company had a policy of promoting on the basis of companywide seniority, providing the competing employees' qualifications were otherwise equal. Bill was "first machinist" in the firm's Plant A when he was offered the job of "plant foreman" in its Plant B. This job was particularly attractive because Plant B was slightly larger than Plant A and, therefore, carried a higher prestige value. Ralph, the first machinist in Plant B, also wanted the foreman's job. Although he had the most plantwide seniority in Plant B, he was not given the job because he had been with the company six months less than Bill, and Bill, therefore, had six months more companywide seniority.

Bill knew that Ralph had counted on getting the job and that several of his new subordinates considered Ralph next in line and better qualified. Fortunately the previous foreman had talked with Ralph before leaving and had tried to explain why he did not get the job. Even so, Ralph resented Bill's presence in the plant and was not too cooperative.

When a machine broke down, Ralph worked diligently on it and did an excellent job of repairing it. Bill, wanting Ralph to know that he appreciated his work, complimented him in front of the other men. "Ralph, thanks for the fine repair job you did on the machine. You demonstrated outstanding skill, knowledge, and experience, and I want you to know I consider you the best qualified first machinist in the company."

Ralph replied, "I should know how to fix that machine, for I helped install it. In fact, I know more about this whole plant than you do, as I've been here longer. In fact, if this company had a fair promotion policy, I would be plant foreman and you wouldn't be here."

Questions

1. What does this case indicate about the problem of promoting from within?
2. What does it show about the difficulty of using seniority as the basis of promotion?
3. How would you evaluate the way Bill handled the situation?
4. What would you do now if you were Bill?
5. What does the case illustrate about the source of personnel?

SUGGESTED READINGS FOR FURTHER STUDY

Brecker, Richard L.   "Ten Common Mistakes in College Recruitment—or How to Try without Really Succeeding." *Personnel* 52 (March-April 1975):19-28.

Dahl, David A., and Patrick R. Pinto.   "Job Posting: An Industry Survey." *Personnel Journal* 56 (January 1977):40-41.

Edson, Andrew S.   "How Other Companies Assess MBA Recruitment: Some Make It Big, Others Stumble." *Management Review* 68 (April 1979):13-14.

Evans, Van M.   "Recruitment Advertising in the '80s." *Personnel Administrator* 23 (December 1978):21-24.

Freund, Madalyn, and Patricia Somers.   "Ethics in College Recruiting." *Personnel Administrator* 24 (April 1979):30-34.

Huseman, Richard C., John D. Hatfield, and Richard B. Robinson.   "The MBA and Fringe Benefits." *Personnel Administrator* 23 (July 1978):57-60.

Kosnik, Thomas J.   "Aiming for the Right Company: Alternative Strategies for Recruitment." *Advanced Management* 44 (Winter 1979):52-57.

Miner, Mary G., and John B. Miner.   *Employee Selection within the Law,* pp. 30-32. Washington, D.C.: Bureau of National Affairs, 1978.

Neuberger, T. S.   "Sex as a Bona Fide Occupational Qualification under Title VII." *Labor Law Journal* 29 (1978):425-29.

Sheibar, Paul.   "A Simple Selection System Called 'Jobmatch.' " *Personnel Journal* 58 (January 1979):26-30 and 56.

Sweeney, Herbert J., and Kenneth S. Teel.   "A New Look at Promotion from Within." *Personnel Journal* 58 (August 1979):531-35.

Taylor, H. Nathaniel.   "Job Posting Update." *Personnel Administrator* 22 (January 1977):45-46.

CHAPTER SEVEN

Selecting Employees

Learning Objectives

After studying the material in this chapter, you should be able to:

1. Explain why selection is so important.
2. Describe the suggested selection procedure.
3. State the important policy decisions that must be made before selection can begin.
4. Explain what selection criteria, predictors, and instruments are.
5. Describe the steps in the selection procedure, telling what is accomplished in each step.
6. Tell how selection decisions are made and communicated to applicants.

Some Important Words and Terms

Criterion
Predictors
Selection technique or instrument
Selection
Job specifications
Selection ratio
"Whole person" concept
Validity
Predictive validity
Concurrent validity
Reliability
Selective perception
Structured interview
Stress interview

Contrast effect
Weighted application blank (WAB)
Biographical information blank (BIB)
Résumé
Intelligence test
Aptitude test
Interest test
Personality test
Achievement or proficiency test
Work sampling
Work previews
Polygraph
In-depth interview
Second injury law

Ability and necessity dwell near each other.
PYTHAGORAS

Progress comes from the intelligent use of experience.
ELBERT HUBBARD

Outline of the Chapter

Sam Able applied for a job on a forestry crew and was told to report for an interview. Following instructions, Sam climbed through knee-deep snow to keep the 8 A.M. appointment—at the top of a 1,600-foot mountain.

Woody Green, the state forester who had arranged the interview, said he had 200 applicants for the job and decided the climb would be a good test of motivation and stamina. Able was the first applicant to show up. He got the job!

Several years ago, a college recruiter for a national firm used an unusual technique for selecting engineering students for visits to his plant. He invited the students in the top 20 percent of the graduating class for interviews. The best ones were invited to dinner and observed as they ordered and ate. Anyone who salted the food before tasting it was rejected for "jumping to conclusions" and not being "analytical."

These cases, of course, are very unusual. Yet they do make some important points about selection. In chapters 5 and 6, we saw:

1. How jobs are designed.
2. How the qualities needed by employees to do the jobs are determined.
3. How a pool of prospective employees is recruited from various sources.

In this chapter, we will see how employees are chosen from that pool to perform certain jobs. Figure 7–1 shows how selection fits into the staffing function.

IMPORTANCE OF SELECTION

You will notice several things about selection in the beginning cases. First, it is a matter of *personal judgment*. Second, in selecting employees, there must be some *criterion* for measuring the extent to which employees perform a given job successfully. Third, there must be some *predictors* that can be used to estimate whether an applicant can and will meet the performance criteria. Fourth, *selection techniques* (or *instruments*) must be used to gather and evaluate information about prospective employees.

Selection can be defined as the process of determining from among the applicants which ones best fill the job specifications and should be offered positions in the organization.

FIGURE 7–1
How employee selection fits into the staffing function

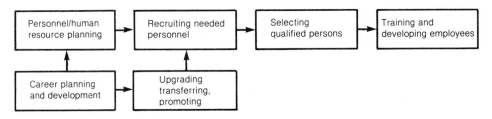

Selection is deciding if an applicant has the personal qualities that match the job requirements. These requirements, given to the personnel department by operating managers, contain (1) the *job specifications*—what is required to do the job—and (2) the *personal qualities* needed for a worker to do the job successfully.

AN EFFECTIVE SELECTION PROCEDURE

Figure 7-2 is a procedure that can be effective for selecting most employees. However, it is based on certain assumptions that may not be true in all cases. Also, it is limited by managerial desires, union demands, public policy, and the environmental conditions affecting the supply of, and demand for, workers.

How Public Policy Influences the Procedure

In *Griggs et al.* v. *Duke Power Company,* the Supreme Court ruled unanimously in 1971 that the company could not require applicants to take the Wonderlic Personnel Test and the Bennett Mathematical Aptitudes

FIGURE 7-2
A suggested procedure for effective personnel selection

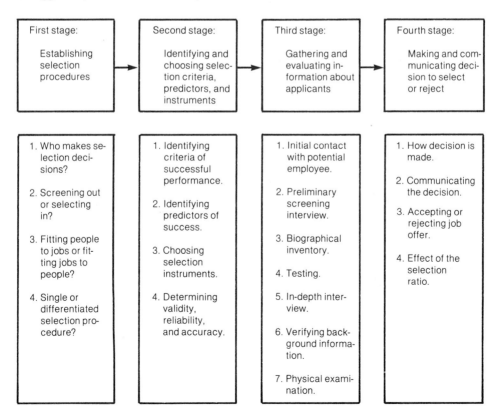

First stage:	Second stage:	Third stage:	Fourth stage:
Establishing selection procedures	Identifying and choosing selection criteria, predictors, and instruments	Gathering and evaluating information about applicants	Making and communicating decision to select or reject
1. Who makes selection decisions?	1. Identifying criteria of successful performance.	1. Initial contact with potential employee.	1. How decision is made.
2. Screening out or selecting in?	2. Identifying predictors of success.	2. Preliminary screening interview.	2. Communicating the decision.
3. Fitting people to jobs or fitting jobs to people?	3. Choosing selection instruments.	3. Biographical inventory.	3. Accepting or rejecting job offer.
4. Single or differentiated selection procedure?	4. Determining validity, reliability, and accuracy.	4. Testing.	4. Effect of the selection ratio.
		5. In-depth interview.	
		6. Verifying background information.	
		7. Physical examination.	

Test, nor require a high school diploma, as a basic measurement of the prospective employee's ability to learn or to perform a job or job category. In essence, the Court laid down the guideline that *any selection criterion must be related to the applicant's ability to perform the job being sought.* The Court said, "The act proscribes not only overt discrimination but also practices that are fair in form, but discriminatory in operation. The touchstone is business necessity. If an employment practice which operates to exclude Negroes cannot be shown to be related to job performance, the practice is prohibited."[1]

As shown in Chapter 4, the Uniform Guidelines on Employee Selection Procedures influence all aspects of selection. In essence, they require employers to validate standard selection procedures. It is more difficult to rely on subjective, covert, or undocumented procedures. Keep this in mind as you study this chapter.

How the Selection Ratio Influences the Procedure

This ideal procedure is also influenced by the law of supply and demand. In essence, the *selection ratio* is:

$$\frac{\text{The number of applicants to be hired}}{\text{The number of applicants available for hiring}}$$

The higher (closer to 1.0) this ratio is, the less selective the personnel officer can be. The lower (closer to 0.0) the ratio, the greater the use of selection techniques in the employment procedure. When the ratio is high, most applicants must be hired, regardless of their performance in the selection procedure.

ESTABLISHING SELECTION POLICIES

The selection procedure is based on several policy decisions that must be made. Some of these will now be discussed.

Who Makes the Selection Decision?

The decision to hire is relatively low on the list of functions desired of the personnel department by line managers (see Chapter 2). As the department has only staff or functional authority, the final decision to hire is usually left up to operating executives, except for lower level, more routine jobs.

---

[1]See 401 U.S. 424 (1971).

Selection is a shared responsibility. In theory, selection involves a division of labor. The *personnel department* (1) does research to establish performance and selection criteria, (2) chooses the selection instrument or techniques to be used, (3) advises on hiring standards, and (4) in the case of public policy, even sets hiring guidelines. The *operating departments* then do the actual selection.

In most organizations, the division of labor works this way:

1. The personnel department does the recruiting, handles the detailed steps in the selection procedure—except for the final employment interview— and then recommends to the operating department that a given individual be interviewed for final selection.
2. The operating managers do the final interviewing and make the decision to select or reject a given applicant.

Current practice. There are many variations of this procedure. For example, many operating executives are now doing college recruiting and preliminary interviewing of scientific, technical, and professional personnel. In that case, the personnel department takes over and processes the information. Also, personnel managers are now being brought in on the final decisions because of public policy and their expertise in the matter. Also, they have an important input into the position, salary, and benefits to be offered to new employees.

Screening Out or Selecting In?

There is much controversy over whether selection should be a *selection* or *rejection* process. The primary reason for this difficulty is that the very nature of selection is predictive. Personnel managers try to predict which applicant has the abilities, interests, and attitudes that best match the job needs.

Screening out. With the present evaluation techniques, it is easier for personnel specialists to determine whether a person *is not* qualified for a given job than whether one *is* qualified. In other words, it is simpler and more accurate to forecast which applicant *will not succeed* than which one *will*. Success results from factors such as ability, training, volition, motivation, and drive, and the absence of these qualities is more obvious than their presence. The entire selection process is designed to reject applicants with factors in their background indicating failure and retaining those with apparent potential for success.

Thus, selection is similar to a series of hurdles that applicants must clear in order to get the job (see Figure 7-3). The hurdles are of different heights and sequence, depending on the organization, the job, and the managers doing the selection. For example, test results may be given more weight than the other factors, making this hurdle higher. In other cases, the interview or physical exam may be given greater weight, and those hurdles would then be higher.

FIGURE 7–3
The selection procedure viewed as a series of hurdles to be cleared before an applicant is selected as an employee

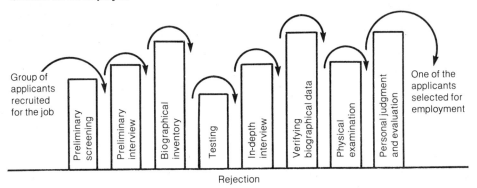

Group of applicants recruited for the job

Preliminary screening

Preliminary interview

Biographical inventory

Testing

In-depth interview

Verifying biographical data

Physical examination

Personal judgment and evaluation

One of the applicants selected for employment

Rejection

Selecting in. Therefore, the selection procedure should be designed so that it will identify individuals with the greatest chances of success. As there is rarely one personal quality that alone assures success, the selection should not be based on one "hurdle." Instead, the selection decision should be based on several predictors of success, considered in combination with each other.

Which approach to use? The screening out approach may be preferable for (1) some routine jobs requiring uniformity of performance on the part of several persons and (2) saving the time and energy of applicants and management.

The selecting in approach is now becoming popular and meets EEO/AA requirements, for it assumes that *a deficiency in one selection criterion can be compensated for by competence in others.* This approach is also preferable for filling jobs that either are complex or depend on the interaction of various abilities.

Fitting People to Jobs or Fitting Jobs to People?

Selection tries to match the personal qualities of applicants with the requirements of the jobs. This matching procedure begins with, and is based upon, an evaluation of an applicant's strengths and weaknesses. The results of this evaluation are then measured against the job standards of the position.

Modify jobs to fit available personnel. However, these standards are not fixed. They vary as job conditions change; so they must be constantly reviewed and updated. Thus, a policy decision must be made either to fit people to existing jobs or to restructure the jobs to fit available people.

For routine jobs, or where several people need to work together on the same job, it is probably better to find people whose qualifications match the job itself. Also, if qualified people aren't available, the job should be altered to accommodate those that are available.

The "whole person" concept. Finally, the *"whole person"* concept should be considered when matching people and jobs. When an employer selects an employee, the whole person is hired—the strengths and weaknesses, personal problems and failures, motivation to work, and nonproductive tendencies. It is impossible to separate the positive factors that lead to productivity in an individual from the negative elements that result in a lack of productivity. However, employees, when properly motivated, may compensate for their weaknesses by developing their strengths, in which case they should become more effective employees.

Using the Same or Differentiated Procedures?

It is usually more effective to use different selection procedures for different sizes and types of institutions, occupations, and levels of employees sought. There is a tendency for the number and variety of selection techniques used to increase with increases in organization size. In general, more than one selection procedure is used as an organization grows. Also, procedures used to select blue-collar and clerical personnel are different from those used in choosing professional, technical, and managerial personnel.

The personnel department of a large chemical firm processes all applicants for production and clerical positions. It performs all the steps except the medical exam. The people chosen are put on a waiting list.

When a worker is needed by one of the production departments, a requisition is sent to the personnel department. The employment supervisor, or an assistant, telephones the top candidate on the list (the best qualified) to come in for an interview. The manager in the production department who will supervise the new employee does the interviewing. If the person is acceptable and passes the physical exam, he or she is put on the payroll.

The same procedure is followed for clerical personnel. On the other hand, the production (or research and development) managers do the recruiting at colleges for professional and technical personnel. Only when someone is invited to the plant for an interview does the personnel officer become involved. Even then, it is only in a service capacity.

ESTABLISHING SELECTION CRITERIA, PREDICTORS, AND TECHNIQUES

There have been many efforts in the past to select people on the basis of some form of character analysis. At one time, *phrenology,* the study of the head's shape, bumps, and irregularities, was used. In Germany and certain other Continental countries, *graphology,* or the interpretation of handwriting, is now extensively used in the selection of managerial personnel.[2] *Astrology* and other mystical techniques of selection have been used in France and some other European areas. Other efforts have been made to study the body structure and so forth. However, these methods are beyond the scope of this study. Attention will be given in this chapter to the more ordinary and practical selection procedures using the more acceptable predictive factors.

Identifying Criteria of Successful Job Performance

One of the most important questions facing personnel managers is what are valid criteria of successful job performance. Considerable effort is now being done to assure *validity*, or that performance criteria are valid indicators of job success. Present research findings are inadequate and sometimes even contradictory.

For example, research conducted to determine the validity of selection criteria found four studies with *scholarship positively correlated with success;* one found it to be *indeterminate;* and two found it *not related (or even inversely related)* to success.[3]

The most valid criterion of successful job performance is the employee's measured performance on the job. Some useful criteria are output per unit of time, quality of production, lost time, labor turnover, time required for training, employee promotability, and employee satisfaction.

Criteria may also be classified as objective and subjective. The *objective criteria* deal with some form of measurable output, quantitative and/or qualitative. Another criterion is using a job sample, which is a test of job performance done under carefully controlled conditions.

Subjective criteria are needed because it is not always possible to obtain objective measures of performance. These criteria attempt to measure performance with subjective estimates of employee proficiency. These are obtained by some form of rating by supervisors and managers.

Identifying Predictors of Job Success

Another selection problem is to isolate *predictors* that can be identified through the use of selection instruments (tests, interviews, references, and so forth) that will correlate with the criterion scores of successful performance. If the predictor correlates highly with the criteria, there is *predictive validity*. That predictor can be successfully used in hiring applicants with the assurance

---

[2]For further details, see Jitendra M. Sharma and Harsh Vardhan, "Graphology: What Handwriting Can Tell about an Applicant," *Personnel* 52 (March–April 1975):57–63.

[3]Robert A. Martin, "Our Primitive Employment Process," *Personnel Journal* 49 (February 1970):177–82.

that they will perform successfully. (The problem of validity will be covered later.)

Some valid predictors.   In general, successful job performance is largely determined by (1) the employee's innate abilities, i.e., intellectual and physical capacities, (2) the modification of these abilities by the total environment, including education, training, and experience, and (3) the person's motivation to succeed, or willingness to pay the price of success. It can be concluded that in many cases ability and motivation are far more meaningful to success than is education.

Specific qualities sought in applicants.   As indicated, personnel managers need to determine through research which personal variables are the best predictors of success for specific jobs. They should establish these as the qualities sought in prospective employees and design a selection procedure that will find out to what extent a given applicant possesses them. Table 7-1

TABLE 7-1
Personal characteristics sought in prospective employees and sources of information about them

Personal characteristics needed to perform job adequately	Sources of information about characteristic
Personal background and past performance	Application blank Interviews School records References
Aptitudes and interests	Application blank School records Psychological tests References Interviews Work records
Attitudes and needs	Interviews Psychological tests References
Analytical abilities	School records Psychological tests Interviews Work references
Skills and technical abilities	School records Training records Interviews Work references Performance tests
Health, energy, and stamina	Medical examination Interviews Work references
Value system	References Interviews

lists some personal qualities found in successful employees and selection techniques used to obtain information about them.

Personal background data include such items as (1) educational institutions attended and courses of study pursued, (2) military service, (3) experience with different tools, machines, or equipment, and (4) work history. These data are considered to be important indicators of past performance and predictors of future performance.

A study by the National Bureau of Economic Research showed that actual job experience in high school had a positive relation to post-high-school employment. It appeared to add as much as 30–35 percent to annual earnings four years after graduation.[4]

Aptitudes and interests indicate our natural abilities, capacities for learning, and desires to do certain jobs.

Attitudes and needs indicate an applicant's frame of mind, emotional and mental maturity, sense of responsibility and authority, and future motivation.

Analytical and manipulative abilities indicate our thinking processes, intelligence level, and ability to use knowledge effectively in performing assigned tasks.

Skills and technical abilities indicate the ability to perform specific operations and technical aspects of a job. These result from education, training, and experience and tend to predict *what one can do* if properly placed, oriented, developed, and motivated.

Health, energy, and stamina indicate the *physical* ability to perform the assigned tasks satisfactorily—especially those involving manual and managerial duties.

A person's *value system* provides clues to motivation, goals, objectives, work values, and perseverance.

There are, of course, other qualities and characteristics that may be considered significant and desirable, but no effort is made to include all of them.

Choosing Selection Instruments

The usual selection instruments, or techniques,[5] used by most personnel managers are (1) preliminary screening or interview, (2) biographical inventory, (3) testing, (4) in-depth interview, (5) verification, and (6) physical examination. These will be discussed in detail later.

Determining Validity, Reliability, and Accuracy

Before any selection technique is used, some problems common to all of them should be studied. These are (1) how valid is it in predicting success on the

---

[4]"Tying Job Experience to High School Experience," *Business Week*, September 10, 1979, p. 21.

[5]While the proper word is probably *instrument*, it will be used interchangeably with *technique* to avoid repetition.

job, (2) does it obtain reliable results under varying conditions, and (3) how accurate is the information obtained from the prospective employee?[6]

How valid is the technique?   In essence, a selection technique is *valid* if it measures the qualities or characteristics it is supposed to measure and predicts success on the job. While there are several types of validity, personnel managers are interested in (1) concurrent validity, (2) predictive validity, and (3) synthetic validity.

Concurrent validity.   *Concurrent validity* is sometimes called the present employee method. In effect, it is the extent to which the results obtained with a selection technique (such as a test) are statistically related to the performance of employees currently on the job. This approach immediately determines the usefulness of a selection instrument.

Predictive validity.   *Predictive validity,* or the follow-up method, is arrived at by using the selection technique on *all* applicants. As the instrument itself is being tested, acceptances or rejections should not be made on the basis of the results ("scores"). Instead, hiring decisions should be made on the basis of other selection techniques. After the employees have been on the job long enough, their performance is statistically correlated with their scores on the selection instrument. This becomes the criterion used to measure successful performance and a predictor for future selection.

This validation technique requires much time before it can be known for certain whether the instrument is useful in predicting success. Therefore, concurrent validation is most frequently used in employment procedures.

Synthetic validity.   Many personnel researchers are now trying to find some general procedure for transferring validation information about an instrument from one setting to another. Small companies particularly attempt to find synthetic validities, for their size makes it difficult for them to establish the more desirable predictive validities of their own.[7]

How reliable is the technique?   A selection technique must also have *reliability,* which means that it gives consistent results under the same, or similar, circumstances, even when administered and interpreted by different people. This means that each time the instrument is used, the same relative appraisal should result. In practice, validity and reliability are actually interrelated. A selection technique that gives consistent results usually has a high validity.

How accurate is the information received from applicants?   A technique is only as valid in predicting success as the information obtained from the applicants. Several studies indicate that information obtained from biographical forms and during the interview tends to be biased in favor of the applicant. One study found substantial disagreement between the applicant's statements and the reference checks on duration of previous employment, reasons for

[6]For excellent discussions of these topics, see John P. Wanous, *Organizational Entry: Recruitment, Selection, and Socialization of Newcomers* (Reading, Mass.: Addison-Wesley Publishing Co., 1980), pp. 137–40, 160–62.

[7]Richard J. Walsh and Lee R. Hess, "The Small Company, EEOC, and Test Validation Alternatives: Do You Know Your Options?" *Personnel Journal* 53 (November 1974):840–45.

leaving, and salary. In fact, 15 percent of the applicants had never worked for the employer named on the form.[8]

GATHERING AND EVALUATING INFORMATION ABOUT APPLICANTS

The usual selection techniques used to obtain meaningful information about applicants are shown in Table 7-2.

As you can see, this stage begins with the available applicants who have been recruited as potential employees. As each instrument is used, some of the

TABLE 7-2
Instruments for gathering information about potential employees

Instruments used to gather data	*Characteristics to look for*	*Applicants who are available as potential employees*
Preliminary screening or interview	Obvious misfit from outward appearance and conduct	
Biographical inventory from application blank, BIB, résumé, etc.	Lacks adequate educational and performance record	
Testing Intelligence test(s)	Fails to meet minimum standards of mental alertness	
Aptitudes test(s)	Lacks specific capacities for acquiring particular knowledges or skills	
Proficiency, or achievement test(s)	Unable to demonstrate ability to do job	
Interest test(s)	Lacks significant vocational interest in job	
Personality test(s)	Lacks the personal characteristics required for job	
In-depth interview	Lacks necessary innate ability, ambition, or other qualities	
Verifying biographical data from references	Unfavorable or negative reports on past performance	
Physical examination	Physically unfit for job	Person(s) left for selection

---

[8]Irving L. Goldstein, "The Application Blank: How Honest Are the Responses?" *Journal of Applied Psychology* 55 (October 1971):491-92.

applicants are eliminated for the reasons shown. (This makes sense, for if a person is obviously unqualified or uninterested in the job or the organization, there is no need to waste anyone's time further.) Finally, if there is more than one qualified candidate remaining, a personal value judgment must be made in selecting the one person from among those remaining.

Initial Contact with Applicant

The steps in selection depend on the recruiting method used. For example, in college recruiting, the initial contact is usually the preliminary interview. With advertising, the initial contact is generally the letter of application. For "walk-ins," there is an initial contact that will result in either a preliminary interview or the completion of an application blank. For higher level personnel, such as managers recruited by consultants, the initial contact might even be at the employment interview.

Preliminary Screening or Interview

Whether formal or informal, there is always some form of preliminary screening of applicants early in the procedure. This is usually done in the preliminary interview, but it may be based on the application form.

Purpose of preliminary interview. This step deals with obvious factors such as voice, dress, physical appearance, personal grooming, educational background, professional training, and—to a limited extent—experience. It ought to be obvious that the applicants should also know something about the organization if they are to be adequately prepared for the preliminary interview.

As this interview is usually done by only one person, there is the danger that the interviewer might select or reject the applicant on some generalized personal basis. This is called *selective perception.*

While doing a case study of an employment agency, I observed that one interviewer had selected significantly more applicants with mustaches than the other interviewers. The interviewer also had a mustache.

There are many ways of overcoming this selective perception, but the most important ones are group interviews and definite criteria for selection.

Compliance with EEO/AA. This interview is where many employers get into trouble by asking questions directly related to sex, race, color, religion, age, or national origin. Unless there are *bona fide occupational qualifications* (BFOQ), where sex or some other characteristic is a valid criterion of job performance, questions that would either directly or indirectly seek information about those characteristics might be deemed discriminatory. As you are faced with the problem not only of *intent* but also of *consequences,* ask no questions that could be construed as a basis for discrimination.

·A representative of the EEOC put it this way: "It is not so much the questions you ask that get you into trouble as what you do with the answers."

Charges of discrimination can be based upon suspected subtle bias in the form of increased qualifications for a job. Therefore, don't ask questions dealing with foreign addresses, membership in organizations, name and address of relatives, type of military discharge, academic background at private schools, arrests and convictions for misdemeanors, Social Security status, height, weight, marital status, or ownership of a house or car. Also, you cannot ask for a photograph or ask whether the person *can* receive a recommendation from a former employer. Table 7–3 shows what questions can and cannot be used.

Why use interviews?   If there are so many problems involved with the interview, why is it the most widely used selection instrument? Surveys show that almost all personnel managers use this method at some stage in the selection procedure.

There are two traits of interviewing that set it aside from the other instruments. First, it is quite flexible and can be used for many different types of job and applicant. For example, the personnel manager can attempt to evaluate personality, including motives, attitudes, and other personal characteristics. Then the operating managers can try to determine technical abilities, experience, and expertise.

Second, this instrument is the only one that provides two-way communication. It permits the interviewer to learn more about the job applicant, while the applicant can learn about the opportunities, challenges, and limitations of the organization.

Types of interview.   Interviews may be either structured or unstructured, directed or undirected, guided or unguided, and patterned or unpatterned. The primary differences are in the type of information sought, the way the questions are asked, the way the answers are interpreted, and the extent to which the questions are related to the specifications of the job to be filled.

Structured interview.   Structured interviews are usually used for particular jobs in specific organizations. These interviews are both standardized and controlled with regard to questions asked, sequence in which they are asked, interpretation of replies, and weight given to factors considered in making the value judgments.

The most popular patterned interview guide is the *McMurry Patterned Interview Form,* shown in Figure 7–4. The questions to the left of the blanks are to be asked of the applicant during the interview, while those below the line are to help the interviewer evaluate the information being presented and to use it in making the employment decision.

Unstructured interview.   In the unstructured interview, the patterns of questions asked, the conditions under which they are asked, and the bases for evaluating the replies are not standardized. As these factors vary between interviewers and between applicants, this type of interview is highly subjective, which may lead to quite different conclusions about a given applicant.

TABLE 7-3
Guidance to lawful and unlawful preemployment inquiries

Subject of inquiry:	It is not discriminatory to inquire about:	It may be discriminatory to inquire about:
1. Name	a. Whether applicant has ever worked under a different name	a. The original name of an applicant whose name has been legally changed b. The ethnic association of applicant's name
2. Birthplace and residence	a. Applicant's place of residence, length of applicant's residence in Nebraska and/or city where employer is located	a. Birthplace of applicant b. Birthplace of applicant's parents c. Birth certificate, naturalization or baptismal certificate
3. Race or color	a. General distinguishing characteristics such as scars, etc.	a. Applicant's race or color of applicant's skin
4. National origin and ancestry		a. Applicant's lineage, ancestry, national origin, descendants, parentage, or nationality b. Nationality of applicant's parents or spouse
5. Sex and family composition		a. Sex of applicant b. Dependents of applicant c. Marital status
6. Creed or religion		a. Applicant's religious affiliation b. Church, parish, or religious holidays observed
7. Citizenship	a. Whether the applicant is in the country on a visa, which permits him to work or is a citizen	a. Whether applicant is a citizen of a country other than the United States
8. Language	a. Language applicant speaks and/or writes fluently	a. Applicant's mother tongue, language commonly used by applicant at home
9. References	a. Names of persons willing or proved professional and/or character references for applicant	a. Name of applicant's pastor or religious leader

Source: Robert L. Mathis and John H. Jackson, *Personnel: Contemporary Perspectives and Applications*, 2d ed. (St. Paul, Minn.: West Publishing, 1979), p. 111. Used with permission of Omaha, Nebraska, Human Relations Department.

TABLE 7-3 *(continued)*

10. Relatives	a. Names of relatives already employed by the organization b. Name and address of person or relative to be notified in an emergency	a. Name and/or address of any relative of applicant
11. Organizations	a. Applicant's membership in any union, professional service, or trade organization	a. All clubs, social fraternities, societies, lodges, or organizations to which the applicant belongs where the name or character of the organization indicates the race, creed, color, or religion, national origin, sex, or ancestry of its members
12. Arrest record and convictions		a. Number and kinds of arrests and convictions unless related to job performance
13. Photographs		a. Photographs with application or before hiring b. Resume with photo of applicant
14. Height and weight		a. Any inquiry into height and weight of applicant, except where it is a bona fide occupational requirement
15. Physical limitations	a. Whether applicant has the ability to perform job-related functions	a. Whether an applicant is handicapped, or the nature or severity of a handicap
16. Education	a. Training an applicant has received if related to the job applied for	a. Educational attainment of an applicant unless there is validation that having certain educational backgrounds (i.e., high school diploma or college degree) is necessary to perform the functions of the job or position applied for
17. Financial status		a. An applicant's debts or assets b. Garnishments

FIGURE 7-4
McMurry patterned interview form

SUMMARY

Rating: 1 2 3 4 Interviewer ______ Date ______

Comments (List both favorable and unfavorable points) ______
In making final rating, be sure to consider not only the man's ability and experience but also his stability, industry, perseverance, ability to get along with others, loyalty, self-reliance, and leadership. Is he mature and realistic? Is he well motivated for this work? Are his living standards, finances, his domestic situation, and the family influence favorable to this work? Does he have sufficient health and physical reserve?

______ Position Considered for ______

Name ______ Telephone Number ______ Is it your phone? ______

Present Address ______ City ______ State ______
Will this location affect his attendance? Is this a desirable neighborhood? Does it appear consistent with income?

Date of your birth ______ Age ______ Have you served in the Armed Services of the United States? ☐ Yes ☐
In some States, legislation forbids discrimination because of age.

(If yes) What were the dates? ______ 19 __ to ______ 19 __ If rejected or exempted, what were the reasons? ______
Discuss military service as a job in chronological order with other jobs. Will this affect his performance on our job?

Why are you applying for this position? ______
Are his underlying reasons practical? Does he have a definite goal?

Are you employed now? ☐ Yes ☐ No; (If yes) how soon available? ______
What are relationships with present employer?

WORK HISTORY: LAST OR PRESENT POSITION Dates from ______ 19 __ to ______ 19 __
If out of work—how long?

Company ______ Division ______ Address ______
Does this check with application?

How did you get this job? ______
Did he show self-reliance in getting this job? Stability of interests? Perseverance?

Nature of work at start ______ Earnings at start ______
Did this work require energy and industry? Close attention? Cooperation?

How did the job change? ______ Earnings at leaving ______
Was progress made? Any indications of strong motivation? Is this in line with what he can earn here?

What were your duties and responsibilities at time of leaving? ______
Did he accept them? Indications of industry? Self-reliance? Perseverance? Leadership?

Superior ______ Title ______ How was he to work with? ______
Was this close supervision? Are there indications of loyalty? Hostility?

What did you especially like about the position? ______
Has he been happy and content in his work? Indications of loyalty, ability to get along with others?

What did you especially dislike? ______
Did he get along well with people? Is he inclined to be critical? Were his dislikes justified?

How much time have you lost from work? ______ Reasons ______
Is he regular in attendance on the job? Are there other interests?

Reasons for leaving ______ Why right then? ______
Are his reasons for leaving reasonable and consistent? Do they check with records?

Part-time jobs during this employment ______
Does this indicate industry? Ambition? Lack of loyalty? Lack of interest in duties of position?

NEXT TO LAST POSITION Dates from ______ 19 __ to ______ 19 __
Any time between this and last job?

Company ______ Division ______ Address ______
Does this check with application?

How did you get this job? ______
Did he show self-reliance in getting this job? Stability of interests? Perseverance?

Nature of work at start ______ Earnings at start ______
Did this work require energy and industry? Close attention? Cooperation?

How did the job change? ______ Earnings at leaving ______
Was progress made? Any indications of strong motivation? Is this in line with what he can earn here?

What were your duties and responsibilities at time of leaving? ______
Did he accept them? Indications of industry? Self-reliance? Perseverance? Leadership?

Superior ______ Title ______ How was he to work with? ______
Was this close supervision? Are there indications of loyalty? Hostility?

Source: Published by the Dartnell Corporation, Chicago. First page only is reproduced with permission. Copyright by the Dartnell Corporation, Chicago.

There is no such thing as a totally unstructured interview. Any experienced interviewer approaches the assignment with some objective in mind and some general understanding of how to achieve the objective. However, in this type of interview, the applicant must do most of the talking and ask most of the questions. Occasionally, an interviewer will talk too much during the interview. This tendency seems to be found more often in college recruiting. One study found that most of the students thought the interviewer talked too much. An examination of 31 tape-recorded interviews showed that the interviewers did 60 percent of the talking.[9]

Stress interview.   The *stress interview* was developed during World War II to select people for espionage activities. It is designed to show how a person acts under pressure. While no meaningful research has validated it for selecting civilian employees, it is frequently used in choosing managerial personnel. Some forms it takes are these:

1. After rapidly firing questions at the applicant, the interviewer suddenly stops and stares at the applicant.
2. The applicant is invited to draw up a chair and sit down, only to find a lamp cord tangled around one of the chair legs.
3. An applicant is invited to smoke, only to find that there is no ashtray.
4. A group of interviewers fires questions at the applicant in an unfriendly, or even hostile, manner.

This method is *not advocated* but is presented as a guide in case you ever face such a situation.

Some problems with the interview.   Interviews have not been found to be very valid or reliable. In general, validity and reliability are increased by structuring the interview and separating information gathering from decisions to hire.

When groups of applicants are being interviewed, the *contrast effect* is sometimes observed. If the previous applicant was "outstanding" and the present interviewee does not *appear* to measure up, there is the danger of rating the individual lower than otherwise. The reverse can also happen. Research indicates that the contrast effect may account for up to 80 percent of the variation in ratings of the "average" applicants when they follow "poorly qualified" or "well-qualified" interviewees.[10]

Biographical Inventory

Personnel managers are now looking for solid evidence of past performance in a person's record, rather than basing their decisions upon such factors as opinion or assumptions. This evidence is available from application blanks, personal data sheets or résumés, work records, school records, and military records.

Application blank.   The application blank is most often used to obtain biographical information. Practically all employers use it to find out about (1)

[9]Calvin W. Downes, "Perceptions of the Selection Interview," *Personnel Administration* 32 (May–June 1969):8–23.

[10]K. Wexley, G. Yukl, S. Kovacs, and R. Sanders, "Importance of Contrast Effects in Employment Interviews," *Journal of Applied Psychology* 56 (February 1972):45–48.

FIGURE 7-5

APPLICATION FOR EMPLOYMENT 991-0070-1L

EXXON

Exxon Corporation and affiliates

PLEASE PRINT

PERSONAL

FULL NAME – LAST | FIRST | MIDDLE | SOCIAL SECURITY NUMBER

PRESENT ADDRESS – STREET | CITY | STATE | ZIP CODE | CONTACT TELEPHONE NO. (INCL. AREA CODE)

LIST PREVIOUS ADDRESS FOR LAST 5 YEARS AND PERMANENT ADDRESS IF DIFFERENT FROM ABOVE

TIME TO CALL ☐ A.M. ☐ P.M.

ALTERNATE CONTACT PHONE NO. (INCL. AREA CODE)

TIME TO CALL ☐ A.M. ☐ P.M.

HOW REFERRED TO EXXON | NO. OF DAYS LOST FROM WORK OR SCHOOL DURING THE PAST 12 MONTHS | IF UNDER 18 YEARS GIVE DATE OF BIRTH

ONLY U.S. CITIZENS OR ALIENS WHO HAVE A LEGAL RIGHT TO WORK AND REMAIN PERMANENTLY IN THE U.S. ARE ELIGIBLE FOR EMPLOYMENT.

U.S. CITIZEN/PERMANENT RESIDENT ALIEN ☐ YES ☐ NO

ALIEN REGISTRATION NO.

IF NO, WHAT IS YOUR VISA STATUS? ☐ Student ☐ Exchange Student ☐ Visitor

Other – Explain

Have you ever applied to Exxon before? ☐ YES ☐ NO | IF YES, WHERE | APPROXIMATE DATE MO. YR.

Have you ever been employed by Exxon Corporation or any affiliate? ☐ YES ☐ NO | IF YES, COMPANY NAME | LOCATION | DATES OF EMPLOYMENT

U.S. MIL.

BRANCH OF SERVICE | FROM (MO./YR.) | TO (MO./YR.) | RANK ON ENTRY | RANK ON DISCHARGE

WHAT KIND OF DUTY (ESPECIALLY IF TECHNICAL IN NATURE)? | WHAT SPECIALIZED TRAINING DID YOU RECEIVE?

IF DISCHARGE WAS DISHONORABLE, PLEASE GIVE DETAILS.

TYPE OF EMPLOYMENT DESIRED ☐ PERMANENT ☐ TEMPORARY ☐ PART TIME ☐ SUMMER | SALARY EXPECTED | DATE AVAILABLE FOR WORK

CAN YOU: Perform shift work? ☐ YES ☐ NO Work overtime (if necessary)? ☐ YES ☐ NO

JOB PREFERRED AND NO. OF YEARS EXPERIENCE IN THIS WORK | GEOGRAPHICAL LOCATION PREFERENCE (IF ANY)

EDUCATION / SKILLS

SPECIALIZED SKILLS (COMPLETE IF APPLICABLE TO POSITION DESIRED) | TYPING WPM | DICTATION WPM | OFFICE MACHINES OPERATED

OTHER MACHINES OPERATED | OTHER SKILLS

NAME & LOCATION OF HIGH SCHOOL. IF NOT HIGH SCHOOL GRADUATE, INDICATE TOTAL YEARS SCHOOLING COMPLETED. | GRADUATION DATE (MO./YR.) | YOUR CLASS STANDING IN YOUR MAJOR | YOUR OVERALL GRADEPOINT AVERAGE

NAME & LOCATION OF COLLEGE/TRADE OR BUSINESS SCHOOL	DATE (MO./YR.) FROM	TO	FIELDS OF STUDY MAJOR	MINOR	GRADUATION DEGREE*	DATE (MO./YR.)	MY STDG. IS 1ST IN CLASS OF 60 EXAMPLE: 1/60	MY AVG. 3.7 ALL A'S 4.0 EXAMPLE: 3.7/4.0
							/	/
							/	/
							/	/
							/	/

**Insert number of college credit hours completed if no degree obtained.*

COLLEGE FINANCING | G.I. BILL % | OWN WORK % | SCHOLARSHIP – EXPLAIN % | OTHER – EXPLAIN %

CHECK QUARTER OF CLASS IN WHICH YOU STOOD | IN HIGH SCHOOL ☐ TOP ☐ 2ND ☐ 3RD ☐ LAST | IN COLLEGE/TRADE OR BUSINESS SCHOOL ☐ TOP ☐ 2ND ☐ 3RD ☐ LAST

ACTIVITIES

LIST SPECIAL ACADEMIC HONORS AND SOCIETIES; SCHOOL, CIVIC OR BUSINESS ACTIVITIES AND OFFICES HELD (EXCLUDE THOSE WHICH INDICATE RACE, COLOR, RELIGION, SEX OR NATIONAL ORIGIN)

SUBJECTS OF SPECIAL STUDY OR RESEARCH, COLLEGE OR OTHER

HOBBIES/LEISURE TIME INTEREST

previous education, including schools, subjects, degrees, and grades or standing, (2) specialized training programs, (3) previous work experience, including employer, location, when employed, duties and responsibilities, salary, and reasons for leaving, (4) membership in job-related associations, and (5) other work-related activities. Figure 7-5 is a well-designed form, free of any ques-

FIGURE 7-5 *(continued)*

SPECIAL EMPLOYMENT NOTICE TO DISABLED VETERANS, VIETNAM ERA VETERANS, AND INDIVIDUALS WITH PHYSICAL OR MENTAL HANDICAPS
Exxon Corporation and many of its affiliates are government contractors. As such they are subject to Section 402 of the Vietnam Era Veterans Readjustment Act of 1974, which requires the contractor to take affirmative action to employ and advance in employment qualified disabled veterans and veterans of the Vietnam Era, and Section 503 of the Rehabilitation Act of 1973, which requires government contractors to take affirmative action to employ and advance in employment qualified handicapped individuals.

If you are a disabled veteran, or have a physical or mental handicap and are scheduled for a personal interview, you are invited to volunteer this information to the employment representative at the time of the interview. You may also provide information on the skills and/or procedures you use or intend to use to perform the job for which you are applying and the nature and type of accommodations which you feel an employer may need to make in order to enable you to perform the job in a proper and safe manner. This information will be treated as confidential. Failure to provide this information will not jeopardize or adversely affect any consideration you may receive for employment.

Give employment record over last 10 years, starting with your present or last employer. Include summer employment. (If space is insufficient, list on separate page or attach resume.) For any unemployed or self-employed periods, show dates and locations.

EMPLOYMENT	DATE – FROM & TO		EMPLOYER'S NAME & ADDRESS – CITY & STATE	POSITION–SALARY	GIVE SPECIFIC REASON FOR LEAVING
	MONTH	YEAR			
	FR		NAME - PRESENT OR LAST EMPLOYER		
			ADDRESS & TELEPHONE NUMBER		
	TO		NAME OF SUPERVISOR		
	FR		NAME		
			ADDRESS & TELEPHONE NUMBER		
	TO		NAME OF SUPERVISOR		
	FR		NAME		
			ADDRESS & TELEPHONE NUMBER		
	TO		NAME OF SUPERVISOR		
	FR		NAME		
			ADDRESS & TELEPHONE NUMBER		
	TO		NAME OF SUPERVISOR		
	FR		NAME		
			ADDRESS & TELEPHONE NUMBER		
	TO		NAME OF SUPERVISOR		

REFERENCES

Give names of three persons to whom you are not related and by whom you have not been employed. These people should have known you for several years.

NAME – INITIALS	LAST NAME	ADDRESS - STREET, CITY, STATE, ZIP CODE	OCCUPATION	YEARS OF ACQUAINT.
A.				
B.				
C.				

Give names of any relatives, including those by marriage, in the employ of Exxon.

NAME	TYPE OF WORK	LOCATION	RELATIONSHIP
A.			
B.			

Names of our employees you know best.

NAME	LOCATION	NAME	LOCATION
A.		B.	

ADD'L. INFORMATION

Have you been convicted under any criminal law within the past 5 years (excluding minor traffic violations)? ☐NO   ☐YES - Give details

May we call your present employer? NOW ☐YES ☐NO LATER ☐YES ☐NO   Are you under technical contract or restriction with a former employer? ☐NO   ☐YES – WHOM? WITH

I authorize investigation of all statements contained in this application for employment. I understand that misrepresentation or omission of facts called for hereon will be sufficient cause for cancellation of consideration for employment or dismissal from the Company's service if I have been employed. I understand that employment is subject to a physical examination in which my health is found to be satisfactory to the Company. I understand that if I am employed evidence of U.S. citizenship or U.S. resident status and a birth certificate or other evidence of date of birth will be required.

SIGNATURE   DATE SIGNED
X

This is to inform you that as part of our procedure for processing your employment application it is understood that an investigative report may be made whereby information is obtained through personal interviews with third parties. This inquiry includes information as to your character, general reputation, personal characteristics, and mode of living, whichever may be applicable. You have the right to make a written request within a reasonable period of time for a complete and accurate disclosure of additional information concerning the nature and scope of the investigation.

991-0070-1L (BACK)

tions that presuppose an intention to discriminate in employment. Notice the questions *not* asked!

As a result of public policy, much progress has been made to revise and upgrade these forms. A much closer relationship between the questions asked and the information sought and the job to be filled is now observed.

Two other sources of biographical data are (1) the weighted application blank (WAB) and (2) the résumé.

Weighted application blank. The *weighted application blank*, sometimes called the *biographical information blank* (BIB), is used to research the relationship between factors in the employee's tasks and the current level of performance. This information is then used for prediction purposes, to see whether future applicants will meet the established criteria for job performance.

For example, the Metropolitan Life Insurance Company developed a program to examine all the possible combinations of 25 intervals of six background factors to identify their predictive ability. The application of the technique to 1,525 sales people found "previous income" the most important variable, with "number of dependents" next.[11]

The WAB consists of a series of statistically correlated and weighted questions concerning the applicant's background. Usually developed and validated by trained professionals, these blanks can be scored and interpreted in much the same manner as other objective instruments.

Research indicates that a careful evaluation of biographical inventories can result in the selection of qualified employees better than other instruments and can also reduce labor turnover. Many firms have found the WAB or BIB to be the single best predictor of success for specialized occupations. In fact, one research study indicated that biographical inventories showed higher validity in predicting job proficiency than psychological tests.[12]

After careful study and experimenting, Standard Oil of Indiana dropped its testing procedure in favor of this form for many of its positions.

Résumé. The *résumé* is a brief summary of the applicant's personal achievements, goals, and abilities. While the organization designs the application blank to gather the most biographical information, the applicant designs the format and content of the résumé. An employment agency indicated the emphasis given to this instrument by saying, "The résumé may be the most important document the applicant will ever write."

How to use these instruments. Personnel experts can use these biographical inventories in many ways. As the forms are usually completed in longhand, they serve as a simple literacy test to see if the person can read, write, and organize and present facts and thoughts clearly.

Some clues to look for when evaluating these documents are (1) a record of achievement, such as upward movement with one employer, or progressive

---

[11]R. Tanofsky, R. R. Shepps, and P. J. O'Neill, "Pattern Analysis of Biographical Predictors of Success as an Insurance Salesman," *Journal of Applied Psychology* 53 (April 1969):137.

[12]James J. Asher, "The Biographical Item: Can It Be Improved?" *Personnel Psychology* 25 (Summer 1972):255ff.

horizontal movement between organizations, (2) responsibility, as shown by positions held, (3) sudden shifts in career movement that might indicate lack of maturity or changed aspirations, (4) degree of mobility, as shown by the number of jobs held compared to years of employment, and (5) reason for wanting the job.

Testing

When the word *testing* is used, most people immediately think of selection and prediction of subsequent job performance. Tests are still one of the major methods of uncovering qualifications and talents that might go unnoticed in other instruments of selection.

A major reason for using testing is that it is the only selection technique that is objective.

Types of test.   While it is essential for each organization to use its own staff to validate the tests it uses, there is no need for it to develop its own tests. There are over 1,000 tests commercially available. Most of them are distributed by a few firms that specialize in developing and using tests.[13]

Tests can be classified on the basis of personal characteristics sought from the applicant. These include intelligence, aptitudes, interests, personality, and achievement (proficiency).

Intelligence tests have been widely used to measure mental ability or general learning ability. There is no good definition of intelligence.

Regardless of the definition, the outstanding feature of these tests is their ability to predict the general capacity for learning and/or problem solving. The most popular intelligence tests are the *Wonderlic Personnel Test, Otis Quick-Scoring Mental Ability Tests,* and *Thurstone Test of Mental Alertness.*

Aptitude tests measure a person's capacity to learn a given job, provided there is adequate training. While there are several types of aptitude or capacity for which tests are available, personnel managers are more interested in those dealing with clerical and mechanical aptitudes.

Clerical aptitude tests include the *Short Employment Tests* (SET) and *Minnesota Clerical Tests.* The mechanical aptitude tests include the *Bennett Test of Mechanical Comprehension* and the revised *Minnesota Paper Form Board Test.*

Probably the most widely used general inventory of aptitudes is the *General Aptitude Test Battery* (GATB), developed by the U.S. Department of Labor for use by state public employment offices.

How valid are aptitude tests in predicting trainability and job proficiency? Ghiselli did a very comprehensive study of the findings of other studies on the

---

[13]For a discussion of some of the types of test available, see O. K. Buros, ed., *The Eighth Mental Measurements Yearbook* (Highland Park, N.J.: Gryphon Press, 1978). This is a basic reference book summarizing practically all the developments in the field of testing. It also provides addresses to write to for further information.

validity of these tests, using the Pearsonian Coefficient of Correlation. His study proved of value in predicting success for managerial occupations, clerical operations, sales, protective services, vehicle operators, trades and crafts, and industrial occupations.[14]

Interest tests are derived from both hereditary and environmental factors. Therefore, they should help predict success on the job if the person's interests and those of the job are matched. The more popular tests designed to discover patterns of individual interest that are associated with success in various types of job are the *Kuder Preference Record* and Strong's *Vocational Interest Blank*.

Personality tests are important because personnel specialists tend to regard personality as basic to success, especially in supervisory or managerial positions. They feel that selected personality characteristics may be even more important than job knowledge or skill, as emotional maturity influences the ability to withstand stress and strain, to be objective, and to gain the respect and cooperation of others.

Among the more popular personality tests are the *Rorschach Test* and the *Murray Thematic Apperception Test* (TAT) and a modification known as the *Thematic Evaluation of Managerial Potential* (TEMP).

Achievement or proficiency tests measure an applicant's knowledge of a given job. In other words, if the personnel department is looking for someone who knows how to do a certain job—now—one of these trade tests is probably preferable. In addition, these tests are sometimes handy for spotting

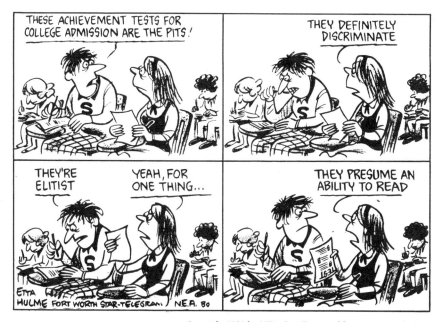

Copyright 1980 by NEA, Inc. Reprinted by permission of NEA.

[14]Edwin E. Ghiselli, "The Validity of Aptitude Tests in Personnel Selection," *Personnel Psychology* 26 (Winter 1973):461–77.

"trade bluffers"—people who claim knowledge and job experience they do not possess.

A specialized form of achievement test is *work sampling,* or *work previews.* Such a test consists of having the prospective employee do a task that is representative of the work actually to be done on the job. It must include the more crucial aspects of job performance in order to be valid. In addition to showing whether the prospective employee is able to do the job, it also provides the latter with realistic job expectations.

One insurance firm, using this instrument, found that 40 percent of its agents survived for 12 months, while only 13 percent of those who had not taken the job sample lasted that long.[15]

Requirements for effective testing.   If an organization is going to use tests, the testing program can be made more productive and rewarding by accepting the following suggestions:

1. Tests themselves should be thoroughly tested.
2. Use tests with discretion and only along with other selection instruments.
3. Use a battery of tests.
4. Use only validated tests.
5. Use tests to separate people into broad groups rather than to choose between two people close together.
6. Set the critical, or cut-off, score in advance.
7. Don't use the raw scores; interpret them.

Effect of public policy on testing.   The EEOC requires that tests:

1. Be developed and administered by competent professionals.
2. Be free of cultural bias.
3. Be validated and related to job performance.[16]
4. Give "great deference" to the EEOC's Uniform Guidelines on Employee Selection Procedures.[17]

Use of the polygraph.   The *polygraph,* a form of test, is being used by business to meet the surge of employee theft.[18] The primary purpose of the "lie detector" in business is to declare the innocence of those under suspicion. There are three polygraph "tests" to keep white-collar thieves out of business in the first place or to find them out once a crime occurs. They are (1) the preemployment security clearance examination, (2) a specific loss examination, and (3) the periodic examination.

---

[15]See Michael A. Raphael, "Work Previews Can Reduce Turnover and Improve Performance," *Personnel Journal* 54 (February 1975):97–99.

[16]*Griggs et al.* v. *Duke Power Company,* 3 FEP Cases 175 (1971).

[17]*Albemarle Paper Company* v. *Moody,* 10 FEP Cases 1181 (1975).

[18]See Victor Lipman, "New Hiring Tool: Truth Tests," *Parade,* October 7, 1979, p. 14ff.

Source: *Baton Rouge* (La.) *Sunday Advocate*, December 12, 1976, p. 4–F.

The test that has been most helpful to businesses is the preemployment examination. Companies request applicants in certain areas of work to take a polygraph examination to determine their integrity and character. They are asked about their past job performance, their physical and mental condition at the time of the test, and their integrity. The test's biggest asset to the employer is its ability to cull potentially bad employee risks before they get in.

In-depth Interview

The *in-depth interview* is often referred to as the employment interview, the preemployment interview, or the diagnostic interview. It is probably the most important part of the whole selection procedure. All the relevant information is brought into focus at that point. Often the final decision to hire an individual is made during that interview.

The factors of aptitude, proficiency, and personality, as measured by energy, drive, social adaptability, emotional control, and conscience, are related to an employee's productivity. These subjects should be openly discussed during this interview. In general, the interviewer tries to find out the applicant's level of maturity, ability to persevere, and degree of self-discipline. Also, the interviewer searches for the right attitude, knowledge, and skills needed for successful performance on the job. In summary, the interviewer attempts to evaluate the person's ability to utilize available resources in solving complex problems.

Verifying Applicant's Information

Somewhere in the selection process, the previously gathered information should be verified by checking the references, running a credit check, and/or checking school records.

Sources used to verify information.   The sources used to verify applicant's information are references, credit checks, and transcripts. The first one is used more than the others.

References.   There are essentially three kinds of reference—personal, academic, and past employment. The first of these are of little value, as they tend to be biased in favor of the applicant. The second are of considerable value if the personnel recruiter develops a relationship with the teachers based on mutual respect and interest.

The most important references, though, are from the applicant's former employers. A measure of the person's actual accomplishments, including productivity, the ability to get along with others, and weaknesses and strengths, may be obtained this way. The potential dangers of work references are (1) "spite references" and (2) failure to reveal shortcomings out of sympathy for the worker.

Credit check.   Although they are declining in popularity because of changing public policy, credit checks can provide a useful source of verification for data given, as well as a source of new information. These checks are subject to the *Fair Credit Reporting Act* of 1970. So an applicant must be notified in writing that such information is being sought. Then he or she is entitled to "full disclosure" from the report received.

Transcripts.   Most employers of higher level employees try to obtain complete transcripts of job applicants' educational background. This information is useful for seeing whether there is a pattern of grades in given courses or subject areas. I have found this to be a good predictor of success for students going into specialized jobs.

How extensively is verification used?   A survey of 38 manufacturing and service organizations showed that 43 percent of them used background checks merely to verify information; 34 percent indicated that such checks gave additional information about the applicant; and 13 percent believed that they uncovered information that would not otherwise have been uncovered.[19] Three out of four respondents said the verification occurred after the interviews.

Like other selection instruments, references are declining in use because of the *Fair Credit Reporting Act* and equal employment guidelines and decisions.

National Bank of Detroit will only "confirm dates and nature of employment. We try not to make judgments or go beyond the basic facts."

---

[19]This study by George M. Beason and John A. Belt, "Verifying Job Applicants' Background," *Personnel Administrator* 14 (November–December, 1974):29–32, provides much research data for this discussion.

General Electric will say whether or not it would rehire a discharged employee, but it won't elaborate.

Uniroyal and ACF Industries try to ease the problem by asking applicants for written permission to check references.

A large utility worries that concern over privacy is "protecting the crooks. We have to hire meter readers who are going into people's homes and we can't get background information on anybody."[20]

What methods used to verify?   Information can be verified in four basic ways:

1. In person—a personal visit with reference giver.
2. By phone—enables prospective employer to listen to the tone of voice and notice pauses or hesitations of reference giver, and follow up quickly on questions, suggestions, or inferences that indicate a problem area. (This is the most frequently used method of verification.)
3. By letter—although letters have a low rate of validity and return, they are still being used.
4. By questionnaire—Nash and Carroll found that the response rate increased from 35 to 85 percent when they used a one-page, objective questionnaire with an individually typed letter signed by one of the authors as "Director of Personnel."[21]

How valid are reference checks?   The research just mentioned found that organizations can improve the usefulness of the reference check by giving careful attention to who gives the reference and the method used to obtain the reference. Only references from former supervisors who are of the same sex, race, and national origin and who had recent opportunity to observe the applicant in a work situation are predictive of the applicant's success in a new job.

Physical Examination

The final step in the information-gathering stage is some form of physical examination. Some employers use a thorough medical history, plus careful observation during interviews, instead of a thorough physical.

Although a physical is usually given as part of the preemployment procedure, it really has several purposes. First, it is designed to screen out individuals who might not be capable of performing the assigned duties effectively. Thus, the intent is to protect prospective employees from possible injury caused by performing a job they were not capable of. Second, the exam can

---

[20]*The Wall Street Journal*, January 6, 1976, p. 1.

[21]See Allan N. Nash and Stephen J. Carroll, Jr., "A Hard Look at the Reference Check," *Business Horizons* 13 (October 1970):47, for further information.

be used to screen out people who might have a high incidence of absenteeism, illness, or accidents. (As shown in Chapter 13, this is particularly true in the case of chemical dependency.) Third, it can prevent hiring people with communicable diseases. Finally, it can be used as a defense against unwarranted claims under workers' compensation laws or in suits for damages.

As current personnel policies are designed to hire more handicapped workers, this creates a dilemma for employers. However, many states have faced up to the reluctance of employers to assume the potentially higher liability caused by hiring those with existing physical impairments. Many states have passed *second injury laws*, under which the present employer's liability is limited to those injuries resulting from the present job. Another fund—usually administered by the state—will provide for earlier injuries.

It is surprising how many applicants are rejected on the basis of physicals. Apparently our new lifestyles are partially responsible.

While doing a case study of a chemical plant in New England, I was told that over 40 percent of blue-collar applicants who reached the physical exam stage of the employment procedure were rejected for "back ailments." Many of the problems resulted from "poor posture."

In Los Angeles, an energy firm found that "a substantial proportion" of young applicants were rejected because of "hearing problems." This was particularly true of former employees of places where music was played.

Which Instruments to Use?

Deciding which instruments, or techniques, to use is difficult. One way of deciding is to see what adverse effects each one might have on different types of applicant. Figure 7-6 summarizes the findings of one researcher. These findings, of course, must be modified to fit the unique conditions of each employer.

MAKING AND COMMUNICATING THE DECISION TO ACCEPT OR REJECT

The next step in the selection procedure is choosing the desired candidate from among the remaining applicants. Whether the selection procedure is regarded as positive *selection* or negative *rejection*, many decisions are made concerning the individual's actual and potential abilities at each stage of the procedure.

How the Decision Is Made

So far, we have looked at the process of gathering information and evaluating it in terms of the applicants' abilities relative to the job to be filled. While

FIGURE 7-6
Several selection procedures and possible adverse impact on different minority members

	Blacks	Females	Elderly	Handicapped
Intelligence and verbal tests	✓ ✓	+	✓	?
Work sampling tests	+	NE	NE	NE
Interview	+	✓ ✓	✓	✓
Educational requirements	✓ ✓	+	✓	?
Physical tests (height, weight, etc.)	+	✓ ✓	?	✓ ✓

✓ ✓ = Fairly established evidence of adverse impact.
✓ = Some evidence of adverse impact.
? = No data which bears direct evidence, but seems likely depending on type of handicap or type of test.
NE = No or little evidence to indicate one way or the other.
+ = Evidence indicates that particular minority group does as well as or better than majority members.

Source: Richard D. Arvey, *Fairness in Selecting Employees,* © 1979, Addison-Wesley Publishing Company, Inc., Table 9-1, p. 236. Reprinted with permission.

decisions have to be made at each step of the way, there comes a time when all the information must be pulled together. Then a decision to accept or reject the applicant(s) is made.

There are two ways of making this decision. First, some mechanized method can be used, whereby the quantifiable data are fed into a computer that is programmed to make the decision. The technology is now available for the computer to make decisions equal to those of personnel specialists—at least for certain jobs.

An experimental model was developed to reduce the judgmental factor in selection. Seven out of eight times, the computer printed out the same final selection decision as an independent consulting psychologist on whether or not to hire applicants for clerical positions.[22]

Finally, however, a value judgment must be made, using knowledge obtained from the various evaluative techniques. This evaluation occurs when the decision is made as to whether the person will be hired or not. (Although not always true, the assumption is made that there is more than one candidate for each job.)

The paradox involved in this step is that the practical art of weighing and evaluating human virtues and limitations must reside with an individual who may have many of the same strengths and weaknesses. This most important step in the selection process, then, is made by a fallible person. The saving

[22]Robert D. Smith, "Models for Personnel Selection Decisions," *Personnel Journal* 52 (August 1973):688–95.

TABLE 7-4
Ratio of acceptances to offers

Engineering (90)	35%
Accounting and business administration (82)	53
Liberal arts graduates (30)	53
Women graduates (65)	50
Black graduates or minorities (66)	48

Source: Frank S. Endicott, *The Endicott Report—1980: Trends in the Hiring of College Graduates in Business and Industry* (Evanston, Ill.:
The Placement Center, Northwestern University, 1979), p. 7.

factor is that the chances of success are enhanced if the procedure has been
effectively handled up to that point, thus furnishing a store of evidence to
serve as a guide to action. Also, most jobs have some crucial indicator or
critical factor, based on research, that serves as the focal point for making the
decision.

Communicating the Decision

When the decision is made not to make a job offer, the rejection may be done
by either the personnel office or the operating executive. Usually it is done by
the personnel department.

When the decision is made to employ the applicant, the job offer may be
made by the operating department. Still the personnel department usually
must give its approval to the terms and conditions of employment.

Ironically, even when the job offer is made, there is always the possibility
that the applicant will reject it. Table 7-4 shows the percentages of acceptances of job offers made to groups of college students. Notice that acceptance
varies from a low of 35 percent to a high of 53 percent.

SUMMARY AND CONCLUSIONS

Personnel selection is the procedure used in judging whether applicants are or
are not suited for positions needing to be filled.

The stages involved in the selection procedure are (1) establishing selection
policies, (2) identifying and establishing selection criteria, predictors, and instruments, (3) gathering and evaluating information about potential employees
and assessing the applicant's suitability for the position, (4) deciding to accept
or reject the applicant, and (5) communicating the decision. The selection
procedure may be considered as either selection or rejection.

The techniques used in the selection process are designed to remove from
further consideration those considered to have the greatest chance of failing,
while leaving the ones with potential for success.

Selection decisions should be based upon several predictors of success in combination with each other. The lower the job level, the greater the use of a single criterion for predicting job performance. Conversely, the higher the job level, the greater the use of multiple correlation procedures. Selection criteria should have validity and reliability.

The personal characteristics usually sought in prospective employees are favorable (1) personal background, (2) aptitudes and interests, (3) attitudes and needs, (4) analytical abilities, (5) skill and technical abilities, (6) health, energy, and stamina, and (7) value system.

Information about personal characteristics can be gathered from application blanks, school records, work records, interviews, references, preliminary interviews, tests, medical examinations, and in-depth interviews.

Those doing employee selection are becoming more interested in past performance as a measure of future performance than they previously were.

Testing is in trouble, but is still one of the best objective measures available.

The in-depth, or diagnostic, interview is one of the most important parts of the whole selection procedure. It can reveal insights that other techniques cannot.

The most valuable references are those from the applicant's previous employers.

Medical examinations are used to (1) screen out those physically incapable of doing the job, (2) prevent employment of those with high incidences of absenteeism, illness, or accidents, (3) prevent hiring people with communicable diseases, and (4) ward off unwarranted claims under workers' compensation laws or suits for damages.

Ironically, after using this elaborate procedure, many applicants reject the job offer.

QUESTIONS

1. Do you think the selection procedure is one of *selection* or *rejection?* Explain your answer.
2. What is the relationship between employee attitudes and productivity? How does this relationship apply to selection? Explain.
3. What is meant by the statement "the matching procedure begins with, and is based upon, an evaluation of the applicant's strengths and weaknesses"?
4. How does public policy affect selection? Explain.
5. Discuss the steps in the suggested selection procedure in the information gathering and evaluating stage. Would you recommend any revision in the steps? If so, what revisions?
6. A common opinion among first-line managers is that because of their interaction with the work group, they should have complete authority over the selection process. Do you agree or disagree? Explain.

7. What do you think of the biographical inventory as a selection instrument? Explain.

8. What do you think of using tests in the selection process? Explain.

9. What advantages do interviews have over other selection instruments? Can you verify from personal experience that interviewers do most of the talking?

PROBLEM

Selection: In Theory and in Practice

The following letter was received from the personnel director of a large chemical company in answer to the question: "What selection techniques do you use?"

> Among the various selection (or rejection) bases we use, the best method for predicting what an employee can and will do is evaluating what one has consistently done in the past. Therefore, a careful review of an applicant's performance history should provide a forecast of what he or she probably will do in the future.
>
> The information normally required on employment applications and résumés has been diluted to the point where they provide basic information only.
>
> An important selection technique, which is currently causing much controversy, is preemployment testing. Despite all of the arguments against testing, it is still one of the best measures we have for providing objective results.
>
> Testing, professionally validated, is a tool of great value, but the greatest value of such testing lies in its administration and use specifically related to the job to be filled. Another great value of a testing program is in obtaining scores from a test battery providing the psychological characteristics of the worker to insure compatibility with the job function and the personnel with whom the employee will be associated. The trend of discounting such testing is causing considerable problems in that the techniques of the personnel interview require considerable training and skill—which most interviewers do not have.
>
> Reference investigations are usually of little value because of the hesitancy of former employers to provide information on former employees. This lack of interest in giving requested information is due to the emphasis being placed by various governmental agencies on the right of privacy of the worker.
>
> This dilution of necessary information is even reaching into the preemployment physical examination, for we get little information from the doctors to help us make employment decisions.

Questions

1. Evaluate this person's assessment of selection.

2. If you were asked to advise this manager, what suggestions would you make?

SUGGESTED READINGS FOR FURTHER STUDY

Bucalo, Jack. "The Balanced Approach to Successful Screening Interviews." *Personnel Journal* 57 (August 1978):420-27.

Byham, William C. "Common Selection Problems Can Be Overcome." *Personnel Administrator* 23 (August 1978):42-47.

Delamontagne, Robert P., and James B. Weitzul. "Performance Alignment: The Fine Art of the Perfect Fit." *Personnel Journal* 59 (February 1980):115-17.

Dyer, Frank J. "An Alternative to Validating Selection Tests." *Personnel Journal* 57 (April 1978):200-203.

Erwin, Frank W. "Comment on Proposed Uniform Employee Selection Guidelines." *Personnel Administrator* 23 (June 1978):41-46.

Gatewood, Robert D., and James Ledvinka. "Selection Interviewing and EEO: Mandate for Objectivity." *Personnel Administrator* 24 (December 1979):51-56.

Latterell, Jeffrey. "Planning for the Selection Interview." *Personnel Journal* 58 (July 1979):466-67 and 480.

Levine, Edward L., Nell Bennett, and Ronald A. Ash. "Evaluation and Use of Four Job Analysis Methods for Personnel Selection." *Public Personnel Management* 8 (May-June 1979):146-51.

Manning, Winton H. "Test Validation and EEOC Requirements: Where We Stand." *Personnel* 55 (May-June 1978):70-73.

Norris, Dwight R., and James A. Buford, Jr. "A Content Valid Writing Test: A Case Study." *Personnel Administrator* 25 (January 1980):40-44.

Perham, John. "New Push for Employee Privacy." *Dun's Review* 113 (March 1979):112-14.

Young, David M., Ernst G. Beier, and Steven Beier. "Beyond Words: Influence of Nonverbal Behavior of Female Job Applicants in the Employment Interview." *Personnel and Guidance Journal* 57 (March 1979):346-50.

CHAPTER EIGHT

Training and Developing Employees

Learning Objectives

After studying the material in this chapter, you should be able to:

1. Explain why training and developing human resources is so important.
2. State some objectives of training and development.
3. Describe the relationship between the personnel department and other departments with regard to development.
4. Tell how to identify development needs.
5. Name some factors involved in designing development programs to make them more effective.
6. List what should be included in development programs for nonmanagerial employees.
7. Outline some methods that can be used in conducting development programs.
8. Explain how to evaluate the effectiveness of a development program.

Some Important Words and Terms

Training	Identification
Education	Law of effect
Development	Vestibule training
Apprenticeship training	Programmed instruction
Training needs survey	Orientation
Problem analysis discussions	On-the-job training (OJT)
Personnel progress report	Cooperative education (coop ed)
Work data analysis	

Chance favors the prepared mind.
LOUIS PASTEUR

Learning maketh the young temperate, is the comfort of old age, standing for wealth with poverty, and serving as an ornament to riches.
CICERO

Outline of the Chapter

IMPORTANCE OF EMPLOYEE DEVELOPMENT
      Relationship between Development and Performance
      What Is Development?
ESTABLISHING DEVELOPMENT OBJECTIVES
      To Help the Organization Grow
      To Adapt to Technological Developments
      To Fulfill Social Responsibility
      To Provide Greater Job Satisfaction
ASSIGNING RESPONSIBILITY FOR DEVELOPMENT
      Role Assigned to Society
      Role Assigned to Unions and Employee Associations
      Role Assigned to Employees
      Role Assigned to Employers
IDENTIFYING DEVELOPMENT NEEDS
      Identifying Who Needs Developing
      Identifying What Needs Developing
FACTORS NEEDED FOR EFFECTIVE DEVELOPMENT PROGRAMS
      Need for Positive Motivation
      Development Must Be Dynamic and Continuous
      Development Involves the Systems Approach
      Overcoming Resistance to Development
      Train the Trainer
CONDUCTING THE DEVELOPMENT PROGRAM
      Training off the Job
      Training on the Job
EVALUATING EFFECTIVENESS OF DEVELOPMENT PROGRAMS
      Approaches to Evaluation
      What Is Evaluated?
      A Cost-effective Approach
INFLUENCE OF EEO ON TRAINING AND DEVELOPMENT

At the end of 1979, many training directors expected development to decline as it usually does in a recession. Yet Kathleen Whiteside, manager of training and development at Detroit's Harper-Grace Hospitals, thought otherwise. She said training had never looked brighter, as they were starting several long-awaited programs. "We'll be doing more in the next year than at any time in the past," she said. The hospitals were planning a pilot program to improve patient care and a comprehensive supervisory skills training program.[1]

Leonardo da Vinci—sculptor, painter, engineer, musician, architect, and scientist—was the supreme example of the Renaissance scholar who believed in broadening the intellectual scope of higher education. Yet it is doubtful that we will ever see another da Vinci simply because, during the 500 years since the Renaissance, knowledge has become so abundant and so complex that no one person can learn and use all of it.

IMPORTANCE OF EMPLOYEE DEVELOPMENT

These two illustrations point up two very important aspects of employee training and development. First, employers now recognize that employee development is an essential part of the staffing function, as shown in Figure 8–1. Second, knowledge is increasing so rapidly and skills must be upgraded so frequently that it is difficult for personnel managers to keep up with training needs.

FIGURE 8–1
How training and development fit into the staffing function

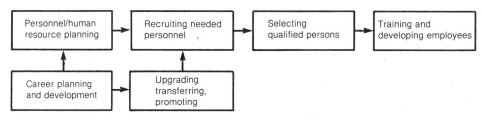

Relationship between Development and Performance

Skills and knowledge can easily become obsolete in the same way as machines or technology. They must be constantly kept up to date if an organization is to survive. It has been estimated that in the future about 20 to 25 percent of an engineer's time must be spent in educational experiences on the job or on the

---

[1]"The Recession's Track Record So Far: Lots of HRD Casualties—as Well as Survivors," *Training/HRD* 16 (December 1979):32.

employer's time.[2] Graduate engineers must spend 10 percent of their time each year extending their knowledge just to keep up with current graduates, and 20 percent if they want to remain of equal value to their employer and society. Finally, general knowledge is increasing at about 10 percent each year.

You can see from these conclusions how vital education, training, and development are to management.

What Is Development?

It is difficult to distinguish between education, training, and development. In reality they are only different aspects of the same idea, which is to develop personnel. However, if an attempt is made to find some distinctions between them, it can be said that:

1. *Training* involves learning specific, detailed, and routine skills and techniques.
2. *Education* is learning general subjects and broad, generalized knowledge.
3. *Development* is the systematic process of education, training, and growing by which a person learns and applies information, knowledge, skills, attitudes, and perceptions.

This chapter covers the overall topics of training and developing employees, especially nonmanagerial personnel. Figure 8–2 shows a suggested development model.

FIGURE 8–2
Model for developing personnel and human resources

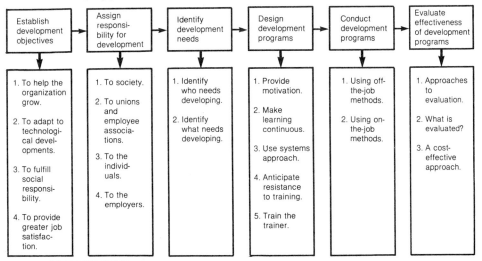

[2]Willis M. Tate, president, Southern Methodist University, "Things Aren't Like They Used to Be," *Proceedings of the 26th Conference of the University Personnel and Management Conference* (Austin: University of Texas, 1964), p. 35.

ESTABLISHING DEVELOPMENT OBJECTIVES

The most effective development programs have objectives that are attainable. These programs must be in harmony with other organizational objectives. They are oriented toward the long and the short run and are closely related to the personal goals of the learner.[3] These programs are finding that training based on the kinds of job that need to be filled is not as important as *developing the kind of people* that the organization will need for future effectiveness.

Some practical objectives are:

1. To help the organization grow.
2. To adapt to technological developments.
3. To fulfill social responsibility.
4. To provide greater job satisfaction.

To Help the Organization Grow

One of the objectives of personnel managers is to see that the resources available to their organizations—private or public—are used efficiently and effectively. Therefore, these managers should be concerned with improving the performance of their employees. This is now true, according to a survey of 1,006 members of the American Society of Personnel Administrators (ASPA). Table 8-1 shows the results of the study, done jointly with Prentice-Hall.

TABLE 8-1
Kinds of training offered by members of the American Society of Personnel Administrators

Type of training program	Percentage offering program
Informal training only	34
Mainly informal	54
In-company classes for special needs	90
Encouraged to attend off-company courses	86
Training for present line supervisors	86
Training for middle and upper management level personnel	73
Presupervisory training	50
Program for upgrading mechanical and specialized skills	40
Program for upgrading basic clerical skills	38
Apprentice program for certain trades and crafts	31
Other special training programs	15

Source: *Employee Training Survey*, by Prentice-Hall, Inc. and the American Society for Personnel Administration in *Personnel Management: Policies and Practices* Report No. 2 (6-12-79). © Prentice-Hall, Inc., Englewood Cliffs, NJ. 1979.

---

[3]E. Arthur Prieve and Dorothy A. Wentorf, "Training Objectives—Philosophy or Practice?" *Personnel Journal* 49 (March 1970):235–40.

While two-thirds of the respondents had some type of formal training, the others had only informal training.

To Adapt to Technological Developments

Human resource development is needed to adjust to rapid technological changes. Not only must new employees be trained, but present ones must be retrained and upgraded. Large numbers of young people without the education or skills required for today's employment are joining the ranks of the unemployed. It is not that they are incompetent but that there are just not enough jobs for their limited skills. The problem is expected to increase.

Research has shown that a steadily increasing level of education and the acceleration of technological change lead to increased stress on formal education by management.[4] Consequently, there are fewer promotional opportunities for lower level employees. This makes it difficult to attract and keep supervisors at that level. It also leads to conflict between supervisors and subordinates. The result of these pressures is to institute—and upgrade—formal programs for personal and organizational development.

The validity of this conclusion is emphasized by the shortage of persons with the basic skills, such as skilled machinists, auto mechanics, welders, and secretaries. With an unemployment rate of around 7 percent in 1980, there were around 1.5 million jobs available in these fields.

To Fulfill Social Responsibility

During the 1960s, there was a change in public policy toward providing employment and promotional opportunities for everyone. Also, considerable emphasis was given to training and developing minority groups. This policy has led to many successful attempts to upgrade the abilities and achievements of these groups.

A study by the Bureau of National Affairs (BNA) in 1976 found that two-thirds of the firms surveyed had special training sessions to implement EEO goals and policies.[5]

One-third of the respondents in the ASPA study had (or were planning) special training programs for women, minorities, and other disadvantaged groups.

---

[4]See Elmer H. Burack and Peter F. Sorensen, Jr., "Manpower Development and Technological Change: Some Considerations for Revised Strategy," *Journal of Management Studies* 8 (October 1971):304–14.

[5]Francine Hall and Maryann Albrecht, "Training for EEO: What Kinds and for Whom?" *Personnel Administrator* 22 (October 1977):25–28.

To Provide Greater Job Satisfaction

Development leads to greater job satisfaction, for employees gain a greater sense of worth, dignity, and well-being as they become more valuable to their employers. They also receive greater income from increased productivity. These two factors will provide a sense of satisfaction in the achievement of personal and social goals. Highly developed employees should cause fewer problems and be more cooperative.

IBM's "career bend" is a program of "enlightened paternalism" that offers near-total security to its employees. The firm claims that in more than 35 years it has never laid off a worker for economic reasons. It retrains workers not needed in one job and assigns them to another. From 1970 to 1975, it retrained and physically relocated 5,000 employees as part of the most extensive corporate education program in the United States. The payoff was in intangible but real benefits such as "loyalty," "hard work," and "satisfaction."[6]

ASSIGNING RESPONSIBILITY FOR DEVELOPMENT

At least four groups are responsible for personnel development. They are (1) *society*, (2) *unions* and other *employee associations*, (3) *individual employees*, and (4) *employers*.

Role Assigned to Society

The responsibility for general education is assigned to society through public and private education. Because of the increasing proportion of the school-age population seeking an education and other factors, formal education is becoming much more expensive.

There are many state and federal programs that cooperate with employers to train and develop present and future employees. Some of the more popular ones are:

1. The *National Apprenticeship Act* of 1937, which sets forth policies and standards for apprenticeship programs.
2. The *Comprehensive Employment and Training Act* (CETA), which replaced many previous programs, such as the *Manpower Development and Training Act* of 1962. It provides federal assistance in training unemployed and underemployed workers, particularly youths without previous work experience.

---

[6]See "How IBM Avoids Layoffs through Retraining," *Business Week*, November 10, 1975, pp. 110–12, for examples of how this program works.

3. The *JOBS* (Job Opportunities in the Business Sector) *Program,* which encourages employers to submit proposals for contracts for on-the-job training for the disadvantaged unemployed.
4. The *Vietnam Era Veterans' Readjustment Assistance Act,* which provides training and education for veterans.

Role Assigned to Unions and Employee Associations

The role of labor organizations is quite formal under *apprenticeship training* arrangements. There is a joint responsibility between labor and management for administering the programs. Many employee associations also provide training and development for their members.

Role Assigned to Employees

The final responsibility for their development ultimately rests with individual employees. Yet outside assistance is needed because stimulation and contact— physical, mental, social—are necessary for normal human development.

Role Assigned to Employers

Developing human resources is also the responsibility of employers. Modern managers feel that increased job specialization and tightened skilled labor markets not only justify this kind of expenditure for personnel training but demand it. American business spends around $40 billion yearly to provide formal education courses for its employees.

Xerox Corporation operates the International Center for Training and Management Development at Leesburg, Virginia. It has a capacity of 1,000 students. All newly hired sales and service employees must take courses in their fields at the center. Courses in management are offered on a voluntary basis to employees who are recommended by their superiors.

Shared responsibilities. Training and development are usually shared responsibilities.[7] In general, the personnel department has overall responsibility for planning the programs and providing the resources. The other departments carry out the programs and do most of the actual development, as shown in Figure 8–3.

---

[7]See E. J. Berne, "Managing Training Activities," *Training and Development Journal* 33 (May 1979):48–50, for further information about this subject.

FIGURE 8-3
How members of Bureau of National Affairs' Personnel Policy Forum share responsibility

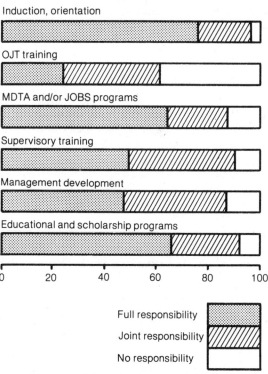

Source: The Bureau of National Affairs, Inc., "The Personnel Department," BNA Policy and Practice Series: *Personnel Management*, Report No. 244 (Washington, D.C.: Bureau of National Affairs), 251:21-22.

A study of manufacturing firms found the majority of them using personnel staff members or full-time training instructors to train both blue- and white-collar employees.[8] In fact, 78 percent of the firms used personnel staff members to train some or all of these employees. Yet 93 percent of them used supervisors and other managers to do the training. Smaller proportions used vocational, technical, or business school teachers and/or college and university professors to do the training. The other developmental activities were carried on by company suppliers of equipment or high school teachers.

Line management's function. Line managers are responsible for establishing a favorable climate in which personnel can develop. Also, many of them actually teach in formal programs, especially orientation and management

---

[8]National Industrial Conference Board, *Personnel Practices in Factory and Office: Manufacturing*, Studies in Personnel Policy No. 194 (New York: National Industrial Conference Board, 1974).

FIGURE 8-4

Responsibility for training among members of the American Society for Personnel Administration

42%	33%	17%	8%
Training done by personnel department	Each division or line department handles its own training	Training done by special department	Training not a separate function

Source: *Employee Training Survey*, by Prentice-Hall, Inc. and the American Society for Personnel Administration in *Personnel Management: Policies and Practices* Report No. 2 (6-12-79). © Prentice-Hall, Inc., Englewood Cliffs, NJ, 1979.

development. Supervisors greatly influence their subordinates' development by telling them when their performance is—or is not—conforming to management standards. If employees are complimented when they do a good job, it should stimulate pride and motivation in them. This is called *reinforcement*.

Staff specialist's function.   The personnel department's function is to provide formal training programs and to maintain the related records. It does not take over the line managers' responsibility for training but helps other managers fulfill that responsibility. The total program for employee development is a joint responsibility. The personnel staff and line managers each perform activities they are best equipped to handle. Figure 8-4 shows how this relationship functions among ASPA members.

IDENTIFYING DEVELOPMENT NEEDS

A major problem with training and development is identifying *who* needs *how much* of *what type* of development. This requires three basic steps, which begin when the employee is hired. These are (1) identifying the skills needed, (2) analyzing employee skills and comparing them with the skills needed, and (3) selecting methods of developing the needed skills.[9] Figure 8-5 expands on these steps.

Identifying Who Needs Developing

There are many specific methods for identifying training needs. However, the most frequently used ones are (1) supervisory recommendations, (2) analysis of job requirements, (3) analysis of job performance, and (4) employee suggestions.

Supervisory recommendations.   There are several ways supervisory recommendations reach the training director.

---

[9]David R. Cook, "Improving Employee Development Programs," *Personnel Administrator* 23 (July 1978):38-40. See "A Model for the Identification of Training Needs," *Public Personnel Management* 7 (July–August 1978):257, for a more behavioral model.

FIGURE 8–5
Model for identifying development needs

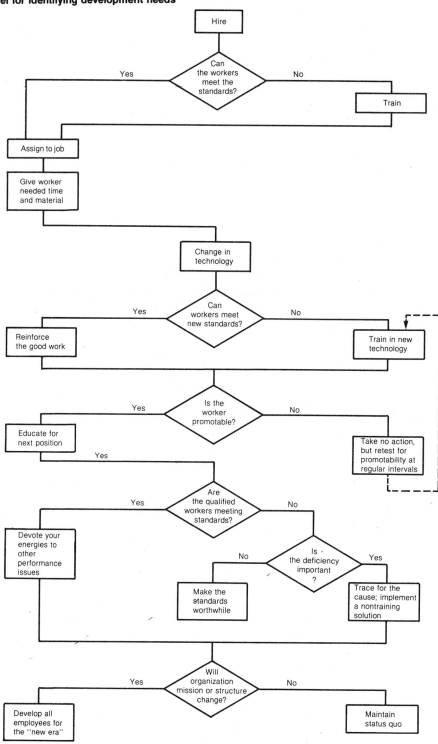

The training and development process.

Source: Dugan Laird, Approaches to Training and Development, © 1978, Addison-Wesley Publishing Company, Chapter 2, p. 13, figure 2.1. Reprinted with permission.

A *supervisor* may *request* that a program be conducted for one or a group of employees.

A *training needs survey* may be conducted by asking supervisors to state their needs on a prepared form. A modification of this is to use the interview method of soliciting training needs from the supervisors.

Problem analysis discussions may also be used. A training specialist meets with a group of supervisors from a given job area and asks them to discuss their specific needs. There is a dual benefit, for not only are the training needs identified, but the supervisors are trained to become more analytical and objective in their study of their problems.

Analysis of job requirements.   As shown in Figure 8-5, the difference between the abilities of an employee or group of employees and the job requirements may indicate a need for training. The important thing is to concentrate on determining training activities that result from—and are expected to correct—the employees' inability to do a job properly.

Analysis of job performance.   Training needs can be indicated by employee performance ratings showing that an employee is not doing the job properly. A form of this method is the *personnel progress report,* usually used to record the progress of new employees. If the report shows that quality specifications or production schedules are not being met, a need for training is indicated.

Through a *work data analysis,* the training director studies production reports to determine trends in unit costs, grievances, safety reports, and other production standards. This might show that an employee, or group of employees, is not performing satisfactorily.

Employee suggestions.   Sometimes employees who know they are not doing a good job will request training. Also, if the employees wish to improve their position through transfers or promotions, they may request training as a stepping-stone to a better job.

Identifying What Needs Developing

A basic need today can be summed up in one word: *adaptability.* In our complex economy, specialized skills become obsolete sooner than they used to. Some *70 percent of the skilled trades found in the United States in the year 1900 do not now exist.* It is a safe prediction that a large proportion of today's skills will become obsolete in the much shorter period between now and the year 2000.

A study of technologically obsolete employees found that many of them could be successfully retrained for relatively high-level technical jobs.[10] Apparently the ability to learn was not a major limiting factor in the process, but the educational background of the workers was.

---

[10]Walter J. McNamara, "Retraining of Industrial Personnel," *Personnel Psychology* 16 (Autumn 1963):233–47.

TABLE 8–2
Courses offered to rank-and-file employees by respondent members of the American Society for Personnel Administration

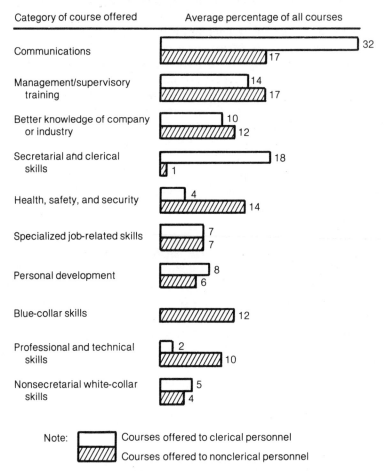

Category of course offered	Average percentage of all courses
Communications	32 / 17
Management/supervisory training	14 / 17
Better knowledge of company or industry	10 / 12
Secretarial and clerical skills	18 / 1
Health, safety, and security	4 / 14
Specialized job-related skills	7 / 7
Personal development	8 / 6
Blue-collar skills	12
Professional and technical skills	2 / 10
Nonsecretarial white-collar skills	5 / 4

Note: ☐ Courses offered to clerical personnel
       ▨ Courses offered to nonclerical personnel

Source: *Employee Training Survey,* by Prentice-Hall, Inc. and the American Society for Personnel Administration in *Personnel Management: Policies and Practices* Report No. 2 (6–12–79). © Prentice-Hall, Inc. Englewood Cliffs, NJ. 1979.

One problem with retraining is that the very employees who most need retraining are the ones who lack the education, training, experience, and aptitudes needed to become the skilled craftsmen, technicians, or professional workers that are most needed.

Table 8–2 shows the courses offered by ASPA members to clerical and nonclerical employees. This should provide a guide to development needs for others.

FACTORS NEEDED FOR EFFECTIVE DEVELOPMENT PROGRAMS

The next step is to design development programs that will satisfy the assessed needs. This step is successful only if based on well-established principles of learning.

What are some learning principles that can be applied to human resource development? In general, it can be assumed that:

1. Development is most effective if it has positive motivation.
2. Continuous development is more effective than infrequent activities.
3. Effective development is based on the systems approach. This approach coordinates all elements of the learning process such as site, selection of learners, teaching methods and personnel, and training aids.
4. Resistance to training is always present.
5. The trainers themselves must first be trained.

Need for Positive Motivation

Like all human behavior, learning is most likely to take place when there is motivation. The motivational process is based upon identification and the law of effect.

Identification. One of the essential aspects of motivation that leads to psychological growth in an organized group is *identification,* whereby a person identifies with someone who has more experience, skill, and power than himself or herself. This identification process continues to be needed for growth (or regression) throughout a person's life.

Law of effect. Superiors are constantly training their subordinates through the *law of effect.*[11] Simply stated, this law says: *behavior that appears to be rewarded tends to be repeated; behavior that appears not to be rewarded, or to be punished, tends not to be repeated.* Superiors are constantly using the law of effect to shape the behavior of subordinates through the use of rewards and punishment. Therefore, supervisors cannot abdicate their role as developers of their subordinates. Even though they may consciously ignore that role, they continue to train their workers one way or another.

Development Must Be Dynamic and Continuous

Learning is, indeed, a lifelong process! Although fantasy, *Through the Looking Glass* reminds us of the rapidly changing tempo of the world when the Red Queen says, "It takes all the running you can do, to keep in the same place."

---

[11]See Edward L. Thorndike, *Human Learning* (New York: Century Co., 1931), for a discussion of this factor in practice.

Therefore, development is a constant need of *all* employees. An organization cannot be static; it *must be dynamic* in creating programs to meet the needs for capable personnel.

This apparently is being done. The Lifelong Learning project estimates that there are around 64 million adults engaging in "deliberate education and learning."[12]

The human resources development department of Reynolds Metals has started a program of continuous employee training, including home study. Nearly all its headquarters supervisory staff receive training in EEO and the firm's EEO policies.[13]

Development Involves the Systems Approach

One special aspect of the systems approach is to teach employees to do the entire job. One study compared the effectiveness of (1) teaching employees to learn the parts of the task, as opposed to the whole task, (2) having them learn the whole job at one time, or (3) using a combination of the whole and part types of learning. The results of this research showed that the more nearly you can teach workers to perform the whole job, the more effective they should become.[14]

Overcoming Resistance to Development

Trainees often view training programs as a threat to their security. They are sometimes openly defensive and refuse to take part in the program. But more often they resist silently and appear to offer full support. In fact, there can even be sabotage.

I was recently teaching a presupervisory program for a large department store. One night shortly after it began, the room where we met was locked, and the personnel manager had the key. When she could not be reached, the group broke into applause. There were many comments such as "I hope it stays locked."

As we stood in the hall, the group members explained to me that the store owner had attended a convention, heard about the value of training, and hurriedly instituted the program. They were attending on their own

---

[12]E. K. Fretwell, Jr., "The Learners of the 1980s: Windex for the University Administrator's Crystal Ball," *National Forum* 60 (Winter 1980):40.

[13]"Chief Executives Report on How Training and Development Pay Off in Their Organizations," *Training/HRD* 16 (October 1979):81.

[14]George E. Briggs and James G. Naylor, "The Relative Efficiency of Several Training Methods as a Function of Transfer Task Complexity," *Journal of Experimental Psychology* 64 (November 1962):505–12.

time, there would be no certificates or other rewards, and the owner did not attend.

Train the Trainer

Many development programs are wasted because of the inability of the person doing the training. One of the great errors of these efforts is to assign the best performers to conduct the program—without training them to be trainers.

Training requires different skills and abilities from operating or even managing. It should be obvious that there should be some instruction in how to instruct.[15]

Figure 8-6 shows the results of an experiment on the effects of instructor

FIGURE 8-6
Employee learning curves

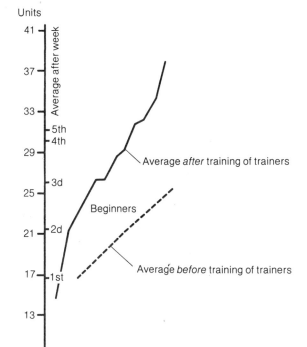

Source: Norman R. F. Maier, *Psychology in Industry*, 3d ed. (Boston: Houghton Mifflin Co., 1965), p. 404. Courtesy of A. Bavelas.

---

[15]See Frank G. Mitchell, "Get More—and Better—Results with a Train-the-Trainer Course," *Training/HRD* 16 (April 1979):24-26, for a model program.

training. Two groups of employees were trained before and after instructor training was introduced. Workers who learned stitching operations after the instructors were trained (top line) learned more rapidly and achieved much higher proficiency than workers who learned before the training methods were adopted (bottom line).

CONDUCTING THE DEVELOPMENT PROGRAMS

There are many ways to conduct education, training, and development programs. The method used will depend on the objective of the program, the type of material to be learned, and the person doing the development.

There are two types of learning involved in employee development—learning theories, concepts, and principles and learning their application. The two types of learning are related and do not have to be separated. In general, (1) the theory is taught off the job, and (2) the applications are learned on the job (OJT).

Training off the Job

Assuming that a knowledge of theory will help employees adjust to changes in the job requirements, how can it best be learned? The usual methods are (1) vestibule training, (2) classroom instruction, (3) programmed instruction, (4) closed-circuit TV, (5) extension courses, (6) assistance from manufacturers, trade associations, and professional organizations, and (7) vocational training.

Vestibule training.   *Vestibule training* is an effective method of giving new employees experience before they go to work in the shop or office. It simulates work conditions in a room near the production area, furnished with equipment similar to that which the employees will use later. While employees are learning new skills, they are not also trying to produce at a given level. Therefore, they should be able to do the actual work more effectively when assigned a job.

This method has the *advantage* of training large numbers of employees in a short period of time without disturbing the actual production routine. It also gives employees a chance to gain preliminary knowledge about the job so they will have confidence when they begin working.

The *disadvantages* are that it requires special instructors and the duplication of shop or office facilities and is relatively expensive.

Classroom instruction.   There is still no good substitute for classroom teaching, where knowledge is transmitted from the instructor in some oral or visual form. Many firms now have training classrooms in which to teach employees the theoretical and background information needed for successful job performance. There, away from production pressures, the teacher and learners can concentrate on the learning experience.

Programmed instruction.   One of the newer training methods for learning theory, principles, and concepts is *programmed instruction.* This type of instruction sometimes involves "teaching machines." The method involves presenting material in a sequential order on film or printed matter. The learners are not allowed to proceed beyond a given point until they have mastered the information needed to perform the job. In other words, they must learn one part of the training program before continuing to the next.

If this method of learning is to be used effectively, it should be based on material that is relatively fixed and can be taught to a large number of individuals over a long period of time.

In studies at over 1,500 companies, programmed learning seemed to offer improved learning at lower cost.[16]

Shell Oil Company has a self-learning approach called PLAN (Programmed Learning According to Need). It involves audiovisual teaching machines, multipart film strips, and coaching.[17]

Closed-circuit television.   Another method of training is the use of closed-circuit TV. This method has the advantage of being available to practically unlimited numbers of people at the same time and at a low cost per person.

For example, several South Carolina companies united and utilized the state's educational TV network to train their middle managers. They used such courses as "Exploring Basic Economics."[18] The program was very effective.

Extension courses.   Extension courses, including correspondence courses, are widely used as an alternative to classroom instruction. Some employers pay all or part of the tuition for job-related courses.

Another variation of this training method is for an academic instructor to go to the firm's premises and conduct regular or special courses for employees.

Some firms provide paid leave for their employees to earn a degree or upgrade their knowledge at the company's expense.

Assistance from manufacturers, trade associations, and professional organizations.   Many employers receive assistance from manufacturers of specialized equipment, trade associations, or other professional organizations. They provide specialists to train the employees doing technical jobs and using special skills and knowledge. Some computer manufacturers train the personnel of companies that purchase or lease their equipment. Makers of scientific instruments offer courses to train scientists to use them.

---

[16]John W. Buckley, "Programmed Instruction in Industrial Training," *California Management Review* 10 (Winter 1967):71–79.

[17]"Programmed Instruction Speeds Training at Shell Oil," *Training/HRD* 17 (February 1980):23.

[18]"TV Teachers Training Plant Bosses Statewide," *Business Week,* August 29, 1964, pp. 64–66.

Xerox Corporation gives half-day courses for "key operators"—office workers who will know how to replace paper, make minor adjustments, and call for service on Xerox copiers—and explain their use to other employees.

Vocational training.   There is currently renewed interest in vocational education, training, and development. This emphasis may be of advantage to employees and employers. Research has shown that vocationally trained workers have a higher labor force participation rate, a higher mean occupational mobility, and a lower mean unemployment rate.[19]

Training on the Job

Although theory and principle are important, the employees must learn how to apply their knowledge to practical aspects of their job. This process involves learning the methods and techniques of actually performing the work and increasing their skill level. The usual methods of training on the job are: (1) orientation, (2) on-the-job training (OJT), (3) apprenticeship training, and (4) internship training.

Orientation.   New employees' development begins with placement on the job for which they were selected. This involves being introduced into the

THE WALL STREET JOURNAL

". . . and watch out for the boss—he likes to sneak up on people."

Reprinted by permission *The Wall Street Journal*

[19]Roger L. Bowlby and William R. Schriver, "Nonwage Benefits of Vocational Training: Employability and Mobility," *Industrial and Labor Relations Review* 23 (July 1970):500–509.

organization through some form of *orientation*. Orientation is quite important, as employee turnover is greatest during the initial period of employment. This is often a time of trial for the new worker, for one will be either accepted or rejected by other employees. Also, the worker decides whether to accept or reject the organization itself.

This problem is particularly acute among scientific and technical personnel. Their technical curricula seem to arouse expectations and to emphasize values and goals that differ from the realities of work life. The result is widespread dissatisfaction among large numbers of scientific and technical employees when they are newly employed.

There are some positive things that personnel managers can do to make orientation easier, to shorten the adjustment period, and to improve the new member's growth and development. Management can (1) assign a mentor to the newcomer, (2) have a formal introduction program to describe the overall activities of the organization, (3) encourage individual recognition, (4) provide pleasing work conditions, and (5) train direct supervisors in human relations.

On-the-job training (OJT).   *OJT* is the most universal form of employee development. It involves actual performance of work duties under the supervision and guidance of a trained worker or instructor. Thus, while learning how to perform the job, one is also a regular employee producing the product or service that the firm sells. This form of training always occurs, whether by formal plan or not.

One study found that nearly a fourth of all training in the construction industry was OJT. Yet the apprenticeship type of training is encouraged in that industry.[20]

The primary *advantages* of OJT are that it results in low out-of-pocket costs, and production is carried on during training. Also there is no transition from classroom learning to actual production.

Poor instruction, excessive waste caused by errors, and the poor learning environment provided by the production area are *disadvantages* of this type of training.

Apprenticeship training.   *Apprenticeship training* blends the learning of theory with practice in techniques. It is used to teach job skills that require long periods of practice and experience. It is generally used in trades, crafts, and other technical fields. If proficiency can be reached only after a long period of classroom instruction and actual learning experiences on the job, this training method should be used. The extent and intensity of training vary among the types of apprentice programs. But they usually consist of around 144 hours per year spent studying theory in formal classes and around 2,000 hours of supervised work experience.

Apprenticeship has not been the total answer to craft training. It has been

---

[20]Howard G. Foster, "Nonapprentice Sources of Training in Construction," *Monthly Labor Review* 93 (February 1970):21-26.

supplemented by the companies through hiring "helpers" who are then upgraded to craftsmen. Also, with the complex and dynamic nature of present production jobs, some firms are instituting their own classroom programs in which theory and principles are taught as supplements to regular job training.

This type of training was formerly used to prevent equal employment for women and minorities. This practice is now under attack.

For example, at the end of 1978, less than 2 percent of the construction trades' registered apprentices were women.[21]

An apprentice program at Kaiser Aluminum's Gramercy, Louisiana, plant designed to increase opportunities for blacks in the skilled trades led to the famous Weber case.

Internship training.   Internship training (sometimes referred to as *cooperative education* or *coop ed*) is another method of coordinating the two types of learning. It is used for professional, managerial, clerical, and sales personnel, along with an educational institution's teaching program. Usually, selected students enrolled in a regular academic program are introduced into a company for a given period of time to gain work experience. Through this training, students gain a better understanding of the relationship between the theory they learn in school and its application. It also gives them a chance to decide whether they like the chosen type of work. But as it is a slow process, both parties should have patience if they expect to achieve the greatest benefit from it.

EVALUATING EFFECTIVENESS OF DEVELOPMENT PROGRAMS

It is necessary to evaluate the effectiveness of formal training programs in achieving their objectives. Training does not always train! Instead, there is usually a high proportion of failures. These can be blamed on such factors as having the wrong objective, using the wrong method, poor instruction, poor training material, and resistance to training.

At best, ineffective development programs may result in a waste of time, effort, and money. At worst, they may result in failure to develop knowledge and skills, which may lead to organizational and personal decline.

Approaches to Evaluation

Probably no other area of the personnel function has been given more attention than evaluating training efforts. There are many techniques that can be used to make an organization operate more smoothly. Fortunately, the costs and benefits are not too difficult to approximate and evaluate.

---

[21]"Labor Letter," *The Wall Street Journal*, February 12, 1980, p. 1.

Use of controls.   The better known and publicly available studies on training program effectiveness show that the use of controls of some type to gauge on-the-job behavior change has become almost standard procedure.[22] Improvement is usually measured by comparing performance before and after training. The primary weakness of these studies is their failure to focus evaluation on both short- and long-term effects.

In evaluating the results of development, the same measures used to identify training needs should be used. For example, if statistical analyses were used to determine the need to develop employees, then essentially the same techniques should be used to determine the effectiveness of the program.

Distinguish between short- and long-range benefits.   In making the evaluation, a distinction must be made between short- and long-range benefits. Some development programs may show quick results, especially if they involve learning of routine skills. Some results, however, may not become evident for years if learning general knowledge is involved.

Objective versus subjective evaluations.   Another evaluation problem is whether there is objective evidence of improvement or a value judgment must be made. When objective evidence is available, it should be used; if not, a value judgment is necessary.

However, there are other complicating factors. First, there are some intangibles that cannot be measured, such as attitudes, opinions, beliefs, and the long-run effects on the worker and management.

A training program was conducted at a hospital to improve supervisory performance. Opinion surveys of the experimental and control groups were done before and after the training. However, during the two months of the program, the board separated merit increases from cost-of-living, granted a 5 percent across-the-board increase, and gave supervisors greater flexibility and discretion in granting the merit increases.

What Is Evaluated?

Most valid evaluation efforts attempt to evaluate at least four things. They are:

1. Reactions—did the participants enjoy the program and think it was effective?
2. Learning—how well did the participants learn the facts, skills, techniques, and so forth?
3. Behavior changes—how did behavior on the job change after the program?
4. Tangible results—did training (1) increase output and improve performance and/or reduce costs, errors, turnover, absenteeism, and so forth? This approach is results-oriented.

---

[22]See Joseph Wolfe, "Evaluating the Training Effort," *Training and Development Journal* 27 (May 1973):20–27, for an excellent presentation.

FIGURE 8–7
A model for evaluating effectiveness of developmental program

Group	Time period		
	1 *Preprogram*	*2* *Program*	*3* *Post program*
Control.................	Test ————————————————→ Test		
Experimental.............	Test ——→ Development ——→ Test		

A Cost-effective Approach

Assuming that the objectives of a development program are precisely stated, the evaluation procedure should try to determine the program's cost and benefits. This cost-effective approach would involve several steps using the method shown in Figure 8–7.

First, the total development costs are obtained. This is done by adding the direct costs of the trainers, materials, and lost output of employees during the training program to the indirect costs, such as a share of the administrative and personnel departments' overhead.

Second, experimental and control groups are set up. The two groups are structured to be as nearly alike as possible in intelligence, education, experience, and job level. Each group is then tested. Testing instruments are based on the objectives of the training and the type of group being developed.

Third, the experimental group is given the training while the control group is held as nearly constant as feasible.

Fourth, after the program is over, both groups are again tested to see whether there were measurable benefits derived from the training. By comparing the before and after performance of each group, an approximation of the effectiveness of the training can be obtained.

An example of this type of evaluation was a Texas Instruments experiment with a one-day "anxiety-reducing" orientation program. The evaluation showed reduced training time, costs, absenteeism, tardiness, waste, and rejects. Figure 8–8 shows the improvement in job performance of the experimental group, as compared to the control group.

Other ways of determining these benefits are through opinion surveys, trainer evaluations, and measurement of job performance or productivity after the training.

In summary, most evaluation studies show that training and development pay for themselves. The programs produce improved performance, higher production, lower turnover, less absenteeism, and more personal satisfaction.[23]

---

[23]Warren H. Schmidt, "How to Evaluate a Company's Training Efforts," *California Management Review* 12 (Spring 1970):49–56.

FIGURE 8–8
Mastery attainment by experimental and control groups

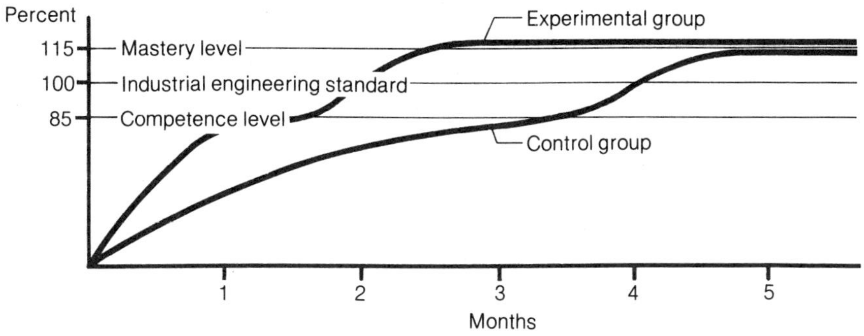

Source: Earl R. Gomersall and M. Scott Myers, "Breakthrough in On-the-Job Training," *Harvard Business Review* 44 (July–August 1966):69. Copyright 1966 by the President and Fellows of Harvard College; all rights reserved.

INFLUENCE OF EEO ON TRAINING AND DEVELOPMENT

A major impact of EEO has been to provide training and development for women and minorities, particularly as a preparation for advancement into management. Evidence indicates that these groups need to develop attitudes and behaviors that will help them take advantage of these new opportunities instead of learning new skills.[24]

Other employees need training in adapting to the new employees. Supervisors and managers need to learn how to update and revise AAPs.

SUMMARY AND CONCLUSIONS

Development is the systematic process of education, training, and growth by which a person acquires and applies information, knowledge, skills, attitudes, and perceptions. As with the other personnel functions, it is becoming more important. The objectives of training and development are to help organizations grow, adapt to technological developments, fulfill social responsibility, and provide employees with greater job satisfaction.

The people or groups responsible for personnel development are society, the organization, unions and other employee associations, and employees themselves. Society performs its function by providing education through private and public bodies.

The four most frequently used methods for identifying development needs are supervisory recommendations, analysis of job requirements, analysis of job performance, and employee suggestions.

In our complex economy, adaptability is very important. Specialized skills,

---

[24]Hall and Albrecht, "Training for EEO: What Kinds and for Whom?"

though necessary and important, are becoming obsolete sooner than ever before.

For development programs to be more effective, (1) there must be positive motivation, (2) they must be dynamic and continuous rather than intermittent, (3) the systems approach must be used, (4) resistance to development must be overcome, and (5) the trainers must be trained.

Job orientation is a vital part of an employee's development. It often means the difference between success or failure in retaining productive employees.

The most popular off-the-job training programs are vestibule training, classroom instruction, programmed instruction, closed circuit television, and extension courses. The usual ways of learning while working are on-the-job training (OJT), apprentice training, and internship training.

In evaluating development programs there is usually an attempt to find out whether (1) participants enjoyed the development program, (2) actual learning occurred, (3) there were job behavior changes, and (4) there were tangible results from the program.

EEO is causing significant shifts in the extent and types of training being done.

QUESTIONS

1. What are the usual objectives of development programs?
2. Do you agree with the following assumption? "You cannot teach people anything; they must learn it for themselves."
3. What are some principles of learning underlying employee development?
4. How would you evaluate a specific development program?
5. What is the relationship between personnel development and social responsibility?
6. Why is self-development so important?
7. How would you determine the development needs of a given organization?
8. What is the *law of effect,* and how does it influence training and development?
9. What are some of the training techniques used in development?
10. How is EEO influencing development? Explain.

PROBLEMS

8-1. Developing a Training Program

If you were a training consultant, how would you set up a training program for the following:

1. Sales personnel for a department store?
2. Research and development employees in a large chemical firm?
3. New unskilled workers on a construction project?
4. Workers to program and use a firm's first electronic computer?

8-2. The New Employee

It was Gayle's first day on the job in an office with 20 other people. She was a 45-year-old mother whose last child was off at college. She has taken an accounting program at a business school and passed "with flying colors." The personnel department had hired her to fill a vacant position in the office.

This was Gayle's first job outside the home. She did not know any of the other employees and the office equipment was new to her. She was obviously upset.

Questions

1. What type of training program would you set up for her?
2. How would you, as the office manager, approach Gayle about training?
3. Could you expect any resistance to training? Explain your answer.

SUGGESTED READINGS FOR FURTHER STUDY

Berger, Lance A. "A DEW Line for Training and Development: The Needs Analysis Survey." *Personnel Administrator* 21 (November 1976):51-55.

Ingalls, John D. "Throw Away Your Job Descriptions and Write Competency Models." *Training/HRD* 16 (April 1979):32-35.

Lukliner, Murray. "Employee Orientation." *Personnel Journal* 57 (April 1978):207-8.

Miller, D., et al. "Human Resources Development Learning Experience." *Training and Development Journal* 32 (March 1978):48-51.

O'Brien, John, and Denise Gubbay. "Training to Inegrate the Multi-Racial Work Force." *Personnel Management* 11 (January 1979):20-21.

Roscow, Jerome M. "Human Dignity in the Public Sector Work Place." *Public Personnel Management* 8 (January 1979):7-14.

Rosenbaum, Bernard L., and Barbara Baker. "Do As I Do: The Trainer As a Behavior Model." *Training/HRD* 16 (December 1979):90-93.

Schwendiman, G., and Rolls, G. "Progress Report on Human Resource Development." *Bankers' Magazine* 160 (Autumn 1977):111-15.

Striner, Herbert E. "Investing to Upgrade the Labor Force." *Business Week*, March 13, 1978, p. 16.

"Talk-Back TV for Training: Worth Waiting For?" *Training/HRD* 16 (September 1979):8-10.

CHAPTER NINE

Management Development

Learning Objectives

After studying the material in this chapter, you should be able to:

1. Explain the relationship between selecting and developing managers.
2. Tell how to identify managerial talent.
3. Describe some special techniques for selecting managers.
4. Explain the need for management development.
5. Name and explain the more popular development methods.
6. Explain the relationship between organizational development (OD) and management development.
7. Explain how to evaluate development programs.

Some Important Words and Terms

Single-criterion measurement
Patrons, or mentors
Combined-criteria measures
Multiple predictors
Selective perception
Assessment centers
Coaching
Planned progression
Job rotation
Temporary assignment
Professional practice programs
Case analysis

Simulation
Role playing
Business gaming
In-basket technique
Laboratory training
T-group training
Sensitivity training
Management by objectives (MBO)
Organizational development (OD)
Change agents
Intervention strategies
Managerial grid

An institution that cannot produce its own managers will die. . . . The ability of an institution to produce managers is more important than its ability to produce efficiently and cheaply.
PETER F. DRUCKER

Outline of the Chapter

The chief executive officer of a large food company committed suicide. During the long time he had run the firm, he had failed to develop anyone to replace him. Instead, he had used autocratic methods which had discouraged subordinates from attempting to develop themselves into possible successors.

At his death, there was no one capable of replacing him; so the board went outside to look for a successor. In the meantime, the company was run by two committees.

The personnel manager of a large hospital was informed of an opening in an executive development program and asked if she would like to send one of her upper-level managers to it. Her answer was, "Yes, we like to invest in our people." She considered the expenses of the entire operation as "contributions to the 'bottom line,'" as they make money for the hospital."

Drucker's statement and these cases emphasize the need for management selection and development.[1] Yet many otherwise progressive organizations fail to provide for these. There are many reasons for this, but the two main ones are (1) not realizing how important they are and (2) considering them a cost rather than an investment in human resources.

DETERMINING THE NEED FOR MANAGERS

As shown in Chapter 5, determining the need for managers involves (1) determining the requirements of the position and (2) deciding where to look for the applicants for the positions to be filled.

Determining Management Requirements

If needed managers are to be found and developed, descriptions of and specifications for the positions to be filled should be determined. Even though it is difficult to determine job descriptions for managerial positions, there should at least be some understanding of the nature of the job to be filled.

What is needed is a clear statement of requirements focused in terms of what the executive will be doing. Table 9-1 shows one such set of requirements stated in terms of dimensions. Notice that these are weighted according to their importance. Then the applicant is ranked on each of these dimensions.

A long lead time is required to educate, train, and develop future managers. Therefore, some effort should be made to forecast future management needs in terms of personnel required for expansion—or contraction—and for replacements.

---

[1]The terms *executive, manager, management,* and *managerial personnel* are used interchangeably to prevent repetition. These terms also include all scientific, technical, and professional personnel.

TABLE 9-1
An example of matching an applicant with the dimensions of a management position

Example			
Position: V.P. Marketing	Applicant's name: N. R. Gee	Date: 1/1/79	
Dimensions	Importance	Applicant ranking	Date ranked
A. Knowledge of			
1. Concepts of marketing as evidenced by study, i.e., academic degree, courses and their uses as evidenced by experience.	5	5	1/15/79
2. Principles of underwriting.	1	3	
3. Management concepts (study, seminars).	2	3	
4. Corporate finance and relationship of marketing to operations.	2	3	
5. The kind of business the position is in.	2	4	
B. Skill in			
1. Communications, particularly speaking and listening.	4	4	
2. Managing managers (experience).	5	4	
3. Planning of multi-department activities.	4	4	
4. Selling.	1	3	
5. Marketing new products.	4	2	
C. Behavior			
1. Connotes by attire and actions desired corporate image; not an excessive drinker or known philanderer.	5	5	
2. No conflicts of interest in business or related involvements.	5	5	
3. Participative manager as opposed to authoritarian.	3	3	
4. Flexible: can swing with shifting priorities.	4	3	
5. Demonstrated high tolerance for ambiguity.	3	?	

Source: Reprinted from the April, 1979 issue of *The Personnel Administrator* with permission of The American Society for Personnel Administration.

Where to Find the Needed Managers

Many openings resulting from expansion are filled by external recruitment. This is particularly true when technological development, innovation, or changing organizational direction bring about the expansion.

During a recent three-year period, 16 out of 62 large industries chose chief executive officers who had been with the firm less than four years.[2]

In organizations with well-developed personnel planning systems, the need for key managerial personnel can be predicted fairly accurately. For example, losses from retirements, promotions, transfers, dismissals, disabilities, and sub-

[2]*The Wall Street Journal*, April 17, 1979, p. 1.

standard job performance can be estimated from past performance, as modified by current situations. There are exceptions, as shown in the beginning case.

HOW TO IDENTIFY MANAGERIAL TALENT

After deciding upon the requirements of the positions to be filled, and the source of potential managers, the next step is to try and identify managerial talent. As shown in Chapter 7, this includes: (1) defining criteria of successful job performance, (2) identifying the traits and qualities that can predict a manager's successful performance in the position, and (3) determining whether a given candidate for the job has those characteristics. A related problem is to predict whether the person will develop those traits and become the manager desired.

Establish Criteria of Job Success

Earlier selection studies undertook to predict managerial effectiveness with a *single-criterion measurement,* such as overall performance ratings by supervisors and other superiors or other indices related to salaries or promotions. Subsequent research has shown that managerial job performance results from the interaction of many factors. These factors include ability, personality, motivation, the institution, the environment, and the situation. Therefore, these factors must be among any criterion measurements used to assess managerial performance.

Some acceptable criterion measures.   Some of the more common criterion measures used in management selection are (1) ratings by supervisors, (2) salary, (3) rank or level in the organization, and (4) rapidity of salary or position progression.

Ratings.   Ratings by supervisors have probably been the most frequently used criterion measure. The superior has the best knowledge of the manager's job behaviors as they contribute to the job performance objectives of the organization. Bias in ratings is a problem, however.

Salary.   Salary level, when statistically corrected for age and/or length of service, has proven to be a valid criterion of success. However, as wage and salary administration has been so "unscientific," there may be "quirks" that do not adequately reflect success.

Rank or organizational level.   Rank or organizational level at least shows that the person has been able to survive and make progress, regardless of the reason. Its main problem is that promotions are sometimes made on the basis of favoritism or "kicking upstairs."

Rapidity of promotions.   The rate at which a person advances in the organization is another measure of success. It shows movement, but care should be used to discount the effect of any *patrons,* or *mentors,* who might have contributed to faster than normal progression. It has long been known that one good way of progressing in an organization is to find someone up the line who will keep an eye on you—and your career progression.

John Chancellor said his "mentor, Reuven Frank, who had done more than anyone to shape (his) career," was responsible for his becoming anchorman on NBC News.[3]

Women are now discovering the importance of patronage, and they are having to learn to play the sponsorship game.[4]

Use of combined criteria. The previously mentioned *single-criterion measures* tend to be less effective when used alone than when used together as *combined-criteria measures*. When used together, particularly when combined into a single overall index, they have proven quite successful.

Standard Oil of New Jersey, after spending years studying various criterion measures, statistically combined organizational level of job held, salary history, and general effectiveness ratings into an overall success index. It has turned out to be very effective in gauging how successful managers will be over the course of their careers with the company.

Determine Predictors of Job Success

Once the measures of success have been established, the problem is to identify the personal traits and qualities that can serve as valid predictors of future success. Although there is no generally accepted list of qualities required to be a successful manager, some are considered significant when evaluating someone for a managerial position. These qualities are (1) intelligence, (2) education, including rank or standing in class and leadership in extracurricular activities, and (3) various aspects of personality.

Intelligence. Research shows that managers usually score higher on intelligence tests than the average person. For example, one study showed that a group of executives had scores that were higher than 96 percent of industrial and business workers studied.[5]

There is some disagreement on this point, for another study showed that the test scores of a group of executives had no statistically significant relationship to their advancement.[6] I think that intelligence is one factor leading to success in management.

---

[3]John Chancellor, "Things Quite Often Go Wrong," *TV Guide*, November 3, 1979, p. 7.

[4]Jacqueline Thompson, "Patrons, Rabbis, Mentors—Whatever You Call Them, Women Need Them, Too," *MBA* 10 (February 1976):26ff.

[5]Robert M. Wald and Roy A. Doty, "The Top Executive—A First-hand Profile," *Harvard Business Review* 32 (July–August 1954):45.

[6]Allen I. Kraut, "Intellectual Ability and Promotional Success among High-Level Managers," *Personnel Psychology* 22 (Autumn 1969):281–90.

Education.   In a study of persons who were rated "promotable," 84 percent had attended college, and 59 percent had degrees, while 75 percent of those rated "nonpromotable" had no college. However, the study also concluded that age and performance can overcome deficiencies in education.[7]

Finally, when 31 different variables were compared with success criteria, the extent of education was the best predictor of executive success.[8]

A Bell System study of 17,000 of its managers who were college graduates indicated a decided correlation between rank in the graduating class and progress in the system.[9] Further, being a graduate of an "above average" college substantially increased promotability. Extracurricular achievements were also related to progress. Those with substantial activities and honors fared better than others.

Various aspects of personality.   Other studies have indicated measurable differences between managers and nonmanagers in certain personality variables. For example, successful managers have been shown to (1) have superior skill in dealing with people and more self-confidence and self-esteem, (2) have better mental and physical health and greater tolerance for frustration, (3) be more firm, positive, and decisive, (4) have mental and emotional strength and judgment, and (5) be innovative and nonconformists.[10]

Use of multiple predictors.   The more successful organizations are now using *multiple predictors* in selecting managerial personnel.

Standard Oil of New Jersey used a biographical inventory and tests to measure intelligence, personality, and attitudes. The biographical inventory was the greatest predictor of success, but a battery of instruments better predicted success in the company. There were correlations as high as .70 between the battery and job-potential measures of managerial success. None of the individual instruments proved that effective.

Some faulty predictors.   A common belief about management selection is that an employee who is highly skilled and has been able to perform technical jobs also has the ability to become a supervisor or manager. This is an invalid

---

[7]Fred Luthans, James Walker, and Richard M. Hodgetts, "Evidence on the Validity of Management Education," *Academy of Management Journal* 12 (December 1969):451–57.

[8]Edwin E. Wagner, "Predicting Success for Young Executives from Objective Test Scores and Personal Data," *Personnel Psychology* 13 (Summer 1960):181–86.

[9]Frederick R. Kappel, "From the World of College to the World of Work," Green Foundation Lecture, Westminster College, April 5, 1962, in *Business Purpose and Performance* (New York: Duell, Sloan & Pearce, 1964), p. 186.

[10]Edwin E. Ghiselli, in "The Validity of Management Traits in Relation to Occupational Level," *Personnel Psychology* 16 (Summer 1963):109–13, states that his research showed that people "who displayed the greatest individuality in managerial behavior were in general the ones judged to be . . . the best managers."

assumption, for *a good producer is not necessarily a potential supervisor or executive.*

Another faulty predictor is *selective perception,* which is noticing traits that we think will satisfy our needs and ignoring those that are unfavorable. Managers are frequently hired on the basis of first impressions or because they have traits that approximate those of the employer.

Develop Techniques for Selecting Managers

The traditional selection instruments tend to be declining in favor for identifying and selecting managers. Interviews have proven to be quite unreliable. Tests are declining in acceptance and validity. And references are unreliable and questionable under public policy. The biographical inventory seems to be a good predictor.

Some techniques being experimented with are (1) simulation exercises, (2) structured and unstructured group interaction exercises, and (3) peer ratings, subordinate ratings, and self-ratings. Techniques which have been found to be successful are (1) assessment centers and (2) computer assistance.

Assessment centers. The assessment center is now one of the most powerful techniques available for identifying managerial talent.[11] It is also used for assessing development needs and for career planning and development.

An *assessment center* is a place where potential candidates for managerial positions are put through a series of interviews, tests, and simulations to determine their promotability and point out weaknesses that need to be corrected through training and development.

Background. AT&T is credited with having the first successful assessment center in this country. It started its management progress study in 1956 to see whether measurements and ratings made in the early phases of a manager's career at an assessment center were valid predictors of future performance. They measured, observed, and evaluated a group of potential managers, including college graduates, who had advanced to the lowest level of management.

The results of the assessments were not made known to operating managers. After about eight years, correlations were made between the predictions from the assessment center and criteria of performance between then and 1965. The predictions were 78 percent accurate for those expected to move fastest in management ranks, and 95 percent for those not expected to move rapidly.

At that time, the Bell System set up over 50 assessment centers throughout the country, using essentially the same techniques used in the original program.

Many other organizations now have such centers.

---

[11]See *Personnel Administrator* 25 (February 1980):24-67, for seven articles covering most aspects of assessment centers.

How assessment centers operate.   In general, the centers use a variety of exercises to simulate the actual conditions found in a manager's position. The most frequently used appraisal techniques are (1) in-basket exercises, (2) leaderless group discussions, (3) simulation, including business games and role playing, (4) psychological tests, and (5) other oral and written exercises, as shown in Figure 9–1.

Five or six managers are gathered into a group and given psychological tests. They complete biographical inventories and participate in intensive interviews with the assessors. They then do the exercises just discussed. Using a variety of criteria to evaluate the potential managers, the personnel managers and consultants make multiple judgments based on their observations and

FIGURE 9–1
How assessment centers operate

*Varied means of judging likely managers include
tape-deck tests, meetings, and written exercises.*

Used by permission of Arnie Ten

FIGURE 9-2
Flow of assessment information

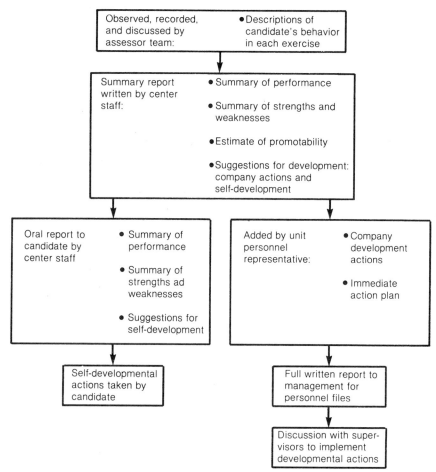

Source: T. A. Jeswald, "Issues in Establishing an Assessment Center," in *Applying the Assessment Center Method,* ed. J. L. Moses and W. C. Byham (Elmsford, N.Y.: Pergamon Press, 1977) p. 65. Reprinted with permission of Pergamon Press, Ltd.

interviews and the test scores. Then assessments are made, as shown on the right side of Figure 9-2. (When used for development purposes, the information tends to flow down the left side.)

Favorable results from using them. Current results indicate that around 25 percent of the examinees score in the "acceptable/or more" category. About 35 percent are "questionable." Some 40 percent are "unacceptable." These ratings are recommendations in the form of briefs prepared on each person and seem to provide relatively valid predictions of managerial ability, as shown in Table 9-2.

The validity and reliability of this technique have been accepted. The *Uniform Guidelines on Employee Selection Procedures* endorsed the concept

ED GRAHAM

"Of the three, I like this fellow."

Source: *Look*, May 3, 1966.

TABLE 9-2
Relationship between assessment rating and progress in management

Assessment rating	Number of assessees	Number receiving two or more promotions	Percent
More than acceptable	410	166	40.5
Acceptable	1,466	321	21.9
Questionable	1,910	220	11.5
Not acceptable	2,157	91	4.2
Total	5,943	798	13.4

Source: Reprinted from the May, 1980 issue of *The Personnel Administrator* with permission of
The American Society for Personnel Administration.

as a viable means of determining validity. Two recent articles by psychologists
from the EEOC and Civil Service Commission indirectly endorsed it.[12]

---

[12]W. A. Gorham, "Federal Executive Aging Guidelines and Their Impact on the Assessment
Center Process," *Journal of Assessment Center Technology* 1 (1978):115–34; and J. O. Taylor,
"The EEOC Guidelines on Content Validity and Their Application to the Assessment Center
Method," ibid., pp. 9–12.

The reliability of the centers also tends to be high. It ranges from .60 to .98, with most over .75.[13] Their reliability has also been accepted by the courts.[14]

Unfavorable consequences of using them.   While these centers are quite sophisticated, this means that they are also quite expensive. Another criticism is the feeling—at least among those who rate low—that a negative rating is "the kiss of death" for that individual in that organization. It has been claimed that what the centers actually measure are the candidate's skill and sensitivity in interpersonal relationships.[15]

Computer assistance.   The computer is now being used to select managers. One such system (see Figure 9-3) is based on the use of information that usually already exists. The "Jobmatch" system used by Citibank (see Chapter 8) is another example of successful use of computer assistance.

FIGURE 9-3
CIS inputs/outputs

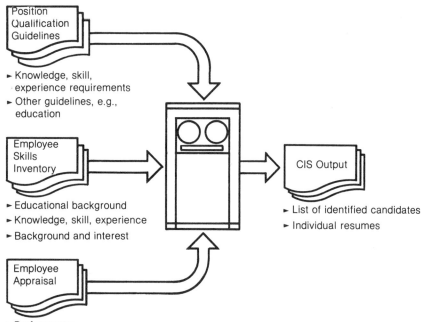

Position Qualification Guidelines

► Knowledge, skill, experience requirements
► Other guidelines, e.g., education

Employee Skills Inventory

► Educational background
► Knowledge, skill, experience
► Background and interest

Employee Appraisal

► Performance
► Promotability
► Potential
► Managerial skills
► Personal qualifications

CIS Output

► List of identified candidates
► Individual resumes

Source: Richard T. McNamar, "Building a Better Executive Team," *California Management Review* 16 (1973):64. Reprinted by permission of the Regents of the University of California.

---

[13]A. Howard, "An Assessment of Assessment Centers," *Academy of Management Journal* 17 (January 1974):115-34.

[14]*Berry, Stokes, and Lant v. City of Omaha.*

[15]See John E. Wilson and Walter Tatge, "Assessment Centers—Further Assessment Needed?" *Personnel Journal* 52 (March 1973):172-79, for an excellent analysis of these criticisms.

REQUIREMENTS FOR EFFECTIVE MANAGEMENT DEVELOPMENT

After being selected, managers need to be further developed because there is always more to learn. Management development programs should result in personal *and* organizational growth.

It is no coincidence that companies dominant in their industries—such as AT&T, Exxon, and IBM—often have the most effective management development programs. In fact, the chief executive officers of these firms all have 20 years or more of service in their firms and are products of such programs.[16]

Factors Influencing Effectiveness

While no two organizations approach executive development in quite the same way, there are some common threads running through the more effective programs. Some of the factors leading to effectiveness are:

1. The program is a deep and integral part of the organization. It involves all levels of management, reflects the organizational climate, and affects the very way the organization works.
2. Top management's support of, and long-term commitment to, the program are unwavering.
3. Management development is a significant part of every manager's job.
4. Development is self-development.
5. Participants view the program positively and enthusiastically.

This last point is quite important. In my years of dealing with management development, I have seen that people selected for development usually have one of two perceptions of why they were chosen. First, they may assume that they are "heirs apparent," being prepared for bigger and better things. These people usually perform well. The second group feel that their performance has been deficient and management is punishing them. These people are difficult to teach and are sometimes even troublemakers.

Who Should Be Developed

The easy answer to who needs to be developed is: all present and potential managers. The best way is to start with top management and work down. But most top managers are not willing to accept their need for further training.

In general, those most in need of development are (1) people being pro-

---

[16]See "How Companies Raise a New Crop of Managers," *Business Week*, March 10, 1975, pp. 44–48, for statements of their management development philosophies.

moted into management positions for the first time, (2) those with technical backgrounds, and (3) managers needing refresher courses. Only the first two will be discussed in detail.

Newly appointed managers.   As can be seen from Figure 9-4, entry-level workers devote most of their time to using technical skills. However, as they progress into first-line supervision and later into middle management, they use managerial skills more and technical skills less.

At several points along this curve, these employees need development. First, it is needed at the job entry level, as most of their time is spent using technical skills. At the supervisory level, the person needs training in supervising nonmanagerial personnel. When the middle management level is reached, the manager begins to manage other managers, which requires more and better administrative skills. This tendency increases the further one rises in the managerial ranks.

Managers with technical backgrounds.   It is sometimes difficult to integrate scientific, technical, and professional personnel into the managerial ranks. Because of their specialized education, technicians tend to think in terms of things; but managers must think in terms of people. The former tend to think in terms of the scientific approach to problem solving, but managers must usually use the artistic approach in dealing with subordinates.

According to James L. Hayes, president of the American Management Association, nearly 500,000 U.S. managers a year take a formal manage-

FIGURE 9-4
The progression of management skills

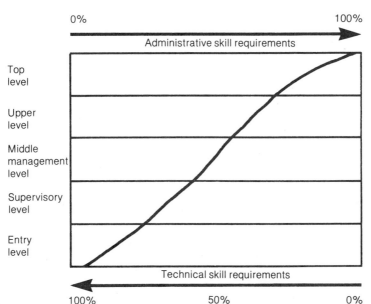

ment education course. These range from two-day seminars to full-year programs. Many are preparing for the "mid-career crunch."[17]

What Should Be Developed

There is no general agreement as to the specific content of formal management development programs. It is assumed, however, that four things should be developed in present and future executives. They are (1) general knowledge, (2) technical knowledge and skills, (3) administrative skills, and (4) attitudes and philosophy.

Two conclusions may be drawn from this observation. First, as one moves upward from a nonmanagerial job to the top management position, the required knowledge expands from general knowledge to attitudes and philosophies. Second, with the exception of attitudes and philosophies, this knowledge can probably be learned better off the job.

METHODS USED TO DEVELOP MANAGERS

There are many methods that can be used to develop managers. These are usually classified as training done (1) on the job, or (2) off the job. Organizational development (OD) involves both types of development and all members of the organization. Therefore, it will be discussed separately.

On-the-Job Development

Every organization uses some form(s) of OJT for managers. Experiential learning is still one of the most effective ways of learning the content of any job, even a managerial one. Yet this method of learning, used alone, is inadequate, for there is little that is creative or innovative.

OJT is an effective method of learning the manager's job for some groups, such as scientific and technical personnel.

In a study of 290 scientists and engineers engaged in research and development, two researchers found that interaction with fellow professionals on the job was a major source of information and motivation.[18]

Among the many OJT methods for developing managers, the most popular ones are (1) coaching, (2) planned progression, (3) job rotation, (4) temporary assignments, (5) management internships, and (6) committee assignments.

Coaching.   *Coaching* involves superiors providing guidance and counsel to subordinates in the course of their regular job performance. Another version

---

[17]Roger Ricklefs, "Back to School: More Executives Take Work-Related Courses to Keep Up, Advance," *The Wall Street Journal*, March 3, 1980, p. 1.

[18]Newton Margulies and Anthony Raia, "Scientists, Engineers, and Technological Obsolescence," *California Management Review* 10 (Winter 1967):44ff.

of this method is the "buddy system." The training department gives little assistance in this respect. The success of this method depends upon the willingness and abilities of the managers themselves.

An unusual and interesting form of this development was engaged in by one administrator who invited her young subordinate to her home four or five times a week to discuss the events of the day with her. During the discussions, she suggested ways for the young woman to grow.

Planned progression. *Planned progression* occurs when the path of promotions that lies ahead of the developing manager is outlined. This is frequently charted through successive levels of the organizational structure. If management considers it too optimistic to chart the progression specifically, it may outline the alternative positions that managers could fill on their way up.

Job rotation. *Job rotation* is a procedure whereby managers receive diversified training through performing jobs of many different types. This may take the form of rotation in nonsupervisory work, in observation assignments, as part of a managerial training program, in middle-level "assistant" positions, and in unspecified rotation in managerial positions.

Charles Garvey, chief executive officer of Exxon, is a product of this type of program. He along with others was rotated among jobs in most of the firm's Baton Rouge refinery operations. This provided him with the breadth needed to manage worldwide operations.

Temporary assignments. A popular method is to put the learners in a short-term *temporary assignment* in a position where they can learn to grow into higher level positions. Other assignments may be made on a more permanent basis but with the expectation that the learners will grow into the next higher job.

Management internships. There are many managers who feel that college graduates need to be more familiar with the pragmatic aspects of the organizational world. To achieve this, many universities now have *professional practice programs,* or *cooperative work programs,* worked out with participating firms. The objective is to provide actual management experience along with academic preparation.

Committee assignments. Committee assignments and task forces can also be used to give managers an overall understanding of the organization. These assignments can be progressively increased in number and importance.

Off-the-Job Development

Regardless of how effective OJT is for developing managers, some development must occur off the job. The most popular methods for doing this are (1) case analysis, (2) simulation, (3) laboratory training, (4) advanced management development programs, and (5) management by objectives (MBO).

Case analysis.   No two people define or use the case method in the same way.[19] But the essential features of *case analysis* are that (1) the teaching material is a written, oral, or visual presentation of actual situations, (2) the teacher leads the participants to develop generally useful concepts, and (3) the case is illustrative of some concept to be learned, an analytical evaluation of some administrative action, or action-oriented in the form of reaching and carrying out a decision.

This method has been criticized on the grounds that it tends to be passive. It does not develop theoretical concepts, nor is it based on rigorous analysis and research. But, when used by a well-trained leader, it can be very effective for developing administrative skills and learning to make and implement decisions.

Simulation.   *Simulation,* an outgrowth of the case method, tends to lead to greater involvement. It can be thought of as a form of vestibule training. The participants perform—or act out—simulated business behavior in reaching and implementing decisions.

Some of the more popular forms of simulation are (1) role playing, (2) business games, and (3) the in-basket technique.

Role playing.   One of the earliest forms of simulation was *role playing.* In essence, the participants act out the roles in a given situation. Then they switch roles, play out the other roles, and evaluate each other's performance. Learning takes place in the playing of the roles. The roles must be realistic and credible in order to be a learning vehicle. But learning also takes place in the evaluation of the role playing itself.

This technique has been found effective in developing administrative skills and in orienting employees into the organization. It also promotes learning to do employee appraisals, and in other interpersonal areas.[20]

Business games.   *Business gaming* is used to learn how to make and carry out decisions. The learning involves taking a simulated business situation, dividing the participants into groups, and letting the groups organize into simulated organizations. Then the groups begin to make decisions. A computer analyzes and presents the results of each team's decision. On the basis of the print-out, the teams make further decisions until the game is stopped.

The main *advantage* of this method is its involvement. The participants begin to think that they are actually running the business.

The primary *disadvantage* is its cost in time and money. It takes from one to three hours for the teams to make their decisions, after taking several hours to be introduced to the game and to organize.

In-basket technique.   The *in-basket technique* grew out of the case method as a learning technique. Participants are presented background mate-

---

[19]This material has been heavily influenced by my experiences with Andrew R. Towl, former director of the Intercollegiate Case Clearing House, Graduate School of Business Administration, Harvard University, for many years. Anyone seeking more knowledge of the use of the case method in executive development should see his book entitled *To Study Administration by Cases* (Boston: Division of Research, Harvard Business School, 1969).

[20]See Melvin Sorcher and Arnold Goldstein, "A Behavior Modeling Approach in Training," *Personnel Administration* 35 (March–April 1972):35–40.

rial on the simulated organization. Then they are given a basket full of assorted information, memoranda, requests, complaints, grievances, and other paperwork requiring managerial action.

The types of learning that take place are ordering of priorities, decision making, interpersonal relationships, and the use of time.

Laboratory training. *Laboratory training* is, in effect, an experiential situation in which participants learn by studying themselves and modifying their attitudes through unstructured discussions, analyses, and observations.[21] This type of training is also known as *T-group training* and *sensitivity training*.

Goals. Among the many goals of this type of training are (1) to gain insight into and awareness of one's own behavior, (2) to become more sensitive to, and increase one's empathy for, the behavior and feelings of others, and (3) to increase one's communicative and interpersonal abilities.

Methodology. The groups are usually unstructured. They have no set agenda and receive little guidance from the leader. They use many of the other techniques, such as experiential learning, role playing, and recording and playing back discussions. Since the change agent does not act as leader, one of the participants must assume the leadership position after the program is opened up by the change agent. As the discussions progress, each person evaluates, records, and feeds back his or her assessment of the behavior of the others.

Evaluating results. Many research efforts have been made to find out the effectiveness of these programs. In one of the most exhaustive efforts, 26 studies of the effect of these sessions were analyzed. It was concluded that the sessions do result in attitude changes—as measured by the participants' self-perceptions. But there was no clear evidence that those attitude changes resulted in improved job performance.[22]

Advanced management development programs. A well-conceived, well-developed, and well-taught university executive development program is probably the most effective management development method available. Although used for only a small percentage of all managers, its influence is very significant. Managers trained by this method tend to become the top executives of their organizations. Also, it tends to be the most progressive and dynamic of all the developmental techniques. As a mid-Victorian educator said, "He who learns from one occupied in learning drinks of a running stream. He who learns from one who has learned all he has to teach, drinks the green mantle of the stagnant pool."

These programs are both praised and criticized. The praise centers on their dynamic and progressive nature, as well as their results. Top managers tend to go to them, and those who attend these programs tend to become the chief executive officers.

---

[21]See Frank T. Paine, "Management Perspective: Sensitivity Training: The Current State of the Question," *Academy of Management Journal* 8 (1965):228–32, for an excellent analysis of the pros and cons of this method.

[22]J. P. Campbell et al., *Managerial Behavior, Performance, and Effectiveness* (New York: McGraw-Hill Book Co., 1970).

The criticisms involve lack of preparation, inadequate selection criteria, and difficulty of evaluating results.[23]

Management by objectives (MBO).   *MBO* is a management technique used for planning, directing, controlling, and appraising employee performance, as well as for management development. (It will be discussed in detail in Part 3.)

In general, managers develop by setting their own objectives and choosing the methods of achieving them. They are evaluated on how well they achieve the objectives.

Evaluating Effectiveness of Methods

As with other aspects of personnel, there is no "one best method" for developing managers. Instead, as shown in the discussions, the method must be chosen according to the learning objective of the manager(s). Table 9–3 shows research findings of the "most" and "least" effective methods for different development objectives.

ORGANIZATIONAL DEVELOPMENT

One outcome of laboratory training programs was that managers were frustrated when they returned to the same organizational climate they had left. Much of what they had gained in improved behavior was wasted in the old organizational relationships. Consequently, organizations began to search for a broader, more innovative, and more integrative way of developing the organization along with its managers. These efforts were called *planned change, organizational renewal,* and *applied behavioral sciences.* Now, however, they are generally called *organizational development,* or *OD.*

TABLE 9–3
Training method effectiveness

Training objective	*Most effective method*	*Least effective method*
Knowledge acquisition	Conference method	Television lecture
Changing attitudes	Sensitivity training	Television lecture
Problem-solving skills	Case study	Movie films
Interpersonal skills	Role playing	Television lecture
Participant acceptance	Case study	Programmed instruction
Knowledge retention	Programmed instruction	Sensitivity training

Source: Reprinted from the January, 1980 issue of *The Personnel Administrator* with permission of The American Society for Personnel Administration.

[23]Reed M. Powell and Charles S. Davis, "Do University Executive Programs Pay Off?" *Business Horizons* 16 (August 1972):81–88.

Approach

Organizational development can be defined as a systematic approach, using the behavioral sciences, to bring about planned changes and innovations within an organization's structure, technology, and human and social processes. It should result in increased organizational effectiveness, health, and self-renewal.

The OD approach tries to create an organization that is more effective, more viable, and better able to achieve both the organization's and individuals' goals. Either internal or external *change agents* are used to bring about improvement.

The difference between management development and organizational development is the "customer." Management development tries to assess, develop, or improve individual managers. Organizational development attempts to improve all of the systems that make up the total organization. Management development usually is a part of the broader organizational development approach.[24]

When Is OD Needed?

The existence of a felt need for a change in the organization is an essential condition for successful use of OD.[25] Management must realize that conditions prevail that prevent the organization from operating in its healthiest and most effective state. Some signs that OD intervention is needed are (1) low collaboration and high competition, (2) a lack of communication, (3) a need to change the motivation of individuals, (4) a need to change structure, roles, climate, and social and cultural norms, and (5) a need to adapt to change.

Methodology

OD uses *intervention strategies* to bring about changes in concepts, values, norms, interpersonal relationships, and organizational climate.

Intervention strategies usually consist of (1) team development and (2) improvement of intergroup relationships.[26] They are concerned with the development of planning and goal-setting processes for individuals, teams, and larger groups. They include educational activities for increasing knowledge, skills, and abilities of personnel at all levels.

---

[24]See Al Gates, "Is There Really any Difference Between OD and Training? *Training/HRD* 17 (May 1980):76, for a different opinion.

[25]Richard Beckhard, *Organizational Development: Strategies and Models* (Reading, Mass.: Addison-Wesley, 1969):17–19.

[26]Warren Bennis, *Organizational Development: Its Nature and Prospects* (Reading, Mass.: Addison-Wesley, 1969).

Team building.   Strategies for developing more effective teams often use an intervention model with three phases. They are (1) collecting information, (2) feedback of data, and (3) action planning based on the feedback. The different phases of the model take different forms in different situations but are common to most team-building activities.

Improving intergroup relationships.   The amount of energy used in unnecessary competition between members reduces organizational effectiveness. Such a condition has a tendency to grow unless action is taken to convert inappropriate competition into collaboration. Intergroup relationship intervention is the strategy most used to remedy low collaboration and high competition conditions. It involves the leaders and group members coming together to reduce misunderstanding and to set up mechanisms for joint collaboration. This should significantly improve the effectiveness of the total organization.

Characteristics of Successful OD Programs

There are certain traits found in most successful OD efforts. In general, the characteristics that make up a successful organizational development program are (1) a long-term commitment to OD efforts, (2) a total commitment to the program by top management, (3) involvement of the whole organization, (4) concerted efforts to change behavior and attitudes, (5) reliance on experience-related learning activities, (6) working primarily with the whole group, and (7) emphasis on action.

Managerial Grid

The *managerial grid* is probably the best known OD method in use. Using various simulations, managers are forced to study the difference between their own behavior and their idealized behavior. It probably is effective in both short-run and longitudinal changes in the attitudes of managers.

Results

Some criticisms of OD are: (1) there is overemphasis upon personal sensitivity and interpersonal relationships rather than on attacking structure, reward system, and other organizational constraints, which can be achieved more effectively using other techniques, (2) OD "graduates" become so engrossed with establishing new behavior patterns that they tend to ignore the responsibilities of their job, and (3) the organization is called upon to fit itself into the OD package, whereas the package should be tailored for each organization, depending upon its needs.[27]

---

[27]See Larry E. Gruiner, "Red Flags in Organizational Development," *Business Horizons* 15 (June 1972):17–24, for these and other criticisms.

Proponents of OD claim that these are not valid criticisms. Whereas the organization can begin either from within or from without, at least it makes an attempt to improve both executives and the organizational climate to which they return from developmental activities.[28]

What conclusions can be reached? First, evaluation of this effort should be incorporated into the original plans for the method, not at the end. Apparently, this method of training is improving both the organizational climate and the performance of managers.

EVALUATING MANAGEMENT DEVELOPMENT

Management development programs are based on the assumption that the time, money, and effort spent on them will result in improved performance. Yet there are few definite estimates of the effectiveness of such programs. Personnel managers have not yet been able to develop effective evaluation techniques to prove whether they are getting full value from their training investments.

Difficulty of Evaluating

First, these programs usually produce maximum benefits only over a long period of time. Therefore, they cannot be expected to lead to changes in the manager's attitudes and skills that will be immediately seen in job performance. (This problem constitutes one of the primary research opportunities for the future.)

Second, evaluations tend to be made by the participants themselves. Since anyone attending such a program is considered to be a "crown prince" or "crown princess," participants tend to say that it was effective. They are afraid to say that the learning did not "take." This might be viewed as a weakness on their part rather than on the part of the program.

An experimental study evaluated a training course in problem solving and decision making involving three levels of management. It found that the participants fervently recommended the course, as they thought it was so worthwhile. Yet the experimental evaluation showed that whatever losses and gains occurred in the experimental group, as opposed to the control group, were not statistically significant.[29]

---

[28]Daniel L. Kegan, "Organizational Development: Description, Issues, and Some Research Results," *Academy of Management Journal* 14 (December 1971):453–62.

[29]Dannie J. Moffie, Richard Calhoon, and James K. O'Brien, "Evaluation of a Management Development Program," *Personnel Psychology* 17 (Winter 1964):431–39.

Process of Evaluating

Figure 9–5 presents a process for evaluating the effectiveness of management development programs. As you can see, there are five essential steps. They are:

1. Establish performance standards expected of participants.
2. Measure their actual performance.
3. Compare actual performance with expected performance.
4. Evaluate the relationship of the two.
5. Determine whether corrective action is needed.

FIGURE 9–5
Evaluation and feedback process

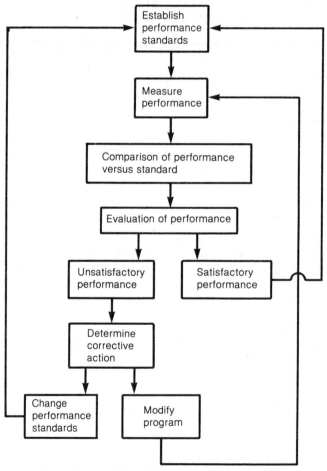

Source: Ralph J. Brown and James D. Somerville, "Evaluation of Management Development Programs: An Innovative Approach," in *Personnel: A Book of Readings,* ed. William F. Glueck (Dallas: Business Publications, 1979), p. 249.

From the figure, you can see that evaluation is based on *measuring the effects of the learning that has taken place*. This can be done by testing the participants before and after training in order to measure knowledge, attitudes, and technical knowledge. Performance is usually measured by performance evaluations before, immediately after, and a considerable time after the training. The evaluations can be done by the participant's supervisor, peers, and/or subordinates. However, the evaluations are usually contaminated because the people doing the evaluations know that the manager has been trained. Therefore they *expect* to find improvement and usually do, whether there has been any or not. These evaluative techniques can be improved by having a control group against which the participants' performance improvement can be measured.

One evaluation of the effectiveness of a training program to improve leadership styles showed that at the completion of the program there was no significant difference between the control group and the experimental group.[30]

On the other hand, using a results-oriented questionnaire evaluation in a British firm, researchers found that a vast majority of participants thought the course had helped them perform in specific areas. Six months later, the superiors were interviewed concerning the managers' performance after training. Half of them perceived positive changes in their subordinates in the areas of study. One-fourth indicated that the techniques used in the program had been introduced into their division by the participants.[31]

EEO AND MANAGEMENT DEVELOPMENT

The EEO laws discussed in Chapter 4 also apply to selection and development of managers. Most employers have accepted their responsibility and are now developing female and minority managers.

Women

Education or training programs for women executives must include "confidence-raising and definitions of professional behavior as well as effective management techniques."[32] These programs must contain these essential elements if the programs are to satisfy the needs of women.

---

[30]Herbert Hand and John Slocum, Jr., "A Longitudinal Study of the Effects of a Human Relations Training Program on Managerial Effectiveness," *Journal of Applied Psychology* 56 (October 1972):412–17.

[31]S. Thobley, "Evaluating an In-Company Management Training Program," *Training and Development Journal* 23 (September 1969):48–50.

[32]Mildred E. Buzenberg, "Training and Development of Women Executives: A Model," *Collegiate News and Views* 29 (Fall 1975):19–22.

"Look sharp, here comes the ol' man."

Used by permission *The Wall Street Journal*

This concept was dramatized by a training program for women managers at the University of Minnesota. The objective of the program was to try to get each woman to understand herself, both as a woman and as an achiever, and to accept the premise that these two qualities are not incompatible. The women were interviewed three months after the residential seminar was over. The effects most often mentioned were "better self-awareness and increased self-confidence."[33]

Minorities

Management development programs need to consider the special needs of minorities. For example, a study of black managers with MBAs found that because of discrimination they became less optimistic over time about their upward mobility in firms run by whites.[34]

---

[33]J. Stephen Heinen et al., "Developing the Woman Manager," *Personnel Journal* 54 (May 1975):282-86.

[34]Gadis Nowell, "Black Businesses and Black Managers: Some Preliminary Findings," *Western Journal of Black Studies* 2 (Summer 1978) 151-56.

SUMMARY AND CONCLUSIONS

The material in this chapter is based on the assumption that, in general, the demand for properly qualified persons to assume managerial positions is greater than the supply of persons available.

The procedure for identifying and selecting managerial talent includes (1) establishing criteria for measuring executive success, (2) identifying predictors to be used in identifying and selecting managerial talent, and (3) using special selection techniques to find out if given applicants have those abilities.

Some commonly used criterion measures are (1) performance appraisals, (2) salary, (3) rank, or position, in the organization, and (4) rapidity of promotions or salary increases. The trend now is away from a single criterion measurement towards a systems approach to selection.

There are certain characteristics that managers have to a higher degree than does the general public. These serve as selected predictors which differentiate the successful executives from others. These are intelligence, education, and certain personality traits.

The assessment center is an effective selection technique. It uses (1) the in-basket technique and management games, (2) structured and unstructured group interaction exercises, and (3) peer ratings, subordinate ratings, and self-ratings.

Some characteristics of effective executive development programs are (1) they are a deep and integral part of the organizational system, (2) top management usually supports them, (3) they are a significant part of every manager's job, and (4) participants view the programs positively. Some reasons why managers resist training include the normal human distaste for change, the resistance to having a mere teacher telling them what to do, and the manner of the training.

Scientists and technical people need to be reoriented to assume managerial responsibilities.

Things that should be developed in present and future executives are (1) general knowledge, (2) technical knowledge and skills, (3) administrative skills, and (4) attitudes and managerial philosophy.

Some of the methods used to develop managers are (1) on-the-job learning experiences, including coaching, planned progression, job rotation, and temporary assignment, and (2) off-the-job methods, such as case analysis, simulation, laboratory training, advanced management development programs, and MBO.

Organizational development (OD) is undertaken by top management to increase the health and effectiveness of the entire organization.

Special attention should be given to developing women and minorities.

QUESTIONS

1. How would you determine the need for managerial personnel?
2. What are some common criteria for measuring successful job perform-

ance? What difficulties do you anticipate in using any single criterion as a measure of successful performance?

3. What characteristics have been found that distinguish successful managers from less successful ones? Do you agree? Explain.

4. Do you think students with high scholastic grades will make better managers than those with average marks? Defend your answer.

5. How is the assessment center being used for making selection decisions?

6. What is executive development? Explain.

7. "In essence, everyone who is in a managerial position or is expected to be in one in the future should be developed." Do you agree? Explain.

8. Are there any special problems that arise in developing technical people? If there are, how can they be resolved?

9. What are some of the popular methods of development, and how are they used?

10. What is your opinion of OD? Explain.

PROBLEM

Outside Help

Because of expansion, the management of a rapidly growing engineering consulting firm had to employ personnel for certain key executive positions. In those firms, the technical qualifications of nonmanagerial employees are normally given more emphasis than their managerial abilities. This eventually leads to a shortage of qualified managers in the firm.

A nontechnical executive from the outside was employed as the assistant to the president. This move was not received very well by the older department heads. It was generally felt that someone from inside the organization should have been placed in the position. Consequently, the new presidential assistant had a hard time obtaining cooperation from her fellow employees.

She remained as assistant to the president for about four years, until she was made a vice president. During that period she was able to convince her fellow employees of her managerial abilities and the need for her services within the business. Her promotion to vice president was "generally well received by all."

Questions

1. What does this problem illustrate about the relationship between type of organization and source of personnel?

2. Why was it necessary—or at least desirable—to go outside for the new manager?

3. What would you have done if you were the president? Explain.

4. What do you think of the way the presidential assistant handled herself?

SUGGESTED READINGS FOR FURTHER STUDY

Bahn, Charles.   "Can Intelligence Tests Predict Executive Competence?" *Personnel* 58 (July–August 1979):52–58.

Coffina, Richard M.   "Management Recruitment Is a Two-Way Street." *Personnel Journal* 58 (February 1979):86–89.

Cook, Mary F.   "Is the Mentor Relationship Primarily a Male Experience?" *Personnel Administrator* 24 (November 1979):82–86.

Hill, Alfred W.   "How Organizational Philosophy Influences Management Development." *Personnel Journal* 59 (February 1980):118–20, 148.

Hodge, B. J., William P. Anthony, and Orson Swindle.   "Management Development: 12 Months Later." *Personnel Administrator* 21 (September 1976):49–55.

Mitchell, Christina.   "Things Carl Rogers Never Told Me." *Personnel Administrator* 24 (May 1979):76–78.

Quick, James C., W. A. Fisher, Lawrence L. Schkade, and George Ayers.   "Developing Administrative Personnel through Assessment Center Technique." *Personnel Administrator* 25 (February 1980):44–46, 62.

Rader, Martha H.   "Evaluating a Management Development Program for Women." *Public Personnel Management* 18 (May–June 1979):138–45.

Tanaka, Hiroshi.   "The Japanese Method of Preparing Today's Graduate to Become Tomorrow's Manager." *Personnel Journal* 59 (February 1980):109–14.

White, Donald D., and Bill Davis.   "Behavioral Contingency Management: A Bottom-Line Alternative for Management Development." *Personnel Administrator* 25 (April 1980):67–75.

Zemke, Ron.   "Using Assessment Centers to Measure Management Potential." *Training/HRD* 17 (March 1980):23–24.

PART THREE

Improving Employee Performance

Any use of human beings in which less is demanded of them, and less is attributed to them, than their full status is a degradation and a waste.

NORBERT WIENER

Employees have now been selected, trained, and developed. Personnel executives must see that they are taken care of and that their needs are satisfied so that they will be productive employees and receive satisfaction from performing their job.

While all sections of this book deal with performance, this part is particularly devoted to improving employee performance. Figure III-1 shows that this activity is essential for an effective personnel system.

The specific topics discussed, and the chapters in which they are covered are:

FIGURE III-1
How various aspects of employee performance fit into the personnel system

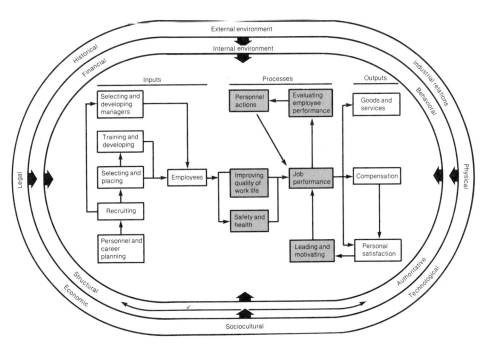

CHAPTER TEN

Improving the Quality of Work Life

Learning Objectives

After studying the material in this chapter, you should be able to:

1. Explain why the quality of work life is so important.
2. Describe how work is organized and managed.
3. Explain why work is becoming less important to workers.
4. Explain what causes job dissatisfaction and how extensive it is.
5. Name some of the efforts now being made to improve job satisfaction.
6. Describe how jobs are designed.
7. Name and explain some current efforts to redesign jobs.
8. Name and explain some current efforts to vary the work schedule.

Some Important Words and Terms

Quality of work life
Work
Job
Occupation
Position
Workaholism
Mid-career change
Job satisfaction
Job design
Job redesign
Job analysis
Job description
Job specification

Job dilution
Job enlargement
Job enrichment
Job rotation
Semiautonomous work teams
Work improvement suggestion systems
Compressed work week
Flexitime
Core time
Job sharing
Job splitting
Group jobs

In order that people may be happy in their work, these three things are needed: they must be for it; they must not do too much of it; and they must have a sense of success in it.
JOHN RUSKIN

Outline of the Chapter

James S. Kuhn, formerly a personnel officer, is now "vice president for individuality" for McDonald's. This office was created to preserve the human touch and maintain the growth and identity of individuals in the chain.

Mr. Kuhn listens to employee complaints and offers advice, when asked for it. He tries to consider an employee's personality and ability in career planning.

The vice president is studying the impact of corporate life on employees' families. This includes writing the workers' spouses and children for suggestions for improvement.

In order to keep in touch with employees, the firm has an annual "Store Day," when managers, from the chairman down, cook hamburgers and clean up.

This case illustrates what one firm is doing to improve the quality of work life for its employees. Many people believe that most jobs and work areas today do not provide a high quality of life for workers.

In general the *quality of work life* refers to the meaningfulness of work to employees, satisfactory working conditions, freedom to make decisions, acceptable working hours, and effective managerial leadership.

This chapter discusses most of these subjects. The quality of managerial leadership will be covered in the next chapter.

HOW WORK IS MANAGED

Most people work for a living. Most organizations require work in order to produce goods or services. Therefore work must be managed effectively if personal and organizational goals are to be attained.

How Work Is Organized

Work must be organized if it is to be productive. This means dividing it into smaller units. To make this discussion meaningful, we must define our terms.

Work is the activity in which we exert physical and/or mental strength in order to do something useful for some form of gain, usually—but not always—monetary reward. It is usually a productive activity, involving physical or mental exertion, scheduled on a routine basis.

A *job* is the specific role or function performed for an employer. A job involves a specific set of tasks, duties, functions, and responsibilities. A problem for personnel managers is the fact that a job usually includes both required and voluntary parts. The *required part* includes those things *all* workers who hold that job must do in order to avoid a charge of negligence or insubordination. The *voluntary part* is composed of the decisions and activities that employees are authorized to make if they choose. This is the part that can be expanded to make the job more meaningful to the firm and to the individual. Rewards are usually based on this part.

An *occupation* is the overall activity in which we engage, which is usually the principal productive activity of our life. It includes the nature of the activities being performed, their level in an organization, the importance of the results, and the skills, aptitudes, abilities, knowledge, education, and training necessary to perform them.

A *position* is a specific job opening that an employer has available. An employee is hired to fill this position.

Jobs and positions are organized into work teams, units, departments, divisions, and others. These, then, make up the organization.

Work Is Becoming Less Important

Eli Ginzberg, a specialist on better ways to use human resources, says hard work is on the way out. He believes that today's higher paid and better educated workers won't tolerate being "ordered around" on the job.[1]

Less emphasis on the work ethic.   Work is now seen by many people as separate from other parts of life. The newer workers consider leisure as important as work. As evidence, the annual hours of work have decreased from around 3,750 to 1,800 during the last century.

Also, people are less dependent on one job, one employer, and work itself as a means of survival and satisfaction. As welfare programs, inheritances, and other sources of income have grown, some people have found that work is not necessary for survival.

Rebellion against "workaholism."   Some industries, such as electronics, investment banking, and consulting, practice *workaholism*. That is, employees are required to work long, hard hours, whether they want to or not. Now workers in those and other industries are rebelling at these conditions, which tend to become counterproductive.[2] These and other workers are refusing to work 10- and 12-hour shifts for six or seven days a week.

Occupational downgrading.   Many bored and discontented workers are "getting out of the rat race" by leaving high-pressure jobs for work that's less boring and more satisfying.[3] To them, success is not worth the price required, so they make a *mid-career change.*

Disenchanted workers.   During the 1960s, millions of employees, especially the young, looked for personal fulfillment through their work, occupation, or even social service. But research by the respected polling firm of

---

[1]"Hard Work on the Way Out?" *U.S. News & World Report,* January 23, 1978, pp. 47–49.

[2]"The Growing Disaffection with 'Workaholism,' " *Business Week,* February 27, 1978, pp. 97–98.

[3]"Getting Out of the Rat Race: How Some Workers Are Doing It," *U.S. News & World Report,* September 19, 1977. pp. 85–86.

In a 'workaholic' office, long hours are often put in even when the job is done.

Kimble Mead for *Business Week.*

Yankelovich, Skelly & White shows that a declining percentage now think this kind of fulfillment is really possible.[4] In 1970, nearly half of those surveyed looked to work as a source of fulfillment. The figure was less than one-half of that in 1978.

A shift in types of jobs. As shown in Chapter 3, machines are now being used to produce goods. There is less emphasis on skilled crafts and a shift to performing services. The unskilled and menial jobs are being filled by immigrants.

Work Is Still Important to Many Workers

In spite of these figures, people still need and want to work. Work plays many roles in their lives, and nothing else can take its place.

A poll of several thousand employees of Burlington Northern Railroad in 19 states found "strong negative feelings" toward the company and the unions among "underworked," "nonproductive," or "extravagantly overpaid" employees. Most favorable feelings came from employees whose jobs required physical effort, mental pressure, or responsibility. Managers and rank-and-filers agreed that "we should have a larger work force but

---

[4]Roger Ricklefs, "Monitoring America," *The Wall Street Journal,* October 10, 1978, p. 26.

TABLE 10-1
Percentage of workers who would go on working

	Go on working	*Quit work*	*Not sure*
Men	76	20	4
Women	67	31	2
Whites	74	23	3
Nonwhites	69	30	1
Earn under $10,000	66	29	5
Earn over $15,000	85	12	2
Age 18–24	90	8	2
Age 40–59	67	31	2
Age 60 or over	52	33	14

Source: Thomas C. Sorensen, "Do Americans Like Their Jobs?" *Parade*, June 3, 1973, p. 15.

fewer managers." Employees worried about the future of the railroad industry but not about being fired or laid off or losing seniority.[5]

We achieve our objectives through work.   Work is the means we use to play the part of provider for our families and to be a useful and productive part of society. It is the method by which we achieve our objectives in life, whatever they may be. If the work we do is in harmony with our abilities, values, attitudes, status, and relationships with other people, we tend to play the role successfully. In playing the role, we adapt ourselves to our work environment.

A study found that garbage collectors didn't feel bad about their low-status jobs. While they were often aware that their jobs were held in low esteem, they didn't let that mar their own self-esteem. The workers seemed to focus mainly on their "extra-occupational status" instead of defining themselves in terms of their jobs. Having a separate sanitation workers' union, as in Detroit, helped bolster self-esteem. The study showed that most collectors liked their work and didn't want it "humanized."[6]

Most employees want to keep on working.   Many studies have shown that employed people want to keep on working, for it makes their lives more meaningful. A study in 1973 found the vast majority of people wanted to continue working.[7] Table 10-1 shows that no more than a third of any group would quit working.

---

[5]See *The Wall Street Journal,* July 15, 1975, p. 1, for details.

[6]*The Wall Street Journal,* September 9, 1975, p. 1.

[7]I have done similar research with first-line supervisors and middle managers since 1965. The answers have varied from a high of 96 percent in 1966 to a low of 63 percent in 1975 for those who would keep on working. The figure for white females has varied from 100 percent to 65 percent. The results for black males is often slightly lower than for white males.

The results for white- and blue-collar workers were similar in 1979. A Gallup survey found that 61 percent of men (working full time) wanted to continue in full-time jobs.[8] Another 27 percent wanted only a part-time job. Only 10 percent said they would not work unless they had to. Only 14 percent of women would quit working, and 40 percent would work part-time.

Meaning of work is related to type of work. The meaningfulness of work varies according to the type of work people do and their level in the organization. In general, work tends to have more meaning to managers and supervisors, skilled workers, and scientific, technical, and professional personnel than to less skilled workers or to those with narrow, specialized jobs.[9]

JOB DISSATISFACTION AND EFFORTS TO OVERCOME IT

There is much difference of opinion over the extent and causes of job dissatisfaction and how to overcome it. *Job satisfaction* results from a combination of the job, the individual, and the environment. Therefore, almost everyone studying the question reaches different conclusions. Part of the problem is that there are so many factors determining whether workers will be satisfied or not. These factors are not always covered in research studies. Some of the factors are age, sex, race, education, religious beliefs, occupation, type of organization, geographic location, and the general environment.

Factors Influencing Job Satisfaction

There are many factors that influence the extent to which workers will be satisfied with their jobs. Some of the more important ones are the following:

1. The individual's vocational choice.
2. Selection and placement of the employee on the job.
3. The total environment of the job.
4. Size and layout of the work area.
5. Type of work performed.
6. Length of uninterrupted effort required to perform the job.
7. Knowledge of the purpose of the work and what is going on around the worker.
8. Personal and social relationships of employees.
9. The employee's fears and anxieties.

---

[8]Associated Press bulletin, October 20, 1979.

[9]John K. Maurer, "Work as a 'Central Life Interest' of Industrial Supervisors," *Academy of Management Journal* 11 (September 1968):329–39; and Frank Friedlander, "Importance of Work versus Nonwork among Socially and Occupationally Stratified Groups," *Journal of Applied Psychology* 50 (December 1966):437–41.

TABLE 10-2
The four-year decline in job satisfaction

	Percent responding "very true"	
	1973	1977
Good hours, pleasant surroundings, and job is free of conflicting demands	38.4%	30.2%
Interesting work with opportunity to develop abilities and freedom to decide how to do the job.................	51.3	41.5
Good pay, fringe benefits, and job security	45.7	33.8
Enough information and authority to get the job done......	63.3	52.4

Data: 1973 and 1977 "Quality of Employment Survey," University of Michigan Survey Research Center; Work in America Institute Inc.
Source: "A Warning That Worker Discontent Is Rising," *Business Week*, June 4, 1979, p. 152.

Extent of Job Dissatisfaction

It is now known that the degree of job satisfaction and dissatisfaction appears to be similar in different parts of the world. In a national comparison of job satisfaction by occupations, the percentage of satisfied workers in the six most highly industrialized countries was essentially the same—about 80 percent.[10] While some studies find satisfaction to be lower, most find it higher.

Dissatisfaction is increasing. Yet dissatisfaction now appears to be increasing, according to a "Quality of Employment Survey" made for the Labor Department by the University of Michigan's Survey Research Center.[11] From 1973 to 1977, various aspects of job satisfaction dropped throughout the country by 11–43 percent of the 1973 figures.

Table 10-2 shows some typical changes. Other findings were that (1) 36 percent of the workers felt that their skills were underutilized, (2) 32 percent thought they were overeducated for their jobs, and (3) more than 50 percent complained about a lack of control over their job assignments and days of work.

Reasons for increasing dissatisfaction. A likely reason for the increasing dissatisfaction is that higher education has created rising expectations in employees. Another reason was given by the person who conducted the poll. He said the results reflect a "decline in the 'quality of life' rather than the 'quality of work.' "[12] Questions about general life situations showed more of a decline than those that were directly related to the job.

---

[10]Alex Inkeles, "Industrial Man: The Relation of Status to Experience, Perception, and Value," *American Journal of Sociology* 56 (July 1960):6.

[11]"Job Satisfaction Drops," *Personnel Administrator* 24 (April 1979):42.

[12]*The Wall Street Journal*, June 5, 1979, p. 1.

This growing dissatisfaction led the U.S. Senate to pass the *Worker Alienation and Technical Assistance Act* of 1972. It provides for research into solutions for this growing problem in our country.

Results of dissatisfaction.   Alienation results in many forms of employee resentment, such as absenteeism, wildcat strikes, and inferior-quality products. This behavior, in turn, affects operating expenses. The entire organization pays a higher price for negative attitudes and their consequences.

A two-year survey of 1,300 workers at ten industrial plants turned up a "significant statistical relationship" between job dissatisfaction and psychologically induced ailments. Workers describing themselves as unhappy with work more often showed real cases of headaches, fatigue, colds, and other common ailments.[13]

Who Are the More Satisfied Workers?

The Michigan study found declines in "virtually all demographic and occupational subclasses." Yet it was found that college graduates liked their work least. They were followed by (1) people under 30 years of age, (2) black workers, (3) semiskilled workers, (4) blue-collar workers, and (5) manufacturing employees.

The findings of several respected studies from 1958 to 1973 *tend* to indicate that:[14]

1.   Whites are more satisfied than blacks.
2.   Older workers are more satisfied than younger ones.
3.   Men are slightly more satisfied than women.[15]
4.   Workers in high-status jobs are more satisfied than those in low-status positions.
5.   Employees who are more professional are more satisfied than those who are less professional.
6.   Workers with a high school education are less satisfied than those with less or more schooling.

The extent of satisfaction seems to have reached a low point with the Lordstown strike of 1972.[16] Now there is much evidence that either there is not that much dissatisfaction or workers have found ways to cope with the

---

[13]This study was done by Joseph Weintraub, a Babson College professor. See *The Wall Street Journal*, December 2, 1975, p. 1, for further details and specific examples.

[14]*Personnel Psychology* 30 (Winter 1977):589–605.

[15]See T. J. Keaveny, J. H. Jackson, and J. A. Fossum, "Are There Sex Differences in Job Satisfaction?" *Personnel Administrator* 23 (March 1978):55–58, for a different conclusion.

[16]For discussion of the causes and consequences of this landmark strike, see Hak C. Lee and John J. Grix, "Communication: An Alternative to Job Enrichment," *Personnel Administrator* 20 (October 1975):20–23.

situation. The answer probably lies somewhere in the middle—there are some boring jobs (see Figure 10-1), but there are many that are not. The effective personnel manager can probably match people and jobs to lessen the effects of this problem.

Efforts to Improve Job Satisfaction and the Work Environment

Personnel and operating managers are trying many methods to improve job satisfaction and the work environment. Some of the more promising ones are:

1. Matching abilities of employees and the job through better selection and placement (as covered in Part 2) and job design and redesign.

FIGURE 10-1
Which jobs are boring?

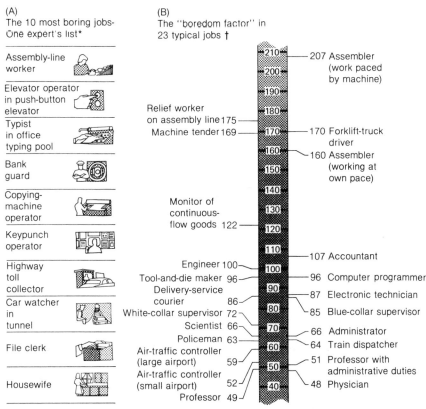

(A)
The 10 most boring jobs—
One expert's list*

Assembly-line worker

Elevator operator in push-button elevator

Typist in office typing pool

Bank guard

Copying-machine operator

Keypunch operator

Highway toll collector

Car watcher in tunnel

File clerk

Housewife

(B)
The "boredom factor" in 23 typical jobs †

207 Assembler (work paced by machine)

Relief worker on assembly line 175

Machine tender 169

170 Forklift-truck driver

160 Assembler (working at own pace)

Monitor of continuous-flow goods 122

107 Accountant

Engineer 100

Tool-and-die maker 96

96 Computer programmer

Delivery-service courier 86

87 Electronic technician

White-collar supervisor 72

85 Blue-collar supervisor

Scientist 66

66 Administrator

Policeman 63

64 Train dispatcher

Air-traffic controller (large airport) 59

51 Professor with administrative duties

Air-traffic controller (small airport) 52

48 Physician

Professor 49

*Which day-to-day tasks involve the most drudgery, the least payoff in satisfaction? Personnel consultant Roy Walters, head of a New Jersey management firm, provides the above list of ten. Jobs are given at random, not necessarily in order of boredom.

†Based on interviews with 2,010 workers performing 23 different jobs, the Institute for Social Research at the University of Michigan drew up "boredom factors" for each occupation—with 100 the average and the higher the rating, the more boring the job.

Source: Reprinted from U.S. News & World Report. "Those 'Boring' Jobs—Not All That Dull," *U.S. News & World Report* (December 1, 1975), pp. 64–65. Copyright 1975 U.S. News & World Report, Inc.

2. Improving work schedules by varying the hours to be worked.
3. Giving more recognition to individual employees.
4. Using newer motivational methods (as will be seen in the next chapter).

DESIGNING AND REDESIGNING JOBS

In *job design*, an effort is made to include technical, social, and psychological variables into the job. *Job redesign* attempts to make the work more meaningful and to help employees perceive that their jobs are important and have status. Some forms of job redesign are (1) job rotation, (2) job enlargement, (3) job enrichment, (4) semiautonomous work teams, and (5) work improvement suggestion systems.

Before discussing these types of job redesign, we need to look at the method used to design jobs.

Method Used to Design Jobs

As shown in Chapter 5, job design begins with an analysis of the job. *Job analysis* consists of (1) identifying the job, (2) determining its features, such as duties, responsibilities, working conditions, and skills and knowledge required, and (3) writing a *job description* or *job specification*. In addition, the social and psychological factors must be considered. Finally, the individual differences of the workers are taken into account.

Next, management must decide if it wants to (1) reduce the scope of the job's content, *job dilution*, (2) increase the number and type of activities in the job, *job enlargement*, or (3) increase the responsibility and authority of the job, *job enrichment*.

Another alternative is to use *job rotation*, whereby employees take turns performing several types of job.

Job Rotation

Job rotation is easier and simpler to use than the other methods. It (1) reduces the time spent on boring and monotonous jobs, (2) makes it easier to staff the less desirable jobs, (3) increases the workers' knowledge and skills, and (4) provides for greater flexibility in scheduling the work.

Job Enlargement

Job enlargement really means adding more and different simple tasks to a specialized job. It may create job interest by providing variety in the job. But it really adds little to challenge the employees' creativity and motivation.

Job Enrichment

Job enrichment is an effort to minimize the undesirable parts of highly repetitive and specialized jobs.

What is included in job enrichment?   In essence, job enrichment increases the content of the job to include (1) a greater variety of skills and knowledge, (2) greater use of employees' abilities and motivation, and (3) greater freedom and responsibility in performing the job.

Table 10-3 shows some of the specifics of what is involved in setting up such a program.

Favorable results.   This technique has shown very favorable results when properly used. For example, ten studies showed that this type of job redesign led to higher quality performance in all cases and increased productivity in four cases.[17]

Bankers Trust Company of New York saved $300,000 in a year by complicating the work of 100 typists. When they were given more responsibility, their work quality and quantity increased.

It has been found that the employees' occupation and job level largely determine whether job enlargement and enrichment lead to improved job performance and personal satisfaction.[18]

Some criticisms.   There have been many criticisms of job enrichment. These include the following:

1. Users have at times neglected some factors that can actually damage the present work climate.[19]

TABLE 10-3
Job enrichment involves:

1. Removing unnecessary details and controls
2. Increasing individuals' accountability
3. Giving each employee a complete natural unit of work
4. Making periodic reports directly available to the workers as well as to the supervisor
5. Introducing new and more difficult tasks
6. Assigning individuals specialized tasks that will help them become more expert in their jobs

[17]Edward E. Lawler III, "Job Design and Employee Motivation," *Personnel Psychology* 22 (Winter 1969):426–34.

[18]Thomas B. Armstrong, "Job Content and Context Factors Related to Satisfaction for Different Occupational Levels," *Journal of Applied Psychology* 55 (February 1971):57–65.

[19]Antone F. Alber, "How (and How Not) to Approach Job Enrichment," *Personnel Journal* 58 (December 1979):837–41.

2. Some employees feel that they are not getting paid enough for increased performance.
3. Unions tend to be opposed.
4. These techniques are more effective in small firms.
5. There is resistance by some supervisors.
6. Some jobs do not lend themselves to this type of enrichment.

Semiautonomous Work Teams

Some employers have had success with using *semiautonomous work teams*.[20] These small groups—of, say, 5 to 15 members—are responsible for much of the planning, organizing, work scheduling, and control over their work. Individual team members are responsible to the group. The group is then responsible to an operating manager.

The Saab-Scania Company of Sweden uses the group basis to assemble engines. Groups must meet weekly quotas, set by management, but have relative freedom to organize the work.[21]

Like other efforts to improve the quality of work life, this method has problems. The two usual problems are worker distrust and permissiveness on the part of management.

The Grain Millers Union accused the 30 workers at Gaines Nutrition Center of being a union that was "unlawfully dominated by management." The NLRB ruled against it and said this was "the best way to organize the work force to get the work out."[22]

Work Improvement Suggestion Systems

Another technique being used to improve productivity and employee satisfaction is the *work improvement suggestion system*.[23] This method removes strict organizational barriers. It allows employees to participate with management in designing the job and streamlining operations. Another form gives monetary rewards for usable suggestions.

---

[20]"Participative Management at Work: An Interview with J. F. Donnelly," *Harvard Business Review* 55 (January-February 1977):117-27.

[21]Kim Hayes, "My Own Engine," *Sweden Now*, April 1976, p. 24ff.

[22]*The Wall Street Journal*, January 11, 1977, p. 1.

[23]Paul S. Greenlaw, "Suggestion Systems: An Old Approach to a New Problem," *Personnel Administrator* 25 (January 1980):49-54.

Reprinted by permission *The Wall Street Journal*

VARYING THE WORK SCHEDULE

Workers have always wanted more free time as their income has risen. For example, in the United States, the average work week dropped from 60 hours to 40 hours between 1900 and 1940. However, the average work week has decreased by only about three hours since then. In fact, almost one out of five workers work over 48 hours per week—especially managers, professionals, salespeople, and the self-employed.[24] Still, workers have gained more free time through the use of longer vacations, more holidays, earlier retirement, more liberal sick leave plans, and now through the use of flexible working hours.

Now there is a great variety of ways of scheduling work so that employees can have more free time.[25] As shown in Figure 10-2, there are essentially three ways of doing this. They are to (1) shorten the work week, (2) let employees have more flexibility in setting their own work hours, and (3) use part-time employees.

---

[24]"The 40-Hour Week Is a Myth for Millions," *U.S. News & World Report*, May 24, 1976, pp. 76–77.

[25]John W. Newstrom and Jon L. Pierce, "Alternative Work Schedules: The State of the Art," *Personnel Administrator* 24 (October 1979):21.

FIGURE 10-2
Ways of providing more free time for workers

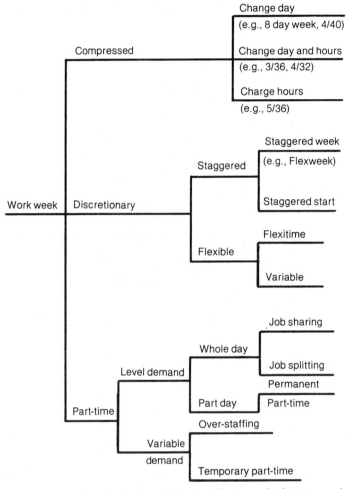

Source: Reprinted from the October, 1979 issue of *The Personnel Administrator* with permission of the American Society for Personnel Administration.

Compressed Work Week

Under the *compressed* (shortened) *work week*, employees work less than the usual five-day week. The usual arrangement is the "eight-day week." Two groups of employees alternate working for four days at ten hours per day (4/40). They are then off for four days.

Other variations of this work schedule are (1) 4/32, (2) 4/36, (3) 5/35, and (4) 5/37½. Some employers even use a work week of three 12-hour days—on weekends only.[26]

---

[26]"A Full-Time Job—Weekends Only," *Business Week*, October 15, 1979, pp. 150–52.

Advantages.   A shortened work week has its advantages and disadvantages. Some of the advantages are (1) increased leisure time for employees, (2) lower absenteeism, (3) improved employee performance, and (4) lower energy use due to not having to drive to and from work five days a week.

Disadvantages.   The shortened work week also has disadvantages. Some of these are (1) increased employee fatigue, (2) difficulty in scheduling overtime, and (3) problems with unions.

About 1,500 building trades workers at a nuclear power plant near Baton Rouge, Louisiana, work four ten-hour days and are off four. They earn overtime for the last two hours each day and for Sunday duty.

Gulf States Utilities will get its plant a year early, absenteeism is half the normal rate, and the employees like the four days off.[27]

Flexible Work Hours

The usual arrangement of flexible hours is *flexitime*. This means that employees have the freedom to choose when to report to work and when to leave. Other terms for this are *flextime, plan-time, adaptable hours, variable hours,* and *gliding time.*

How flexitime operates.   The basic intention of a flexitime system is to give employees flexibility in choosing their starting and ending working hours in a given day. This arrangement is shown in Figure 10-3. Under a typical schedule, employees can arrive at work anytime between 7:00 and 9:30 A.M. and leave work any time between 3:00 and 6:00 P.M. However, during the *core time* between 9:30 A.M. and 3:00 P.M., all workers must be present on the job. This excludes the lunch break. Employees must complete the required number of total work hours per day, week, or month.

In some situations, where management must be assured of having an adequate number of employees on hand, workers are required to begin work at about the same time each day for a given period. This introduces the idea of team flexibility as opposed to individual flexibility.

Experiments at the Social Security Administration found that flexitime increased productivity and worker morale.[28]

Managers' reactions to flexitime.   In general, managers have reacted favorably to flexitime. The chief benefits to the employer are (1) better morale, (2) increased productivity, and (3) better quality. Table 10-4 shows the reaction of 100 managers at Control Data Corporation after three years' experience with flexible hours.

Employees' reactions to flexitime.   Employees tend to favor flexitime, too. They have more time (1) with their families, (2) for leisure, and (3) to handle

---

[27]*The Wall Street Journal*, March 18, 1980, p. 1.

[28]Cary B. Barad, "Flexitime under Scrutiny: Research on Work Adjustment and Organizational Performance," *Personnel Administrator* 25 (May 1980):69-74.

FIGURE 10-3
A typical working day under flexitime

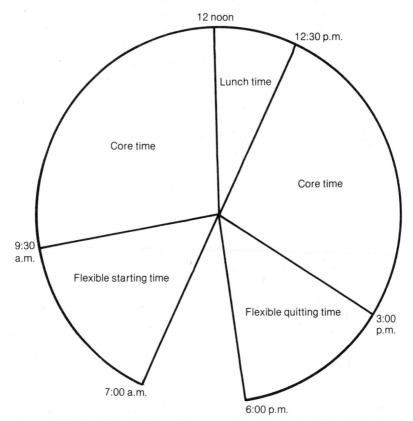

Source: Adapted from Robert J. Kuhne and Courtney O. Blair, "Changing the Workweek: Flexitime,"
Business Horizons 21 (April 1978):40. Copyright, 1978, by the Foundation for the School of Business at Indiana University. Used by permission.

TABLE 10-4
Summary of managers' reactions to flexible work hours program (*N* = 100)

	Increased	*Unaffected*	*Decreased*
Employee's driving time	3%	25%	72%
Sick leave utilization..................	4	80	16
Tardiness...........................	10	43	47
Productivity........................	51	46	3
Absenteeism........................	23	69	8
Supervisor-subordinate relationship	14	73	13
Employee's leisure time..............	74	24	12

Source: Reprinted from the January, 1978 issue of *The Personnel Administrator* with permission of The
American Society for Personnel Administration.

TABLE 10-5
Summary of nonexempt employees' reactions to flexible work hours program
($N = 286$)

	Increased	Unaffected	Decreased
Driving time	24%	19%	57%
Pressures and frustrations of trying to get to work on scheduled time	13	14	73
Need to leave work before quitting time..	13	27	60
Leisure time	59	22	19
Morale...........................	85	10	5
Attitudes toward the company	65	18	17
Productivity.......................	66	23	11
Need to supervise employees (control)....	30	24	46
Cooperation and coordination between departments......................	41	35	24
Cooperation and coordination between shifts............................	49	38	13
Abuses	21	13	66

Source: Reprinted from the January, 1978 issue of *The Personnel Administrator* with permission of The American Society for Personnel Administration.

personal business.[29] The reactions of Control Data employees to the plan are shown in Table 10–5.

Limitations on use of flexitime. There are several disadvantages of flexitime that must be considered. They include: (1) it is hard to use on assembly-line work or multiple shift jobs, (2) car pools cannot be used easily, and more heating and lighting will be needed, (3) record keeping is more complicated, (4) scheduling problems may occur, and (5) employees may resent the loss of overtime.

Using Part-time Workers

A third way of varying work schedules is to use part-time employees. There are many ways of doing this, but only three will be discussed here: (1) job sharing, (2) job splitting, and (3) permanent part-time workers.

Job sharing. Under *job sharing*, a single full-time job is divided and shared by two (or more) employees. Each worker does all the work called for in the job description. The workers who have benefitted most from job sharing are (1) women, (2) retired workers, and (3) students.[30]

---

[29]William H. Holley, Jr., Achilles A. Armenakis, and Hubert S. Field, Jr., "Employee Reactions to a Flexitime Program: A Longitudinal Study," *Human Resource Management* 15 (Winter 1976):21–23.

[30]Michael Frease and Robert A. Zawacki, "Job Sharing: An Answer to Productivity Problems?" *Personnel Administrator* 24 (October 1979):35–39.

Jean Farmer and Carole Olsen share a single teaching position at Garton School in Des Moines. Each woman teaches two days one week and three the next. They coordinate by phone.[31]

Job splitting. *Job splitting* is dividing the single job into its parts and letting two (or more) workers do different parts.

Permanent part-time employees. Some jobs do not require a full-time worker because of their limited content. This system employs permanent part-time employees who work less than a whole day or week.

The Dartnell Institute of Business Research found that between 63 and 90 percent of firms have people who work less than the standard work week. Larger firms use them more than small ones.[32]

A few firms have *group jobs* that are given to a group or family. The group is responsible for seeing that the job is done.

SUMMARY AND CONCLUSIONS

The quality of work life needs to be improved for many jobs in many work environments. Work seems to be declining in importance for many people. It is still needed for certain groups. Job satisfaction is also declining for most employees. The more progressive personnel managers are now attempting to improve the quality of work life and raise the satisfaction level.

Many methods are being used. These include efforts to (1) make the work more meaningful, (2) organize workers into smaller, more cohesive groups, (3) let employees and groups make more decisions about what they do and how they do it, and (4) vary the work schedule to suit the workers' needs.

The less meaningful work is being done by machines where possible. In other cases it is being performed by immigrants.

Jobs are being designed and redesigned to make the work more meaningful. This is being done by (1) job rotation, where employees perform several different jobs, (2) job enlargement, or having more activities included in the job, (3) job enrichment, or having greater responsibility for performing the job, (4) semiautonomous work teams, which have greater general control over the work, and (5) work improvement suggestion systems.

Work schedules are being varied by (1) compressing the work week, (2) having flexible work hours, and (3) using part-time workers.

Some general conclusions that can be reached are:

1. Job satisfaction varies with the extent to which the needs of the individual

---

[31]"Two People, One Job—How Teachers Do It," *U.S. News & World Report,* April 4, 1977, p. 80.

[32]"Short Work Week for Some," *Personnel Administrator* 24 (October 1979):45.

worker can be satisfied in a job situation. Therefore, workers whose needs are satisfied on the job are more likely to remain on the job as productive employees than those whose needs are not satisfied.

2. The greater the intrinsic value of the work being performed, the more satisfying it is to the individual performing it. That is, the employee gets more satisfaction out of doing a job he or she views as important.

3. The greater the satisfaction-yielding characteristics of a specific job, the less need there is for external motivation. Conversely, the less satisfaction-yielding the job, the greater the need for external motivation and the greater the chances for disrupted working relationships.

4. The greater the status attributed to work, an occupation, or a specific job, the more satisfaction yielding it becomes to the performer.

QUESTIONS

1. Do you see evidence that work is becoming less meaningful or necessary for some people? Explain.

2. Do you view job satisfaction as declining or increasing? Explain.

3. What suggestions do you have for improving job satisfaction?

4. Evaluate some of the present efforts to overcome job dissatisfaction.

5. Distinguish between *(a)* job rotation, *(b)* job enlargement, and *(c)* job enrichment.

6. How successful do you think the use of semiautonomous work teams will be?

7. What are the reasons for and against *(a)* the compressed work week and *(b)* using flexible working hours?

PROBLEM

The Recalcitrant Orderly

The following events were narrated by the head nurse in the emergency room of a large hospital.

"I've had a problem with one of the employees in the emergency room. He has a very bad attitude in general about his job and fellow employees. He was hired as a male aide, or orderly. He acts as though he were doing the hospital a favor by working for it. He gripes about everything he has to do. He tries to give the impression that he is too good to do certain things and that certain jobs are beneath his dignity. He gripes about the pay and the working hours, and he talks about his fellow employees behind their backs. When you ask him to do something, he comes back with, 'Why don't you do it yourself?'

"We tried to talk with him about the different job descriptions of an orderly and a nurse and to explain to him that when I ask him to do something, it's usually because I'm busy doing something he's not allowed to do, such as giving medications.

"He has had several years of college, and this may be why he feels he's better than an orderly, but, still, no one made him take the job, and the hospital is giving him an opportunity to earn some money while he goes to college."

Questions

1. What does this case tell you about the growing dissatisfaction with work?
2. How do you explain this employee's attitude?
3. What would you suggest doing to improve his performance?

SUGGESTED READINGS FOR FURTHER STUDY

Atwood, Caleb S.   "A Work Schedule to Increase Productivity." *Personnel Administrator* 24 (October 1979):29–33.

Baker, H. Kent.   "The Hows and Whys of Team Building." *Personnel Journal* 58 (June 1979):367–70.

Benschel, Jane G.   "Expect Coalitions to Break Up." *International Management*, September 1979, pp. 27ff.

Bernard, Keith E.   "Flexitime's Potential for Management." *Personnel Administrator* 24 (October 1979):51–55.

Copperman, Lois F.   "Alternative Work Policies in Private Firms." *Personnel Administrator* 24 (October 1979):40–44.

Dubin, R.   "Industrial Workers' World: A Study of the Central Life Interests of Industrial Workers." *Social Problems* 3 (1956):131–42.

Foy, Nancy, and Herman Gadon.   "Worker Participation Contrasts in Three Countries." *Harvard Business Review* 54 (May–June 1976):71.

Glueck, William F.   "Changing Hours of Work: A Review and Analysis of the Research." *Personnel Administrator* 24 (March 1979):44–47, 62–67.

McCarthy, Maureen.   "Trends in the Development of Alternative Work Patterns." *Personnel Administrator* 24 (October 1979):25–28, 33.

Schnur, Glenn J.   "Here Comes Flextime." *Management Accounting* 60 (June 1978):50–52.

Swart, J. Carroll.   "What Time Shall I Go to Work Today?" *Business Horizons* 18 (October 1975):19–26.

CHAPTER ELEVEN

Leading and Supervising Employees

Learning Objectives

After studying the material in this chapter, you should be able to:

1. Describe the prevailing theories of leadership.
2. Explain the styles of leadership used by managers.
3. Describe the communication process.
4. Explain how to improve communications with employees.
5. Describe the current theories of motivation.
6. Explain how to motivate employees to perform more effectively.
7. Explain some ways to improve employees' self-perception and make them feel more important.

Some Important Words and Terms

Leadership
Behavioral theory of leadership
Contingency theory of leadership
Authoritarian leadership style
Participative leadership style
Free-rein leadership style
Communication
Encoding
Decoding
Feedback
Grapevine
Nonverbal communication (body language)

Motivation
Maslow's hierarchy of needs
Herzberg's motivation-hygiene theory
Hygiene factors
Motivating factors
McClelland's achievement theory
Achievement motive
Equity theory
Expectancy theory
Reinforcement
Punishment
Theory X
Theory Y

Nature has given to men one tongue, but two ears, that we may hear from others twice as much as we speak.
EPICTETUS

Leadership appears to be the art of getting others to want to do something you are convinced should be done.
VANCE PACKARD

Outline of the Chapter

In the play *My Fair Lady,* Prof. Henry Higgins takes Eliza Doolittle, a flower girl from the gutters of London, and through personal coaching and guidance converts her into a polished and cultured "lady." Then he tries to send her back to the gutter, but she balks. Later, when he recognizes her true value, he asks her to marry him.

The modern counterpart of Eliza is Doris Smithers, who began working as a cashier in a supermarket. The manager recognized her potential and trained her for bookkeeping. She then badgered her boss into sending her to a management training program. Afterwards she was given more and more responsibility, even before she thought she was ready for it. Eventually, she became the first woman manager of a Shopwell grocery store and is now a highly successful businesswoman.[1]

That's what this chapter is all about—leading and supervising individuals to perform more effectively so that they can reach organizational and personal objectives. The previous chapter looked at the general work environment of the group. This one studies individual managers and employees and how they relate to each other.

Figure 11-1 shows that leading and supervising employees includes (1) using managerial leadership, (2) communicating with employees, (3) motivating them, and (4) improving their self-perception.

USING MANAGERIAL LEADERSHIP

Personnel managers need to use effective managerial leadership if they want to succeed in their job. There are many definitions of leadership, but they all boil down to one fact: If people follow you, you're a leader; if they don't, you aren't. A working definition is: *Leadership* occurs when you influence another person to work to achieve a desired objective.

The leader-follower bond is one of the oldest, most basic of human relationships. The manager-subordinate interaction represents a much newer—and less romantic—relationship.

FIGURE 11-1
A model for maximizing personnel potential

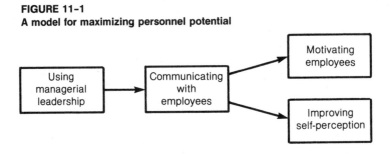

[1]Doris Smithers, "How I Got My Job," *Redbook*, March 1976, pp. 80–82.

"Leadership is of the spirit, compounded of personality and vision; its practice is an art. Management is of the mind, more a matter of accurate calculation of statistics, of methods, timetables, and routine; its practice is a science. Managers are necessary; leaders are essential."[2]

Theories of Leadership

Several theories of leadership, or perspectives on it, have been developed. Only the behavioral and contingency theories are discussed here.

The traitist theory of leadership was popular for a long time. Now, though, few management scholars accept this theory as a valid predictive model.

The behavioral theory.   Intensive research at Ohio State University and the University of Michigan developed the *behavioral theory of leadership.*[3] It emphasized identifying, studying, and measuring the influence of the leader's behavior on employee satisfaction and performance.

This theory appeals to managers, for it is easy to understand and apply. But it doesn't include the effect of environmental factors on leadership behavior.

The contingency theory.   Fiedler's *contingency theory of leadership* attempted to carry the leadership theory beyond that oversimplified model.[4] He indicated that any leadership theory must do more than account for the interaction between personality and the leadership situation. It must also deal with the way in which situational changes affect leader behavior and organizational performance.

In essence, this theory says that different situations, in different environments, with different groups of followers (subordinates) require different leadership styles.

Factors Influencing Leadership

As these theories show, there are many variables affecting the leadership style. However, as Mary Parker Follett explained, there are three critical leadership factors—the leader, the followers, and the situation.[5]

These factors help determine the effectiveness of managerial leadership. Yet no one of them can be studied in isolation, for each, in turn, affects the others, as shown in Figure 11-2.

---

[2]Attributed to Field Marshall Sir William Slim, commander of the famous 14th Army in Burma during World War II, and later governor-general of Australia.

[3]See R. M. Stogdill and A. E. Coons, eds., *Leader Behavior: Its Description and Measurement* (Columbus: Ohio State University, Bureau of Business Research, 1957).

[4]Fred E. Fiedler, "New Concepts for the Management of Managers" in *Man and Work in Society,* ed. E. L. Cass and F. C. Zimmer (New York: Van Nostrand Reinhold Co., 1975), pp. 207-19.

[5]Mary Parker Follett, *Freedom and Coordination* (London: Management Publications Trust, 1949), pp. 47-60.

FIGURE 11–2
The relationship between the leader,
subordinates, and the situation

Leader's qualities and abilities. Studies in leadership have often focused on the leader's personality traits or personal characteristics—such as height, appearance, intelligence, and dominance. For example, according to the "great man" theory, which sees leaders as objects of hero worship, the charisma of the leader is essential.

President Franklin D. Roosevelt, crippled with polio, gave us hope in the depths of the depression in 1933 when he said that "The only thing we have to fear is fear itself."

President John F. Kennedy, young, handsome, and expressive, gave us a national mission—to put a man on the moon in the 1960s. This fired our imagination and stimulated our performance for years.

People's personal abilities and personality may be either beneficial or harmful to them as leaders. Considerable effort has been devoted to the problem of relating personal abilities and characteristics to leadership ability.

One of the most valid of these studies found that the most important qualities were (1) supervisory ability, (2) intelligence, and (3) initiative.[6] Of these three, supervisory ability and intelligence were relatively more important.

Subordinates and their qualities and abilities. The type of employee being supervised will influence the leadership style used. In general, workers with less education, training, and experience require more leadership and supervision. Higher-caliber employees are more adaptable to a more participative type of leadership.

---

[6]Edwin E. Ghiselli, *Explorations in Managerial Talent* (Pacific Palisades, Calif.: Goodyear Publishing Co., 1971).

The situation and its characteristics.   There are two important factors included in the situation—(1) the position(s) involved and (2) the environmental factors.

The position factor.   The position factor is the meaning that an organization and its members give to a task, function, or position.

You saw in Chapter 9 that managers hold positions with different amounts and types of authority and responsibility, have different types and numbers of subordinates, and are found in differing locations. These factors are involved in determining the leadership role those managers play. For example, personnel managers and operating managers play different roles.

The environmental factor.   The environmental factors include the internal and external circumstances and conditions within which the leader and followers interact. Different environments call for different leadership roles and personality characteristics. People who are unable to adapt their leadership style to their present situation may have little success until they find themselves in a situation that suits their style.

Harry S Truman was well suited to the situation when he was president from 1945 to 1953. Strong, quick, decisive action was needed to meet the fast-breaking crises involved in ending World War II, rebuilding Europe and Asia, and containing communism.

President Eisenhower, on the other hand, was needed to lead the quiet period from 1953 to 1961. The small-town boy who became a great "war hero" during World War II, president of a great university, and head of NATO was a popular "father figure" who helped maintain the "peace and prosperity" of those years.

Styles of Leadership

There are many styles of leadership managers can use to influence their subordinates. Some managers use a great deal of power and influence over their subordinates, while others use very little. As you can see in Figure 11–3, the manager's use of power and influence declines and the subordinates have greater freedom as the manager's behavior shifts to the right.

At least three leadership styles have been identified from this relationship. They are the (1) authoritarian, (2) participative, and (3) free-rein styles.

Authoritarian style.   The *authoritarian style* (also called *bureaucratic, autocratic,* or *dictatorial*) stresses the use of authority and is task-oriented. The manager makes the decisions, tells subordinates what to do, and uses organizational and position authority and economic rewards to get them to perform. This style may be useful in situations where quick decision making and action are needed, or where employees are relatively untrained, unskilled, and unmotivated.

FIGURE 11-3

Continuum of manager-nonmanager behavior

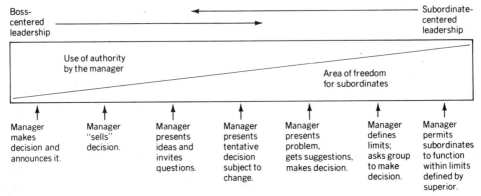

Its disadvantages are its emphasis on rules, regulations, and orders and its disregard for subordinates' ideas. However, remember that it *can* be effective.

One of the most frequently quoted comments of Vince Lombardi's players is: "He treated us all the same—like dogs." Yet Lombardi was one of the winningest coaches in professional football. Today, his players look back on his leadership style with respect and admiration.

Participative style. The *participative style* (also called *democratic* and *employee-centered*) is people-oriented and stresses employee participation in decision making. The manager presents problems to the group, gets input from them, and then decides. He or she encourages a free flow of communication within the group.

One *advantage* of this style is that subordinates require only limited supervision because they are willing to perform their assignments. Some *disadvantages* of this style are slower decision making and limited control by the leader.

Free-rein style. The *free-rein style* (also called *laissez-faire*) is used by the manager who leaves subordinates almost entirely on their own. The manager and nonmanagers jointly make decisions within the limits set by the organization. This style is used by organizations emphasizing creativity, such as small advertising agencies, research laboratories, and university faculties.

One difficulty of this style is that all group members must understand the goals and seek to attain them. In general, this managerial style tends to be more effective for professional subordinates. Managers do not give excessive direction to professionals but rather interact with them and allow them to make their own decision.

Choosing a leadership style. You can see that none of these styles is effective at all times, for managers must be concerned with *people* and *performance*. The ideal manager would use the leadership style that was best for the people as well as production.

Effect of contingency theory.   Various conditions exist that may influence the style of leadership and influence the manager's actions. According to the contingency theory, the appropriate answer to the question, "Which leadership style is best?" is: "It depends." It depends on the characteristics of the manager, the subordinates, and the situation.

The late Douglas M. McGregor tried to use the free-rein style as president of Antioch College. He tried to practice "good human relations" in order to eliminate discord and disagreement and cause the faculty and staff to like him. He hoped to serve as an "advisor" to the school and avoid some of the unpleasantness of making difficult decisions.

His desire did not work out in practice; so he had to tell the alumni and faculty in his final message: "I couldn't have been more wrong. It took a couple of years, but I finally began to realize that a leader cannot avoid the exercise of authority any more than he can avoid responsibility for what happens to his organization."[7]

A problem situation may require immediate attention and may have to be handled without consulting subordinates. With less time pressure, participative decision making may be desirable. If there must be a reduction in employment, you would probably be autocratic in deciding which employees to terminate, even if you usually allowed them to participate in decision making.

Effect of followers.   Some followers possess neither the ability nor the desire to assume responsibility and make decisions.

Paul Lawrence reported to the 50th Anniversary Symposium of the Hawthorne Studies that his research indicated that automobile assembly line workers did not want more responsible jobs. Instead, they wanted a specified amount of work to be done in a given period of time, good pay, and plenty of free time.[8]

When appropriate for the situation, the participative or free-rein style of leadership is preferred for job satisfaction.

Finally, consistency in leadership style appears to be more related to managerial effectiveness than the style used. In a series of opinion surveys, it was found that managers who failed to follow a consistent leadership style were graded far below the ones who were consistent, regardless of the style used.[9]

---

[7]Douglas M. McGregor, "On Leadership," *Antioch Notes*, May 1954, p. 3.

[8]Paul Lawrence, "Individual Differences in the World of Work," in Cass and Zimmer, *Man and Work in Society*, pp. 19-29.

[9]Phillip Sadler, "Leadership Style, Confidence in Management, and Job Satisfaction," *Journal of Applied Behavioral Science* 6 (March 1970):3-20.

COMMUNICATING WITH EMPLOYEES

Communication is involved in every aspect of a successful personnel program. *Communication* is the process of transmitting meanings, ideas, and understanding of a person or a group to another person or group.

Importance of Communicating

"Good communication . . . is the lifeblood of any enterprise," said the chief executive of a major corporation in a survey conducted by the International Association of Business Communicators (IABC).[10] Yet only two-thirds of the 50 U.S. and Canadian corporations surveyed had a formal communication program with clearly defined objectives.

The importance of communication was also reflected in another IABC survey in 1979, which found that 34 percent of the firms surveyed spent over $100,000 for employee communications media.[11]

The Communication Process

Communicating is a human activity, not a technical or mechanical process. Consequently, while I will try to explain it as a process, communication is really a human technique that varies with the people, positions, and situations involved.

As shown in Figure 11-4, communication is a cycle of interrelated stages that includes (1) an idea, thought, or mental impression, which (2) is translated, encoded, or put into symbols, which then (3) are transmitted to someone else, who (4) receives them and (5) retranslates or decodes them back into an idea. Yet communicating is not complete until there is some form of response.

FIGURE 11-4
The communication process

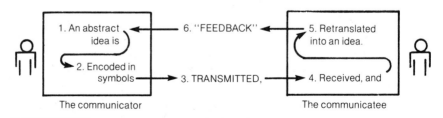

---

[10]"Corporate Communications," *Personnel Administrator* 24 (July 1979):111.
[11]"More Spent on Communication," *Personnel Administrator* 24 (December 1979):48.

Idea stage. In the idea stage, there are no words involved. There are thoughts, perceptions, sentiments, observations, reflections, or feelings that must be translated into symbols such as words, sounds, or gestures before they can be shared with another person or group.

Encoding stage. These ideas are transformed into a form of symbolic language (written, spoken, or gesture) called *encoding* or translating. The most frequently used symbols are words. This step is difficult, for we can't always find the symbol we need. We have all had occasion to say, "I can't say what I mean," or "I can't put it into words," or "You know what I mean."

Transmitting and receiving stages. The symbols must then be transmitted through some medium to their intended receiver. This medium will inevitably be subject to some "static," "noise," "filtering," or other interference, so that the exact symbols are not always received.

Decoding stage. Even though the person may receive the correct symbols, the retranslation, or *decoding*, of the message may result in quite different ideas, depending on the condition of the receiver. Also, the decoding can be no more perfect than the encoding.

Feedback stage. Frequently, communication ceases at the point where the message has been encoded, transmitted, received, and decoded. Yet, in superior-subordinate relations, the process must be repeated in reverse. Otherwise, we have no way to determine whether the decoded idea corresponds with the idea as it existed before encoding. This step requires *feedback*.

It can be seen from the above discussion that communication is a socializing process, involving a communicator (sender), a message (meaning), and a communicatee (receiver). As communication is the interchange of understanding, mental and emotional meanings are transmitted from one person or group to another by means of symbols. Each is compelled to think in terms of *who* says *what, to whom, how, when,* and *with what effect.* Thus, good communication is ultimately the result of clear thinking—and attentive listening.

Communication Channels

In any organization, there are at least three types of communication. They can be classed, on the basis of the nature of their flow, as (1) vertical, (2) horizontal, and (3) informal.

Vertical channels. Vertical channels are used when managers and subordinates communicate. As shown in Figure 11-5, vertical communication includes both a downward and an upward flow of messages through the organization structure. Organization charts tend to show the vertical channels of communication as well as the flow of authority and responsibility.

Face-to-face communication between the superior and subordinates is best for (1) improving motivation and aspiration, (2) advising what is to be done, (3) telling subordinates the consequences of their performance, and (4) providing feedback to—or from—management.

FIGURE 11-5
Vertical communication between manager and subordinates

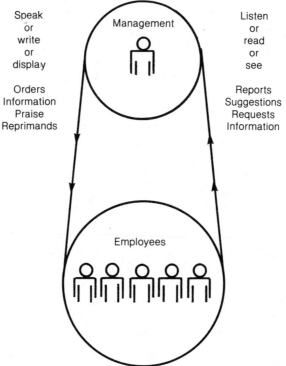

Horizontal channels.   Horizontal channels are used by managers on the same level to coordinate their activities. It also works the same way for non-managers on the same level. Horizontal and diagonal (or lateral) flows of communication transmit a large amount of information in any organization, as shown in Figure 11-6.

Informal channels.   Informal communication channels are known as the *grapevine.* The grapevine is quite effective. It (1) provides current news quickly, (2) is more free and open, and (3) flows between persons who know each other well.

Methods of Communicating

In choosing the proper method to use in communicating with employees, two questions must be answered: (1) What is to be communicated? (2) How is it to be communicated?

What to communicate?   Factual information, opinions, and attitudes are

FIGURE 11-6
Horizontal communications between people on the same level

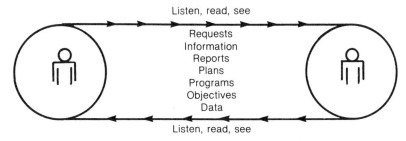

communicated. An example of a *fact* is an inspector telling a supervisor that "Arwen's production meets the quality specifications exactly." An example of an *opinion* is the statement, "I believe that Justin will grow with the job." An example of an *attitude* is a comment about a subordinate's attitude at work, such as "Jay is really committed to his work."

How to communicate? There are many ways of communicating, including verbal (oral and written) and nonverbal means.

Oral communication. Oral communication is the most direct form of communication. It is used by managers for discussions, conferences, and meetings. In order to be effective, oral communication should be a two-way street. The speaker should know the subject and organize it well; the receiver(s) should know how to listen. Some familiar examples are: sales talks, interviews, speeches, press conferences, and telephone communications.

Baker Industries, Inc., used telephone conference calls to discuss the energy situation. Managers and nonmanagers at five divisions in four states were free to ask the president any questions they wanted to about energy.[12]

Written communication. Written communication is used by managers at all levels in performing their basic managerial functions. In planning, managers communicate information such as objectives, goals, plans, and procedures. In organizing, job descriptions must be written. In directing, memos should be written to superiors and subordinates. In controlling, written reports may be submitted by a subordinate. Familiar examples of written communications to people outside the company are letters, annual reports, and press releases.

As shown in the previous chapter, *question boxes* and *suggestion systems* are forms of written communication.

---

[12]"Phone Link to the Top," *Personnel Administrator* 24 (October 1979):46.

"... and don't forget, Johnson, employee communications is a two-way street."

Source: Reprinted from the July, 1979 issue of *The Personnel Administrator* with permission of the American Society for Personnel Administration.

General Electric's Space Division offers "Suggestion Dollars" to any employee who mails in a suggestion. The $2 certificates can be cashed whether the suggestion is used or not. There is no limit to the number of certificates an employee can acquire.[13]

Nonverbal communication. *Nonverbal communication* is conveying a message without using speech or formal language. Instead, the message may be sent by eyes, eyebrows, facial expressions, tones of voice, hand positions, speech inflections, and body movements (sometimes called *body language*).

Requirements for Effective Communication

There are two related, but independent, requirements for improving communication. First, management must want to communicate with others. Second, some practical techniques should be developed. The following are suggested:

---

[13]"Idea Spur," *Personnel Administrator* 24 (October 1979):48.

1. Stress fairness, openness, and straight talk.
2. Encourage and expedite feedback and response from the receiver.
3. Improve listening, for it is more than merely being able to repeat the message. It involves attempting to understand the meaning of the message. When listening, try to fit your thoughts into the sender's framework.
4. Use as many different channels and appeal to as many senses as is feasible.
5. Repetition and some redundancy may be needed to overcome some barriers.
6. Select words carefully, avoid emotionally loaded terms, and encourage the "you" attitude.

MOTIVATING EMPLOYEES

Chris Evert Lloyd, the 2–5 favorite, lost the 1977 Wimbledon Tennis Championships to Virginia Wade in the semifinals. She explained her defeat by saying, "I could not reach deep inside myself and pull out what I needed to win."

She said she had seen "fire in Virginia's eyes" as the two came out on the court. "I think Virginia wanted to win worse than I did. . . . I couldn't get psyched up. . . . I was emotionally drained. After my matches with Tracy Austin and Billie Jean King, *I could not motivate myself.*"[14]

This story shows the need for, the difficulty of, and the process of motivation.

What Is Motivation?

Since managers must get things done through others, motivating subordinates to perform well is of major concern to most managers.

The words *motivating* and *motivation* are derived from the word *motive,* which is a drive, impulse, or desire that *moves* one toward a goal. A *motive* is an inner state that directs a person to seek to satisfy a felt need. *Managerial motivation* is the process by which managers stimulate employee behavior and direct it toward achieving desired personal and organizational goals.

Role of Motivation

As shown in earlier chapters, performance results from the interaction of physical, financial, and human resources. The first two are inanimate. They are translated into productivity, or performance, only when the human element is

---

[14]Associated Press story from Wimbledon, England, June 30, 1977. Emphasis added.

introduced. However, the human element introduces a variable over which management has only limited control.

When dealing with the inanimate factors of production, management can predict the input-output relationship. It can then vary the factors as it chooses in order to achieve a desired rate of production. In dealing with employees, however, the intangible factor of will, volition, or freedom of choice is introduced. Thus workers can—and do—increase or decrease their performance as they choose. This human quality leads to the need for positive motivation.

Performance results from ability and motivation.   Many managers expect self-motivation to do too much of their job. They assume that anyone can be motivated—if they try hard enough. This is not true, for performance occurs when people are motivated to use their abilities to do something, or:

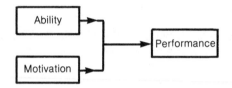

As seen in Figure 11–7, ability determines what employees *can do;* motivation determines what they *will do.* If performance were a function of ability alone, the relationship would be simple. An employee's output would vary directly with increases in ability. As ability increased, performance would increase directly and proportionately, as shown by performance curve 1 in Figure 11–7.

FIGURE 11–7
Relationships between ability, motivation, and performance

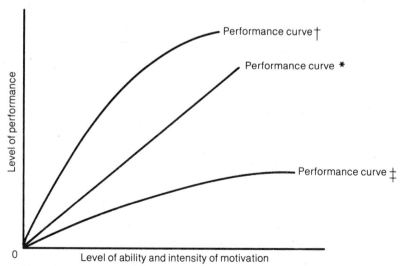

*Result of increasing ability and strong positive motivation.
†Level of performance expected with a given increase in ability but disregarding motivation.
‡Result of increasing ability but with a strong negative or weak positive motivation.

However, motivation is also necessary to encourage output. Hence the performance curve is related to the type and extent of motivation. It can be seen from performance curve 2 that where there is strong positive motivation, the employee's output steadily increases. Where there is strong negative motivation—or weak positive motivation—the person's performance level will be low, regardless of changes in ability, as shown by performance curve 3.

Other factors influencing performance.   In addition to ability and motivation, there are many factors influencing a person's performance. Refer back to Figure 11-3. You will see that the *societal* (total) and *organizational environments* affect the behavior of both managers and nonmanagers.

A few of the societal factors are (1) technology, (2) the social, political, educational, and economic systems, (3) cultural and religious beliefs, (4) personal problems, and (5) the communications system.

Can you see why motivation is so complex, hard to understand, and difficult to effect?

A study was undertaken to determine how some of these variables affected employee job performance and personal satisfaction. About 775 scientists and technicians employed in a large midwestern business organization were asked to rank 17 variables for both dimensions on a questionnaire.

The results indicated that (1) personal accomplishment, (2) praise for good work, (3) getting along with co-workers, (4) company location, and (5) receiving credit for ideas had a greater impact on *personal satisfaction* than on their job effort.

However, (1) knowing what was expected of them, (2) having a capable supervisor, (3) having challenging work and responsibility, (4) being kept informed, and (5) participating in decisions were all given more importance for their effects on *performance.*[15]

Employees are already motivated.   Most of us assume that everyone must be stimulated to do what we want them to do. In reality, this is not true. Most people have a natural, built-in motivation.[16] From a practical point of view, managers need to appeal to that self-motivation. They should look for signs of declining motivation and use positive methods to encourage performance.

Theories of Work Motivation

It is difficult to condense and compare the prevailing theories of work motivation, as they are based on different assumptions and often focus on different dimensions of performance. Complicating the problem is the fact that theorists often give different names to the same concept.

---

[15]P. F. Werniment, P. Toren, and H. Kapell, "Comparison of Sources of Personal Satisfaction and of Work Motivation," *Journal of Applied Psychology* 54 (February 1970):95–102.

[16]Read Don Spiegel, "How NOT to Motivate," *Supervisory Management* 22 (November 1977):11–15, for a fascinating discussion of how managers *demotivate* employees.

In general, the theories can be classified as follows:

1. *Prescriptive models* try to tell management *how to motivate* employees. Examples are (a) Taylor's scientific management, (b) the human relations model, and (c) McGregor's Theory Y.
2. *Content models* are concerned with the question of *what causes behavior.* The most popular of these theories are (a) Maslow's hierarchy of needs, (b) Herzberg's motivation-hygiene theory, and (c) McClelland's "need for achievement" theory.
3. *Process models* deal with *how behavior originates and is performed.* These include the (a) equity, and (b) expectancy theories.

Maslow's hierarchy of needs. Abraham Maslow developed a theory based on the concept of a hierarchy of needs.[17] Figure 11–8 shows that the hierarchy of needs progresses through five basic levels:

---

[17]These needs were introduced by A. H. Maslow in *Motivation and Personality* (New York: Harper & Bros., 1954) and modified by Douglas McGregor in *The Human Side of Enterprise* (New York: McGraw-Hill Book Co., 1960).

1. *Physiological needs* include the need for food, drink, sex, shelter, clothing, rest, sleep, and respiration.
2. *Safety,* or *security, needs* are the need for protection against danger— attack, the elements, job layoffs, and other dangers.
3. *Belonging,* or *social, needs* involve association and interaction with others in groups for love, friendship, affection, and acceptance.
4. *Esteem, status,* or *ego needs* are related to self-respect, the respect of others, prestige, recognition, and ego satisfaction.
5. *Self-actualization,* or *realization, needs* motivate us to seek self-development, self-expression, creativity, and self-fulfillment through becoming what we are capable of becoming.

As shown in Figure 11–8, these needs are arranged in an order of priority in which lower level (physiological) needs are satisfied before higher level needs are activated. A lower level need does not have to be completely satisfied before a higher level one becomes involved. However, once a particular need has been completely satisfied, it is no longer an effective motivator.

An example familiar to you is an employee's earnings. As soon as those earnings are high enough to provide the employee with the basics for survival and shelter (satisfying physiological and safety needs), he or she begins to seek the association and respect of others on the job (to satisfy social and esteem needs).

In attempting to satisfy self-actualization needs, individuals should have levels of aspiration equal to or higher than their abilities and developmental level. If one's level of aspiration does not increase, one's motivation will be limited.

A friend of the great Danish sculptor Albert Thorvaldsen, looking at a piece of sculpture that seemed to be perfect, said, "Now you must be satisfied with this great production." The artist answered that this was not

FIGURE 11–8
Order of priority of human needs

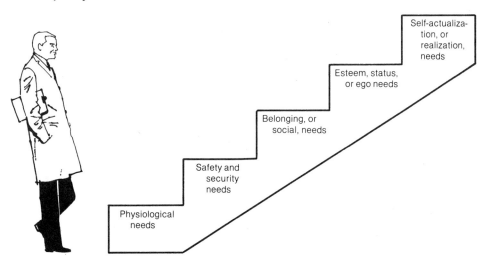

true because "I must be going downhill when I find my work equal to my aspirations."

Herzberg's motivation-hygiene theory. Herzberg's motivation-hygiene theory assumes that the relationship between job factors such as personal attitudes and performance cannot be studied in isolation but must be studied together.[18] In a study of relatively well-educated employees, he found that there are two sets of job attitudes and factors.

The first-level factors are objective elements that, if present, will not lead to motivation but will contribute to job satisfaction. If they are not present, they lead to dissatisfaction and possibly negative motivation. These he called *hygiene factors*, as shown in Table 11-1.

The second set of factors includes employees' perceptions and introspections of themselves, or of their attempts to define their need and value systems. This second group is referred to as *motivating factors*.

Herzberg stated that providing and maintaining the proper hygiene factors is necessary to satisfy the lower level needs and thereby obtain minimal employee performance and satisfaction. Providing the proper motivating factors is necessary to achieve the participative attitude that produces outstanding employee performance.

McClelland's achievement motive theory. McClelland's achievement theory is quite extensive and involved. His greatest contribution is in developing the *achievement motive*.[19] According to him, every motive, except seeking pleasure and avoiding displeasure or pain, is a learned one.

TABLE 11-1
Motivating and hygiene factors according to Herzberg's motivation-hygiene theory

Motivating factors	Hygiene factors
Achievement	Company policies and administration
Responsibility	Quality of technical supervision
Recognition	Interpersonal relationships
Advancement	Salary
Work itself	Job security
Possibility of growth on the job	Working conditions
	Fringe benefits
	Job status
	Personal life

---

[18]Frederick Herzberg et al., *The Motivation to Work*, 2d ed. (New York: John Wiley & Sons, 1959).

[19]David C. McClelland, *Studies in Motivation* (New York: Appleton-Century-Crofts, 1955).

He identified three needs that motivate behavior. They are (1) power, (2) affiliation, and (3) achievement. All people have these needs, but they have them in differing degrees.

An oversimplified conclusion is that (1) the need for achievement can be learned, and (2) by appealing to it, management can call forth the self-motivation present in the employee.

Equity theory. Equity theory assumes that people are motivated by the desire to be treated equitably and fairly.[20] Employees are willing to exchange their inputs of time, effort, and production for outcomes such as compensation and other tangible and intangible rewards. Motivation comes from comparing one's inputs and outcomes with those of others. As long as a worker perceives that there is equity in the way she or he is paid and treated, performance will be satisfactory.

If employees think they are being treated inequitably, they will withhold or perform at a reduced level.

Expectancy theory. One of the best known of these theories is the expectancy theory.[21] According to this theory, employees' motivation is the force driving them to achieve some level of job performance. This force or effort depends upon their perception of the likelihood that certain outcomes will result from their effort and the value they place on those outcomes.

For example, if employees believe that they will be paid higher wages if they perform at a high level than if they do not, and if the higher income is of value to them, they will produce more. In achieving the high level of performance, the worker gains satisfaction, which, in turn, influences future efforts. If the employee also receives the expected higher income, it will provide satisfaction, which, in turn, will tend to make future incomes appear more valuable.

The *Porter-Lawler theory* is also based on the expectancy theory of motivation.[22] It is a future-oriented expectancy theory that emphasizes the anticipated response or outcome. It assumes that managers particularly rely upon these future expectations rather than on past learning, as you can see from Figure 11-9. As employees perceive that performance (6) leads to intrinsic (7A) and extrinsic (7B) rewards and satisfaction (9), that the rewards have value (1), and that effort will probably be rewarded (2), they will exert the effort (3) to perform (6).

Reinforcement theory. An overgeneralization is that reinforcement theories are based on the *stimulus-response relationship*. B. F. Skinner tested the stimulus-response model and emphasized the reinforcement aspect.[23] He dis-

---

[20]J. S. Adams, "Toward an Understanding of Inequity," *Journal of Abnormal and Social Psychology* 67 (November 1963):425ff.

[21]Victor H. Vroom, *Work and Motivation* (New York: John Wiley & Sons, 1964), pp. 192–210.

[22]Lyman W. Porter and Edward E. Lawler III, *Managerial Attitudes and Performance* (Homewood, Ill.: Richard D. Irwin, 1968).

[23]B. F. Skinner, *About Behaviorism* (New York: Alfred A. Knopf, 1974).

FIGURE 11-9
The Porter and Lawler motivational model

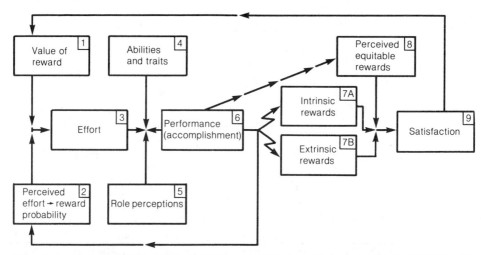

Source: Lyman W. Porter and Edward E. Lawler III, *Managerial Attitudes and Performance* (Homewood, Ill.: Richard D. Irwin, 1968), p. 165. Used with permission.

tinguished *reinforcement,* which is the presentation of an attractive reward following a response or the removal of an unpleasant or negative condition following a response, from *punishment,* which is the reverse of reinforcement.

Motivation results from efforts to achieve reinforcement and avoid punishment. Training, development, and growth occur through reinforcement or focusing behavioral responses on what should be done.

Goal-setting theory.   Management-by-objectives (MBO) is based on the goal-setting theory. This technique will be covered in the next chapter.

Using Expectancy Theory to Motivate Different Behaviors

There are many types of behavior that management tries to motivate. For example, managers try to motivate employees to (1) join the organization, (2) maintain regular and prompt attendance, (3) perform properly, and (4) remain with the organization.

The motivation tends to be different for each of these behaviors. In general, the motivation to join an organization depends upon (1) the attractiveness of the organization and (2) the expectancy of being accepted.[24]

From a practical point of view, salary and working conditions are relatively more important in *attracting a new employee* than in motivating performance.

---

[24]John P. Wanous, *Organizational Entry: Recruitment, Selection, and Socialization of Newcomers* (Reading, Mass.: Addison-Wesley Publishing Co., 1980), pp. 91-94 and 98-99.

Since 1957, I have used questionnaires to survey what junior and senior personnel majors looked for in their first full-time job. In 93 percent of the surveys, "wages and salary" ranked first.

Motivators such as achievement, recognition, and challenging work serve better to *motivate performance*—at least for professional, technical, and other white-collar employees.

Contests and financial rewards have been found effective in *motivating attendance*.

Employee benefits can be used to *retain employees*, as will be seen in Chapter 17.

IMPROVING EMPLOYEES' SELF-PERCEPTION

If people are as important as this text has shown, what can personnel executives do to help them grow—as individuals? There are several things that can be done, including developing a more enlightened attitude toward the role of individuals in an organization. While these attitudes have been called by many names, the most frequently used are the *factor-of-production, human relations,* and *human resources* philosophies. The last, which is now generally accepted by personnel managers as the proper approach in dealing with employees, tends to incorporate the better elements of the previous two systems of thought.

Factor-of-Production Approach

The classical approach, which regarded employees as merely another economic factor of production, reached its peak of acceptance during the 1930s. It tended to be used by the owner-entrepreneurs of some business firms, as well as by many managers of nonbusiness activities, such as government units.

To a certain extent, this system of thought provided the background for Douglas McGregor's *Theory X*, which stated that the average human being (1) was lazy, (2) disliked work, (3) shunned responsibility, and (4) had to be coerced into effective performance.[25] Most personnel managers have abandoned this concept along with any conclusions they may have drawn concerning its relevance to employee behavior.[26]

---

[25]If you have not already read it, you should read McGregor's *The Human Side of Enterprise,* pp. 33–47, for a fuller explanation of Theory X and Theory Y.

[26]Yet a survey of over 400 graduate and undergraduate business students at Pennsylvania State University found that a majority of them believed that most people "have no ambition," "dislike responsibility," and "are not very bright." See "Surprise! Theory Xers Outnumber Theory Yers," *Training/*HRD 16 (April 1979):13.

"Now then, what makes you feel that we're dehumanizing you, 624078?"

Reprinted by permission *The Wall Street Journal*

Human Relations Approach

The Hawthorne experiments and early research by behavioral scientists emphasized the concept that "people are human and like to be treated as such." The model for this management method was:

Employee participation → Job satisfaction → Increased productivity

In its purest form, this model was similar to McGregor's *Theory Y*, which stated that it is generally accepted that (1) work is normal, (2) people need and desire to work, and (3) the intellectual and productive capabilities of employees are only partially utilized.

Employees in a large retail firm were tested on their perceptions of their supervisors' behaviors. Subordinates who perceived their supervisor as possessing Theory Y assumptions of employee behavior tended to be better satisfied with their jobs than others.

Human Resources Approach

Now, the human resources approach, which views the productivity of employees as an economic resource of an organization, is popular.[27] While their per-

---

[27]This is an oversimplified model of the human resources approach to human administration. For a more intensive and explicit presentation of this approach, see Raymond E. Miles, "Human Relations or Human Resources?" *Harvard Business Review* 43 (July–August 1965):148–63.

formance is measured by the economic criteria of productivity, efficiency, effectiveness, costs, and profitability, the employees themselves, in their relationships to other members of the organization, are viewed as having dignity, worth, and value.

When 254 managers were given a test to determine how they felt about the present attitudes of employees, most responded that employees tend to resist change, and that the behavior of today's employees is influenced by a complex blend of social, economic, psychological, and biological factors.

These tests indicated that managers today do not believe in either Theory X or Theory Y but rather try to combine them to meet various situations.[28] This is the approach favored by most managers today.

SUMMARY AND CONCLUSIONS

One of the greatest needs in personnel work is for effective managerial leadership, communication, and motivation.

Leadership occurs when one causes another person to work toward some specific goal. The leadership process is an interaction between the leader, the followers, and the situation.

Different styles of leadership used by different managers vary from the manager-dominated to the cooperative approach. But the three most popular leadership styles are the (1) authoritarian, (2) participative, and (3) free-rein.

An important part of managerial leadership is communication, whereby the meanings, ideas, and understanding of a person or a group are conveyed to another person or group. Communication starts with (1) a wordless idea or thought, which (2) is translated or encoded into symbols, which (3) are transmitted to someone else, who (4) receives them, (5) retranslates or decodes them back into an idea similar to the meaning meant by the sender, and (6) sends feedback to the sender.

Among the many ways of communicating are verbal (oral and written) and nonverbal means. Effective communication ultimately results from clear thinking and attentive listening.

Leadership also includes motivating, which is the process by which managers achieve the best performance by convincing subordinates that their personal needs can best be satisfied by working within the organization.

The most popular motivation theories are Maslow's hierarchy of needs, Herzberg's motivation-hygiene concept, McClelland's achievement motive theory, equity theory, Vroom's expectancy theory, the Porter-Lawler expectancy model, Skinner's reinforcement theory, and goal-path theory.

Maslow's hierarchy of needs says that low-level needs must be satisfied

---

[28]This research was reported by Louis A. Allen in "M for Management: Theory Y Updated," *Personnel Journal* 52 (December 1973): 1061-67.

before high-level ones are activated. Once a particular need has been completely satisfied, it is no longer an effective motivator.

Herzberg found that the real motivators are related to achievement, responsibility, advancement, growth on the job, and the satisfaction of self-esteem and self-actualization needs.

Equity theory assumes that people are motivated by their wish to be treated equitably in their work situation. If they perceive that there is equity, they will be positively motivated.

Reinforcement theory is based on the expectation that (1) behavior that is rewarded tends to be repeated, and (2) behavior that is not rewarded, or is punished, tends not to be repeated.

Expectancy theory says that people are motivated by (1) the outcomes they expect from given inputs and (2) the belief that those outcomes can be attained by a given behavior pattern. This theory should help personnel managers to (1) attract new employees, (2) maintain employee attendance, (3) improve performance, and (4) retain employees.

The unresolved question facing personnel managers is whether employees have traded a satisfaction of the spirit, which their work formerly afforded them, for economic assurances that they did not previously enjoy. That is, have they substituted material benefits for a more intangible satisfaction of indefinable longings?

It can be concluded from the material in the chapter that: *Managerial effectiveness depends on the interdependence of the members of the work group and the interaction of the manager with the subordinates.* Therefore, effective managers are those who stay psychologically close enough to maintain helpful contacts with subordinates, yet maintain sufficient distance to deal objectively with poor performance. Successful managers will also use the leadership and communication techniques that are most effective in motivating improved performance.

Finally, for an organization to be most successful, its personnel executives need to use various motivational theories to develop the full potential of the members of the organization.

QUESTIONS

1. Explain how an individual's goals may conflict with organizational goals. How may they be compatible?
2. What are the factors that affect a given leadership situation? Discuss the relationships between these factors.
3. What are the most popular leadership styles? Explain.
4. What role is played by *expectations* and *perceptions* as far as leadership and motivation are concerned?
5. What are the main themes of the following selected motivational theorists: (*a*) Maslow? (*b*) Herzberg? (*c*) McClelland? (*d*) Porter and Lawler?

6. What is communication? Explain the process.

7. What are the stages involved in the communication process? Explain.

PROBLEMS

11–1. The Overworked Maids

The assistant housekeeper of a small hospital gave the following example as her greatest supervisory problem.

"We have seven maids and five orderlies working with us. All of them do acceptable work, but some do better work than others. Two of our maids, Mary and Jane, do much better work than the others and are more dependable. For this reason, some of the other maids and orderlies take advantage of them, and this has really become a problem. As we make rounds to check on different areas of the hospital, maybe a bathroom or room isn't as clean as it should be. We then send Mary or Jane to do the job over. So some of the other workers do their work only halfway, knowing that Mary or Jane will be sent to do it over.

"We didn't realize that this wasn't being fair to any of the maids until we had a meeting and discussed the problem. Now we must do something."

Questions

1. What would you suggest doing to motivate the maids and orderlies?
2. What was the message conveyed to the workers when their unsatisfactory work was turned over to Mary and Jane?
3. What message did Mary and Jane receive?
4. Can you apply any of the motivation theories to this case? Explain.

11–2. The Reluctant Office Worker

Bob has worked in the office for four years. He is quite capable, personable, and willing to receive supervision and correction. But he continually fails to comply with suggestions for improvement and disregards the office's rules, procedures, and policies. It is apparent to everyone that his attitude is friendly, and he cooperates with everyone. He seldom has a personality clash or disagrees with anyone.

The job Bob has involves dealing with the public; so he could hurt the firm if he wanted to. He spends too much time on personal business, as he owns part interest in a restaurant and manages it at night. He uses his office time for this and other personal affairs instead of doing his job.

The manager frequently talks to Bob, and he readily promises her that he will improve. Yet, as soon as she is gone, he goes back to his usual ways.

Questions

1. What would you do if you were the manager?
2. How would you do it?
3. How do you motivate this type of employee?

SUGGESTED READINGS FOR FURTHER STUDY

Appelbaum, Steven H.   "Human Resources Development: A Foundation for Participative Leadership." *Personnel Administrator* 24 (March 1979):50–56.

Archer, Earnest R.   "The Myth of Motivation." *Personnel Administrator* 23 (December 1978):57–64.

Curley, Douglas G.   "Employee Sounding Boards: Answering the Participative Need." *Personnel Administrator* 23 (May 1978):69–73.

Davis, Keith.   *Human Behavior at Work.* New York: McGraw-Hill Book Co., 1977.

Denzler, Richard D.   "People and Productivity: Do They Still Equal Pay and Profits?" *Personnel Journal* 53 (January 1974):59–63.

Grazulis, Cheryl.   "Communicating Corporate Attitudes through Annual Reports." *Personnel Administrator* 24 (July 1979):51–55.

Hughes, Charles L.   "If It's Right for You, It's Wrong for Employees." *Personnel Administrator* 24 (December 1979):39–44.

Kirkpatrick, Donald L.   "Communications: 'Everybody Talks about It but . . .'" *Personnel Administrator* 23 (January 1978):46–50.

Loffreda, Robert.   "Employee Attitude Surveys: A Valuable Motivating Tool." *Personnel Administrator* 24 (July 1979):41–43.

Schindler, John A.   *How to Live 365 Days a Year.* Englewood Cliffs, N. J.: Prentice-Hall, 1954.

Thompson, Donald B.   "Many Fail Management's Sternest Test." *Industry Week,* March 1979, pp. 91–94.

CHAPTER TWELVE

Evaluating Employee Performance

Learning Objectives

After studying the material in this chapter, you should be able to:

1. Explain the role of performance appraisals in a personnel system and show why appraisals are increasing in importance.
2. Discuss why appraisals are used.
3. List what is included in performance appraisals.
4. Name and describe the popular methods of appraising performance and explain why each is used.
5. Suggest ways to improve performance appraisals.
6. Describe some personnel actions resulting from appraisals.
7. Name the groups needing career counseling and explain their needs.

Some Important Words and Terms

Performance appraisal

Peer ratings

Subordinate appraisals

Simple ranking

Rank order

Paired comparison

Forced distribution

Traditional rating scales

Behaviorally anchored rating scales (BARS)

Job dimensions

Anchors

Forced-choice method

Essay method

Critical incidents method

Management by objectives (MBO)

Self-fulfilling prophecy

Halo effect

Horn effect

Bias

Inflation of ratings

Central tendency

Reliability

Upgrading

Seniority Merit

Super-seniority

Synthetic seniority

Career counseling

Career development workshops

Always dream and shoot higher than you know you can do. Don't bother just to be better than your contemporaries or predecessors. Try to be better than yourself.
WILLIAM FAULKNER

Outline of the Chapter

In 1813, General Lewis Cass, the Commanding Officer of the 27th Infantry Regiment, United States Army, submitted to the War Department what has since become famous as the earliest recorded instance of a formal evaluation report. It has also been cited frequently as a humorous example of performance rating, for General Cass characterized each of his men in picturesque but archaic terms as, for example, "a good-natured man" or "a knave despised by all."[1]

The system today may be a little more formal, the language a little less striking and colorful, and the forms more advanced and complex. But the purpose and problems of performance appraisal are still the same.

The purpose is for one person to evaluate the job performance of another person. The problems are also still the same, namely (1) how to keep personal judgments and biases from influencing the appraisal and (2) how to use the results in future personnel actions. This chapter will discuss these and other aspects of performance appraisals.

ROLE OF PERFORMANCE APPRAISALS IN A PERSONNEL SYSTEM

Employers and employees are constantly using some form of formal or informal performance evaluation. For example, employees use it when they discuss how other employees perform. Managers use it when they praise or criticize an employee, make a salary adjustment, or promote one person over others.

Growing Importance of Performance Appraisals

Most employers have developed formal programs for improving employee performance, growth, and development. It is also one of the most frequently used techniques. According to a survey by the Bureau of National Affairs, 93 percent of the firms surveyed have appraisal programs. Yet only 10 percent of the personnel executives of those firms felt that their appraisal programs were effective.[2]

Now, most employers are trying to improve their appraisal programs as they are being used more, and for more purposes.

What Are Performance Appraisals?

Performance appraisal is the process an employer uses to determine whether an employee is performing the job as intended. *Merit rating, efficiency rating, service rating,* and *employee appraisal* are some other frequently used terms for performance appraisal.

---

[1]F. M. Lopez, *Evaluating Employee Performance* (Chicago: Public Personnel Association, 1968), p. 27.

[2]John D. Colby and Ronald L. Wallance, "Performance Appraisal: Help or Hindrance to Employee Productivity?" *Personnel Administrator* 20 (October 1975):38ff.

How Performance Appraisals Operate

First, if production can be measured, there is less need for employee appraisal. Each person can be judged according to the amount produced. However, if the work performed cannot be measured, the personal characteristics that lead to favorable behavior and increased performance must be appraised.

You should be able to understand performance appraisal better by referring to Figure 12-1. Notice that (1) employees have personal qualities, which lead to (2) job behaviors, which result in (3) work performance, which the manager (4) appraises, so that (5) personnel actions can be taken.

FIGURE 12-1
How performance appraisals operate

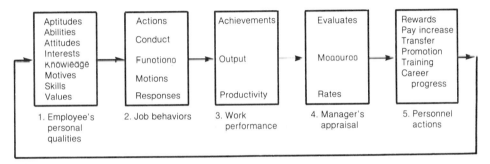

Aptitudes Abilities Attitudes Interests Knowledge Motives Skills Values	Actions Conduct Functions Motions Responses	Achievements Output Productivity	Evaluates Measures Rates	Rewards Pay increase Transfer Promotion Training Career progress
1. Employee's personal qualities	2. Job behaviors	3. Work performance	4. Manager's appraisal	5. Personnel actions

The theory assumes that there are personal abilities and qualities that lead to behaviors that result in performance, and that these can be perceived and measured, or evaluated. Some of these personal qualities are work quality, reliability, cooperativeness, job knowledge, initiative, attitude, safety consciousness, attendance, learning ability, health and physical condition, adaptability, judgment, responsibility, and skill.

A second assumption is that the manager can objectively evaluate employees' productive contributions on the basis of their personal characteristics and job behaviors. One of the most valid criticisms of employee appraisals is that objective evaluations cannot be made, as the ratings are usually subjective and deal with other qualities not related to performance.

WHY DO APPRAISALS?

Figure 12-2 shows that there are two overall purposes of performance appraisals. First, they can be used for making administrative decisions. Second, they can be used for employee career planning and development. The purpose of the appraisals will determine the (1) bases for comparison, (2) techniques to be used, (3) role of the supervisor, and (4) distribution to be made of the evaluations. Whether done for administrative or development purposes, appraisals can also serve the secondary purpose of motivating employees.

FIGURE 12-2
Purposes of employee performance appraisals

	Purpose of employee performance appraisal	
	Employee development	Administrative
Definition of purpose	Performance improvement through advising employee what is expected	Information for decisions about: salary adjustments transfers promotions reduction-in-force
Basis for comparison	Performance relative to predetermined standards of performance (absolute standard)	Performance relative to other similar employees (relative standard)
Technique of appraisal	Results-oriented appraisal	Employee ranking
Role of supervisor	Counselor	Judge
Distribution of evaluation information	Employee and supervisor	Employee, supervisor, personnel folder, others involved in administrative actions listed above

Source: Robert J. Hayden, "Performance Appraisal: A Better Way," *Personnel Journal* 52 (July 1973):610. Reprinted with permission, *Personnel Journal*, copyright July 1973.

For Administrative Purposes

When used for administrative purposes, appraisals (1) serve as a basis for granting merit salary adjustment, (2) help in selecting people for transfers, promotions, and demotions, (3) validate selection techniques to meet EEO requirements, (4) determine the employee's training needs, and (5) provide a basis for reducing the work force.

When done for these purposes, the evaluation is based on comparing the performance of one employee with that of other workers. The role of the supervisors and other managers, including the personnel manager, is to judge the employee's performance. As shown in the figure, the evaluation results are distributed to several people.

For Development Purposes

Appraisals may also be made—or used—for development purposes. In this case, they provide employees with (1) information about the performance expectations (standards of performance) of their supervisor, (2) feedback regarding subsequent performance, (3) advice, coaching, or counseling to help them meet expectations that have not been achieved, and (4) a basis for career planning and development.

When appraisals are used this way, the basis of comparison is the employee's actual performance against absolute work standards. The role of the supervisor is that of a counselor, mentor, guide, or instructor. The results of the evaluation are given to the supervisor and the employee.

For Motivational Purposes

The mere process of using a valid, objective appraisal system should have a motivational effect on employees. It should foster initiative, develop a sense of responsibility, and increase the employees' efforts toward achieving personal and organizational goals. Performance evaluation also gives employees a better understanding of job responsibilities, relationships with co-workers, the work expected of them, and their training needs.

The process also aids appraisers by providing them with a greater understanding of their subordinates' job behavior, the job itself, and each employee's strengths and weaknesses.

WHO SHOULD DO THE APPRAISING?

The people and groups who usually do the appraising include (1) the immediate supervisor, (2) employees' peers, (3) employees themselves, and (4) subordinates.

Immediate Supervisor

Rating of employees by their superior is the traditional and most frequently used approach. In fact, this is a part of all managers' responsibility that they cannot avoid. Also, supervisors are in the best position to know the job requirements, to observe employees at work, and to make the best value judgments.

Yet there are indications that peer ratings, self-appraisals, and subordinate appraisals offer insights that are not available elsewhere.

A Conference Board study found that almost 95 percent of the respondents listed their immediate supervisor as one of the appraisers. Other people listed as appraisers were self (about 13 percent of the time), groups or committees (6 percent), and personnel staff (6 percent).[3]

---

[3]*Appraising Managerial Performance: Current Practices and Future Directions*, Conference Board Report no. 723 (New York: Conference Board, 1977), p. 26.

Peers

The *peer rating* method is frequently called the "mutual rating system." In effect, each employee evaluates each of the other members of the work group by secret ballot.

A modification of this system is used at TRW, Inc. Performance evaluations are made by executives' supervisors as well as by their peer groups. Before making a decision about an executive's need for development, possibilities for promotion, or the like, the supervisor talks to the people who regularly work with the executive to see what they think about his or her performance.[4]

Employees Themselves

A new trend is to let subordinates, especially managers, rate themselves. This method encourages personal career planning. These ratings are usually not a part of the employee's regular performance evaluation. There are exceptions, though.

At Citibank, the senior vice president simply hands subordinates their own blank evaluation forms and asks them to fill in their ratings. According to one vice president, "It's amazing how honest people are. They put in things that are detrimental to their own progress and promotion." The procedure has a built-in safeguard, as the vice president makes a final review of the ratings.

Subordinates

Some firms are now using *subordinate appraisals,* whereby subordinates rate their superiors. This is useful in trying to develop better superior-subordinate relationships. It is also helpful to supervisors who want to improve their human relationships.

HOW SHOULD APPRAISALS BE DONE?

The greatest criticism of these systems is a lack of understanding of how performance is appraised. There are many procedures used and many ways of classifying them. But the most useful classification is to divide (1) those that compare the employee with other employees from (2) those that compare the

---

[4]Herbert E. Meyer, "How They're Doing," *Fortune,* January 1974, p. 106.

PRISCILLA'S POP

employee to absolute work standards. The first is called the *ranking method,* the second the *rating method.*

By Comparing with Other Employees

When appraisals are used for administrative purposes, it is desirable to compare an employee against others. This helps the appraiser to make the difficult decisions.

Ranking systems are well suited to this purpose, for they compare employees directly with each other. They are fairly easy to develop, they yield consistent results, and they are easily understood.

Yet these systems tend to measure only overall performance, not specific behaviors. Therefore, they are not very useful for development purposes. They do not tell employees how well or poorly they are doing relative to job standards. Hence they provide little meaningful feedback to help an employee with career planning.

The usual methods are (1) simple ranking, (2) paired comparison, and (3) forced distribution.

Simple ranking.   In using the *simple ranking* (sometimes called the *rank order*) method, the evaluator arrays the employees from the best to the poorest on some performance dimension.

Paired comparison.   With the *paired comparison* method, every employee is paired with every other worker in the group. Then the supervisor must decide which of the two subordinates in each pair is more valuable to the firm. This procedure is repeated until each person has been paired with every other employee and each one's rank relative to every other person has been determined. The main disadvantages of this system are that it is complex and the volume of work is great. Yet research has shown that this method is more reliable than simple ranking.

Forced distribution.   Under the *forced distribution* method, the rater is forced to place the employees in a few groups—say three to six—according to their performance. The purpose of this technique, which is similar to "grading on the curve," is to overcome any tendency for evaluators to be either too lenient or too severe in their ratings. However, it can lead to an invalid assessment unless the group of individuals actually represents a "normal distribution" in performance and/or potential.

The advantage of this method is that all the values cannot be stacked at one end of the scale. Instead, there must be a distribution of the individuals over the entire curve, from "best" to "worst." Also, this system is useful when the performance of several employees is nearly the same.

At a progressive hospital, the evaluators can allocate no more than 20 percent to the highest category on the scale, around 70 percent to the middle of the scale, and about 10 percent to the lowest group.

By Comparing Against Established Work Standards

For development purposes, it is better to use methods that evaluate the employee's performance against established work standards. In using these methods, the appraiser evaluates each person against several specific items concerning traits, attitudes, skill, knowledge, job behaviors, or work results. Thus each person is told how well he or she is doing on a specific item, rather than on overall performance.

The most popular of these methods are (1) the traditional rating scales, (2) behaviorally anchored rating scales (BARS), (3) the forced-choice rating method, and (4) management by objectives (MBO), which will be covered separately.

Traditional rating scales.   As shown in Figure 12–3, the *traditional rating scales* use numbers, graphic scales, or multiple-step scales. The degrees are expressed in positions, numbers, or terms, with the rater circling, checking, or putting a number in a position.

These methods of rating have built-in possibilities for error, such as the rater's being (1) opposed to some personal attribute of the ratee, (2) unable to translate estimates of competence into a scale or number, or (3) unable to translate value judgments into numbers or points on a scale. Also, the scales tend to be a continuum, with the values ranging from a negative end to a positive end. The midpoint should be average. However, as there is a human tendency to give a negative meaning to anything that is average, there is constant pressure to rate people between average and superior, rather than along the entire scale.

Behaviorally anchored rating scales (BARS).   *Behaviorally anchored rating scales* were designed to be used as a behaviorally based evaluation tool.[5] They are a technique for specifying the actual job behaviors needed to obtain objectives.

---

[5]Craig E. Schneier and Richard W. Beatty, Jr., "Developing Behaviorally Anchored Rating Scales (BARS)," *Personnel Administrator* 24 (August 1979):59–68. This is one of the best articles on this subject.

FIGURE 12-3
Examples of graphic and numerical rating scales

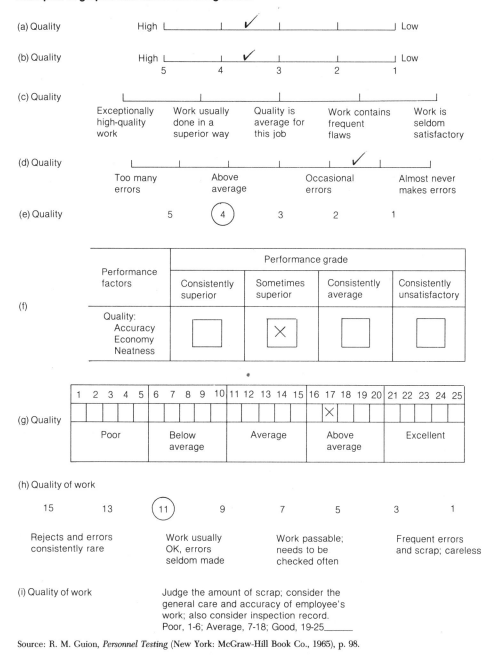

Source: R. M. Guion, *Personnel Testing* (New York: McGraw-Hill Book Co., 1965), p. 98.

FIGURE 12-4
Example of a behaviorally anchored rating scale—Job dimension: planning, organizing, and scheduling project assignments and due dates

7 [ ] EXCELLENT	Develops a comprehensive project plan, documents it well, obtains required approval and distributes the plan to all concerned.
6 [ ] VERY GOOD	Plans, communicates, and observes milestones; states week-by-week where the project stands relative to plans. Maintains up-to-date charts of project accomplishments and backlogs and uses these to optimize any schedule modifications required.
	Experiences occasional minor operational problems, but communicates effectively.
5 [ ] GOOD	Lays out all the parts of a job and schedules each part; seeks to beat schedule and will allow for slack.
	Satisfies customers' time constraints; time and cost overruns occur infrequently.
4 [ ] AVERAGE	Makes a list of due dates and revises them as the project progresses, usually adding unforeseen events; instigates frequent customer complaints.
	May have a sound plan, but does not keep track of milestones; does not report slippages in schedule or other problems as they occur.
3 [ ] BELOW AVERAGE	Plans are poorly defined; unrealistic time schedules are common.
	Cannot plan more than a day or two ahead; has no concept of a realistic project due date.
2 [ ] VERY POOR	Has no plan or schedule of work segments to be performed.
	Does little or no planning for project assignments.
1 [ ] UNACCEPTABLE	Seldom, if ever, completes project because of lack of planning and does not seem to care.
	Fails consistently due to lack of planning and does not inquire about how to improve.

Source: Reprinted from the August, 1979 issue of *The Personnel Administrator* with permission of The American Society for Personnel Administration.

There are five to ten scales in a set—one scale for each job dimension. *Job dimensions* are the broad groups of duties, activities, and responsibilities that make up the job.

Figure 12-4 is an example of a scale for one dimension of a manager's job, called "planning, organizing, and scheduling project assignments and due dates."

Note that BARS are vertical scales, with several anchors listed. *Anchors* are brief statements of actual worker behavior on the job. They indicate the specific degrees of job performance. There are usually seven to ten of these statements. They vary from the poorest performance level at the bottom to the highest level at the top. In the scale shown, the statements of behavior vary from "unacceptable" performance at the bottom to "excellent" performance at the top.

BARS are developed in a series of small group meetings between employees and their supervisors. The relevant job dimensions are identified. Then actual performance of the job is observed. From these meetings and observations, the anchors are prepared.

BARS are quite useful in developing plans in MBO systems. They provide statements of the desired behaviors needed to reach objectives.

Some studies have shown that BARS can provide better results than other rating methods by reducing rater errors.[6] Moreover, they are based on job analysis, which makes them more job-oriented. However, they have not lived up to their early promise.

Forced-choice rating method.   The *forced-choice rating method* is quite popular at present. In general, this plan includes several pairs of statements concerning job performance. There are two comments that appear to be equally favorable to the employee and two that appear to be equally unfavorable. These two sets of statements and one other irrelevant statement are grouped together. From each group of observations, the rater must choose one statement that is most descriptive of the person under consideration and one that is least descriptive.

Although the rater does not know it, only one of the favorable statements is really meaningful as far as job performance is concerned, and only one of the unfavorable ones really counts against the employee. These results have been predetermined from research with similar jobs and employees and have been found to be valid predictors of success. Because the rater does not know which of the responses really counts in favor of or against the employee, there is less bias in the rating process. An example of a forced-choice list is given in Figure 12–5.

FIGURE 12–5
Example of a forced-choice list

Most Descriptive	Least Descriptive	Item
☐	☐	Reviews work of subordinates and provides assistance as needed.
☐	☐	Follows up on all delegated assignments to ensure conformance with operating procedures.
☐	☐	Requests employee opinions and uses them when conditions permit.
☐	☐	Meets deadlines on work assignments.
☐	☐	Praises those whose workplace behavior has earned recognition.

Source: Richard Henderson, *Performance Appraisal: Theory to Practice* (Reston, Va.: Reston Publishing, 1980), p. 148.

---

[6]J. Campbell et al., "The Development and Evaluation of Behaviorally Based Rating Scales," *Journal of Applied Psychology* 57 (February 1973):15–22.

The method does have disadvantages. Because it is so complex and involved, it is difficult to use the findings as a basis for counseling employees. Also, informed raters can "see through" the form and still bias their evaluations. Another problem is that appraisers object to the intended secrecy of the method and try to bias their appraisals in order to fight the system.

Other methods.   Some other popular methods are the (1) essay, (2) critical incidents, and (3) checklist methods.

Using Management by Objectives (MBO)

Over half the firms surveyed by the Conference Board in 1978 used *management by objectives* as an appraisal system. It received the "greatest vote of confidence expressed for any of the approaches."[7]

Bases of MBO.   MBO is based on the concepts that (1) managers who are strongly attached to a goal are willing to expend more effort to reach it than others, (2) whenever we predict that something will happen, we will do everything possible to make it happen (this is known as a *self-fulfilling prophecy*), and (3) subordinates prefer to be evaluated according to criteria that they perceive to be realistic and standards that are viewed as reasonably attainable.

Under this method, subordinates participate in setting the goals and identifying the criteria that will be used to evaluate them. Some of the goals may be measurable in quantitative terms (such as sales volume, production volume, expenses, or profits). Others may be assessed qualitatively (on the basis of customer relations, a marketing plan, or employee development).

Elements of an MBO program.   In essence, management by objectives stresses the importance of managers' (with the aid and concurrence of their immediate superiors) setting specific objectives that they intend to reach in the next period and then measuring performance against the standard of those objectives.

In the more successful applications, the approach extends beyond a focus on the objectives-results-objectives applications into a process of ongoing career planning and development, carefully integrated into the institution's overall development program.

In general, the process involves the following steps:

1.   Top management sets *organizational objectives*.
2.   These are translated into *goals* by the managers at the next lower organizational levels.
3.   Managers at the next lower level develop their own *specific goals* and submit them to their supervisors for discussion of whether they are feasible and how they will be achieved.

---

[7]Harry B. Anderson, "The Rating Game: Formal Job Appraisals Grow More Prevalent but Get More Criticism," *The Wall Street Journal* May 23, 1978, p. 23.

4. At the end of a given period—usually a quarter or a year—each subordinate manager's *actual performance* is compared with predetermined goals.
5. Managers are *evaluated* on the basis of their actual performance relative to the objectives set.
6. This evaluation is discussed with them, and they are *rewarded* on the basis of their goal and the amount of progress they made toward it.
7. The process starts over for the next period.

Advantages and disadvantages.   The advantages of using MBO to develop subordinates appear to far outweigh the disadvantages. While both sides are presented, only the highlights are covered.

Advantages.   The primary advantage of MBO is its appeal to managers' need for creative expression, recognition, new experiences, and self-esteem. It challenges subordinates' *creativity* through inducing them to find better ways to perform their duties. They achieve *recognition* according to how high their goals were and how close they came to achieving them. *New experiences* can be gained by using the methods developed to achieve the goals and objectives. *Self-esteem* results from the sense of challenge in setting the goals and the feeling of satisfaction that comes from meeting challenges.

Other advantages are that (1) people tend to increase their efforts when they know their performance is being appraised and rewarded, (2) the existence of specific, clear-cut goals makes it easier to appraise and reward performance, and (3) management is able to spot deficiencies in the organization sooner.

Disadvantages.   The main disadvantages revolve around the possible overemphasis on the individual rather than the group. This tendency may encourage undue competition, "buck passing," and short-range production to the detriment of group cohesiveness, managerial responsibility, and such factors as morale, employee development, and long-range organizational development.

Evaluating MBO's effectiveness.   While MBO is still very popular, there are some problems with it. Yet, where tried conscientiously, it does seem to lead to improved management. In one study, there was a test before the program and a retest two years later measuring responsibilities and goals, delegation, knowledge of performance, assistance as needed, and motivation. The researchers concluded that, regardless of the organizational level of the supervisors and subordinates involved, the use of MBO led to increased managerial activity and favorable results.[8]

In spite of those impressive results, a survey by *Fortune* revealed that only 181 of the top 500 firms claimed to use MBO. Of those, somewhere between 36 and 50 companies had MBO-based programs that were considered "suc-

---

[8]P. P. Fay and D. N. Beach, "Management by Objectives Evaluated," *Personnel Journal* 53 (October 1974):767–69.

cessful." And only 10 companies had programs that were considered "highly successful."[9]

MAKING PERFORMANCE APPRAISALS MORE EFFECTIVE

As performance appraisals are so important and used so extensively, management should try to improve them. Some of the ways of making them more effective are (1) improving their validity and reliability, (2) using multiple appraisals, (3) training the appraisers, (4) basing the appraisals on specific work standards, (5) providing better feedback, and (6) relating them to EEO.

Improving Their Validity and Reliability

Like most other personnel techniques, performance appraisals have the problems of validity and reliability.

The validity problems. Performance appraisals are intended to evaluate the performance and potential of employees. Yet they may not be valid indicators of what they are intended to assess because of a variety of limitations on their use.

The greater the reliance on objective measurements of performance, the greater the validity of the evaluation. When more subjective criteria are used, the evaluations become less valid for decision making and career guidance.

A study of three groups of salespersons chosen from 20 randomly selected departments in a retail store indicated that there was no relationship between dollar sales volume (the success criterion used) and any of the job functions on which the employees were rated.[10]

The most common sources of error are the halo effect, bias, inflation of ratings, and the central tendency.

Halo effect. The *halo effect* (and its counterpart, the *horn effect*) is the tendency of evaluators to base assessments of *all* performance dimensions—which are presumed to be independent of each other—on the raters' overall impression of the person being evaluated. In essence, the halo effect is the tendency to generalize from a predetermined overall impression to the appraisal of specific behaviors and performance.

Bias. Many otherwise valid appraisals are invalidated by *bias* on the part of the appraiser. The bias may occur for many reasons, including racial, educational, or interpersonal conflict. While it is difficult to deal with bias, the

[9]Fred E. Schuster and Alva F. Kindall, "Management by Objectives—Where We Stand Today: A Survey of the Fortune 500," *Human Resource Management* 13 (Spring 1974):12-13.

[10]Robert J. Paul, "Employee Performance Appraisal: Some Empirical Findings," *Personnel Journal* 47 (February 1968):109-14.

more descriptive methods offer less chance for overt bias. Bias may also be a factor of time. Recent impressions are more likely to bias appraisals. There is a tendency to forget or overlook more distant events. Consequently, recent information about an individual may have an undue influence on evaluations.

Inflation of ratings.   Another limitation on appraisals is the tendency to inflate ratings. Sometimes there is a gradual *inflation of ratings* over time. In some organizations, there may be inflation by certain raters at all times.

Central tendency.   *Central tendency* occurs when evaluators avoid using the extremes of rating scales. In other words, there appears to be a tendency for ratings to cluster around some intermediate point on the rating scale.

Reliability problems.   Appraisals may lack *reliability* as well as validity because of the inconsistent use of differing standards and lack of training in appraisal techniques. Failure to follow up on the use of appraisals is another problem.

Using Multiple Appraisals and Different Timing

Because of bias and the halo effect, it may be more useful to use multiple rather than single evaluations. While the ratings of one supervisor may not be valid, the overall pattern of several ratings does provide an indication of overall performance and potential for development. Therefore, the use of multiple ratings enables the organization to interpret the ratings of each appraiser, who may be known to be typically "easy to please" or "difficult to please."

In one large hospital, the supervisor, department head, and vice president evaluate each employee as a basis for training and development activities.

Appraisals can also be improved by being done several times a year rather than just once. This overcomes the bias of recency.

Appraisals are also more effective if they are made at a different time from salary adjustments. If ratings are tied to pay periods, supervisors tend to adjust the ratings to the salaries they think subordinates should have.

The hospital mentioned above separated merit increases from cost-of-living adjustments. Supervisors were asked to rate their subordinates as a basis for granting merit increases. Over 97 percent of the nurses were rated "excellent" by their supervisors. The explanation given to the personnel officer was the nurses "deserve[d] a large increase."

Training the Appraisers

In general, managers are poor at evaluating their employees' work. According to a poll of 360 business and government managers, over two-thirds of them said their employers failed to recognize and reward their achievement adequately.[11]

Supervisors need training to develop the insights, skills, and techniques needed for evaluating the performance of others. They need help in (1) developing results-oriented performance standards, (2) doing the evaluating, and (3) conducting the appraisal interviews.

General Telephone and Electronics Corporation (GTE) started a uniform system of job reviews in 1979. It hired a consultant to develop a two-day course to improve the managers' ability to evaluate their people. Around 400 managers, including the chairman and chief executive, took the course and were then appraised by their subordinates.[12]

Basing Appraisals on Specific Job Standards

It has been said many times and many ways in this chapter: Appraisals are more effective if they measure an employee's performance in terms of how well specific job standards are met.

Figure 12-6 shows an example of how this technique improved appraisals.

FIGURE 12-6
Performance appraisal before and after a job standards program was instituted

EMPLOYEE'S JOB TITLE: Consumer Banking Officer

APPRAISAL BEFORE STANDARDS:

Sybil has continued to perform in an exemplary manner. Her performance has been continually marked by strong initiative and profound devotion to her job. She has repeatedly demonstrated an inherent ability to discern problems and recommend good, sound, logical decisions. She has proven to be oriented toward the betterment of the department by watching for potential problems and bringing them to my attention.

December, 1975

APPRAISAL AFTER STANDARDS:

Sybil has averaged 127 walk-in interviews the last six months; standard is 110. A very good performance. Delinquency collections have been a high point. She averaged .6% in number, compared to a standard of 1.25%. She was consistently a leader among her peers and frequently led in this particular category. Her cross-sells of bank services were down. She averaged 11 per month, while standard was 14. From a quantity standpoint, an excellent performance overall.

Sybil has good rapport with her customers and fellow employees. Her loan knowledge—this is a new area of responsibility—is coming along nicely, but she still needs to work on real estate loans.

December, 1978

Source: "MJS: Management by Job Standards," *Personnel Journal* 58 (August 1979):540.

---

[11]*The Wall Street Journal,* April 22, 1980, p. 1.

[12]"Training Managers to Rate Their Employees," *Business Week,* March 19, 1980, pp. 178-83.

Providing Better Feedback

The results of the evaluation, along with suggestions for improvement, should be communicated to the subordinates as soon as is feasible. As shown in the last chapter, most managers need improvement in their communications, and this area is no exception. (For an example, see Problem 12-1, "Pete's Confusion," at the end of this chapter.)

Appraisal interviews have not been very effective in the past. Yet the skill with which the supervisor handles the appraisal feedback is the key factor in determining whether the appraisal program is effective in changing employee behavior or not.

Research has indicated that, among middle managers in a large manufacturing firm, those who took some form of constructive action as a result of performance appraisals did so because of the way their superiors had conducted the appraisal feedback interview and discussion.[13]

In general, these interviews should tell the employee at least three things: (1) exactly how performance has related to the job standards, (2) what is needed to improve any deficient behaviors, and (3) the expected results of improvement—or failure to improve.

Relating Appraisals to Equal Employment Opportunity Guidelines

The Civil Rights Act permitted the use of valid performance appraisals as a basis for making management decisions. Later, the *Uniform Guidelines on Employee Selection Procedures* explained when and how appraisals could be used.[14]

Essentially, appraisals can be used if (1) they are done under standardized conditions, (2) ratings are based on specific, objective, and observed job behaviors, (3) they are valid and reliable, and (4) the appraisal method is based on a valid job analysis, especially functional job analysis.

PERSONNEL ACTIONS RESULTING FROM APPRAISALS

The usual personnel actions resulting from performance appraisals are (1) salary adjustments, (2) movement in the organization, and (3) career counseling. Each of these is discussed in other parts of this book. However, the aspects associated with appraisals will be summarized here.

---

[13]H. H. Meyer and W. B. Walker, "A Study of Factors Relating to the Effectiveness of a Performance Appraisal Program," *Personnel Psychology* 14 (August 1961):291-98.

[14]See D. B. Schneier, "The Impact of EEO Legislation on Performance Appraisal," *Personnel* 55 (April 1978):24-34.

Salary Adjustments

As will be discussed in Chapters 15 and 16, merit salary adjustments result from either informal or formal performance evaluations. As shown in the last chapter, motivation is improved when rewards are related to performance. Therefore, for merit increases to serve as a motivator, they must be based on well-developed and administered performance appraisals.

Movement Within the Organization

Appraisals may result in movement within the organization. Progression and growth are usually provided through upgrading, transferring, and promoting. While the selection aspects of these were covered in Part Two, the career development phases are discussed here.

Upgrading through training and development. Increased job requirements often lead to situations in which present job holders can no longer perform their jobs. That is, the educational or skill demands have increased beyond their capacities. If performance evaluation indicates that they can be developed, employees can be upgraded. *Upgrading* involves retraining the workers so that they will be able to perform the increasingly complex functions. When used effectively, this procedure results in improving and enhancing the individual's productive abilities.

An organization used conventional ledgers, journals, and office machines to keep its books. It decided to use a computer service. The woman who kept the books was not qualified to perform the new job. She was given a leave of absence to take courses at the local university to prepare herself to learn the new system. When the change was made, she successfully made the transition.

Transferring. Employees can also progress within the organization by being transferred from one position to another. This usually happens when a person has greater capabilities, as shown by performance ratings, than those required by the position held, or when the transfer puts that person in line for greater potential advancement. Essentially, a transfer involves the movement of an employee without special regard for either a change in pay or increased responsibilities, although these may be included.

Transfers are usually considered a positive move toward career improvement. Yet, as shown in the following case, a transfer can also be regarded as punishment.

A study of around 500 midwestern business executives indicated a positive reaction to transfers. While 64 percent of the managers were neutral about transferring the first time, their reaction tended to become negative with the second move. In general, the reaction to transfers was more favor-

"I know we don't have an office in Alaska. That's why I'm transferring you there."

Reprinted by permission *The Wall Street Journal*

able among managers with a great desire to reach the top, those in the higher organizational ranks, and those who had moved often. Finally, the respondents felt that their transfers were not a part of careful career management, and that they were not adequately consulted before the transfer.[15]

Promoting. Although increases in salary are sometimes considered promotions, this is not necessarily true. A promotion is a movement to a higher position, in which responsibilities are increased and there is greater status or prestige. Frequently, promotions result in higher titles or job classifications.

Why use promotion? Promoting from within motivates employees, especially when it results from performance evaluation. Some organizations take pride in providing opportunities for their workers to develop and advance. This tends to satisfy the egoistic needs of the employees by permitting them to

[15]William F. Glueck, "Managers, Mobility and Morale," *Business Horizons* 17 (December 1974):65–70.

enjoy the rewards that come from doing more challenging and interesting work with higher pay and better working conditions. Also, advancement opportunities usually lead to higher productivity. As employees have little motivation to work harder if the better jobs are to be filled from outside, it is the personnel executive's responsibility to seek, train, and reward meritorious service.

Bases for promoting.   Promotions may be based on (1) *seniority*, that is, an individual's length of service, (2) *merit*, that is, a person's ability to perform a job better than others, or (3) a *combination* of the two.

In theory, promotions based on merit are more desirable from a motivational and developmental point of view. They cause employees to produce more in order to demonstrate their ability, or merit. Merit promotions are based on managerial judgment and usually result from appraisals.

For lower level jobs, however, particularly where unions or public policy is involved, seniority is becoming the more frequently used basis for promotion. The reason for this trend is that seniority is more objective, does not involve as many value judgments, and does not lead to as many personal conflicts as other bases for promoting.

Yet there are problems involved, for there are many types of seniority and many ways it can be lost or modified. Seniority may be based on one's position in the organization, whether companywide or departmental, or it can be based on an occupational classification. Finally, there is *super-seniority*, often given to union officials and some minority groups. And there is *synthetic seniority*, often given to workers on military leave.

Career Counseling

As shown in Figure 12-2, one of the primary purposes of employee appraisals is to help employees to develop. Therefore, career counseling is a direct action resulting from evaluation.

Career counseling is helping employees attain the sequence of jobs they want in the organization, in order to progress in their chosen career.

What is involved.   Figure 12-7 shows how career counseling works. First, the supervisor and employee reach an interpersonal, or psychological, "contract" about what job duties and performance standards are expected from each. Next, the employee develops by performing the work under the supervisor's guidance. Then the supervisor performs the formal appraisal. Finally, there is an interview during which the results of the performance appraisal are discussed. The supervisor encourages and helps the employee to do a self-analysis and establish career goals and development plans. The supervisor also helps by suggesting training and development programs and activities.

Using career development workshops.   Several companies have supplemented career counseling with *career development workshops*. At these workshops, individuals are given assistance in evaluating their own abilities and

FIGURE 12-7
Performance appraisal task model

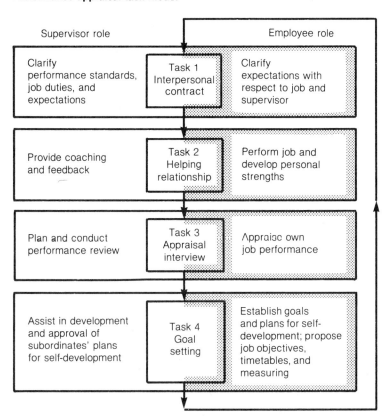

Source: John D. Colby and Ronald L. Wallace, "Performance Appraisal: Help or Hindrance to Employee Productivity?" *Personnel Administrator* 20 (October 1975):38. Reprinted with permission of *The Personnel Administrator;* copyright 1975 by the American Society for Personnel Administration.

interests. They are also given information about various job and career possibilities within the company.

These workshops are particularly important to new entrants into management ranks. As a group, new entrants have a very low perception and expectation of how far they can rise in the organization. While most entrepreneurs and executives have a high achievement drive and possess a need for power, some minorities, women, diasabled, and older workers need to have these traits instilled in them, as they may have been denied the right to use these traits in the past. This is one of the functions of these workshops.

TRW, Inc., set up a career achievement workshop based on the concept of developing a "need for achievement." The workshop emphasizes individuals' need to make decisions concerning their own career. In these workshops, the conventional concept of working on weaknesses is discarded. Participants are encouraged instead to work on their strengths. This enables them to expand upon their uniqueness and behave with more self-confidence and self-esteem. A corollary objective is to instill in them the willingness to take more prudent risks.

Apparently the workshops are proving to be successful, as 80 percent of the employees who have attended have done something later to advance their careers. In fact, 20 percent of them received promotions within eight months of attending. Another benefit to the firm was reduction in turnover of employees.[16]

There are several groups needing special career guidance and counseling. They include (1) new entrants into management (who may have been promoted as a result of the appraisals) and (2) managers with special problems.

Counseling the new managers.   The newer entrants into management ranks, though quite different from each other, have certain traits in common. These young people, minorities, and women tend to have different expectations, goals, and value systems from previous managerial groups. Personnel managers and supervisors need to give much time and effort to guiding the careers of these groups, for they will be an integral part of management in the future.

Young people.   It is difficult to draw firm conclusions about the young people now becoming managers. Their attitudes, motivations, and values are quite different from those of older managers. The previous reward systems, including money, praise, and promotion, do not appear to be working as well with this group. Commitment to a given organization appears to have been replaced by identification with their profession. The organization is merely a stepping-stone to achieving success in their occupation or profession. While these employees are generally well educated, they are beginning to question the value of their education, as well as some of the things they learned. As a group, they are more mobile and less inclined to remain with one organization very long. However, they want to be mobile at their own chosen time; so they do not hesitate to reject transfers, particularly to less desirable jobs and locations.

These managers need career counseling in making their expectations conform more to the realities of the economic and organizational environments. They need to be encouraged to think and act like managers and to accept the organizational climate in which they are to work.

Women and minorities.   From several years of case research, I have concluded that there are certain "pivotal" positions that lead either to the top or to a plateaued position. Along with the pivotal jobs, there are committee assignments, public relations activities, and training and development programs that tend to be predictive of upward mobility in the same organization. The more progressive organizations are now using career planning, develop-

---

[16]R. D. Brynildsen and W. S. Curra, "Program Aims to Mesh Company's, Employees' Goals," *Industry Week*, March 22, 1973, pp. 46–50.

ment, and counseling to see that women and minorities are given the opportunity to move into these pivotal positions so that they can grow beyond them.

What can personnel managers do to help guide and develop the careers of these groups? Much of the career guidance for women and minorities now involves (1) raising their level of expectation, (2) making them dissatisfied with the position they now hold, and (3) encouraging and assisting them to prepare for higher level positions.

Counseling managers in unique situations. The second broad group needing special career counseling and development are managers with special problems. These include (1) those with special abilities, who are being groomed for fast promotion, (2) those with unwarranted expectations, who tend to be overly mobile, (3) those who have plateaued in a given position, and (4) those being terminated.

"Fast-track" managers. Several leading companies have special programs to accelerate the progress of "bright young people" with potential for becoming top executives. These programs usually involve offering them the kind of challenge, recognition, and ego satisfaction they seek.

A study of personnel planning practices in 220 major U.S. corporations indicated that over 31 percent of them had personnel planning and career development programs for these executives, while 42 percent recommended the use of this technique.[17]

While this technique has pitfalls, the programs do provide benefits to both the organization and the individuals. The evidence shows that the technique is a practical method for providing the talent needed for future growth and development.

"Supermobile" managers. A variation of the "fast-tracks" are the "supermobiles," who have "rising expectations" that increase faster than the organization can satisfy them. The ambitions of this group are usually formed before the firm hires them, but many development programs inadvertently encourage their ambitions. While these executives are more easily developed than others, they are also more difficult to retain.

The personnel executive can assist this group by helping them keep their expectations in line with reality. Also, this group needs to be guided in coping with the stress resulting from the discrepancy between expectations and achievement.

"Plateaued" executives. Career planning and development are especially important during a period of no growth or slow growth. Rapid growth during the 1950s and 1960s tended to solve the problem of most employers. An expanding work force provided for the expanding quantity and quality of young executives, but this is not necessarily happening now.

---

[17]James W. Walker, "Tracking Corporate Tigers in the Seventies," *Human Resource Management* 12 (Winter 1972):18–24.

A study of nine companies found a large number of managers who, in the judgment of their organizations, had "plateaued." These individuals had little or no likelihood of being promoted or receiving substantial increases in duties or responsibilities.[18]

Plateauing is inevitable and has occurred in the past. But it was more gradual. Those seeking advancement had opportunity to do so, while those who did not desire to rise could be gradually bypassed by their more ambitious colleagues. Now, the declining rate of growth and an increasing number of ambitious candidates have increased the competition for a stabilizing—or even decreasing—number of positions. Consequently, the managers who advanced rapidly during past growth periods are now in the middle and upper-middle levels of management, competing for the relatively few positions at the top. The problem is that these individuals still have many productive years before normal retirement. Yet their career progress has been slowed through no fault of their own.

Outplaced managers.   Many managers (and many more nonmanagers) are being terminated as their employers reduce their work force. These *outplaced managers* require much specialized career counseling and other assistance in finding another job. This will be covered in the next chapter.

SUMMARY AND CONCLUSIONS

Performance appraisals are always used, either formally or informally, for making personnel decisions and for developmental purposes. Formal appraisal systems are effective, and their value is increased when they are used as a motivator of employee performance and as a guide to career development. Performance appraisals are used primarily among white-collar and salaried personnel, especially the scientific, technical, professional, and managerial employees.

Merit ratings, as such, are being used less than goal-setting methods, such as MBO programs. Also, more emphasis is being given in performance appraisals to evaluating the employee's actual level of job performance, as measured against preestablished work standards, rather than to appraising the personal qualities that should lead to future productivity.

As with other personnel selection, development, and reward techniques, the traits used in performance rating must be validated for the individual organizations and jobs involved and cannot be used indiscriminately.

The most popular appraisal methods are (1) ranking methods, such as paired comparison and forced distribution, and (2) rating methods, such as traditional rating scales, behaviorally anchored rating scales, and MBO.

---

[18]E. Kirby Warren, Thomas P. Ference, and James A. F. Stoner, "Problems in Review," *Harvard Business Review* 53 (January-February 1975):30–38 and 146–48.

Appraisals can be more effective if they are based on actual job standards and performed by trained supervisors. They must conform to EEO regulations. Real progress results from an effective appraisal interview.

Some personnel actions resulting from appraisals are (1) salary adjustments, (2) movement within the organization through upgrading, transfers, and promotion, and (3) career counseling.

Some groups needing special career counseling are (1) new entrants into management, including young people, minorities, and women, and (2) managers in unique situations, such as "fast-tracks," "supermobiles," "plateaued" managers, and "outplaced" managers.

QUESTIONS

1. Why are performance appraisals becoming more popular?
2. What are the advantages and limitations of performance appraisals? Discuss.
3. What purposes do performance appraisals serve?
4. How would you describe the most popular methods of performance appraisal in use today?
5. Evaluate the use of MBO for appraisal purposes. Do you think this method is superior to the others? Defend your answer.
6. Should seniority or merit be used as a basis for promotion? Defend your answer.
7. How can performance appraisals be made more effective?
8. What personnel actions usually result from appraisals?
9. What groups especially need career counseling? Why?

PROBLEMS

12-1. Pete's Confusion

An operating unit of a refinery was inefficient. When the unit's manager retired, Ted was sent in to make it more effective, including reducing the work force. One of the employees he talked to was Pete Cassity.

Pete was 53 years old and had a high school education and 25 years of service. For the 12 years that performance appraisals had been used, Pete's had always been "poor" or "fair."

Ted decided to keep Pete but felt that his performance had to improve or he should be terminated. The following discussion took place.

"Pete," said Ted, "I have decided to keep you this time because of your seniority and invalid wife. But your performance must improve or you will be the first to go next time."

"What's wrong with my work?" asked Pete in surprise. "I've always done what I was told to do! You're the first person in 25 years who's ever said I wasn't doing my job right!"

"But, Pete, that can't be true! You've signed every one of your evaluations, and they said you were only doing 'fair' or 'poor' work."

"Well, isn't that okay?"

Questions

1. How would you answer Pete?
2. How do you explain the fact that Pete was permitted to do "fair" or "poor" work for so long?
3. What does the case say about employees' reactions to the usual appraisals?

12-2. The Excellent Employees*

On January 15, Mr. Bush told the division chiefs that merit ratings were to be prepared on all employees in the department. He asked Bill to train the supervisors and division chiefs in the proper procedures to be followed in making the ratings. This was done on January 22. Bill reminded the chiefs that they should collect the completed rating forms from their subordinates and send them to him by March 15, the deadline.

On March 5, Bill sent a memo to the chiefs, to remind them of the deadline date. On March 15, none of the forms had been turned in. When he asked for them, Bill was told that time had simply slipped by, but that he would have his forms within 10 days.

On March 25, when Bill reviewed the forms, he found that 587 of the 675 employees had been rated as "excellent." Bill suggested that each supervisor be asked to write a letter explaining these "excellent" ratings. Mr. Bush agreed, but said that if the supervisors presented satisfactory reasons for their actions, he would have to accept the ratings as it was not proper to ask them to reverse their judgment.

All the letters said that the employees—on the basis of the criteria which Bill had discussed in the training session—were "excellent" and had been performing above-average work.

Questions

1. In your opinion, what caused the problem? Explain.
2. What would you have done differently if you were Bill?
3. What would you do now if you were Bill? Mr. Bush?

*See the cases at the beginning and end of Chapter 2 for other details.

SUGGESTED REFERENCES FOR FURTHER STUDY

Duemer, Walter C., Nancy Frye Walker, and James C. Quick. "Improving Work Life through Effective Performance Planning." *Personnel Administrator* 23 (July 1978):23–26.

"Evaluating the Performance of Public Organizations: A Method for Developing a Single Index." *Journal of Health and Human Resources Administration* 2 (February 1980):343ff.

Forbes, R. J., and E. M. Anaya. "Appraiser and Appraised." *Management Today*, January 1980, pp. 33–39.

Fritz, Roger J. "Self-Appraisal for Results." *Personnel Administrator* 22 (August 1977):26–28.

Henderson, Richard. *Performance Appraisal: Theory to Practice*. Reston, Va.: Reston Publishing, 1980.

Kearney, William J. "Behaviorally Anchored Rating Scales—MBO's Missing Ingredient." *Personnel Journal* 58 (January 1979):20–23.

McMaster, John B. "Designing an Appraisal System That Is Fair and Accurate." *Personnel Journal* 58 (January 1979):38–40.

Morano, Richard A. "An Rx for Performance Appraisals." *Personnel Journal* 58 (May 1979):306–7.

Muczyk, Jan P. "Dynamics and Hazards of MBO Application." *Personnel Administrator* 24 (May 1979):51–61.

CHAPTER THIRTEEN

Handling Difficult People Problems

Learning Objectives

After studying the material in this chapter, you should be able to:

1. Explain the role of counseling in the personnel program.
2. Name and discuss the areas requiring counseling.
3. Make suggestions for improving counseling.
4. Explain the need for discipline.
4. Define what discipline is.
6. Explain who has the authority for administering discipline.
7. Describe how discipline is administered.
8. Understand the unique problems of discipline in nonbusiness areas and in disciplining professional employees.

Some Important Words and Terms

Counseling	Occupational stress
Outplacement	Discipline
Chemical dependency	Judicial due process
Alcoholism	Respondent conditioning
Cross-addiction	Operant conditioning

Good order is the foundation of all good things.
EDMUND BURKE

A stern discipline pervades all nature, which is a little cruel that it may be very kind.
HERBERT SPENCER

Outline of the Chapter

The employees of a private clinic consisted of an office manager—who also performed the personnel function—a receptionist, two nurses, a lab technician, and a typist. The receptionist, who was married and had three children, was quite capable in her work and got along with everyone, including the patients. She did an outstanding job for several months.

But then she began receiving many phone calls from her husband, who was an alcoholic. At times, he kept her on the phone for long periods. At those times, she would ask one of the other employees to answer the other lines for her.

The office manager counseled with her about the problem, and it would improve—for a while. After about six months, the receptionist could no longer even make appointments for patients or handle incoming calls as she should. So the doctors called the employees into one of their meetings and asked what they thought about the situation. It was decided that, because of the receptionist's inability to carry out her duties, which was affecting the clinic in various ways, she should be discharged.

This unusual case illustrates the two personnel activities covered in this chapter—counseling and disciplining difficult employees.

ROLE OF COUNSELING

Managerial counseling is designed to help employees do a better job by providing them with an understanding of their relationships with their superiors, fellow workers, and subordinates. Counseling is now accepted as an important part of management. It operates at all levels and with all subordinates and is not restricted to any one level of supervision.

While counseling is not new, it has been improved as our knowledge of human behavior has expanded.

What Counseling Involves

Counseling operates in a conversational setting between two people. When a third party comes into the picture, it is no longer counseling, but a conference. Counseling is always a one-to-one relationship. One can talk with another person, draw that individual out, and point him or her in the right direction.

Counseling and guidance also involves two-way communication. While it is desirable to convey meaning to subordinates, it is likewise important to learn from them what the manager needs to know in order to be of assistance.

Benefits of Counseling

There are many benefits received from effective counseling, both to those being counseled and those doing the counseling.

As counseling reduces anxiety, fear, and distrust, it tends to develop, fortify, and strengthen working relationships, so that misunderstanding and apprehension can be cleared up. It tends to get disturbed relationships back on a two-way, cooperative basis. Counseling can also improve interpersonal relationships and make the interactions more pleasant. It is a way of at least being able to sit down and talk to other persons and tell them quite frankly where they stand.

Employees of Kennecott Copper Corporation who discussed problems with the firm's counselors had a decrease of 75 percent in work compensation costs and 55 percent in health care costs. Their attendance improved 52 percent.[1]

Some Problems Involved in Counseling

Like other managerial activities, providing counsel and guidance has many problems. To the extent that these problems are recognized and judiciously overcome, the process should be most effective.

Fear on the part of the counselor. One of the first problems involved in counseling is fear on the part of the counselor. This fear adversely affects performance and verbal behavior. It also leads to reluctance to tell others of their weaknesses and shortcomings—and reluctance to see our own.

Conflict of values. Another problem is that counseling may involve a conflict of values. People have a value system that provides them with a shock absorber to cushion them against the ugly realities of life. When counseling threatens subordinates' value systems, it threatens them personally. Employees' cultural backgrounds have much to do with their attitudes toward their superiors and colleagues and the roles they assume as members of the work team.

Complementarity of symptoms. Finally, there is the problem of complementarity of symptoms. If a subordinate has an alcohol problem and is counseled to overcome it, periods of depression may follow. In other words, even when counseling is successful, the employee may not be completely cured.

There may also be an escape into other problem areas. There is evidence that students, as well as employees, are turning from drugs to alcohol.

Who is to do the counseling? Figure 13-1 shows that counseling (and discipline) is very much a personnel activity. Yet not all managers are effective counselors. To be effective, they need special talents and training in listening, patience, objectivity, and helping people without trying to "run their life for them."

AREAS REQUIRING COUNSELING

Counseling is involved in all aspects of personnel management. It begins with the selection process and does not end until the worker leaves the organiza-

---

[1]"Employee Counseling Pays Off," *Behavioral Sciences Newsletter*, November 13, 1978.

FIGURE 13–1
Responsibility for counseling and discipline in the Bureau of National Affairs' Personnel Policy Forum companies.

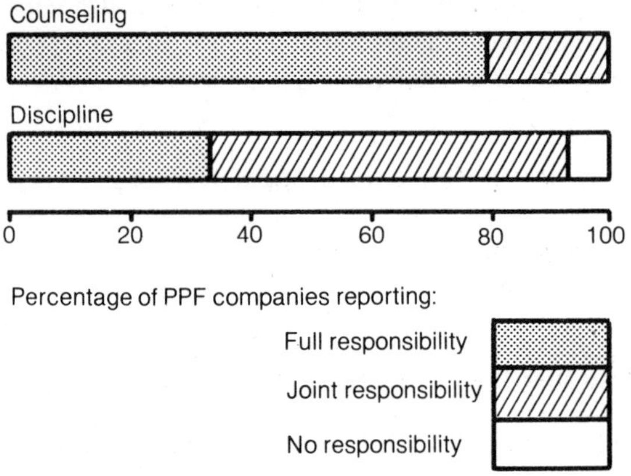

Counseling

Discipline

```
0      20      40      60      80      100
```

Percentage of PPF companies reporting:

Full responsibility

Joint responsibility

No responsibility

Source: "The Personnel Department," BNA Policy and Practice Series: *Personnel Management* (Washington, D.C.: The Bureau of National Affairs, Inc., No. 243, p. 251:23.

tion, if then. Yet there are certain areas where counseling is practices more frequently than in others. These include (1) job-related activities and (2) personal problems.

Job-related Activities

While all aspects of the job are subject to counseling, the most prevalent ones are (1) performance, (2) discipline, (3) safety, (4) conflict, (5) retirement, and (6) outplacement.

Performance.   Management is responsible for informing employees of their progress. Knowing how they are doing is one of the greatest desires of today's workers. Motivation is based on setting goals, stimulating employees to achieve them, and informing them of their progress. The key factor is the follow-up appraisal interview, as discussed in the previous chapter.

According to the theory of appraisal interviews, the line manager, after appraising the performance of subordinates, should discuss the results with them to help them see their strengths and weaknesses more clearly. This procedure should motivate the subordinates to build on their strengths and minimize their weaknesses.

Disciplinary cases.   As will be seen later in this chapter, there are times when counseling does not succeed and disciplinary action is required. An early, and important, part of discipline, however, is counseling the involved workers. Personnel managers must establish the borderline between these two aspects of their job, if it is necessary to make a distinction.

Safety and industrial health. As will be shown in the next chapter, the entire area of safety requires considerable counseling and guidance, as it is largely a matter of attitudes. The role of the personnel manager is primarily one of assisting operating managers to perform this function.

Conflict. When conflict arises in a work situation and cannot be resolved between the parties, the personnel manager may have to step in. Therefore, it is important for her or him to know when, and how, to intervene.[2] There are many sophisticated techniques now being used to intervene in conflict.[3]

Retirement. As will be shown in Chapter 17, there is now a "retirement revolution." It has been sparked by recent developments, especially the prohibition on forced retirement before age 70. Employees need considerable preparation for retirement, especially about the benefits coming to them. The personnel manager is primarily responsible for this type of counseling.

The Bureau of National Affairs (BNA) surveyed the members of ASPA to find out the impact of that revolution. It found that 36 percent of the respondents had a preretirement counseling program.[4] Some of the topics covered include (1) financial planning, (2) earning money after retirement, and (3) health problems.

---

[2]See Derek Sheane, "When and How to Intervene in Conflict," *Personnel Management* 11 (July 1979):32–36, for guides on when and how to intervene.

[3]See "Teaching How to Cope with Workplace Conflict," *Business Week*, February 18, 1980, pp. 136–39, for some methods used to learn how to cope.

[4]"ASPA-BNA Survey no. 39: Retirement Policies and Programs," *Bulletin to Management*, January 24, 1980, p. 1.

Reprinted by permission *The Wall Street Journal.*

A survey of 1,500 physicians treating older patients found that career-oriented men suffer rapid physical decline after retirement "four times more frequently than career-oriented women."[5]

Outplacement.   A relatively new area needing counseling is *outplacement,* which is the term for people who are laid off or terminated.

Counseling involuntary terminations.   One of the most difficult problems faced by managers is firing an employee for unsatisfactory performance. This task often falls to the personnel manager. Actually, the counseling should begin before termination. But, if counseling fails and termination is inevitable, suggestions can be given for seeking another job and preparing for the psychological stages of adjustment.[6]

Counseling those whose jobs are terminated.   Pushed by unions and the threat of federal legislation, many firms are trying outplacement counseling for workers who lose their jobs through reductions in the work force.

Goodyear Tire & Rubber Company, which idled 1,200 hourly workers when it closed two plants in February 1980, tried an experiment to find jobs

---

[5]*Business Week,* March 23, 1979, p. 100.

[6]Dennis J. Kravetz, "Counseling Strategies for Involuntary Termination," *Personnel Administrator* 23 (October 1978):47-54.

for union members and salaried personnel. Trained counselors would help them look for work for at least a month after the plants closed.[7]

Personal Problems

Personal crises, physical and mental illness, alcoholism, and drug abuse are personal problems. Yet, when they spill over into the work area and influence behavior and performance, they become management problems. Then personnel managers become responsible for identifying and assisting the troubled workers.

Extent of these problems.   There are few employers with formal programs for counseling employees with these problems. In a 1978 BNA survey of ASPA members, only 65 respondents said they had such programs. As shown in Table 13-1, the main problems found were (1) personal crises over marital, family, financial, or legal problems, (2) alcoholism, (3) drug abuse, and (4) emotional illness. Notice that all of the problems had increased between 1970 and 1978.

Table 13-2 shows the methods used to deal with problem employees. It is interesting that most of the employers provided in-house counseling for all the problems except drug addiction. The personnel department was involved in this counseling in four out of five cases.

Personal crises.   Employees do get into—or have—trouble away from the job (see the opening case). But the guideline followed by most personnel

TABLE 13-1
Employee problems

	Production/ service	Clerical/office	Technical/ professional	Managerial
Alcoholism................	7.7 (3.2)	3.8 (1.9)	4.6	4.6 (1.9)
Marijuana abuse	4.8 (1.2)	2.8 (0.7)	3.1	2.1 (0.1)
Prescription drug abuse	2.4	1.6	2.0	1.8
Hard-drug addiction........	1.5 (0.4)	0.7 (0.1)	0.6	0.5 (0.1)
Emotional illness requiring psychiatric treatment	2.8 (1.4)	2.4 (1.4)	3.0	2.3 (1.3)
Personal crisis situations (e.g. marital, family, financial, legal) which interfere with job performance	10.9	7.2	6.1	5.8

Note: Figures are percentages of employees with indicated problem. Figures in parentheses are results of 1970
  survey.
Source: Reprinted by special permission from *Bulletin to Management*, copyright 1978 by The Bureau of
  National Affairs, Inc., Washington, D.C.

---

[7]Tom Bailey, "Industrial Outplacement at Goodyear: Part I. The Company's Position," *Personnel Administrator* 25 (March 1980):42ff.

TABLE 13-2
Methods used to deal with problem employees

	Alco- holism	Mari- juana abuse	Pre- scription drug abuse	Hard drug addiction	Emo- tional illness	Personal crises
Consultation with supervisor . . .	55	40	32	26	43	55
Discipline short of discharge . . .	35 (49)	15 (17)	12	8 (11)	9 (16)	12
Discharge.	29 (25)	28 (27)	15	25 (33)	9 (7)	9
In-house counseling	45 (67)	20 (21)	22	15 (18)	43 (43)	55
Referral to outside agency.	60 (65)	38 (21)	31	35 (20)	55 (67)	58
Other (Please describe)	14	8	6	8	9	8
No Response	12	37	48	48	28	18

Note: Figures are percentages of companies using specified method for each problem. Figures in parentheses are results of 1970 survey.
Source: Reprinted by special permission from *Bulletin to Management,* copyright 1978 by The Bureau of National Affairs, Inc., Washington, D.C.

managers is: Steer clear of personal problems except to the extent that they adversely affect the employee's or others' work.

A second guideline is to restrict counseling to the employee's job performance. Table 13–3 suggests some ways of doing this. Notice that most of them involve setting performance standards and then being firm in enforcing them.

There are many outside agencies that handle these problems, and they should be used.

Alcoholism.   Two prominent health problems facing personnel executives are alcoholism and drug addiction, now called *chemical dependency.* They have received wide attention because of their noticeable and negative effects on job performance and because they are so widespread and growing in severity.

Alcoholism costs industry about $15.6 million annually in absenteeism and medical costs.[8] These costs result from the fact that these problem workers (1) have about three times as many accidents, (2) are absent around three times as frequently, and (3) require almost three times as much in sickness payments as average workers. Other losses resulting from (1) inefficiencies and slowdowns, (2) interpersonal problems, and (3) the necessity to discharge highly trained and skilled employees cannot be estimated.

Alcoholism was long viewed as essentially a moral issue calling for social censure and punishment. In 1956, the American Medical Association recognized *alcoholism* as a disease resulting from drinking alcoholic beverages to the point where functioning is impaired. It is the fourth greatest cause of serious illness in the country, according to the AMA.

In spite of the above facts, supervisors go to great lengths to protect alcoholic employees, even refusing to give performance records during "bad

---

[8]Philip Goldberg, *Executive Health: How to Recognize Health Danger Signals and Manage Stress Successfully* (New York: McGraw-Hill Publications, 1978), p. xi.

TABLE 13-3
How to approach a troubled employee

1. Establish levels of work performance you expect.
2. Be specific about supportive behavioral criteria, e.g. absenteeism, poor job performance, and others.
3. Be consistent.
4. Try not to diagnose the problem.
5. Restrict criticism to job performance.
6. Be firm.
7. Be prepared to cope with the employee's resistance, defensiveness, or hostility.
8. Try to get the employee to acknowledge the problem.
9. Show him he cannot play you against higher management and/or union.
10. Point out the availability of counseling services.
11. Discuss drinking only if it occurs on the job or the employee is obviously intoxicated.
12. Get a commitment from the employee to meet specific work criteria and monitor this with a plan for improvement based on work performance.
13. Explain that the employee must decide for himself whether or not to seek assistance.
14. Emphasize the confidentiality of the program.

Source: Reprinted from the June, 1979 issue of *The Personnel Administrator* with permission of The American Society for Personnel Administration.

times," failing to record symptoms until they become chronic, and considering such employees to "have a bit of a drinking problem."

Experience has shown that, where an enlightened and consistent policy toward alcoholic employees had been worked out, the problem has been reduced. Such a policy usually recognizes that alcoholism is a disease. Then managers attempt to (1) identify the symptoms by which the alcoholic can be recognized early (see Table 13-4), (2) set up steps to assist such employees, and (3) set limits of tolerance—including immediate discharge if the employee doesn't take treatment. The better company programs have two advantages. They can detect alcoholism early and can force workers to take treatment or lose their jobs. They have been quite successful.[9]

One especially difficult aspect is *cross-addiction*, where alcoholics are addicted to other chemical substances.[10]

---

[9]See Roger Ricklefs, "Drinkers at Work: Firms Act to Uncover the Secret Alcoholics, Make Them Get Help," *The Wall Street Journal*, December 1, 1975, pp. 1 and 12, for details about these programs and the experience of firms using them.

[10]According to Edward L. Johnson, manager of the employee assistance program at Firestone Tire & Rubber Co., as quoted in "Ways Employers Can Help Drinkers, Drug Addicts," *U.S. News & World Report*, August 27, 1979, p. 61.

TABLE 13-4
Early signs of alcoholism

1. Excessive tardiness for work, with invalid or improbable excuse.
2. Increasing frequency and length of absences, especially on Mondays.
3. Slackening work pace.
4. Declining quantity and quality of performance.
5. Increasing frequency and intensity of arguments with colleagues.
6. Poor, "fuzzy," or irrational decisions.

Source: Extracted from "One Time Too Many," A case written by Karen Arnold and Leon Megginson for the Intercollegiate Case Clearinghouse.

Drug abuse.   While it is still less prevalent than alcoholism, drug abuse is increasingly posing a problem for personnel managers. Drugs are more difficult for industry to contain, for when the dope addict gets into an organization, the "pusher" is often not too far behind—or the drug users may sell drugs to other workers to provide money for their own drugs.

Of 95 addicts in various rehabilitation centers in New York City, (1) 91 admitted using drugs during working hours, (2) 68 confessed to criminal behavior at work, including stealing from the employer and fellow employees, and (3) 48 had sold drugs to other employees.[11]

The drug problem is found all the way from the last employee hired up to and including senior executives who have been with the firm for a long time.[12] Companies are increasing their security departments, running drug screens on applicants, instituting companywide education programs, helping those who are discovered to be on drugs prove themselves, and hiring or rehiring employees certified to be ex-addicts. Yet many of these procedures are not proving very effctive.

As shown in Table 13-3, the most frequent way of handling these employees is referring them to outside agencies.

Physical illness.   Counseling in the area of physical health involves seeing that employees continue to stay well while on the job. Also, if off-the-job activities are harming employees' performance, then management should advise them how to improve their work performance.

Heart-related diseases alone result in an annual loss of about 32 million work days and $8.6 billion in wages.[13]

One particularly difficult area of counseling is knowing when a physical impairment reaches the stage at which an individual is no longer employable

[11]See Jerome Siegel and Eric H. Schoof, "Corporate Responsiveness to the Drug Abuse Problems," *Personnel* 50 (November–December 1973):8–14.

[12]Linda Gutstein, "Drug Addicts Worry Industry," *Parade*, February 14, 1971, pp. 4–5.

[13]Goldberg, *Executive Health.*

or when one must take sick leave. Judgment is needed to decide when reduced efficiency can no longer be tolerated and corrective action must be taken.

Mental and emotional illness. The American Medical Association recognizes mental illness as one of the top four diseases. It is also one of the most complex and pressing health problems in the nation. The mentally ill occupy half of all hospital beds in the country. In fact, social and psychological reasons account for over half the cost of delivering all medical care in the United States. It is estimated that one-fifth of all employees are, or will be, victims to some degree of mental disorder.[14]

Emotional problems are caused by many intangible, complex, and interrelated factors. Some result directly from external environmental factors or interpersonal conflicts, which in the work situation are referred to as *occupational stress* (which will be discussed in the next chapter).

An indication of the severity of these external pressures is given by the fact that *of the four primary causes of illness*—heart trouble, mental illness, cancer, and alcoholism—*three are directly related to stress and strains found in the work environment,* and even the fourth one—cancer—may be indirectly caused by these factors.

Regardless of the sources of these problems, to the extent that they interfere with job performance, they are subject to personnel counseling. Where feasible, managers may counsel employees about possible improvements in their behavior or suggest seeking professional advice, depending on the severity of the problem.

One study has shown that counseling is an effective method of aiding the emotionally disturbed person. It has resulted in reducing absenteeism and tardiness while increasing morale and productivity.[15]

NEED FOR DISCIPLINE

It has been seen that counseling does not always work. Therefore, discipline is sometimes needed to achieve effective performance by both managers and nonmanagers.

Employees prefer to work with a well-organized, well-trained, and well-disciplined group rather than with one that is not. It has been shown that employees want to be supervised on "an adequate scale," "not too much—but also not too little," for they benefit from discipline and suffer from disorder.[16] Successful supervisors know how to find this middle road that allows their subordinates to know exactly what they may and may not do.

---

[14]Robert L. Noland, *Industrial Mental Health and Employee Counseling* (New York: Behavioral Publications, 1973), pp. 11-12.

[15]Gerald H. Graham, "Recognizing Emotional Disturbance Symptoms," *Personnel Administrator* 15 (July–August 1970):3-7.

[16]Irvin H. McMaster found that the supervisor's training is a key to success, as is timing, or knowing when to discipline. "Unusual Aspects of Discipline," *Supervision* 36 (April 1974):19.

Behavior Needing Discipline

A study by the BNA's Personnel Policies Forum found that the greatest disciplinary problems in the firms studied were (1) absenteeism and/or tardiness (79 percent) and (2) poor productivity, work habits, and/or attitudes (11 percent).[17]

Absenteeism. The most frequent disciplinary problem is absenteeism. This has always been a problem, but it is apparently increasing at present. Some of this loss of work is unavoidable for many reasons. Yet the avoidable part is substantial and needs to be controlled.

If the loss of work is the result of negligence or lack of responsibility, the personnel manager may correct it through counseling. If it is caused by illness, it may be referred to the medical staff. If, however, it is caused by mental illness, it may require outside professional treatment.

Safety. Partly for humanitarian reasons and partly as a result of OSHAct, safety violations are now being treated as a major, or even intolerable offense, depending on the severity of the infraction. Some of the most severe penalties are being imposed for the more flagrant and repeated violations.

In a study of five electric utility firms, seven levels of managers were asked to rate cases involving violations of rules by hourly workers on a diciplinary action scale. Cases involving safety violations were judged more severely by all levels of management.[18]

Meaning of Discipline

When asked what discipline is, most people will say that it means imposing penalties for "wrong" behavior. But there is also a positive element. As the word *discipline* is derived from words meaning "pupil" and "to teach or train," its root meaning is *instruction* or *training*. Discipline, then, even when it is punishment, is punishment intended to correct wrong behavior and train the individual to perform correctly.

The term *discipline* is used in this book to mean self-discipline, the necessary condition for orderly behavior, and the judicial due process of punishing employees for unacceptable behavior.

Self-control. The first meaning of the word maintains that discipline is training that corrects, molds, strengthens, or perfects. It is evident that self-discipline is extremely important in administrators, managers, and supervisors. If they do not have control, how can they instill it in their subordinates?

Conditions of orderly behavior. The second meaning regards discipline as the condition necessary to obtain orderly behavior in an organization. This

---

[17]*Employee Conduct and Discipline*, Personnel Policies Forum Survey No. 102 (Washington, D.C.: Bureau of National Affairs, 1973), p. 1.

[18]Philip Shaak and Milton Schwartz, "Uniformity of Policy Interpretation among Managers in the Utility Industry," *Academy of Management Journal* 16 (March 1973):77–83.

implies keeping order and control among a group of workers by using methods that build morale, *esprit de corps,* and obedience, which is one of the most basic elements in organizational structures. If these standards of behavior are to be effective, the members of the organization have to accept them and adhere to them.

Judicial due process.   Discipline is also a *judicial due process* for punishing a person as a result of an unacceptable act. Its function is not to change past behavior but to prevent a recurrence of the act in the future.

As applied to personnel management, this process involves (1) establishing "laws," or rules of behavior, (2) setting penalties for violating those rules, with progressive degrees of severity, and (3) imposing the penalties upon violators only after determining the extent of guilt and taking into consideration any extenuating circumstances.

The due process concept is based on four requirements that are usually upheld by arbitrators. They are: (1) the employer has the right to have a well-disciplined, cooperative work force, (2) managers have the authority to administer discipline when rules are violated, (3) the rules must be "reasonable," and (4) employees must have a clear idea of what is expected of them.

Positive versus Negative Discipline

As you can see, discipline can be (1) positive and activating or (2) negative and restraining. In either case, discipline is the force that prompts an individual or group to observe the policies, rules, regulations, and procedures that are necessary to attain objectives.

Positive discipline.   Positive discipline is based on the principles of respondent conditioning and operant conditioning. *Respondent conditioning* operates on the theory that anything consistently paired with something else will eventually produce the same response as the first thing. ("Pavlov's dog" is a familiar example.) *Operant conditioning* is based on the concept of increasing the frequency of an action and following it up as quickly as feasible with a reward.

A classic example of positive discipline that has been in effect for several years at a plywood mill in Canada is shown in Table 13-5.

Negative discipline.   Negative discipline involves force or an outside influence. This type of discipline need not be extreme and is best used *only* when the positive type fails. Force will often cause a person to change outwardly but not mentally or emotionally.

Based upon the contingency approach, personnel managers will vary the type of discipline used to suit the situation and their subordinates.

AUTHORITY FOR ADMINISTERING DISCIPLINE

Usually the policies, rules, and regulations for employee behavior are established by top and middle management with the assistance and guidance of the

TABLE 13-5
How a plan of discipline without punishment works

1. When an employee does something meriting punishment, there are casual, private reminders from the departmental supervisor in a friendly but factual manner.
2. If a second transgression occurs within four to six weeks, the reminders are repeated.
3. A third occurrence within a "reasonable time" (usually four to six weeks) leads to another discussion, this time with a shift supervisor involved. At this point, an attempt is made to determine the roots of the employee's problem. For example,
   a. Does the worker like the job?
   b. Is the worker unable to tolerate the work routine?
   c. Are there personal or domestic problems?
   d. Is the worker able and willing to abide by the rules in the future?
4. If a fourth incident occurs within six to eight weeks, the worker's supervisor and the plant superintendent have a "final" discussion with the individual.
   a. The worker is informed that another incident will result in termination.
   b. A record of this discussion is sent to the worker's home.
5. Continued "good performance" over a period of several months leads to a clearing of the record.
   a. One step at a time.
   b. In reverse order.
6. Applying Skinner's "reinforcement" principle, when there is *any* improvement the supervisor lets the worker know it is appreciated.

Source: John Huberman, "Discipline without Punishment Lives," *Harvard Business Review* 53 (July–August 1975):7.

personnel manager (see Figure 13-1). Yet they tend to be enforced by the first-line supervisor.

Role of the Personnel Manager

Although not universally true, the general rule is that (1) at lower levels of discipline, involving only a warning, the first-line supervisor has final authority, (2) at the middle level, involving suspensions, line supervisors and managers have the final authority, while (3) at the top levels, involving discharges, the authority is about evenly split between line managers and personnel managers. In general, *as the severity increases, the role of the first-line supervisor decreases and the role of the personnel officer increases.*

The personnel manager's role is greater in small companies than in large ones and greater in nonbusiness organizations than in business firms.

In general, persons in higher levels of management take a stronger, perhaps more punitive, position on matters of discipline than those at the lower levels. One explanation in that first-line supervisors are more inclined than top management to give consideration to individual circumstances and behavior. Also, supervisors are somewhat reluctant to follow rules in a strict fashion for fear of losing the cooperation of subordinates if they are too severe.

Role of the Supervisor

Effective supervisors are usually considerate of their subordinates and rely heavily upon favorable personal relationships to accomplish the job of maintaining a high level of performance. For fear of destroying these personal relationships, supervisors tend to be reluctant to impose severe disciplinary action that is established at the top. On the other hand some top managers become so isolated from the workers—and supervisors—that they lose touch with reality and may place the blame for poor discipline on the supervisors.

Formal grievances in a large paper plant indicated that the workers were bitter about traditional "bread-and-butter" issues such as rates of pay, fringe benefits, and work standards. However, top management felt that the grievances were due to a "lack of understanding" and it was the supervisors' job to correct it. Even after an opinion survey determined the true reason for the dissatisfaction of the workers, the plant manager still thought the supervisors were partially at fault.

Still, personnel officers need to train and counsel supervisors that (1) every job should have a certain margin for error, (2) overemphasis on avoiding errors stifles initiative and can encourage subordinates to postpone decisions or avoid them altogether, and (3) a different way should not be mistaken for a wrong way.

Discipline really begins with hiring. Supervisors who are involved at that stage are usually more effective.

A survey of personnel directors in 66 of the largest U.S. cities found that the supervisors were involved in hiring in the cities with effective disciplinary systems. They were not included in hiring decisions where there were ineffective systems.[19]

Role of Unions and Arbitrators

The role of unions in applying discipline cannot be ignored, as will be seen in Part 5. Management's right to discipline employees has been modified to the extent that unions have grown. Not only do they serve as catalysts for the adoption of new ideas concerning the disciplinary process, they have also contributed significantly to the development of that process through negotiating the labor agreement and using its grievance procedure.

Some of the major principles that unions and arbitrators insist on are: (1) a discharge can occur only for just cause, (2) the burden of proof should be on the employer rather than on the individual, (3) formal procedures should be used, and (4) management actions must meet the due process test (see Table

---

[19]James A. Belohlav and Paul O. Popp, "Making Employee Discipline Work," *Personnel Administrator* 23 (March 1978):22–24.

TABLE 13-6
Factors used to determine whether management has "just cause" for discharging an employee

1. Did the employee have prior warning that his or her conduct would result in discipline, including possible discharge?
2. Was the misconduct related to the safe, efficient, and orderly operation of the organization?
3. Was an investigation held?
4. Was the investigation fair and objective?
5. Did the investigation obtain circumstantial evidence that the employee was guilty?
6. Was the disciplinary decision nondiscriminatory?
7. Was the discipline reasonably related to the seriousness of the offense and the employee's record with the organization?

Source: Leon D. Boncarosky, "Guidelines to Corrective Discipline," *Personnel Journal* 58 (October 1979):698.

13-6). These changes have substantially added to the burdens of the first-line supervisor.

HOW DISCIPLINE IS ADMINISTERED UNDER THE JUDICIAL DUE PROCESS

As you will remember, the due process of discipline includes:

1. Establishing rules of conduct.
2. Setting specific penalties for violating them.
3. Imposing the penalties impartially.

Establishing Rules of Conduct

As with any other judicial process, rules of behavior should be predetermined and announced. If employees are expected to adhere to the rules and regulations, then they must know what they are and what freedom they have under them. In most organizations, there is some form of statement of expected conduct. Such formal rules were found in 85 percent of the companies participating in the BNA study cited earlier. As expected, the larger organizations followed this practice more frequently than the smaller ones.

Setting Up Specific Penalties

In unionized organizations and in many public ones, there will be stated penalties for infraction of the rules.

Even in those organizations without formal rules, there are instructions as to expected behavior, and employees know that they will be formally or informally appraised on their conduct in performing their job.

Some guidelines for making and applying rules are: A rule must be (1) necessary, (2) widely applicable, (3) consistent with organizational policies and objectives, (4) communicated to everyone, (5) clear and understandable, (6) reasonable, and (7) enforceable. Further, penalties should fit the rule violation.

Types of penalty.   The type and variety of penalties used, as well as the manner in which they are employed, are usually limited by contract, by fear of entry of a union, and/or by governmental action.

The main types of penalty are the following:

1. *Oral warning*—not placed on the employee's record.
2. *Oral warning entered on the employee's record*—helps avoid the charge of gathering evidence after the fact.
3. *Written reprimand*—usually given by a manager higher than the immediate supervisor and may be challenged by the employee.
4. *Suspension*—usually consists of a layoff lasting from a few days to several months.
5. *Discharge*—constitutes a break in service and wipes out the worker's seniority.

A discharge is almost always subject to the grievance procedure and arbitration. Most arbitrators tend to be influenced by (1) whether the facts upon which the discharge was based were accurate, (2) whether the penalty was excessive in relation to the offense, and (3) the individual's past record.

Some other penalties used are *demotions, transfers,* and *withholding benefits* such as promotions, raises, and bonuses.

It should be remembered when imposing penalties that employees want to know that their treatment will be equal under equal conditions and that *it is the offensive action that is being punished and not the offenders themselves.*

Using a graduated code of penalties.   Unions and most personnel managers favor some type of graduated code of penalties that become increasingly severe after the first violation. One of the main advantages of this arrangement is that it tends to be standardized and consistent. (Refer to Table 13–7 to see how this operates in practice.)

Imposing the Penalties

Following an established procedure includes determining "guilt" and imposing the penalty. The usual procedure involves the following steps:

1. Investigate the facts.
   a. Interview witnesses, including the charged employee, and obtain signed statements.

TABLE 13-7
Shop rules typical in unionized plants

Rules	1st offense	2d offense	3d offense
1. Stealing private or company property...........	Discharge		
2. Material falsification of any company record	Discharge		
3. Gambling on company property.................	Discharge		
4. Fighting on company property..................	Discharge		
5. Refusal to obey orders of supervisor	Discharge		
6. Deliberate destruction or abuse of company property	Discharge		
7. Reporting to work or working while under the influence of intoxicating beverages and/or narcotics or other drugs or having possession of same on company property.....................	Discharge		
8. Possession of weapons on company premises	Discharge		
9. Immoral conduct on company property	Discharge		
10. Sleeping during working hours.................	Discharge		
11. Absent three consecutive days without notification.	Voluntary termination		
12. Willfully punching somebody else's timecard......	Discharge		
13. Leaving premises during working hours without permission................................	Discharge		
14. Personal work on company time	Written warning	2 Days layoff	Discharge
15. Personal conduct at work dangerous to others.....	Written warning	2 Days layoff	Discharge
16. Solicitation for any cause during working time without permission..........................	Written warning	2 Days layoff	Discharge
17. Distribution of literature during working hours or in areas of work without permission	Written warning	2 Days layoff	Discharge
18. Repeated failure to punch time card.............	Written warning	2 Days layoff	Discharge
19. Visiting other departments during working hours without permission..........................	Written warning	2 Days layoff	Discharge
20. Stopping work before break time, lunch time, or quitting time or not performing assigned work.....	Written warning	2 Days layoff	Discharge
21. Posting, removal, or tampering with bulletin board notices without authority	Written warning	2 Days layoff	Discharge
22. Threatening, intimidating, coercing, or interfering with employees or supervision at any time........	Written warning	2 Days layoff	Discharge

Receipt of any combination of five (5) of the above offenses within a one (1) year period will result in the employee's
    automatic discharge.
Written notices or warning or other disciplinary action shall not be used as a basis for further discipline after the employee
    has maintained a clear record of conduct for one year.
Source: *Employee Conduct and Discipline,* Personnel Policies Forum Survey No. 102 (Washington, D.C.: Bureau of National Affairs, 1973), p. 30.

TABLE 13-7 (continued)

Rules	1st offense	2d offense	3d offense
23. Poor or careless workmanship	Written warning	2 Days layoff	Discharge
24. Leaving early and/or failure to be at assigned work area at the start or end of shifts, breaks, and/or meal periods	Written warning	2 Days layoff	Discharge
25. Using abusive language or making false or malicious statements concerning any employee, the company or its products	Written warning	2 Days layoff	Discharge
26. Distracting the attention of others or causing confusion by unnecessary shouting, catcalls, or demonstrations in plant	Written warning	2 Days layoff	Discharge
27. Littering or contributing to poor housekeeping, unsanitary or unsafe conditions on plant premises . .	Written warning	2 Days layoff	Discharge
28. Negligence of safety rules or common safety practices	Written warning	2 Days layoff	Discharge
29. Restricting output or intentional slowdown	Written warning	5 Days layoff	Discharge
30. Unexcused absence	Written warning		
31. Unexcused tardiness	Written warning		

    b.   Review the documentary evidence.

    c.   Visit the site of the incident.

2.   Ascertain guilt.

3.   Determine the appropriate penalty.

    a.   Examine the applicable company policy and collective bargaining agreement.

    b.   Investigate how other similar cases have been handled.

    c.   Review the employee's file.

4.   Apply the penalty as judiciously as feasible.

AREAS WITH UNIQUE DISCIPLINE PROBLEMS

Two areas requiring special consideration are (1) nonbusiness organizations and (2) professional employees.

Discipline in Nonbusiness Organizations

Discipline is a problem not only in business firms but also in government, the military, unions, sports, and volunteer organizations.

Federal agencies are now required under Title VII of the *Civil Service Reform Act* to have a formal appeals system regarding adverse actions against employees. The agencies are thus responsible not only for disciplining employees, but also for receiving and adjudicating appeals. As an added protection, the appeals have to be decided at an administrative level higher than the level that took the adverse action. It was felt that this added appellate responsibility would cause agencies to reevaluate their disciplinary policies and practices, thus improving all stages in the process of dealing with employees in trouble.

Employees are given three options. They can (1) appeal first to their own agency, (2) appeal to the Civil Service Commission, or (3) go to their agency first and then appeal to the commission. Experience shows that an increasing number are using the third alternative, with their appeals going through local, regional, and national appeals offices up to, and terminating in, the Board of Appeals and Review.

Unions can punish their members for many activities, including actions during a strike. The members also file grievances against their local leaders all the way to the national convention.

The late George Meany, when head of the AFL-CIO, called that organization's Massachusetts chiefs to Washington and ordered them to rescind an antibusing resolution they had passed at their state convention. If they did not, they would be suspended.

In *professional sports,* players and managers can be disciplined by outside authorities.

Disciplining Professional Employees

Professional employees, such as scientists, computer specialists, engineers, accountants, and health care specialists, are now presenting personnel managers with disciplinary problems. They tend to lack genuine grievance procedures; so they show their militancy in different ways.

As shown in Table 13-8, their problems are different from other employees'. As their performance is hard to state and measure, it leads to controversies.

SUMMARY AND CONCLUSIONS

A certain number of employees in all organizations will have personal difficulties that result from strain. Sometimes these are connected with the job, but

TABLE 13–8
Incidents resulting in disciplinary action against professional employees

Incident	Number	Percent of Total
Job performance	50	42
Absenteeism and tardiness	36	30
Insubordination	23	19
Other	11	9
Totals	120	100

Source: Reprinted from the March, 1979 issue of *The Personnel Administrator* with permission of The American Society for Personnel Administration.

equally often they are based on home problems, relations with fellow employees, the general makeup of the individual, or the pressures caused by the complexities of present-day living. To meet the needs of such people, personnel executives need to become familiar with counseling needs and techniques.

Yet employee counseling must not detract from normal grievance procedures and the regular channels of authority and responsibility. Also, it is essential that adequate machinery exist for adjustment of differences arising from work conditions, as contrasted with individual personality problems. Some firms have had success in achieving positive results through broad educational programs, often undertaken jointly with the union.

Although counseling is very important (probably *because* it is), it is extremely difficult. Therefore, either specially trained counselors should be used, or personnel managers should have special training in order to know not only how to counsel but, more importantly, when to do it and when not to.

Almost all managers, regardless of their position in the organization's hierarchy, are involved to some extent in providing counseling and guidance. Managers have the right and the responsibility to become involved when employees' personal problems begin to have a noticeable negative effect on their work or that of other employees.

The two areas that require counseling are job-related activities and personal problems. The job-related activities are performance, disciplinary cases including absenteeism, safety, conflict, retirement, and outplacement.

Some of the personal problems requiring counseling and guidance are (1) personal crises, (2) chemical dependency, including alcoholism and drug abuse, and (3) physical, mental, and emotional illness.

For best results, managers should restrict counseling to the employee's job performance and make the counseling and guidance as specific as possible. Then the employee has something concrete to work on in improving job performance.

Discipline is necessary to perform the personnel function. It may be (1) positive, providing freedom of self-expression and emotional satisfaction, or (2) negative, involving force or outward influence.

Formerly, discipline involved unilateral punishment. The manager had almost complete control over employees. Now, under the judicial due process, there must be predetermined—and preannounced—rules and penalties for violations.

The disciplinary problems most frequently encountered are absenteeism, tardiness, and poor productivity, work habits, and/or attitudes.

Penalties for violating rules are applied on a graduated basis as the severity of the offense increases or as the frequency of the offenses increases. As the severity of the offense—and penalty—increases, the authority for applying discipline shifts from the supervisor, to higher level line managers, to the personnel executive.

Discipline in nonbusiness organizations takes different forms, especially in public organizations where there are more appeals procedures.

QUESTIONS

1. What is the role of counseling in personnel management? Why is it so important?
2. What benefits can you expect from effective counseling? Explain how and why the benefits arise.
3. "Counseling should avoid personal problems." What is the reasoning behind this statement? What is the limitation of the statement from the manager's point of view? What is the reasonable boundary in dealing with an employee's personal life in counseling?
4. What are the different roles and areas of counseling, if any, provided by the immediate supervisor and a professional counselor?
5. Do you think that drugs are as great a problem in industry as shown in this chapter? Explain.
6. What is discipline? Why is discipline so important in organizations?
7. To what extent is the concept of self-control important as a means of discipline?
8. How is discipline administered by the judicial due process?
9. What are the major disciplinary problems in organizations today?
10. Who should administer discipline? Explain.

PROBLEMS

13-1. The Indispensable Nurse

The nature of the organization's operations determines what is an acceptable or an intolerable offense for disciplinary purposes. What is acceptable in one type of industry might not be in another. A head nurse in a large hospital explained the following situation.

"I am responsible for staffing units for best coverage on the 3-to-11 shift. Saturday, when staffing was short, we had an unusual number of admissions because of an explosion about 10 miles away. The house was very busy, especially on medical units. There were four employees on each unit, except for one unit that had five people—three nurses and two nurses' aides. The intensive care unit desperately needed another nurse.

"Joe Blow, my only male nurse on duty, was versatile and could care for male patients. I asked Mr. Blow to work on the busy unit. He became very angry and said that if he was not needed on his assigned unit, he would go home and come back when he was needed. I gave him every opportunity to work, explaining that he was my choice because he was flexible, knowledgeable, and good with the male patients. He became hostile and said I was unfair, that I always asked him to do extra work because he was the only male in the house. This may have been true, as male nurses are in the minority.

"He was so upset that I could not reason with him. I told him it was his decision if he left and not mine, but I felt that he would be making a mistake. I also informed him that it would mean termination if he left a nursing unit understaffed.

"Mr. Blow clocked out and left. He was terminated at that time."

Questions

1. What would you have done if you were the head nurse? Explain.
2. Why do you think Mr. Blow acted the way he did?
3. Would his behavior have been acceptable under other circumstances? Explain.

13-2. The Young Librarian

Jo Ann was the assistant librarian in a medium-sized government agency. It was her first job after she finished school, and she had been in the department for about two years when she was promoted into a supervisory position. After about a year, she reported the following problem:

"I was the youngest employee in the department when I was hired. I soon found out that it is hard to supervise employees who are older as well as more experienced, even when they have less education. I have overcome most of my supervisory problems, but I still find it hard to treat everyone fairly or spread my time evenly. I think the main problem is keeping peace between the other employees.

"One employee in particular doesn't seem to want to get along with anyone in the department. She takes separate lunch and coffee breaks. Every time we plan some sort of social event for the department, she can't agree with anyone else. If her ideas aren't used, she gets mad and won't have anything to do with whatever is planned. Her attitude toward me and the other employees makes it hard for me to treat her fairly. It is really hard to know the best way to handle such situations."

Questions

1. What would you advise Jo Ann to do?
1. How should she do it?

SUGGESTED READINGS FOR FURTHER STUDY

"BNA's Quarterly Report on Job Absence and Turnover." *Bulletin to Management,* September 14, 1978.

Fair, Ernest W. "Discipline: Wise or Otherwise." *Supervision* 40 (February 1978):19ff.

Foster, James A. "Humor and Counseling: Close Encounters of Another Kind." *Personnel and Guidance Journal* 57 (September 1978):46-49.

Gandz, Jeffrey. "Resolving Conflict: A Guide for the Industrial Relations Manager." *Personnel* 56 (November-December 1979):22-25.

Gersunny, Carl. "A Devil in Petticoats and Just Cause: Patterns of Punishment in Two New England Textile Factories." *Business History Review* 50 (Summer 1976):131ff.

Hutchins, David E. "Systematic Counseling: The T-F-A Model for Counselor Intervention." *Personnel and Guidance Journal* 57 (June 1979):529-31.

Oberle, Rodney L. "Administering Disciplinary Actions." *Personnel Journal* 57 (January 1978):29-31.

Sinick, Daniel. *Counseling Older Persons: Careers, Retirement, Dying.* New York: Human Sciences Press, 1977.

Wijting, Jan B. "Employing the Recovered Drug Abuser—Viable?" *Personnel* 56 (May-June 1979):56-63.

Witte, Robert, and Marsha Cannon. "Employee Assistance Programs: Getting Top Management's Support." *Personnel Administrator* 24 (June 1979):23-26, 44ff.

CHAPTER FOURTEEN

Maintaining Employee Safety and Health

Learning Objectives

After studying the material in this chapter, you should be able to:

1. Explain why employee safety and health are so important.
2. Describe the *Occupational Safety and Health Act* (OSHAct).
3. Explain how OSHAct influences employee safety and health.
4. Describe some of the most prevalent occupational health problems.
5. Show how employees can be protected from occupational health problems.
6. Explain the factors influencing safety and accidents.
7. Explain how safety management can help protect employees.

Some Important Words and Terms

Safety
Occupational safety
Occupational health
Occupational Safety and Health Act
  (OSHAct)
Occupational Safety and Health
  Administration (OSHA)

Compliance officers (COs)
Worst first
Preventive medicine
Stress
Safety management
Incidence rate

No man is an island, entire of itself; . . . any man's death diminishes me, because I am involved in mankind; and therefore never send to know for whom the bell tolls; it tolls for thee.
JOHN DONNE

Outline of the Chapter

In 1978, there were 4,760 job-related deaths in firms with over 10 employees.[1] There were about 5.66 million injuries, and 38.2 million lost workdays. This means that about one out of every 11 workers is injured on the job each year.

An earlier estimate was that a worker is injured on the job *every 14 seconds* and one killed *every 37 minutes* of the average workday.[2]

The Occupational Safety and Health Administration (OSHA) fined five firms $62,730 when the roof of the $8.5 million stadium in Rosemont, Illinois, collapsed. OSHA cited the firms for 8 willful violations and 14 serious violations of the Occupational Safety and Health Act (OSHAct). One of the charges was that there was not adequate temporary bracing of the arches in the roof.[3]

These figures provide a rough estimate of the importance of occupational safety and health to employees, employers, and society. The case illustrates the growing role of OSHA in forcing employers to be more safety-conscious.

This chapter will look at the background of safety and health problems, discuss the role of OSHAct, and show some ways of improving employee safety and health.

GROWING AWARENESS OF OCCUPATIONAL SAFETY AND HEALTH

Personnel managers realize that the safety and health of their employees is a matter of good economics as well as a humanitarian concern. Unconcerned employers suffer decreased performance and increased medical and insurance costs as a direct result of their indifference to safety and health policies.

What Is Occupational Safety and Health?

The term *safety* is an overall term that can include both safety and health hazards. In the personnel area, however, a distinction is usually made between them.

Occupational safety refers to the condition of being safe from suffering—or causing—hurt, injury, or loss in the workplace. *Safety hazards* are those aspects of the work environment that can cause burns, electrical shock, cuts, bruises, sprains, broken bones, and the loss of limbs, eyesight, or hearing. They are often associated with industrial equipment or the physical environment

---

[1]"Workplace Injuries and Illnesses Up Slightly in 1978," ASPA's *Occupational Safety & Health Review,* December 1979.

[2]"Surprisingly Higher Cost of a Safer Environment," *Business Week,* September 14, 1974, pp. 102–3.

[3]"OSHA Fines Five Firms in Connection with Stadium Roof Collapse," *Occupational Safety & Health Review,* December 1979.

and involve job tasks that require care and training. The harm is usually immediate and sometimes violent.

Occupational health refers to the condition of being free from physical, mental, or emotional disease or pain caused by the work environment. *Health hazards* are factors in the environment that, over a period of time, can create emotional stress or physical disease.

What Has Been Done

Interest in occupational safety and health is not new. Employers have been trying to improve the work environment for a long time—at least a century. What is new is the sense of urgency and commitment and the growing role of the government.

Society has shown its interest by passing many laws such as workers' compensation, the *Coal Mine Health and Safety Act*, the *Atomic Energy Act*, and the *Toxic Substances Control Act* of 1976.

Industry has shown its concern by forming safety organizations like the National Safety Council, the American Society of Safety Engineers, and the National Fire Protection Association.

Employers have provided air conditioning and ventilation systems in plants and offices, greater control of toxic materials, improved soundproofing, better illumination, and clean washrooms and cafeterias. The leading companies have usually included certain safety and health standards among their manufacturing and other operating standards.

Many industrial diseases, such as anthrax, silicosis, and phossy-jaw, have almost disappeared, although science has discovered or even caused new ones, such as radiation hazards and asbestosis.

Since accident protection is regarded as cheaper and more socially responsible than compulsory accident insurance, the new emphasis on safety has led to changing concepts in engineering and the establishment of personnel safety programs. However, problems in industrial safety and health have not gone away—despite technological progress—but have been magnified.

Balancing Safety and Health With Efficient Operations

The problem involved in providing safety and health in the work setting is one of degree. That is, how much safety should be provided, what should be done to protect health, who should pay for the protection, and what will be the effectiveness of providing safety and health?

Few people disagree with OSHAct's purpose of providing a safe and healthful workplace. Therefore, the basic thrust of this material is *not* how to do away with OSHAct or other safety and health activities. Instead, the problem is: How can employers balance the need for a safe, healthy work environment for their employees against the need for effective and economical operations?

This type of cost-benefit analysis must be considered by employers, employees, unions, and society as well. Society must choose the least costly method for achieving certain objectives in trying to reduce occupational illness and injuries—and the production of goods and services.

The real problem is: The costs involved are objective and easily quantifiable, but the benefits are subjective and difficult to measure.[4]

OSHACT'S ROLE IN MAINTAINING SAFETY AND HEALTH

OSHAct was passed December 29, 1970, and went into effect April 28, 1971. Industrial injuries and occupational disease were increasingly rapidly. The act was drawn up because of the failure of state governments, labor, and management to provide safe and healthy working conditions.

Employees complained about the way the law was being interpreted and applied. There were meaningless and costly standards, and the inspectors would give no advice or assistance—just write citations. Congress has since changed the law, and OSHA has relaxed some of the less meaningful rules and standards. OSHAct now promises a significant improvement in health and safety on the job.

Its Purpose

The purpose of the law is "to assure so far as possible [for] every working man and woman in the nation safe and healthful working conditions and to preserve our human resources." This is to be done by:

1. Encouraging employers and employees to reduce hazards in the workplace and to improve or expand existing safety and health programs or start new ones.
2. Establishing specific responsibilities for employer and employees.
3. Setting mandatory job safety and health standards.
4. Providing an effective enforcement program.
5. Providing for procedures for reporting job injuries, illnesses, and fatalities.
6. Encouraging the states to assume the fullest possible responsibility for administering and enforcing their own occupational safety and health programs. State programs are to be at least as effective as the federal ones.

---

[4]Edward Ginter, "Communication and Cost-Benefit Aspects of Employee Safety," *Management Accounting* 60 (May 1979):120-28.

Who Is Covered

The act covers every employer in a private business affecting interstate commerce (except as shown later). Federal, state, and local governments and employers covered by other federal safety and health laws are exempt.

Rights and Responsibilities of Employers

The *responsibilities of employers* are to provide (1) a workplace free from safety and health hazards, (2) safe tools with which to work, (3) equal standards for all employees without regard for race, sex, religion, or national origin, and (4) compliance with established standards.

Some of the *employer's rights* are to:

1. Request and receive proper identification of OSHA personnel prior to inspection of their workplace.
2. Be advised by OSHA personnel of the reason for the inspection.
3. Participate in the walkaround inspection of the workplace with the compliance officers and in the opening and closing conferences with them.
4. Borrow money from the Small Business Administration to comply with OSHA standards.
5. Have a free visit from a consultant who will give them practical advice about the job site's safety and health.

Rights and Responsibilities of Employees

The act *requires employees* to comply with occupational safety and health standards, as well as all rules, regulations, and orders issued under the law that apply to their own actions and conduct.

Some of the *employees' rights* are to:

1. Request the OSHA area director to conduct an inspection if they believe a hazardous condition exists in their workplace.
2. Request information from their employer on safety and health hazards in their work area, on precautions they need to take, and on what they must do if they are involved in an accident or exposed to toxic substances. (This will probably be an important aspect of safety and health during the 1980s.)

Administration of the Act

The law is administered by the *Occupational Safety and Health Administration* (OSHA) in the Department of Labor. OSHA (1) develops standards, (2) conducts inspections, (3) sees that the standards are followed, and (4) enforces actions through citations and penalties. There is now a special assistant to help small firms comply with the law.

The National Institute for Occupational Safety and Health (NIOSH) (1) conducts research into the causes and prevention of illness and injuries, (2) develops safety and health standards, and (3) develops educational programs.

The Occupational Safety and Health Review Commission settles contested enforcement actions between OSHA and the employers, employees, and/or unions.

Setting standards.   OSHA has issued (1) general industry, (2) construction, and (3) maritime industry standards. Most employers can find the standards that apply to them in the general industry grouping.

OSHA enforces the safety and health standards by (1) conducting compliance inspections, (2) reporting violations, (3) proposing correction of violations, and (4) imposing penalties.

Compliance inspections.   OSHA standards are enforced through compliance inspections made by specially trained *compliance officers* (COs). These inspections can be initiated by OSHA or result from complaints by employees. OSHA decides which industries and firms to inspect. The COs have the right to enter a workplace without advance warning to the employer and to inspect the premises.

In 1978, the Supreme Court decided in *Marshall* v. *Barlow's, Inc.*, that employers are not required to admit OSHA inspectors without valid search warrants, as it violates the Fourth Amendment. Despite this and other challenges, the inspectors are rarely kept out.

In 1979, Congress voted to exempt firms with ten or fewer employees from safety inspections if they are in relatively safe industries. Nearly 80 percent of American businesses would be exempted by this provision. In 1980, efforts were made to exempt workplaces with safety records that fall below the national average, as determined by state workers' compensation records. This would exempt 4 million workplaces, or over 90 percent of those now covered by the law.

SHOE

Reprinted by permission of the Chicago Tribune-New York News Syndicate, Inc.

Reporting violations.   The COs have the authority to impose penalties for violations of the standards. It would be very difficult to enforce compliance of the law without this right.

OSHA can impose a fine as high as $20,000 and/or a year in prison for the second conviction of a serious willful violation resulting in the death of an employee. The penalty for falsification of records is $10,000 and six months in prison. A penalty fine as high as $1,000 per day may be imposed without going to court.

About a third of the 58,000 inspections conducted by the agency in 1979 resulted in citations for serious hazards.[5]

Enforcement priorities.   OSHA inspectors are empowered to investigate firms selected for inspection according to the following priorities:

1.   Whenever catastrophes and/or fatalities are reported.
2.   Whenever an employee complains to OSHA about unsafe or unhealthful conditions.
3.   Whenever it is apparent that an injury rate for an industry is higher than the national average.

Obviously, all businesses cannot be inspected with any degree of frequency. Consequently, a system of *worst first* has been devised. Under this policy, 95 percent of OSHA inspections will be directed toward "high-risk" industries. The targeted industries are these: longshoring, meat and meat products, roofing and sheet metal, lumber and wood products, and miscellaneous transport.

Evaluating OSHAct's Effectiveness

In evaluating the effectiveness of the law, we need to look at some criticisms of it first and then look at some of its achievements.

Some criticisms.   Some specific criticisms of OSHAct are that (1) the standards are complex, vague and often hard to understand, (2) the matter of jurisdiction is confusing, (3) record keeping is burdensome, and (4) compliance is costly.

Standards.   Employers claim that the standards are too complex and too vague. They are difficult to interpret and hard to comply with. It is claimed that some sections are too general to explain completely how precautions should be taken.

A task force set up by the president to study safety and health estimated that "only 25 percent of accidents could be prevented through compliance with OSHA rules."[6]

---

[5]"Restraining OSHA: It's Just a Matter of Time," *Business Week*, May 5, 1980, p.110.

[6]"Accident Statistics That Jolted OSHA," *Business Week*, December 11, 1978, p. 63.

An effort is now being made to change from equipment and specifications standards to performance standards.

Jurisdiction. Another problem of major concern is jurisdiction, or who has control over what actions. The act allows certain federal agencies that exercise statutory authority to continue to prescribe or enforce standards and regulations affecting occupational safety and health. In addition, some states have now complied with the requirements of the law and are beginning to assume responsibility for enforcing it. Some of these state laws are quite different from the federal ones.

Record keeping. Many managers contend that record keeping is the most burdensome aspect of the law. It requires so much time, effort, and money. Employers with 11 or more employees are required to keep records as shown in Figure 14-1. These records include:

FIGURE 14-1
Record keeping required by OSHA

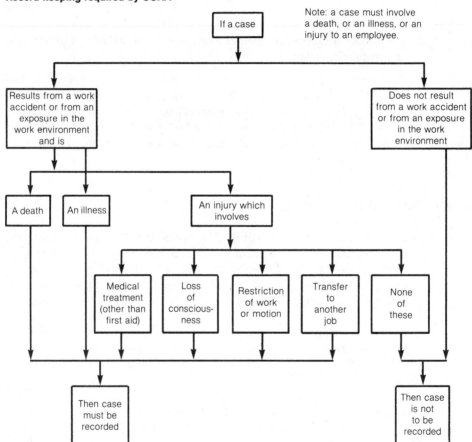

Source: U.S., Department of Labor, Bureau of Labor Statistics, *What Every Employer Needs to Know about OSHA Recordkeeping* (Washington, D.C.: Government Printing Office, 1979), p. 3.

1. OSHA No. 200—a log and summary of occupational injuries and illnesses.
2. OSHA No. 101—a supplementary record of each injury or illness (see Figure 14-2).

FIGURE 14-2

OSHA No. 101   Form approved
Case or File No. _____   OMB No. 44R 1453

Supplementary Record of Occupational Injuries and Illnesses

EMPLOYER

1. Name _____

2. Mail address _____
              (No. and street)   (City or town)   (State)

3. Location, if different from mail address _____

INJURED OR ILL EMPLOYEE

4. Name _____ Social Security No. _____
    (First name)   (Middle name)   (Last name)

5. Home address _____
     (No. and street)   (City or town)   (State)

6. Age _____   7. Sex: Male_____ Female_____ (Check one)

8. Occupation _____
      (Enter regular job title, *not* the specific activity he was performing at time of injury.)

9. Department _____
    (Enter name of department or division in which the injured person is regularly employed, even
    though he may have been temporarily working in another department at the time of injury.)

THE ACCIDENT OR EXPOSURE TO OCCUPATIONAL ILLNESS

10. Place of accident or exposure _____
           (No. and street)   (City or town)   (State)
    If accident or exposure occurred on employer's premises, give address of plant or establishment in which
    it occurred. Do not indicate department or division within the plant or establishment. If accident oc-
    curred outside employer's premises at an identifiable address, give that address. If it occurred on a pub-
    lic highway or at any other place which cannot be identified by number and street, please provide place
    references locating the place of injury as accurately as possible.

11. Was place of accident or exposure on employer's premises? _____ (Yes or No)

12. What was the employee doing when injured? _____
                  (Be specific. If he was using tools or equipment or handling material,
_____
            name them and tell what he was doing with them.)

13. How did the accident occur? _____
               (Describe fully the events which resulted in the injury or occupational illness. Tell what
_____
happened and how it happened. Name any objects or substances involved and tell how they were involved. Give
_____
full details on all factors which led or contributed to the accident. Use separate sheet for additional space.)

OCCUPATIONAL INJURY OR OCCUPATIONAL ILLNESS

14. Describe the injury or illness in detail and indicate the part of body affected. _____
                                  (e.g.: amputation of right index finger
_____
            at second joint; fracture of ribs; lead poisoning; dermatitis of left hand, etc.)

15. Name the object or substance which directly injured the employee. (For example, the machine or thing
    he struck against or which struck him; the vapor or poison he inhaled or swallowed; the chemical or ra-
    diation which irritated his skin; or in cases of strains, hernias, etc., the thing he was lifting, pulling, etc.)
_____

16. Date of injury or initial diagnosis of occupational illness _____
                                (Date)

17. Did employee die? _____ (Yes or No)

OTHER

18. Name and address of physician _____

19. If hospitalized, name and address of hospital _____
_____

    Date of report _____ Prepared by _____
    Official position _____

These records must be kept for five years. The summary part of OSHA No. 200 must be posted in the work area by February 1 of the following year.

Cost.   Cost is also an important object of criticism. The economic impact of the law must now be considered by the Review Commission when issuing standards, as well as when an appeal is filed.

The commission ruled that Continental Can did not have to spend $32 million for engineering controls to reduce noise when protective equipment would protect the employees' hearing.[7]

OSHA's attempt to lower acceptable noise levels for all work sites from 90 to 85 decibels illustrates the cost problem. A study of OSHA in 1976 estimated that it would cost $18.5 billion to do this with engineering controls.[8]

While labor unions are in favor of the tougher standards, management, being cost-conscious, is in favor of the more lenient 90 decibels—or using earplugs.

Some achievements.   Safety experts have long complained about the apathy of employees and management toward safety. OSHAct changed all that. When it had been in effect for one year, the Conference Board found that almost three out of five firms had issued stronger safety policies and had more numerous policy statements concerning safety.[9] The general consensus of the companies was that OSHAct had succeeded in fostering an increased awareness of safety and health in both employees and management. In fact, management has no real alternative to compliance with the law.

A study of 800 companies with over 500 employees each was conducted to   see how their health care programs had been affected. A marked increase was   noted, as preemployment physical examinations increased from 63 to 71 per cent. The percentage of work-related periodic medical exams increased from 40 percent to 53 percent.[10]

These statistics are most encouraging, especially as this is preventive medicine, which saves more lives than curative medicine.

But the real question is: How effective have the compliance officers, consultations, and penalties been? The evidence is mixed. Figure 14–3 shows that the rate of injuries, illnesses, and fatalities declined from 1973 to 1975. Then it began to rise. The number of workdays lost per 100 full-time workers increased each year.

---

[7]Frank R. Barnako, "Enforcing Job Safety: A Managerial View," *Monthly Labor Review* 98 (March 1975):36–39.

[8]"OSHA's Deaf Ear to Tighter Noise Control," *Business Week*, March 26, 1979, p. 30.

[9]Donald J. Petersen, "The Impact of OSHA on Management—A First Look," *Conference Board Record* 10 (October 1973):22–25.

[10]Seymour Lusterman, "Industry's Role in Health Care," *Personnel Administrator* 19 (March–April 1974):39.

FIGURE 14-3
How OSHAct has affected occupational safety and health

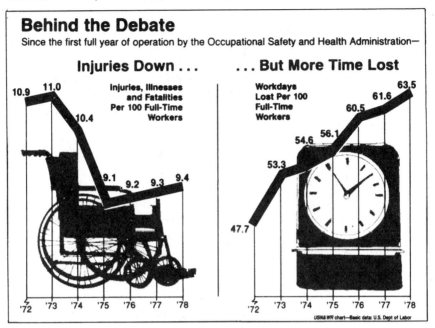

Behind the Debate

Since the first full year of operation by the Occupational Safety and Health Administration—

Injuries Down . . .   . . . But More Time Lost

Injuries, Illnesses and Fatalities Per 100 Full-Time Workers

10.9   11.0
10.4
9.1   9.2   9.3   9.4

Workdays Lost Per 100 Full-Time Workers

63.5
61.6
60.5
56.1
54.6
53.3
47.7

'72 '73 '74 '75 '76 '77 '78   '72 '73 '74 '75 '76 '77 '78

USN&WR chart—Basic data: U.S. Dept of Labor

Source: "Troubled OSHA Faces Further Loss of Power," reprinted from *U.S. News & World Report*, February 11, 1980, p. 79. Copyright 1980, U.S. News & World Report, Inc.

PROTECTING EMPLOYEE HEALTH

No longer are accidental deaths and injuries the overriding concern of personnel managers. Now they are concerned instead about occupational diseases, which are the primary killer of U.S. workers.

Extent of the Problem

In 1972, the U.S. government calculated that around 100,000 people die each year of occupational diseases, and 390,000 are disabled.[11] It is also estimated that the total cost of all environmental diseases may be $35 billion each year. Over $1 billion is now spent each year just in direct payments to victims of black lung disease.

Suspected occupational health hazards tend to be found in combination with noise, heat, and other forms of stress. These hazards can be acute or

---

[11]"Is Your Job Dangerous to Your Health?" *U.S. News & World Report*, February 5, 1979, p. 39.

chronic and can appear after a long latency period even if the original exposure occurred briefly. They can be difficult or impossible to diagnose early or with certainty.

The effects of these hazards—unlike those of safety hazards—may be slow, cumulative, irreversible, and complicated by nonwork factors. While an unguarded blade in a circular saw may present a severe and immediate danger, it is often difficult to anticipate the severity of imminent danger contained in a brief exposure to a potential carcinogen that can take years to cause a tumor or death. However, the probability of dying from cancer may be even higher than that of being injured by the saw.

Affected Occupations

Miners, construction and transportation workers, and blue-collar and lower level supervisory personnel in manufacturing industries experience a greater incidence of both occupational disease and injury than others. However, occupational health problems are not limited to industrial or agricultural workers. They affect white-collar workers and corporate executives as well.

Dentists are being studied for the possible effects of x-radiation, mercury, and anesthetics on them. They have the highest suicide rate of any professional group and a higher incidence of diseases of the nervous system, leukemia, and lymphatic malignancies. *Operating room nurses* suffer several times the miscarriage rate of other nurses and give birth to a larger proportion of children with congenital deformities. *Cosmetologists* (beauticians) display excessive cancer, respiratory, and cardiac disease. *Administrators* are far more likely to develop coronary disease than scientists and engineers.

From Noise

The UAW union calls the problem of noise the single greatest health hazard of the workplace.[12] Exposure to constant high noise levels can damage workers' hearing, make them irritable and inefficient, and drown out warning cries of impending danger.

Another area where "noise" is a problem is workplaces where loud music is played for long periods of time. This would include skating rinks, rock concerts, and some cocktail lounges. But even "background" music can make employees irritable without their knowing why.

From Heart Ailments

Only 25 percent of heart ailments, the leading cause of death in the United States, can be explained by known physiological and environmental factors,

---

[12]T. B. Copeland, "Clamoring for Action," *Newsweek*, July 7, 1975, p. 52.

such as overweight, hypertension, serum cholesterol, and cigarette smoking.[13] Quite possibly, a substantial proportion of the 75 percent of heart disease risk that is presently unaccounted for could be related to work and its attendant hazards, particularly *stress*.

From Cancer

Another occupational disease is cancer. It is the second leading cause of death in the United States, and its incidence has risen rapidly with industrialization. In 1900, only 4 percent of deaths was attributable to cancer; by 1968, the proportion was 16 percent.

It is not presently known how much cancer is occupationally related, but there seems to be a general consensus among cancer researchers and environmentalists that probably one-half of this figure is complicated by occupational factors. The experience of chemical and asbestos workers, underground uranium miners, and rubber workers, as well as other occupational groups, indicates that "excess" cancer of various types is indeed occupationally related.

In coke-oven plants, for example, studies show that because of coal tar pitch emissions, workers are ten times more likely to get cancer than other workers. The industry is expected to spend over $800 million to meet OSHA's new standards.[14]

There is growing evidence that asbestos may also increase the chances of lung cancer.

From Respiratory Diseases

Chronic diseases of the respiratory system are becoming major causes of death and disability. Chronic bronchitis and emphysema are the fastest-growing diseases in the United States, doubling every five years. Much of the respiratory disease that plagues the workers is job-related.

Asbestos workers risk developing a chronic lung ailment, asbestosis, also known as "white lung disease."

Around 5,000 California shipyard workers filed a $1 billion suit against 15 asbestos manufacturers. They charged the firm with "a conspiracy to withhold and distort evidence of health dangers associated with asbestos."[15]

---

[13] *Work in America: Report of a Special Task Force to the Secretary of Health, Education, and Welfare* (Cambridge, Mass.: MIT Press, 1973), p. 79.

[14] "Is Your Job Dangerous to Your Health?" p. 41.

[15] "$1 Billion Asbestos Suit Alleges Industry Cover-up," *Occupational Safety & Health Review*, December 1978.

FIGURE 14-4
Relationship between stress and performance levels

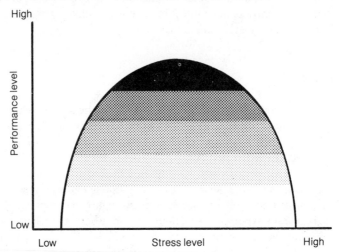

Source: Reprinted from the August, 1979 issue of *The Personnel Administrator* with
permission of The American Society for Personnel Administration.

From Stress

Stress can be defined as a state of bodily or mental tension resulting from
factors that tend to alter an existing equilibrium.

One authority has stated that all the physical and mental demands we make
cause stress.[16] Stress tends to be related to change. Therefore, it can be either
helpful or harmful. In fact, as shown in Figure 14-4, some stress is needed for
us to perform effectively. But a point is reached where it begins to restrict
performance.

Harmful aspects of stress. The harmful aspects of stress seem to be present in the workplace to a great extent. As you have seen in the previous
discussion, there are now increasing pressures in most jobs, occupations, and
industries. There are also many strains brought to the job from outside the
work area. New value systems are causing many problems. Figure 14-5 shows
how the new job demands and value systems are combining to cause greater
stress, especially on managers.

As more women become managers, they are expected to have more stress-
related problems. According to the head of the Life Extension Institute,
women are beginning to have more heart diseases, ulcers, and other diseases
traditionally associated with male executives.[17]

---

[16]"Secret of Coping with Stress: Interview with International Authority Dr. Hans Selye,"
U.S. News & World Report, March 21, 1977, p. 51.

[17]"Stress Has No Gender," *U.S. News & World Report*, November 15, 1976, p. 73.

FIGURE 14-5
Relationship between new job demands, new management values, and greater management stress

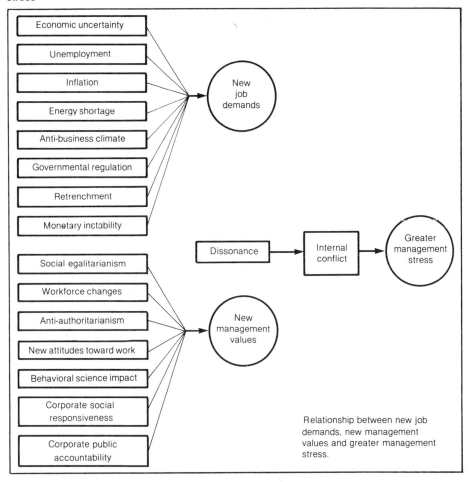

Source: Reprinted from the November, 1978 issue of *The Personnel Administrator* with permission of The American Society for Personnel Administration.

Peggy Lancaster, a principal and creative director of an ad agency, said, "I don't know any woman who doesn't have some form of stress or some kind of physical result of it."

Coping with stress. There are two ways of coping with occupational stress—self-management and organizational assistance.[18]

---

[18]John D. Adams, "Guidelines for Stress Management and Life Style Changes," *Personnel Administrator* 24 (June 1979):35-38.

Self-management.   Self-management includes good nutritional habits, exercise, relaxing, separating work and nonwork life, and personal planning, including life, career, and time management.

Organizational assistance.   Organizational assistance includes counseling, identifying and changing stress-provoking norms, team building, and periodic physical exams that include setting clear goals and performance standards.

Many employers are now providing *physical fitness* programs for employees. These are quite helpful for those with heart problems. They also help relieve depression and reduce boredom.

PepsiCo Corporation's headquarters has jogging tracks, a football field, a baseball diamond, and courts for basketball, tennis, and volleyball.

From Alcoholism and Drug Abuse

As shown in the previous chapter, alcoholism and drug abuse are now major illnesses that personnel managers must cope with.

How to Maintain Employee Health

In addition to providing more efficient performance, health services act as an effective employee benefit and help in recruiting. Yet they do have drawbacks, including rising costs and the search for qualified medical personnel.

For valid health standards and care, the hazards must be identified, and special procedures used to prevent their occurrence. But the main problem is obtaining adequate data about employee health.

Monsanto Chemical is planning a computerized system to "keep tabs on the health of its 50,000 employees at 200 plants." Their medical histories and exposure to various substances, data on products the firm makes, and government regulations will be kept in the computer to detect cause-and-effect relationships between exposure to substances and diseases.[19]

Occupational health problems can be most effectively dealt with through the practice of *preventive medicine*. But this is exceedingly underdeveloped in the United States. Preventive medicine needs a different kind of approach—one that emphasizes the reduction of exposure to potentially harmful substances.

PROTECTING EMPLOYEE SAFETY

Occupational safety is a condition involving *relative* freedom from danger or injury. Although totally safe conditions are theoretically possible, they are rarely found in the organizational world. Therefore, what I am referring to in this discussion is how the employer can maintain conditions in which employees will not only *be* safe but also *feel* safe.

Factors Influencing Safety

There are several factors affecting occupational safety. They are not independent but influence each other.

Organization size. The smallest and largest organizations tend to be the safest places to work. Companies with under 20 employees or over 1,000 are considerably safer than those in between. Statistically, the most dangerous organizations are those with 50 to 1,000 employees.[20]

Type of industry. As you will see later from Figure 14-6, the type of industry has a great deal to do with the safety and health of the workplace. To understand and improve safety, personnel managers should compare their record with the average for the industry in which they are operating.

Human variables. Many human variables, both personal and occupational, influence safety. However, only management attitudes and style, job satisfaction, and personal characteristics will be discussed.

Management attitudes and style. Several studies have shown that management attitudes and style influence the way employees think about safety. Some attitudes and styles encourage subordinates to take individual responsibility for safety, while others may encourage a belief that safety is management's responsibility.

A study of firms with low work accident frequency and severity rates found top managers highly interested and involved in safety programs.

---

[19]*The Wall Street Journal,* October 10, 1978, p. 1.

[20]New York State, Department of Labor, Division of Research and Statistics, *Injury Rates in Factories—New York State,* 1966.

They also supported and actively participated in safety activities. It also showed that first-line supervisors with a wide span of management had a higher injury rate than those with a narrow span.[21]

Job satisfaction.   There is also a relationship between job satisfaction and safety. Job design programs discussed in Chapter 10 may have a positive effect on safety as well as making employees happier.

A study at one plant showed a close link between job satisfaction and a low injury rate.[22]

Personal qualities.   Safety engineers are convinced that accidents often result from individual personal qualities. Patterns of accident frequency have shown that there are accident-prone people who can be identified during the selection procedure.

Studies show that accidents tend to be caused by people who (1) have tendencies toward emotional insecurity, low motivation, and egocentric aggressiveness, (2) show hostility toward themselves, (3) are single, and (4) are between the ages of 20 and 24.[23]

It appears from the progress made thus far that a short test to determine accident-proneness is possible. Further studies are being conducted with this objective in view.

Causes of Accidents

Accidents do not just *happen;* they are caused. Among the many causes are human factors (such as those just mentioned), environmental causes, and technical causes.

Human factors.   Resistance to safety rules is bound to occur, and personnel executives should be prepared for it. Unsafe personal acts, such as removing safety devices or making them inoperable, horseplay, fighting, poor attitudes, and improper operation of equipment lead to accidents.

Environmental factors.   Some of the environmental causes of accidents are climatic variables, such as disorderly housekeeping, poor ventilation, and improper or inadequate lighting and job-related stress or tension.

Technical factors.   Technical causes of accidents include unsafe chemical, mechanical, or physical conditions such as defective tools and equipment, unsafe mechanical construction or design, lack of—or improper—personal protective equipment, and inadequate mechanical guards for machines or work areas.

---

[21]Rollin H. Simonds, "OSHA Compliance: Safety Is Good Business," *Personnel* 50 (July–August 1973):30–39.

[22]George Clark, "Safety after the Revolution," *Job Safety and Health* 3 (May 1975):5–8.

[23]See Simonds, "OSHA Compliance," pp. 30–39; and L. F. Senger, "Workman's Compensation Costs," *Best's Insurance News,* Fire and Casualty ed. 63 (February 1963):89.

Safety Management

As shown earlier, effective *safety management* begins with top management's commitment and dedication to improving safety. This includes (1) assigning definite responsibility for the program, (2) identifying and measuring the problem, (3) training and educating *all* employees, and (4) communicating the need for safety and motivating employees to strive for it.

Assigning definite responsibility for safety. There is a trend toward shifting responsibility for safety matters—like other personnel activities—upwards within a company to the personnel manager, who is now usually a vice president. Also, the more progressive companies are centralizing the safety function at the corporate level, apparently in an effort to achieve more uniformity in safety and health standards throughout the organization.

The personnel manager tends to have a safety committee to (1) help set policies, (2) help enforce them, (3) train and educate the workers, and (4) communicate with and motivate employees. There is also usually a safety engineer to help improve the technical aspects. Unions also play an important role in seeing that everything possible is done to prevent accidents.

Identifying and measuring the problem. If personnel managers are really to understand the magnitude of the safety question, they must be able to identify the problem areas and measure their frequency and severity. This has been standardized so that organizations can compare their rates with national and industry figures. Although several statistics are computed, the most frequently used ones are the accident and illness *incidence rates* established by the National Safety Council, as shown in Figure 14-6.

Notice the incidence rate, on the left, for the *number of injuries or illnesses* per 100 full-time employees working 40 hours per week for 50 weeks, or 200,000 employee hours. This incidence rate is computed as follows:

$$\text{Incidence rate} = \frac{\text{Number of injuries and illnesses} \times 200{,}000}{\text{Number of employee hours worked in the period}}$$

The rate on the right is for the *number of days away from work.* This incidence rate is computed as follows:

$$\text{Incidence rate} = \frac{\text{Number of work days lost} \times 200{,}000}{\text{Number of employee hours worked in the period}}$$

Training and educating employees. Managers are responsible for seeing to it that all employees know (1) their job, (2) how to use the equipment and facilities, (3) the hazards of the work area, (4) how to control or deal with the hazards, (5) safety rules, and (6) first aid.

Not only should new workers be trained, but older ones should be retrained when equipment and methods change.

Communicating with and motivating employees. There should be constant communication with employees to encourage them to think and act safely. Also, campaigns should be held to motivate employees to try to improve safety.

FIGURE 14-6
Incidence rates, by industry, 1978

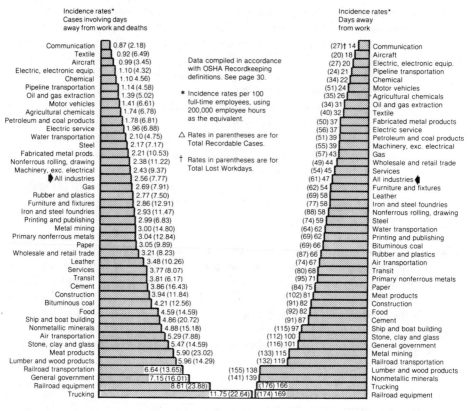

Source: *Accident Facts*, 1979 Edition, National Safety Council.

Dow Chemical Company found about 30 off-the-job disabling injuries for every one employee injured at work. Management went to work persuading employees and their families to think about safety constantly. The main thrust was to create a family and community awareness of safety through the use of the slogan "Life Is Fragile—Handle with Care," including the logo shown in Figure 14–7, the version used in French-speaking parts of Louisiana. Within a year, employee-disabling injuries were found to be drastically reduced, which meant savings to the company.[24]

SUMMARY AND CONCLUSIONS

One of our most basic needs is safety. Top managers—including personnel managers—are now paying more attention to safety than ever before. Organi-

---

[24]"Life Is Fragile—Handle with Care," *Job Safety and Health* 3 (August 1975):4ff.

Copyright 1969 by NEA, Inc. Reprinted by permission of NEA.

FIGURE 14-7
Logo of the Dow Chemical Company safety campaign (French version)

zations have organized to get the job done. Management seems to be giving added force to its commitment to safety and health, from both humanitarian and cost points of view.

There is a need, though, to balance the human and material benefits of better employee safety and health against the cost involved. This requires a balancing of scarce resources.

The purpose of OSHAct is to ensure safe and healthful working conditions for everyone. Therefore, the law covers every employer in a business affecting interstate commerce. The law is enforced by the Department of Labor's Occupational Safety and Health Administration. Its functions are to develop standards, conduct inspections, see that standards are followed, and enforce actions where the standards are not met.

Some management criticisms of OSHAct are (1) vague and complex standards, (2) confusion over jurisdiction, (3) the volume and detail of statistics and record keeping, and (4) the cost. Its achievements include a lower incidence of injuries, illnesses, and deaths. But more time has been lost from work.

The most prevalent employee health problems are (1) noise, (2) heart ailments, (3) cancer, (4) respiratory diseases, and (5) stress. Occupational health care is shifting from curative to preventive medicine. Interest in employee fitness programs is now high.

Employee safety is influenced by (1) the employer's size, (2) the type of industry, (3) management attitudes, (4) job satisfaction, and (5) employee qualities. Accidents are caused by human, environmental, and technical factors.

Safety management includes (1) assigning responsibility, (2) identifying and measuring the extent of the problem, (3) training and developing employees, and (4) communicating with and motivating employees about safety.

OSHAct was a much-needed piece of legislation. But, as is the case with any law, its success lies in how vigorously it is enforced. And, with this law in particular, it is essential that there be cooperation from both management and labor. It seems that it has now been achieved. It is to be hoped that lives will be saved, our human resources will be enhanced, and our economic well-being will be improved.

QUESTIONS

1. How would you differentiate between occupational health hazards and safety hazards?
2. What are the major occupational diseases in the United States?
3. What can be done to prevent or minimize them?
4. How are accidents, illnesses, and deaths measured? Of what value are the results?
5. What are the objectives of OSHAct? Whom does it cover?

6. How would you evaluate the effectiveness of OSHAct?
7. What should be included in an effective safety program?

PROBLEMS

14-1. The Disobedient Painter

Joe is a painter in an automobile repair shop. You have given him a mask and other protective equipment to be used when painting, but Joe doesn't like to wear it. Several times you have caught him painting without the mask, and each time, you have cautioned him about the hazard of not using it. Each time, he has promised to wear it. You warned him that you would discipline him the next time you caught him without it. That time came today.

Questions

1. What are you going to do? Explain.
2. What can a manager do to encourage the use of safety equipment?

14-2. The Four E's of Accident Prevention

A safety engineer speaking to an ASPA chapter made the following statement:

> Although volumes could be written on how to improve safety, the only thing needed is to use the "4 E's of accident prevention." They are:
>
> 1. *Engineering*—design and build safety into all machines, muffle all unnecessary noises, and maintain enough space for safe operation.
> 2. *Education*—teach all personnel the proper procedures for safe operation.
> 3. *Enforcement*—enforce *all* the safety rules to prevent careless accidents from happening.
> 4. *Enthusiasm*—promote enthusiasm in employees regarding safe procedures and policies.

Questions

1. Do you think these four components are sufficient for accident prevention? Explain.
2. What else might be needed?

SUGGESTED REFERENCES FOR FURTHER STUDY

Aikin, Olga. "What Is 'Reasonable' on Safety?" *Personnel Management* 11 (November 1979):54.
Anderson, Rebecca Cogwell. "Preventing Health Problems in Pregnant Workers." *Personnel Administrator* 24 (November 1979):43–44.

Corn, Morton. "An Inside View of OSHA Compliance." *Personnel Administrator* 24 (November 1979):39–42.

" 'Job Burnout': Growing Worry for Workers, Bosses," an interview with Cary Cherniss, an expert on job stress. *U.S. News & World Report*, February 18, 1980, pp. 71–72.

Larson, K. Per. "How Companies Can Rein In Their Health Care Costs." *Personnel Administrator* 24 (November 1979):29–33.

Martin, Alan. "Tuning In to Hearing Hazards." *Personnel Management* 11 (November 1979):43–46.

Notkin, Herbert, and Leland V. Meader. "The American Health Care System." *Personnel Administrator* 23 (May 1978):18–23.

Pyle, Richard L. "Corporate Fitness Programs: How Do They Shape Up?" *Personnel* 56 (January–February 1979):58–67.

"Reducing Stress through Preventive Management." *Human Resource Development* 18 (Fall 1979):15ff.

Schuler, Randall S. "Effective Use of Communication to Minimize Employee Stress." *Personnel Administrator* 24 (June 1979):40–44.

PART FOUR

Compensating
Employees

*By dealing loyally and punctually with subordinates in all engagements which he
makes with them and allowing a liberal scale of pay—that is how the ruler gives
encouragement to people in the public service.*
CONFUCIUS

Employee compensation concerns everyone in the economy—from the president, who
is responsible for protecting the health and safety of the country (including its economic welfare), to the lowest paid individuals, who must use their wages as a means of
subsistence.

As you can see from Figure IV-1, compensation is an important part of the
personnel system. Wage and salary administration is highly subjective. Many value
judgments are involved in determining what should be paid to employees as compensation for their knowledge, education, training, time, and effort. Yet, from a practical
point of view, there must be rules, regulations, and policies applied to this sensitive
area of personnel management.

The ideas covered in this part include (1) the role of compensation, (2) some
of the factors that influence an employer's compensation policies, (3) how rates of pay
are set for different jobs, (4) how rates of pay are determined for individual employees,
(5) the use of financial rewards as motivators of employee performance, and (6) the
growing problem of providing employee benefits.

These topics are covered in the following chapters:

15. Wage and Salary Administration
16. Using Financial Incentives to Motivate Employees
17. Providing Employee Benefits and Services

FIGURE IV-1
How compensation fits into the personnel system

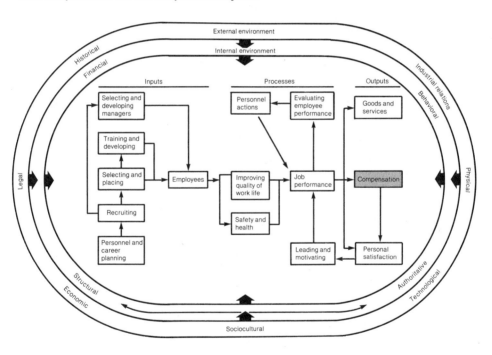

CHAPTER FIFTEEN

Wage and Salary Administration

Learning Objectives

After studying the material in this chapter, you should be able to:

1. Describe what is involved in wage and salary administration.
2. Explain why compensation is so important to employees, employers, and the nation.
3. Name and explain the roles played by compensation.
4. State your position on some of the more important compensation policy issues.
5. Name and describe the most significant factors affecting compensation policies and practices.
6. State why formal job evaluation is used.
7. Describe the job evaluation process.

Some Important Words and Terms

Wages
Salary
Wage and salary administration
Law of the wage share
Law of effect
Single rates
Rate ranges
Time wages
Day work
Incentive wages
Wage packages
Nonexempt workers
Exempt employees

Minimum wage
Overtime pay
Domino effect
Teenwage
Prevailing wage rates
Going wage rates
Wage and price guidelines
Cost-of-living adjustments (COLAs)
Consumer price index (CPI)
Uncapped cost-of-living adjustments
Job evaluation
Wage and salary surveys

Tell me and pay me what I'm worth. Tell me where I can go and help me grow there.
ANONYMOUS

What have workers wanted through the ages?
Shorter hours and higher wages.
What have employers wanted for aye?
Longer hours and lower pay.
SAMUEL PEPYS

Outline of the Chapter

Several managers were invited to submit a short statement of their philosophy of wages. Of the ones received, the following was representative of what practicing managers think the basis for employee compensation should be.

"Employees feel that their worth to the employer is measured in a great part by the earnings they receive. It is important to make the employees aware that to a large degree their earnings are a direct result of the work they perform. Thus the employer should make sure that each employee understands why he or she does or does not receive an increase. The employee deserves the truth concerning these matters. Many employers grant wage increases almost entirely on the basis of longevity, but I feel that productivity and cooperation are equally—or more—important. It is to the employers' advantage, as well as the employees', to pay personnel as much as possible under the circumstances."

The quotations and case illustrate the importance of wage and salary administration and what it is all about. This chapter will cover some of the problems involved in determining employees' earnings.[1]

WHAT WAGE AND SALARY ADMINISTRATION INVOLVES

The term *wage(s)* has at least two meanings: (1) the payment, usually of money, for labor or services or (2) the money usually paid on an hourly, daily, or piece rate basis for chiefly physical work. A *salary* is usually paid for services requiring special training or abilities, in a fixed amount, and for a longer period of time, especially by the month. However, in this book, the term *wage* is used to refer to the general idea of income, not the restricted sense of pay to hourly employees.

As mysterious as it may sometimes appear to employees, *wage and salary administration* is simply the creation of a system of orderly payments that is equitable to both the employee and the employer and motivates employees to exert an acceptable effort in the performance of their job.

If this aim is to be achieved, there must be an efficient and effective program of compensation that is *internally equitable* and *externally competitive*, as shown in Figure 15–1. As you can see, several steps are involved in accomplishing this goal.

First, management needs to have well-conceived and clearly understood

---

[1]Total earnings are based on the interaction of the basic wage rate and the length of time worked (or the units of production, in the case of incentive systems). However, this chapter will deal only with the wage rate and/or total compensation and will not become involved with the period of time worked, or the units produced. These will be covered in Chapter 16.

FIGURE 15-1
How wage and salary administration operates

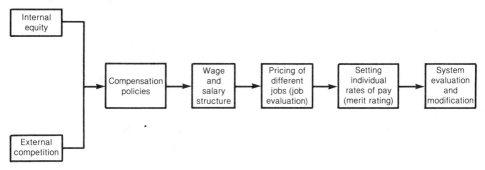

compensation policies, including the source of funds to pay the wages. Second, overall wage and salary structure should be set up. Third, differentials are determined for the various jobs and job ranges, including specific wage rates or ranges. Fourth, an appraisal of each employee's performance determines his or her salary within the range. Fifth, procedures for evaluating and modifying this process should be established.

IMPORTANCE OF COMPENSATION

Compensation is important to personnel managers for many reasons. Of all personnel problems, paying employees is perhaps the most perplexing one. It involves many emotional factors, as will be shown in the following discussion.

To Employees

Compensation is the primary—and often the only—source of income for employees and their family. Also, the concept of equity demands that employees be "fairly" compensated for the work they perform and the benefits they provide for the employer.

Compensation is also important because it determines our status in the social system. Our income is a measure of our worth to ourselves, our fellow workers, our family, and society.

Thus employees' absolute level of income determines their standard of living, while their relative income indicates their status, prestige, and worth.

Many authorities claim that compensation has only limited value in motivating employees, as higher needs are more important. This question is discussed in detail in the next chapter.

To Employers

The amount a firm pays its employees in the form of wages, salaries, and fringe benefits is quite important, as this cost factor interacts with total revenue to determine the firm's financial success. According to the economic *law of the wage share*, the ratio of employee wages to total business income has remained practically constant at approximately 50 percent since the turn of the century.[2]

Therefore, the primary way for employees to increase their earnings is to increase the company's sales and profits. A firm's compensation policy should be to pay wages high enough to attract, motivate, and retain qualified employees and, at the same time, low enough to insure adequate profits to attract new capital, expand productive facilities, and permit consumer satisfaction (at a reasonable price).

To the Nation's Economy

The nation also has an interest in the compensation problem. Most overt complaints of workers focus on their absolute and relative wage rates. Consequently, most strikes and grievances are over some aspect of wages. Also, the new employees discussed in Chapter 3—especially the professionals—are turning to militant labor unions. The reason is almost always compensation.[3]

Second, there is the ever present danger of inflation. If wage rates increase faster than increases in employee productivity, unit labor costs go up, and the inevitable result is a wage-price spiral. As you can see from Table 15-1, this has been happening for more than two decades. As wage rates increased faster than productivity, unit labor costs rose, and the consumer price index (CPI) increased at about the same rate. The same trend is found in manufacturing industries, even with all their automation (see Figure 15-2).

TABLE 15-1
The cost-push effect of rising wages on inflation (average annual rates of growth)

	(1) *Wage rises* *(percent)*	*(2)* *Productivity rises* *(percent)*	*(3)* *Unit-labor* *costs (1 − 2)* *(percent)*	*Inflation* *(Cpi)* *(percent)*
1960-1964	4.4	3.6	0.9	1.2
1965-1969	6.2	2.6	3.6	3.8
1970-1974	7.4	1.2	6.2	6.7
1975-1978	9.2	2.3	6.9	6.9

Source: Warren T. Brookes, "Do Wage Increases Cause Inflation?" *Human Events*, April 7, 1979, p. 17.

---

[2]Sidney Weintraub, "A Law That Cannot Be Repealed," *Challenge* 10 (April 1962):17–19.
[3]David J. Thomsen, "Compensation and Benefits," *Personnel Journal* 59 (January 1980):21.

FIGURE 15–2
The rising cost of labor (over two decades)

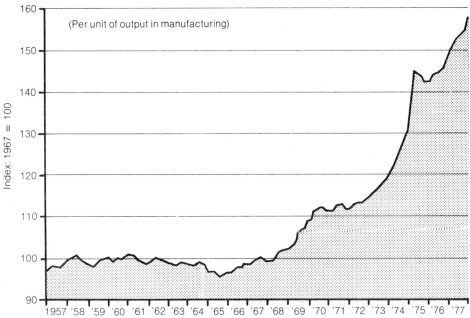

Source: *The Wall Street Journal,* March 14, 1978, p. 48.

Finally, compensation accounts for 75 to 80 percent of the nation's income. This is a drastic change from 1929, when it accounted for only 58 percent of the total. During this period of time, employees in business and government have increased from 78 percent to 86 percent of the total number of persons in the overall labor force.

ROLES PLAYED BY COMPENSATION

The previous discussion should help you understand the roles played by compensation. Employees are compensated for three reasons:

1. As equity, or pay for past service.
2. As a stimulus to improved performance in the future.
3. As a reward for joining and remaining with the organization.

There are several other services performed by compensation, including (1) attracting better employees, (2) reducing labor turnover, (3) and compensating employees for performing work they would otherwise not do.

As shown in Chapter 11, the *exchange theory* says that employees are willing to exchange their service for material and psychological rewards. In general, (1) the wage or salary performs the equity function, (2) financial

FIGURE 15-3
Types of employee compensation and how they are determined

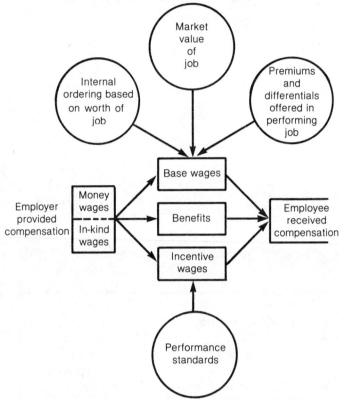

Source: Richard I. Henderson, "Influencing Employee Behavior through Compensation,"
in *Management of Human Resources*, ed. E. L. Miller, E. H. Burack, and Maryann
Albrecht, p. 237. © 1980, Prentice-Hall, Inc., Englewood Cliffs, New Jersey. Reprinted with permission.

incentives motivate for extra performance, and (3) employee benefits reward
for loyal service. This is shown in Figure 15-3.

The Equity Role

According to the *equity theory of motivation,* subordinates believe that the
employer's pay system—consisting of salaries, wages, bonuses, dividends, interest payments, and so forth—equitably rewards them for their efforts and
contributions. The process by which equity or inequity is perceived involves
the inputs and outcomes of the individual and "others." That is, employees
compare the rewards they receive from their investment in the job with the
rewards others receive from their investments.

Possible *inputs* are: education, experience, training, skill, seniority, and effort. Possible *outcomes* are pay, benefits, satisfying supervision, congenial colleagues, status symbols, and intrinsic rewards.

The Motivational Role

Compensation also satisfies the *expectancy theory of motivation,* as it serves as a motivator to future initiative and effort. However, there are many motivational factors influencing employee behavior, and it is impossible to identify and isolate any one variable as the specific stimulus to such behavior. The motivational role of compensation, however, is based upon the *law of effect.* This law states that employee behavior that appears to lead to reward tends to be repeated, while behavior that appears to lead to punishment tends not to be repeated.

This role will be discussed in detail in Chapter 16.

The Maintenance Role

Compensation is one of the *maintenance factors* in the two-factor theory of motivation. Employee benefits help keep employees from being dissatisfied, as you will see in Chapter 17.

Practical Objectives

Some practical objectives of any compensation program are to (1) create internal equity among positions, (2) ensure external competitiveness of earnings in the industry and communities in which the organization operates, and (3) reward individual performance.[4]

ESTABLISHING COMPENSATION POLICIES

There are several policy decisions the personnel manager must make at this point. They include:

1. Who is to be responsible for wage and salary administration.
2. What type of wage rate to use.
3. Whether to pay by time worked or by level of performance (productivity).

---

[4]Ray G. Foltz, "Compensation Communications," *Personnel Administrator* 25 (May 1980):22.

4. Whether to provide a fixed package of compensation for all employees, or to use variable (or flexible) packages for different individuals.
5. Whether salaries should be paid to all employees.
6. Whether to try to keep salaries secret or have an open policy.

Who Is Responsible for Wage and Salary Administration?

Wage and salary administration is a shared responsibility, as shown in Figure 15-4. Except for executive compensation and incentive and bonus plans, the personnel department has considerable responsibility. Even in those areas the operating managers depend upon personnel people for advice and assistance.

What Type of Wage Rate?

There are two ways of paying for a given job. First, a *single rate* can be paid to everyone who performs the job, regardless of the level of performance. Second, a *rate range* can be set whereby employees are paid different rates depending on how well they perform.

Who uses which type?   The use of single rates is growing in many industries (such as automobiles, trucking, steel, trade, and services) and occupations (including the crafts, production workers, and maintenance personnel). Rate ranges are used for most office and plant workers. Almost all government workers are paid this way, and they prefer it.

Unions' attitudes toward rates.   Generally, unions prefer single rates rather than rate ranges for the same type of job. In essence, they want to eliminate wage variations among workers doing the same or similar work.

When unions do accept wage ranges, it is largely for the purpose of securing higher wage rates than could be obtained under a single rate. Even then, the workers are expected to progress from the minimum to the maximum rate according to seniority or tenure.

The major disputes between the union and management are over (1) the amount of the wage rate that should be based on merit and (2) what criteria should be used in measuring merit. Difficulty arises when an employee is passed over for a merit increase within the range. When that happens, the union usually files a grievance and forces management to grant the increase. The net effect is that progression within the wage range becomes automatic, or semiautomatic, so that the maximum rate is reached by all employees in the minimum amount of time.

The union's argument for automatic progression based on length of service is that workers achieve merit with the passage of time through improvement in their productive ability. In general, when wage rates are based on seniority, age, or experience, attention is diverted away from job performance.

FIGURE 15-4
Personnel department responsibility for wage and salary administration in the Bureau of National Affairs' Personnel Policy Forum companies

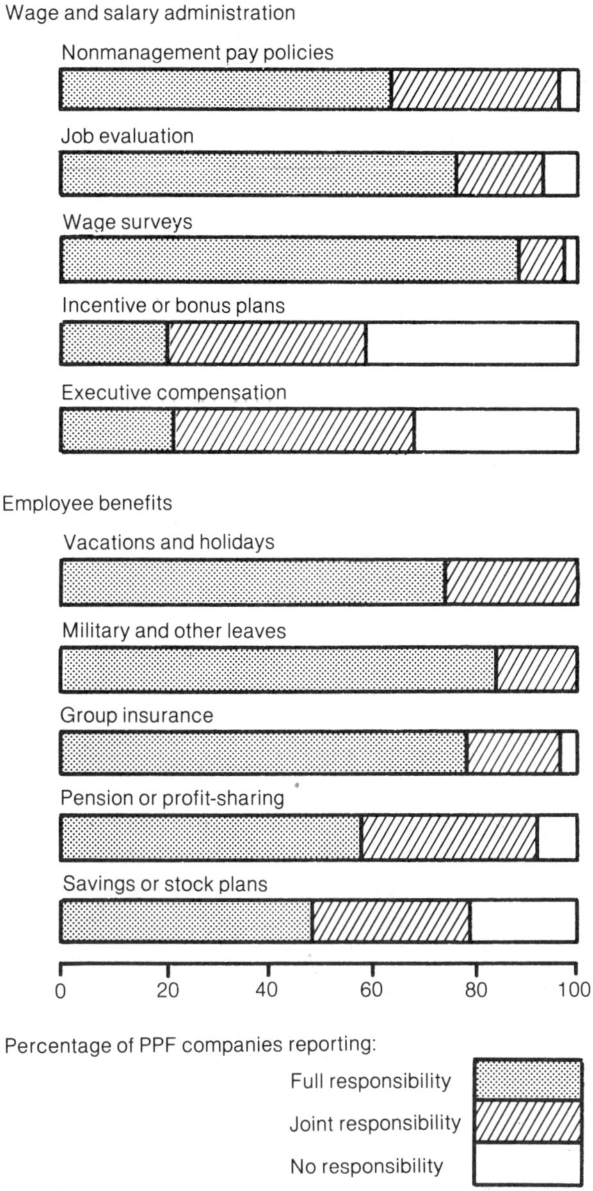

Wage and salary administration

Nonmanagement pay policies

Job evaluation

Wage surveys

Incentive or bonus plans

Executive compensation

Employee benefits

Vacations and holidays

Military and other leaves

Group insurance

Pension or profit-sharing

Savings or stock plans

0   20   40   60   80   100

Percentage of PPF companies reporting:

Full responsibility

Joint responsibility

No responsibility

Source: "BNA Policy and Practice Series:" *Personnel Management* (Washington, D.C.: The Bureau of National Affairs, Inc., No. 244), p. 251:22-23.

Pay for Time Worked or for Performance?

Essentially, there are only two bases for compensating employees. One is to pay for the amount of time the worker spends on the job, or the *input of time into the job*. The other is to pay for the amount of goods or services produced, or the *output from the job*. The first of these is called *day work* (or *time wages*) and tends to perform the equity function. The second, *incentive wages*, tends to perform the motivation function.

Use a Fixed or Variable Package?

During the last quarter-century, the use of wages and salaries to reward employees has given way to *wage packages*, in which benefits and nonwage items account for over a third of the total. Under this arrangement, each employee is given a stated amount of compensation. Then he or she must determine how the dollars are to be allocated for salary and for each type of benefit.[5]

This concept is based on the belief that employees will be better motivated and more satisfied if they have an opportunity to develop their own income arrangements. Indications are that employees favor this approach.

A study in a large aerospace firm found that over three-fourths of the workers would change the composition of their wage package if they could.[6]

Salaries for Everyone?

An extension of the "equal pay for equal work" argument is being used by some union leaders to justify paying hourly paid workers a guaranteed salary. They argue that it is inequitable for some employees to receive steady income by the month or year regardless of attendance or level of performance, while others are entitled only to payment by the hour or units produced.[7]

Arguments against salaries for everyone center around possible increases in absences. Several such plans are already in effect, as shown in Table 15-2. In general, the absence rate increased around 15 percent, which amounted to about 1 percent of the firms' payroll.

---

[5]System Development Corporation, a computer software firm, has developed a program to help employees to choose from among several alternatives. See J. R. Schuster, L. D. Hart, and Barbara Clark, "EPIC: New Cafeteria Compensation Plan," *Datamation* 17 (February 1, 1971):28–30.

[6]See Jay R. Schuster, "Another Look at Compensation Preferences," *Industrial Management Review* 10 (Spring 1969):1–18, for further details.

[7]See "Should Blue-Collar Workers Be Salaried?" *Business Management* 21 (March 1966):43ff., for these arguments.

It was also found that, although the supervisors were initially reluctant to assume added responsibilities (they had to administer the program), the change was taken in stride. In fact, Avon claimed that the changes increased the desirability of accepting supervisory positions.

According to Black and Decker's experience, the objective of developing a sense of unity among employees was reached, along with the achievement of historically good management-employee relations. At another plant, a 5 percent increase in employment since 1966 was matched by an 80 percent increase in productivity.

Secret or Open Pay Policies?

Historically, private employers have been very reluctant to discuss details of nonunion salaries. But surveys show that employees want to know more about compensation policies and practices.[8]

A survey by the Bureau of National Affairs (BNA) found that nearly three-fourths of the respondents had a written statement of their basic compensation policies (concerning such matters as paying competitive salaries, pay raises, and when they could be expected). But only two-thirds of these firms made their policy known to all employees.[9]

Many believe that more openness in these policies would result in higher employee motivation by bringing about more equitable pay systems. For example, another study showed a direct relationship between the type of pay system and pay satisfaction.[10] Satisfaction declined as the amount of information available declined.

FACTORS AFFECTING COMPENSATION POLICIES AND PRACTICES

The major factors that affect an organization's compensation policies and practices are:

1. Governmental factors.
2. Collective bargaining.
3. Standard and cost of living.
4. Comparable wages.
5. Supply and demand.
6. Ability to pay.

---

[8]Foltz, "Compensation Communications."

[9]Mary G. Miner, "Pay Policies: Secret or Open? And Why?" *Personnel Journal* 53 (February 1974):110ff.

[10]Paul Thompson and John Pronsky, "Secrecy or Disclosure in Management Compensation?" *Business Horizons* 18 (June 1975):67-74.

TABLE 15-2
Some results of changing from wage to salary basis of paying blue-collar employees at selected companies

Company	Union status	Date of change-over	Objective of changeover	Treatment of time clocks	Absence rate for workers affected by plan°			Employee reaction	Employer appraisal
					Before	After	Current		
Avon Products	Nonunion	1972†	Eliminate distinctions in treatment of office and factory employees	Removed	4.1%	4.4%	4.2%	Some preimplementation resistance from management; favorable post-implementation reaction, including that of supervisors	There were no specific gains, but management is satisfied that the approach is an essential part of its philosophy
Gillette	Nonunion	1955	Provide a logical alternative to improved sick leave	Retained	4.6	4.7	4.7	Generally favorable reaction, but initial minor concern about loss of status of clerical employees	Management is satisfied with the results

Company	Union status	Year	Objective	Plan status				Introduction	Response
Black and Decker	Nonunion	1971	Improve employee relationships, with consequent benefits to operational effectiveness	Removed	1.5‡	2.3	2.0	Introduction of plan a contribution to favorable attitudes; some supervisory concern over payment decisions	Response generated by the plan has allowed continued productivity improvements
Kinetic Dispersion	Union (UAW)	1962	Eliminate distinctions and provide security of income	Retained	§	§	§	Plan welcomed, but misused initially	Management is reasonably satisfied, although problems were far more severe than anticipated
Polaroid	Nonunion	1966	Unify hourly and salaried employees	Retained until 1972	5.0	6 0	6.0	Benefits of plan well accepted, but no fundamental change of attitude	Management is not unhappy and considers program now controlled

*Basis of measurement may vary, so figures are not comparable between companies.
†Weekly salary plan was introduced in 1972, but 1968 changes equalized treatment in most cases.
‡This applies for sickness only.
§Rates were not measured; substantial increase occurred after changeover.
Source: Robert D. Hulme and Richard V. Bevan, "The Blue-Collar Worker Goes on Salary," *Harvard Business Review* 53 (March–April 1975):108. Copyright © 1975 by the President and Fellows of Harvard College; all rights reserved.

Effective personnel managers recognize that these factors influence their decisions and these managers will evaluate the resulting positive and negative effects. Obviously, no one of these factors operates alone in determining the overall rate. Instead, they operate concurrently, some in one direction and others in the opposite direction. Thus the policies and practices selected are the result of pressures operating in various directions.

Governmental Factors

One of the strongest and most persistent pressures upon compensation policies and practices is the large number of government rules, regulations, executive orders, and laws. All states have laws pertaining to unemployment compensation, workers' compensation, and other aspects of employee compensation.

Fair Labor Standards Act.   The *Fair Labor Standards Act* (FLSA), passed in 1938 and amended several times since, is the basic wage and hour law of the land. It establishes the minimum wage, overtime pay, equal pay, and child labor standards for over 50 million full-time and part-time workers.

Coverage.   The law covers all employees of enterprises having workers engaged (1) in interstate commerce, (2) in producing goods for interstate commerce, and (3) in handling, selling, or working on goods that have moved (or will move) in interstate commerce. Also covered are employees in laundries, construction, health-care institutions, and educational institutions. Federal employees and some state employees are also covered. It applies to retail firms that have annual gross sales of over $325,000. Domestic service workers are covered if they work over 8 hours a week or earn over $100 a year.

These employees are called *nonexempt workers.*

Exempt employees.   Executives, administrative and professional employees, outside sales personnel, and other selected groups are exempted from the wage and overtime provisions of the law. They are referred to as *exempt employees.*

Basic wage and hour standards.   The basic *minimum wage* is now $3.35 an hour, before any overtime is added. *Overtime pay* of not less than one and one-half times the employee's regular rate must be paid for all hours over 40 in a given work week.

There are provisions for employing full-time students at rates lower than the minimum wage.

Child labor provisions.   For most nonfarm jobs, 14 is the minimum working age. Workers 14 and 15 can work on nonhazardous jobs for no more than three hours on a school day, eight hours on any other day, and 40 hours per week. Those 16 and 17 years old can work in nonhazardous jobs for unlimited hours.

Equal pay provisions.   The law prohibits wage differentials based on sex in jobs requiring *substantially* equal skill, effort, responsibility, and working conditions.

Source: U.S., Department of Labor, Wage and Hour Division, *Handy Reference Guide to the Fair Labor Standards Act,* Publication 1282 (Washington, D.C.: Government Printing Office, 1978).

The law does permit differences based on valid factors such as seniority, merit, and incentive systems.

Administration of the law. The Wage and Hour Division of the Labor Department administers the law for most employers. It also enforces the *Davis-Bacon Act,* the *Walsh-Healey Act,* and the *Age Discrimination in Employment Act.* the Civil Service Commission enforces the law for most federal employees.

Possible negative effects. It is claimed that increasing the level of an existing minimum wage has a *domino effect* on industry by increasing the cost of labor. First, the pay level of *all* employees increases, for differentials must be maintained. Second, the marginal workers are forced out of the labor force; employers cannot afford to pay them the higher wage if their productivity does not warrant it. Third, marginal employers are eliminated; they cannot produce at a level where revenues will provide for the higher wages. Finally, there are changes in production techniques, improvements in labor and management efficiency, and adoption of other productive factors.

There seems to be a definite correlation between changes in factor costs and minimum wage changes in low-wage industries.[11]

---

[11]See David E. Kaun, "Minimum Wages, Factor Substitution and the Marginal Producer," *Quarterly Journal of Economics* 69 (August 1965):478–86, for an excellent analysis of these factors.

A report by the Center for Study of American Business at Washington University, St. Louis, indicated that more than 300,000 jobs for teenagers were priced out of the labor market by recent hikes in the federal minimum wage.[12]

The president of Marriott Corporation said that recent increases in the minimum wage had "wiped out about 1,500 jobs." The company cut costs by combining jobs and mechanizing.[13]

Efforts are being made in Congress to permit employers to pay 16-to-19-year-old workers at a rate less than the minimum wage. So far, the *teenwage*, as it is called, has failed to pass.

Walsh-Healey Act.   The *Walsh-Healey Act*, passed in 1936, covers employees working on any government contract exceeding $10,000. It sets labor standards that require that (1) the *prevailing wage rate* in the area,[14] as determined by the Secretary of Labor, be paid covered workers and (2) no less than time and one-half be paid for all hours over eight worked in one day or over 40 hours in a given week.

Davis-Bacon Act.   The *Davis-Bacon Act*, passed in 1931, covers employees of construction firms with government contracts or subcontracts in excess of $2,000. It also requires payment of the prevailing wage.

Wage and price guidelines.   Another aspect of government regulation of wages has been the use of *wage and price guidelines* as a basis for wage adjustments. These guidelines are based on the assumption that inflation is the result of the wage-price-wage (or price-wage-price) spiral. Consequently, it is assumed that increases in the basic wage rate should be restricted to less than price increases.

In 1980, the pay guidelines set by the Council on Wage and Price Stability (COWPS) had a "7.5 percent-to-9.5 percent limit." They did permit employers without cost-of-living adjustments (COLAs) to bring their pay scales up to those of firms with them.

These guidelines force some painful decisions on personnel managers.[15] Although the guidelines are supposed to be voluntary, a Washington, D.C., Court of Appeals ruled in 1979 that the president can use the government's purchasing policies to force government contractors to obey them.[16]

---

[12]Cited in *U.S. News & World Report*, May 10, 1976, p. 8.

[13]"How the Minimum Wage Destroys Jobs," *Fortune*, January 1979, pp. 101–3.

[14]There are two phrases that are confusing—*prevailing wage rates* and *going wage rates*. Most personnel managers in business firms distinguish between *going wages*, or those currently being paid because of the condition of the labor market, and *prevailing wages*, or those set by the Secretary of Labor and based on the prevailing union rates in the area. This distinction is not made by governmental organizations, which use the term *prevailing wages*.

[15]See H. Hoover Yount, "Pay Guideline Maximization Approach to Salary Administration," *Personnel Administrator* 24 (June 1979):69–72.

[16]*Personnel Management—Policies and Practices*, Report Bulletin 6 (Englewood Cliffs, N.J.: Prentice-Hall, 1979), Section II, p. vii.

Government compensation policies and practices.   Government compensation policies and practices are similar to those of private employers. Job evaluation, salary surveys, and merit systems are extensively used. The government uses wage ranges and COLAs more than private employers, but makes less use of incentive wage plans and bonus programs.

How EEO affects compensation.   Public policy now requires equal pay for employees engaged in the same type of work.

Laws requiring equal pay.   Until the passage of the *Equal Pay Act* of 1963, which amended the FLSA, public policy on equal pay was found only at the state level. This law is now enforced by the EEOC.

Equal pay legislation is only a part of public policy prohibiting discrimination in pay. Title VII of the *Civil Rights Act* of 1964 prohibits differences in pay based on race, color, religion, sex, or national origin. The *Age Discrimination in Employment Act* prohibits discrimination against persons from 40 to 70 years of age. The *Vocational Rehabilitation Act* protects the handicapped against pay discrimination.

In addition, many state laws and local ordinances similarly prohibit pay discrimination.

Results of EEO requirements.   The results of this public policy have been mixed. As can be seen from Figure 15-5, the earnings of black workers rose from about 70 percent of white workers' in 1967 to about 85 percent in 1978. But those of women actually decreased relative to men's earnings. Women's earnings were about 63 percent of men's in 1967 but declined to 59 percent in 1978. They are now up to about 61 percent.

Collective Bargaining

Collective bargaining affects all the factors involved in determining the overall wage rate. When a union is involved, basic wages, fringe benefits, job differentials, and individual differences tend to be determined by the relative strength of the organization and the union.

This is now debatable. For example, one study found that from 1952 to 1958 there was a high correlation between union power and wage changes.[17] Another study indicated that unions had widened the pay differential between skilled and unskilled employees.[18]

However, there are many who reason that the gains in employee productivity achieved through mechanization (as well as a shortage of skilled personnel), caused wage increases.[19] Therefore, wages would have risen even without unions.

[17]Martin Segal, "Unionism and Wage Movements," *Southern Economic Journal* 28 (October 1961):174–81.

[18]Sherwin Rosen, "Unionism and the Occupational Wage Structure in the United States," *International Economic Review* 11 (June 1970):269–86.

[19]See Kenneth O. Alexander, "Unionism, Wages, and Cost-Push," *American Journal of Economics and Sociology* 24 (October 1965):389–95.

FIGURE 15–5

Blacks' relative earnings are increasing, but women's are not

Median usual weekly earnings of wage and salary workers who usually work full time, in current dollars, by sex and race, May 1967-May 1978

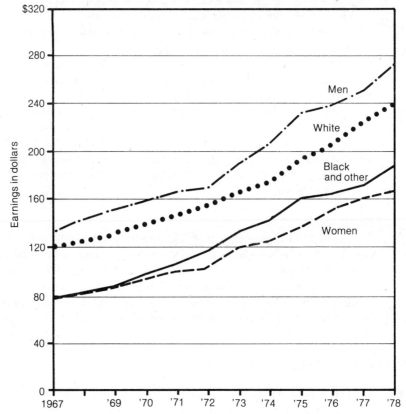

Source: *Monthly Labor Review*, August 1979, p. 35.

However, it is clear that wage changes under union conditions are less sensitive to high unemployment than under nonunion conditions. Regardless of the role unions play in determining wage rates, collective bargaining does seem to cause the basic wage rates in a community to become more nearly uniform. The union philosophy of equal pay for equal jobs, which tends to minimize ability and performance as factors in individual pay, leads to this result.

Cost of Living

After World War II, the cost of living tended to increase faster than employees' income. Therefore, the main demand of the United Auto Workers in 1948 was *cost-of-living adjustments* (COLAs) to employee wages. GM agreed to this, and so did many other employers.

Who is covered. The arrangement was popular until the early 1950s. Then interest in COLAs declined, for wage increases were greater than inflation. This has changed during the escalating inflation of the last decade. Now about 9 million workers in the automobile, communications, electrical, mining, steel, transportation, and rubber industries, among others, have COLA arrangements. So do many government employees.[20]

Most employers are affected by inflation whether they have formal COLA agreements or not. They must try to keep their employees' earnings related to the inflation rate. This is not always possible.

Professors' salaries rose 6 percent during the 1977–78 academic year, while the CPI rose 9 percent.[21]

How COLAs operate. The usual COLA in auto, steel, and trucking companies is a 1¢-per-hour increase in wages for every 0.3-point rise in the *consumer price index* (CPI). Some COLA agreements state that the wage increase is limited to a specified rate during a given period. However, there is now a trend toward having *uncapped cost-of-living adjustments*, whereby earnings can increase just as much as inflation, without any maximum or limit.

The National Education Association estimates that 32 of its affiliates have negotiated "unlimited raises pegged to inflation."[22]

Difficulties with COLAs. There are many difficulties—from an equity point of view—in using this method of income determination. First, the way the CPI is determined insures inequity for some workers. It is designed for urban wage earners and clerical workers. Second, as it is an abstract measurement, it does not actually measure employees' real cost of living. Third, it provides a common adjustment for employees covered, regardless of their performance. This means that it is inequitable to the better producers. Finally, it implies a constant standard of living, with employees merely maintaining their existing positions.

Comparable Wage Rates

Another factor affecting wage policies is comparable wages. An employer's policies and practices will, voluntarily or involuntarily, tend to conform to the wage pattern in the industry and in the community.

Industry rates. Employers will tend to conform to the wage pattern in their industry for several reasons. First, competition demands that competitors adhere to the same relative wage level. Second, various government laws and

---

[20]*U.S. News & World Report*, May 5, 1980, p. 14.

[21]*The Wall Street Journal*, March 27, 1979, p. 1.

[22]*The Wall Street Journal*, April 29, 1980, p. 1.

administrative and judicial decisions tend to result in conformity. Third, unions encourage this practice so their members can have "equal pay for equal jobs" and in order to eliminate geographical differences. Fourth, trade associations encourage uniform wage structures by providing wage information, including wage and salary surveys, to their members.

Finally, the inherent economics of related industries results in uniform wages. Functionally related firms of comparable size in the same industry require about the same number of employees with the same skills and experience. This reality results in considerable uniformity in wage and salary rates and compensation practices within a given industry and considerable diversity between industries. However, some industries do appear to be "high-wage" industries, while others may be characterized as "low-wage."

Employees at three U.S. Steel fabricating plants agreed to accept a modified wage freeze from 1981 to 1983 after the company threatened to close the plants because they were losing money. Employment costs were averaging $3.50 an hour more than at competing steel fabricators.[23]

Area rates. It is difficult for employers to pay rates that are substantially lower—or even higher—than those paid by others in the area. The pressure for uniformity is greater when labor becomes scarce than when it is plentiful. However, a company may choose to pay more in order to become known as a desirable place to work.

Occupational rates. An organization's compensation package should be related to, and comparable for, the various occupations. This is particularly true for managerial and administrative personnel, professional and technical workers, sales personnel, and—to a certain extent—clerical employees.

Probably the classic example of using occupational rates is the federal government's practice of tying the wages and salaries of its employees to comparable wages in similar occupations around the country.

Using wage and salary surveys to determine comparable wages. *Wage and salary surveys* provide much useful information that can help in determining compensation policies and practices. This information helps employers keep their pay rates and practices in line with others and prevents costly errors. The surveys are particularly helpful in keeping employee benefits competitive.

Area surveys are done by groups such as chambers of commerce and personnel associations. *Industry surveys* are performed by groups such as trade associations and the Bureau of Labor Statistics. *Occupational surveys* are an important service of most professional groups, like ASPA. Its salary survey is highly respected and widely used.

To be most useful, surveys must (1) include enough of the major employers

---

[23]*U.S. News & World Report,* December 24, 1979, p. 79, and January 14, 1980, p. 74.

"A computer breaks down and right away you want a raise!"

Source: Kaufman in *The Christian Science Monitor.* Used by permission.

to be representative, (2) be done frequently and currently so that the data reflect significant changes, and (3) be accurate and in a usable form.[24]

Market Conditions

The basic laws of economics, including the law of supply and demand, must be considered in establishing wage rates. Regardless of the other factors involved, an overriding consideration is the supply of employees relative to the demand for their services. Therefore, this relationship will determine wage rates, for they are the price the employer must pay, as the following headlines show:

Secretaries Get Better Pay, Broader Work, As Demand Outpaces Supply.[25]

Salary Spiral: Demand for Pathologists and Toxicologists Sends Pay Upwards.[26]

Ability to Pay

Regardless of other factors, wage rates are ultimately dependent on the employer's ability to pay. As previously indicated, wages constitute the most

---

[24]See Burce R. Ellig, "Salary Surveys: Design to Application," *Personnel Administrator* 22 (October 1977):41–48, for an excellent discussion of points to consider when preparing, conducting, summarizing, analyzing, and using a salary survey.

[25]*The Wall Street Journal,* January 29, 1980, p. 1.

[26]*The Wall Street Journal,* January 22, 1980, p. 1.

important cost item for most firms. This item, in turn, tends to establish the selling price of the product and thus influences the firm's profitability. It has also been pointed out that employees tend to receive a relatively fixed proportion of gross national product, of value added by manufacture, and of the company's sales. Therefore, there must be revenue before there can be wages. Moreover, there must be profit to the owners if the firm is to survive and wages continue.

Ability to pay is now becoming important in nonprofit organizations as revenues are not increasing as rapidly as costs.

USING JOB EVALUATION TO PRICE JOBS

If employees are to be fairly rewarded for their productive contribution, there should be a careful evaluation of the worth of each job in an organization. If feasible, the evaluation should be done in such a manner that the *relative* value of the jobs is reflected in the relative wage rates for the jobs. This does not mean that labor market factors such as shortages of employees with specific skills, experience, aptitude, education, and training can be ignored. However, these are usually included within the upper and lower job rates as determined by some form of job evaluation.

Whenever different wage rates are paid for two or more positions, job evaluation is used, consciously or unconsciously, because *job evaluation* means determining the relative value of jobs to the employer. Consequently, in order to determine the earnings and income of employees in given jobs most equitably, and to minimize inequities, complaints, grievances, and the resulting low morale, some type of formal job evaluation procedure should be used.

Value of Job Evaluation

Like most other personnel practices, job evaluation has its advantages and disadvantages. In general, the advantages of the system outweigh the disadvantages.

Reasons for using job evaluation. As far as wage and salary administration is concerned, an effective job evaluation program, efficiently administered, should provide several benefits. It helps to:

1. Develop a fair and equitable scale of wages, especially for new employees.
2. Determine the relative value of each job to the organization as a basis for determining wage increases for existing personnel.
3. Provide information for determining the qualifications needed in making selections, promotions, demotions, job changes, or transfers.
4. Satisfy EEO requirements.

The technique can also be used in the area of labor relations and negotiations. It can assist in (1) setting wage rates for new job classifications, (2) meeting grievances with facts rather than opinions, (3) limiting bargaining issues to factual matters concerning the job, and (4) establishing a method of rating employees fairly according to the skill and production requirements.

Some problems in using job evaluation.   Although it is feasible to obtain a reasonable degree of equity by using job evaluation, efforts to achieve a greater degree of precision in measurement have not been particularly rewarding. Some specific problem areas are that:

1. The worth of all occupations cannot be precisely measured with the same yardstick.
2. It is difficult to measure the worth of scientific, technical, professional, and managerial jobs.
3. It is difficult to separate the individual's contribution from the job being evaluated.
4. Unions tend to be opposed.

Union opposition tends to be declining, however, as more white-collar and professional personnel join unions.

In 1978, only 33 out of 108 AFL-CIO and independent unions had provisions for job evaluation in their contracts (up from 26 in 1971). Eleven of those were in government, professional, and technical unions (up from 1 in 1971).[27]

Steps in Job Evaluation

Four steps are usually involved in arriving at the specific job rates. These include (1) performing a job analysis, (2) grading the jobs, (3) assigning a price to each job, and (4) administering the resulting program.

These four steps are related to each other as shown in Figure 15-6. The process of *job analysis* results in *job descriptions,* which are refined into *job specifications.* These specifications define the requirements for performing the work and serve as the basis for hiring personnel. Job specifications are also used in *grading* the jobs. This step involves determining the relative worth of jobs and results in *job classifications.* The *pricing* step uses these grades, plus the company's basic wage scale, to determine the wage ranges for all the jobs to be evaluated. Then, in *administering* the program, some form of employee appraisal is used to evaluate the performance of workers performing those jobs and to assign them a specific rate of pay somewhere between the minimum and maximum rates. This figure becomes their rate of pay until they are rated again, the value of the job changes, or there is a general wage increase.

---

[27]Harold D. James, "Union Views on Job Evaluation: 1971 vs. 1978," *Personnel Journal* 58 (February 1979):80–85.

FIGURE 15-6
Steps in the job evaluation procedure

Step	Procedures and products used	Resulting product
STEP 1: *Analysis*	Job analysis → job description →	Job specifications°
STEP 2: *Grading*	Job specifications + Job evaluation and appraisal of the worth of job → job ratings →	Job grades
STEP 3: *Pricing*	Job grades + overall wage rate →	Job wage rates, or ranges
STEP 4: *Administering*	Job wage rates or ranges + appraisal of perform- ance or qualities of each employee →	Individual wage rate

°These specifications can be used as the basis for performing the job evaluation procedure, or they can be used to prepare
  a statement of the personal qualifications needed in a person to perform the job. This statement then becomes the basis
  of the recruitment and selection procedure.

Job analysis.   As shown in Chapter 5, job analysis describes the duties, responsibilities, and working conditions of a job and the interrelationships between the job as it is and the other jobs with which it is associated. This analysis results in a job description, which is a written statement describing the content, duties, and essential requirements of the job or position. When this detailed statement is modified to include the personal requirements needed in a person to perform the job satisfactorily, it is called job specifications.

Job grading.   After the job specifications are determined, the actual process of grading, rating, or evaluating begins. A job is rated or graded in order to determine its value relative to the other jobs in the organization that are subject to evaluation. There are many evaluative methods used, but the most popular ones are the point, factor comparison, job classification, and ranking methods.[28] As you can see from Table 15-3, the point system is the one most widely used.

Nonquantitative systems.   *Ranking* and *job classification* are nonquantitative systems. They make no use of devices such as points, scores, or any other objective quantity in the evaluating process. Essentially, they involve a simple procedure of arranging the jobs in descending order of importance and assigning appropriate numeric values to each job.

Quantitative systems.   The *factor comparison* and *point* methods do use quantitative measurements. Each of these methods breaks the job down into its component parts. These parts are the factors that affect the performance of

---

[28]See Elaine Wegener, "Does Competitive Pay Discriminate?" *Personnel Administrator* 25 (May 1980):38–44 and 66, for a discussion of these methods.

TABLE 15-3
Job evaluation procedures used

Evaluation method used	Number of employers using the method (N = 172)
Point system	53
Factor comparison	33
Job classification	24
Ranking	14
Simple	9
Forced-choice	5
Market pricing	12

Source: Adapted from *Job Evaluation Policies and Procedures,* Personnel Policies Forum Survey no. 113 (Washington, D.C.: The Bureau of National Affairs, Inc., 1976), p. 4.

the work, which is the basis of the job itself. The list of such factors usually includes (1) education, (2) skill, (3) initiative, (4) responsibility, (5) job conditions, (6) physical and mental effort, and (7) experience.

Then each of these factors is appraised and a numeric value assigned to it. These fractional appraisals are added into a total score for the job, and the scores are then ranked. Finally, the jobs are grouped together into job ranges, classifications, or hierarchies.

Establishing job hierarchies. Regardless of what method is used in the evaluation procedure, job hierarchies are usually established. These hierarchies may have a vertical basis or a horizontal one. When the vertical scale is used, the grading is done on the basis of the *abilities* a person needs to perform the job. When grading on the vertical scale, the company tries to rank and evaluate the jobs on differing levels of responsibility needed, types of ability and knowledge required, working conditions, or some similar factors.

When the horizontal scale is used, the grading is based on the level of *performance* required to satisfy the position needs. An effort is made to appraise the relationship of the jobs on the same responsibility level according to the mental and physical abilities, skill, education, and experience required.

Job pricing. Pricing involves converting the *relative job values* into *specific monetary values,* or translating the job classes into rate ranges. Here again, value judgments must be used, in spite of the statistical techniques.

As shown in Figure 15-6, pricing involves applying the organization's overall wage rate to each of the job grades in order to convert the job values established through the grading process into specific monetary rates of job pay. Through various processes, the analyst arrives at a *specific rate* of pay for each job. This figure becomes the beginning wage for the worker who performs the job. More often, the analyst sets up a *wage rate range,* with a minimum and maximum figure for each job grade or classification.

Administering the procedure. After the wage rate, or wage range, for each job is established, the specific wage rate within the range must be determined for each employee. Through various procedures of personnel evaluation, as discussed in Chapter 12, the individual employee progresses over a period of time from the lowest point on the wage scale to the highest. The employee's rate of progression through the wage range depends on (1) seniority, (2) productivity, or (3) characteristics that are assumed to lead to productivity. This procedure involves the very important process of merit rating, which will be discussed in the next chapter.

An Example of Job Evaluation

A personnel manager selected 12 jobs (as shown in column 1) to be evaluated and serve as key jobs to compare others with (see Table 15-4). The jobs were analyzed and descriptions and specifications prepared. Then the jobs were graded on the basis of skills, responsibility, experience, education, knowledge, and effort required (column 2). The jobs were grouped into job grades (column 3) on the basis of point ranges (column 4). Then a survey was made of salaries paid by members of the local ASPA chapter for those job grades. The minimum, average, and maximum salaries were tabulated (column 5). The organization's pay curve was applied to each of the job grades (column 6). Finally, the minimum and maximum rates were established for each job grade.

Employees hired to perform job H would be paid between $21,150 and $25,850. The exact amount would be determined by merit rating (covered in the next chapter).

Employees making less than the minimum for the job (at the time the system is installed) should have their rate increased up to the minimum. Those making more than the maximum should receive smaller periodic increases until their salary is within the range.

TABLE 15-4
Establishing rate ranges with job evaluation, using salary survey results and the point system

(1) Selected job	(2) Point value for each job	(3) Job grade	(4) Point range	(5) Pay ranges for comparable jobs according to survey			(6) Organization's pay curve	(7) Established job rate range
				Mini-mum	Average	Maxi-mum		
A.........	28							
B.........	34	I	25–39	$16,500	$18,100	$19,200	$18,000	$16,200–19,550
C.........	38							
D.........	43							
E.........	51	II	40–59	18,100	20,370	22,500	20,200	18,180–22,250
F.........	57							
G.........	61							
H.........	70	III	60–79	21,200	23,750	26,100	23,500	21,150–25,850
I.........	81							
J.........	88							
K.........	94	IV	80–99	22,300	26,500	28,800	26,300	23,670–28,950
L.........	98							

SUMMARY AND CONCLUSIONS

Employee compensation is important (1) to the individual for it provides the source of purchasing power, (2) to the organization for it is usually the largest single expense, and (3) to the nation for it accounts for between 75 and 80 percent of national income.

Compensation has three primary functions: (1) to reward employees for work performed for the organization, (2) to stimulate them to improve future performance, and (3) to reward them for being members of the organization. Compensation is also needed to attract better employees, reduce labor turnover, and motivate employees to do work that they otherwise would not do.

The law of effect states that employee behavior that appears to be rewarded tends to be repeated, while behavior that appears not to be rewarded—or to lead to punishment—tends not to be repeated. Although money, in general, does have a positive effect on performance, the degree and type of stimulus will vary according to individual needs and perceptions.

An organization's compensation policies are determined by the interplay of three factors: (1) what it is willing to pay, (2) what it is able to pay, and (3) what it is compelled to pay. In the long run, what the organization is willing to pay is determined by the inexorable laws of economics, especially the law of supply and demand.

Some of the pressures that determine the organization's compensation policies and practices are (1) governmental factors, (2) the collective bargaining procedure, (3) the standard and cost of living, (4) comparable wages, (5) the supply of and demand for workers, and (6) what the employer is able to pay.

The basic wage and hour law is the *Fair Labor Standards Act* of 1938, commonly called the Wages and Hours Law. The *Equal Pay Act* of 1963 amended the FLSA to require that women be paid the same as men for the same general type of work.

The price for individual jobs is determined by job evaluation. It consists of (1) doing a job analysis, (2) grading the jobs, (3) assigning a wage rate, or wage rate range, to each job, and (4) administering it. The point system is the most popular method of job evaluation.

QUESTIONS

1. Can a satisfactory solution, that is, one considered equitable by all concerned, ever be found to the compensation problem? Explain.
2. What roles are played by compensation?
3. "An organization's compensation policies are determined by: willingness to pay, ability to pay, and compulsion to pay." Isn't the third factor the only really important one? Explain.
4. What possible disadvantages might there be to cost-of-living clauses in wage agreements? Is such an agreement equitable to the employee? The company?

5. "There must be profits before there can be wages." Do you agree that this is true for a private business?

6. What is your reaction to granting wage differentials to people performing the same job? What are the basic issues involved in the argument?

7. What is the difference between "equitable wage payment" and "equal wage payment"? Discuss the conflict between the two issues.

8. Wage differentials are both an economic and noneconomic motivating force. Do you agree? Explain.

9. From your reading and observation, to what extent are wage differentials based on race, sex, and age decreasing? To what extent do you think they *should be* decreased?

10. What is the best basis for determining wage differentials for different jobs? Explain.

PROBLEM

The Unhappy Supervisor

Joe Johnson, a programmer, was discussing his salary situation with Wanda Walker, his supervisor. Joe was unhappy because he had not received a raise for the next year, while inflation had increased 15 percent. He knew that some of the other programmers had received "substantial" increases—up to 18 percent.

Wanda tried to explain that a job evaluation program had recently been started. Before that, Joe's salary had been permitted to "increase too rapidly" and was "way above" the salary range for his job. Some of the other employees were below the range for the job. Instead of cutting his salary back to the job range, they were just going to give him smaller increases until the range caught up with him. Some of the lower paid people were being brought up to the range as quickly as feasible.

Joe said he still did not understand.

Questions

1. How would you persuade Joe to accept the decision?
2. Would you have handled the situation differently? Explain.
3. Is this a valid use of job evaluation results? Explain.

SUGGESTED READINGS FOR FURTHER STUDY

Belcher, David W. "Pay Equity or Pay Fairness?" *Compensation Review* 11 (Second Quarter 1979):31–37.

Beyer, Richard E. "One-Way Analysis of Variance: Sample Sizes Unequal." *Personnel Administrator* 23 (November 1978):63–69.

Field, Robert L., and Gary A. Vogt. "Ways to Pay Your Key People Well." *Personnel Administrator* 24 (May 1979):37-40.

Finkin, Eugene. "How to Figure Out Executive Compensation." *Personnel Journal* 57 (July 1978):371ff.

Gomez-Mejia, Luis R., Ronald C. Page, and Walter W. Tornow. "Development and Implementation of a Computerized Job Evaluation System." *Personnel Administrator* 24 (February 1979):46-54.

Green, Robert J. "Career Alternatives and Compensation Potential." *Personnel Administrator* 23 (December 1978):27-30.

Thomasen, D. J. "Eliminating Pay Discrimination Caused by Job Evaluation." *Personnel Journal* 55 (May 1978):11-22.

Weber, Arnold R. "How Guidelines Could Affect Four Key Elements in 1979 Labor Talks." *Dun's Review* 113 (January 1979):9.

White, William L. "Impact of the Anti-Inflation Program on Executive Compensation." *Personnel* 56 (July-August 1979):12-21.

Worrell, Allan K. "Salary Administration Simplified." *Management Review* 68 (March 1979):42-45.

CHAPTER SIXTEEN

Using Financial Incentives To Motivate Employees

Learning Objectives

After studying the material in this chapter, you should be able to:

1. Discuss whether financial incentives do or do not motivate employees.
2. Explain the motivational effects of:
   a. Merit increases
   b. Incentive wages
   c. Profit sharing
   d. Bonuses
   e. Companywide productivity sharing systems
3. Describe what is needed for financial incentives to motivate.

Some Important Words and Terms

Merit increases
Lump sum increases
Incentive wages
Piecework plans
Productivity sharing plans
Profit sharing

Deferred profit-sharing plan
Employee stock ownership plan
   (ESOP)
Bonus
Companywide productivity sharing
   system

Money motivates most people some of the time and some people all of the time.
SAUL W. GELLERMAN

Outline of the Chapter

Scanlon Plan
Rucker Share-of-Production Plan
Kaiser Long-range Sharing Plan
Evaluating the Motivational Effects of These Systems
WHAT IS REQUIRED FOR FINANCIAL INCENTIVES TO MOTIVATE

Wu Jinghua has been named the "outstanding worker" at the Peking Glassware Factory several times. Each time, she has received a bonus of 7 yuan (about $4.30). She says the prospect of increasing her 40-yuan-a-month salary with the bonus makes her work harder.

Workers who suggest money-saving ideas at the Peking Heavy Electric Generator Plant earn cash bonuses equal to a month's salary.[1]

These and many other examples show that what Adam Smith said over 200 years ago is still true: The promise of higher earnings causes people to be more productive. As shown in Chapter 11, *while money has rarely been regarded as the sole motivator, it is still a potent one.*

The previous chapters have developed the need for setting equitable wage rates for jobs and individuals. This chapter will show that, while time payments are one way of relating earnings to individual employees, there are other motivational methods that achieve the same goal, only more equitably. They include:

1. Merit increases.
2. Incentive wages.
3. Profit sharing.
4. Bonuses.
5. Companywide productivity sharing systems.

MOTIVATIONAL THEORY OF COMPENSATION

No one of these methods is totally effective in stimulating performance and rewarding productivity. And no one of them is the *only* effective incentive. Instead, in any incentive situation, there are pressures to produce and pressures to withhold production. Nonfinancial incentives, especially those related to our higher level needs, may be more effective than financial rewards.

Figure 16–1 shows that the rate of production results from (1) pressures that encourage output and (2) those that discourage it. The actual level of performance can be increased by (1) reducing the effectiveness of the forces above the line, (2) increasing the effectiveness of the forces below the line, or (3) both at the same time.

---

[1]Kenneth H. Bacon, "Managing in China," *The Wall Street Journal,* June 18, 1979, p. 22.

FIGURE 16-1
Forces affecting rate of production under incentive systems

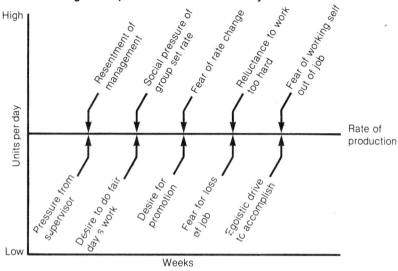

Source: Mason Haire, *Psychology in Management*, 2d ed. (New York: McGraw-Hill Book Co., 1964), p. 167.

We will now look at some empirical evidence that compensation (1) *does motivate* and (2) *does not motivate*, and evaluate the findings.

Compensation Does Motivate

Many classical writers, as well as contemporary theorists, have emphasized the motivational value of compensation. Research on this subject has shown that financial rewards are a strong stimulus to production. Yet there are some contrary findings, which will also be presented.

One study showed that when people believe their efforts will lead to the desired reward, they will produce.[2] It also showed that few individuals would engage in extended activities unless they believed that there was a connection between what they did and the rewards they received.

Another study found that when the basic income of any group of employees did not permit satisfaction, the workers turned to overtime, slowdowns, and other means of meeting their needs.[3]

A Ford Motor Company survey revealed that its employees were primarily concerned with wages, job security, and fringe benefits. An experiment

---

[2] Melvin J. Lerner, "Evaluation of Performance as a Function of Performer's Reward and Attractiveness," *Journal of Personality and Social Psychology* 1 (April 1965):355-60.

[3] Sylvia Schimmin, "Extramural Factors Influencing Behavior at Work," *Occupational Psychology* 36 (July 1962):124-31.

with job enrichment at one of its plants showed no change in absenteeism or quality of work. Moreover, these workers were ready to swap their "enriched" jobs for "another nickel an hour."[4]

As shown in Chapter 10, *there is not necessarily any direct and positive correlation between the motivation to perform and job satisfaction.* High motivation and performance can be associated with high satisfaction, but they can also be associated with low satisfaction—or entirely unrelated to satisfaction. A study by Schwab found that *the type of pay system may have a positive impact on motivation but a negative one on satisfaction.*[5] The research indicated that this finding might make the personnel manager's job even more difficult. As a policy change may have conflicting effects on different employee attitudes and behaviors, these managers must establish personnel priorities. For example, to what extent is the organization willing to trade off decreased employee satisfaction for higher motivation to perform?

Compensation Does Not Motivate

In many instances, the economic motive is no longer considered important. Many believe that employees have risen above the mundane demands of a physical existence and now have higher desires. For example, one outstanding authority said, "In the terms in which we are speaking there is no such thing as an economic motive."[6] A British sociologist concluded that it was impossible to find a direct statistical relationship between the application of incentive schemes and increased output.[7]

It has been claimed that in actual organizational situations, as well as in experimental laboratories, psychological rewards may be more significant than material incentives.[8] This appears to be true even for members of the Academy of Management.[9]

Evaluating the Motivational Effects of Compensation

There is no simple answer to the question, "Does money motivate?" Instead, it can be concluded that *until employees satisfy their physiological and safety*

---

[4]Richard D. Denzler, "People and Productivity: Do They Still Equal Pay and Profits?" *Personnel Journal* 53 (January 1974):59–63.

[5]Donald P. Schwab, "Conflicting Impacts of Pay on Employee Motivation and Satisfaction," *Personnel Journal* 53 (March 1974):196–200.

[6]Mason Haire, *Psychology in Management,* 2d ed. (New York: McGraw-Hill Book Co., 1964), p. 34.

[7]Hilde Behrend, "Financial Incentives as the Expression of a System of Beliefs," *British Journal of Sociology* 10 (June 1959):137–47.

[8]Stanley Sloan and David E. Schrieber, "Incentives: Are They Relevant? Obsolete? Misunderstood?" *Personnel Administrator* 33 (January–February 1970):52–57.

[9]Louis J. Shuster, "Mobility among Business Faculty," *Academy of Management Journal* 13 (September 1970):325–35.

Incentives to perform.   Reprinted by permission *The Wall Street Journal*

needs, compensation does serve as a motivator. Above that level, money (espe-cially time wages) tends to decline in importance.

A study was conducted to determine to what extent management could rely on *either* intrinsic *or* extrinsic rewards to produce job satisfaction *and* productivity. The results indicated that the employees perceived direct and indirect economic (extrinsic) rewards as more important than the intrinsic ones. Three of the four categories judged most important—working condi-tions, security, and compensation—are extrinsic, and the only intrinsic reward was self-actualization.[10]

There are some general requirements for financial incentives to be effec-tive. These apply to every type of financial incentive and to every level of position that may be covered by a financial incentive plan. Some of these are as follows:

1.   Employees should know what the goals and rewards are.
2.   The goals must be understandable and attainable.
3.   There must be a direct relationship between an individual's reward and performance.
4.   The rewards must be significant and certain.

---

[10]William E. Reif, "Intrinsic versus Extrinsic Rewards: Resolving the Controversy," *Human Resource Management* 14 (Summer 1975):7.

5. An employee must have the tools to accomplish work expectations.
6. The incentive system cannot be in conflict with the employee's other vital interests.
7. The financial incentive system must be compatible with overall job requirements, the work environment, and management's style.[11]

In summary, people who have high achievement needs will be high producers with or without financial incentives; those with low achievement needs must have the monetary stimulus. According to *expectancy theory,* employees' attitudes toward their job and pay result from the difference between what they receive and what they expect.

USING MERIT INCREASES TO MOTIVATE EMPLOYEES

As shown in the previous chapter, *merit increases*—wage increases based on ability and merit, rather than upon seniority or a time interval—have great potential value for motivating employees. When raises are based on seniority, or are automatic, there is a tendency to do just enough to get by and not to exert more effort than is necessary.

The merit basis of wage determination is generally accepted by managers. A group of managers was asked to identify the factors that were "legitimate pay determinants" in an effective compensation program. As shown in Table 16-1, they thought a third of base pay should be based on "individual job performance."

Also, EEOC and OFCCP have accepted the merit pay system.[12] However, as shown in the previous chapter, questions are being raised about the validity of job evaluation procedures.

TABLE 16-1
Percentage of base pay that should be allocated to base pay objectives

Base salary objectives	Percentage of base pay allocated to objective
Relative job worth	55
Individual job performance	33
Reward for personal contributions (loyalty, dedication, integrity) ...	12

Source: Reprinted from the May, 1978 issue of *The Personnel Administrator* with permission of The American Society for Personnel Administration.

---

[11]Robert E. Sibson, *Increasing Employee Productivity* (New York: AMACOM, 1976), p. 178.

[12]James T. Brinks, "Is There Merit in Merit Increases?" *Personnel Administrator* 25 (May 1980):59-64.

Why Use Merit Increases?

Compensation based on merit increases assumes that it produces the highest benefit in terms of motivation, performance, and productivity. Therefore, merit compensation programs are designed to identify, appraise, and reward employees for making outstanding contributions toward the organization's goals. If this is true, then salary increases should be directly related to the individual's achievements relative to established objectives.

Definite criteria by which to determine merit are needed if inequities in rates are to be prevented. Some factors that serve this purpose are training, experience, know-how, attendance, promptness, accident rate, ability to get along with other workers, and production (which reflects the others).

Evaluating the Motivational Effects of Merit Increases

Many firms are now trying to relate compensation to performance. But in most large organizations, particularly public ones, employees are caught in a highly structured and bureaucratic system where individualism is discouraged. Instead, employees are in "lock step"—that is, everyone receives essentially the same increase.

Some critics of the merit system say it has a built-in bias in favor of high performers and against others.[13] They say that high producers not only receive high pay but also are given more opportunities for management development programs. This gives them a double reward while doing nothing for highly motivated marginal performers.

Yet merit plans can motivate employees to perform, develop positive attitudes, and have greater job satisfaction, if (1) they are kept simple, so that employees can understand that their compensation is directly related to their performance, (2) the plans receive support from top management and supervisors, and (3) the programs are flexible.

An unusual form of merit increase is the *lump sum increase.* Eligible employees are given the choice of receiving their increase in (1) the usual regular payments or (2) one lump sum, paid in advance. The lump sum serves to communicate and motivate by dramatizing the amount of the increase. Between 40 and 90 percent of employees given the chance choose the lump sum.[14]

Aetna, American Can, B. F. Goodrich, Clark Equipment, J & L Steel, Timex, and Westinghouse have introduced such programs—with generally good results.

---

[13]Frederick S. Hills, "The Pay-for-Performance Dilemma," *Personnel* 56 (September-October 1979):23–31.

[14]Charles A. Smith, "Lump Sum Increases—A Creditable Change Strategy," *Personnel* 56 (July-August 1979):59–63.

USING INCENTIVE WAGES TO MOTIVATE EMPLOYEES

The fact that there is a great variety of incentive wage plans makes it difficult to define the term precisely. However, *incentive wages* can be defined as the extra compensation paid for all production over a specified amount that results from an employee's use of above average skill, effort, or concentration when performed in a predetermined manner with standard tools, facilities, and materials.

Objectives of Using Incentive Wages

The main objectives of using incentive wage plans are (1) to lower the unit cost of production by increasing productivity, (2) to increase employees' earnings through individual merit and accomplishment (if the increase is due to application of skill or devotion of more concentrated effort to the task), and (3) to reduce overhead expense per unit produced.

Advantages and Disadvantages of Incentive Wages

Like other personnel management techniques, incentive wages have potential advantages and disadvantages. Both are presented for your evaluation.

Advantages of incentive wages.   The many advantages of incentive wage plans can be condensed into one statement: Management benefits from this system through greater production. There is (1) more efficient use of facilities, which (2) leads to reduced unit cost of goods or services produced, which (3) means greater profits.

There are many advantages to employees, but they are all included in one statement: A worker receives increased earnings in direct proportion to increased productivity.

Disadvantages of incentive wages.   There are certain serious disadvantages and limitations to the use of incentive wage plans. The most serious one is that these plans can be applied only in particular cases. It is not advisable to use them where delays are frequent and beyond the control of the worker, or in highly automated plants. They also tend to require greater quality control, for the emphasis shifts from quality to quantity.

The workers also find disadvantages in the incentive system. Some of these are (1) the danger of rate cuts is always present and (2) beginning or handicapped workers might not receive an acceptable income.

Finally, it is always possible that an incentive plan may inadvertently achieve the opposite effect to that which was planned. Through errors in the measurement systems, through faulty reward systems, or because of the traits of the managers involved, the system may result in decreasing performance rather than increasing it.

Declining Use of Incentive Wages

During and immediately following World War II, an increasing number of companies turned to incentive pay plans as a method of improving production and increasing employee income. There has been a slight decline in the percentage of workers on incentive since that time.

Extent of use. A study of 7 million workers in 1945–46 found that about 30 percent of the plant employees in manufacturing industries were paid on an incentive basis.[15]

A similar study of 11 million production and related employees in all of the nation's manufacturing industries in 1958 found that 27 percent of such workers were paid on an incentive basis.[16]

From 1961 to 1963, the Bureau of Labor Statistics did an occupational wage survey in 212 standard metropolitan statistical areas.[17] It found that 26 percent of the plant workers in manufacturing were on incentive, as compared to 27 percent in 1958 and 30 percent in 1945–46. Only 18 percent of the plant workers in retail industries, 13 percent in wholesaling, and 12 percent in service industries were paid on an incentive basis.

Trends in use of incentives. A more recent study matched industries, where possible, with those in earlier studies that used incentives. The results showed that the proportion of production and related workers paid under incentive plans was virtually unchanged for most of the matched industries. As indicated in Table 16-2, there were substantial declines in the proportion of incentive workers in cigar manufacturing and in certain machinery manufacturing industries.

It is difficult to determine whether declines in the incidence of incentive workers were caused by changes in (1) policies on the method of wage payment, (2) employment among establishments with no policy changes, or (3) the ratio of direct to indirect workers as new and improved methods of manufacturing were introduced.

Effects of Using Incentive Wages

There are so many variables influencing employee performance that it is difficult to separate the results obtained by using incentive wages from those obtained through other factors. For instance, it was found during the Hawthorne studies that the Second Relay Assembly Control Group increased its

---

[15]Joseph M. Sherman, "Incentive Pay in American Industry, 1945–46," *Monthly Labor Review* 65 (November 1947):535–37.

[16]Earl Lewis, "Extent of Incentive Pay in Manufacturing," *Monthly Labor Review* 83 (May 1960):460–63.

[17]John H. Cox, "Wage Payment Plans in Metropolitan Areas," *Monthly Labor Review* 87 (July 1964):794–96.

TABLE 16–2
Comparison of incentive-paid production and related workers in selected industries over periods of time*

Industry	Most recent survey		Earlier survey	
	Percent	Year	Percent	Year
Work clothing.............................	82	(1968)	80	(1961)
Men's and boys' shirts, except work, and nightwear.............................	81	(1964)	81	(1956)
Men's and boys' suits and coats..............	74	(1967)	71	(1958)
Footwear, except rubber....................	70	(1968)	71	(1957)
Cigars..................................	57	(1967)	75	(1955)
Leather tanning and finishing	53	(1968)	50	(1959)
Cotton textiles...........................	34	(1965)	36	(1954)
Farm machinery	34	(1966)	32†	(1958)
Wool yarn and broadwoven fabrics	27	(1966)	30	(1957)
Synthetic textiles.........................	26	(1965)	29	(1954)
Office and computing machines	24	(1966)	31†	(1958)
Service industry machines	18	(1966)	33†	(1958)
General industrial machinery.................	16	(1966)	32†	(1958)
Construction and related machinery...........	13	(1966)	12†	(1958)
Metalworking machinery	13	(1966)	24†	(1958)
Industrial chemicals	5	(1965)	4	(1955)
Fertilizers...............................	1	(1966)	2	(1956)
Cigarettes...............................	‡	(1965)	3†	(1958)

*It is not possible to make precise comparisons of the proportions of incentive workers among industries or between the "most recent survey" and the "earlier survey" because the estimates from industry surveys include some sampling error. Thus differences of a few percentage points should not be considered real.
†See L. Earl Lewis, "Extent of Incentive Pay in Manufacturing," *Monthly Labor Review* 83 (May 1960):460-63. Estimates obtained from the May 1958 study of the incidence of wage incentives in all manufacturing establishments are not precisely comparable with most recent studies that have a minimum establishment size cutoff.
Source: George L. Stelluto, "Report on Incentive Pay in Manufacturing Industries," *Monthly Labor Review* 92 (July 1969):52.

productivity an average of 12 percent when placed on an incentive plan. But "it was quite apparent that factors other than the change in wage incentive contributed to that increase."[18]

The importance of financial incentives depends on the intensity of an individual's needs. When the need is great, people will do things they dislike for the sake of money. As it is practically impossible to simulate this need, experimental studies cannot approximate reality.

While these difficulties are recognized, an effort is made to show the effects of incentives on productivity, labor costs, employee earnings, and other factors.

---

[18]F. J. Roethlisberger and William J. Dickson, *Management and the Worker* (Cambridge: Harvard University Press, 1939), p. 158.

Effects on productivity.   As one of the primary objectives of using incentive wages is to increase performance, the question may rightly be asked, "To what extent have they increased employee productivity?"

One of the most comprehensive studies of the effects of incentive plans was conducted in 1959. It included 29 industries and 305 plans, most of which had been instituted during the 1950s. The study showed that productivity had increased an average of 63 percent.[19]

A controlled study of the effect of piecework in the corrugated shipping container industry found that 16 of 18 operations displayed statistically significant increases in productivity after the use of monetary incentives began.[20] The average increase in efficiency under the plan was 58 percent. Productivity per production employee increased 75 percent, on the average.

In summary, productivity is typically around 20-25 percent higher with a properly developed and administered wage incentive plan. Direct labor costs decrease around 10 to 25 percent as a result of incentives.

Effects on employee earnings.   The differential in earnings between incentive workers and time workers generally varies from 0 to about 40 percent. In general, incentive earnings of employees are around 20 percent higher than hourly earnings.

In the comprehensive study of 1959, the average increase in employee earnings attributed to the influence of incentives was 21 percent.

In summary, incentive wages increase earnings by around 20 percent in most cases.

Other effects.   Incentive wages tend to reduce the rate of labor turnover. However, since incentive coverage is only one of the many factors involved in the turnover of personnel, conclusions drawn from turnover statistics should be judged with considerable caution.

Other effects of incentive wage plans are (1) decreased costs through better methods, (2) fewer employees on the payroll, (3) cost control, (4) performance measurement, (5) accurate scheduling, and (6) spotlighting of poor management practices.

Unions and Wage Incentives

In general, unions are opposed to incentive wage plans, for they tend to differentiate between workers and destroy the group relationship in a shop. Yet there are wide variations in attitude toward these wage programs. In the

---

[19]John H. Dale, "Wage Incentives and Productivity," as reported in "Increase Productivity 50% in One Year with Sound Wage Incentives," *Management Methods* 15 (February 1959):38-42.

[20]Donald L. McManis and William G. Dick, "Monetary Incentives in Today's Industrial Setting," *Personnel Journal* 52 (May 1973):387-92.

textile, apparel, and (to a limited extent) metal goods industries, payment by results is the custom and is accepted by the union.

Unions do not seem to object to incentive wage plans themselves. They do oppose the potentially disruptive effect. These plans emphasize the individual rather than the group and give management a basis for appraising one worker's work in relation to another's. Unions tend to accept the plans that share the gains in productivity arising from all factors, not just the increase in human application. The union must also have a voice in introducing and administering the plan before it will accept it.

When—and Where—Can Incentive Wages Be Used?

Several conditions are needed before such systems can be applied:

1. The work should be standardized and working conditions uniform. Otherwise, there will be inequities in wage payments.
2. The volume of work performed by each individual worker, or group of workers, should be easy to measure.
3. There should be no division of labor within the process for which incentives are paid. If this were the case, one worker could detain or slow up another so that the second worker's earnings would depend upon the effort of the first person as well as his or her own.
4. Production processes should be independent of one another so that one process will not retard another.
5. The materials should come to workers in a uniform condition and in such a manner that workers can control the volume and rate of flow of the work. This requirement tends to eliminate the use of such schemes in highly automated plants.

Look at Table 16–2 again. Notice that the workers control the flow of work in the industries at the top, and incentives are used. At the bottom, machines control the work flow, and incentives are not used.

Requirements for the Successful Use of Incentive Wages

There are several requirements for an incentive plan to succeed once it is introduced:

1. The standard of performance should be reasonably attainable, so that average employees can achieve it with "normal" effort.
2. The rate of pay should be such that employees can achieve an incentive bonus that will make their pay exceed the pay of workers on straight time by about 20 percent.
3. The standard of performance and rate of pay per unit should be modified only when technological changes in the machines, methods, or materials, or changes in living costs require it.

4. The plan should be designed by a professional who can prevent some of the problems from occurring.
5. The plan should be easily understood. Workers' satisfaction with incentive plans is positively related to their understanding of the system. A simple plan will probably be accepted by employees, whereas a complex system may be mistrusted by them.

In a survey of nearly 4,400 workers in six factories where some type of incentive pay program was used, only a small percentage of employees could explain the bonus system. Nor could they calculate the bonuses they earned each day. As the workers could not understand the system and were unaware of the amount of money they earned, it was inevitable that the incentive program "had little motivating power with which to improve productivity."[21]

There are many ways of learning whether an incentive plan is effective. One method is to analyze the distribution curve of the average incentive earning percentage of all the employees in the plan. This should be checked monthly. If the distribution curve is in a normal bell shape, everything is all right. However, if the curve tends to approximate a straight line, the incentive program is in trouble.

What Plan to Use?

There are so many plans available that it is difficult to select the one to use. However, they can be classified into two types: (1) *piecework plans,* where employees are paid according to the number of units produced, and (2) *productivity sharing plans,* where workers are paid according to the amount of time saved in producing a given quantity.

In a study to evaluate employee preferences for alternative forms of job compensation, it was found that piecework incentives were preferred more by the relatively skilled workers. Also, the incentive value of such plans was greatly improved after employees had successful direct experience with them.[22]

Plans based on an individual's performance have more motivating effect than group plans. As you can see from Figure 16-2, employee output and earnings increase as the size of the work group decreases. Also, workers paid individually had higher average output than other groups. Apparently, incentive wages have greater effect when individuals feel they control their own earnings.

---

[21]Bernard M. Bass, *Man, Work, and Organizations* (Boston: Allyn & Bacon, 1972), p. 45.

[22]See Lyle V. Jones and Thomas E. Jeffery, "A Quantitative Analysis of Expressed Preference for Compensatory Plans," *Journal of Applied Psychology* 48 (August 1964):201-10, for similar statements.

FIGURE 16–2
Average piece rate earnings of workers with work groups of various sizes

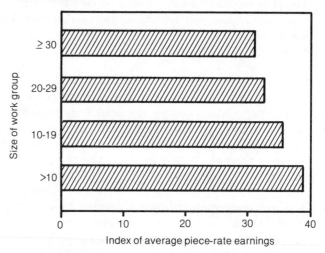

Source: R. Marriott, "Size of Working Group and Output," *Occupational Psychology*, 23 (1949):47.

Evaluating the Motivational Effect of Incentive Wages

Do incentive wage systems serve to stimulate increased productivity? Evidence indicates that they appear to result in higher productivity than time-based systems. These increased levels of productivity appear to result from a positive motivational effect of the incentive pay systems. However, evidence also indicates a negative effect on employee satisfaction and group cohesiveness.

These generalizations were tested in a large-scale research project in a consumer goods organization in the Midwest that used three different pay systems for its operative employees—individual piece rates, group incentive rates, and hourly rates. As shown in Table 16–3, the hourly paid group had significantly greater satisfaction than either of the incentive groups, and employees on piecework had higher satisfaction than those on group incentives. But the performance-reward probability was highest among the piecework employees and lowest among the hourly paid workers. In summary, persons *paid by the hour were best satisfied with their pay, while those paid by the amount of output were the most highly motivated to perform.*

USING PROFIT SHARING TO MOTIVATE EMPLOYEES

Another financial incentive that can be used by management to motivate employees is sharing profits with them. This method is desirable because it

TABLE 16-3
Relationship between pay satisfaction, motivation, and basis of wage payment

	Adjusted° averages		
	(n = 128)	(n = 84)	(n = 61)
Pay satisfaction	Piece	Group	Hourly
MSQ	7.20	6.21	8.69
JDI	4.10	3.89	6.44
	Averages°°		
	(n = 128)	(n = 84)	(n = 61)
Motivation	Piece	Group	Hourly
Pay valence	2.88	2.85	2.24
Performance-reward probability for pay........	4.46	3.95	2.03

°Averages adjusted for any differences in pay and job level, age, tenure and sex.
°°Scaled 1 (low) to 5 (high).
Source: Donald Schwab, "Conflicting Impacts of Pay on Employee Motivation and Satisfaction," *Personnel Journal* 53 (March 1974):196-99. Reprinted with permission of *Personnel Journal*, copyright March 1974.

removes some of the barriers to cooperation between management and non-management groups in a firm.

Objectives of Profit Sharing

Profit sharing is based on a combination of ethical idealism and hard practicality. It links employees' self-interest to the firm's success in the following way: there is (1) the wage relationship, (2) a profit relationship, and finally (3) partnership. Of course, the last stage or two are not always achieved. Managers are often forced to subordinate the ideal concepts of this practice to the more practical concern for profitability. This latter can best be achieved when employees increase their output and efficiency.

Definition of Profit Sharing

The term *profit sharing* means different things to different people. In fact, the term has been broadened so greatly that it is now a very confusing concept. It is often used to refer to such plans as cost-of-living adjustments, guaranteed wage arrangements, health provisions, incentive wage plans, bonus payment plans, stock purchase plans, pensions, and production bonus systems.

Regardless of the definition used, there are two tests that can be used to determine whether a given arrangement is profit sharing:

1. Does the extra compensation paid to employees bear some recognizable relationship to the firm's profit?

2. Does management announce to its employees in advance that profits will be shared with employees?

In view of these two criteria, *profit sharing* is defined as the prearranged distribution of a specified percentage of a firm's profits to the workers.

Types of Plan

The most popular plans are (1) cash, (2) deferred, and (3) a combination. Under the *cash plans,* profits are distributed directly to the employees as current compensation, as soon as profits are determined. The payment may be in the form of a check, stock, or even cash, and it may be made annually, semiannually, quarterly, monthly, or at even shorter intervals, if feasible.

Under a *deferred profit-sharing plan,* the incentive earnings are credited to the employee's account, to be paid upon certain contingencies at a later date. These occurrences are retirement, severance, withdrawal from the plan, disability, and death. These must be approved by the Internal Revenue Service (IRS).

Finally, some plans provide for part of the earnings to be paid in cash and part deferred. These are called *combination* plans.

Extent of Use

It is difficult to state exactly how many plans are in effect, or how many personnel are involved, because of the difficulty of classifying the compensation programs. However, it is known that about a fifth of the largest companies have some such plan. One estimate places the number at around 200,000.[23]

Banks and retail and wholesale establishments use these plans more than manufacturers or insurance companies. In general, large firms use the deferred plans, and small ones use the cash programs.

Effects of Using Profit Sharing

Historically, it has been accepted that profit sharing would work among the higher managers and probably among middle management, but not for the individual workers as they could not understand the relationship between their added effort and the resulting profit. This belief is still held by many managers. But there is a growing belief that the plans are advantageous for all levels of personnel if profits can be traced to employee productivity and the time interval between doing the work and receiving the benefits is not too long.

---

[23]"Employee Wrath Hits Profit-Sharing Plans," *Business Week,* July 18, 1977, p. 25.

Benefits.   The Profit Sharing Research Foundation found that profit-sharing firms outperformed other firms by "substantial and widening percentages" from 1952 to 1969.[24]

Limitations.   Probably the main limitation of this incentive device is the lack of understanding of what profit is and what causes it. Employees see sales increasing and expect profits to be high. Then when management is required to use large amounts of those profits for the replacement of machinery and equipment, or some other contingency, the workers feel cheated and resentful. Therefore, for any profit-sharing plan to be successful, there should be a close correlation between what the workers expect to receive and what they actually receive.

Other limitations are that (1) the rewards vary greatly, depending on the business and market conditions and (2) the financial reward is too far removed in time from employee performance to serve as a strong stimulant to productivity.

Participants in profit-sharing plans at Marriott Corporation and Tappan Company sued the firms when the asset value of profit-sharing funds tumbled about 40 percent in 1973 and 1974—although that was about the same as most pension and profit-sharing funds.

Sears, which has the nation's largest profit-sharing plan, instituted a noncontributory pension plan in 1979 to "provide assured and predictable retirement benefits."[25]

Evaluating the Motivational Effect of Profit Sharing

In summary, effective profit sharing can be considered a motivational tool that can raise productivity significantly in our society, through the incentive of increased compensation and participation—the end result being the achievement of higher social goals.

Employee Stock Ownership Plans (ESOPs)

ESOPs are a modification of profit sharing.[26] In general, the ESOP borrows money, purchases a large block of the employer's stock, and allocates it to the employees on the basis of salary and/or longevity. Each year the firm places a portion of its profits in the ESOP fund, which, in turn, uses the money to pay

---

[24]Bert L. Metzer, "Share Profits—Don't Freeze Them," *Personnel Journal* 51 (January 1972):54–62.

[25]"Employee Wrath," pp. 25–28.

[26]W. Robert Reum and Sherry Milliken Reum, "Employee Stock Ownership Plans: Pluses and Minuses," *Harvard Business Review* 54 (July–August 1976):133–43.

off the loan. As the employees do not actually receive their shares until they retire or leave the company, the employees do not pay tax on it until they are in a lower tax bracket, and even then they must sell the stock before it is taxed as capital gains.

The benefits to the company are that it (1) provides a source of needed capital, (2) boosts company cash flow, (3) raises employee morale and productivity, (4) provides new employee benefits, and (5) encourages wider public ownership of its stock.

Some of the possible disadvantages are that, as employees become owners, (1) management may find itself unable to make tough decisions that the workers oppose, and (2) the workers may be putting a lot of faith in the employer for which they work, sharing losses as well as gains. However, these plans are now growing in popularity.

Believing that the railroad industry is uniquely suited to employee ownership, Northwest Industries sold its Chicago and Northwestern Railroad to its employees in 1969. While it is not possible to quantify the benefits of this employee ownership, it has been claimed that "there is a new spirit in the company which is bound to benefit it."[27]

USING BONUS PLANS TO MOTIVATE EMPLOYEES

Another financial incentive that can be used to stimulate employees to improve performance is any one of numerous *bonus* arrangements. These differ in varying degrees from profit-sharing arrangements and incentive wage plans. But there are essentially two types, (1) those that are tied to production and (2) those that are not prearranged or based on a proportion of the business profits or directly related to productivity.

Types of Bonuses

The first kind of bonus is one directly or indirectly tied to productivity. A study of 444 firms found around 65 percent paying a salary plus some type of incentive payment, including bonuses, for sales representatives.

Conley Mill Works, employing 22 blue-collar and 5 white-collar people with supporting staff personnel, installed a plan providing a 5 percent bonus, based on each worker's gross earnings for the month, for every 10

---

[27]Johyn McClaughty, "Employee Ownership—A New Way to Run a Railroad," *Management Review* 63 (August 1974):36–38.

percent rise in shipments. Sales went up, labor costs went down, and earnings increased, for (1) the workers received the bonus immediately after earning it, (2) the reward was large enough to be significant, and (3) the bonus was paid at a different time from the regular salary so that it was considered a "special bonus for exceptional performance."[28]

Included in the second group are (1) awards for exceeding production quotas, (2) gratuitous payments (not directly associated with production) at Christmas or the end of the year or some other period, and (3) many others. Usually this bonus arrangement has only an indirect relationship to the employee's productivity, for the amount and continuity of the bonus are uncertain. These details are left to the discretion of management.

Effects of Using Bonuses

There are two factors limiting the motivational value of this type of bonus. First, if one is granted periodically, employees view it as a right and take it for granted when it is received. If it fails to materialize, there is resentment toward management. Yet, if the bonus is not granted regularly, it is not anticipated and so comes as a windfall. In either case, production tends not to be increased as a result of the bonus.

One study found that most employees did not like bonuses. They found them a very unstable way to be rewarded for their efforts because they could not understand the basis of the bonus.[29]

However, some plans of this type do have an indirect stimulating effect through improving morale and cooperation.

Some companies are now using a bonus system to encourage attendance. If employees put in a full work week, they will receive a fixed bonus, such as 10 percent of their earnings.

Bonuses have usually been paid only by private employers. Now, however, some government agencies, with the approval of Civil Service, are offering cash performance bonuses. They are called *Work Planning/Performance Review*.[30]

---

[28]Richard I. Henderson, "Money Is, Too, an Incentive: One Company's Experience," *Supervisory Management* 19 (May 1974):20-25.

[29]"Has the Bonus Carrot Lost Its Savor?" *Management Review* 58 (January 1969):40-46.

[30]"How Does the U.S. Treasury Reward Its Outstanding Workers? With Cash, Of Course," *Management Review* 68 (November 1979):47.

USING COMPANYWIDE PRODUCTIVITY SHARING SYSTEMS TO MOTIVATE EMPLOYEES

With the exception of merit increases, all the systems mentioned have been difficult to install and maintain. Also, technological changes have made it difficult to measure individual or even unit performance. Finally, the previous systems have tended to be based on competition rather than cooperation between individuals and units.

For these reasons, interest has shifted to *companywide productivity sharing systems*. These plans tend to be similar in that they offer everyone in the company or plant the chance to earn a bonus or some form of extra compensation based on some measure of organizational performance. The bonus is usually a percentage of the base rate of each employee, so that bonuses are equal for those receiving equal wages or salary.

The plans usually have (1) a system of departmental and plant screening committees to evaluate cost-saving suggestions and (2) some direct incentive paid to employees to improve efficiency.

The best known of these plans are the (1) Nunn-Bush Shoe Company Plan, (2) Scanlon Plan, (3) Rucker Share-of-Production Plan, (4) Kaiser Long-Range Sharing Plan, and (5) Lincoln Incentive Compensation Plan. Only the first four will be described, for the Lincoln Plan is really a combination of individual piece rate and group incentive plans.

Nunn-Bush Shoe Company Plan

The Nunn-Bush plan is one of the oldest and most successful of these plans. It was installed over 40 years ago as a basis of sharing productivity and guaranteeing annual incomes. The plan has much cooperation between management and employees, although there is no union.

Scanlon Plan

Joseph Scanlon, a union representative, developed this plan in 1937 to help reduce costs in a steel mill. Since then, it has been used in other organizations, including union and nonunion plants. The plan is as much a union-management cooperative venture as a compensation or motivating vehicle.

The usual results of these programs are (1) employee willingness to accept technological change, including methods and equipment, (2) greater willingness of employees to help one another, (3) greater awareness of company problems among employees, (4) a better workplace and work climate, usually free of loafing, (5) less overtime, grievances, and waste, (6) better administration of seniority clauses pertaining to promotions, layoffs, transfers, and recalls, and (7) more employee insistence on efficient management.

Some problems are (1) management's—particularly supervisors'—fear of loss of authority, (2) problems caused by changes in product mix, the proportion of direct or indirect workers, and determining the ratio going to employees and the company, and (3) the difficulty of installing the plan in large organizations.

Rucker Share-of-Production Plan

While the Scanlon plan is difficult to put into operation, especially if it is to replace or be added to incentive wage plans or profit-sharing plans, the Rucker plan has been successfully added to them. The Rucker plan is a much more sophisticated program based on a careful analysis of the historical relationships between the productive value created by the firm and the total earnings (direct and indirect compensation) of employees. Also, there are fewer adjustments in these plans than in the Scanlon plan because of the careful analysis that goes into the original plan.

Kaiser Long-range Sharing Plan

This program was worked out between the union and the company as a means of providing motivation to save on labor, materials, and supply costs. It is similar to the Rucker plan in that it was based on a careful study of company costs. The plan is quite complex, having some 16 objectives, including protecting employees against unemployment resulting from technological change.

Evaluating the Motivational Effects of These Systems

It is difficult to evaluate the motivational effect of these plans, as there are so many of them, they are so varied, and usually there are so many organizational changes made when the plans are introduced. However, in one case, employee earnings increased 14 percent per year, compounded.[31]

Experience with the Kaiser plan indicates that productivity increased fairly rapidly at first but tended to decline over time.

A survey of 21 plants having Scanlon plans indicated employee satisfaction with this way of assessing organizational efficiency and compensating employees.[32]

In essence, these plans do increase cooperation but apparently do not have

---

[31]Robert J. Schulhof, "Five Years with a Scanlon Plan," *Personnel Administrator* 24 (June 1979):55ff.

[32]R. K. Goodman, J. H. Wakeley, and R. Ruh, "What Employees Think of the Scanlon Plan," *Personnel* 49 (September–October 1972):27.

TABLE 16–4
Financial incentives and criteria for improving performance

Type of incentive	(1) Related to behavior	(2) Immediacy of reward	(3) Certainty of reward
Merit increases	Sometimes	Sometimes	Sometimes
Negotiated increases.	No	No	No
General increases	No	No	No
Production increases.	Sometimes	No	No
Cost-of-living increases.	No	No	No
Length-of-service increases . . .	No	No	No
Profit-sharing plans	Sometimes	No	No
Bonuses and commissions.	Yes	Sometimes	Yes
Individual incentive plans	Yes	Yes	Yes
Group incentive plans	Yes	Yes	Yes

Source: Reprinted by permission of the publisher from Harold F. Rothe, "Does Higher Pay Bring Higher Productivity?" *Personnel* 37 (July–August 1969):25. © 1969 by American Management Association, Inc.

the same degree of motivational value as individual incentive programs because the connection between performance and compensation is broken.

WHAT IS REQUIRED FOR FINANCIAL INCENTIVES TO MOTIVATE

In order to be effective in motivating employees to produce more, an incentive system must meet certain criteria. The critical ones appear to be (1) that the system be related to some behavior such as better performance or higher productivity, (2) that the reward received through the plan be received quickly, and (3) that the payment be certain if a particular behavioral pattern is displayed. If these criteria are considered jointly by personnel executives in designing their compensation programs, performance should improve, as shown in Table 16–4.

For example, money seemed to be the prime motivator of several electronics engineers who switched jobs. This observation was particularly surprising because they left companies that were considered to be among the most "enlightened and progressive." But, when the cause of the job changes was investigated, it was found that the engineers had been motivated, not by money itself, but by its importance as equitable and timely recognition of their contribution to their firm's total effort.[33]

SUMMARY AND CONCLUSIONS

Do financial incentives motivate? Research findings seem to indicate that they do. In general, financial rewards tend to be the prime motivator up to the

[33]Allan Young, "On the Line," *Personnel Administration* 29 (March–April 1966):60.

point where the safety-security needs are met. Beyond that point, other motivators tend to become stronger.

People with low achievement needs will probably be motivated by financial rewards more than those with high achievement needs.

Using ability and merit as the basis for granting salary increases has great potential for motivating employees to increase output and efficiency. Yet it is sometimes difficult to use this method because of limited financial resources and the difficulty of determining "merit."

The main objectives of incentive wage plans are to (1) lower unit cost, direct labor costs and overhead by increasing production and (2) increase earnings of employees through individual merit and accomplishment.

With a properly developed and administered wage incentive plan, the output per hour should increase around 20 percent, while employee earnings should increase by about the same amount.

Unions, in general, oppose wage incentive plans, for they tend to hurt group relationships.

Profit sharing is in essence a system under which employees are motivated to improve performance and reduce costs so that profits increase. Then they share in those profits according to a preannounced and fixed formula. It is effective when profits increase, but not when they fall or disappear. Employee stock ownership plans (ESOPs) are being used as a profit-sharing technique.

Another financial incentive that can be used to stimulate employees to improve performance is any one of numerous bonus arrangements. Their effectiveness is reduced, however, if they are not in some way related to performance.

The five best-known companywide productivity sharing systems are the (1) Nunn-Bush Shoe Company Plan, (2) Scanlon Plan, (3) Rucker Share-of-Production Plan, (4) Kaiser Long-range Sharing Plan, and (5) Lincoln Incentive Compensation Plan.

What conclusions can be reached from this discussion? First, most managers want to relate employees' compensation to their performance in order to motivate them. However, financial rewards, such as merit salary increases, incentive wages, profit sharing, and bonuses, are limited in supply and can be used only to a restricted extent in motivating employees by promising to satisfy their material needs. Conversely, intrinsic rewards, such as interesting and challenging work, recognition, and achieving self-actualization, give satisfaction within themselves and can be used to an unlimited extent.

Second, employees have different capacities for job performance, and those capacities are being only partially utilized. Hence, regardless of the experience, training, or similar factors involved, some personnel will be better performers than others. Therefore, in order to motivate them to produce at a superior level, compensation must be provided that is related to their performance.

Third, individual performance does tend to vary with the economic rewards. The greater the reward relative to the employee's economic needs, the greater its motivational stimulus to increase productivity and improve performance. But there is a point beyond which financial increases will have less and less effect as a motivator.

Fourth, financial rewards have psychological as well as economic value. They can (1) serve as status symbols, (2) satisfy the ego, and (3) signify achievement, recognition, and advancement.

QUESTIONS

1. How does money induce people to increase their productivity, and how do people relate their wage to the level of productivity?
2. Why is the concept of *differential* payments important for an equitable and motivational reward system?
3. What is necessary for merit increases to motivate?
4. What is the objective of an incentive wage system? Do you think this type of wage system functions well in contemporary American industry? Why or why not?
5. What are the advantages and disadvantages of the incentive wage system from the company's and the individual's points of view?
6. Why do certain industries use incentive wages more than others?
7. What is profit sharing, and what is the philosophy underlying the scheme?
8. Do bonuses motivate? Explain.
9. What is the motivational value of companywide productivity sharing systems? Explain.

PROBLEM

The Reluctant Sales Reps

"I just don't know what we're going to do about our sales reps," said Annie Sinclair, a partner in Commercial Sales. "During the spring and summer, they usually tend to their contractor accounts. But when housing starts slow down in the fall and winter, they forget about those contractors. Most of the contractors have to call in their orders because they haven't heard from our representative in weeks. What would you suggest?"

Commercial Sales is owned and managed by Bob and Annie Sinclair and two other partners. The company sells and installs fireplaces, metal doors, siding, and garage doors. It has one location from which it serves customers anywhere within a 100-mile radius. There are six sales reps—five men and one woman.

The sales reps try to generate sales by visiting housing contractors and individuals and by answering individual inquiries about Commercial's products. Recently the woman sales rep was hired to call individuals whose names appeared in the newspaper listing of building permits to try to set up appointments for a sales rep to show them what products in home comfort Commercial has to offer.

At present, the sales reps receive an 8 percent commission on contractor sales and a 10 percent commission on sales to individuals. The female sales rep receives a salary plus a 1 percent commission on all sales she helps generate by her telephone calls.

The problem is that during the cold and rainy months, when housing starts are slow, the sales reps neglect their contractor accounts. Sales to individuals rise because more people want fireplaces put in during the cold weather. Then the sales reps try to persuade the customer to purchase other Commercial products. Mrs. Sinclair said an individual may buy $3,000 worth of products, while the usual contractor sale amounts to about $500. But the contractor sales are repeat sales, while individuals buy only once. "Not only are the contractors having to call the office to place their orders—which puts an overload on the office staff—but we are even losing sales because of this problem," said Mrs. Sinclair. "As long as sales keep growing as fast as they are now, we're fine. If things ever slow down, though, these lost sales will present a real problem."

Questions

1. If you were the sales manager of Commercial Sales, what would you suggest to the partners as a possible solution? Explain.
2. What does this case suggest about the use of financial incentives?

SUGGESTED READINGS FOR FURTHER STUDY

"Awards for Federal Employees Found Ineffective." *The Office*, May 1979, p. 24.

"Be Generous." *Economist*, December 16, 1978, p. 93.

Cook, Frederic W. "Book-Value Stock as an Employee Stock Ownership and Incentive Device." *Compensation Review* 9 (Third Quarter 1977):11–19.

"Every Employee an Owner? Old Idea Gets a New Boost." *U.S. News & World Report*, June 9, 1975, p. 68–69.

Flamion, Allen. "The Dollars and Sense of Motivation." *Personnel Journal* 59 (January 1980):51ff.

Forbes, Wallace F., and Donald P. Partland. "Pros and Cons of Employee Stock Ownership Plans." *Business Horizons* 19 (June 1976):5–12.

Goodman, Isidore. *ESOP's Updated*. Chicago: Commerce Clearing House, 1978.

Hewitt, Garth. "Letting Employees Have Their Share." *International Management* 34 (December 1979):35–37.

Lawler, Edward E., III. "Workers Can Set Their Own Wages—Responsibly." *Psychology Today* 10 (February 1977):109–10 and 112.

Sherman, George. "The Scanlon Concept: Its Capabilities for Productivity Improvement." *Personnel Administrator* 21 (July 1976):17–20.

CHAPTER SEVENTEEN

Providing Employee Benefits and Services

Learning Objectives

After reading the material in this chapter, you should be able to:

1. Discuss how and why benefit programs have grown so rapidly.
2. Explain some of the special considerations, such as extent of use, cost, and difficulty of defining and classifying benefits.
3. Explain the provisions of the legally required benefits: Social Security, unemployment compensation, and workers' compensation.
4. Name and explain some of the most popular voluntary programs.
5. Describe some of the problems with retirement programs and how they are being corrected.
6. Explain how the programs can be made more effective.
7. Explain how EEO laws affect benefit programs.

Some Important Words and Terms

Employee (fringe) benefits
Social Security
Medicare
Unemployment compensation
Experience rating
Workers' compensation
Second injury fund
Sabbatical leaves
Sick-leave pool

Supplemental unemployment benefits (SUBs)
Health maintenance organizations (HMOs)
Fixed-contribution pension plan
Individual retirement account (IRA)
Fixed-benefit pension plan
Vested interest
Cafeteria benefit plan

Sugar in the gourd and honey in the horn.
I was never so happy since the hour I was born.
"Turkey in the Straw," an American Folk Tune

Outline of the Chapter

BACKGROUND
      How Benefits Have Grown
      Why Benefits Have Grown
SOME SPECIAL CONSIDERATIONS
      Problem of Definition
      Extent of Use
      Cost of Programs
      Problem of Classification
LEGALLY REQUIRED BENEFITS
      Social Security
      Unemployment Compensation
      Workers' Compensation
VOLUNTARY PROGRAMS
      Pay for Time Not Worked
      Supplemental Unemployment Benefits
      Health Protection
      Other Benefits
RETIREMENT
      When Should Employees Retire?
      How Much Help to Give Retirees?
      Financing Retirement Programs
      How ERISA Protects Pension Funds
REQUIREMENTS FOR MAKING BENEFITS MORE EFFECTIVE
      Develop Attainable Objectives
      Invite Employee Participation
      Communicate More Effectively with Employees
      Control Costs
HOW EEO REGULATIONS AFFECT BENEFITS
      Sick Leave
      Retirement

447

"Happy Birthday" means different things to different people. To many employees, it means a paid holiday or double pay if they must work that day. Several supermarkets in the Los Angeles area provide free psychiatric treatment for their clerks and families. Some other benefits now being received are hairpieces for bald persons, free apartment furnishings for single nurses, steak once a week aboard ships of the U.S. Coast and Geodetic Survey, day care centers for working parents, tension-releasing areas—such as gyms and chapels—dental care, auto insurance, and legal services.

These are only a few examples of the many and varied compensation provisions commonly referred to as *employee benefits* or "fringe benefits." These items are increasing in importance as part of the compensation package because more and costlier benefits continue to be major goals of today's employees.

The purpose of this chapter is to review the background of employee benefits, analyze their objectives, discuss the types of benefits, estimate the extent of their use and the cost to employers, and suggest ways to improve their use.

BACKGROUND

While some of today's programs designed to protect employees from the basic hazards of life are relatively new, the inability to produce because of age or disability is not a new problem. The basic hazards have been of concern for hundreds of years.

How Benefits Have Grown

Employee benefits began when the first *accident and death benefit plans* were offered in the early 1900s, following the passage of *workers' compensation laws.*

Benefits also expanded in the 1930s when the government became interested in the *physical and economic security* of employees, as demonstrated by the *Social Security Act* of 1935. Also, as a result of (1) the Hawthorne experiments, which concluded that job satisfaction led to increased employee production, and (2) union pressure, many employers introduced benefits designed to "make the workers happy." These included *paying for time not worked.*

The next expansion of these benefit programs occurred during World War II, largely as a result of the freezing of wage rates. Desperate for labor, companies began to compete for the scarce workers by means of expanded employee benefits—usually *extra compensation in the form of some good or service employees needed.*

Since then, the emphasis has been on benefits like pensions, retirement plans, insurance provisions, shorter work hours—for the same pay, and underwriting the changing lifestyles of employees, including mental health care, dental care, legal services, and day care centers for the children of working parents.

Benefits have grown rapidly in recent years, and the growth shows no signs of slowing down. After allowing for inflation, benefits have increased twice as fast as wages and salaries. They are predicted to reach 50 percent of payroll by 1985.

Why Benefits Have Grown

Many factors have caused this change in the nature of compensation. Only a few of them will be discussed here. They are increased real wages, changing lifestyles, and governmental influences.

Increased real wages. Increases in productivity have resulted in increased real wages for most employees. This has permitted choices in the way the workers' share is distributed. Part of the productivity increase, for example, has been taken in increased leisure in the form of vacations and holidays as well as shorter hours. However, productivity and real wages are now declining.

Changing lifestyles. Changing lifestyles lead to increased use of benefits instead of (or in addition to) wages or salaries. Working parents need child-care centers. More educated workers want more leisure and more assured income. Prepaid legal services are required because more people are now suing—and being sued. And the pressures of modern life are causing many people to need psychiatric treatment.

Governmental influences. The influence of governments in the allocation of compensation has been felt in social legislation, such as (1) workers' compensation, (2) the Social Security program, including unemployment compensation, (3) laws protecting pensions, and (4) health and safety protection.

Another important factor has been income tax legislation. High income tax rates for both employers and employees have encouraged the expansion of benefit programs. Because much of the employers' cost of such programs is deductible for income tax purposes as a business expense, they have had an incentive to institute benefit programs. Also, it is to the employees' benefit to receive these nontaxable benefits instead of taxable income.

During the 1978 coal miners' strike, the members' order of priority was (1) health benefits, (2) pension benefits, and (3) wages. Instead, only 6 percent of the 37 percent increase was for fringes. The rest was for wages, which were taxable. The miners refused to accept the contract until they got what they wanted.

SOME SPECIAL CONSIDERATIONS

Some current problems with employee benefits—from the personnel managers' viewpoint—are (1) how to define them, (2) the extent of their use, (3) their increasing cost, and (4) how to classify them.

Problem of Definition

The term *employee benefits* is so broad that it might easily extend from steady employment at fair wages to the payment of tuition for employees attending university management courses, or from comprehensive safety programs to interplant athletics, or from free meals to free psychiatric or legal assistance. However, a working definition is: *Employee benefits* are the rewards and services provided to employees in addition to regular earnings.

Extent of Use

All employers use fringe benefits; the only question is the extent of their use by individual industries and firms. According to the Chamber of Commerce of the United States, the *highest fringe benefit payments* are found in (1) chemicals, (2) primary metals, (3) petroleum, (4) banks, and (5) public utilities. Employers *making less extensive use of the plans* are (1) the textile products and apparel industry, (2) hospitals, (3) trade, and (4) department stores. See Figure 17-1 for a comparison of these and other industries.

Cost of Programs

Another problem with these programs is their escalating cost. In 1978, the cost for all employers was estimated at $350 billion, 250 percent greater than in 1967. The cost for the average employee was $5,138, or 36.9 percent of total payroll cost.[1]

Problem of Classification

There is no uniform method of classifying employee benefits. Yet it is desirable to have some procedure for classifying them for comparative and analytical purposes. The system followed in this text is that used by the Chamber of

---

[1]*Employee Benefits, 1978* (Washington, D.C.: Chamber of Commerce of the United States, 1979).

URE 17-1

ployee benefits as a percentage of payroll, by industry groups, in 748 companies, 1977

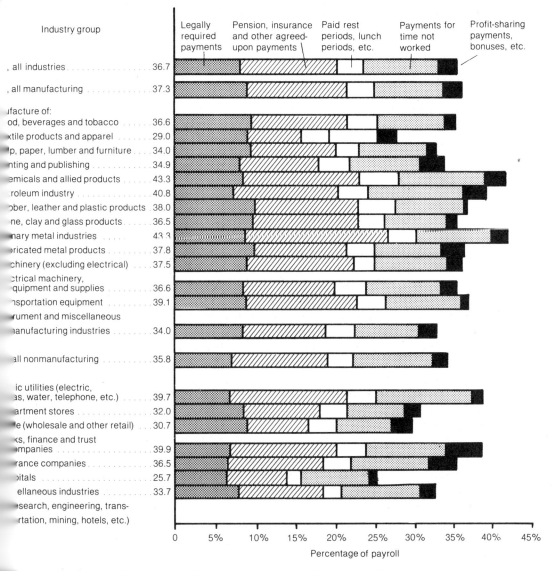

Industry group	
, all industries	36.7
, all manufacturing	37.3
facture of:	
od, beverages and tobacco	36.6
xtile products and apparel	29.0
p, paper, lumber and furniture	34.0
nting and publishing	34.9
emicals and allied products	43.3
roleum industry	40.8
ober, leather and plastic products	38.0
ne, clay and glass products	36.5
nary metal industries	43.3
ricated metal products	37.8
chinery (excluding electrical)	37.5
trical machinery, quipment and supplies	36.6
sportation equipment	39.1
rument and miscellaneous manufacturing industries	34.0
all nonmanufacturing	35.8
ic utilities (electric, s, water, telephone, etc.)	39.7
artment stores	32.0
e (wholesale and other retail)	30.7
ks, finance and trust mpanies	39.9
rance companies	36.5
itals	25.7
ellaneous industries search, engineering, trans- rtation, mining, hotels, etc.)	33.7

Employee Benefits, 1977 (Washington, D.C.: Chamber of Commerce of the United States, 1978), p. 10.

Commerce, namely, (1) the legally required benefits and (2) voluntary programs.

LLY REQUIRED BENEFITS

The benefits that are legally required by state and federal laws include (1) Social Security, (2) unemployment insurance, and (3) workers' compensation.

Social Security

Social Security is the basic method U.S. employers use to provide for continued income when family earnings stop because of death or are reduced through disability or retirement.

Who and what is covered.   When the *Social Security Act* was passed in 1935, Social Security covered only the *worker* upon *retirement*. In 1939, the law was changed to pay survivors when the worker died, as well as certain dependents when the worker retired.

Social Security covered only workers in industry and commerce when the program began. In the 1950s, coverage was extended to include most self-employed persons, most state and local employees, household and farm employees, members of the Armed Forces, and members of the clergy. Today almost all workers except railroad and U.S. government employees are covered by the act.

Disability insurance benefits were added in 1957, giving workers protection against loss of earnings due to total disability.

The program was expanded in 1965 with the enactment of *Medicare,* which assured hospital and medical insurance protection to *people 65 and over.* Since 1973, Medicare coverage has been available to *people under 65* who have been entitled to disability checks for two or more consecutive years and to people with permanent kidney failure who need dialysis or kidney transplants.

Now nearly nine out of every ten workers are earning Social Security protection, and one out of every seven people in the country receives monthly benefit checks.

Benefits.   In general, workers, their living or surviving spouses, and children under 18 (22 if full-time students) receive benefits when the worker dies, becomes disabled, or retires.

Since 1972, benefits increase automatically as the cost of living goes up.

Under this program, retired persons who are covered can start receiving retirement checks as early as age 62. Workers who become "severely disabled" before age 65 can receive disability income. If a covered worker dies, certain members of the family can receive a lump-sum payment and regular monthly income checks.

Financing.   Benefits are financed by a payroll tax paid by both employer and employees. The tax rate and base are subject to congressional change. They are now scheduled to increase for both employer and employee as shown in Table 17–1.

Self-employed people must pay the entire cost themselves. Their rates will increase from 9.30 percent in 1981 to 10.75 percent in 1990.

Some problem areas.   Two of the main problems with Social Security are shown in Figure 17–2. As you can see, the benefits are paid from the incoming payroll taxes. But most people believe that either the tax rates or the taxable earnings will have to be lower than proposed for the future. This will mean that the income will be less than the benefits being paid.

FIGURE 17–2
Future problems for Social Security

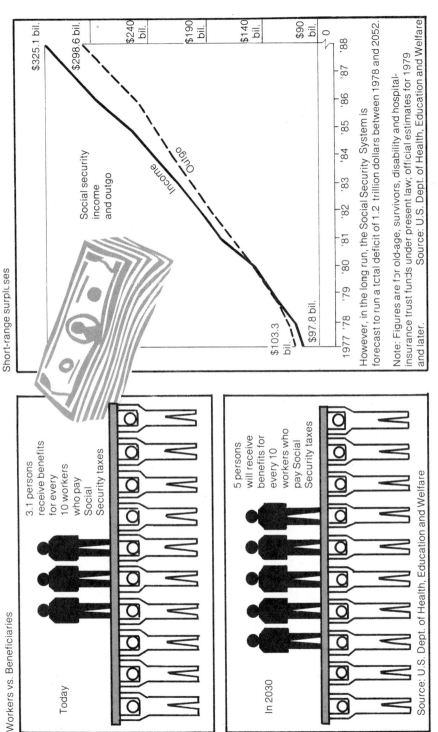

Workers vs. Beneficiaries

Today

3.1 persons receive benefits for every 10 workers who pay Social Security taxes

In 2030

5 persons will receive benefits for every 10 workers who pay Social Security taxes

Source: U.S. Dept. of Health, Education and Welfare

Short-range surpluses

Social security income and outgo

Income

Outgo

$325.1 bil.

$298.6 bil.

$103.3 bil.

$97.8 bil.

$240 bil.

$190 bil.

$140 bil.

$90 bil.

0

1977 '78 '79 '80 '81 '82 '83 '84 '85 '86 '87 '88

However, in the long run, the Social Security System is forecast to run a total deficit of 1.2 trillion dollars between 1978 and 2052.

Note: Figures are for old-age, survivors, disability and hospital-insurance trust funds under present law; official estimates for 1979 and later.

Source: U.S. Dept. of Health, Education and Welfare

Source: "Social Security: Will It Be There When You Need It?" reprinted from *U.S. News & World Report*, April 30, 1978, p. 27. Copyright 1978 U.S. News and **World Report, Inc.**

TABLE 17-1
Social Security taxes, 1981-1989

Year	Tax rate for employer and employee (percent)	Taxable earnings	Maximum tax
1981	6.65	$29,700	$1,975
1982	6.70	31,800	2,130
1983	6.70	33,900	2,271
1984	6.70	36,000	2,412
1985	7.05	38,100	2,686
1986	7.15	40,200	2,874
1987	7.15	42,600	3,046
1988	7.15	42,600	3,046
1989	7.15	49,800	3,561

Source: Social Security Administration.

Also, as Figure 17-2 shows, the number of workers supporting each person receiving benefits is declining. Between now and the time you retire, the number of people receiving benefits will double. But those working and paying the tax will increase by only a third. This "intergenerational transfer system" has been called the "ticking time bomb" by a former Secretary of the Treasury.[2]

Unemployment Compensation

Unemployment compensation was also set up by the *Social Security Act* of 1935. The tax is collected by the U.S. government. Most of it is returned to the states, which set the conditions and pay the benefits. The rest is used for administrative expenses.

Benefits are paid to unemployed workers under certain conditions. They must (1) have worked for a covered employer, (2) be willing and able to work, and (3) have been terminated under certain specified conditions. The amount and duration of benefits vary from state to state and with each individual case.

The program is financed by taxes on the employer (in most states). The amount of the tax varies according to the individual firm's *experience rating,* which is based on how many of its former employees are receiving payments. The tax is imposed on the first $6,600 paid in wages to each employee annually. The experience rating factor encourages a firm to minimize its labor turnover.

The amount of compensation received by eligible workers, which varies from state to state, is determined by their previous wage rates and periods of employment. Usually the benefits are received for 26 weeks, but this is sometimes raised to 52 weeks in periods of emergency. There is currently an effort

---

[2]William E. Simon, *A Time for Truth* (New York: Reader's Digest Press, 1978).

to set federal standards requiring minimum benefit levels at 50 percent of a worker's weekly wage.

There are criticisms, even by the General Accounting Office, that this form of compensation—especially in the states where it is close to regular take-home pay—encourages laid-off workers to remain jobless longer than they otherwise would.[3]

Workers' Compensation Laws

All states now have *workers' compensation laws.* Before the states began to pass these laws (then called workmen's compensation) in the early 1900s, injured employees had to sue their employer if they were injured. Not only was this costly, but few suits were won. Under common law, the workers assumed the risk of death or injury when they took a job. Also, the employer was not responsible for contributory negligence.

Provisions. The state laws now establish what are essentially no-fault insurance programs. These are strictly state laws, and each one differs. In general, though, they provide that the employer is liable for paying medical and hospital bills, and for part of wages lost by the employee because of industrial illness or accidents. There is a fixed scale of payments—so much for the loss of a leg, arm, eye, and so forth. Also, the percentage of salary to be paid is stated.

The entire cost is paid by the employer, either through approved insurance companies or through special funds set up by the firm or a state fund.

Coverage. To receive benefits, a worker must be employed by a covered employer, in a covered occupation. The law is compulsory on employers except in New Jersey, South Carolina, and Texas. Even in those states, if an employer is not under the law, the common law defenses mentioned above are lost, and the danger of lawsuits is greater.

Benefits. For the employee who is the head of a household, workers' compensation is probably the most important of all benefits received, as it guarantees a continuation of income if one is disabled or dies. Also, the expenses for medical care and rehabilitation to return the employee to a productive life are paid by the insurance.

A secondary benefit of the system is the promotion of occupational safety and health through the economic incentives forced upon the employer. If the incidence of work injuries is low, the employer has a high *experience rating.* This improvement is reflected in a reduction of the insurance cost. Thus, efforts by employers to create safer work environments can reduce the total personnel costs of their organization.

As many employers are reluctant to hire the handicapped because they fear an increase in workers' compensation insurance costs, some states have passed *second injury fund* laws. These set up a state agency to reimburse employers

---

[3]"Jobless Benefits So Generous, GAO Says, That Many Recipients Quit Seeking Jobs," *The Wall Street Journal,* August 29, 1979, p. 2.

FIGURE 17-3
Workers' compensation benefits as a percentage of take-home pay

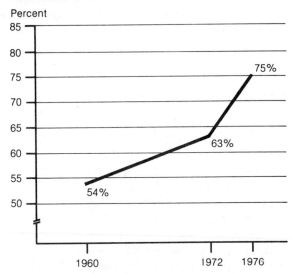

Source: "Modern Workers' Compensation" *Journal of American Insurance* 51 (Winter 1975–76):16.

or their insurance carriers for part of the workers' compensation costs when a handicapped employee is injured on the job.

As shown in Figure 17–3, workers' compensation benefits replace about 75 percent of the typical worker's spendable earnings, on the average.

Federal workers' compensation.   The U.S. government also has a program to help federal workers hurt or made ill on the job. It is administered by the Office of Workers' Compensation Programs in the Labor Department.

VOLUNTARY PROGRAMS

The voluntary programs will be covered under the following headings: (1) pay for time not worked, (2) supplemental unemployment benefit funds, (3) health protection, and (4) retirement income plans.

Pay for Time Not Worked

One of the main problems facing personnel managers today is the increasing emphasis on absence from the job, at the employer's expense. This practice takes several forms, namely, vacations, holidays, and time off for other reasons such as sick leave, jury duty, and compassionate leave. The long-range trend has been toward reducing the total number of hours worked each year. I have estimated that the work year has decreased from around 3,700 hours in the

19th century to about 1,800 now. This trend is expected to continue at an increasing rate.

Paid vacations.   The original reason for granting paid vacations was to permit employees to improve themselves through rest and relaxation so that they could become more productive workers. Now, however, vacations are regarded as deferred wages. Payment for unused vacation time is therefore made to employees when they terminate their employment.

Five-week periods away from the job are now commonplace. Moreover, in industries such as steel, some employees are now granted *sabbatical leaves*. These are three-month vacations designed to permit the workers to rest, relax, and become more productive employees.

Paid holidays.   Most managers feel that workers will be more productive if they are permitted time off to celebrate holidays. This practice gives employees time to rest, relax, and get away from the routine of the job without fear of financial loss. Therefore, they should be better workers because of the improved morale and job satisfaction generated.

Many employers are now giving employees a holiday on their birthday.

Paid sick leave.   Sick leave is granted to employees to relieve them of the worry of financial loss resulting from conditions beyond their control. However, this arrangement can easily be abused. The feeling that the employees have that much time coming to them seems to be prevalent. Therefore, frequently employees will take the time off, even if it is not entirely necessary. As a consequence, many organizations require a doctor's certificate as a proof of illness or they will not pay the first day or two of illness.

Bonus for not taking leave.   Some employers now even pay a bonus to workers for *not* taking their sick leave time.

Parsons Pine Products cut absenteeism by one-third by giving "well pay" instead of "sick pay." An employee gets an extra day's pay for every month in which he or she works every day.[4]

Sick-leave pool.   Another variation of this is the *sick-leave pool*.[5] Employees are allowed to pool some of their compensated sick-leave days in a common fund. Then they can draw upon the fund if protracted illness uses up their remaining time off.

Supplemental Unemployment Benefits

Many firms provide *supplemental unemployment benefits* (SUBs) to employees. These payments are additions to their unemployment compensation payments and are designed to stabilize employment.

---

[4]*The Wall Street Journal*, April 2, 1978, p. 1.

[5]Hoyt W. Doyel and John D. McMillan, "Low Cost Benefit Suggestions," *Personnel Administrator* 25 (May 1980):55.

SUBs are based on the concept of employees' working and drawing wages as long as they can. When they can no longer work, they receive unemployment compensation from the state and other benefits from the company.

These benefits, added to the state unemployment compensation, will provide the unemployed workers with up to 95 percent of their straight-time pay for a 40-hour week, after taxes, for the first four weeks of layoff. After that, they are assured of a slightly lower percentage of their straight-time pay.

Health Protection

Another group of benefits provides for medical and hospital attention, pay while the employee is sick, and benefits in case of the death of the employee.

Health care insurance.   Group medical, surgical, and dental plans are very popular with employees but expensive for management. Most public employees, and around 35 million employees of private firms, are covered by some form of health-care insurance plan. These group plans are financed by the employer through an insurance company. The employer is increasingly paying the total cost of the premiums.

Many employers are turning to *health maintenance organizations* (HMOs). HMOs are composed of many groups of health-care personnel, such as doctors, nurses, and technicians, who provide complete medical care for the entire family. They are financed by a fixed flat fee, paid by the employer and employee each month.

Life insurance.   Life insurance is one of the oldest and most popular benefits for both public and private employees. These group plans provide for death benefits to the beneficiaries upon an employee's death.

The amount of coverage is usually based on the employee's income. A popular amount is two or two and a half times the base annual salary. The employee pays part of the cost for most programs. However, there is a trend here also for the employer to pay the total cost.

Other Benefits

Some other popular benefits are (1) payment of transfer costs, including sale of homes, (2) employee discounts and group purchase plans, (3) stock purchase plans, (4) tuition refunds, (5) educational benefit trusts, and (6) career management programs.[6]

RETIREMENT

Over the past several decades, there was a trend toward early retirement in the United States. Government, unions, and managers cooperated to create

------

[6]Ibid.

new jobs for younger employees by encouraging and providing for early retirement of older workers. As there was an excess of workers, it was thought socially desirable to create jobs for the younger ones by making early retirement attractive to the senior employees.

Now several factors are causing a reversal of this trend.[7] These include (1) population changes, with the work force now getting older, (2) increased governmental action, including raising the mandatory retirement age, (3) inflation, which is eroding retirement benefits, and (4) problems with Social Security.

Now personnel managers face several problems with retirement policies and practices. They are (1) when to retire workers, (2) how much help to give, before and after retirement, (3) financing retirement programs, and (4) protecting retirees' pensions.

When Should Employees Retire?

There are really two aspects of the question of the timing of retirement: (1) at what age should workers retire, and (2) should retirement be voluntary or mandatory?

Early or late?   Workers now face the dilemma of deciding whether to retire at an early age or wait until they are older. This is not always an easy decision.

Early retirement.   Early retirement is nothing new. Miners have been able to retire at age 55 for some years now. Auto workers, regardless of age, can retire after spending 30 years in the shop. Military personnel can retire after 20 years of service. Many of these early retirees pursue a second career.

Early retirement has been made feasible by the existence of private pension plans in addition to Social Security. The result has been that the years male workers spend outside the labor force have increased from 15.2 in 1900 to 32.4 in 1975.[8] The figure for female workers would be around 40, as they have a greater life expectancy.

Later retirement.   In general, the older one gets, the less attractive retirement gets. Also, the thought of what to do with one's time, declines in emotional and physical health, and fear of what inflation can do to retirement benefits encourage employees to take later retirement.

One survey of workers aged 46–74, both male and female, found that 63 percent were willing to retire, and 14 percent were unwilling. Those who did not want to retire (1) liked their job, (2) liked their workplace, (3) felt they did better work than younger employees, (4) visited friends more

---

[7]Kenneth P. Shapiro, "The Reversing Early Retirement Trend," *Personnel Administrator* 25 (April 1980):77–79.

[8]Mark Lipton, "An Unmentionable Personnel Problem of the 1980s," *Personnel* 56 (September–October 1979):60.

"Now that I've retired, I have time for all the things I dreamed of doing, but I forget what they were!"

Reprinted by permission *The Wall Street Journal*

often, (5) earned more, and (6) worried less about their health than those who did want to retire.[9]

Mandatory or voluntary?   There is considerable controversy over whether or not there should be a mandatory retirement age. Here are some of the factors involved.[10]

For mandatory retirement. Those favoring fixed retirement programs

---

[9]Mary E. Hopkins and Marcia W. Wood, "Who Wants to Retire?" *Personnel Administrator* 21 (October 1976):38–41. Similar results were found at the Veterans Administration outpatient clinic in Boston, where 13 percent of the men planned "never to retire." "They Want to Go on Working," *Modern Maturity*, October-November 1978, p. 5.

[10]Thomas A. Litros, "The Battle over Retirement Policies and Practices," *Personnel Journal* 58 (February 1979):102–10.

claim they (1) are simple and easy to administer, (2) make room for younger, more productive employees, and (3) are a humane way of easing out unproductive workers.

For voluntary retirement. Voluntary programs are favored because (1) physical and mental abilities cannot be judged by age, (2) many older workers perform better than younger ones, and (3) forced retirement reduces the nation's ability to produce goods and services at a time when they are needed.

One study found that more retirees than currently employed workers, more men than women, and more people in the North Central area than in the West South Central area favored mandatory retirement.[11]

How Much Help to Give Retirees?

Personnel managers are now giving great attention to preparing employees for retirement. This takes two forms: (1) giving preretirement assistance and (2) providing part-time employment after retirement.

Preretirement assistance. A survey of 800 companies by the Conference Board showed that 88 percent of the companies gave preretirement assistance to their employees. Over 96 percent of them gave some type of postretirement assistance, even if it was only sending a list of publications with the pension check. As shown in Table 17-2, most of the preretirement assistance took the form of providing financial information.

Another problem personnel executives face is deciding what kind of assistance to give retiring employees. For example, an outstanding study of 200 retired employees showed a variation between (1) the information sought by employees before retirement, (2) the problems faced after retirement, and (3) the information they then sought from the organization. Health was seventh on the list of preretirement information sought. Yet it became the most serious

TABLE 17-2
Preretirement assistance given by 800 companies

Employees are offered	*Percentage of companies offering*
No preretirement assistance.............	12
Financial information only..............	46
Financial and health information only	21
Financial information, plus written counseling in other areas	8
Financial information, plus personal counseling in other areas	13

Source: J. Roger O'Meara, "Retirement—The Eighth Age of Man," *Conference Board Record* 11 (October 1974):59-64.

---

[11]Ray Hemming, ed., "What's the Right Age for Retirement," *Retirement Living* 17 (April 1977):22-25.

TABLE 17–3
Seriousness of retirees' problems

Problems	Rank of seriousness
Health	1
Money and financial matters	2
Too much free time	3
Lack of personal and social contacts	4
Food and nutrition	5
Transportation................................	6
Housing	7

Source: William H. Holley, Jr. and Hubert S. Field, Jr., "The Design of a Retirement Preparation Program: A Case History," *Personnel Journal* 53 (July 1974):529. Reprinted with permission of *Personnel Journal*, copyright July 1974.

problem of the retirees after retirement (see Table 17–3) and so was the number one subject of questions then.

Some employers are providing more concrete assistance. Some firms pay for college courses to prepare employees for new careers.

Pitney Bowes reimburses employees over 50, and their spouses, up to $300 a year for tuition, books, and fees for approved courses or individual instruction.[12]

Part-time employment. Many factors are causing employers to provide ways for retiring personnel to keep working part time. As you can see from Table 17–4, most employers in the ASPA/BNA survey did this.

Other retirees are finding new careers after retiring.[13]

TABLE 17–4
Flexible retirement arrangements

Type of arrangement	Percentage of companies
Employees may "taper off" working hours prior to retirement	15
All employees eligible	7
Certain employees eligible..............	8
Employees may continue working on consultant basis after retirement........	52
Employees may be recalled for temporary work after retirement.................	62

Source: Reprinted by special permission from *Bulletin to Management*, copyright 1980 by The Bureau of National Affairs, Inc., Washington, D.C.

---

[12]"Second Careers," *Personnel Administrator* 24 (December 1979):47.

[13]"New Careers for Retirees," *Modern Maturity*, February–March 1979, pp. 57–59.

Financing Retirement Programs

During the last two decades, there have been dramatic improvements in retirement benefits for working Americans. These benefits are now provided by over 80 percent of major American employers. Around four out of five of these are financed entirely by the employer.[14]

There are two basic types of plans—(1) fixed-contribution plans and (2) fixed-benefit plans.

Under a *fixed-contribution pension plan,* the employer puts a fixed amount into a fund for the employees to use. These programs include (1) thrift plans, (2) profit sharing, (3) *individual retirement accounts* (IRAs), and others. The amount received by an employee will be determined by what happens to interest rates, inflation, and other factors.

Under *fixed-benefit pension plans,* the amount of pension to be received at retirement is a fixed amount, which is stated in advance. The amount to be received is usually based on the employee's salary. These plans may be either set up in a trust fund or based on purchased insurance annuities.

How ERISA Protects Pension Funds

There are two basic problems in protecting employees' pension benefits. The first involves seeing that the funds retain their purchasing power. Inflation is now threatening to destroy the value of these funds.

The second problem is to see that the funds are actually available when needed. The *Employee Retirement Income Security Act* of 1974 (ERISA or the Pension Reform Law) tries to do this. It requires that all private firms with retirement programs meet federally imposed standards. Companies are not required to have a plan, but, if they do, the plan must be financially sound and easily understood by the plan participants. Also, firms with plans that cover 100 or more employees must submit detailed descriptions of the plans and annual reports to the Department of Labor.

What the law provides. The law does provide considerable protection to employees covered by a pension plan. Some of the benefits are:

1. Anyone is eligible for the plan, regardless of age.
2. Employees must be given a *vested interest* in (nonforfeitable right to) the pension within 5 to 15 years, depending on conditions.
3. Employers are responsible for keeping the fund solvent.
4. A surviving spouse must receive 50 percent of the employee's retirement benefits.
5. A federal agency, the Pension Benefit Guaranty Corporation (PBGC), insures the right of employees and retirees in the fund even if the firm goes bankrupt.

---

[14]Mary Miner, *Pension Plans and the Impact of ERISA* (Washington, D.C.: Bureau of National Affairs, 1977), p. 12.

6. Employees not covered by a pension program can set up an individual retirement account (IRA) or a similar plan.
7. Employees must be provided with information and details about the program in language that "the average employee can understand."

Employers have several alternatives under the law. These vary from having no plan at all to having a fixed-benefit pension plan with a general benefit level providing predictable benefits to employees.

Who administers it.   The act is the primary responsibility of the Administrator of Pension and Welfare Benefit Programs in the Department of Labor. Plans must be submitted to the administrator for approval. Yet the plans must also be approved by the Internal Revenue Service (IRS) in the Treasury Department, and the PBGC must approve the plans it insures.

Some problems with the law.   The law has some crucial problems, but efforts are being made to overcome them. Retirement experts say that workers and their representatives will find managers of pension plans struggling to find ways of providing the benefits already promised.

Firms discontinuing plans.   The law was passed to protect and guarantee retirement benefits for over 30 million workers and to encourage the creation of new plans for over 40 million other workers not covered. But indications are that it may be working in the opposite direction. There have been 11,000 new plans added since the law was passed in 1974. But 16,500 plans have folded, partly because of the act's tougher standards. These plans were primarily in small firms, where help for retirees is needed most.

The General Accounting Office found that ERISA was a factor in 41 percent of the cases where firms with less than 100 employees dropped their plans between 1975 and 1977.

Communicating benefits.   The act has for the first time legally required clarity in communication of on-the-job benefits to employees.[15] It places the responsibility for clear, concise communication of benefit plans on the shoulders of management. Management must take nothing for granted in assuring a shared understanding of plan intent and detail.

A positive spinoff of that action will be that the employees will gain a better understanding of exactly what the organization is doing for them.

A New York-based public relations and consulting firm has added two "pioneers in language simplification" to its staff. Both are lawyers. They'll help corporate clients to do such things as write employee benefit plans in understandable language.

------

[15]See Rudolph Kagerer, "Do Employees Understand Your Benefits Program?" *Personnel Administrator* 20 (October 1975):29–31.

REQUIREMENTS FOR MAKING BENEFITS MORE EFFECTIVE

Personnel managers can improve the use of employee benefits if they will (1) develop attainable objectives and strategies, (2) invite employee participation, (3) communicate better with employees, and (4) control costs.

Develop Attainable Objectives

Managers need to decide what they want to achieve through the use of benefits. Most employers know that maintaining a labor force requires more than just paying employees for productive service. They believe that indirect compensation helps attract and keep workers. In addition, employers use benefits to (1) improve morale and loyalty, (2) lower turnover and absenteeism, (3) reduce the influence of unions, and (4) increase employee income by reducing taxes.

A Roper poll showed that 44 percent of workers would prefer new and better benefits to pay increases. The two leading benefits—cost-of-living adjustments and dental insurance—would tend to increase earnings.[16]

It is impossible to achieve all the objectives at the same time. Only by deciding which ones are most important and concentrating on them can employers make benefits more effective.

Invite Employee Participation

Managers are not known for their knowledge of what employees want. They would be well advised to find out, however, before introducing new benefits or increasing old ones.

One effort to do this is to use the *cafeteria benefit plan.* With this plan, employees can pick and choose from among many benefits—within a fixed dollar limit and including the legally required benefits.

The American Can Company offers a selection of benefits to 700 salaried employees in its Consumer Tissue and Towel Division. After reducing its program to the minimum it thought all employees should have, it gave the workers the chance to "trade off" benefits in five areas.[17]

---

[16]*The Wall Street Journal,* February 22, 1977 p. 1.

[17]"New Life for Flexible Compensation," *Dun's Review* 112 (September 1978):66–70.

**In a benefits cafeteria, employees get a choice of extras to add
to a core plan that includes insurance, vacations, and pensions.**

John Lane for *Business Week*

Communicate More Effectively with Employees

It has been assumed that benefits have some motivational value in stimulating
employees to greater job satisfaction. Yet these programs appear to have little
or no incentive value but do have a great potential for dissatisfaction.

Studies show that employees do not know what benefits are provided or
understand their provisions. Moreover, in nearly every case of poor understanding, it was found that the employees did not appreciate the benefits, nor
did they believe they compared favorably with the benefits provided by other
firms.

Shell Oil Company spent $153 million on various benefit programs for its
employees, only to find out that they did not appreciate them. It wasn't that
the firm was not spending enough, but that it was not taking enough credit
for the benefits. Its "Red Book" explained the benefits, but the employees
did not read it. A new Red Book was printed that clearly indicated to employees the amount the firm was spending on their "invisible paycheck." It
also explained exactly what the employees were getting and what it would
cost them if they tried to obtain the benefits on their own.[18]

---

[18]"Extra Benefits: A Two-Way Street," *Nation's Business* 62 (September 1974):55–56.

Many other progressive personnel managers are now trying to make benefits more effective by informing workers of the dollar-and-cents value of their benefits.

Before the government began regulating benefit plans in 1974, 60 percent of a group of firms had formal programs to inform workers, in writing, of the benefits they were entitled to. Now 97 percent of them do this.[19]

Control Costs

Personnel managers are now making vigorous efforts to control the cost of benefits. Some firms are trying to do this through collective bargaining, even if it means taking a strike.[20] They also do it through Congress.[21]

A more feasible way is to compare costs for different types of benefit with other firms in the same industry. This can be done by referring to figures prepared by the Chamber of Commerce (see Figure 17-1), the Conference Board, and the Bureau of Labor Statistics.

HOW EEO REGULATIONS AFFECT BENEFITS

EEO laws affect nearly every aspect of the benefit program. But only two will be specifically mentioned, for they are causing personnel managers the most problems. They are (1) sick leave and (2) retirement.

Sick Leave

Until a few years ago, there was much controversy over whether pregnancy is a disability, resulting in paid sick leave. In December 1976, the Supreme Court decided that pregnancy was not considered a disability or sickness. Opponents argued that pregnancy *is* a disability and so should be covered, as many ailments limited to men were, in the insurance plan.

In 1978, Congress amended Title VII of the *Civil Rights Act.* It required employers to make the necessary adjustments in their benefit plans to assure that pregnant workers are granted the same benefits as workers suffering from other disabilities.[22]

AT&T has amended its benefit program so that pregnant employees can take paid sick leave as long as they're certified by doctors as unable to

---

[19]*The Wall Street Journal*, March 20, 1979, p. 1.

[20]"A Pension Stand Costs Westinghouse a Strike," *Business Week*, July 30, 1979, pp. 32-33.

[21]"Rescuing 2,000 Pension Plans," *Business Week*, April 20, 1980, pp. 62-66.

[22]See Paul S. Greenlaw, "Some Further Implications of Pregnancy Discrimination Act," *Personnel Journal* 59 (January 1980):36-43.

work. It also permits unpaid leave of up to six months for fathers, as well as mothers, to care for a newborn child.[23]

Retirement

As already shown, private employers cannot force employees, except for "seasoned executives" and tenured professors, to retire before age 70. Government cannot force employees, so long as they are able, to retire at any age. Most employers are conforming to the law.

One survey found that 56 percent of firms were not even using the "executive exemption."[24] Another survey of 582 firms found 45 percent of salaried employees continuing to work past 65.[25]

SUMMARY AND CONCLUSIONS

Employee compensation is now a complex and integrated package. This makes it difficult to classify wages and employee benefits separately.

Benefits are increasing in importance as part of the compensation package because more and costlier benefits continue to be major goals of today's employees. The trend is for the employer to pay an increasing share, especially for health and retirement programs.

The legally required benefits include (1) Social Security, (2) unemployment insurance, and (3) workers' compensation. Social Security, the basic method of providing for retirement, is in trouble because of escalating costs and number of recipients.

Voluntary programs include (1) pay for time not worked, (2) supplemental unemployment pay, (3) health protection and insurance provisions, and (4) retirement.

Helping employees cope with retirement problems is becoming of growing concern to personnel managers. Some problems are (1) when to permit retirement, (2) how much help to give, (3) providing pensions for retirement, and (4) protecting pensions.

ERISA, or the *Pension Reform Act*, provides protection to present employees covered by a pension plan.

Benefits are quite costly (about one-third of basic payroll), and alert managers are using research and various control devices to maintain a competitive position in regard to them.

---

[23]*The Wall Street Journal*, April 23, 1979, p. 5.

[24]*The Wall Street Journal*, March 4, 1980, p. 1.

[25]"They Stay, Too," *U.S. News & World Report*, February 25, 1980, p. 101.

What choices do personnel executives have? An obvious—but not very feasible—alternative is to reduce such benefit plans. However, in addition to the practical problems involved, the absence of benefits would turn away prospective employees, even though their presence may not attract new employees.

A second possible solution is to publicize company benefits through reports, bulletin boards, house organs, and others.

A modification of this publicity aspect is to provide an increased awareness of benefits by making employees choose which ones they want. These flexible benefits, or the "cafeteria" approach to benefits, have the advantage of forcing the employees to become aware of their benefits and to choose how they would like to receive them.

Finally, some form of control can be exercised over the expansion of these benefits. This is the approach most companies are now taking.

Regardless of management's perception of employee benefits, they are here to stay. In order to attract and hold competent employees, an organization must offer benefits that compare favorably with those offered by competitors. The great need is to balance the cost with the returns received in improved job performance and employee satisfaction. This requires a different approach to benefit planning and decision making from that followed by most employers in the past.

For employee benefits to be most effective, they must be geared to the preferences of employees. In general, as employees' income, age, and length of service increase, their attitude toward benefits becomes more favorable.

QUESTIONS

1. What are employee benefits? Why and how did they come into such extensive use?

2. Why is stabilized employment desirable from the points of view of the individual and management? What employee benefits would you apply to achieve that purpose?

3. What are the primary intentions of the legally required as opposed to the voluntarily arranged employee benefit programs?

4. Would you advocate letting all employees determine their own "compensation package"? Explain.

5. If employee benefits are not effective in motivating employees, then why do employers continue to use them?

6. Would you, as a personnel manager, favor early retirement for the employees of your institution? Explain.

7. How would you go about preparing them for retirement?

8. How would you, as a personnel manager, try to make your benefit program more effective? Explain.

PROBLEMS

17-1. The Transferee

The personnel policy manual of a progressive firm stated that the company would reimburse employees for such items as moving furniture and household goods, transportation of employee and family, lease cancellation costs, alterations, and real estate agent fees of 6 percent on the sale of a house.

The manual did not specify the time after transfer in which these expenses would be paid. It had been assumed by management that most transfer expenses would be closed out by the end of six months. However, expenses had been paid after more than a year in several cases where employees could not sell their houses because of a depressed market.

Will Gill accepted a lateral transfer to one of the operating divisions, which became effective February 1, 19 . He actually assumed the new duties on February 23. He started repairing and painting his house on weekends in order to make it salable. As his children were in school, he did not want to move until early in June.

Gill bought a home near the new job in June and relocated his family. He then discovered that, because of termite damage, he would have to have extensive foundation repairs to his old house before he could sell it. By then, the housing market was at a standstill, and only a few prospective buyers even looked at the house.

In early February of the next year, he received an offer on the house. Assuming that the company would pay the 6 percent realtor's fee, he figured that he could sell the house for the price offered and lose only a few hundred dollars of equity.

He contacted the division manager to make sure that the firm would pay the realtor's fees. The matter was passed by letter to the company's executive offices, where the request was refused on the grounds that over a year had passed since the effective date of transfer. It was still slightly less than a year since the actual transfer had taken place.

Gill felt that the company had let him down, as its decision had caused him to lose several thousand dollars in equity on his house.

Questions

1. Do you think the firm should have paid the expense even after more than a year? Explain.
2. If you answered "yes," what should be the limit? Should an employee wait until the market goes up? Explain.
3. How would you rewrite the policy statement in this matter?

17-2. Sick Leave

As the firm was progressive and expanding, it held regular supervisory training programs to meet the constant need for new supervisors. John was among those in one of the programs.

During the second phase of the training program, a severe throat infection caused John to be absent. The doctor advised him not to return to work until all traces of the infection had disappeared. He also advised John to "get plenty of rest" and to "avoid getting chilled." The firm provided 30 days of sick leave per year, if an employee was under a doctor's care.

During his recuperation, and a week after getting sick, John came to visit with some of the employees in his work area. Jill Carter, his supervisor, chatted a while with him. John looked physically fit and said, "With the exception of a little sore throat, I feel fine." John told Jill that the doctor would tell him in four days if it was all right to return to work.

After John left, Jill discussed his visit with one of the other supervisors, commenting that when she was going through the training program, it would have taken a lot more than a sore throat to keep her home from work.

Questions

1. Should John have visited the plant if he was unable to work? Explain.
2. Evaluate Jill's comment.
3. What should a sick leave policy provide for?

SUGGESTED READINGS FOR FURTHER STUDY

Clutterbuck, David. "Career Planning Helps Workers Beat Retirement." *International Management* 33 (June 1978):55–56.

Diotte, Alfred P., and Douglas M. Soat. "Employees' Attitudes toward Retirement." *Personnel Administrator* 24 (February 1979):26ff.

"The Efficacy of Preretirement Preparation Programs for Industrial Workers." *Journal of Gerontology* 30 (September 1975):595–600.

"Employee Benefits: A $4 Billion Cost." *Nation's Business* 67 (November 1979):114–16.

Holt, Lawrence J. "Retirement: A Time to Enjoy or Endure?" *Personnel Administrator* 24 (November 1979):69–73.

Huseman, Richard C., John D. Hatfield, and Russell W. Driver. "Getting Your Benefit Programs Understood and Appreciated." *Personnel Journal* 57 (October 1978):560–66.

Pati, Gopal C., and Randall C. Jacobs. "Mandatory Retirement at 70: Separating Substance from Politics." *Personnel Administrator* 24 (February 1979):19–24.

Scheible, Paul L. "Changes in Employee Compensation, 1966 to 1972." *Monthly Labor Review* 98 (March 1975):13.

"Social Security: Coping with the Long-Term Shortfall." *Management Review* 68 (February 1979):60–61.

Yaffe, Rian M. "Changing Retirement Patterns: Their Effect on Employee Benefits." *Personnel Administrator* 24 (February 1979):29–33.

PART FIVE

Industrial Relations

Unions have developed together with corporations a supplementary constitutional system which provides a maximum degree of accommodation between management, as the government of the day, and unions, as the opposition.
BENJAMIN SELEKMAN

Labor unions are one of the most powerful groups in the United States, and they influence all aspects of personnel and human resources management, whether an employer is unionized or not. Directly or indirectly, the decisions of personnel managers are made with the unconscious realization that those decisions will be subject to review and approval—or disapproval—by union officers or recruiters. Consequently, the scope of personnel managers' decisions has been considerably narrowed.

As shown in Figure V-1, industrial relations forms a part of the legal-authoritative environment. As such, it greatly constrains the performance of the personnel function.

The material in this part examines the way unions and other employee associations influence the performance of the personnel function. Among the consequences of unionization are (1) the widening gap between management and the individual employee, (2) more formal management policies and procedures, and (3) more employee satisfaction from union membership than from the employer. The material also shows what happens when the union enters. The following chapters are included:

18. How Industrial Relations Affect Personnel Management
19. Recognizing and Dealing with the Union

FIGURE V-1

How industrial relations fits into the overall personnel management system

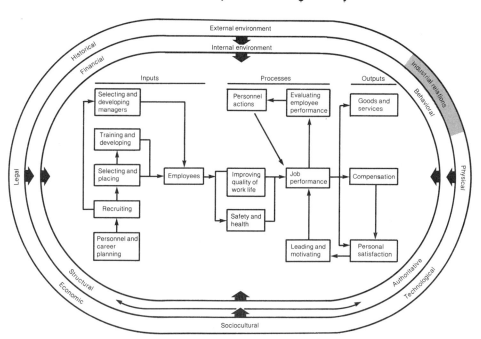

CHAPTER EIGHTEEN

How Industrial Relations Affect Personnel Management

Learning Objectives

After studying the material in this chapter, you should be able to:

1. Tell how unions have developed in the United States.
2. Describe the different types of union.
3. Name and explain the laws that form the legal framework of unionism.
4. Explain the trends in union membership and organizing.
5. Name the objectives of unions and the methods used to achieve them.

Some Important Words and Terms

Yellow-dog contract	Section 7
Craft union	Unfair labor practice
Industrial union	Featherbedding
General labor union	Closed shop
Employee association	Union shop
Local union	Agency shop
Business representative	Open shop
Union steward	Section 14(b)
National (or international) union	Right-to-work laws
Independent union	Union members' bill of rights
Affiliated union	

A philosopher handed a stick to each of his children. "Now, break your stick over your knee," he said to them. Each one, in turn, broke the stick.

Again he handed each of them a stick. This time he said, "Bind the seven sticks together into a bundle." They did as he asked. "Now try to break the sticks," he said to each of them in turn. None of them could break the bundle of sticks.

"Remember," he said, "in union there is strength."

AESOP, "The Bundle of Sticks"

Outline of the Chapter

"The foreman keeps saying this is a rule, and that's a rule, and if you don't do this or that, you could be suspended for two days with no pay. I don't know where he gets the rules from all the time. We never had anything given to us about those rules or any other rules. I would really like to know what the rules are."[1]

The fable and case explain why employees join unions. They also show the need for personnel managers to work with other managers to train supervisors to use basic human relations in dealing with employees.

As shown throughout this book, unions and employee associations have tremendous influence on personnel management. They directly or indirectly affect almost every aspect of the personnel function, in almost all organizations—public or private.

DEVELOPMENT OF UNIONISM

Unions have been active since the beginning of the United States. But their main growth and strength have been seen during the last century.

Emergence of National Unions

The Knights of Labor was organized shortly after the Civil War. It did not last long because business was too powerful.

In 1881, the original American Federation of Labor (AFL) was organized. It was reorganized in 1886 and has remained dominant since then.

By the beginning of World War I, unions were powerful enough to get the *Clayton Act* of 1914 passed. This law declared that unions were not to be considered illegal conspiracies in restraint of trade under the *Sherman Antitrust Act* of 1890. During the war, labor was given its own separate department in the president's cabinet.

The unions' position declined during the 1920s. Employers began to encourage employees to set up employee representation plans. This led to independent and company-dominated unions to replace national unions. Management used the *yellow-dog contract* as a means of breaking the unions. Under such contracts, employees would not be hired unless they agreed not to join a union.

The prevailing opinion was that government should be a neutral observer in the industrial relations field. Yet the *Railway Labor Act* of 1926 was passed to give railroad employees (and later airline employees) the right to be represented by unions in negotiations (collective bargaining) with employers. In

---

[1]A. A. Imberman and Ralph C. Lasher, "The New Labor Law Amendments and Your Nonunion Plants," *Business Horizons* 21 (August 1978):56–58.

1932, the *Norris-LaGuardia Anti-injunction Act* outlawed the yellow-dog contract.

Increasing Government Involvement

The Great Depression, while harming the country and management, helped unions.[2] The period of real growth of unionism began in 1935 with the *National Labor Relations Act* (NLRA). This law (commonly called the *Wagner Act*) required companies to bargain collectively with the union, which represented employees—who now had the right to participate in union activities. The government, under President Roosevelt, ceased being neutral and became an active participant in industrial relations.

Period of strife. At first, managers did not believe that the Supreme Court would uphold the legality of the act. The Court had earlier said that Congress could not pass laws affecting manufacturing within a state. Many businessmen accepted the law and learned to live with it. Others took a "wait and see" attitude, while others actively fought it. There followed one of the truly bloody periods in the history of union-management relations, particularly in the automobile and steel industries.

In 1937, in an effort to organize the employees of Ford Motor Company, Walter Reuther and a group of unionists did battle with the firm's guards at an overpass between buildings at the Ford River Rouge Plant. That bloody struggle, in which 16 union leaders (including six women) were badly beaten, eventually led to the unionization of Ford.[3]

Period of union growth. When the act was upheld by the Supreme Court in *NLRB* v. *Jones and Laughlin Steel Company,* the unions gained much prestige, strength, and power. Union membership increased from about 3 million in 1932 to around 9 million in 1939.

There was a power struggle in the AFL over union membership. The conflict was over whether workers with similar skills in the same craft should form their own union, or if all employees in one industry were to be organized by the same union. The latter group won and formed the Congress of Industrial Organizations (CIO), which operated independently of the AFL until 1955.

During World War II, the right of employees to join unions was changed to a requirement under union shop and closed shop agreements. Because of this, and for other reasons, Congress passed the *Labor-Management Relations Act*

---

[2]See "The Ruins Gave Rise to Big Labor," *Business Week,* 50th Anniversary Issue (September 1979).

[3]See Roger Rapoport, "The Battle of the Overpass," *The Wall Street Journal,* May 25, 1967, p. 12, for further details of this unfortunate incident.

(LMRA) in 1947—over President Truman's veto. The purpose of this law (commonly called the *Taft-Hartley*) was to make the *Wagner Act* more "even-handed" in dealing with both labor and management.

Period of stability.   The government became less active in industrial relations during the 1950s, under President Eisenhower. Two results were (1) a decline in union membership and (2) the merger of the AFL and the CIO. There were charges of corruption in some unions. In 1959, the *Labor-Management Reporting and Disclosure Act*, also called the *Landrum-Griffin*, was passed.

Emergence of Government Unions and Employee Associations

The 1960s saw a vital shift in unionism. Executive Order 10988, issued by President Kennedy in 1962, gave government employees the right to engage in union activities. This effectively amended the LMRA, which had exempted public employees from its coverage. In 1978, this order, as amended, was included in Title VII of the *Civil Service Reform Act*.

Because of these and other actions, public employee unions and associations are among the fastest-growing unions.

Presently, there is a move to affiliate the independent unions (10.7 million members) with the AFL-CIO (13.6 million) into a unified labor movement.[4] Another trend is for unions to merge. Almost a third of these groups have been affected by a merger in the last two decades.[5]

Present Position of Strength and Influence

Unions are now one of the most powerful institutions in the country. This position rests upon three facts: (1) the public supports them, (2) politicians favor them, and (3) they have large financial resources.

The public supports unions.   Unions are now generally accepted by the public. Various polls indicate that most Americans approve of labor unions "in general." But they also place union leaders near the bottom of their confidence list. This in no way implies that people approve or disapprove of the specific actions of individual unions and their leaders. Instead, it indicates that the principles of unionism are accepted by the public.

Nearly four out of five graduating seniors at James Madison University thought workers should have the right to join a union. Slightly more thought they shouldn't be forced to join.[6]

---

[4]"If Labor Movement is United—The Impact," *U.S. News & World Report,* December 3, 1979, pp. 76–79.

[5]Arnold R. Weber, "Merger: Union Style," *Wall Street Journal,* May 14, 1979, p. 20.

[6]"Labor Letter," *The Wall Street Journal,* October 16, 1979, p. 1.

Yet this acceptance seems to be declining. For example, a study in 1972 found that seven out of ten people questioned felt that unions were big enough or even too big.[7] As you can see from Figure 18-1, public approval of unions is at a 43-year low. Now, only 55 percent of those polled approve of unions. This is a big drop from 76 percent in 1956.

The National Labor Relations Board reports that the percentage of certification elections won by unions declined from 53 in 1973 to 46 in 1977. The number of decertification elections increased threefold in the last decade.

FIGURE 18-1
Unions seem to be losing favor with the public

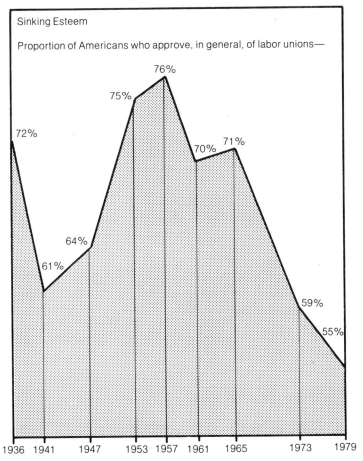

Source: "How Unions Try to Clean Up Their Image," reprinted from *U.S. News & World Report*, October 22, 1979, p. 69. Copyright 1979, U.S. News + World Report, Inc.

---

[7]"Trouble Plagues the House of Labor," *Business Week*, October 28, 1972, pp. 66–76.

Union efforts are viewed as being against the public interest. Six out of ten people blame union demands and steadily rising labor costs for "causing the United States to price itself out of world markets." Many also think that unions help cause inflation.

Politicians favor unions.   It has been estimated that around 60 percent of the members of Congress are favorable to unions. Many of those owe their election to union efforts. For example, unions spent over $8 million in 1978 to help elect friendly members.

President Carter stated that he owed his election to unions, especially the National Education Association (NEA). Many state, county, and city officials owe their election to unions.

This support for unions may also be declining as the conservative political trend continues.[8]

Unions have large financial resources.   Unions are also powerful because of the financial resources they control—or can control. Pension funds resulting from union-management agreements now total around $250 billion in assets. By 1985, pension funds will in essence control most large corporations. While unions do not have direct control over these funds, they are trying to get it.

Unions also have large sums on deposit in many banks. They can exercise power by threatening to withdraw those funds.

The Amalgamated Clothing and Textile Workers Union used this power in its effort to unionize J. P. Stevens & Co. It forced Stevens' chairman, James D. Finley, to resign as director of Manufacturers Hanover Trust with the threat of withdrawing $1 billion from the bank.[9]

TYPES OF UNION AND THEIR LEADERSHIP

In general, unions can be classified according to (1) type of member, (2) scope, and (3) degree of independence.

According to Membership

There are essentially four types of union, depending on their standards for membership. They are as follows:

1. *Craft unions* have members with uniform skills needed to do a particular type of work, regardless of where the person is employed. An example is the International Brotherhood of Electrical Workers (IBEW).

---

[8]See Kenneth Kovach, "Do We Still Need Labor Unions?" *Personnel Journal* 58 (1979):849–50.

[9]"More Unions Brandish Money as a Weapon," *Business Week*, February 26, 1979, p. 47.

2. *Industrial unions* accept members from an entire industry, regardless of their skill, job, or occupation. An example is the United Steel Workers (USW).
3. *General labor unions,* such as the United Mine Workers of America, accept members representing many types of industries and skills.
4. *Employee associations* are usually composed of professionals who choose to have the organization negotiate for them. An example is the National Education Association (NEA), which represents 1.8 million schoolteachers.

According to Scope

Unions are similar to our system of government. The basic unit is the local. These may be grouped into regional, state, national, and international groups.

Local union.   The *local* operates within a relatively small area. This permits its members to have more direct contact with its officers and the employers. The members' interests are better protected this way.

These locals may join with others to form regional labor councils. An example is where several craft locals form a building trades council.

The Chicago and Cook County Building Trades Council's union affiliates represent over 100,000 government and private-industry workers.

Then there are often state organizations.

Officers.   The leadership of a local usually includes a president, a vice president, and a secretary-treasurer. In addition, there are several committees headed by chairpersons.

Business representative.   There is usually a full-time *business representative,* or one of the officers serves in that capacity. The other officers have regular jobs with employers in the area. The duties of the representative include (1) negotiating and administering the local labor agreement and (2) helping the members in other ways.

Union steward.   The *union steward* is the link between the members and their supervisor and managers. The steward files grievances with management and reports results to the member(s). In effect, this person serves as the employees' advocate against their adversary, the employer.

National union.   Locals in the same craft or industry then band together into a *national* (or *international*) union. It may be a loose federation of relatively free locals, or it may exercise tight control. In general, national unions (1) set standards of membership and contract provisions, (2) provide financial and professional assistance, (3) assist with negotiations, and (4) provide printed materials.

While the local representative (and other officers) negotiate the local contract, the national officers negotiate with the management of large firms and also assist the locals with advice and research.

The national's offices are operated much like large businesses. They have full-time paid officers and staffs.

According to Degree of Independence

A union may be independent or affiliated with a national union or the AFL-CIO. If the union is *independent,* it operates on its own and is not affiliated with a larger national or international union. The independent union may be only one local, representing the employees of only one firm, or it may be a national union not *affiliated* with the AFL-CIO. It is not bound by the jurisdiction of any other group. Over 10 million workers belong to independent unions. Table 18–1 shows the relative strength of the AFL-CIO and the independents.

TABLE 18–1
Membership in the AFL-CIO and independent unions in 1979 (millions)

Members of Unions affiliated with AFL-CIO............	13.6
Members of unions independent of AFL-CIO...........	10.7
Including:	
Teamsters Union..............................	2.30
National Education Association.................	1.80
United Auto Workers..........................	1.50
United Mine Workers..........................	0.23
United Electrical Workers......................	0.17

Source: U.S. Department of Labor, Bureau of Labor Statistics.

Union Leaders

Union leaders are as different as managers and employees. But certain conclusions can be reached about them.

1. Most of them have come up through the ranks and have less formal education than the managers they deal with.
2. Few college graduates make it to the top.

Lane Kirkland is the first president of the AFL, CIO, or AFL-CIO with a college degree.

3. The more educated young people go into national unions as staff experts rather than into operating (line) activities.

Many of the brightest college activists of the 1960s are now moving up in union staffs. Hundreds of well-educated young men and women are now exerting direct and indirect influence on unions. Many of them are children of managers and professionals who believe the problems of the 1960s cannot be solved "unless the labor movement becomes a strong progressive force for social change."[10]

4.   There are few women in leadership positions.

The number of official positions held by women has jumped 73 percent over the last 20 years—to a total of 55 positions. There were two women union presidents in 1976 (none in 1956), but only seven secretary-treasurers, down from eight in 1956.[11]

5.   Union leadership must be improved if unions are to improve their public image.

A survey by the University of Michigan's Survey Research Center found that union members rank "Internal union administration" as their top concern—over money issues and "quality of work life."[12]

LAWS DEALING WITH INDUSTRIAL RELATIONS

As shown in Chapter 4, the basic federal labor law of the land is the *National Labor Relations Act,* as amended by the *Labor-Management Relations Act,* the *Labor-Management Reporting and Disclosure Act,* and others. The basic law for government employees is Title VII of the *Civil Service Reform Act.*

National Labor Relations Act

It is difficult to condense the provisions of the NLRA into a few statements. But it essentially does three things: (1) permits workers to form or join unions of their own choosing without fear of prosecution under the antitrust laws, (2) limits the rights and discretion of management by having working conditions determined bilaterally at the bargaining table rather than unilaterally at the place of occurrence, and (3) limits the rights of unions.

Rights of employees.   Under *Section 7* of this act, as amended, employees have the right:

1.   To self-organization.
2.   To form, join, or assist labor organizations.

---

[10]"Young-Turk Network: New Force in Unions," *U.S. News & World Report,* March 19, 1979, p. 79.

[11]*Wall Street Journal,* October 3, 1978, p. 1.

[12]*The Wall Street Journal,* June 19, 1979, p. 1.

3. To bargain collectively through representatives of their own choosing.
4. To act together for the purpose of collective bargaining or other mutual aid or protection.
5. To refuse to exercise these rights, unless the union and employer have a valid union shop or agency shop agreement requiring employees to join the union.

Restrictions on management's rights.   There are some things that management may not do under the law. It is an *unfair labor practice:*

1. To interfere with, restrain, or coerce employees in exercising their rights under Section 7.
2. To dominate or interfere with the formation or administration of unions, or to contribute financial or other support to them.
3. To discriminate in regard to hire or tenure of employment or any term or condition of employment is such a way as to encourage or discourage membership in any labor organization.
4. To discharge or otherwise discriminate against employees for filing charges or testifying in the administration of the act.
5. To refuse to bargain collectively with the representatives chosen by the majority of the employees in the appropriate bargaining unit.

Restrictions on unions' rights.   Certain limitations were also placed on the rights of unions. It is an unfair labor practice for a union:

1. To coerce employees into participating in union activities, or restrain them from doing so freely.
2. To force employers to discriminate against employees in violation of the act.
3. To restrain or coerce employers in their choice of people to bargain for them.
4. To refuse to bargain in good faith with the employer.
5. To attempt to force the employer to recognize the union when another union is already the certified representative of employees.
6. To engage in *featherbedding*, or receive pay for work not done.
7. To engage in, or cause employees of any employer to engage in, a strike or labor boycott where the purpose is to force management into illegal or undesirable acts.
8. To charge excessive fees or dues if there is a union shop agreement.

The act also limits the union's right to engage in organizational or recognition picketing.

Administration of the law.   The judicial powers of the act are vested in a five-person National Labor Relations Board (NLRB). Its administrative duties are handled by an independent general counsel. All six members are appointed by the president.

The primary responsibilities of the NLRB are:

1. To set up procedures for elections to determine the employees' choice of a bargaining agent.

2. To determine whether a majority of the workers want a union to represent them.
3. To investigate and prosecute complaints of unfair labor practices under the law.

The representation elections, as well as the investigation of unfair labor practices, are supervised by the general counsel. The judicial decisions involving unfair labor practices are made by administrative law judges and reviewed by the board in Washington.

Labor-Management Relations Act

In addition to amending the NLRA, the LMRA (1) gave management certain rights, (2) provided for right-to-work laws, (3) set up the Federal Mediation and Conciliation Service, and (4) provided for national emergencies.

Rights of management. The LMRA granted management the following rights that it had not had under the NLRA:

1. To refuse to bargain with supervisory personnel.
2. To have freedom of speech, as long as there is no threat of reprisal or force, or any promise of benefit, during a representation election.
3. To seek a representation election if it does not believe the union represents the employees.
4. To sue the union for breach of contract when unlawful strikes and boycotts are used.
5. To receive a 60-day notice of the union's intent to terminate a contract.

Right-to-work laws. Another effect was to prohibit the closed shop agreement—except in some specific instances—and to limit the union shop agreement in states that prohibited it. The net effect of this was quite significant. Under the *closed shop* agreement workers *had* to join the union before getting a job; so employers could not choose their own employees but had to accept those chosen by the unions. Under the *union shop* agreement, employers have the right to hire the people of their choice, and only then do the employees have to join the union. A variation of the union shop is the *agency shop* agreement, whereby workers may choose not to join the union, but must pay the equivalent of union dues to the union to serve as their "agent." Under an *open shop* agreement, employees may choose to join or not join the union.

Section 14(b) gave states the right to pass laws prohibiting the union shop. These state *right-to-work laws* take priority over the federal law. They are now found in 20 states (see Figure 18-2) but are a favorite target of unions.

These laws are quite controversial. People who favor them say that they (1) increase economic growth, wages, and income and (2) give individual employees "freedom of choice."

Opponents say that the laws (1) depress wages, (2) threaten unionism, and (3) permit "free riders" who benefit from the union without paying for it. Figure 18-3 suggests that these laws may have a "chilling effect" on union membership.

FIGURE 18-2
States with and without right-to-work laws

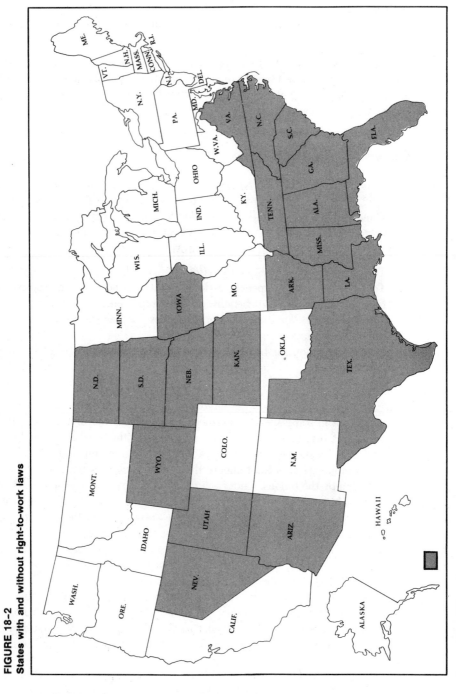

Source: Adapted from information furnished by the National Right-to-Work Council.

FIGURE 18-3
Right-to-work laws may affect union membership

Part of the sunbelt's allure for industry

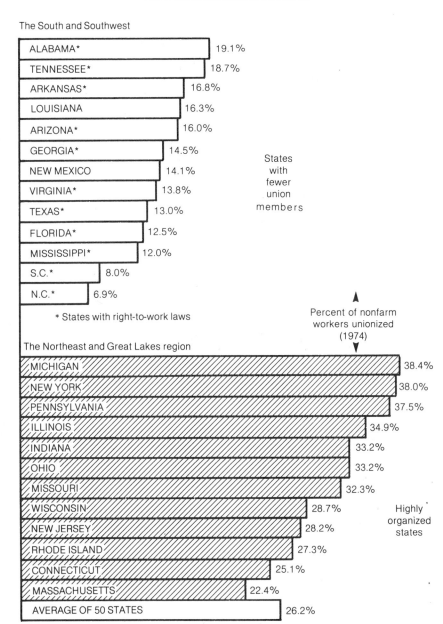

The South and Southwest

State	Percent
ALABAMA*	19.1%
TENNESSEE*	18.7%
ARKANSAS*	16.8%
LOUISIANA	16.3%
ARIZONA*	16.0%
GEORGIA*	14.5%
NEW MEXICO	14.1%
VIRGINIA*	13.8%
TEXAS*	13.0%
FLORIDA*	12.5%
MISSISSIPPI*	12.0%
S.C.*	8.0%
N.C.*	6.9%

States with fewer union members

* States with right-to-work laws

Percent of nonfarm workers unionized (1974)

The Northeast and Great Lakes region

State	Percent
MICHIGAN	38.4%
NEW YORK	38.0%
PENNSYLVANIA	37.5%
ILLINOIS	34.9%
INDIANA	33.2%
OHIO	33.2%
MISSOURI	32.3%
WISCONSIN	28.7%
NEW JERSEY	28.2%
RHODE ISLAND	27.3%
CONNECTICUT	25.1%
MASSACHUSETTS	22.4%
AVERAGE OF 50 STATES	26.2%

Highly organized states

Data: Bureau of Labor Statistics

Note: Louisiana now has a right-to-work law.
Source: "No Welcome Mat for Unions in the Sunbelt," *Business Week*, May 17, 1976, p. 109.

According to a recent Research Corporation opinion poll, the public favors right-to-work laws. From 61 to 74 percent of the general public, and from 43 to 72 percent of union members, favor laws under which workers can't be required to join a union or pay dues.[13]

Other provisions. The act set up the Federal Mediation and Conciliation Service (FMCS). The FMCS tries to prevent strikes and works to help settle them when they do occur. It can only persuade the union or management to prevent or stop a strike, but has no right to force them to.

The law also provided for the President to protect the national health and safety for a period of 80 days. When these are threatened by a strike, the President can have the attorney general seek an injunction from the courts to prevent (or stop) the strike. If the strike is not settled in 60 days, the NLRB is required to hold a secret-ballot election to see whether the employees are willing to accept the employer's last offer. Then the injunction is lifted— whether the vote is "yes" or "no." It is then up to Congress to decide what to do.

Labor-Management Reporting and Disclosure Act

Because of allegations of corruption and abuse of workers by some unions, Congress passed the *Labor-Management Reporting and Disclosure Act* (LMRDA). The goal of the law was to regulate the internal affairs of unions, particularly their relationship with their members. It gave union members a *bill of rights*. This permitted members to (1) attend and participate in union meetings, (2) vote on business, including elections and whether to strike or not, (3) nominate or be a candidate for union office, and (4) examine the union's books.

It speeded up the election process by using regional organizations rather than the centralized NLRB. In the building and construction industry, a pre-hire union contract was permitted. With this contract union membership could be required after seven days rather than the usual 30-day waiting period.

Finally, management is prevented from making illegal payments to a union to influence its negotiations for an agreement for its members; and union members are protected from possible coercive and abusive actions by a few unscrupulous labor leaders.

Title VII of the *Civil Service Reform Act*

Title VII of the *Civil Service Reform Act* gave employees of the federal government most of the same rights and privileges enjoyed by other employees in

---

[13]*The Wall Street Journal,* May 6, 1980, p. 1.

FIGURE 18-4
Membership of national unions and associations, 1930-1978.*

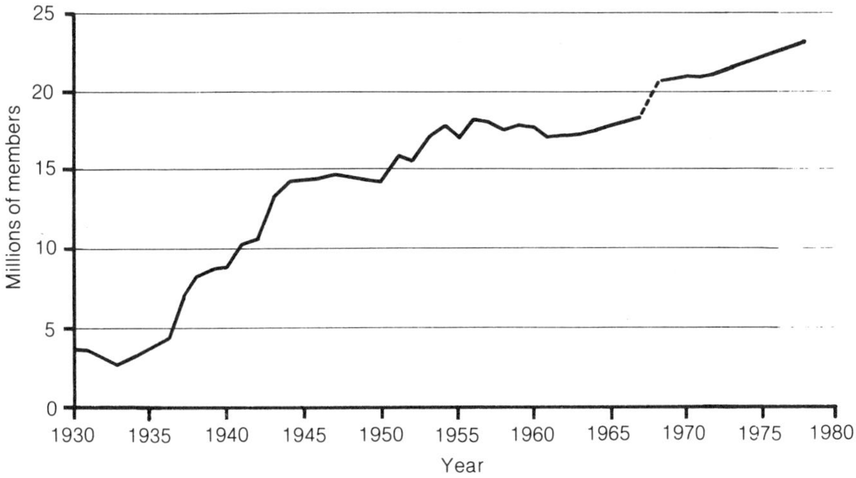

*(Exclusive of Canadian membership.) The dashed line beginning in 1967-68 indicates that employee associ-
ations that bargain collectively were first reported then.
Source: U.S. Department of Labor, Bureau of Labor Statistics.

private industry, except the right to strike. It set up the Federal Labor Relations Authority and gave it many of the same duties and responsibilities as the
NLRB. Federal employers are now required to arbitrate unresolved grievances.

TRENDS IN UNION MEMBERSHIP AND ORGANIZING

There are two clear trends in union membership. First, the rate of growth is
declining. Second, there is a search for new types of members.

A Slow Growth in Members

As you can see from Table 18-2, the growth in union and employee association membership appears to be stabilizing. The growth during the last ten
years was only 2.5 million, which is about the growth in the total labor force
in a single year.

As you can see from Figure 18-4, the greatest gains in union membership
occurred from 1933 to 1944 and from 1950 to 1956. There was steady growth
from 1962 to 1967 as government employees began to unionize. The organizing of members of professional associations caused the increase from 1967 to
1978.

In 1935, there were 3.5 million union members. By the end of 1978, there
were 20.5 million members of unions and 2.8 million members of professional
associations, for a total of 23.2 million members of unions and associations.

TABLE 18–2
Membership in national unions and employee associations*

Year	Number (millions)	Percentage of total labor force	Percentage in nonagricultural establishments
1968	20.7	25.2	30.5
1970	21.2	24.7	30.1
1972	21.7	24.3	29.8
1976	22.8	24.5	29.1
1978	23.2	23.0	27.0

*Includes total reported membership, excluding Canadian but including other areas outside the United States.
Source: U.S. Department of Labor, Bureau of Labor Statistics.

You will notice in Figure 18–5 that, while the number of union members has been increasing, the percentage of all employees who are union members has declined over the last two decades. In 1935, around 7 percent of the total labor force, and 13 percent of employees in nonagricultural firms, were union members. These figures increased to around 26 and 36 percent by the mid-1950s. But by 1978, only about 22 percent of the total labor force and 27 percent of nonagricultural employees were members.

It is interesting to see which industries are the most heavily unionized. As you can see from Table 18–3, there is a great difference in the extent of unionization.

FIGURE 18–5
Membership of national unions and associations as a percentage of total labor force and of employees in nonagricultural establishments, 1930–78.*

*(Exclusive of Canadian membership.) The dashed lines beginning in 1967–68 indicate the fact that employee associations that bargain collectively were first reported then.
Source: U.S. Department of Labor, Bureau of Labor Statistics.

TABLE 18-3
Industries ranked by the degree of union organization

75 percent and over

1.	Transportation	4.	Paper
2.	Contract construction	5.	Electrical machinery
3.	Ordnance	6.	Transportation equipment

50 percent to less than 75 percent

7.	Primary metals	13.	Manufacturing
8.	Food and kindred products	14.	Fabricated metals
9.	Mining	15.	Telephone and telegraph
10.	Apparel	16.	Stone, clay, and glass products
11.	Tobacco manufactures	17.	Federal government
12.	Petroleum	18.	Rubber

25 percent to less than 50 percent

19.	Printing, publishing	23.	Machinery
20.	Leather	24.	Chemicals
21.	Furniture	25.	Lumber
22.	Electric, gas utilities		

Less than 25 percent

26.	Nonmanufacturing	31.	Local government
27.	Textile mill products	32.	State government
28.	Government	33.	Trade
29.	Instruments	34.	Agriculture and fishing
30.	Service	35.	Finance

Unions Are Now Organizing New Types of Members

Union leaders are now varying their organizing efforts to benefit from the economic, social, and political environments. They are planning for the labor movement to strive for a new meaning to American life. This will require adjusting to changes in the coming period. Thus the size, power, militancy, and economic demands of unions will increase. The "union mix" will include the new workers entering the labor force, in spite of their distrust of unions.

The drive for new members will probably occur, where legally permitted, among (1) public employees—including teachers, police, and firefighters, (2) professionals—including teachers, medical personnel, athletes, dentists, and lawyers, (3) persons in the service industries, (4) agricultural workers, (5) white-collar employees, (6) women, (7) minorities, and (8) young workers.

Public employees. The main source of union growth is public employees. As a result of government recognition, public employee unions have become the fastest-growing labor organizations in the country. Around two out of every five public employees are now unionized.

Guests at the NLRB's gala 40th anniversary dinner in Washington in 1975 were handed leaflets by representatives of the NLRB employees' union charging the agency with "unfair labor practices," "bad-faith negotiations," and "inadequate pay rates."

Many states have followed the federal example by passing laws permitting state, local, and municipal workers to engage in union activities.

Professionals.   Traditionally, professors and teachers, doctors and nurses, athletes, lawyers, and other professionals have thought of themselves as just that—professionals—and, as such, "above" union activities. Yet when these groups found themselves falling far behind union members in rewards and benefits during the 1960s, they adopted union methods.

The AFL-CIO acquired its first doctors' union as the 4,500–member New York State Federation of Physicians and Dentists joined the American Federation of Teachers.[14]

In March 1980, the players of all 26 major league baseball teams voted to strike if their demands were not met. Only one player voted against the strike, on religious grounds.

College and university faculty members are finding certain trade union concepts, such as bargaining over salaries and job security, to their liking.[15] Three organizations—the American Association of University Professors (AAUP), American Federation of Teachers (AFT), and National Education Association (NEA)—are currently competing to represent this level of academic personnel. Regardless of which one wins, university administrators can expect greater efforts on the part of all three to represent their faculties as bargaining agents. This may change with a March 1980 Supreme Court decision.

Full-time professors at private colleges now have no legal right to form unions. The NLRB had treated them as "employees," but the Court ruled that they were "part of college management."

These new organizing activities will apparently be an irresistible force for several reasons. There will also be increased militancy, for unionism has become acceptable to the middle- and upper-middle-class employees and professionals.[16]

Employees of service industries.   The unions are increasing their activities in the service industries, which are rapidly expanding. This is particularly true in retailing, including the food service industry—especially restaurants.

In 1978, the 730,000-member Retail Clerks International Union merged with the Amalgamated Meat Cutters & Butcher Workmen, with 500,000 members. The new United Food & Commercial Workers will rank as one of the largest U.S. unions.

---

[14]*The Wall Street Journal,* April 22, 1980, p. 1.

[15]"Faculty Unionism in Institutions of Higher Education," *Monthly Labor Review* 97 (April 1974):48–50.

[16]For an explanation—with examples—of these attitudinal changes, see "Labor: Doctors, Nurses, Teachers—Why More Are Joining Unions," *U.S. News & World Report,* November 10, 1975, pp. 61-62.

THE WALL STREET JOURNAL

SCHWALB

"If the union gets the contract it's demanding, I suggest we quit management and join it!"

Reprinted by permission *The Wall Street Journal*

Agricultural employees. Unions have now organized agriculture, especially in the vast grape, lettuce, citrus, and cotton-growing industries of California. The state's *Agricultural Labor Relations Act,* which was passed in 1975, is expected to serve as a model for other states where millions of field laborers present a tempting target for union organizers.

White-collar employees. Special organizing units have been set up to recruit white-collar employees. This is a fertile field for unions, for research indicates that in a sample of clerical and sales personnel, over half identify themselves as "working-class people" and not as "managerial personnel."[17] Another study on the attitudes of clerical workers found that their feelings toward their organizations have become much less favorable in the areas of basic employment conditions, personnel practices, and communications.[18] Many clerical jobs have become dull, routine, and unrewarding—almost like assembly-line operations—and there has been increased depersonalization and fragmentation of many work organizations.

Women. From 1956 to 1976, women's membership in unions, including employee associations such as the NEA, increased from 1.1 to 4.3 million.[19] Women accounted for about half the growth in union membership. More than one in every five union members were women in 1976.

The female delegates to the 1975 AFL-CIO national convention organized

---

[17]John Shea, "Would Foremen Unionize?" *Personnel Journal* 49 (November 1970):926–31.

[18]See Erwin S. Stanton, "White Collar Unionization: New Challenge to Management," *Personnel Journal* 51 (February 1972):118–24, for some ideas on preparing for the entry of the union and what you can do about it.

[19]"Labor Letter," *The Wall Street Journal,* October 3, 1978, p. 1.

the Coalition of Labor Union Women (CLUW). Its membership increased from 3,000 in 1977 to around 11,000 in 1980.[20]

Minorities.   Black employees are also being recruited by union organizers. Yet there appears to be considerable racial discrimination, which is forcing blacks to consider organizing along racial lines or rejecting the collective bargaining process altogether. To overcome this, the courts have directed the unions to take affirmative action through apprenticeship and membership programs to meet racial goals.[21]

Fully two-thirds of nonunion minority workers say they would vote to unionize, compared to one-third of all nonunionized workers.[22] Nearly a third of all black workers are union members, compared to 30 percent of Hispanics and 26 percent of whites.

Young workers.   Young employees are posing problems for union-management relations. They tend to be better educated than their older colleagues and to have different values. A problem this poses for personnel managers is that they also seek different settlements from collective bargaining, which will lead to more rejections of agreements.

Another problem for personnel is that even the younger managers are ripe for unionization.[23]

UNION OBJECTIVES AND HOW THEY ARE ACHIEVED

The main reason why unions are needed is that individual workers are helpless in the face of the economic and social power of large groups, such as companies and governments. Therefore, workers must act as groups, not as individuals. That is why unions have adopted part of Longfellow's *Song of Hiawatha* as their motto:

> All your strength is in your union;
> All your danger is in discord;
> Therefore be at peace henceforward,
> And as brothers live together.

Basic Principles of Unionism

This motto has been translated into the three basic principles upon which unionism is founded. If any one of them is threatened, the union will fight

---

[20]*The Wall Street Journal*, March 18, 1980, p. 1.

[21]"Significant Decisions in Labor Cases: *Rios* v. *Steamfitters Local 638; United States* v. *Steamfitters Local 638,*" *Monthly Labor Review* 97 (November 1974):59-60.

[22]*The Wall Street Journal*, June 19, 1979, p. 1.

[23]"The Boom in Executive Self-Interest," *Business Week*, May 26, 1976, p. 16ff.

back. They are (1) in unity there is strength, (2) equal pay for the same job, and (3) all terms and conditions of employment should be based on seniority.

This last principle is now being challenged by equal employment opportunity efforts. Several court decisions have upheld seniority. But EEO leaders hope the Weber case may change this.[24]

Practical Objectives

These principles form the basis for the practical objectives unions have for their members. These goals have almost always been (1) higher pay, (2) shorter hours of work on a daily, weekly, or annual basis, (3) improved physical, social, and psychological working conditions, and (4) improved security, both of the person and of the job.

For example, a union usually opposes automation if it threatens the job security of its members. There are times, though, when *not* to automate may cause the firm to go bankrupt. Then a compromise must be worked out.

For example, New York's major commercial printing firms were losing business to more efficient firms. The union signed a ten-year contract allowing them to introduce automated techniques in the composing room. In return, all regular full-time printers employed at that time were given lifetime guarantees of jobs.[25]

How Unions Achieve Their Objectives

How do unions accomplish their goals? The usual methods used are (1) organization, (2) recognition as the bargaining agent, (3) collective bargaining, (4) union security clauses, (5) processing grievances, conciliation, mediation, and arbitration, (6) strikes and the threat of strike, (7) boycotts, and (8) union labels. These will be discussed in detail in the next chapter.

SUMMARY AND CONCLUSIONS

At present, unions are one of the major power blocs in the United States. Directly or indirectly, managerial decisions in all organizations are influenced by the effect of unions. Consequently, management's freedom of action has been considerably narrowed.

---

[24]See Amal Nag, "Slipping Back: Recession Threatens to Erode Job Gains of Women and Minorities," *The Wall Street Journal*, January 7, 1980, pp. 1 and 14.

[25]See "Printers, New York City Printing Firms Tentatively Agree on 10-Year Labor Pact," *The Wall Street Journal*, October 28, 1975, p. 4, for details of this and a similar earlier agreement.

Now management, instead of acting alone to reward or punish employees, must operate through the union. Decisions affecting employees are now made collectively at the bargaining (and arbitration) tables, instead of individually by the supervisor when and where the need arises. Wages, hours, and other terms and conditions of employment are largely decided outside of management's sphere of discretion.

Unions may now be losing favor with the public—and even with politicians. Yet they still have tremendous financial resources and political influence.

The different types of union are (1) craft unions, (2) industrial unions, (3) general labor unions, and (4) employee associations. These begin with the local, which can be either independent or affiliated with a national or international union.

Union leadership is still dominated by white males with relatively little education. But this too is changing as the bright young militants of the 1960s move into management and union leadership positions.

The basic labor law is the NLRA, which protects employees' right to union activities by making certain management and union actions "unfair labor practices." The law is administered by the NLRB. The LMRA tends to protect management and the workers, while the LMRDA protects workers against both union and management. Title VII of the *Civil Service Reform Act* gives federal employees similar protection.

Traditional union membership is declining; so unions are organizing new groups. A growing number of public, white-collar, and professional employees, as well as minorities, women, and young people, are becoming union members. Therefore, personnel executives should focus clearly on the specific needs and concerns of their own work force instead of "doing what others are doing." Second, as career dissatisfaction is a factor that contributes to militancy, management should provide as much guidance and assistance as feasible.

Finally, personnel managers need to realize that militancy is increasing among this new group of employees, and that they must constantly search for methods of combating it.

It is felt that the basic objectives of unions have been met. However, as a result of this, the following have occurred: (1) the gap between management and the individual employee has widened, (2) there has been a broadening of the scope of collective bargaining, with a consequent limitation of managerial rights, (3) unilateral action has given way to collective action, (4) rank-and-file employees have tended to get more satisfaction from union membership than from their employers, and (5) loyalty has shifted from organizations—and their managers—to unions and their leaders.

Now there is a need to change the philosophies, precepts, strategies, and tactics of industrial relations. The function of unions should now be to maintain the advantages already achieved and, at the same time, to accept joint responsibility and leadership in striving to solve some of the problems currently facing the country.

QUESTIONS

1. What are the new organizational goals of unions today as far as organizing employees is concerned?
2. What are the most important laws affecting industrial relations, and what does each attempt to do?
3. How would you describe the stages of union development *(a)* until 1935, *(b)* from 1935 to 1960, and *(c)* from 1960 to the present.
4. What do you see happening in industrial relations at the present time?
5. *(a)* What are the objectives of unions? *(b)* How do unions achieve these objectives?
6. Can you suggest ways to bring more women and minorities into positions of union leadership? Explain.
7. Discuss the pros and cons of the union shop and of right-to-work laws.
8. How do you explain the present slow growth in union membership?

PROBLEM

Division of Labor

The following letter was written by the personnel manager of an industrial firm in 1962.° He had just been reading H. F. Merrill's *Classics in Management,* which included a treatise written by Charles Babbage in 1832 entitled "Economy of Machinery and Manufacturers."

> The division of labor that existed in Charles Babbage's time is now in real trouble. Although it is true that more production can be obtained with workers doing only one phase of a complicated manufacturing process, automation has now taken over most hand-operated jobs. The jobs that are left do not lend themselves to individual crafts or specialists. In the modern automated plant, practically the only hand jobs left are maintenance, and, in most cases, the person responsible for fixing things needs to be a jack-of-all-trades. Automation will turn history back to the handyman, or else maintenance will be contracted out to service people.
>
> For example, we recently had a problem in our plant with cleaning the burner on a 50-gallon water heater. The heater originally cost $250. After employees belonging to seven different craft unions (operator, insulator, pipe fitter, instrument man, sheet metal workers, electrician, and carpenter) had worked for over eight hours, the job was still not complete. At that time, the total labor cost was already $270.
>
> The shop steward informed the maintenance supervisor that the craftsmen would have to work overtime to insure hot water in the change house, because it was in the contract.

°Notice the historical nature of this problem. This degree of specialization is not common now.

A local plumber had quoted a firm price of $15 to clean and adjust the burner. If the company had allowed the plumber to do the job, however, the workers would have gone on strike.

Questions

1. What is your evaluation of the sentence, "Automation will turn history back to the handyman, or else maintenance will be contracted out to service people"? Is this happening with maintenance?
2. How would you evaluate the problem from the point of view of (a) management, (b) a union leader, and (c) an employee?
3. How would you attempt to resolve the dilemma faced by management?

SUGGESTED READINGS FOR FURTHER STUDY

Chamot, Dennis. "Professional Employees Turn to Unions." *Harvard Business Review* 54 (May-June 1976):119-27.

Goodfellow, Matthew. "Proposed Labor Law Amendments: Their Possible Effect." *Personnel Administrator* 23 (June 1978):27ff.

Hammerman, Herbert, and Marvin Rogoff. "Unions and Title VII of the Civil Rights Act of 1964." *Monthly Labor Review* 99 (April 1976):34-37.

Hatkoff, Stanley D. "To What Lengths Should Medical Institutions Go in Preventing Unionization?" *Personnel Administrator* 23 (March 1978):17ff.

Helfgott, Roy B. *Labor Economics*, p. 117ff. New York: Random House, 1974.

Marcus, Robert J. "The Changing Work Force: Implications for Companies and Unions." *Personnel* 48 (January-February 1971):8-15.

Phillips, Madison. "Developing Healthy Management Attitudes." *Personnel* 54 (September 1977):68-70.

Schiavoni, Michael R. "Employee Relations: Where Will It Be in 1985?" *Personnel Administrator* 23 (March 1978):25-29.

Swanson, Stephen C. "The Effect of the Supreme Court's Seniority Decisions." *Personnel Journal* 56 (December 1977):625-27.

Tavernier, Gerard. "Industrial Relations in the 80's." *International Management* 34 (January 1979):25-28.

CHAPTER NINETEEN

Recognizing and Dealing
with the Union

Learning Objectives

After studying the material in this chapter, you should be able to:

1. Tell how the union organizing campaign begins, and how it is run.
2. Describe how a union becomes certified as the bargaining agent for an organization's employees.
3. Explain the collective bargaining procedure.
4. Explain how the agreement is enforced.

Some Important Words and Terms

Representation authorization card
Exclusive bargaining agent
Certification election
Bargaining unit
Collective bargaining
Quid pro quo
Cardinal demands
Whiplash
Good faith
Impasse

Sticking point
Mediation
Arbitration
Strike
Lockout
Cost-of-living adjustment (COLA)
Lifetime guarantee of jobs
Agreement
Grievance procedure
Grievance mediation

People don't ask for facts in making up their minds. They would rather have one good, soul-satisfying emotion than a dozen facts.
ROBERT KEITH LEAVITT

Outline of the Chapter

John Weinacker bought the Quality Supply Company four years ago. The firm, which distributed bottled gas, had three employees, a secretary and two truck drivers.

A week after John took over, Jay Williams, the local representative for the Teamsters union, visited him. John remembered Jay from his college days, but their paths had seldom crossed since then.

Jay: John, I'm here to see about some back wages you owe your drivers. Our union signed a contract with this company four months ago, but they are still getting nonunion wages. You owe each of them close to $800.

John: Jay, when I took this business over last week I didn't assume any liabilities for back wages owed, and I didn't assume any union contract.

Jay: I don't know about that, and I don't care. I'm going to see that these men get paid, even if we have to strike.

John: I have no contract with your union. If these men fail to report for work without good reason, I won't consider it a strike. I'll consider them "absent without leave" and fire them.

Jay: We'll see about that. You know how highly unionized this town is. You'll be hearing from me soon.

Jay walked out. John felt a little shaken as he called his lawyer. After being reassured that he could not be held responsible for the back salaries owed, he felt more relaxed. He knew he could hire two new drivers if the present ones tried to strike, as business was slack and there was considerable unemployment. He would just have to fire them.

Nothing more was heard from Jay until a week later when he walked directly into John's office, dropped a union contract on John's desk, and said flatly, "Sign it!" John scanned it briefly.

John: I can't do it, Jay. I'd go broke if I had to live with this contract. I just can't afford group insurance, retirement programs, and a lot of the other benefits in this contract, as desirable as they are. I'm paying close to the union scale now, and as soon as I get my feet on the ground, I'll give the drivers periodic raises—if they deserve them. That's the best I can do.

Jay: You'll have to do better than that because, if you don't sign the contract, we'll strike your place.

John: As I said before, if my drivers fail to show up for work without a good excuse, I'll fire them.

Jay: Well, we'll see about that.

Jay hesitated a moment as if to say something else, then picked up the contract, and walked out.

That afternoon, one of the drivers came in to talk with the new owner. He said he didn't want to join the union but Jay and the other driver had pressured him into it.

This case points up the emotional, as well as economic, nature of industrial relations. The drive to unionize an organization is socially and psychologically upsetting.

FIGURE 19-1
Example of a representation authorization card

> ## COMMUNICATIONS WORKERS of AMERICA, A.F.L.-C.I.O.
>
> Name _____
>   (Please Print)   First   Middle   Last
> Address _____
>   Street
>
> _____
>   City   State   Zip Code
> Tel. No. _____ Job Title _____
>
> I am an Employee of_____ ,
>
> Department _____ , Section _____ , Shift_____
> and I hereby designate the Communications Workers of America, as my
> collective bargaining representative.
>
> Date _____ Signature _____
>
> FORM O-100   **REPRESENTATION AUTHORIZATION**   150
> 1-77

Many people claim that the entry of a union is evidence of mismanagement. This is not true! In certain industries and in some areas, unions tend to be very strong, regardless of the actions of management.

This chapter outlines some of the factors that contribute to improving industrial relations in a given organization.

THE ORGANIZING CAMPAIGN

The unionizing process begins in a firm when an organizer starts trying to get employees to join the union. This usually starts, as in the opening case, with one or more employees signing a *representation authorization card* (see Figure 19-1) designating the union as their bargaining agent. This goes on until a majority have signed the cards and management accepts the union, or until 30 percent of the workers have signed them and an election is held.

There are many reasons why unions succeed in organizing workers. But the main one is the employer's neglect of the employee's economic and social needs.

Factors Leading to Unionization

In general, there are four factors responsible for unionization. They are (1) chaotic working conditions, (2) poor internal communications, (3) mishandling of employees by supervisors, and (4) management's lack of time or desire to listen to employees.[1]

Chaotic working conditions. Operating managers try to get production out. But all too often they ignore the employees' problems. Few things are more disturbing to lower level employees than this neglect. Management should realize that these day-to-day problems are going to be found in the plant and should take quick corrective action. Otherwise, employees will be very sympathetic to the union organizer's promises.

Poor internal communications. Most employees like to know what is going on in the organization. But supervisors, who are usually more interested in production, tend to disregard this. Many employers fail to provide employees with policy manuals or employee handbooks. So the workers do not know what is expected of them. People object to rules that are not set down in black and white, unrealistic job assignments, benefits that are too complicated, or management plans for them that are secret. The union organizer promises to clear away the fog because a union contract has the answers in writing.

A plant in the Chicago area built a new brick wash house with heat and hot water to replace a leaky metal one without those comforts. Over the weekend, the employees' personal things were moved to the new building—without their knowledge. They were so upset that they invited the union in.

Uninterested or abusive supervision. There are times when supervisors seem not to care what happens to the employees, or even abuse them. They neglect to provide things such as raises, benefits, or recognition for work well done. Abuse can be physical or emotional. The organizer will promise to correct that.

An employee was careless about arriving at work on time. The supervisor warned him that the next time he was late he would be fired. He was not tardy for several weeks. One morning he was an hour late. The supervisor discharged him without letting him explain. The other employees organized a union, for the man had taken his wife to the hospital and then hurried on to work as fast as he could.

No time to listen. One of the major reasons for unionization is management's failure to listen to employees, especially personal gripes. Also, many useful suggestions can be obtained by listening to employees. If management doesn't have time to listen to employees, then the union will.

The operator of a unit in a refinery warned the supervisor several times that pressure was building up because the equipment was defective. He was ignored until there was an explosion. The supervisor blamed it on the

---

[1]A. A. Imberman and Ralph C. Lasher, "The New Labor Law Amendments and Your Nonunion Plants," *Business Horizons* 21 (August 1978):56ff.

operator. Management fired him without hearing his side of the story, and a union was voted in.

Why Employees Join a Union

There are no simple explanations of why workers join or reject a union, for motivation is very complex. Also, environmental pressures are constantly shifting. These pressures influence workers first in one direction and then in another. One sure reason is the emotionalism usually found during the organizing drive.

Reasons why workers join a union.   The main reasons for joining unions derive from the workers' search for:

1. Steady employment or income.
2. Rationalization of personnel policies.
3. A voice in decisions affecting their welfare.
4. Protection from economic hazards beyond their control.
5. Recognition and participation.

A further reason is: compulsion or coercion.

Steady employment or income.   Probably the most basic desire of employees is for security, especially economic security. Therefore, to the extent that the union can convince workers that it (better than management or anyone else) can assure them steady jobs or income, they will probably join the union.

Rationalization of personnel policies.   As shown earlier, if management is viewed by employees as acting in an arbitrary manner, they will tend to join the union. Workers prefer that employment practices be governed by set rules. They may feel that there will be less favoritism and discrimination with a union.

A voice in decisions affecting their welfare.   Workers may join unions in order to be able to communicate their frustrations, aims, feelings, and ideas to their superiors. They also seek an outlet when advancement in the organization is blocked.

Protection from economic hazards beyond their control.   Workers are subjected to many hazards beyond their control, such as sickness, accidents, and death. Many of them cannot plan for or cope with these personal tragedies. The workers feel that the union can force employers to help them to overcome such adversities.

Recognition and participation.   One of our basic needs is to be accepted by the group, to belong, and to get along with others. Becoming a union member may help workers gain respect in the eyes of their peers. If a worker's parents and neighbors have belonged to unions, this will influence the worker to join the union.[2] Recreational and social activities associated with unions provide an added incentive for some workers.

---

[2]Robert Hershey, "Predicting Outcomes of Union Representation Elections," *Personnel Administrator* 21 (1976):42.

Compulsion.   Some workers are compelled to join the union in order to get a particular job or in order not to be treated as a social outcast. Certain union security provisions, such as the union or agency shop, require union membership in states without right-to-work laws.

Reasons why workers do not join unions.   The main reasons why workers do not join unions are (1) lack of a compelling reason and (2) identification with management.

Lack of a compelling reason.   Some employees simply lack a valid reason for joining unions. They consider their wages adequate, their working conditions satisfactory, and their other needs reasonably well met. They feel they can progress on their own abilities, which they consider superior to those of the group, and are satisfied with their work.

Research has shown that organizers find it easier to organize white-collar employees working on machines (such as keypunch operators) than to attract those doing more creative and less mechanized duties.[3]

Identification with management.   Some employees tend to identify themselves more closely with management and therefore shun unions. In the past, white-collar, scientific, technical, and professional employees have thought and acted like managers or hoped for promotion into supervisory and management ranks. This, too, is now changing.

Employee traits influence decision.   There seem to be some actual differences between "pro-union" and "pro-company" employees. A study found three needs that seemed to differentiate the two groups: (1) achievement, (2) endurance, and (3) sympathy.[4]

Pro-company employees.   These employees possessed the characteristics that management accepts and rewards. They had greater need for perfection and success (achievement) and a higher drive for endurance. This kind of person identifies with management and management with him or her.

Pro-union employees.   These workers had a significantly greater need for personal attention and sympathy. Employees who try to satisfy these needs on the job may become disturbed when these needs are not satisfied. Union organizers use these situations to their advantage by (1) making the company look cruel and unfeeling, (2) making the union appear to care about workers' personal problems, and (3) guaranteeing them a grievance procedure.

Role of Supervisors

The importance of supervisors in the organizing drive cannot be overstressed. They serve as the link between the employees and the employer by identify-

---

[3]See Everett M. Kassalow, "Occupational Functions of Trade Unionism in the United States," *White-Collar Report,* January 9, 1961, p. 7, for further findings.

[4]Joseph P. Cangemi, Lynn Clark, et al., "Differences between Pro-Union and Pro-Company Employees," *Personnel Journal* 55 (September 1976):451.

ing workers' needs and trying to satisfy them. If they do not do this, the link will break, and the union will become the missing link for the employees.

RECOGNIZING THE UNION AS THE BARGAINING AGENT

Union membership and an organization by themselves are of little value. Only when the employer recognizes the union as the *exclusive bargaining agent* does it become effective. This means that the union has the *sole* right to represent *all eligible employees*—whether they are union members are not—in their dealings with the employer.

How Unions Get Recognized

There are many ways a union can be recognized by management. First, management can voluntarily recognize it. Second, the employees can vote for it in an NLRB certification election. Third, the NLRB can issue a bargaining order because of the employer's unfair labor practices.[5]

The usual way, though, is through a secret-ballot *certification election* conducted by the NLRB (see Figure 19-2). This involves several steps, including:

1. Determining the bargaining unit.
2. Campaigning before the election.
3. Holding the election.
4. Certifying the union as the bargaining agent.

Determining the Bargaining Unit

A union, the employer, or a group of employees can file a petition for an election with the regional director of the NLRB. A union must get 30 percent of the employees to sign authorization cards before it can petition for an election.

How determined. An examiner holds a hearing to see if the NLRB has jurisdiction and if there is sufficient interest to warrant holding an election. At this time, the order in which the choices will appear on the ballot is determined (if there is more than one union involved). One space is then provided for "no union."

The *bargaining unit* is also defined at that time. This unit is a group of employees recognized as the appropriate unit to be represented by the union for bargaining purposes. This decision is usually based on (1) the preference of the employees, (2) past practices in the organization, (3) similar working conditions, jobs, and skills, and (4) common practices in the industry.

---

[5]Ira Gould, "The Propriety of Issuing *Gissel* Bargaining Orders Where the Union Has Never Attained a Majority," *Labor Law Journal* 29 (October 1978):631.

FIGURE 19-2
Notice of an NLRB certification election and sample ballot

15-RC-6434

<u>VOTING UNIT</u>

Those eligible to vote are all truckdrivers, machine operators, forklift drivers, straddle truck operators, mechanics, mechanics helper, carpenters, carpenters assistant, machine feeders, machine take-off men, shipping and receiving clerks, chipper operators, saw operators and laborers employed by the Employer at its New Orleans, Louisiana facility, who were employed during the payroll period ending April 11, 1979; excluding plant leadermen, salesmen, office clerical employees, guards and supervisors as defined in the Act.

<u>TIME AND PLACE OF ELECTION</u>

<u>DATE</u>: Friday, May 18, 1979   <u>TIME</u>: 4:00 p.m. to 4:45 p.m.

<u>PLACE</u>

Sales Trailer
Employer's Premises

UNITED STATES OF AMERICA
National Labor Relations Board
OFFICIAL SECRET BALLOT
FOR CERTAIN EMPLOYEES OF
R. N. TEMPLEMAN, INC.
New Orleans, Louisiana

Do you wish to be represented for purposes of collective bargaining by -

GENERAL TRUCK DRIVERS, CHAUFFEURS, WAREHOUSEMEN & HELPERS LOCAL NO. 270, A/W INTERNATIONAL BROTHERHOOD OF TEAMSTERS, CHAUFFEURS, WAREHOUSEMEN & HELPERS OF AMERICA, IND. ?

MARK AN "X" IN THE SQUARE OF YOUR CHOICE

YES	NO
☐	☐

DO NOT SIGN THIS BALLOT. Fold and drop in ballot box.
If you spoil this ballot return it to the Board Agent for a new one.

Source: Provided by the regional NLRB office in New Orleans, Louisiana.

By law, supervisors, managers, and professional personnel are excluded from the bargaining unit. Guards can belong to their own unit, but not to that of any other group.

Who is to be included?   The unit generally includes those workers who petitioned for the election, and their co-workers. This is an important aspect of collective bargaining. The unit chosen largely determines whether the union will win the election or not.

Another aspect of this question is who is to be excluded from the bargaining unit. The general rule is to include those with a common interest with their fellow employees and to exclude those whose interests more nearly approach those of management. The union tries to select a bargaining unit that it thinks will vote for it. Management just as strongly tries to structure the bargaining unit to vote against the union.

An AFL-CIO local wanted to become the bargaining unit for the eligible employees at Louisiana State University. The school officials wanted to include clerical and other white-collar employees in the bargaining unit, for they could be expected to vote against the union. The union wanted only food service, custodial, and other blue-collar workers. The union got its way and so won the election.

Campaigning for the Election

Campaigning can be very active, bitter, and even violent. (Refer to the Ford Motor Company organizing drive in the previous chapter.)

The union's approach.   How does the union approach employees during the campaign? In general, it offers them what the employer has failed to provide. It promises better wages, hours, working conditions, job security, and protection from the arbitrary acts of management.

The organizer tries to keep the union's activities from management, provides workers with good communication, and emphasizes person-to-person contacts. The union hopes management won't do the same.

One study found that the unions won over four-fifths of elections where there was no personal contact between the employer and employees, over half where there was personal contact, but only a third where the firm used both written and personal communications.[6]

Management's approach.   Management has the right to try to talk the workers out of voting in favor of the union until 24 hours before the election. But they cannot promise a reward or threaten reprisal. (See Appendix A for

---

[6]Edward Curtin, *White-Collar Unionization*, NICB Studies in Personnel Policy No. 220 (New York: National Industrial Conference Board, 1970).

things that can be done when the union enters and Appendix B for what cannot be done.)

The NLRB threw out a pro-management vote in an election because the firm provided beer and liquor within 150 feet of the polling area.[7]

Some specific things management can do to lessen the chances of unionization are (1) upgrade current policies and relationships—especially communications, (2) conduct attitude surveys and employee interviews, (3) use suggestion boxes to receive anonymous complaints, (4) use media—such as bulletin boards and company newsletters—to keep the employees informed of what is going on, and (5) train supervisors to be more sensitive to employee needs.

Many employers are now using the services of labor relations consultants. These experts help managers correct weaknesses in the personnel program. They particularly try to improve communications. They have helped reduce union victories from over 60 percent in the mid-1960s to 51 percent in 1973 and 46 percent in 1978.[8]

Holding the Election

The NLRB then proceeds to hold the election within 30 to 60 days, during which time both sides try to influence the employees' decision.

The NLRB not only supervises the election, but provides ballots, boxes, watchers at the poll, a count of the votes, and the certification of the union if it wins the election.

Certifying the Union as the Bargaining Agent

To win an election, the union must obtain over 50 percent of the votes of those voting. If it does, it is certified as the exclusive bargaining agent for *all* the employees in the bargaining unit. After the union is certified as the bargaining agent, it begins negotiating an agreement with the employer.[9]

NEGOTIATING THE AGREEMENT

Collective bargaining is the heart of industrial relations. It is through that procedure that the terms and conditions under which the two parties will live

---

[7]*The Wall Street Journal,* April 11, 1978, p. 1.

[8]See Douglas Martin, "Labor Nemesis: When the Boss Calls In This Expert, the Union May Be in Real Trouble," *The Wall Street Journal,* November 11, 1979, pp. 1 and 39, for these and other details.

[9]Although the word *contract* is often used in this context, the proper one is *agreement.* Section 502 of the Taft-Hartley Act prohibits requiring an *individual employee* to render labor or service without his or her consent. However, the two terms will be used interchangeably in this text.

together are determined. *Collective bargaining* is (1) the mutual obligation (2) of representatives of the employer and employees (3) to meet at reasonable times and places and (4) confer in good faith (5) over wages, hours, and other terms and conditions of employment.

As you can see, this becomes a power struggle. As such, it is a social and psychological, as well as a legal and economic, process. Therefore, the same behavioral theories apply to it as apply to other aspects of personnel.

Developing a Bargaining Strategy

Each bargaining session is different, depending on the negotiators and the situation. Yet there are some useful suggestions that can be made at this time. Management should never *concede* anything to the union but should allow itself to *be persuaded.* Labor negotiators will perceive themselves as inferior if concessions come from management. Gifts are not made to equals when the receiver is in no position to make gifts in return.

Other suggestions are:

1. Prepare continually for negotiations.
2. Prepare a list of demands comparable to that which the union usually presents; then bargain on each issue on a *quid pro quo* (something in return for something) basis.
3. Don't plead inability to pay for a requested benefit unless you are prepared to open your books to the union.
4. Determine in advance which are your *cardinal demands*—those for which you are willing to take a strike rather than yield.
5. Don't belittle your employees, for you must "live with them" when the negotiating is over.

The Bargaining Procedure

Bargaining can take place between the union and (1) a single employer, (2) several employers in a given area, (3) a sector of an industry, or (4) a whole industry. By a wide margin, most agreements are negotiated between one employer and one or several unions.

When there is more than one union representing its employees, management negotiates with each of them individually. This sometimes leads to the *whiplash,* which means that as each union settles, the next union asks for the same settlement—plus a little more. This means that the last union is in a strategic position; it can stop the entire operation by calling its members out on strike.

Selecting the target for bargaining. The union uses care in choosing the company against which it will focus its bargaining strategy. Usually, one of the larger firms is chosen, for the agreement with it will set a precedent for the entire industry. The very small firms are highly dependent upon the patterns set by the larger firms. They are in a relatively weak bargaining position and usually can do little to resist the demands of a large and powerful union.

The bargaining teams. The employer's bargaining team usually consists of three or four members. The personnel director is almost always on the team and may be the chief negotiator. Other members will include the plant manager, the operating superintendent, and occasionally a lawyer or other technical advisor.

The union team is usually larger, including from five to seven representatives. The shop stewards or committeemen, the officers of the local, and representatives of the regional or national organization are on the team.

When and where to bargain. The law requires bargaining only during "normal work periods." But, if negotiations are reaching a crisis, both parties may wish to bargain for longer periods of time. However, as one of the tactics of the union is to wear management down, it has been found that this is not desirable except on special occasions.

It is legal to bargain on the employer's premises. But experience has shown that the union will make management "pay" for exercising this right. Instead, it is much more desirable and feasible to meet at some neutral place, usually a hotel or motel.

How to bargain. The law requires bargaining *in good faith*. This means that, while the employer does not have to accept the union's demands, it must listen to them and make valid counteroffers. This is one of the stickiest areas of industrial relations.

Impasse

Collective bargaining is a give-and-take process, with both sides offering many proposals in the form of demands. These are countered by counteroffers or proposals from the other side, also in the form of demands. During the early history of collective bargaining, management did not submit demands but merely answered the union's. It was found that management was giving up everything and getting nothing in return. In bargaining now, each side both gives and receives.

However, a point may be reached where neither side is willing to yield on a point. This point is called the *impasse*. An example of negotiating over wages will best illustrate this point.

How the impasse occurs. Under the bargaining theory of wages (see Chapter 15), the relative strength of the union and the employer determines wage rates. As shown in Figure 19–3, the union has a lower limit on its demands, and the employer has an upper limit. These are *sticking points* beyond which they will not go. When the firm's sticking point is higher than the union's (first condition), bargaining, or haggling, takes place. When the union's sticking point is higher than management's (second condition) there is no basis for practical bargaining, and an impasse is reached.

FIGURE 19–3
The collective bargaining process under conditions of practical bargaining and impasse

---

First condition: Range of practical bargaining

Union demands: *Company offer:*

Upper limit
  on demands $10.50/hr
                        ⎧ . . . . $9.50 ⎫ Sticking point
                        ⎨ Range of practical bargaining   ⎬
Sticking point . . . . ⎩ $8.50 . . . . ⎭
                                                          $7.50 . . . Lower limit on
                                                                        company offer

Second condition: Impasse; no area for practical bargaining

Union demands: *Company offer:*

Upper limit
  on demands . . . . $10.50/hr.
Sticking point . . . . $9.50 . . . .
                        No Area for practical bargaining
                        . . . . $9.00 . . . Sticking point
                                                          $7.00 . . . Lower limit on
                                                                        company offer

---

What to do when impasse occurs.   There are three alternatives when impasse occurs: (1) mediation or conciliation, (2) arbitration, or (3) a strike or lockout.

Mediation or conciliation.   The Federal Mediation and Conciliation Service (FMCS) offers its services when a major strike is about to occur. During the preliminaries and negotiations, the FMCS is available for mediation between the two negotiating parties. If a strike or lockout occurs, the mediator will meet with both parties to try to find out what they really want and what they are willing to concede. Usually a face-saving solution is found that brings the parties together and ends the strike.

There seems to be a growing desire to settle labor disputes without work stoppages, as there are many economic and other disadvantages to strikes. Instead, there is a growing trend to use mediation and conciliation as an alternative to strikes. Conciliation is essentially the same as mediation.

Arbitration.   Arbitration is the process by which management and the union submit a dispute to an outsider to settle and agree to abide by the decision. Both sides present their arguments to the arbitration panel, which includes a union, a management, and a neutral member. The panel weighs the evidence and makes a decision, which is usually a compromise.

In states that permit collective bargaining for public employees but prohibit strikes, *binding arbitration* is required. *Fact-finding* and/or *voluntary arbitration* are required in other states. Yet many public unions do strike, even in states where it is not permitted.

Reprinted by permission of the Chicago Tribune-New York News Syndicate, Inc.

The strike.   If all else fails, the union has the right to strike, and the employer has the right to use the lockout. A *strike* occurs when employees withhold their services from their employer in order to get something. They frequently tell the public why by picketing with signs that accuse the employer of being "unfair." A *lockout* occurs when the employer prevents employees, as a group, from coming onto the premises.

In general, union leaders do not like to use the strike. It is costly, carries a certain amount of stigma for those walking the picket line, and is potentially dangerous to the union because of the possible loss of membership and power if the strike fails.

Local 366 of the Brewery Workers Union struck the Adolph Coors Company in April 1977. The local was joined in a boycott by a number of other groups opposed to the Coors family policies.

The issues were never primarily economic: management claimed that the average employee earned more than $20,000 a year. The key issue was whether Coors would have a union shop. Also, some human relations issues—such as mandatory polygraph tests and requirements that employees display public loyalty to the company—were involved.

Management claimed that about 70 percent of the strikers returned to work shortly after the strike began. In late 1978, Coors employees overwhelmingly rejected the local as their bargaining agent.[10]

As shown in Figure 19-4, the number and severity of strikes increase during the summer and when business is good. Yet only a very small percentage of some 12,000 contracts being renewed annually result in strikes.

---

[10]*The Wall Street Journal*, January 19, 1979, p. 1.

FIGURE 19–4
Strikes vary by season and business cycle

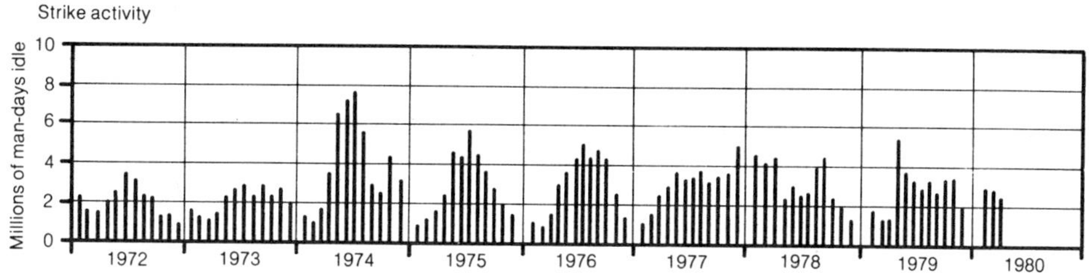

Source: U.S. Department of Labor reports, as depicted in the *The Wall Street Journal*, August 25, 1975, and March 1, 1980.

Although the strike itself is the technique resorted to when all other methods of resolving differences fail, the *threat of a strike* is a continuing factor in almost all negotiations. Both the union and management act as if one could occur.

In 1979, the United Automobile Workers had around $280 million (enough for a ten-week strike) in its strike fund. General Motors had stockpiled a large number of cars. No strike or lockout took place.

Some current bargaining issues. In addition to the usual wage issues, unions are currently asking for (1) expanded pension benefits, (2) a shorter work week (with two and one-half times the base rate for overtime, rather than one and one-half times), and (3) improved "quality of work life."[11] They are also asking for a "catch-up" in wage adjustments in contracts with *cost-of-living adjustments* (COLA).

Emphasis is being placed on *retirement benefits*—especially earlier retirement based on years of service alone, not age plus service—and *better pensions*. Portability of private pensions is being demanded.

Employers are becoming more militant in asking unions to give back some key benefits and yield on work rules that restrict worker output.[12] Finally, management is "trading off" *lifetime guarantees* of jobs for union members in exchange for the right to automate operations—or otherwise increase effectiveness (refer to the case of the New York printers cited in Chapter 18).

Agreement Is Reached

Finally, agreement is reached. A memorandum of agreement is prepared and signed by both parties. However, it is not binding until the workers accept it and top management signs it.

---

[11]"Hot UAW Issue: 'Quality of Work Life,'" *Business Week*, September 17, 1979, pp. 120–21.

[12]See " 'Give-Backs' Is a Fighting Word in Union Bargaining," *U.S. News & World Report*, April 17, 1978, pp. 82–84.

Content of agreement. Each union and organization has its own set of agreements on which the contract is based. But the typical *agreement* includes at least the following subjects:

1. Purpose and intent of the parties.
2. Scope of the agreement.
3. Management rights.
4. Union security and dues checkoff.
5. Other responsibilities.
6. Adjustment of grievances.
7. Provisions for arbitration.
8. Disciplinary procedures.
9. Rates of pay.
10. Hours of work, including overtime and special time.
11. Work rules.
12. Benefits, including vacations, holidays, insurance, and pensions.
13. Health and safety provisions.
14. Employee security and seniority provisions, including promotions, lay-offs/recalls, and transfers.
15. Duration and reopening date.

Approval or rejection of agreement. After it is signed, the union representatives must "sell" the agreement to the members to be ratified by them. While this step was taken for granted for many years, there is now a trend toward rejecting the agreement. The newer types of employees and union members are more militant and independent. They are more likely to reject the contract than the traditional members.

LIVING WITH THE AGREEMENT

The process is not over even with the signing of an agreement. It must be communicated to those affected by it, and machinery must be set up to interpret and implement the settlement as grievances arise from it.

Handling Grievances

It is human nature to complain about things that displease us. Some employees may be dissatisfied with some aspects of their job and will complain about it. Workers also complain about supervisory practices, including attitudes, behavior, and decisions. A common cause of complaints is a supervisor who plays favorites, does not keep promises, or is too demanding of subordinates.

The grievance procedure in unionized organizations. The form and substance of the *grievance procedure* depends on the size of the industry and the size and structure of the employer and union. The procedure tends to conform to the structure of the employer and union, with a step at each level from the supervisor to the chief executive officer. A typical grievance proce-

FIGURE 19–5
Example of a typical grievance procedure

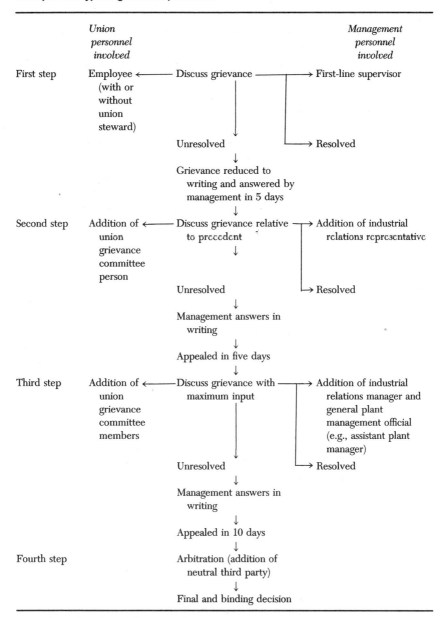

Source: From *The Labor Relations Process* by William H. Holley, Jr. and Kenneth M. Jennings. Copyright ©
1980 by The Dryden Press.A division of Holt, Rinehart and Winston, Publishers. Reprinted by permission
of Holt, Rinehart and Winston.

dure is shown in Figure 19–5. As you can see, if satisfaction cannot be obtained within the organization, it goes outside to arbitration.

The arbitration procedure has become more formal and legalistic, costly, and time consuming. Therefore, many personnel people have sought a viable alternative. *Grievance mediation* is one such possibility. It brings in an outside mediator to help interpret the contract terms. It is voluntary, informal, and preventive in nature.[13]

Now, many workers are complaining to the NLRB that the unions are not defending their rights vigorously enough. The number of such complaints has tripled over the last ten years.[14]

Handling complaints in nonunion organizations.   Many nonunion employers have established procedures for handling complaints that are in many ways comparable to formal union grievance procedures. Many of these permit complaints to go from the immediate supervisor to committees composed of higher level executives, usually under the responsibility of the personnel officer, and to review committees consisting of the top executives or neutral third parties. However, arbitration is not usually provided for. The main purposes of these arrangements are to assure fairness in employee relations and to improve employee attitudes, rather than to interpret personnel policies and practices.

The National Industrial Conference Board found that about half of 800 companies surveyed had complaint programs for nonunion employees. Two-thirds of the firms without unions had such systems. The main purpose was "to stave off unionism."[15] These arrangements are frequently found in the public sector.

Role of Supervisors

The supervisors' attitudes toward subordinates are important in living with the contract. For example, one study showed that supervisors who had high consideration for subordinates had low grievance rates. Also, supervisors who processed grievances faster had fewer to process.[16]

A training program was conducted for both supervisors and union stewards in a large organization handling around 3,000 grievances per year. It resulted in a decline in the number of grievances per 100 employees from 17 to 7, and the percentage settled at the first step increased from 33 to 54 percent.[17]

---

[13]Mollie H. Bowers, "Grievance Mediation: Another Route to Resolution," *Personnel Journal* 59 (1980):132–36.

[14]"On Trial: A Union's Fairness," *Business Week*, August 13, 1979, pp. 76–78.

[15]*The Wall Street Journal*, February 19, 1980, p. 1.

[16]Philip Ash, "The Parties to the Grievance," *Personnel Psychology* 23 (Spring 1970):13–37.

[17]J. C. Pettefer, "Effective Grievance Administration," *California Management Review* 12 (Winter 1970):12–18.

Many company grievance plans follow union models.

Source: Used by permission of Marc Nadel.

SUMMARY AND CONCLUSIONS

When the union enters, it affects personnel management in many ways. It starts a series of emotional, economic, and procedural events that change the way management operates.

The first thing the personnel manager should do is to improve all aspects of the personnel function. Communications should be improved, especially listening to employees to see what their gripes are—and then doing something to correct them.

Many employers are hiring labor relations experts as consultants to help prevent unionization. They are usually quite successful.

When 30 percent of the employees in the bargaining unit have signed authorization cards, the union can ask the NLRB to hold a secret-ballot certification election. If over half of the eligible employees vote for the union, it becomes the exclusive bargaining agent for all of the employees. If not, it cannot file for another election for a year.

After the union is certified, it begins negotiating with the employer for a contract. Representatives of both sides must bargain in good faith over wages, hours, and other terms and conditions of employment. While no contract is legally required, one usually results from the bargaining.

If an impasse is reached during the negotiations, an outsider can serve as a mediator to help the parties clarify positions and reach agreement. If this fails, the union can strike, or the employer can lock the employees out. Neither side likes to use these strong measures. Public unions and employers use arbitration if it is illegal for the workers to strike.

After an agreement is reached, the employees must ratify it. The newer employees are less willing to accept this than the older workers. Many contracts are now turned down by the more militant members.

When the agreement is ratified, the problems are not over. It must be lived with by both sides. This requires interpretation of its meaning and application. When an employee has a complaint about its interpretation, an effort is made to solve it with the first-line supervisor. If this fails, the formal grievance procedure is used. If the grievance is not settled in the organization, it goes outside to an arbitrator, who makes a binding decision.

What conclusions can be reached about industrial relations? First, some degree of conflict is always present in every union-management relationship. Second, the trend in labor relations has been away from conflict and toward a more accommodating and cooperative relationship. Third, the absence of a union puts a heavier burden on supervisors and managers, as shown in these comments by a practicing personnel manager:

> Personnel management is quite different in unionized operations. Unionization leaves little flexibility for the personnel managers, for the agreement covers practically all aspects of the employee-employer relationship. In nonunion plants, a greater load is placed on line supervision to manage people, as well as production. Line managers carry the larger load of personnel management in those operations. The results are in most cases gratifying, but there is a need to police their actions to insure that there is reasonable consistency in administering company policies and rules—or a union will enter!

APPENDIX A: THINGS EMPLOYERS CAN DO WHEN A UNION TRIES TO ORGANIZE THEIR EMPLOYEES

1. Keep outside organizers off the premises.
2. Inform employees from time to time of the benefits they presently enjoy (avoiding veiled promises or threats).
3. Inform employees that signing a union authorization card does not mean they must vote for the union if there is an election.
4. Inform employees of the disadvantages of belonging to the union, such as the possibility of strikes, serving in a picket line, dues, fines, assessments, and one-man or clique rule.
5. Inform employees that management would prefer to deal with them rather than have the union or any other outsider settle grievances.
6. Tell employees what they think about unions and about union policies.
7. Inform employees about any prior experience they have had with unions and whatever they know about the union officials trying to organize them.
8. Inform employees that the law permits them to hire a new employee to replace any employee who goes on strike for economic reasons.
9. Inform employees that no union can obtain more than they as employers are able to give.

10. Inform employees about how their wages and benefits compare with unionized or nonunionized concerns where wages are lower and benefits less desirable.
11. Inform employees that the local union will probably be dominated by the international union, and that they, the members, will have little say in its operations.
12. Inform employees of any untrue or misleading statements made by the organizer. They may give employees the correct facts.
13. Inform employees of any known racketeering, Communist, or other undesirable elements that may be active in the union.
14. Give opinions on unions and union leaders, even in derogatory terms.
15. Distribute information about unions such as disclosures of corruption.
16. Reply to union attacks on company policies or practices.
17. Give legal position on labor-management matters.
18. Advise employees of their legal rights, provided they don't engage in or finance an employee suit or proceeding.
19. Declare a fixed policy in opposition to compulsory union membership contracts.
20. Campaign against unions seeking to represent the employees.
21. Tell employees they do not like to deal with unions.
22. Insist that any solicitation of membership or discussion of union affairs be conducted outside of working time.
23. Enforce plant rules impartially, regardless of the employee's membership or activity in a union.
24. Tell employees, if they ask, that they are free to join or not join any organization, so far as their status with the company is concerned.
25. Administer discipline, layoffs, grievance procedures, and the like without regard to union membership or nonmembership of the employees involved.
26. Treat both union and nonunion employees alike in making assignments of preferred work, desired overtime, and so on.
27. Tell employees that their *personal* and *job* security will be determined by the economic prosperity of the company. Profits are an important essential in this picture.

Source: Curtis Tate, L. C. Megginson, Charles R. Scott, Jr., and Lyle Trueblood, *Successful Small Business Management,* rev. ed. (Dallas: Business Publications, 1978), pp. 212–15.

APPENDIX B: THINGS EMPLOYERS CANNOT DO

1. Engage in surveillance of employees to determine who is or is not participating in the union program, attend union meetings, or engage in any undercover activities for this purpose.
2. Threaten, intimidate, or punish employees who engage in union activity.
3. Request information from employees about union matters, meetings, and

so on. Employees may of their own volition give such information without prompting. Employers may listen but not ask questions.

4. Prevent employee union representatives from soliciting memberships during nonworking time.
5. Grant wage increases, special concessions, or promises of any kind to keep the union out.
6. Question a prospective employee about an affiliation with a labor organization.
7. Threaten to close up or move the plant, curtail operations, or reduce employee benefits.
8. Engage in any discriminatory practices, such as work assignments, overtime, layoffs, promotions, wage increases, or any other practices that could be regarded as preferential treatment for certain employees.
9. Discriminate against union people when disciplining employees for a specific action, and permit nonunion employees to go unpunished for the same action.
10. Transfer workers on the basis of teaming up nonunion employees to separate them from union employees.
11. Deviate in any way from known company policies for the primary purpose of eliminating a union employee.
12. Intimate, advise, or indicate, in any way, that unionization will force the company to lay off employees, take away company benefits or privileges enjoyed, or make any other changes that could be regarded as a curtailment of privileges.
13. Make statements to the effect that they will not deal with a union.
14. Give any financial support or other assistance to employees who support or oppose the union.
15. Visit the homes of employees to urge them to oppose or reject the union in its campaign.
16. Be a party to a petition or circular against the union, or encourage employees to circulate such a petition.
17. Make any promises of promotions, benefits, wage increases, or anything else that would induce employees to oppose the union.
18. Engage in discussions or arguments that may lead to physical encounters with employees over the union question.
19. Use a third party to threaten or coerce a union member, or attempt to influence votes through this medium.
20. Question employees on whether or not they have affiliated or signed with the union.
21. Use the word *never* in any predictions or attitudes about the union or its promises or demands.
22. Talk about tomorrow. Employers may talk about yesterday or today when they give examples or reasons, instead of tomorrow, to avoid making a prediction or condition that might be interpreted as a threat or promise by the union or the NLRB.

QUESTIONS

1. Why do managers of small firms tend to be "antiunion"?
2. Why do workers join a union? Why do they reject the union?
3. Do you believe that union power will increase or decrease in the future? Explain your answer.
4. How are supervisory relationships with employees affected in a unionized organization?
5. How can a personnel manager prepare to handle grievances more effectively?
6. How would you describe the preparations you would make for bargaining with labor unions?
7. How do you distinguish between arbitration, mediation, and collective bargaining?
8. Is the strike the most powerful means of achieving union goals? How would you explain the significance of the strike to management, the union, the workers, and the nation's economy?

PROBLEM

The Union Enters*

Two weeks passed with no word from the union. John decided if he was going to keep the union out, he would have to get rid of the driver who wanted the union. As business was slow, John laid him off "until things pick up again." John would have to drive the other truck himself if it were needed.

Shortly after being laid off, the driver found a permanent job, so John was not bound to hire him back.

John was quite successful during the next four years. He was now employing 13 people and had arranged to buy a similar firm in a neighboring city.

John had heard nothing more from the union. Each time he hired a new driver, he tried not to hire those who expressed favorable attitudes toward the union. He was firmly convinced that he could not possibly make any profit if his drivers were unionized.

Recently, Jay walked in for their first meeting in four years.

John: Hello, Jay. How've you been?

Jay: Okay, and from the looks of your business, you've been doing okay, too. You've got five trucks going full time, and you'll have three more when you get your new distributorship. That'll make eight drivers. The last time I was here, you told me you were too small to afford a union. Now that you're the biggest supply company in the city, I think your men had better be working under contract.

---

*See the case at the beginning of the chapter for earlier details.

Questions

1. What do you think of Jay's approach to organizing the drivers in the first part of the case? In the second part?
2. What do you think of John's approach to the union representative in the first part of the case? What do you think his approach will be this time?
3. Were John's actions legal? Explain.
4. What would you do now if you were John?

SUGGESTED READINGS FOR FURTHER STUDY

Bohlander, George W.   "Fair Representation: Not Just a Union Problem." *Personnel Administrator* 25 (March 1980):36–40, 82.

Constantino, George E., Jr.   "Defining Line and Staff Roles in Collective Bargaining." *Personnel Journal* 58 (October 1979):689–91.

Goodfellow, Matthew.   "How to Lose an NLRB Election." *Personnel Administrator* 21 (September 1976):42 ff.

Hopkins, James H., and Robert D. Binderup.   "Employee Relations and Union Organizing Campaigns." *Personnel Administrator* 25 (March 1980):57–61.

Kilgour, John H.   "How to Respond to an Impending Strike." *Personnel Journal* 58 (February 1979):98–101.

―――――.   "Wrapping the Package of Labor Agreement Costs." *Personnel Journal* 56 (June 1977):298 ff.

Kristol, Irving.   "Understanding Trade Unionism." *Wall Street Journal*, October 23, 1978, p. 24.

Rand, James F.   "Creative Problem-Solving Applied to Grievance/Arbitration Procedures." *Personnel Administrator* 25 (March 1980):50–52.

Raskin, A. H.   "Show 'Em the Clenched Fist!" *Forbes*, October 2, 1978, pp. 31–32.

Stessin, Lawrence.   "Expedited Arbitration: Less Grief over Grievances." *Harvard Business Review* 55 (January–February 1977):129 ff.

Veglahn, Peter A.   "Arbitration Costs/Time: Labor and Management Views." *Labor Law Journal* 30 (January 1979):49–57.

PART SIX

Planning for the Future

The future enters into us, in order to transform itself in us, long before it happens.
RAINER MARIA RILKE

You have now learned what personnel management is and what personnel managers do. You have seen the latest developments as far as the personnel functions are concerned.

Now we will look at some of the changes expected in the environment in which personnel management operates. These changes are not necessarily the ones you or I would wish to see. Instead, they seem to be the results of past and present trends.

After studying the expected changes, we will look at what is needed to prepare for them, including personnel research and evaluation.

CHAPTER TWENTY

Personnel Management in Perspective

Learning Objectives

After studying the material in this chapter, you should be able to:

1. Estimate the environment in which the personnel function will be performed.
2. Describe some of the challenges facing you as a future personnel manager.
3. Explain what type of personnel research is needed and show how it can be done.
4. Explain why evaluating a personnel program is so important.
5. Describe some methods of evaluating personnel programs.

Some Important Words and Terms

Scientific approach	Personnel audit
Laboratory investigation	Absenteeism
Experimental study	Absence rate
Descriptive study	Turnover rate
Predictive study	Unavoidable separations
Diagnostic study	

I learned the most amazing truth yesterday. I can scarcely wait for tomorrow.
ALBERT EINSTEIN

Outline of the Chapter

In a speech several years ago, Keith Davis identified four basic, funda-
mental truths that are affecting management in the 1980s. They are: We
are (1) a service economy, (2) a knowledge society, (3) a more socially
concerned, humanistic society, and (4) a fast-changing, unstable social
and economic system.

He concluded by saying that future managers will need to be better
prepared than ever. They will need more behavioral, social, political, and
system understanding. They, as well as their employees, will face lifelong
learning as they attempt to deal constructively with all the changes that are
taking place.[1]

TABLE 20–1
Some significant changes expected by 1984 by 1,500 ASPA conferees

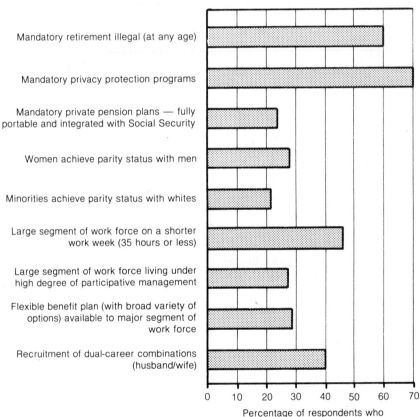

TIMETABLE — SOME SIGNIFICANT CHANGES

Percentage of respondents who
expect these major changes
to take place within next 5 years

Source: Reprinted from the November, 1979 issue of *The Personnel Administrator* with permission of The
American Society for Personnel Administration.

---

[1]Keith Davis, "Some Basic Trends Affecting Management in the 1980s," University of Minnesota College and Graduate School of Business, Alumni Lecture Series, May 7, 1976.

Table 20-1 shows the results of a survey of some significant changes expected by 1984 by 1,500 participants at the annual conference of ASPA in Milwaukee, July 17-20, 1979.

Keith Davis' thoughts and the ASPA survey tend to confirm the conclusion reached in the preface of this book: performing the personnel function in the future will be very much more difficult and complex—but also more challenging and rewarding.

First, we will explore some of the changes expected in the environment and in the personnel functions to be performed. Then we will see what will be required of personnel managers to carry out their duties and responsibilities, including the use of personnel research and evaluation of personnel programs.

EXPECTED CHANGES IN THE ENVIRONMENT

The basic hypothesis of this text has been: *If one understands employee behavior, one can predict that behavior; if one can predict behavior, one can direct and control it.* As management's objective is to direct employee activities, it logically follows that there is a need to predict them. Yet, in order to predict, it is necessary to understand the cause-and-effect relationships leading to employee behavior. Therefore, the purpose of the material in this book has been to help you understand employee behavior so that you can better perform the personnel function.

The conclusions reached in this book were based on five premises:

1. As personnel and human resources management is inherent in all management positions, it is the primary function and responsibility of all managers, regardless of the nature of their activities or their place in the organization.
2. The technical aspects of personnel are no longer assigned to lower levels of managerial activity. Instead, they must also be viewed as part of the activities to be performed by personnel executives at the highest levels.
3. The performance of these functions must deal with employees as they actually exist in the work environment, not in the idealistic state that management would prefer.
4. Since organizations do not exist in isolation, personnel management cannot be understood outside the context of the total economic, technological, political, and social environment in which it is performed.
5. The people involved have changed. The personnel activities are performed by more capable and professional administrators. The same generalization is true of managers and employees outside of personnel.

On the basis of these premises, the previous chapters have tried to present the latest theoretical and technical thoughts in the field. Little effort has been made to present the techniques and practices required to implement those findings. Instead, the objective has been to evolve some generally useful concepts that you can apply in the context and environment in which you find yourself as a manager.

Changing Work Environment

The performance of the personnel management function will change drastically during the next decade because of a changed work environment, resulting from several trends. The most important of these are that (1) employees are achieving a position of economic independence; (2) the government is becoming increasingly involved in the employer-employee relationship; (3) unions are shifting from economic to quasi-political positions; (4) an overwhelming technological revolution is occurring; (5) organizational life is becoming increasingly complex; (6) managerial frontiers are shifting from the realm of increasing physical production to that of improving interpersonal relationships and social responsibility; and (7) the knowledge of human behavior is increasing at a rapid rate.

Effective personnel managers will not only be influenced by this changing environment, but they will also modify it to improve their own performance.

Higher quality of work life.   An important current trend is improving the quality of work life. Therefore, *personnel executives must become change agents and begin to act creatively and voluntarily* instead of reluctantly reacting to outside change agents.

Changing attitudes will call for greater *acceptance of leisure as a valid activity, a rejection of authoritarianism, a growing belief in the values of participation and involvement, and a greater respect for individual dignity.* The emphasis must be based on greater consideration for the rights and needs of the individual employee. All-inclusive programs and uniform plans will no longer meet the needs of people in organizations.

Improving social responsibility.   Changing public attitudes will demand that personnel managers become more involved in problems of social responsibility. Personnel work will take on a new community relations dimension; managers will find that they must deal with activist groups much as they have dealt with unions in the past. The major point that personnel managers must keep constantly in mind and impress upon those groups is that *only a thriving, profitable company can provide new jobs and meet social responsibilities;* for the smaller the profit a company makes, the smaller the effort it can make toward meeting public goals. Even public institutions must become more cost-effective—if they are to be accepted by the public.

Changing Organizational Environment

Organizational relationships will also undergo drastic changes. Not only will *organizational planning and development* (OD) be emphasized, but greater consideration will be given to the human resource, the role of the personnel specialist, and the first-line supervisor.

Increasing importance of human resources.   As organizations are in reality human organisms, the financial and physical resources are relatively unproductive until combined with the human resources. Therefore, future performance of the personnel function will be based not on the "factor of production" or the "human relations" philosophy but on the "human resources" concept. This means that employees will be treated with human dignity and worth, but their output will be judged by the economic criteria of efficiency and effectiveness. Management will no longer assume that the cause-and-effect relationship is:

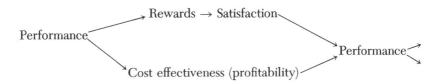

Increasing organizational pressures.   Organizations will become larger, more interrelated, and more complex. The matrix and project organizational relationships will probably be used more frequently, as they are so adaptable to complex and changing situations.

Social groupings will be minimized because of mechanization, and employee isolation will increase. A sense of alienation, isolation, loneliness, frustration, and impotence will result.

New authority for personnel managers.   As work has become more complex, as employees have become more capable, and as work and decision making have become more centralized, personnel managers have been given greater authority. *Functional authority is tending to replace staff authority as the dominant authority-responsibility relationship.*

New status for personnel managers.   A basic assumption of this book is that the selection and use of human resources is of greater concern to organizations than the management of financial and physical resources. It is people who determine the use of nonhuman resources. Yet too few employers are presently planning for human resources in any but a very short-term way. Therefore, the role (and number) of personnel executives will expand, and their image will improve, during this decade.[2]

The position of personnel directors as staff advisors to line personnel will change to directors of personnel and human resources who guard the people investment through centralized leadership and evaluation. These directors will probably report directly to the chief executive officer and be involved with planning all activities affecting personnel—directly or indirectly. These people will not be personnel managers with a new title but executives with training in information systems, budgeting, and organizational theory, as well as expertise in the use of the behavioral and management sciences.

---

[2]Donald E. Klinger, "Changing Role of Personnel Management in the 1980s," *Personnel Administrator* 24 (September 1979):41–48.

Table 20–2 shows the implications of these and other changes for the personnel function, according to the survey of the 1979 ASPA conferees.

TABLE 20–2
Implications of expected changes for the personnel profession during the 1980s

IMPLICATIONS FOR THE PERSONNEL PROFESSION

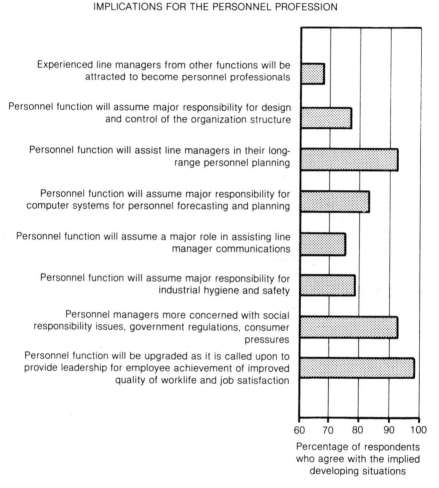

Percentage of respondents
who agree with the implied
developing situations

Source: Reprinted from the November, 1979 issue of *The Personnel Administrator* with permission of The American Society for Personnel Administration.

EXPECTED CHANGES IN PERSONNEL FUNCTIONS

In addition to these modifications of the work and organizational environment, the specific personnel functions will also change drastically. While it is impossible to discuss all expected changes in the limited space available, some of the more significant ones will be discussed.

Planning for, Recruiting, Selecting, and Developing Employees

Personnel executives will deal with a changed work force. All aspects of building and developing the work team will change. *Possibly the greatest change will occur in validating recruitment, selection, and development criteria to provide more objective bases for better and more defensible decisions.*

Changes in the labor force.   Many factors, including the previously mentioned ones, will result in drastic changes in the size and composition of the nation's labor force. These changes will greatly influence the performance of the personnel function in each organization.

First, the labor force will begin to shrink from about 1983 on. High school graduating classes will decline by 2 to 3 percent each year, and retirements will increase by around 6 percent per year. This will probably result in work force declines of around 1 to 2 percent annually.[3]

This labor force will be composed of (1) a declining proportion of younger and older workers, (2) an increasing proportion in the "prime working age" group, the 35-44-year olds, (3) an increasing number and percentage of women, especially working mothers, who will be found in all job categories, (4) about the same proportion of blacks, but in higher level positions, and (5) an increasing number and proportion of Hispanics.

The *demand* for this labor force *will continue to shift toward service-producing industries and away from goods-producing industries.* The greatest increase in demand will come from the service industries—except household service—with government following. Declines will occur fastest in agriculture and mining. There will also be occupational shifts away from blue-collar and farm jobs and toward white-collar and service ones, especially the professional, technical, and clerical positions.

Recruiting and selecting employees.   For legal and economic reasons, *human resource planning* and *career management* will become more important and sophisticated. Organizations must have affirmative action programs—based on defensible planning—for recruiting minorities, women, disabled workers, and older workers. EEO/AA are now accepted as a legal part of personnel. But it is important to accept them as ethical or even moral obligations.[4]

More objective and analytical methods, including the computer, will be used.[5] New supply sources for personnel will also be used. Temporary personnel—including retired and skilled blue-collar workers—will be used exten-

---

[3]Warren T. Brookes, "Coming: A Severe Labor Shortage in 1980s," *Human Events*, February 10, 1979, p. 24.

[4]Vernon E. Jordan, "Human Resources Perspectives for the '80s," *Personnel Administrator* 24 (October 1979):75–82.

[5]Grant H. Morris, "Navigating the Backwaters: Personnel and Data Processing," *Personnel Journal* 58 (July 1979):476–80.

sively in technical and professional, clerical, janitorial, and maintenance activities. This will avoid the "fixed" expenses of hiring full-time people. Finally, selection will be handled increasingly through the employment agencies, especially for clerical, professional, and managerial personnel.

Public policy will prevent subjective selection. Instead, *more valid objective selection criteria based on extensive research will result in improved selection.*

Electronic data processing will increasingly be used in selection, particularly in obtaining, analyzing, and evaluating data hitherto unavailable.

Providing management succession. The supply of managers relative to the demand will improve during the decade. However, there will be three pressure points. First, management jobs will become so much more demanding that those who wish to progress in management will need to develop themselves continually to keep from becoming obsolete. Second, the new entrants into the management ranks have different value systems, aspirations, lifestyles, and perceptions of their function. They will tend to question, challenge, and modify existing patterns of authority-responsibility relationships and behavior. Third, career management will become an important and essential part of personnel planning and management progression.

Maximizing employee potential. Education, training, and development will be modified, becoming more dynamic and continuous. Potential employees will remain outside the work force for longer periods of time while receiving additional formal education. Yet, even after they are hired, they will need longer, more complex, and more specialized and individualized development and career guidance. Nonmanagerial—as well as managerial—personnel must spend from 10 to 20 percent of their time on the job in personal development.

It has been predicted that personnel managers may eventually spend around 40 percent of their working time in training—just to keep up with the rapid changes being brought about by science and technology. As the educational system does not change as quickly as an organization's technological development, new and different training programs must be created to develop employees to meet future needs, including how to cope with change itself. Ultimately, education will be a continual, lifetime, integrative process.[6]

Improving Employee Performance

The declining productivity of American workers has been cited as one of the greatest problems of the 1980s.[7] This trend will make the management of

---

[6]See James M. Mitchell and Rolfe Schroeder, "Future Shock for Personnel Administration," *Public Personnel Management* 3 (July–August 1974):265–69.

[7]Fred E. Shuster, "Human Resources Management: Key to the Future," *Personnel Administrator* 23 (December 1978):33–35 and 66–68.

human resources even more important. If we are to maintain our present material level, some way must be found to increase employee productivity. That is one challenge facing personnel managers during the 1980s.

Improving the quality of work life.   The two prevailing concepts of work will be the *leisure and pleasure concept* and the *human needs concept.* The former, which will be accepted by the mass of employees, views work as a way of providing funds to buy leisure time in which to have pleasure. *Job enrichment* programs will increase in importance as a motivational and developmental technique.

OD, MBO, semiautonomous work groups, job sharing and splitting, and similar efforts will be used to improve the quality of work life. The annual hours of work will decline, and probably the four-day week will become a viable alternative for those who choose it. Almost certainly, the 40-hour, five-day work week will be reduced.

Motivating and leading.   Although *motivation* will continue to be important, the higher level personnel would have a greater degree of "self-motivation" from the expanded job content and higher educational levels. Consequently, emphasis will be placed on using incentives that will stimulate the employees through appealing to their self-fulfillment needs, particularly their desire for achievement, accomplishment, and pride of workmanship.

The use of *management by objectives* and behaviorally anchored rating scales to evaluate employee performance will become more popular. *Performance appraisals must be validated and become more objective if they are to be used.*

Although the need for individualism will continue to be felt, and nonconforming individualists will be sought—and rewarded—for their excellence and creativity, the pressure for conformity will be even greater.

Legal issues.   Two major legal issues that will affect employee performance are (1) *sexual harassment* and (2) *privacy of employees.*

The present trend is for employers to be held responsible for seeing that women employees are not sexually harassed. If they are, the employer may be sued for civil rights violations and workers' compensation because of adverse effects on the employees' health.[8] The EEOC has issued interim guidelines encouraging employers to deal affirmatively with the issue.[9]

The Department of Labor, Congress, and the courts are now vigorously seeking ways to provide employees greater privacy in the workplace—especially as far as their personnel records are concerned. This will be one of the big issues of the 1980s.[10]

---

[8]"Sexual Harassment Lands Companies in Court," *Business Week,* October 1, 1979, pp. 120-22.

[9]*Washington Vantage Point,* April 1980, pp. 2-3.

[10]*Washington Vantage Point,* April 1980, pp. 1-2, and "Big Crusade of the '80s: More Rights for Workers," *U.S. News & World Report,* March 26, 1979, pp. 1-2; Joann S. Lublin, "Privacy at Work, "*The Wall Street Journal,* May 12, 1980, p. 26; and Alan F. Westin, "What Should Be Done About Employee Privacy," *Personnel Administrator* 25 (March 1980):27-30.

Compensating Employees

Although less emphasis will be given to *money per se* as an incentive to improve performance, financial gain will continue to be a motivational factor. However, as a stimulus to perform better, its value will be in satisfying the social, ego, and achievement needs rather than the economic ones. Greater use will be made of companywide group bonus plans, rather than individual ones. Less use will be made of incentive wage plans because of the difficulty of administering them, especially in terms of relating productivity to individual effort.

Performance appraisal methods and instruments must be "EEO-proof."[11] This means that they must be job-oriented appraisals using predetermined and validated standards.

The *Fair Labor Standards Act* will be extended to most of the remaining uncovered organizations regardless of whether they are engaged in business or not. Wage differentials between white and nonwhite and male and female employees will decline as women and nonwhites move up from the entry-level jobs they now hold.

Equal pay for comparable work—or worth—will be a big issue during the decade. The chairperson of the EEOC said it will be "*the* EEO issue of the 1980s."[12]

Employee benefits will continue to expand in number and cost—especially toward lifetime employment and early retirement. However, there will probably be more emphasis on individualized "packages" rather than on giving all workers the same benefits.

Industrial Relations

Union power will probably stay about the same, but emphasis will be on quasi-political activities such as legislation, executive orders, and administrative decisions instead of the more traditional economic approaches of collective bargaining and striking. Compulsory arbitration will be used more in public organizations. *Organizational and recruiting efforts will be directed at public, professional, and agricultural employees, especially white-collar, female, and black workers.* Bargaining demands will concentrate: on reducing the hours worked, "isolation" pay, dental care, and additional personal benefits provided during working hours. Union membership will continue to decline as a percentage of the work force.

The changing composition of the work force will cause nonunionized workers to seek affiliation with professional and learned societies. These groups will serve as their agents for establishing terms and conditions of employment.

---

[11]Robert J. Greene, "Thoughts on Compensation Management in the '80s and '90s," *Personnel Administrator* 25 (May 1980):27-28.

[12]ASPA, *Fair Employment Digest,* December 1979, p. 1; see the March 1980 *Digest* for further details of this proposal.

NEED FOR PERSONNEL RESEARCH

Leonardo da Vinci said: "Those who are enamoured of practice without science are like a pilot who goes into a ship without a rudder or compass and never has any certainty where he is going. Practice should always be based upon a sound knowledge of theory." This statement illustrates the truth that performing the personnel function requires more than mere techniques and tools for working with people. An effective ongoing personnel program is based on a practical philosophy, using well-established theoretical knowledge and practical application. This knowledge is constantly being expanded by researchers in the behavioral science and personnel fields.

Yet even more research is needed in the personnel area.

Why Personnel Research Is Needed

Current personnel research is quite varied in scope, methods, and techniques used. However, the common thread found in all the organizations doing it is that they attempt to study human behavior by using scientific procedures.

Characteristics of the Scientific Approach

The scientific approach has much to offer personnel executives in the study of employee behavior. It is generally agreed that there is no single scientific method. Instead, there are several methods that can be and are used; so it is better to say that there is a *scientific approach*. It tends to have the following characteristics:

1. *Procedures are public,* which means that a scientific report contains a complete description of what was done. This enables other researchers in the field to follow each step of the investigation as if they were actually present.
2. *Definitions are precise,* and the procedures used, the variables measured, and how they were measured are clearly stated.
3. *Data collection is objective;* so there should be no bias in collecting information and interpreting results.
4. *Findings are replicable,* so that any researcher in the field can test the findings or results of a study by reproducing them under similar conditions.
5. *The approach is systematic and cumulative,* so that a unified body of knowledge can be developed. Thus, a major purpose of the behavioral science approach to personnel is to develop an organized system of verified hypotheses about employee behavior.
6. *The purposes are explanation, understanding, and prediction,* so that if one determines the "why" and "how" and is able to provide proof, one can

then predict the particular conditions under which specific events will occur. *Prediction is the ultimate objective of personnel research!*

These characteristics constitute the objective, systematic, and controlled nature of the scientific approach, which enables others to have confidence in the outcome of the research.

Characteristics of Personnel Research

In addition to understanding the characteristics of the scientific approach to doing research, personnel executives should also understand the characteristics of personnel research. There are two dimensions that determine the level, validity, and usefulness of this type of research. They are (1) the degree of control exercised by the researcher, and (2) the level of its outcome.

Degree of control. One way of classifying personnel research is by the degree of control exercised by researchers. When a study is described as a *laboratory investigation,* this implies that the researchers made their observations and recorded their data in a highly controlled situation. When a researcher does an *experimental study,* using an experimental group and a control group, it is usually a laboratory study.

Researchers, government officials, and others are becoming concerned about the ethical dilemmas involved in doing big, complex social experiments with humans. They are asking questions like these: Must the subject be told the purpose of an experiment, even if it biases the results? Can researchers keep information about a person confidential from government agencies that might use it to the person's detriment? What obligation is there to make sure that subjects don't suffer when the experiment ends?[13]

In a *field study,* the only control involves selecting time, place, and subjects for making observations, recording data, and analyzing it. When *library research* is used to solve a problem, it is implied that the researcher seeks a solution by gathering and synthesizing observations made by others.

Level of outcome. A second way of classifying personnel research is in terms of its level of outcome. A study concerned only with what something is like is called *descriptive* (most personnel research is done at this level). When the outcome is used to anticipate the future, it is called *predictive.* If it seeks an answer to the question of "why"—that is, looking for a cause-and-effect relationship—the study is described as *diagnostic.* You can see that description is usually the first step to both prediction and diagnosis.

---

[13]See Alan L. Otten, "Ethical Quandaries," *The Wall Street Journal,* September 18, 1975, p. 20, for further details.

Who Does the Research?

Personnel research is not being done very extensively at present, but this is expected to change in the near future.

ASPA's Personnel Research Committee found, in a small random sample of its members, that only about half of them were conducting personnel research studies.[14] Most of those dealt with training program effectiveness, as shown in Table 20–3. Figures from outside sources were used for comparative purposes by 62 percent of those doing research.

An exhaustive survey done several years ago found that private, nonresearch firms conducted about 39 percent of all personnel research; universities conducted 34 percent; the federal government, 22 percent; and private business, only 5 percent.[15] The larger firms, such as American Telephone & Telegraph, General Electric, General Motors, IBM, Sears, and Texas Instruments, do more of their own research.

The primary responsibility for personnel research is usually assigned to the personnel department. Some is done by research and development departments.

Personnel research tends to be done by industrial psychologists, most of whom have their doctorates. Much research is now being done by personnel graduates.

Sources of Data

Many data sources were used by the ASPA members, including (1) government agencies, such as the Bureau of Labor Statistics (BLS), and federal, state, and local employment service offices, (2) reporting services, such as BNA, Conference Board, and Commerce Clearing House, (3) employer associations, such as the U.S. Chamber of Commerce and the American Management Association, (4) consulting firms that conduct their own surveys, (5) industry trade associations, and (6) universities, such as the University of Michigan's Institute for Social Research.

Areas of Research

A survey of 44 companies doing research found that 98 percent were doing research on selection, 75 percent on opinion measurement, 30 percent on

---

[14]BNA's *Bulletin to Management,* March 22, 1979, p. 1.
[15]Cecil Goode, *Personnel Research Frontiers* (Chicago: Public Personnel Association, 1958).

TABLE 20-3
Personnel research studies

| | Percentage of companies | | | | | |
| | By industry | | | By size | | |
Research topic	Manufacturing	Nonmanufacturing	Nonbusiness	Large	Small	All companies
Training program effectiveness						
Studies being conducted............	14	39	18	35	17	24
Studies conducted previously........	9	12	18	19	8	12
Effectiveness of recruiting sources						
Studies being conducted............	11	27	27	35	11	21
Studies conducted previously........	9	21	14	22	9	14
Reliability of performance evaluations						
Studies being conducted............	3	24	18	16	13	14
Studies conducted previously........	0	15	27	11	13	12
Validity of selection techniques						
Studies being conducted............	6	18	18	27	4	13
Studies conducted previously........	9	21	9	14	13	13
Impact of employee publications or other communications media						
Studies being conducted............	6	9	5	5	8	7
Studies conducted previously........	3	12	18	19	4	10
No personnel research studies reported	71	42	36	41	60	52

Source: Reprinted by special permission from *Bulletin to Management*, copyright 1979, by The Bureau of National Affairs, Inc., Washington, D.C.

training and development, 20 percent on appraisal, 18 percent on motivation, 16 percent on organizational effectiveness, and 10 percent on other subjects, including counseling.[16]

Table 20-3 shows the effects of EEO/AA on personnel research. Three of the top four subjects being studied deal with it.

While these are the areas actually being researched, what are the fields needing more research? One study of personnel executives found that their estimates of research needs were (1) selection of minority groups, (2) placing and training the disadvantaged, (3) turnover, (4) evaluation and training and development, (5) performance appraisal, and (6) opinion surveys.[17]

Methods Used

As indicated earlier, there are many methods used. First, the method actually selected will depend on the degree of *realism* sought. If this is desired, then some form of field research such as *surveys, field experiments,* or *case studies* will be used because of their natural and regular conditions and realistic setting.

Second, the *scope* of the research will determine the method used. The field research mentioned is broader in scope, for it permits researchers to measure many factors that might be missing in a laboratory setting.

The degree of *precision* required also influences the choice of methods. Laboratory research ordinarily is more precise in measurement than is typically possible in the field. The use of multiple observations and repeated measurements allows the researcher to obtain more accurate information about the variables being studied.

The degree of *control* also influences the method used. In the laboratory, researchers have much greater control over what happens, whereas in the field there are many disruptive factors.

Evaluating Personnel Research

Very little research has been done to evaluate personnel research. However, what has been done indicates that personnel research, so far, has had very little significant impact on top management. Also, it is estimated that as few as 15 corporations actually use their research facilities as fully as they could.[18]

---

[16]W. C. Byham, *The Uses of Personnel Research*, Research Study no. 91 (New York: American Management Association, 1968).

[17]Dean Berry, *The Politics of Personnel Research* (Ann Arbor: University of Michigan, Bureau of Industrial Relations, 1967).

[18]Byham, *The Uses of Personnel Research.*

EVALUATING PERSONNEL PROGRAMS

This text has stressed the importance of establishing objective plans, policies, and procedures that will lead to effective personnel programs. Yet these actions will not necessarily give effective results. Instead, they must be evaluated periodically to see that satisfactory results are being obtained. This is called a *personnel audit* or *evaluation of the personnel function.*

The *personnel audit* is a systematic, formal procedure used to measure the costs and benefits of the total personnel program and to compare its efficiency and effectiveness with the organization's objectives and past performance, as well as the performance of similar effective organizations.

Purposes of Evaluation

Personnel audits are done to (1) justify, or increase, the department's budget, (2) improve the personnel function by providing a method for deciding when to add new programs or to drop old activities, (3) provide feedback from employees and operating departments on how effectively personnel is performing, (4) help personnel to do its part to achieve the organization's objectives, and (5) evaluate progress in meeting EEO/AA goals.

In general, the evaluation of a personnel program will often provide the basis for making improvements in it. Successful personnel managers are able to familiarize themselves with the practices of other organizations and with the findings from studies conducted by professionals. The results of research studies are so widely publicized through journals, special reports, and professional meetings that information to improve personnel practices is available to anyone who is interested. Therefore, personnel managers should utilize findings from personnel research studies, as well as information obtained from appraisals of their own programs, to improve those programs.

Sources of Information for Evaluation

Personnel managers are often surprised at the great amount of data available from existing records. Some of these are (1) personnel budgets, (2) recruitment cost data, (3) employment interview records, (4) transfer requests, (5) EEO/AA complaints, (6) training and development cost figures, (7) accident records, (8) performance evaluation records, (9) production records, (10) data on wages, salaries, and benefits, (11) wage survey records, (12) unemployment compensation data, (13) grievance records, (14) attitude survey results, (15) turnover records, (16) absenteeism records, and (17) injury and illness reports and OSHA inspection reports.

In addition, special surveys can generate even more data.

Methods of Evaluation

According to a recent survey, four out of five of BNA's Personnel Policy Forum members periodically evaluate the effectiveness of their personnel programs.

As you can see from Table 20-4, they use many and varied methods of appraisal. The method most often used is comparison of actual results against established goals—including MBO. Periodic audits, surveys, meetings, discussions, and interviews are quite effective in correcting problem areas, as they tend to discover the *cause* of problems. The more statistical analyses can tell the extent of a problem but not its cause.

Comparison with other employers.   As shown throughout the book, personnel managers can compare the results of their activities with other employers in the area or industry. This can be done for such functions as safety and health (Chapter 14), compensation (Chapter 15), benefits (Chapter 17), and industrial relations (Chapters 18 and 19).

Using checklists.   The personnel department—or a consultant—can prepare a list of important personnel activities to be performed. The checklist usually requires the analyst to check "yes" or "no" beside the listed activity. The list may also include items designed to see whether existing personnel policies are being followed or activities performed. The items on the checklist

TABLE 20-4
Personnel evaluation methods used by members of BNA's Personnel Policies Forum

	Percentage of companies°		
	Total	Larger	Smaller
Evaluating departmental results against goals..................	33†	37	23
Periodic audit of policies, procedures...................	25	25	26
Surveys, meetings, discussions, and interviews	20	19	23
Analysis of turnover figures	16	15	19
Analysis of grievances...........	8	9	10
Analysis of cost of performing various personnel functions	6	7	5
Analysis of training effectiveness...	5	5	5
Analysis of accident frequency	5	6	4
Feedback from managers.........	5	5	5

°Figures total more than 100 percent because most companies used more than one method.
†Includes 7 percent of companies specifying an MBO program for the personnel department.
Source: *Labor Policy and Practice—Personnel Management* (Washington, D.C.: The Bureau of National Affairs, Inc., 1975), pp. 201-2.

are usually grouped by personnel functions, such as personnel planning, career management, or safety and health.

A checklist is a very simple and elementary approach to evaluation. While checklists do provide a format that is relatively easy to prepare and record, interpretation is quite difficult. About one out of five employers with formal audits uses the checklist approach.

Using statistical methods.   The statistical methods of examining and analyzing the organization's employment data are the most frequently used and most effective means of doing personnel audits. This approach is much more sophisticated and lends itself to greater analysis than other methods.

Using management by objectives.   MBO is now being used by personnel managers for many personnel functions, such as training and development and employee evaluation. It also promises to be a very effective method of evaluating the overall personnel program.

EEO/AA audits.   As shown throughout this text, EEO/AA are requiring special attention from personnel managers, including periodic audits.

Employers must maintain records for these programs in specified formats for examination by compliance investigators. Also, many employers have learned to keep current as much information as possible about past EEO/AA performance in order to avoid last-minute crises in data-gathering projects.

Figure 20–1 shows how Citibank, one of America's largest banks, performs this audit. The audit begins with identifying the crucial personnel areas to be audited. Then the bank randomly chooses branch banks to be studied. The audit procedure follows the diagram shown in the figure. The review is conducted by a personnel practices review unit, which audits all branches every year.

Bank personnel believe the audit has substantially improved its personnel program.

What Is Evaluated?

Statistical analyses can be done with many sets of data that serve as indicators of personnel effectiveness. The most popular ones are (1) complaints and grievances, (2) illnesses and injuries, (3) absences, and (4) turnover.

Complaints and grievances.   Data on complaints and grievances provide a basis for evaluating how well personnel management is meeting its objectives. While these are not the direct responsibility of the personnel department, they do reflect failures on the part of line supervision. Thus, an analysis of the number and type of grievances may suggest ways of improving the personnel program.

Illnesses and injuries.   The safety and health records mentioned in Chapter 14 provide a basis for studying the physical (and psychological) environment in which personnel work is performed. They may indicate failures in personnel programs, such as training and development.

FIGURE 20-1
Personnel compliance audit process at Citibank

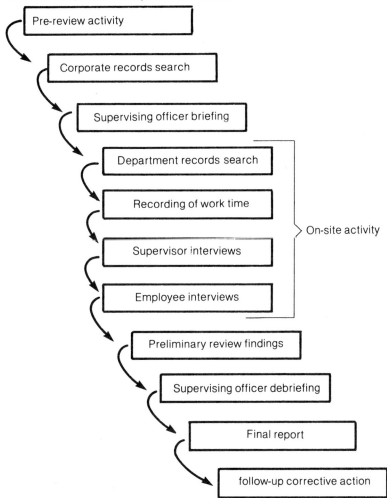

Source: Paul Sheibar, "Personnel Practices Review: A Personnel Audit Activity," *Personnel Journal* 53 (March 1974):213.

Absenteeism.   The term *absenteeism*, as used by the Labor Department, is the failure of employees to report for work as scheduled, whether such failure is excused or not. Scheduled absences, such as vacations, holidays, and leaves of absence, are not counted as job absence.

Management tries to reduce absenteeism because of its costs and the operating problems it causes. Costs to the employer include (1) the costs of benefits, which continue even when workers are absent, (2) overtime pay, which may be necessary for the worker who is doing the job for the missing worker, (3) underutilization of facilities, and (4) production drops due to understaffing.

There may also be increased break-in costs for replacements, substandard production, a need for more help from supervisors and peers, and increased inspection costs.

How absence rate is computed.   The standard formula recommended by government bodies and used by over 70 percent of those who compute absenteeism is:

$$\frac{\text{Number of worker days lost through}}{\text{Average number of employees} \times \text{Number of workdays}} \times 100$$

Thus, if 400 worker days are lost in a month with 22 workdays, through absences at an organization that employs 800 workers, the *absence rate* is:

$$[400/(800 \times 22)] \times 100 = 2.27 \text{ percent}$$

Most employers calculate absenteeism rates on a monthly basis. Some compute it annually. Most employers compute it by department or division. Most also separate long-term absences from short-term ones.

Research studies raise questions about the use of absence rates, especially aggregate measures of absenteeism, to appraise the personnel function. Some people even suggest abandoning the measure. It is more useful to pursue research designed to identify absence-prone persons, work groups, working conditions, and communities, with a view to designing strategies to reduce absenteeism. When this is done, management can concentrate on workers with high absence rates. Action can then be taken to improve health, if the cause appears to be illness; or, if health is not a factor, counseling, discipline, and so on can be used.

Comparing absence rates with other employers.   BNA's quarterly *Bulletin to Management* uses the above formula to report average monthly (and annual) absence rates by region, industry, and size of employer. Therefore, personnel managers can compare their rates with those of comparable organizations—as well as with their own past experience.

Turnover.   The term *turnover rate* refers to the extent of movement of employees in and out of an organization. Current and past turnover rates for a department or an organization can be important indicators of the efficiency with which the personnel function is performed by operating managers and supervisors, as well as by the personnel department.

Computing turnover rates.   The Department of Labor uses the following formula for computing turnover rates:

$$\frac{\text{Number of separations during the month}}{\text{Total number of employees at mid-month}} \times 100$$

If there were 32 separations during a given month, and the total number of employees at mid-month was 800, then the turnover rate would be:

$$(32/800) \times 100 = 4 \text{ percent.}$$

Over half of all employers figure turnover rates by this formula. Most other employers use a similar method that results in figures similar to those based on the above formula. Separate rates may be computed for different departments or divisions of an organization. Separate rates may also be computed for different types of turnover such as quits, discharges, deaths, retirements, layoffs, and transfers, or for avoidable and unavoidable separations.

Unavoidable separations include illness, death, marriage, transfers, promotions, and termination of temporary employment. If these are subtracted from all separations, the remainder is the number that are avoidable. These are the ones personnel managers should concentrate on reducing.

Comparing turnover rates with other employers.   BNA reports median turnover rates by region, industry, and size of organization. Therefore, personnel managers can make comparisons with similar institutions. During the last three years, the highest rates have been in the finance industry, in the West, and in smaller companies.

Taking Corrective Action

The evaluation of the personnel function is of little use unless the results are used to correct deficiencies in the personnel program. Analysis of the data may indicate that procedures for carrying out some of the personnel functions need revision. It is even possible that whole programs need revision if they are to meet the objectives that have been established for them. Finally, policies for each of the personnel functions should be examined to see if they are adding to the effectiveness of the entire personnel program.

SUMMARY AND CONCLUSIONS

Some of the trends and problems facing personnel managers of the future have been presented in this chapter. It has been shown that performing the personnel function will be very much more difficult and complex—but more challenging and rewarding. It will demand more capable managerial personnel because more highly educated, skilled, and developed employees will be supervised. Personnel executives will need more scientific and technical knowledge themselves in order to operate more effectively. Also, new horizons for performing service to the organization, employees, and society will become available.

The role of personnel research, some research methodologies, and uses of research were discussed. It was shown that future personnel people must do more meaningful research if they are to be effective.

The need to evaluate the overall personnel program, some methods of doing the evaluating, and some measures of effectiveness were discussed. It was concluded that evaluation is useless unless corrective action is taken.

How the factors in the environment in which personnel is performed will be, or should be, handled is the question now facing us. Perhaps we'll become so efficient that the necessary jobs individuals must perform will occupy such a small percentage of their time that finding fulfillment and satisfaction through work will dwindle in importance, and leisure-time satisfaction will become the main objective. Until such a time arrives, personnel executives must continue to harmonize individual needs with organizational needs. This has never been an easy task nor does it appear that it will be in the future.

Herein lies the challenge of managing personnel and human resources—to deliberately shape and enhance management knowledge so that it will prove most useful to all in the modern, postindustrial society.

QUESTIONS

1. What is your estimate of the future of personnel management? Try to show where you differ with the author in his projections.

2. To the best of your knowledge, have any of his predictions proven to be erroneous? Explain.

3. Has the need for personnel research been overestimated? Explain.

4. Are the evaluation procedures discussed really feasible in an ongoing personnel program? Explain.

SUGGESTED READINGS FOR FURTHER STUDY

Brown, Barry. "Pinpointing Your Personnel Problems." *Personnel Administrator* 24 (January 1979):26–28.

"Challenges of the '80s." *U.S. News & World Report*, October 15, 1979, pp. 45–80.

Lorber, Lawrence. "Job Segregation and Wage Discrimination under Title VII and the Equal Pay Act." *Personnel Administrator* 25 (May 1980):31–34.

Odiorne, George S. "Personnel Management for the '80s." *Personnel Administrator* 24 (December 1979):77–80.

Rieder, George A. "The Role of Tomorrow's Manager." *Personnel Administrator* 24 (December 1979):27–31.

Schiavoni, Michael R. "Employee Relations: Where Will It Be in 1985?" *Personnel Administrator* 23 (March 1978):25–29.

Short, Larry L. "Now You Can Micro-Computerize Your Personnel System." *Personnel Journal* 58 (March 1979):154–56.

Turner, Ian. "Chips with Everything—How New Technology Affects You . . . in Personnel." *Personnel Management* 11 (June 1979):34–36.

Werther, William B., Jr. "Management Turnover: Implications of Career Mobility." *Personnel Administrator* 22 (February 1977):63–66.

Zechar, Dale. "Personnel Odyssey 2002." *Personnel Administrator* 22 (August 1977):30–32, 63.

PART SEVEN

Cases for Applying What You Have Learned

CASE 1. OK! WHO'S PASSING THE BUCK?*

EXECUTIVE VICE PRESIDENT: Good morning! As you know, the purpose of this staff meeting is to get on top of some of our *supervision and management* problems. You've all had time to look into the situation insofar as your respective divisions are concerned, so you should be prepared to discuss the problems and recommendations for resolving them. Let it all hang out, as they say, and tell it like it is! Joe?†

MANUFACTURING: Well, we're still having problems with *orientation*. Personnel is doing a pretty fair job of orienting new employees to the company, but our new people are not being oriented to the manufacturing division. I think personnel should develop, schedule, and conduct orientation sessions designed specifically for manufacturing employees.

TRANSPORTATION: I agree with Joe. We need a similar program for transportation personnel.

TREASURER: Me too.

BUDGET: Same here.

INDUSTRIAL RELATIONS: Why not have personnel assume responsibility for orienting all new employees to all units at all levels of the company organization?

ENGINEERING: We'll buy that.

MARKETING: We're not on top of the *employee suggestion and awards program*. Marketing hasn't received an employee suggestion or presented an award since 1965! We think personnel should come up with some meaningful direction and guidance to encourage more use of the program.

RESEARCH AND DEVELOPMENT: It seems to me that personnel isn't fully involved in the area of *disciplinary actions*. We have three potential and two active cases in R&D now and personnel hasn't made a move to step in and take over. We think they should be more aggressive in matters of this kind.

ENGINEERING: Our *safety and accident prevention* program is a complete flop! Perhaps if personnel prepared a detailed safety plan for each of our divisions . . .

PLANNING: And conducted safety meetings, at least weekly, for all personnel . . .

ENGINEERING: . . . we could improve our accident record.

MANUFACTURING: I wonder if personnel couldn't do a better job of *employee counseling*. Our employees are continually complaining about the lack of counseling, and

---

*R. C. Burkholder, "As You Were Saying—OK! Who's Passing the Buck?" *Personnel Journal* 51 (November 1972):846–47. Reprinted with permission, *Personnel Journal*, copyright © November 1972.

†The names of most organizations and persons mentioned in the cases in this book are fictitious, although the organizations, persons, and situations are real.

our supervisors and foremen simply don't have the time to do it. I believe personnel should assume full responsibility for all employee counseling.

PURCHASING: Something has to be done about *job descriptions!* I'm not exaggerating when I say that at least 80 percent of our employees in purchasing are operating under outdated or inaccurate job descriptions. I'd like to suggest that personnel schedule some time to review, analyze, and update each and every employee's job description as soon as possible.

TREASURER: Our biggest problem has to do with *performance standards and evaluation.* Personnel hasn't established performance standards or evaluated the performance of our employees since I don't know when. Don't you think they should provide this service at least once a year?

PUBLIC RELATIONS: I think one of our major problems lies in the area of *directing and coordinating* our efforts and activities. The old left hand and right hand, you know. We'd like to see personnel look into the situation—across the board— and come up with some proposals for our people to work with.

BUDGET: I agree with PR, but our people simply don't or won't *communicate*—internally *or* externally—and I think personnel should do something about it.

TRANSPORTATION: How do you fellows feel about *delegation?* Some of our people in transportation delegate too much; others don't delegate at all. I'd like to make a recommendation that personnel see to it that our employees delegate properly and effectively.

LEGAL: I don't know if this is a matter of recruitment, orientation, or training, but I think personnel will have to do something about the fact that too many of our people lack the necessary education, background, experience, or inclination to make good and valid decisions. *Decision making* is . . .

MARKETING: Speaking of *training*, our people are being overtrained. Train, train, train! I'm always approving the attendance of marketing personnel at some kind of training session or other! Why can't personnel establish quotas . . . or something?

PLANNING: Our people aren't getting enough training, and I think employee morale, along with work performance, is suffering as a result. We think personnel should see to it that planning people are included in more in- and out-of-company training sessions.

INDUSTRIAL RELATIONS: We're getting plenty of training, but it's not always the right kind . . . or the wrong people got it . . . or it wasn't needed in the first place . . . or . . .

ENGINEERING: I agree with industrial relations.

PURCHASING: What did he say?

RESEARCH AND DEVELOPMENT: I don't know, but doesn't personnel have the responsibility for determining who needs what training and how, when, and where to get it?

MANUFACTURING: I'd like to suggest that personnel develop a company program which will provide all employees with the scientific, technical, administrative, and clerical training they need—no more, no less.

EXECUTIVE VICE PRESIDENT: You getting all this, Harvey?

PERSONNEL: Yes, sir. I'll put my staff on it first thing in the morning.

Questions

1. What does the case show about the overexpectations other managers sometimes have of the personnel officer and staff?
2. If you were the personnel officer, how would you begin ("first thing in the morning") to implement the suggestions made?
3. What order of priorities would you set up?
4. What assistance would you request from the line managers?

CASE 2. THE NEW WORK FORCE

Tom Jackson, personnel officer in one of Trappy Oil Company's refineries, sat reviewing his just completed meeting with Bob Jay, who had recently been promoted to the position of department head.

Bob had received an M.S. degree in chemical engineering from one of the state colleges seven years earlier. Since joining Trappy, he had progressed rapidly in the plant and had successfully performed jobs of increasing responsibilities. In his new position, his primary responsibility involved the operation, maintenance, and safety of a number of the processing units of the plant. There were about 15 other engineers, around 155 unit operators and mechanical craftsmen, and 15 first-line supervisors in the department.

Bob had been in his new job less than a week when Bill Lockey, first-line supervisor of one of the units, came in to see him about a "personnel" problem. The supervisor, who was obviously upset, told Bob that he was fed up with the people that the company was hiring for him to run his part of the plant. Bill angrily stated that, "If the company gives me one more college graduate to do our job, I can't guarantee the safety and operation of my unit. That damn Jones you gave me last week failed to check the meters last night, and we have run all day making off-spec product. We're lucky to be here today."

Bob was surprised. As he had not worked closely with Bill before, he did not know exactly what weight to place on his comments in view of the nature of the outburst. He asked Bill to write up the incident for him, and he would review it and decide what action should be taken about it. Bill agreed and stormed out of Bob's office.

Bob had scheduled conferences with each of his first-line supervisors to discuss their feelings about the "new work force." He received widely varying opinions on the worth of the new group, ranging from "They are lazy and never had to work a day in their life" to "They have done things in better ways than we have done them before." Bob had talked to a number of his fellow department heads about the new workers and had also received from them quite varied opinions on the effectiveness of the "new work force."

Bob did not have the responsibility for selecting potential new employees, as this task was done by the personnel officer. However, in his new position, he would be responsible for actually selecting any new employees he might need from a list of "qualified" applicants furnished by the personnel department. So he decided to call the personnel officer to discuss the firm's hiring policies.

Tom Jackson had told Bob that in the last few years the company had undertaken a fairly intensive hiring plan in the plant. This was due to the large number of operators and mechanical craftsmen who were retiring. During World War II, Trappy had greatly expanded its work force—as had all the other refineries. Following the war, there were some layoffs, but most of the employees hired during the war were retained as a matter of company policy. The "overstaffing" resulting from that policy—plus automation in the industry—resulted in a 25- to 30-year period during which employees who quit, were fired, or retired were not replaced.

"Now," said the personnel oficer, "this group of employees is reaching the age where they can take early retirement. Many new people are having to be hired and trained in a short period of time."

Bob also learned from the personnel officer that about 65 percent of the firm's process and mechanical employees had been replaced during the last four years—primarily because of retirements. However, nearly a third of the new employees who had two years experience had quit or been fired. The most surprising statistic was that the average education level of the new employees was about three years of college. Many of them had degrees, primarily in education, the social sciences, and biological sciences. The statistics also showed that the pay of the blue-collar workers in the refinery was significantly higher than the pay in the professional fields of most of the graduates.

Questions

1. How do you explain the trends in the refinery?
2. What does the case show about the historical development of personnel management?
3. What does it show about the new work environment?
4. What does it show about the effects of technological development?
5. What would you do now if you were the personnel officer?

CASE 3. TO DO OR NOT TO DO?

The AAA Corporation was a large national chemical company. The company's research department was located at one of its manufacturing locations on the East coast. The department, charged with the responsibility for providing the new technology needed to stay competitive in that rapidly changing industry, had about 300 employees, 80 of whom were professional employees with degrees in either chemical engineering or chemistry.

The company's employee relations department did all the on-campus recruiting for the company, including the research department. Any department needing personnel would then screen the application blanks, academic records, and interview reports of employment prospects that recruiters had interviewed on the college campuses and choose the individuals it wanted to hire. Because of the high standard of technical expertise that the research department maintained, it made the decision on which candidates to invite to visit the department for further evaluation. During the visit, each candidate was interviewed by at least four of the professionals, including a young engineer, a more experienced technical expert, a middle-level manager, and one of the four top managers in the department. Based upon these interviews, the applicants' academic records, their experience level, and the quality of the colleges involved, a decision was made that the candidates were either "qualified" or "not qualified" for the type of work to be done. If a candidate was rated as "outstanding," an offer of employment was made during the visit. Otherwise, offers of employment were made only after reviewing and comparing the evaluations of all the candidates that had visited the department.

The department had a reputation as a top scientific organization because of its record of technical accomplishments during its 30 years of existence. Its top management was "very proud of this record and the reputation for technical excellence that the department enjoys." The manager of the department, Bob Jones, and his three assistants, Fred Smith, Jay Lord, and Bill Shaw, attributed the success in part to "the policy of recruiting only top technical people from highly rated schools."

Although the size of the technical staff in the department had stayed fairly constant at about 80 for a number of years, the department usually hired three to five new technical personnel each year to replace those employees that had transferred to other parts of the company, who retired, or had left the company. Last year the department needed to hire four chemical engineers.

According to the employee relations manager, "The company has been very active over the last few years in recruiting and hiring female employees." It had an aggressive and successful AAP, as it did a lot of business with the government. The manufacturing plant (where the research department was located) had been successful in meeting affirmative action goals recruiting both professional and nonprofessional female employees. The research department had also been very successful in hiring qualified women in the nonprofessional jobs. However, the department to date has not been able to hire a female engineer or chemist. They have no women in the total professional staff of 80.

"Recruiting female professionals has been a difficult task as the national proportion of female chemical engineers, the primary degree required in the department, is less than 2 percent. Based upon this fact, we have set a goal of eventually hiring at least two female professionals, with a goal of hiring at least one this year."

Overall, the company was meeting its goals—which had been established in compliance with the laws—of hiring women; so the research department was not receiving pressure from the government on its deficiency of women professionals. However, Bob Jones was receiving pressure from the company's employee relations manager to hire a female professional. Actually the department had made employment offers to two female chemical engineers in each of the last two years, but both had declined the offers. In fact, one of those two had accepted employment with another department of the firm. The four candidates who had received the job offers were "outstandingly qualified," and the competition for their employment had been intense.

This year, in seeking four new chemical engineers, Bob had invited 25 candidates, including five females, to visit the plant. Several of the women did not appear to be qualified—based on their campus evaluations alone—but Bob had invited them anyway to get a better personal evaluation of their qualifications.

Three of the current candidates—all males—had been rated as "outstanding" and were offered jobs during their visit. All three had accepted the offers. Of the other 22 applicants, seven—including one female, Betty Craig, a senior at a small engineering school in the Midwest—had been evaluated as being "qualified" for employment in the department. Betty was ranked fourth out of the seven.

At that time, Bob called a meeting of his three assistants and the employee relations manager to discuss their views on what action should be taken in filling the other vacancy. With only one opening left, the normal procedure would have been to offer the job to the candidate who had the next highest evaluation. However, because of the conflict between their normal, seemingly objective, procedure and their desire to hire a woman professional, Bob wanted to get their advice before making his decision. Betty had been interviewed by Bob when she visited and had indicated that she would accept a job in the department if it were offered. So Bob knew that he had a certainty of fulfilling his affirmative action goal if he decided to offer her the job.

Fred Smith, who had been in the department since it was formed 30 years ago, thought that Betty should not get the next offer. If the next three applicants turned down the offer, then he agreed that Betty should get the job. He pointed out that the success of the department and the company had been "based on the high degree of technical expertise that the department has maintained—and that goal should override the affirmative action goal. Thus, the offer should be made to the person who has been objectively judged as being the best qualified of the remaining possibilities. Otherwise, the company will be practicing 'reverse discrimination.' "

Jay Lord, recently promoted into his job, recommended that Betty be given the job as she had been "evaluated as meeting the qualifications and thus could not jeopardize our technical reputation. Also, our evaluation procedure should be changed as it is biased in favor of men and is not distinctive enough to select between candidates rated so close."

The third assistant manager, Bill Shaw, agreed that Betty was qualified, but he concurred with Fred that the three people over her on the list of qualified applicants should be offered the position first. He also expressed a concern that to hire a person near the bottom of the qualified list might cause some future risk of an unusual nature. "If she does not turn out to be a good performer, we might have great difficulty in releasing her as the only female professional in the department. On the other hand, one of the male applicants would pose no problem in releasing if he should happen not to perform satisfactorily." He recommended that they wait and try to hire a woman who was clearly "outstanding" from a well-established college to minimize this problem. He knew that they had been unsuccessful in doing that in the past but suggested that they make an unusually high salary offer to the next clearly outstanding female applicant to ensure their success.

Bob was quiet through most of the discussion. He was in agreement to some extent with both the pros and cons presented but knew that he would have to make the decision himself considering the effect on the company, the department, and the applicants involved, as well as the effect on his career.

Questions

1. Evaluate the firm's recruiting procedure.
2. Would you propose any changes in it? Explain.
3. Discuss the validity of the arguments made by each of the three assistant managers.
4. How would you resolve the apparent conflict of goals imposed by different parts of the company?
5. Do you think the procedure used for selecting professional employees is a fair method? If not, how would you change it?
6. What concepts about female employees surface in the case?
7. Assuming that you are the employee relations manager, propose a solution and defend it.

CASE 4. AFFIRMATIVE ACTION IN THEORY AND IN PRACTICE*

The Apex plant, an operating facility of Petrochem Corporation, was one of many plants operating as part of the petrochemical complex of the Gulf coastal region. Much of the industrial growth in this region was relatively recent so Apex, like many other plants in this area, was a modern growth-oriented facility.

The Firm's Affirmative Action Plan: Background

During recent years, Petrochem Corporation had taken a firm stand as an "equal opportunity employer," and Apex was working under an affirmative action plan (AAP) with the goal of achieving within five years a work force mixture which matched that of the recruiting area in both ethnic background and sex.

To achieve this work force distribution at both the exempt and nonexempt levels while maintaining its basic entry standards, Apex recruited extensively at black universities and vocational schools. The plant also maintained close contact with other state universities, private employment agencies, the state employment agency, local high schools, and various civic and community groups. However, the prime source of both minority and female applicants had been, and continued to be, referrals by the Apex plant employees themselves.

Although the plant had considered offering training courses for applicants who fell below minimum standards, this approach had been avoided since previous experience had shown that job applicants tended to view acceptance into the training courses as tantamount to a job offer. However, the plant had worked through the local school board in providing various cooperative and adult education courses. The plant also maintained an active summer hiring program which was used to identify potential minority group employees.

Apex's in-house program for minority groups consisted of compiling a work history for each minority group member and then assessing promotional potential. Additional training needed, as well as potential openings, were identified. Any time openings actually did develop, the affirmative action list was reviewed for potential candidates.

All AAPs were reviewed and updated on a quarterly basis. First-line supervisors were responsible for individual training and development while upper-level management scrutinized departmental compliance with the goals set.

---

*Prepared by Linda Calvert, University of Houston, Clear Lake.

The Affirmative Action Plan: Application

When Charles Gunn, age 22, was hired, he was the third black technician to be employed in the Alpha unit. Carl Myers, the first black hired, was then supervisor of D shift; the second black hired, Henry Sherman, was a technician on C shift. Exhibit 1 gives a partial organizational structure for the Alpha unit.

Prior to joining Petrochem, Charles had completed three years in the U.S. Army as a radio operator. He had entered the military immediately after high school because he figured his low C average in high school would not be sufficient to see him through college.

The personnel manager placed Charles on the A shift of the Alpha unit with Raymond Crane as his supervisor and Warren Sayles, another technician, as his "trainer." Raymond had been hired three years earlier as a technician immediately after he finished college. With his strong technical background, he had "done extremely well" and two years later was promoted to supervisor—six months before Charles was hired.

Warren, the trainer for A shift, had had about three years of college and was unquestionably the best technician on that particular shift. When Warren found out that he would be training Charles, he expressed some "apprehensions about training a black," since he had never worked side by side with a black before. However, he had trained several other technicians and said he would do his best.

When Charles reported to Alpha unit, Raymond introduced him to the other technicians, showed him his locker, gave him some study guides, and turned him over to Warren. (The study guides were basically a list of questions which the trainees should be able to answer once they had learned the unit operations from the trainer.)

Since Charles Gunn, the new technician, was told to spend this training period "in his trainer's back pocket," Warren and Charles were almost inseparable for the next five months. Charles asked questions; Warren answered. They went over the extractive and recovery systems, schematics of the pro-

EXHIBIT 1

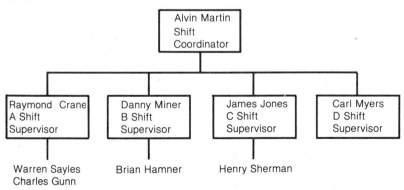

cess, start-up and shut-down procedures, reading and sampling methods, and procedures for logging information.

About once a month Warren and Charles sat down to evaluate the progress Charles was making. In the first of these sessions, Warren noted that Charles was not making any progress at all. After two or three months, Warren noted slight—but not satisfactory—progress.

After five months, Charles was still only taking samples, a procedure normally picked up in the first few weeks of training. Warren felt that Charles was not putting forth the effort needed to learn the job. Charles agreed that he needed to improve but did not agree that he was not putting forth satisfactory effort. The reports passed along to Raymond during this period reflected Warren's evaluation of Charles but did not contain any of Charles's reactions.

About six months after Charles had started to work, Warren went on vacation. Although supervisors normally assign a trainee to someone else if their trainer goes on vacation, Raymond neglected to make such a reassignment for Charles.

Meanwhile Henry Sherman, the other black technician, had been placed on temporary duty with A shift, and, thus, "Charles gravitated rather naturally to Henry." It was during this period that Charles began to grasp just how far behind the other technicians he really was. However, with Henry using simplified examples and then applying them to the unit processes, Charles began to grasp things that had completely escaped him before. By the end of a week, Charles understood the extractive process of the unit—the most difficult part of the unit to learn.

Within a couple of days after Warren returned from vacation, Warren and Charles again sat down for an evaluation session and again Warren reiterated Charles's lack of progress. But Charles was not satisfied this time. For the next few days he thought things over and asked questions of the other technicians to make sure that he really did understand the extractive process. Finally, he went back to Warren, and, at the end of Warren's first week back from vacation, they held their first meeting with Raymond.

Charles felt that he understood the extractive process of the unit, but Warren did not agree. The session boiled down to bickering and was finally brought to a close with Raymond's nonchalant, "You guys will just have to work this thing out yourselves."

Things simmered along for the next three or four days with Charles still dissatisfied but uncertain about what to do next. Things came to a head the next Monday morning when Alvin Martin, the shift coordinator, ran into Charles. Since Alvin rarely saw the technicians, he tried to use any chance meeting with them to get a quick reading on "the mood of the troops."

Alvin's question, "How are things going?" was all Charles needed to pour out his frustrations.

Alvin reacted by immediately setting up a meeting with Raymond and Charles. In this meeting Raymond stated that Charles was at best "a marginal performer" or perhaps even "a slow learner." Charles countered with charges of discrimination in his training. Raymond came back with the fact that if

Charles had, indeed, learned the extractive process of the unit, then he must have been getting proper training. Not willing to back down, Charles explained that Henry had taught him this particular part of the unit while Warren was on vacation.

Charles left the meeting with the understanding that his performance was, in fact, deficient in several areas, and he would need to work on these things. Alvin and Raymond then continued "hot and heavy" for the next several hours.

Charles had told a story "heavily steeped in racial overtones." Though he admitted that Warren had answered all his questions without irritation, Charles felt that Warren had not volunteered as much information as he had to the other technicians. (Later talks with the other technicians tended to confirm this statement.)

At that point, though, the hostilities were pretty firmly entrenched, and Alvin felt that a change had to be made—but what? Since Henry had proven that Charles could learn, and since Charles worked well with Henry, a move to C shift was pretty tempting. Or, there was D shift, run by Carl Myers, the only black supervisor.

Alvin finally decided that moving Charles to C or to D shift was simply an easy way out and represented, at best, a temporary solution. Charles was transferred to B shift.

Charles's new supervisor was Danny Miner, who had a two-year technical degree and had taught mathematics and drawing at a vocational-technical college. Danny had worked around blacks on a "give-and-take" basis nearly all of his life and had no real apprehensions about Charles joining his shift. On Charles's first day, Danny sat down and explained what he expected of Charles, and what Charles could expect from him.

During that week, he and Charles did what is known as a "walk through" of the unit. Starting at the front door and going to the back door, Danny and Charles went through the unit with Charles explaining everything that he could about the unit. Danny could see Charles had a lot of problems but that he did understand the extractive process—again the most difficult part of the unit's work.

Danny continued to ask questions and listen. He used Carl as a sounding board—trying to find out more about Charles, trying to find the best way to work with him. In his conversations with the new employee, Danny soon found out that he had only taken General Math and Algebra I in high school, had made a D in chemistry, and had avoided physics.

In the military service, Charles had had problems when he started in the school for radio operators, but he eventually caught up and did well. Danny concluded that Charles could learn but simply had to be brought along more slowly than the other technicians.

After the first week, Danny decided to turn Charles over to Brian Hamner for training. Brian was not "the best technician in the unit," according to the personnel manager. In fact, he was average in just about every sense of the word. He was methodical—neither too fast nor too slow. He was dependable, somewhat of a stickler for detail, and had plenty of patience.

Although this assignment worked out well, there was some subsequent talk of rotating Charles to other technicians to improve his technical skills. However, the decision was made to work with both Brian and Charles on technical skills rather than singling Charles out for special training.

After four years, Charles was "not considered supervisory material," according to the personnel manager, but he was an "average" to "above average" performer and was taking some correspondence courses to upgrade his technical skills.

Questions

1. Evaluate Apex's affirmative action plan.
2. Was Charles properly placed? Explain.
3. What does this case illustrate about the problems of developing minority employees?
4. (*a*) Evaluate the training program set up for Charles. (*b*) How could it have been improved?
5. How do you explain Raymond's attitude?
6. Why work with both Brian and Charles instead of "singling" Charles out for special training?
7. Evaluate the way Danny handled Charles.
8. What would you suggest doing now, if you were the personnel manager?

CASE 5. A CHALLENGING JOB*

Data Systems Management, Incorporated (DSM), was formed 12 years ago in a major U.S. city. The company grew slowly for two years, but then revenues doubled each year for the next six years. DSM was principally engaged in designing complete electronic data processing systems for corporate customers and then installing and operating the systems. The firm effectively became the customer's data processing department under long-term contracts of five to eight years. At the time of this case, the company employed over 1,000 people, with approximately 70 percent of them being systems engineers.

Recruiting and Interviewing

The firm's recruiting policy was to bring in either fully qualified systems engineers—who also possessed management and leadership capabilities—or to

---

*Prepared by James Donald Powell, North Texas State University.

hire individuals who had these qualities and the aptitude to become competent systems engineers.

Lee Williams was attracted to the company by its reputation for high-caliber personnel, by the glamour of the computer field, and an ad in the largest daily newspaper in the firm's home city. (See Exhibit 1.) Williams was a veteran of seven years in the U.S. Air Force and had an MBA from a large midwestern university.

EXHIBIT 1
DSM's employment advertisement

DSM is a young, growing, successful computer company that can offer you an outstanding business opportunity NOW. DSM is interested in individuals that are skilled in *or meet the qualifications to be trained in:*

1. Commercial systems design and programming.
2. Computer operations.
3. Recruiting.

DSM needs men and women who are willing to do whatever it takes, as long as it is fair and honest, to get the job done. *You must be flexible in your working hours and be willing to travel and relocate.*

DSM is a great environment for men and women with leadership experience and maturity who are trustworthy, unselfish, results-oriented, self-reliant, and have a record of success. Your future at DSM is limited only by your ability.

After completing and mailing a detailed application form and biographical questionnaire, Williams was visited by a recruiter from the firm's personnel office, who, although she had been with DSM only two weeks, was very adept at answering William's questions about the firm. After a two-hour interview and the completion of a 30-minute computer programming aptitude test, Williams was told that he had passed the first hurdle and would be flown to company headquarters for a "team interview."

That interview was conducted by three systems engineers and the personnel manager, who questioned Williams for approximately three hours about virtually all facets of his background or personality that might bear on his success with the company, including his aspirations, successes, failures, and self-doubts. At the conclusion of this interview, Williams was introduced to Morton Benson, head of DSM's systems engineer trainee program, who questioned him briefly and then made a job offer.

After Williams quickly accepted, he was told that it was company policy for each hire to take a fairly detailed aptitude and personality test. This test was designed to be a final check on the suitability of the job applicant. Williams was told that in about two weeks, when the test results were back, he would be sent a formal contract.

At the end of two weeks, Benson called Williams. The following conversation occurred.

Test Results

BENSON: Lee, the results of your test are back and we have a problem. Some of your answers indicate that you would probably have trouble functioning effectively in our environment.

WILLIAMS: What specifically were the problems areas, Mr. Benson?

BENSON: Well, according to the results (see the Appendix for the test results), you rate low in "social dominance," which indicates that you might be hesitant to make decisions that might be unpopular, though correct. The other area of concern is that the test indicates that you prefer "structured situations," and we just don't have many of those in DSM.

WILLIAMS: On that last point, Mr. Benson, I think the test reflected more the military environment in which I have been during the last seven years rather than my real preferences.

BENSON: What about the "social dominance" problem?

WILLIAMS: I think the test question that related to that area was, "Would you take the initiative in bringing life into a dull party?" I had difficulty answering that one for there wasn't an answer on the test for what I would actually do at a dull party. I wouldn't attempt to bring it to life, I would *just leave*. Another question asked, "Would you mind returning merchandise to a department store?" I admit that I don't like to return things that I've bought, but I don't feel that the dislike can be generalized to include business situations.

BENSON: Let me ask you a specific question along that line. Today I have to tell two new employees, who haven't even gotten their families settled here in town, that they leave tomorrow for an extended stay at one of our west coast projects. Would it bother you to tell someone that sort of news?

WILLIAMS: Not if there were no other way to handle the situation.

BENSON: Well, let me tell you this. That personality test was administered to the top people in our company. Their personality profiles serve as the basis for judging all the new people who take the test. We feel that a person who scores low on particular aspects of the test will be at a competitive disadvantage in the company. I hired one man, who is in the training program now, in spite of his test results, and that guy is in my office every other day for something.

WILLIAMS: All I can tell you is that I feel that I can compete against the company people I met in the team interview. I just don't think I'll be at a disadvantage.

BENSON: O.K., Lee, I'll get a contract in the mail to you and will see you when you get here.

First Assignment

Williams' first month with DSM was spent in self-study, as he had much to learn about computers and the health insurance field, in which he was to concentrate. Then he was assigned to a customer account in a midwestern city. The assignment came as a mild shock, as he had assumed that he would initially be staying at company headquarters. He had leased a home and settled his family in a town near DSM's home office.

Following company policy, Williams took his wife and child with him (at company expense).

Williams was put in a five-person systems team responsible for installing a data processing system in a health insurance firm. Although the actual computer programming and processing were done back at company headquarters, Williams and the others were responsible for learning the customer's business and acting as an interface between the system designers and the customer.

The work was challenging and Williams felt that he was gaining valuable experience. But after several months, the pace began to have its effects on Williams' family. He often worked 75 to 90 hours each week and typically worked seven days per week for weeks on end. His wife, in unfamiliar surroundings and left virtually alone in caring for their small child, began to question Williams about the real value of such a job. Williams wondered if the company's rising profits were the result of accomplishing "twelve-person jobs with five-person teams."

Toward the end of the project, after Williams had been with the company about eight months, he received his first appraisal interview. He was told that he had "done excellent work on the project." As evidence of management's appreciation, he was given an $800 bonus. He was then told to take a couple of weeks off to get his family settled at his new assignment.

Programming School

Williams' next assignment was to go back to the home office for schooling in computer programming. As with the previous project, the pace was set so that the men were forced to work extremely hard just to keep up. Williams was trying very hard to learn how to program, but he made some concessions to his family's desire for attention. Although he knew he was falling behind in his classwork, he would occasionally spend Sunday with his family, rather than at the office.

Although Williams knew that he needed help, he hesitated to ask, since the instructor was Morton Benson, the man who had hired him—reluctantly. Williams remembered Benson's comment about the man who "was in my office every other day" and was determined to succeed without Benson's help. When at last he had to admit failure, Williams was asked to see the personnel manager.

Resolution

Williams was told that inability to program was an insurmountable handicap to advancement in the company, and, for that reason, it would be a disservice to him for the firm to retain him as an employee. He was temporarily assigned to another part of the company and was asked to work out a program of work/job hunting for approximately six weeks, after which he would be terminated with two-weeks' severance pay.

Questions

1. Evaluate the firm's recruiting and selection procedure.
2. Would you suggest any changes? Explain.
3. Should Williams have been hired? Defend your answer.
4. From the test results, how would you describe Williams?
5. Evaluate the placement policies of this firm.
6. Was the decision to terminate Williams the right one? Explain.
7. What would you have done in this case if you had been in Williams' place?

APPENDIX: LEE WILLIAMS' APTITUDES AND PERSONALITY TEST RESULTS

Mr. Lee H. Williams   Systems engineer trainee

I. Motivation and Job Interest

The incentives or motivations of this man (see Exhibit 2) point him toward the business world, for he has a very tough-minded, highly economic, and investigative attitude. He is interested in communications and here we look at the persuasive interest. Computational and scientific job interests are not particularly strong. But the detail and the literary interests seem well developed. He is interested in words as is noted by the very high literary interest.

II. Capacity for Work

Mr. Williams's aptitudes are quite high. He had seven problems correct on the math test, which is a "fair" performance, but he did very well on all of the other capacity tests. Speed of thinking is first-rate, the judgment factor is well developed, and persuasiveness looks good. This man's insight into people is quite well developed.

EXHIBIT 2

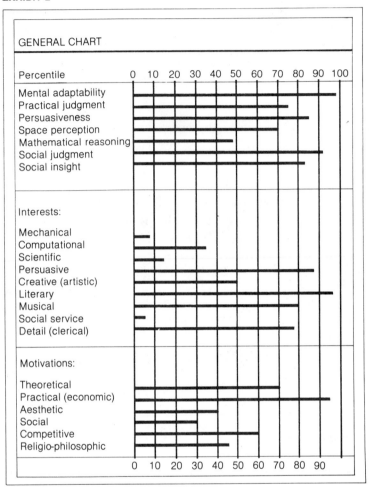

GENERAL CHART

Percentile	0 10 20 30 40 50 60 70 80 90 100
Mental adaptability	
Practical judgment	
Persuasiveness	
Space perception	
Mathematical reasoning	
Social judgment	
Social insight	

Interests:

Mechanical
Computational
Scientific
Persuasive
Creative (artistic)
Literary
Musical
Social service
Detail (clerical)

Motivations:

Theoretical
Practical (economic)
Aesthetic
Social
Competitive
Religio-philosophic

0 10 20 30 40 50 60 70 80 90

III. Personality and Temperament

The lines at the top of the personality and temperament chart (see Exhibit 3) suggest indications of a self-sufficient temperament but not a very tough one. Social independence is low, as he is eager to please, and he may be somewhat hesitant in his decisions simply because of this desire to please. There is quite a "dip" in dominance between stability and self-confidence. In our estimate, he tends to be overly cautious with people. We do not pick up indications of strong aggressiveness or of strong self-assurance. He comes across as composed and controlled; he is not jumpy, edgy, or impulsive. While not highly rated as far as thoroughness is concerned, we do note his detail interest. He may not love the routine of the job, but he will cope with it.

EXHIBIT 3

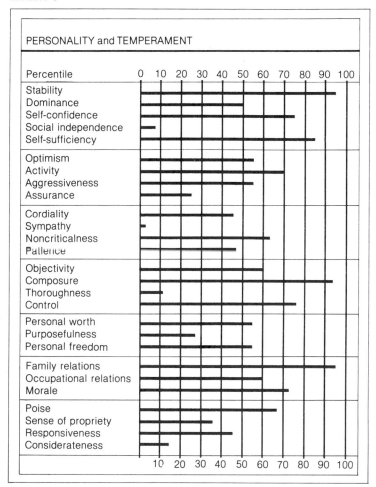

PERSONALITY and TEMPERAMENT

The estimate of personal worth is neither high nor low but seems about right considering his education and experience. Low sympathy (1 percent) means he tends to be cautious with people. He is perhaps a bit reserved with them. While not withdrawing from them necessarily, he is the kind of person who seems to have been hurt somewhere, and he will tend not always to extend himself in an emotional way. As compensation for low sympathy, he does have very high scores in social judgment and social insight.

IV. Conclusions

This is a very bright man with a strong motivation for business. He is a well-composed type of person, very self-sufficient in manner.

We think a problem may show up in two areas. First, the personality pattern where there is an underdevelopment of dominance, and a relatively low social independence factor. A person may appear pleasant and well poised in a face-to-face relationship, but this can conceal a tendency to be somewhat edgy about decisions, about exerting force in face-to-face situations, and can conceal the tendency to be somewhat more concerned with what other people think than is necessary.

The other problem area is the aggressiveness-assurance one. We think he will tend to want a situation where he has a well-structured program in front of him and will tend to feel somewhat less easy in a situation or job climate less well-structured where he is expected to reach out and set the tempo and to establish the dimensions of the job. He is apt to be more concerned than he should be about the interpersonal relationships and less concerned with the objectives of accomplishing a given objective or target.

We do not, therefore, feel this individual measures up to the standards that have been set for your systems engineer trainee program.

CASE 6. LOUIS KEMP

The personnel officer of a division of the state government received a phone call from the manager of a local office, who was having a problem with Louis Kemp.

Earlier the manager had engaged in extensive recruitment efforts to fill a vacancy in her operations. Finally, the personnel officer had recommended a Mr. Kemp after interviewing him in the home office. After an interview with the local manager, Mr. Kemp was hired at the usual rank and salary for that position.

The new employee had a B.A. degree in social science, was 29 years old, and at the time of his employment was unmarried. His experience during the preceding four years had been wholly on jobs that required little or no responsibility. He had worked on a seismograph crew "off and on" for the past two years as a rodman. He had been employed at a cotton gin as a ticket clerk helper for two seasons prior to his employment with the seismograph company.

As the office was small, the manager had only three subordinates, and the line of supervision was direct from her to the employees. After Kemp was employed, he was reluctant to talk to the manager or other employees about the operations of the office and other matters pertaining to the job. For that matter, he was reluctant to talk about any other subject with them. At the completion of his initial training period, the quality and quantity of his work failed to meet the minimum standards set by the manager. She discussed the problem with Kemp and attempted to offer assistance in solving his problem.

In the meantime, Kemp had married the daughter of one of the local business-persons.

It was soon apparent to the manager that Kemp needed further training. His lack of knowledge about the activities of his new employment lengthened the time required for him to meet the expected job standards. Therefore, a program of training and development was designed with this factor in mind. However, after three or four months, the manager decided that this was not the answer.

Kemp continued to insist that he liked his work but would give no reason for not meeting the expected job goals. The manager requested the aid of her district supervisor and assistance from the staff personnel at the home office. After they interviewed Kemp, a joint conference was held with the manager. This interview and the conference resulted in a decision to try an entirely new approach with the recalcitrant employee. Kemp would be given free rein and full responsibility for the job; the manager and supervisors would follow up on the results of the experiment after a period of several months. The results showed no improvement.

During this two-year period of employment, Kemp was sometimes assigned other office duties which were entirely different from his routine ones. It was noted that his attitude on these days seemed somewhat better. After 30 months, it was evident that some decisive action was necessary.

Questions

1. As manager, what would you do now?
2. Upon what criteria should a person be selected and developed?
3. What is the relationship between selection, development, and motivation?
4. Evaluate the development program utilized by this manager.
5. As personnel officer, what would you recommend to the manager?

CASE 7. THE PEPPER BUSH*

Sherman Kent, an electrical engineer and a graduate of one of the foremost universities in the Southwest, determined that his future lay in operating a restaurant. This idea evolved by accident over a period of time when Sherman did the cooking for hunting and fishing trips with friends. He used jalapeno pepper liberally to flavor the food and combined it with cheese to form a spread to enhance the flavor of meat.

---

*Prepared by William V. Rice and Robert McGlashan, University of Houston at Clear Lake City.

His hunting and fishing companions suggested that he should market his product. As the discussions became more serious, they agreed to back him financially if he would establish and manage a restaurant specializing in hamburgers with the special recipe jalapeno cheese sauce. Thus, the Pepper Bush was born.

Sherman opened the small restaurant in a suburban community of approximately 15,000 near a large metropolitan area in the spring of 1973. While he was the operating partner, two other partners helped finance the business by securing a small loan from a local bank. He secured a building with a seating capacity of 50 and equipped it to serve the usual line of short-order food services. Though he specialized in hamburgers with the special jalapeno and cheese sauce, he also served the usual line of hamburgers, french fries, beverages, and so forth. His principal competition was franchise food operations such as McDonald's and Burger King.

By the summer of 1975, business had increased to an expected gross of $125,000 and Sherman was thinking of expanding. Financing could be secured from the bank, and a newer and larger site could be found in the vicinity of the present restaurant.

The personnel policies of the Pepper Bush could be described as highly unstructured. When Sherman opened the restaurant, he hired a cook, three waitresses, and a dishwasher by running ads in the local papers. He did much of the cooking himself and performed all of the management functions. In 1975, his employees consisted of two cooks, five full-time waitresses, two part-time waitresses, and three dishwashers.

One of the cooks, Alvin Marsh, also served as assistant manager. Alvin was one of the first employees hired and had been with Sherman throughout the two-and-a-half-year existence of the Pepper Bush. He served as manager in Sherman's absence and for the previous six months had been actively involved with Sherman in hiring new employees. When a vacancy occurred, one of the employees would bring a friend to Sherman to be interviewed, or Sherman would run an ad in the local paper.

The interview was relatively brief, no formal application was required, and the applicant was either hired on the spot or told immediately that he would not be hired. Turnover of employees had been remarkably small. Two of the waitresses had been at the Pepper Bush since it opened. Sherman stated that the low turnover rate was due to the fact that he took a personal interest in each of his employees and took into account individual differences. For example, he did not require any uniform dress. Most of the waitresses wore jeans and a blouse, and the male help could wear their hair as long as they desired. He also allowed a "very flexible schedule of work," with the various classes of employees working out their own substitutions, as long as each category was covered during the appropriate hours.

Sherman had no formal job descriptions and his training consisted of on-the-job training. For example, all waitresses were expected to be able to work the cash register, wait tables, clean the tables, and, on the last shift, clean up for the night. But, if the waitresses were too busy, the cook might also work the cash register or clean the tables. All employees were expected to do whatever needed doing.

The proposed expansion would complicate Sherman's personnel problems. The "personal touch," the paternalistic attitude which Sherman had taken toward his employees, (the average age of the 10 full-time employees was 21), was a luxury he could afford. But, if he expanded, and he expected to at least double the number of employees within the next six months, would he need a more formalized organizational structure? Sherman and Alvin also discussed the overall personnel problems.

Questions

1. Should Sherman and Alvin continue the present unstructured informal personnel policy if they did not expand?
2. How would the proposed expansion impact on this policy?

CASE 8. THE VALUE OF RECOGNITION

ABC Chemical Corporation was a large American manufacturing firm. The plant involved in this case was one of its largest. The primary product of the plant sold well, as its quality was high, and the capacity of the plant, though large, was continually oversold.

A large department was headed by a technical director who had several assistants, each of whom was in charge of a given phase of the department's activities. One of these assistants, Mr. Roberts, was in charge of a group of chemists and chemical engineers whose primary duties related to purifying and processing an important by-product. The employees in this group reported directly to Mr. Roberts. He, in turn, reported to the technical director. Research problems, product development, quality, and the like were handled by the personnel in this group, reviewed by Mr. Roberts, and passed along to the technical director. The group members also served as supervisors for the operating crews of the by-product plant.

Jo Brown, a chemical engineer, was a member of the group. She became completely absorbed in the research work in that area and set out to "learn everything there was to know about it." At the start of the project, she was pleased with the potential it held and would half-jokingly say, "I'm going to make myself an expert in this field."

Elaborate research was conducted for about a year, and Jo thought the results she achieved were well worth the effort. However, after about six months, Jo sensed that her work was being taken for granted and that her superiors had not given the project the importance that it deserved. Jo did not let this lack of recognition affect her work, however; and the quality and value of her work and research findings remained high. She expressed her feelings to some associates but since they were not as close to the problem as she, their replies were more humorous than serious. This reaction did not help Jo's feelings one bit, but she increased her efforts and did an excellent research job.

She reported the results completely and thoroughly in a well-written and well-documented report. As was the practice in the group, all copies of the report were delivered to Mr. Roberts, who was to review the report, present it to the technical director, and arrange for necessary meetings to discuss practical applications of the findings.

Jo waited about a month for some action to her work; but none came. She was given some other minor assignments and helped in routine work. She found it difficult to approach Mr. Roberts concerning the report and was put off time after time.

Mr. Roberts was called out of town on a business trip, and Jo was assigned the duty of pinch hitting for him while he was gone. One day the technical director gave Jo the key to Mr. Roberts' desk and asked her to get a file which he knew was there. When Jo opened the desk, she saw all the copies of her report lying there, apparently unread. This discovery caused Jo considerable trauma, since she was confident that by this time some of the copies of the report had been delivered to the technical director and other company officials.

Jo's feeling of worth was reduced to nothing and with it went her feeling of pride in her work. She was so shaken by this experience that she resigned from the company.

She was immediately hired by a competitive concern where her success in her chosen field has been outstanding.

Questions

1. *a.* What were the main motivational needs of Jo Brown?
   b. Which one apparently motivated her the most?
2. *a.* What does this case explain about the motivation of scientific, technical, and professional personnel?
   b. How does this tend to differ from the motivation of rank-and-file employees?
   c. What does this portend for management in the future?
3. Would you say that Jo is self-motivated? Explain.
4. How would you have handled the situation if you had been Mr. Roberts? Explain.
5. Would you say that the same motivational factor stimulated Jo to begin the research as stimulated her at the time of her failure to be recognized (i.e., did her motivation change as the work progressed)? Explain.
6. Would you have acted any differently if you had been Jo? Explain.

CASE 9. JACK MORAN

Jack Moran, a long-time employee of the Practical Public Utility Company, had achieved his position (normally one held by a technical graduate) through the ranks, was recognized as quite competent in his field of activity, and was respected by his associates.

After 15 years of service, although his performance was not noticeably affected, there were indications that Jack's domestic life was unhappy. It was company policy not to let these matters be of concern unless they interfered with an employee's efficiency or were of such nature as to hurt the company's reputation.

However, in addition to the evidences of domestic troubles, it began to appear that Jack was drinking too much. Besides some obvious physical evidences, frequent one-day absences from the job, particularly following a week-end, pointed to the possibility of abnormal drinking.

Jack and his wife obtained a divorce, and he remarried shortly thereafter. Jack was then transferred to an area where the company had recently opened a new office.

During the next year, a number of instances occurred which indicated that he was continuing to drink to excess and that his new marriage was not working out satisfactorily. In one of these cases, he actually assaulted his wife during a brawl in public. Due to the circumstances (both the place and those present), the scene caused some concern to the company; such a display by one of its employees certainly would not help its public image. As a result, the company felt that Jack should be removed from this assignment, so he was returned to the home office.

Before being given another assignment, Jack was given a warning by Frank Moore, the head of the department. This warning was the strongest that could be given short of dismissal, and Jack's attitude was that of very sincere appreciation for having been given another chance. Although the new assignment constituted a lowering of his position and status, no change was made in his rate of compensation.

For a period of nearly a year, Jack's conduct and job performance improved. His reputation in his new assignment was growing more favorable, and outwardly it appeared that the problem no longer existed; it was known, however, that it did exist. Jack's drinking began to get out of hand. He and his second wife were estranged, divorce action was in progress, and she was making quite a nuisance of herself, both in pestering Jack and Jack's supervisor, Henry Blane. It appeared to the latter that in her conversations with him her only aim was to belittle Jack in the eyes of the company. Henry was not particularly disturbed by the telephone calls and had said nothing about them to Jack.

Jack, too, was apparently taking things in stride until suddenly, without warning, he failed to appear for work one morning. He was presumed to be sick, although no formal notification had been made. The next afternoon, Henry was notified by the police in a city some 200 miles away that Jack had been picked up in a condition which indicated that he was suffering from acute alcoholism.

After several weeks of hospitalization and rest at home and on the advice of company medical authorities and Jack's personal physician, Jack returned to work. His wife agreed to a reconciliation if Jack would do something about his drinking problem. Continued employment was, at this time, made conditional on Jack's total abstinence from alcoholic beverages and his promise to seek help if he needed it from an agency such as Alcoholics Anonymous or the state alcoholic treatment center.

Jack joined a local AA group, and, for approximately a year now, the company has not had a more loyal employee. Even though an assignment of lesser responsibility had to be given, there was no complaint from Jack, and his performance has been excellent. Inasmuch as Jack has been performing a job much less demanding than his former position, Frank Moore and the personnel manager decided his salary would have to be reduced to a level more comparable with the job he has been doing.

Questions

1. *a.* When should the company have been concerned with Jack's drinking?
   b. Should it have become concerned?
   c. Evaluate the company policy, or lack of policy, concerning alcoholic employees.
2. Should Frank Moore have done more than warn Jack? Explain your answer.
3. Would you recommend Jack for promotion again? Why or why not?
4. *a.* What does this case illustrate about alcoholism as a progressive illness?
   b. What does it show about discipline as a judicial process?
   c. Explain how the due-process concept was or was not followed in this case. (Refer to Chapter 13, if needed.)
5. Was the firm ethically "right" in making his continued employment conditional upon the two circumstances? Explain.
6. Would you treat this type of illness differently from physical illness? Mental illness? Explain why.

CASE 10. THE CASE OF SAM SAWYER*

Sam Sawyer was a top-rated operator in a building devoted to a five-stage batch process involving material with a high percentage of caustic soda. The five stages in the process were located on five separate floors. In addition to controlling temperatures carefully on various pieces of equipment and making sure that the time cycles were closely controlled, the operators moved the material in open buggies from one stage to the proper chute located in the floor and dumped the material through the chute to equipment on the floor below, where the next stage took place.

Because of the corrosive nature of the material, eye protection in the form of close-fitting goggles had been provided for a number of years. Up until a year ago, the safety rules only required that goggles be worn when removing material from equipment, since it was during the unloading operations that the greatest possibility of injury existed. The wearing of goggles at other times was up to the discretion of the operator.

At two stages in the process, the material was light and fluffy, and there were occasional backdrafts through the chutes causing it to fly. There had been three cases of minor eye irritations from this cause. Consequently, the safety rule was changed about a year ago, and operators had been required to wear goggles whenever they were near exposed material.

David Watts, who had been supervisor for two years, had come to the plant three years ago directly from engineering school. Prior to becoming supervisor, he had worked on all stages of the operation and had gotten along well with all the men. He felt "very kindly toward them" because they had taught him the "tricks of the trade" so that by the time he became supervisor he had a thorough knowledge of the operations.

Watts' shift supervisor was very safety-minded, believing that "all personal injuries can be prevented." He was quite insistent that safety rules "be followed to the letter."

Sam Sawyer, the oldest operator in point of service, had been working on this particular operation for 20 years and was an outstanding operator on all five stages. Because of his years of experience and his excellence as an operator, he was looked up to by the rest of the men. He had an outstanding safety record, which was one of the best in the plant, as he had had only one minor injury in all his years of service.

When the new safety rule went into effect about a year ago, Dave Watts was bothered because everyone went along with it except Sam, who resisted the change in the rule. This caused some difficulty in selling the rule to the other men because they respected his opinions. His main contention was that

---

*Prepared by Bruce Gunn, Florida State University.

it was unnecessary to wear goggles except when unloading equipment. However, after much discussion he agreed to go along with the rule.

During the past six months, Dave caught Sam without his goggles on on four occasions. He had a strong feeling that Sam was not complying with the safety rule fully and that his opinions were unchanged. Dave suspected that Sam was complying with the rule only while he was around. On half a dozen occasions he had had the feeling that Sam had put the goggles over his eyes when the supervisor came on the floor. Prior to the rule change, Sam had worn his goggles around his neck when they were not needed, but he started wearing them pushed up on his forehead. The supervisor's doubts were confirmed three days ago when he came upon Sam unexpectedly and saw him bob his head to shift the goggles from his forehead to his eyes.

Question

1. What would you do if you were the supervisor?

CASE 11. THE UNION BLOW*

The union first tried to organize the employees of Southern Offshore Fabricators (SOF) in 1963. After a national union organizer had persuaded enough employees to sign cards in support of the union, an election was held in 1964. The vote was seven to one against the union.

In February 1975, the union again petitioned for an election to certify it as the exclusive bargaining agent in three of the seven divisions of SOF, and contended that each division was a bargaining unit. The firm took the stand that there should be only one bargaining unit, and it should include all seven of its divisions because of the close relationship between what happened in one division and its effects on the others. In March, the company appealed to the National Labor Relations Board (NLRB), which ruled in its favor.

The NLRB gave the union 30 days in which to gain support from 30 percent of the employees in all seven divisions. If the union failed to gain such support, it would have to wait at least six months before repetitioning.

The union began its campaign to gain support by inducing workers in different areas from which all the employees came to visit employees at their homes with and without the union representatives. The union also encouraged union sympathizers to "talk union" during breaks on the job.

To combat union influence, the company planned meetings with 20 to 30 employees at a time. Prior to these meetings, the personnel manager met with the specialist in charge of employee benefits. To determine what was to be

---

*Prepared by Laura Badeau of Louisiana State University.

said at the meetings, these two people went over every written page in the company files describing employee benefits and discussed those things unwritten but understood.

During the meetings with employees—each of which lasted two to three hours over a period of seven weeks—three representatives of management sat down and "talked Southern Offshore Fabricators" to the employees. Although taking personnel away from the job lowered production, management felt the cost was necessary to preserve the continued effective functioning of the company.

From these meetings, management learned things that had never reached the front office before.

To learn and exchange information, supervisors were meeting every month with the employees, but only about half of them had been relaying what they had learned to their superiors. For example, the handling of pay raises was found to be unsatisfactory to employees out in the field. People were being bypassed for raises and then not being told why. Raises were not based on seniority at SOF but on initiative, ability to learn fast, and performance. Promotions, too, were not based on seniority. Instead, management reviewed a prospective manager's ability, job performance, and popularity with the other employees.

In these meetings, management explained that the union could not dictate how things were going to be run at SOF. All present employee benefits would be put aside, and management and the union would negotiate what future benefits would be. According to the employees, the union was talking about raising the present pay rate of $6.65 up to $7.75-$8.50 per hour. Management showed the workers copies of union contracts with other steel fabricating and offshore companies in the area. These unionized employees were being paid at the same wage rate as SOF's employees. Management asked how could the union do better at SOF.

After about two weeks of these meetings, attitudes and questions started to change as the grapevine relayed what management was saying. Employees began to realize that what was being told them by the union organizers, and how the union was going to provide such extras, were two different matters.

Management continued explaining in further meetings that SOF was a service company to the oil industry and had to operate 24 hours per day, seven days per week. Jobs were awarded in this industry through competitive bidding. Working under union conditions would mean uncertainities about meeting deadlines and being caught by a contract's penalty clause. When bidding on jobs, the company would have to stipulate that it could meet deadlines, "providing there would be no union interference." According to management, SOF had to be available to oil companies as needed, and the union would keep management from making firm commitments

SOF had a history of few layoffs. In 1969-70, when the Secretary of the Interior discontinued offshore federal leases in the Gulf of Mexico, the situation was so critical that the company could have laid off 500 workers. Instead, it made work for all except 125 people. Also, management reminded the workers that it usually found chores for its employees to do when work was slow.

To paint a clearer picture, management explained that a competitor, McDuff & Company, had been one of the better steel fabrication and offshore companies in the southern area. Ten years earlier, the company employees had unionized, with the result that the firm was no longer considered a competitor in the field. Because of strikes and walkouts, McDuff had been unable to serve the industry. Before McDuff unionized, employees were not laid off when work was slow; after unionization, layoffs became common. Management felt it had no control over its employees. Thus, when there was no work, why should management keep these people on the payroll? Consequently, the better skilled workers migrated to other companies where there was year-round employment.

The efforts of management were successful. When the union had to petition all seven divisions of SOF, the union did not have the 30 percent support necessary for an election. On September 15, 1975, the union was notified by the board that there would be no election. Management never knew whether the union could have gained the necessary support in the three divisions first petitioned. Management was aware, however, that the union probably had difficulty in effectively reaching employees in all seven divisions because employee homes were spread over a relatively large geographical area. It was also felt that many who signed cards in support of the union had probably left the company by the time the board requested the payroll of those eligible to vote. Turnover, especially of younger employees in the fabricators division, has been relatively high in the last few years. Management also inferred that many who signed union cards were new employees who were not yet concerned with the long-term welfare of the company.

As a result of the meetings held, several changes were brought about. Before the meetings, pay raises had been initiated by superintendents in the divisions, and there was no set time period for evaluation. The superintendents could evaluate employees whenever they wanted to, and favoritism played a part in such decisions. Afterwards, pay raises were initiated by leadermen (pushers). Every three months, a superintendent and the leadermen evaluated a worker. If one was not given a merit raise, the employee was told why.

Although meetings were no longer held with employees, a suggestion box system for grievances and constructive ideas was put into effect.

Management still waited, however, wondering when a sign of unionism would next appear on the scene.

Questions

1. Evaluate management's approach to the union's efforts.
2. What would you have done differently in view of the law?
3. How do you explain the change in employee attitude?

CASE 12. THE DISCHARGE OF SLEEPING BEAUTY*

Company: Reynolds Metals Company, Corpus Christi, Texas
Union: Aluminum Workers International Union, AFL-CIO

On August 6, 1974, Allen Walston was discharged for sleeping while on duty. He filed a grievance two days later, protesting his discharge and requesting full reinstatement with back pay. The grievance was not resolved, and the case went to arbitration in accordance with Article VI of the union-management contract. The parties agreed that the grievance was properly before the arbitrator and jointly identified the issue as: Was the discharge of Allen Walston for proper and just cause? If not, what is the appropriate remedy?

Background

Walston began working at the Reynolds plant in April 1969. Five years later at the time of his discharge, he was a trainee under area foreman, Ben Chavez. He had received no written warnings in the three months preceding his termination.

On August 4, two days before his discharge, Walston was working the "graveyard" (midnight–8:00 A.M.) shift. Chavez needed to see him and thus paged Walston twice using the public address system. Walston did not respond. Sometime later he did appear and said that noise had kept him from hearing the call. Chavez tore up the written reprimand he had intended to give Walston for sleeping on the job. He did, however, counsel Walston about failure to appear when paged. He also discussed Walston's generally poor work record with him, as he had already done on several previous occasions.

On August 6, Walston again worked the graveyard. He was taking aspirin and Dristan, as he had sinus trouble. Chavez saw Walston at 5:45 A.M. when the employee came to the office for a piece of equipment. Then about 30 minutes later, Chavez and general foreman Clarke (in the hospital at the time of the hearing) found Walston in a prone position on top of a tool locker, his head on a makeshift "pillow."

The locker was located on the third and highest floor of a filter building across the street from Walston's work area. No other employees were in the locker area because no work was being done there on this particular night. There was a snack bar used for coffee breaks on the same floor, about 50 to 75 yards from the tool locker. Coffee breaks were generally taken about 6 A.M.,

---

*Prepared by I. B. Helburn of the University of Texas at Austin and Darold T. Barnum, Associate Professor of Labor Relations, Division of Business, Indiana University Northwest, Gary.

with employees allowed to be away from their worksites for approximately ten minutes.

After finding Walston on the locker, Chavez called plant security and had Walston escorted to the office. There Chavez asked for an explanation of the incident, but Walston gave him none. Chavez then told the employee that he was being discharged for sleeping on the job and that he could pick up his formal termination notice from personnel when that office opened in the morning. The security guard escorted Walston directly to his locker to collect his belongings, and from there, off the plant grounds. Walston was the first employee Chavez had fired in his 18 years as a foreman at Reynolds Metals.

On August 8, Walston filed a grievance through his union, but it was denied by the company. The case was arbitrated on December 19, 1974.

Company Position

The company claimed the right to discharge under Article XXIII of the agreement because Walston's sleeping was deliberate. It maintained that premeditation was shown by the resting place, the pillow, and the deep sleep in which Walston was found.

Chavez testified that upon finding Walston he first called Walston's name several times while standing next to him. Walston did not respond until after Chavez had shaken him four times. Then Walston sat up and said, "I'm sick." At that point the foreman called plant security.

Chavez further testified that Walston was resting his head on an army field jacket stuffed with rags. Chavez said that he had never seen the jacket before, that with the warm August weather there was no need for a jacket, and that there had been no rags in the building or work area. Chavez also noted that Walston had what appeared to be a jacket with him when he finally left the plant grounds, and that the "pillow" was gone the next day when Chavez checked the area.

The foreman knew that Walston had been taking medicine for his sinus trouble, but noted that he had not asked to go to First Aid. Had he done so, permission would have been granted.

Regarding the incident two nights earlier, Chavez said that when Walston did appear he looked as though he had been sleeping. The warning was torn up because the foreman hoped that talking to Walston and giving him the benefit of the doubt would encourage him to do better. The company attorney claimed that another employee, whom the company would not name nor call to testify, later reported that Walston had indeed been sleeping in a pickup truck.

Chavez also testified that Walston was "irresponsible, lackadaisical, and lazy" and that he needed much more supervision than other "problem" employees. The company attorney said that Walston was disliked by fellow employees because of his poor performance.

The company agreed that employees did doze on coffee breaks when they were in the snack bar or the operations shack, and that such employees were simply awakened and sent back to work without being disciplined. It was argued, nevertheless, that such dozing was different from Walston's deliberate and premeditated sleeping, and that Walston's behavior was serious enough to warrant discharge. The company cited an arbitration decision in another company, in which the arbitrator upheld the discharge of an employee found sleeping in a tractor he was supposed to be operating.

Union Position

The union responded that Walston had not preplanned his pillow, hid himself, or purposely fallen asleep.

Walston said he left his work area about 0 A.M. He took five to seven minutes to walk from his worksite to the locker area, stopping to tell other employees he was going to rest rather than to have coffee, and to call him if he was needed. He wanted the rest rather than the coffee because of his sinus condition, which was bothering him considerably, particularly since earlier in the evening he had had to use a pistol-grip compressed air hammer.

Walston admitted to resting on the tool locker, but would only say that it was possible he was sleeping, although he did not think so. He said he did hear his name being called but did not feel Chavez shake him.

Walston denied having a jacket as a pillow, saying that his head was resting on a piece of cloth and some rags that he found on the locker. This piece of cloth had neither buttons nor sleeves. He further testified that he could not have recovered a jacket from the tool locker since he was escorted by plant security from the time Chavez found him until he left the grounds.

Also, the union argued that since Chavez had not seen Walston lie down, he could not say the bed had been deliberately made. And, no company employee had ever been terminated for sleeping on the job.

Walston claimed that on the August 4 shift, he had not heard Chavez call him because of the noise of some nearby pumps, which obscured the public address system. When he was told by Henry Cooper, a fellow employee, that Chavez wanted to see him, he went directly to the office. Cooper's testimony supported Walston's story.

Finally, the union pointed out that in the arbitration decision cited by the company, the discharged employee had not been taking medicine and had been given one written warning and two short suspensions in the two weeks prior to dismissal. Thus, the circumstances did not apply to the Walston case. Although the union did not dispute the company's right to discharge under Article XXIII, they argued that proper and just cause was lacking and that full back pay and allowances were due.

Selected Agreement Provisions

The following provisions of the agreement are pertinent to the Walston case:

Article V, Section 1: In the event an employee in the opinion of the company has acted in such a manner as to deserve discharge he may be immediately suspended and the chairman of the Grievance Committee, or his designated representative, shall be informed of the reason for the Company action. Such notice will be given on the same day as notice is transmitted to the employee involved.

Article V, Section 2: Should the employee, within five (5) working days of the suspension, believe that he should not be discharged, he and/or his Union Representative may present his complaint in writing to the Company Personnel Representative (third step of the grievance procedure), who will give the matter prompt and thorough consideration.

Article V, Section 3: Should it be found upon investigation as provided in Article VI hereof that an employee has been unjustly treated, such employees [sic] shall be immediately reinstated in his former position without loss of seniority and shall be compensated for all time lost in an amount based on his average straight time hourly rate of pay for the pay period next preceding such suspension, or other such adjustment as may be mutually agreed to by the Company and the Union, or determined to be proper by an arbitrator.

Article VI, Section 1: Failing satisfactory adjustment by the Director of Labor Relations, the grievance may be submitted to arbitration by either party.

The decision of the arbitrator shall be final and binding on all affected parties.

Article X: The following understandings shall apply to plant working rules number 9 to 17, inclusive: When an employee receives a warning under one of the aforementioned working rules, he may have this warning removed from his record if he does not receive another warning under any of the aforementioned rules within three months after the date of this warning.

Article XXIII: It is recognized that, subject to the provisions of this Agreement, the operations of the plant and the direction of the working force including the rights to hire, lay off, suspend and discharge any employee for proper and just cause are vested exclusively with the Company.

Plant Working Rules (part of contract): For those persons who fail to properly conduct themselves, the following penalties have been established and will be enforced. Violations of rules 1–8 will result in discharge for the first offense. Violations of rules 9–17 will draw a written warning for the first offense, and discharge for the second. Violations of rules 18 and 19 will draw written warnings for the first and second offenses, and discharge for the third.

1. Fighting.
2. Refusal to obey orders.
3. Possession of a lethal weapon.
4. Possession or use of drugs or alcoholic beverages in the plant.
5. Theft.
6. Moral offenses.
7. Willful destruction of company property.
8. Deliberately tampering with or punching another employee's time card.
9. Violation of a safety regulation which could result in injury.
10. Failure to wear prescribed safety equipment.
11. Loafing.
12. Poor work.

13. Leaving work area without permission of foreman.
14. Leaving operating post without proper relief or without permission of employee's foreman.
15. Horseplay.
16. Failure to have badge in possession.
17. Soliciting funds without consent of Company.
18. Unexcused tardiness.
19. Absence without leave.

Questions

1. What must the company prove to have the discharge upheld?
2. What must the union show if Walston is to gain full reinstatement with back pay?
3. Evaluate the arguments of each side.
4. As arbitrator, how would you rule? Why?
5. As management, how would you attempt to prevent a similar arbitration case in the future?

CASE 13. "FRIENDLY VISITS" FROM THE EEOC*

The Synco Rubber Corporation was established during the Second World War in response to the critical shortage of natural rubber which developed when the United States was cut off from its suppliers in Malaya and the East Indies. The U.S. government had immediately created the Rubber Reserve Company to accelerate research and development of a synthetic rubber. During the next decade of its existence, Synco used this research to grow to a position of eminence in the production of synthetic rubber. When the government placed Synco up for bids in the mid-fifties, it was understandable that the bidding was very competitive. In the end, however, the several independent and friendly, but competitive, companies that had managed Synco for the government succeeded in securing its ownership.

Synco retained its home office building and main plant in Trevor City, a Southern city with a population of 200,000 which is growing due to recent industrial expansion in the area. The management of the corporation also remained relatively intact after the formal change in ownership, and very little change in management practices or personnel policies was felt by the workers out in the rubber plant operation.

In general, four main categories of jobs were present in the plant operation:

---

*This case was prepared by Lee D. Stokes of Louisiana State University, Baton Rouge, under the supervision of Leon C. Megginson. From Robert D. Hay, Edmund R. Gray, and James E. Gates (eds.), *Business and Society: Cases and Text* (Cincinnati: South-Western Publishing Co., 1976), pp. 236–239. Reproduced with permission.

operators, laboratory technicians, maintenance craftsmen, and laborers. Shortly after the change in ownership, several local unions were organized by the men in the various job categories, and these unions were readily accepted by Synco's management as an example of good faith in their workers. Each union represented a craft or occupation, and each union entered into collective bargaining on its own resources.

The first three job categories, i.e., operators, laboratory technicians, and maintenance craftsmen, had been traditionally filled with white job applicants due to educational and cultural demands. The laborer jobs had always been filled with black job applicants due to these same demands and pressures. Over the earlier period of government ownership, this practice of having "racial job categories" had inadvertently become an implicitly accepted fact of life by management and workers alike. Management was concerned with "more pressing matters" when "formal" ownership changed hands, so the white and black workers remained segregated in all areas that did not directly interfere with completion of their jobs, i.e., dressing rooms, eating facilities, drinking fountains, etc. In fact, when a single intelligence test was installed as a "general" hiring procedure in 1958, only white applicants for jobs were given the test. It was not until 1961, when Al Royens was hired as training and employment manager, that blacks could also receive the hiring test.

Early in 1966, Bob Kiligan was promoted from labor relations manager to industrial relations director. Bob had joined Synco's management team in 1961 at the age of 28 after working for the Teamsters Union as an organizer while he worked on his Master's Degree in Industrial Relations at one of the better universities in the East. During one of his frequent visits to one of the owner companies, Felbs & Dobbs Company, Inc., the subject of Synco's hiring procedures was discussed and Bob decided that a complete employment test battery should be developed for Synco. Shortly thereafter, Felbs & Dobbs sent in a test specialist to develop the battery. The specialist set up the battery during a period of one week based upon his objective observations and his intuitive, but well-trained, feelings concerning the various job categories at Synco's rubber plant operation. Both Bob Kiligan and Al Royens were pleased with their "more professional looking" test battery.

About a year later, Bob Kiligan received a visit from a representative of the Equal Employment Opportunity Commission (EEOC). The representative was a black lawyer in his late twenties, and he seemed quite friendly and open in his manner. He informed Bob that complaints had been filed in his office by two of Synco's laborers charging racial discrimination in Synco's promotion policies. Both of the employees, Sy Washington and Willie Nord, claimed that they had applied for different job categories when the job openings were advertised on the company bulletin board, a practice initiated by Al Royens to implement the policy of "promotion from within." They felt that they had been consistently passed over for these promotions in favor of white workers with the same qualifications as their own. Bob Kiligan assured the EEOC representative that he would look into the matter immediately and inform him in writing of the results of his investigation.

After the government representative had left his office, Bob decided to handle the investigation personally. He had the reputation of doing things "himself," and he put all of his "lone wolf" experience into putting together the facts available. The company records showed that Sy Washington had been employed as a laborer by Synco since 1956 and that he had indeed applied for several promotion opportunities over the last two years. Although the employment tests were one of the main criteria used in promotion decisions, Washington had never received any tests due to the fact that there were no tests when he was hired in 1956. Washington had been turned down for promotion each time he applied due to "just satisfactory" work ratings and the fact that his supervisor did not consider him to be "too bright."

Willie Nord, who was several years younger than Washington at age 25, had been employed as a laborer in 1961 and had received the hiring test in use at that time. Nord's applications for promotion opportunities over the last two years had been turned down due to his low test scores and his supervisor's evaluation that Nord was also not "too bright" and had to be supervised constantly.

Kiligan then checked the personnel folders of the men who had been accepted for promotion. He noted that all of these men had done well on the original test or the new test battery and that each had received many excellent ratings from their supervisors before they had been promoted.

In meeting with the supervisors of the two laborers, Kiligan inquired if they had been approached by the men themselves or their union representative concerning the fact that they had not received any promotions. Both of the supervisors remembered comments by the men that they were upset due to being consistently passed over for promotion, but neither supervisor had been approached by the laborers' union questioning this consistency. Neither supervisor had felt that the discontent shown by the men was serious enough to warrant an "upward" communication. The supervisors reiterated their positions that neither Washington nor Nord was "bright" enough to deserve a promotion into another job category.

When Bob Kiligan arrived back at his office, he called Al Royens into his office and told him that he wanted all of the present employees to have a chance to take the new employment test battery. Al immediately set about accomplishing this task and completed it sooner than expected due to the fact that many of the old employees who had not been tested did not want to take the test battery regardless of its importance as a promotion criterion.

Bob Kiligan wrote the EEOC office concerning the results of his investigation and the actions he had taken to test all of the plant workers who were interested in being tested. He also informed the EEOC that the concerned laborers had taken the test battery and that their scores on the battery when combined with their supervisor's ratings still showed them to be unsuitable for promotion to a better paying job category. He assured the EEOC that all the employees who had been promoted had received much higher scores on the test battery and much better work ratings by their supervisors before they had received promotions. Kiligan ended the letter by expressing his feelings that the introduction of standard testing and ratings for all employees had corrected all possible deficits in Synco's promotion policies and that the present system was fair and nondiscriminatory.

A year and a few months went by without a reply from the EEOC. Neither the laborers' union nor the concerned employees themselves were heard from concerning the promotion matter. Both Sy Washington and Willie Nord, however, had tried again, unsuccessfully, to be promoted. Bob Kiligan left Synco to accept the position of industrial relations director in another company, and he was replaced by Glenn Doyle.

Doyle was an "old hand" at industrial relations as he had consistently worked in one area or another concerned with industrial relations ever since he had received his law degree late in the thirties. He had the reputation of being tough, but fair, in all of his dealings with both individual employees and their unions.

One morning Glenn Doyle was studying the facts of an arbitration outcome when the lawyer from the EEOC called for an appointment. Doyle granted the appointment for an afternoon later in the week, and after he hung up the phone, he called in Al Royens to see what he knew about the matter. Al gave him the facts of the case that he had been involved with, and Doyle obtained the rest of his information from the reports and letter written by Bob Kiligan. Glenn then phoned some of his friends in industrial relations positions in other companies to obtain information about the lawyer who was to "visit." With all of this information at his disposal, Glenn formulated his strategy for dealing with the matter.

Later that week, Glenn Doyle and Al Royens both greeted the lawyer from EEOC when he arrived, and all three men went into Glenn's office. Again the young lawyer was as congenial as could be expected under the circumstances, and he quickly got down to business.

> Mr. Doyle, our office has investigated the discrimination complaints filed by two of your employees, Mr. Nord and Mr. Washington, and we have also taken into account the comments and actions described in a letter to our office from Mr. Kiligan, your predecessor. In the EEOC's opinion three separate and indisputable facts stand out in this case. First, the segregation apparent in your dressing rooms, washrooms, and eating and drinking facilities tends to support an atmosphere of discrimination at Synco. Second, there are no blacks employed by Synco in anything other than menial-type jobs, and this also supports contentions of discrimination in your corporation. Third, we have noticed that the tests used as promotion criteria have not been shown to be relevant to job performance at Synco.

The young lawyer sat forward in his chair a little, looking directly into Glenn Doyle's eyes, and smiled in a friendly manner before he said, "When all of these facts are combined, we feel the evidence weighs heavily that our clients have been discriminated against at Synco in terms of promotion opportunities, if not in other areas also. Now what the EEOC wants to know is this: What does Synco plan to do to assure fair opportunities for our clients, to repay these two men for the personal injury and economic loss they have suffered, and to assure that the same situation does not occur again with other minority employees?"

Questions

1. How would you answer the question?
2. What is your evaluation of the way the company had handled the situation? Explain.
3. What should it have done differently?
4. What do you think of the way the EEOC representative handled himself? Explain.
5. What do you think of the way Bob Kiligan handled the situation? Explain.

CASE 14. WHAT DETERMINES WAGES?

The following letter was received from the vice president of personnel of a medium-sized insurance company in answer to the question: "How do you actually determine your rates of pay?"

Dear Professor:

Regardless of the type of wage plan to be adopted, whether based upon a time-basis of payment or one related to output, certain parameters can be established. Minimum wage rates have been established by governmental regulations through such acts as the Fair Labor Standards Act, the Walsh-Healey Act, and the Davis-Bacon Act. At the opposite end of the spectrum, it can be said that maximum wage rates are largely determined by management's philosophy toward the sharing of gains or its largesse.

In situations where labor is a direct cost, as in some service organizations, the extent of competition is a primary factor influencing the wage rate employed by the firm. An item not often considered directly is the efficiency of management itself. An inefficient management might find the resulting low profits sufficient cause to maintain a low wage rate.

The cost of living within contiguous areas is another force exerting an influence on the level of wages. Within a given community, the wage paid for a given type of work will, like water, seek its own level. In order to attract workers, the organization must, therefore, meet the local competition for the type of labor it seeks. If the firm is to maintain competition within its industry, and market its product outside its local community, the wage level paid within the firm's industry will influence the wage rate decision.

Benefits other than the basic wage are as much a part of the cost of labor as the basic wage rate itself. If the firm's situation is such that there is only a given amount available from the sale of its product to pay wages, then the extent to which benefits are paid must be a determining factor in the establishment of the basic wage rate. Management's philosophy toward workers will include a desire to reward past service, efficiency, or cooperation in some cases. From this desire there might arise individual differences in wage rates within given job descriptions.

Finally, the labor contract in force between the firm and the union is an additional component in the wage rate decision. It is true, however, that competition within the community for workers will force the nonunion company to approximate the unionized competitor in wage rate. In addition, a nonunion firm may, in its desire to remain nonunion, approximate the going union rate.

These items have been found to play a dominant part, in the past few years, in shaping any wage plan which we put into effect.

Sincerely yours,
Gayle M. Ross
Vice President, Personnel

Questions

1. *a.* Whose right is it to set wages?
   b. Explain.
2. *a.* Assuming (1) a natural human dignity and (2) a competitive market with labor mobility, what influence should labor unions exert in the shaping of wage rates?
   b. Explain.
3. *a.* Differentiate between (1) internal and (2) external pressures which determine the wage rate in this firm.
   b. What are some pressures the vice president did not mention?
4. What influence does the employee's wage rate have on job performance?

Name Index

593

Subject Index

This book has been set in 10 and 9 point Laurel roman, leaded 2 points. Part and Chapter numbers are in 14 point Vega roman; Part and Chapter titles are in 18/26 point Vega medium roman. The size of the type page is 27 picas plus 3 picas marginal by 47½ picas.